WHEN THERE IS NO WIND, ROW

*One Woman's Retrospective on the
Most Transformative Changes
Over the Past 50 Years*

a memoir by
PAULA N. SINGER

Copyright © 2016 by Paula N. Singer
All rights reserved.

No part of this publication may be reproduced, distributed or transmitted in any form or by any means, including photocopying, recording, or other electronic or mechanical methods, without the prior written permission of the publisher, except in the case of brief quotations embodied in critical reviews and certain other noncommercial uses permitted by copyright law. For permission requests, write to the publisher, addressed "Attention: Permissions Coordinator," at the address below:

Swallow Lane Publishing
Lyman, Maine 04002

Editing by Steve Hrehovcik
Cover design by Elaine York, Allusion Graphics LLC
Interior design and formatting by JT Formatting

Publisher's Cataloging-In-Publication Data
(Prepared by The Donohue Group, Inc.)

Names: Singer, Paula N.

Title: When there is no wind, row : one woman's retrospective on the most transformative changes over the past 50 years : a memoir / by Paula N. Singer.
Description: First edition. | Lyman, Maine : Swallow Lane Publishing, [2016]
Identifiers: LCCN 2016915083 | ISBN 978-0-9976598-0-1 | ISBN 978-0-9976598-1-8 (ebook)

Subjects: LCSH: Singer, Paula N. | Feminists–United States–Biography. | Women–United States–Social conditions–20th century. | Women–United States--Social conditions–21st century. | Sex discrimination in employment–United States–History–20th century. | Sex discrimination in employment–United States–History–21st century. | Women lawyers–United States–Biography. | Maine–Biography. | Massachusetts–Biography. | LCGFT: Autobiographies.

Classification: LCC HQ1413.S56 A3 2016 (print) | LCC HQ1413.S56 (ebook) | DDC 305.42092–dc23

Dedicated to my daughters,
Beth and Samantha,
and my granddaughters,
Grace and Rose

With the admonition in the words of George Santayana,
"those who cannot remember the past are condemned to repeat it."

And to my husband, Gary,
without whom the last half of my story could not have happened.

TABLE OF CONTENTS

	Prologue	i
Chapter 1	I Am Woman, See Me Soar!	1
Chapter 2	Women and Politics Make Strange Bedmates	9
Chapter 3	Women Need Not Apply	22
Chapter 4	My Family Roots Run Deep	31
Chapter 5	Growing Up In Kennebunk: The Only Village in the World So Named	44
Chapter 6	A Great Public School Teacher	52
Chapter 7	Being Smart—A Curse or Blessing	58
Chapter 8	More Exceptional Gifts	67
Chapter 9	One College Semester at a Time	73
Chapter 10	It Wasn't All Work	83
Chapter 11	Who's Afraid of Computers?	90
Chapter 12	My Responsibilities Expand	101
Chapter 13	More High-Tech and High Hopes	109

Chapter 14	Trials of a Divorced Woman	120
Chapter 15	My Next Challenge: Law School	128
Chapter 16	I Wanted to Practice Law	139
Chapter 17	How to Make a Silk Purse from a Sow's Ear	149
Chapter 18	Exploring Big Worlds at Arthur D. Little	161
Chapter 19	International Taxes—Learning an Exotic Language	175
Chapter 20	An Unconventional Law Practice	185
Chapter 21	Spreading the World with Taxes	199
Chapter 22	A Maze of Tax Laws for My Foreign National Clients	209
Chapter 23	Some Unconventional Tax Planning	220
Chapter 24	Computers and the Law Don't Always Compute	231
Chapter 25	Gary Has a Great Idea	240
Chapter 26	Launching Our New Business: Windstar	248
Chapter 27	Windstar Grows Its Product Line	258
Chapter 28	Our Creative Funding—When 2+2=22	270
Chapter 29	David Slays Goliath, How Sweet It Is!	282
Chapter 30	Courses, Seminars and Conferences Keep Me Current	292
Chapter 31	Teaching the IRS about International Taxation	303
Chapter 32	The IRS, the Agency Everyone Loves to Hate	315

Chapter 33	Advocating for Tax Reform	326
Chapter 34	Born 10 Years Too Soon	334
	Epilogue	340
	Appendices	343
	Acknowledgments	366

PROLOGUE

Twenty years from now, you will be more disappointed by the things that you did not do than by the things you did do. So, throw off the bowlines. Sail away from the safe harbor. Catch the trade winds in your sails. Explore. Dream. Discover.

– Mark Twain

If "the pill" and publication of Betty Friedan's *The Feminine Mystique* and her subsequent founding of the National Organization for Women (NOW) hadn't intruded on the 1960s, the progress of women may never have happened. But it did, played out against a backdrop of a country staggering out of control as it grappled with the paralyzing effects of war protests, assassinations and civil unrest during this conflict-ridden era.

Against this dire background, as a teenager, I had my own worlds to conquer. By age 16, I had reached some adult decisions—I would go to college, then to law school and have a career in law. While I didn't know how I would do it, I had no doubt that I'd achieve my dreams. Dreams that saw me as someone in control of my destiny. And, like Maria in one of my favorite films, *The Sound of Music,* I'd climb every mountain and forge every stream to reach the far shore of my journey. I started to pay more attention to events around me. As I began this journey, it became obvious from my personal experiences how many unfair accepted practices favored first boys over girls, then men over women.

In school I became aware of how social customs encouraged more opportunities for boys and minimized those for girls, as in both academic and sports options. Even more glaring, as I matured, I saw other accepted practices where men dominated business careers and political offices at the expense of women.

While I still had a lot to figure out, I made up my mind about one thing. I had no intention to allow the winds of prejudice and injustice of a male-dominated society to prevent me from continuing on my journey. I refused to let islands of ignorance or submerged shoals of hidden practices I couldn't see stop me.

I never let up on my dreams and I found just the encouragement I needed when I entered law school. It came in the form of a poster which read, "When There Is No Wind, Row." I taped the poster on the wall beside the desk where I studied in the law library. I never put it into words before, but this poster explained how I had accomplished so much with so few resources. I kept that poster and followed its advice throughout my careers.

I use the plural "careers" because I had many. I always described my career path as "tacking," a nautical term used in sailing. When I had a headwind, I couldn't sail directly into the wind. Instead, I'd have to tack left, to port, and right, to starboard to make headway. I moved forward, but slower than if I had the wind in my sails.

I never had the wind in my sails. Most of the time, I had a headwind, so I tacked. And when there was no wind, I rowed.

Difficult as my zigzag route was, it obliged me to learn skills that would shape my future.

I entered the University of Maine in Orono in 1962 without enough funds to complete my freshman year. But I had the resolve to find a way to get my degree. I planned to continue my education at the law school in Portland—later named the University of Maine School of Law—after getting my BA. But when I approached the pre-law adviser, all he said was, "If they let you in, they won't give you any student aid."

At that time, women attending professional schools couldn't get financial aid. Since I was both female and poor, and by then supporting my mother, this was a very strong headwind. So I tacked to my first career out of college—programming computers in the insurance industry.

It took a hard fought battle, but in 1972 Congress passed Title IX of the Civil Rights Act. It made it possible for women to receive financial aid for professional schools. At last I could fulfill my dream of attending law school.

At age 30, I applied to law school and was accepted. Three years later I had earned my Juris Doctor degree, my first step toward the practice of law. But law firms weren't hiring women of my age. So I tacked again to my next career with the prestigious Cambridge-based consulting firm, Arthur D. Little, Inc., with offices around the world.

I tacked to a new course at age 40 when I joined a tax law firm, where I proceeded to become an expert in international tax matters and a rainmaker, the term used for a lawyer who brings in new business. After four years, I became a partner with the firm—later named Vacovec, Mayotte & Singer LLP—with a distinguished reputation for international tax expertise.

At 50, I tacked again, co-founding Windstar Technologies, Inc. with my husband, Gary Singer. We named the company after our sailboat "Windstar." But we had no time for sailing after we founded Windstar.

As a result of my tacking, I became a participant in the three most transformative changes in the past 50 years—the computer revolution, the women's rights movement and the globalization of the economy.

A colleague once asked me if I had planned my career path this way. I replied, "No, I just took the best opportunity—sometimes the only opportunity—available to me at the time. But I couldn't have planned it better if I'd tried."

The nautical theme began early in my life at age 2.

CHAPTER 1

I Am Woman, See Me Soar!

*Challenges are what makes life interesting
and overcoming them is what makes life meaningful.*

– Joshua J. Marine

"I am woman, hear me roar" is the first line of the song *I Am Woman*. In 1975, it became the anthem of the women's liberation movement and the theme song for the United Nation's International Woman's Year.

With her moving lyrics, Helen Reddy stirred the conscience of the country about the unfair treatment of women. A decade earlier Betty Freidan's book *The Feminine Mystique* started the feminist movement by exposing "the problem that had no name." When the book was republished in 2001 for the fifth time, the New York Times book review said it "changed the world so comprehensively that it's hard to remember how much change was called for."

• • •

Betty Friedan (1921 – 2006) With her publication of *The Feminine Mystique* in 1963, Betty Friedan is credited with sparking the second women's rights movement in the 20th century. The first was the struggle for voting right in the early 1900s won with ratification of the 19th Amendment to the Constitution. As co-founder and president of the National Organization for Women (NOW), Friedan lobbied for new laws to help working women, such as national day care. She said, "Men are not the enemy, but the fellow victims. The real enemy is women's denigration of themselves."

• • •

I could relate to the power of the song and its uplifting message. I began my careers when few doors opened for women no matter what their intelligence or talent. I endured slights, condescending attitudes and insults from decision makers who saw men as the bread winners and women only as wives and mothers.

I cringed when I heard, "A woman's place is in the home." But I smiled when I saw the bumper sticker, "A woman's place is in the House—and the Senate."

I Am Woman proclaimed our rightful place in business, relationships and career opportunities.

But as the lyrics of the song recognize, we still had "… a long, long way to go." I knew, no matter what patriarchal barriers blocked my path, I'd have to soar over them.

Women Were Supposed To Be Sexy

I was a tomboy when I was young and liked to wear dungarees and climb trees. But in the 50s and 60s, girls couldn't wear pants in school. Even in the winter. The Kennebunk middle school I attended was about a mile from my home. The winters in Maine were cold with lots of snow. I wore my dungarees under my dress for the walk to school. But I had to remove them when I got to school. We didn't have a room to change in. I took them off in the corridor in front of my locker before going to home room. I put them on again in the corridor after classes for the walk home. You can imagine the stares I got from some of the boys.

The summer after my freshman year at college I worked as a waitress at the Howard Johnson's restaurant on the Maine Turnpike exit to Kennebunk. We lived on Fletcher Street and I biked the mile to work. I wore the required orange and turquoise uniform and white nurses' shoes with thick high heels. I wasn't used to wearing high heels, and they hurt my feet.

My customers would say, "You walk like your feet hurt."

I replied, "They do."

When they asked why I wore high heels, I explained it was company policy. I guess high heels made our legs look sexy. Howard Johnson's got a surprising number of comment cards that said, "Let the waitress ware low-heeled shoes." As a result, the local management sent the requests to upper management who gave me a dispensation to wear low-heeled shoes.

In the 70s, the miniskirt became very popular. I never wore a miniskirt. It wasn't because I didn't have great legs. I did. I had a pretty good figure, too. When I was 17, I was a finalist in the annual summer bathing suit beauty contest held at the Colony Hotel in Kennebunkport. I didn't wear miniskirts because I viewed them as one more fashion to make women sex objects. When I was at work, I didn't want to distract the men with what I wore. And I didn't have long hair either. Long hair became popular too, because girls felt long hair was sexy. But long hair required more time. I had enough to do before leaving for work without spending extra time on my hair.

In the 80s, women began to wear pant suits, but not in the legal community. Lawyers were more conservative. My law partner Maureen Mayotte and I began to wear pant suits sooner than the female lawyers at the downtown firms. We could get away with it. Our office was in the suburbs and we were partners. We had flexible work policies too. Our female associates who were new mothers brought their babies to work, maybe a first in the Boston area.

Navigating the Waters as a Career Woman

During the 60s, men had careers, but women had to be content with jobs—strange, because in the 20s and 30s, women did have careers. Black and white movies starring Rosalind Russell, Katherine Hepburn and Bette Davis depicted high powered women matching wits with men.

In the 40s, women played a decisive role in building war armaments. Rosie the Riveter made a stunning presence in ads supporting the war effort.

But in the 50s, attitudes shifted. "Career woman" became a dirty word. Even in the late 60s when I worked at Union Mutual Life Insurance Company as a computer programmer, women who were mothers faced pressure from some fellow employees to stay at home and care for their children.

As a way to demonstrate the unfair treatment of women on a larger scale, Gloria Steinem went undercover as a Playboy bunny. She wrote about her experience in a national magazine.

• • •

Gloria Steinem (1934 –) Wearing a "bunny" suit and floppy ears, Gloria Steinem gained notoriety in 1963 with her expose of behind the scene unfair treatment of women at the New York City Playboy Club. She catapulted into prominence as a writer, editor and outspoken political activist for women's rights. In 1971, she founded *Ms. Magazine* and, in 1992, she created the "Take Our Daughter to Work Day" to show girls they should be proud of being smart.

WHEN THERE IS NO WIND, ROW

• • •

The most disconcerting behavior I encountered was from men who treated me as if I wasn't there. It happened the first time in my senior year honor's course in college. Two classmates and I became involved in a discussion with our professor about war. I commented, "More people are killed by automobiles in the United States each year than were killed in World War II." Fifteen minutes later, as if an original thought, our professor made exactly the same comment. My two male classmates looked at me bewildered.

I encountered this problem when I worked with a certain manager at Union Mutual. To overcome this frustration I found it necessary to take with me one of the young men who reported to me when I met with this manager. As questions came up, I gave the answers and the young man repeated my answers. I felt like a ventriloquist. I don't think the manager had a clue about what went on.

Another time at Union Mutual, I had an informal conversation over his cubical partition with Tom, a colleague in the Pension Department. An underwriter came by, hung over the petition and asked Tom a question. Tom didn't know the answer, so he asked me. I gave him the answer. He gave the same answer to the underwriter. "Tom's" answer satisfied the underwriter, so he had several follow-up questions. Each time I gave Tom the answer, and he repeated it to the underwriter. The underwriter thanked Tom, never acknowledged my presence and walked away.

After the underwriter left Tom said, "I don't believe what just happened."

I said, "Believe it. It isn't the first time this has happened and it won't be the last."

A similar event took place more than a decade later. I was on a telephone conference call at my law firm with a male partner speaking with his client who had substantive questions about taxes.

Once again I provided detailed answers. The client spoke only to my partner. It's obvious the client heard my voice over the phone. But to him, I didn't exist.

When the call ended, the partner said, "He didn't even acknowledge you. Doesn't that make you mad?"

I replied, "If I got mad every time something like this happened I'd be a very bitter person. I just ignore it. Besides, I've been insulted by better people than him."

The Challenging Life of A Married Full-Time Student

By the early 60s, more than 50 percent of American women were married by age 20. When I married my first husband Wayne Goodrich in 1964, I was 20 and a junior at the University of Maine in Orono (UMO). Wayne was also a full-time student at UMO, studying for his master's degree.

While a student wife, I studied to earn a BA in history. But as the wife of a student, I also worked to earn my PHT for "Putting Hubby Through." I joined the Mrs. Maine Club for student wives for mutual support and camaraderie. If there were any other full-time married female students at UMO at the time, I never met them. When our husbands graduated, we all received our PHT certificate.

At one club meeting, I discovered how powerful the culture to minimize women had become. A large number of women accepted their subservient role without complaint and quit college when they got married.

I urged the student wives to complete their college educations. I told them, "You may have to support your family on your own someday." They all looked at me as if I came from outer space.

Many of young wives learned this painful truth years later when their marriages ended in divorce. As divorced mothers with children, they only had the meager wages they could earn without a college degree.

At the time, courts awarded alimony in only 15 percent of divorces. Unpaid child support could be collected only with legal action and the assistance of a lawyer.

A Working Mother Gets Little Respect

Still lacking adequate funds, I changed my major at UMO to history and government and took enough credits to graduate a semester early in 1966. I joined New England Mutual Life Insurance Company as a computer programmer trainee in Boston, Massachusetts. Most programmers at that time had degrees in math, history or music. It would be a long time before schools offered a degree in computer science.

Wayne had a job as a stock broker at Hayden Stone in Boston. Following a training program in New York City, he accepted a transfer to the Portland, Maine, office. So we decided to start a family, and I stopped taking the pill.

After I got pregnant, I discovered Massachusetts law restricted pregnant women from working past their sixth month. So after my sixth month, I had to leave the company. I moved back to Kennebunk, Maine, where Wayne and I grew up. We scrambled to get our apartment ready for our new family, which now also included my mother. I was 23.

When Wayne's training program ended, I drove down to pick him up in our VW bug. I was eight months pregnant with our daughter, Beth.

In 1968, when Beth was six months old, I went back to work as a waitress and chambermaid to pay a hospital bill. At the end of the tourist season, I started to look for a full-time job. In December I began work as a computer programmer at Union Mutual Life Insurance Company in Portland.

Some were surprised to discover I was a mother. At a meeting with the head of the Actuarial Department, I saw a picture of his wife and children and commented about my daughter.

He said, "You're married?!"

I said, "No."

"But you have a child,"

I said, "I was married but now I'm divorced." By 1973 Wayne and I realized our marriage didn't satisfy either of us, so we decided to separate and then divorced.

Then he asked, "But who takes care of your daughter?" "My mother. She lives with me."

"Oh, that's good."

"Yes, it is."

He concluded, "I mean for your daughter."

I thought it was good for my mother and me too.

CHAPTER 2

Women and Politics Make Strange Bedmates

The size of your dreams must always exceed your current capacity to achieve them. If your dreams do not scare you, they are not big enough.

– Ellen Johnson Sirleaf

In the 60s, women were expected to support the politics of their husband. But I was more liberal than my husband, Wayne. I learned this the hard way.

In 1965, I attended an anti-Vietnam war protest meeting at UMO. The University of California Berkley organized the protest and linked participants on college campuses around the country by radio hook-up. Wayne got upset because he supported the war, as did most people at that time.

When we moved back to Kennebunk, I joined the Republican Party after Wayne became active in politics.

Real Politics Are for Men

In 1968, Wayne became a delegate, and I served as an alternate, to the Maine Republican State Convention. Wayne had set up campaign headquarters around the state for presidential candidate Richard Nixon. He hoped it would help get him chosen as a delegate to the Republican National Convention in Florida. Wayne was running against a doctor who had given a large amount of money to the GOP. The doctor had the support of party leaders.

When we arrived at the convention in Augusta, we went straight to the smoke-filled motel room where the Republican power brokers were selecting the delegates who would win. They shooed me away. Real politics were for men, not women.

I wandered out to the exhibit area where the county organizations had their tents. I spotted Pug Chase in the Lincoln County tent. Pug held the high profile position of county road commissioner. He was also the uncle of a good friend. I met Pug when I attended the town meeting in Whitefield Junction with my friend that spring.

I threw my arms around him and said, "Hi, Pug. I need your help." He gave me a startled look. After I reminded him who I was, we visited the other tents together to drum up support for Wayne.

When we filed into the auditorium for the votes, I took a seat where I could watch the reaction of the GOP leaders. Much to their bewilderment, the vote between Wayne and the doctor by a show of hands was too close to call. They asked for a standing vote. When they called the vote for Wayne, the delegates from the rural counties, who were in the back of the room, all stood up. The GOP leaders hadn't expected their authority to be challenged. I heard one of them say, "What's going on?"

When they tallied the count, Wayne had lost by only a few votes. The result even surprised Wayne. As we were leaving, I said to him within ear shot of the puzzled GOP leaders, "I drummed up lots of votes for you, didn't I?"

It would be 40 years before a woman became a creditable candidate for president of the United States. In 2016, Hillary Clinton became the first female presidential candidate for a major political party. But Clinton did much more to promote women's rights than run for president.

• • •

Hillary Clinton (1947 –) When actress Meryl Streep introduced Secretary of State Hillary Clinton during the 2012 Women In the World Conference, Streep said Clinton not only meets heads of states, but also women leaders in grassroots organization in each country. One supporter pointed out, her picture with these activists is more than a remembrance of their meeting. "It will be my bullet-proof vest." As a result, leaders around the world know "Women's Rights are Human Rights" is a vital part of American policy.

• • •

Over the years, many of my clients asked if I'd ever consider running for public office. I did hold a public office in the 70s. Kennebunk town officials appointed me to the budget board in 1971 for a three-year term. I was the board's first female member.

Our major issues each year centered on the school budget and how much to budget for "winter roads." One time, all six male board members showed enthusiastic support for a new snow-moving truck with a snow-blower attached. I pointed to the message on a band across the brochure cover, "Not recommended for municipalities on the ocean," and said, "Last time I checked, Kennebunk was on the ocean."

Another time, they voted to buy a new eight-cylinder police car over my protests. I argued for a V6 to save gas. The year after the purchase, the town garage replaced the V8 engine with a V6. It was 1973, and everyone had to wait in long lines at the gas station for their ration because of the Saudi oil embargo.

Long Overdue Changes in Attitudes and Helpful Legislation

Historic changes for women occurred in the 60s. We began to push back on laws restricting *our* rights. This resistance won us more freedom. The pill, introduced in 1960 for menstrual pain, soon became a hit but for another reason. In 1963, when my doctor prescribed it for my debilitating cramps, he said, "There's one side effect. You can't get pregnant." In 1965, the U.S. Supreme Court, in *Griswold v. Connecticut*, overturned a state law outlawing contraception for married couples. Seven years later in 1972, the Supreme Court, in *Eisenstadt v. Baird*, struck down a state law prohibiting the sale of contraceptives to unmarried persons.

The pill freed women more than any legislation or court case ever could. Attitudes began to change. The U.S. Supreme Court struck down a state law requiring pregnant teachers to leave work after their third month. This led to the repeal of other restrictive employment laws for pregnant workers.

In 1963, Congress passed the Equal Pay Act (EPA) to "prohibit discrimination on account of sex in the payment of wages by employers." In 1964, Congress passed Title VII of the Civil Rights Act banning sex discrimination in employment, along with race discrimination. Maine's Senator Margaret Chase Smith played a pivotal role in passing the bill.

• • •

Margaret Chase Smith (1897 – 1995) Maine's Margaret Chase Smith became the first woman to serve in both the House and Senate. As a senator in 1950, she gave her "Declaration of Conscience" speech in opposition to Senator Joseph McCarthy's persecution of anyone suspected of links to the Communist Party. In the mid-40s, she cosponsored the Equal Rights Amendment and broke new ground as the first woman placed in nomination for the presidency by the Republican Party.

• • •

A conservative southern Senator had added sex discrimination to Title VII as a joke and delaying tactic. His stunt backfired when the bill became the law of the land.

But the Equal Employment Opportunity Commission (EEOC) refused to enforce the rules against sex-segregated practices in employment. Employers remained unaware of the law or ignored it for years.

When I hunted for a job in 1966, newspaper ads still listed all high paying jobs under "Help-Wanted: Male." As a result, women began filling the ranks of teachers, nurses, administrators and other "traditional" female occupations.

I encountered a number of sex discriminating practices on job interviews.

In 1966, Dr. Edwin H. Land, the founder of Polaroid, refused to see me for a scheduled interview when he realized I was a woman. I later learned from a friend who worked at Polaroid that Dr. Land became very supportive of female employees by 1969. Too late to help me.

Another personal example of the discrepancy between men and women occurred when I got my first job out of college as a computer programmer. I started with a salary of $4,000. A man hired the same day for the same job got $5,000.

The list goes on. By the late 60s, every interviewer asked, "Are you on birth control?" I failed to get a job with a bank in Portland in 1968. The interviewer told me, "We really don't want to hire a woman."

It took a while, but the job prospects for women changed when businesses introduced affirmative action programs almost a decade after Congress passed Title VII banning sex discrimination.

A New Kind of Organization and New Magazine for Women

In 1968, when protests to the EEOC failed to result in enforcement of Title VII and the EPA, Betty Friedan co-founded the National Organization for Women (NOW). Friedan gained renown when she started the woman's liberation movement with her 1963 book *The Feminine Mystique*. NOW's purpose was "to take action to bring women into full participation in the mainstream of American society now ... in truly equal partnership with men." As a result of pressure from NOW, an EEOC decision ruled sex-segregated want ads were illegal. NOW opened chapters around the country and began supporting "consciousness-raising" efforts where women—and a few men—got together to discuss the problems encountered by women because of their gender. I joined NOW and participated in consciousness-raising meetings.

In 1971, Gloria Steinem co-founded *Ms. Magazine*. The title "Ms." for the magazine came from the new way to identify women. Before "Ms." a woman's title defined her marital status as married, with "Mrs." followed by her husband's name, or single, with "Miss" followed by her surname.

While women's magazines at the time covered topics like saving marriages, raising babies and using the right cosmetics, *Ms. Magazine* addressed more serious issues for women—domestic violence, sexual harassment, date rape and the decriminalization of abortion. *Ms.* also broke new ground when it became the first magazine to rate presidential candidates on their support for women's issues. *Ms. Magazine* continues today as an important resource for women.

I became an early subscriber and read it cover to cover every month. I also began using "Ms." as my title. "Mrs." didn't seem appropriate in a work setting, and, since I wasn't single, neither did "Miss."

Engrossed in Ms. Magazine, 1975

Congress Gets a Conscience with the Civil Rights Act

In 1972, Congress passed Title IX of the Civil Rights Act banning sex discrimination in education. Title IX is best known for requiring equal access for women into college sports programs. But Title IX also gave women access to student aid for professional schools.

Long-time feminist activist and congresswoman Bella Abzug helped to pass Title IX.

• • •

Bella Abzug (1920 – 1998) Famous for wearing wide-brimmed hats to distinguish herself for the firm's secretaries, Bella Abzug began practicing law in the 1940s. She won a seat in Congress and was one of the first to submit a bill in support of gay rights, the Equality Act of 1974. As a prominent feminist activist, she developed the Women's Caucus to get women involved in all phases of planning and development of United Nations conferences.

• • •

I couldn't go to law school right after college in 1966 because of the lack of student aid for women. They might have to let me in but they weren't going to pay me to be there. I began law school in 1975 when I was 31, thanks to Title IX and federal guaranteed student loans.

In 1972, Congress also passed the Equal Rights Amendment (ERA). Its objective: "Equality of rights under the law shall not be denied or abridged by the United States or any State on account of sex." An earlier version had been introduced to Congress in 1923. Although the ERA had widespread support, it failed to gain required passage by three-quarters of the states.

To paraphrase Helen Reddy again, we still had a long, long way to go.

The Last Bastion of Male Chauvinism

The more strident women liberationists referred to men who refused to change their attitudes toward women as "male chauvinist pigs." I never used the term. I liked men and had empathy for people who, all of a sudden, discovered their world had changed.

In 1985, I attended a tax seminar given by several major accounting firms. By coincidence, that morning the newspaper had a story with the headline, "Major Accounting Firms: The Last Bastion of Male Chauvinism." One speaker talked about the article. He spoke about the good opportunities for women in the accounting firms where his daughter now worked. But he said, "There are few experienced women in the pipeline for advancement into the ranks of management."

I met him at the break and told him I had been part of first group of female tax specialists hired by a major accounting firm in the mid-70s. I explained that, after a few months, I still hadn't learned about their training programs. So I asked a senior tax specialist about it. He told me about the requirements to get a Master of Laws (LL.M) in Taxation at Boston University and to become a Certified Public Accountant (CPA).

While all the men had received this information, the women hadn't. I went to the man in charge of administration and told him he needed to give the same information to the women. I ended my story by telling the seminar speaker, "And that is why there are so few experienced women in the pipeline."

Women and Their Influence on the Law

In the 80s and 90s, women made up a small but growing minority in the legal profession. In 1981, President Ronald Reagan appointed the first woman to the Supreme Court, Sandra Day O'Connor. She served as the sole woman on the Court for more than a decade until President William Clinton appointed Ruth Bader Ginsberg in 1993.

Justice O'Connor retired in 2005. We now have three female justices on the Supreme Court thanks to President Barack Obama. He appointed two female justices: Justice Sonia Sotomayor in 2009 and Justice Elena Kagan in 2010, still a minority of three, but a very articulate, vocal minority who would be heard.

By the 90s, women had begun making inroads in the state courts. For the first time in the history of the Massachusetts Appeals Court, an all-woman panel of appellate judges sat on the bench together. The justices sit in panels of three and rotate, so the composition of a panel changes on a regular basis. At one point on that same day, women made up all of the key participants—the three justices, the clerk, the court officer and the two attorneys.

But women remained a small minority of the tax lawyers. After I entered private practice in 1985, I joined the International Fiscal Association (IFA) to find experts in the tax laws of other countries. IFA's membership—5,000 when I joined but now more than 10,000—consists of international tax lawyers and accountants from over 90 countries. At the very first meeting I attended, the Global Congress in Amsterdam in 1988, of the 1,500 participants only 15 of us were female.

At the conference I became friendly with a female lawyer from Bogota, Columbia. She was a very pretty, young woman and a divorcee. A persistent tax lawyer from Cyprus pursued her, so she drafted me to serve as her chaperone. I'm not a night person, but wherever she went after hours I remained with her, much to her pursuer's annoyance. I did my job well and kept him at bay for the duration of the conference.

While the ranks of women in accounting firms have grown, women still comprise less than a third of tax lawyers.

Our law firm, Vacovec, Mayotte & Singer may have had the distinction as the first law partnership in the Greater Boston area, other than women only firms, with a female majority—Maureen Mayotte and me. In 1990, the firm had the opportunity to have the firm's name affixed to a room in the rehabbed Massachusetts Bar Association headquarters. Our partner Ken Vacovec was the association's president that year. As a nod to the "traditional" role of women, Maureen and I chose the kitchen. I sent our choice to the MBA with the message "… in recognition of the fact that, at a time when there were few female partners in area law firms, Ken Vacovec had guts enough to have two of them." Female lawyers represent only about 20 percent of equity partners in law firms today.

A Pushback on Affirmative Action

In the 90s, twenty years after affirmative action policies had been implemented, men began to view themselves as victims of these policies.

Businesses and colleges adopted affirmative action policies in the 70s to give special consideration to groups who had been excluded from opportunities because of their sex or race. After Union Mutual implemented their policy, a vice president told me I had been identified as one of the women qualified for advancement into upper management. I told him, "You're two years too late. I sold my house and I'm leaving for law school." I began planning for law school two years before when I learned I didn't get a management job because two men reporting to the position refused to work for a woman. I had gone too far to turn back.

In 1995, my law partner Ken Vacovec voiced his support for affirmative action when he was interviewed by *Lawyers Weekly* as president-elect of the Massachusetts Bar Association. Ken and the MBA supported affirmative action, but the interviewer did not. The paper published two editorials the following week, one against and one for affirmative action.

The author of the first letter, a long-standing MBA member, described affirmative action as "dubious exercises in allocating individual rights from one person to another based on a 'pseudo protected status.'" He was critical of Governor William Weld's nomination of Margaret H. Marshall to the Supreme Judicial Court. He described Weld as dangling "only female and minority candidates from his pool of potential nominees before he ultimately fished a white female out of the barrel."

At the time she was appointed, Margaret Marshall was Harvard University's general counsel, the first woman to hold that position. Not a bad "catch" by the governor!

• • •

Margaret Marshall (1944 –) Born in South Africa, Margaret Marshall moved to the United States to escape political persecution. She was the second woman appointed to the Massachusetts Supreme Judicial Court, the oldest court in the United States. She served as chief justice for 11 years, the first woman to hold that position in its 300-year history. During her 14 years on the bench, she wrote more than 300 opinions, many of them groundbreaking.

• • •

The second letter was mine—"Vacovec's Partner Defends Affirmative Action." I explained the reasons for the policy with a litany of the discrimination I had faced. I made it clear I didn't support quotas noting, "In the 1970s, my law school limited the number of female students with a 25-percent quota." I ended with, "When quality public education is available once again for those among us who lack other educational opportunities and employers make their decisions based on merit, we will no longer need affirmative action remedies and programs. Until then we do."

My law school dean took me to task for my quota comment. But I had the statistics to back up my statement and sent them to him. I still have those statistics.

Without that quota, law school classes following the passage of Title IX might have had a majority of women, many of them older. As it was, there were only two women over 30 in my law school class, and I was one of them. One of the lucky ones.

CHAPTER 3

Women Need Not Apply

I am thankful for all of those who said no to me. It's because of them I'm doing it myself.

– Albert Einstein

Along with the diploma I received when I graduated from the University of Maine in Orono in 1966 came the burden of student loan debt. Although $2,200 might not seem high today, it exceeded 50 percent of the salary for my first job.

Today, 70 percent of young people leave school with student loan debt of on average $35,000. In 1966 the percent of those with student debt was so small it wasn't even tabulated. Most often, the few students with loans owed only a few hundred dollars. But I had so many loans they had to list some in the margins of the debt summary I received from the university. I would be over 40 when I made the final payment on my undergraduate and law school loans.

I became desperate to find a job. It didn't matter that I graduated in the top of my class. As a woman seeking employment, I soon discovered a barrier that kept high-level jobs beyond my reach.

Job Opportunities Were Segregated by Sex

I was surprised and frustrated when I checked the classified section of the Boston newspapers and discovered the ads segregated by sex. Jobs under "Female" listed positions for teachers, nurses, secretaries and Girl-Friday administrative positions. Jobs for "Male" offered all the good, higher-paying jobs with career potential.

In my first week of searching, I answered an ad for the best "female" position, a Girl-Friday job and managed to get an interview. It wasn't my first preference for employment. But I felt it offered a hope for advancement once I proved my abilities. As part of the interview I had to take a typing test. I could type but not fast enough. Worse, I didn't take shorthand.

Hollywood showcased the plight of intelligent women relegated to lower level jobs in the comedy *9 to 5*, starring Jane Fonda, Lily Tomlin and Dolly Parton.

• • •

Dolly Parton (1946 –) The most honored female country singer, Dolly Parton is also a songwriter, businesswoman, humanitarian, author and actress. She starred with Jane Fonda and Lily Tomlin in the 1980 film *9 to 5*, as office workers who take revenge on their sexist, egotistical, lying and hypocritical bigot boss. Her record "9 to 5" was a hit song that year. The movie struck a nerve with working women and made it one of the 20 highest grossing comedies, earning $3.9 million in its first week.

• • •

The woman interviewer sensed my frustration. She told me, "With your college grades you should be looking for a higher level job." I felt encouraged when she gave me the name of an employment agency. With high hopes I made an appointment for the next day.

My enthusiasm faded when I got to the agency. It consisted of two rooms on the second floor of an old building. The secretary greeted me and led me into the next room where she introduced me to a disheveled older man with fly-away hair and wire-rimmed glasses. He took a quick glance at my resume and wasted no time getting right to business. As I sat down, he explained the arrangement and said, "You'll pay my fee from your first salary check."

It sounded reasonable enough. I thought, "I hope he has some good openings." He did.

I watched as his fingers flipped though his card file of potential employers. He paused each time he found a job with qualifications matching my credentials and muttered without looking up at me, "They won't interview a woman."

At last he found two prospects. He arranged for interviews that week.

He scheduled my first interview at the Polaroid Corporation in Cambridge. The position looked promising: executive assistant to Dr. Erwin Land, the company's founder and president. I arrived at Polaroid's impressive art deco building on Memorial Drive and thought, "This would be a great place to work."

Dressed in my only suit, I walked up the steps to the entrance. Just as I opened the door, a young woman grabbed the door and blocked my entry. Somewhat embarrassed, she told me, "Dr. Land refuses to interview a woman."

Stunned and without saying a word, I turned and walked back down the steps. I wondered if this is the kind of impenetrable barrier I would continue to encounter as a woman looking for a high-level job. I still relive that painful memory whenever I drive by that building.

Years later on a train to New York City, by coincidence, I shared a seat with a singer with the Metropolitan Opera. We swapped stories about the lingering prejudices and unfairness toward women in the workplace. I told her about my appalling experience at Polaroid. To my amazement she said, "I can tell you who got that job. My brother!" What are the odds of such a meeting?

My second interview was scheduled with John Hancock Insurance Company at 9:00 a.m. the following day. I arrived on time with the upsetting Polaroid experience still fresh in my mind. I introduced myself to the Personnel Department receptionist. She phoned the personnel officer and told him I had arrived for my appointment. She hung up and said, "He is very busy and can't see you now."

I settled in a seat in the reception area and began reading a book I brought with me. Every hour or so, I walked over to the receptionist to remind her about my appointment. Each time she told me the personnel officer was busy and would fit me in as soon as possible. At noon, I think she took pity on me and invited me to have lunch with her in the company cafeteria.

Finally, at 4:00 p.m., wanting to avoid the MTA during rush hour and not willing to give up, I walked over and asked the receptionist to make an appointment for the next day. She checked with the personnel officer and said, "Oh, he can see you now."

I guess he figured I wasn't going to go away. When I entered his office, he stood up, greeted me and managed an apology, "I'm sorry for keeping you waiting."

I said, "That's OK. I read *Moby Dick*."

He glared at me and said, "Are you being sarcastic?"

I said, "No. I started reading *Moby Dick* on the T this morning and finished it while waiting." I took the book out of my purse to show him. "You didn't expect me to sit out here from 9 in the morning till 4 o'clock doing nothing did you?"

The interview went downhill from there.

I "Bridge" New Programming Opportunities

The next day I met with my employment agent and described the disastrous two interviews. I said, "You didn't tell them I'm a woman, did you?"

He shrugged and said, "They didn't specify a man, and you have the credentials they wanted."

Holding my tongue in check, I replied, "Do me a favor. Tell them I'm a woman before you set up an interview. Otherwise, I'm going to waste a lot of time." He scheduled my next interview at New England Mutual Life Insurance Company for the following Monday. He told them I was a woman.

The interview went well, and I felt thrilled when they offered me a job in the Personnel Department. But the personnel officer said, "We need computer programmers. We don't have enough applicants to fill the growing number of jobs." I assumed he meant men. "From what I see on your resume, I'm sure you can do the job."

I didn't even know what a computer was. At the time, almost no one did. Eager to try anything I agreed to interview with the vice president of Data Processing. He was a young man in his early 30s. I sat and waited while he scanned my resume. He leaned back in his chair sizing me up. I expected him to ask me traditional questions of applicants like what my goals and aspirations were and how I could help the company. Instead he said, "I see you've listed bridge as a hobby."

Surprised and a little relieved, I said, "Yes, I played bridge several times a week in college."

He began questioning me about bidding conventions. "Do you play Blackwood?"

I said, "Yes."

He said, "Describe it."

Without missing a beat I explained, "It's a four-no-trump bid used to ask your partner for the number of aces in his hand. A response of five clubs means zero or four aces. Five diamonds means one ace, five hearts means two and five spades means three."

He smiled and said, "Yes. Very good."

To my delight we had a spirited chat about the intricacies of playing bridge for a few minutes. At last, he got around to describe the duties of a computer programmer. I told him, "This all sounds new to me, but I believe I have the skills to learn the job. Given the opportunity, I'm sure I could do very well."

I must have impressed him enough because Personnel offered me the computer programmer trainee position. They also said they would keep the job in the Personnel Department open for me for three months in case I changed my mind. I didn't.

I was elated when they told me my annual salary would be $4,000. Strange as it seems, thanks to my knowledge of bridge, I began my computer career.

We Moved Back to Maine

In 1966, both my husband Wayne and I had found jobs we liked in Boston. Me at New England Mutual. Wayne at Hayden Stone, a brokerage house. Later that year Wayne had an offer to transfer to his company's office in Portland, Maine, so we decided to start a family. We found a place to live in Kennebunk.

We decided it would be best if I continued working at New England Mutual while he trained in New York City. I arranged to live with friends in Tewksbury. By then I was pregnant and could only work through my sixth month of pregnancy. State law didn't allow me to work longer.

Two events would change society's view of pregnant women. One: The Supreme Court struck down a law requiring pregnant teachers to leave work after their third month. The second: Lucille Ball's *I Love Lucy* episodes showed her pregnant and about to give birth.

• • •

Lucille Ball (1911 – 1989) Best known for her television show *I Love Lucy*, Lucille Ball started at RKO in B-movies. She became the first women to own a production company, *Desilu*, co-owned with her husband and co-star Desi Arnez. Desilu produced other TV shows including *Star Trek* and *Mission Impossible* and laid the groundwork for syndication. She broke new ground as an actress, both by depicting her multicultural marriage—Desi was "Hispanic"—and her very real pregnancy in historic *I Love Lucy* episodes.

• • •

I moved back to Kennebunk and Wayne joined me two months later. Our daughter Beth was born that November.

Serious problems arose when Beth was six months old. Wayne had an emergency stay at a hospital, and we had bills we couldn't pay. Bill collectors began to call us.

I realized I had to go back to work fast to pay the bills. So I contacted the owner of the Sundial Hotel, a summer hotel at Kennebunk Beach where I had worked during high school, and got a job as a chambermaid. I started my day at 8:30 in the morning. I took a second job as a waitress at Nunan's Lobster Hut in Cape Porpoise. Cape Porpoise is a picturesque section of Kennebunkport with a working fishermen's dock. It was the site of a minor naval skirmish near the end of the American Revolutionary War.

The days were long and exhausting. I didn't have a car, so Wayne dropped me at the Sundial before he went to work in Portland. Captain Nunan, the owner of the Lobster Hut, picked me up there just before lunch and gave me a ride to the restaurant. Without a ride home between lunch and dinner, I sat at a booth and read. Wayne picked me up around 8:30 p.m. And when he couldn't, Captain Nunan drove me home.

Captain Nunan epitomized an authentic old salt. After years of schooner fishing on the Grand Banks off the coast of Maine, he opened his restaurant in 1953. His business began as a few picnic tables where he served customers boiled lobsters. The first building consisted of an oversized hut. As business improved over the years, he added new sections. The air conditioning consisted of a sprinkler on top of the tarpapered roof.

Captain Nunan wrote the daily per pound price of lobster on a blackboard outside the restaurant. One day he wrote, "Too hot to work." Tourists stopped to take pictures of the sign. While I enjoyed the time off, I missed the tips.

Nunan's had the reputation as the best lobster restaurant in Maine. Word-of-mouth kept business booming. Customers came from all around the country. One visitor from Wisconsin said, "A friend told me if I ever visited Maine, I had to eat lobster at Nunan's."

One night I was waiting on group of six young men. Someone pointed out to me one was George Bush. The Bush family has a summer residence at Walker's Point not far from Nunan's. The group was boisterous and demanding and I was waiting on lots of other customers too. I didn't understand the extent of the disrespect for us year-round residents until a teenage visitor from Canada told me, "You know, summer residents refer to you as 'townies from the bunk.'"

When George asked for more butter, I had become frazzled from all their demands and brought him hard, cold butter patties for his rolls. I plunked down the butter paddies. As I hurried to wait on my other customers, it struck me he probably wanted drawn butter for his lobster, but I didn't have time to correct my error. I don't remember if they left a tip.

When the tourist season ended, Wayne and I decided I should continue to work so we could buy a home. I hoped my skills as a computer programmer would help me get interviews even though I was a woman.

CHAPTER 4

My Family Roots Run Deep

*You don't choose your family.
They are God's gift to you as you are to them.*

– Desmond Tutu

My father and mother, Paul Noyes and Grace Smith Noyes, were born at the turn of the last century. Their families—Noyes and Smith—have deep roots in New England dating to the early 1600s. Several ancestors came over on the Mayflower, including Plymouth Colony governor William Brewster and settlers Thomas Rogers and Stephen Hopkins.

I can trace my father's genealogy back even further. He has royalty in his bloodline. They included Charlemagne, Emperor of the Holy Roman Empire until 814 and England's King John, the archrival in the tales of Robin Hood. But I think my most fascinating ancestor was King John's mother, Eleanor of Aquitaine, wife of Henry II. Katherine Hepburn portrayed her in the 1968 movie *The Lion In Winter*.

• • •

Katherine Hepburn (1907 – 2003) Named the greatest female star in Hollywood history by the American Film Institute, Katherine Hepburn became the epitome of the "modern woman." On and off the screen she demonstrated her intelligence and independence. She displayed her assertive personality by wearing trousers long before they became fashionable for women. She won four academy awards for Best Actress including for her portrayal of Eleanor of Aquitaine in *The Lion In Winter*.

• • •

Eleanor of Aquitaine lived to age 82. Historians claim she had a youthful look all her life. I think I got her genes. I'm flattered when people show surprise when they learn my age and say I look at least 10 years younger.

My father told me his mother was one-half Passamaquoddy Indian, one of the Wabanaki tribes of New England. During King Philip's War (1675-1678), the Wabanakis captured Smith ancestors in the raids called the York Massacres and forced them to go to Canada. While some stayed with the Indian tribe in Canada, others preferred to become "redeemed" to Maine.

My grandmother's Indian ancestry was evident from old photos. She had jet black hair and high cheekbones. I inherited her high cheek bones and deeper Indian skin coloring. My friends refer to these characteristics as my "unusual physiognomy." My grandmother had a college education at a normal school, the term for a teacher's college at the time. A remarkable feat for a woman in the late 1800s. Another pioneering trait I inherited from her: sailing into uncharted waters.

My mother had an unusual story about when the nurse in the hospital brought me to her. She told the nurse I couldn't be her baby because I didn't look like the other newborn infants. I had a much darker complexion. It took some convincing, but the nurse assured my mother I was her child. Later I grew blond curls, and my mother felt better because I didn't look so different.

My Father's Family

My father was a direct descendent of Nicolas Noyes, who sailed from England to America in 1634 with his brother James. Along with other passengers on the ship they founded Newbury, Massachusetts. Many descendants of the two Noyes brothers still live there.

Another settler on that same ship, Percival Lowell, is also an ancestor. Lowell was one of the 600 descendants of the royal families of Europe who settled in the United States. The city of Lowell, Massachusetts bears his name.

My father grew up in Hancock, Massachusetts with his seven siblings. He saw considerable family tragedy in his younger years. His oldest brother fought in World War I and died of mustard gas poisoning after returning home. A younger brother died in a motor cycle accident. His mother was institutionalized for seizures, a condition treatable today with medication. She died after 20 years in an institution and is buried on its grounds in a grave marked only by a number.

My father, front center, with his mother, father and five siblings

After his father died, my father came to Maine with four siblings. He was 17. My father and a sister went to live with an aunt. Two younger siblings went to live at the Home for Little Wanderers. I never knew any of my father's siblings.

As I grew up, I saw my father as a hardworking and industrious man. He had a natural intelligence, even though he never graduated from high school. He told me when he reached 10 years old he went to work to help support the family. This became a common practice in the early half of the 20th century when child labor was legal. His school teacher tutored him through eighth grade.

My Mother's Family

My mother's families, the Smiths, and the Lombards on her mother's side, both have long histories in Maine. The Smiths settled on the ocean in Biddeford Pool. The Lombards, who came to Maine from

Touro, Massachusetts, settled on the ocean just across the Saco River in Ferry Beach. My mother's ancestors also include the Newcombs, distant ancestors of President George W. Bush's family.

The Smiths moved inland to farm in Hollis in the late 1700s. Though far removed from the events leading up to the American Revolution, they no doubt learned of the battles of Lexington and Concord and the famous ride of Paul Revere. Lesser known to history, a young seventeen-year-old named Sybil Ludington made a similar ride but much farther. And she didn't get caught by the Red Coats as Revere did.

• • •

> **Sybil Ludington (1761 – 1839)** At age 16, Sybil Ludington became a heroine of the Revolutionary War. When British troops threaten to attacked the area near Danbury, Connecticut, a rider came to warn the farmers. He stopped at the Ludington household because Sybil's father was a colonel of the local militia. Since most members of the Colonel's regiment were farmers away for planting, they needed someone to warn them. The task fell to Sybil who rode twice the distance of Paul Revere's famed ride and managed to gather most of the militia to defend their homes.

• • •

In 1900, my mother's father moved from Hollis to Kennebunk. In 1903, he bought and began operating a dairy on Route 1 named Wonderbrook Farm. A shopping center and small businesses have replaced the farm's meadows of hay with grazing cows. The old farm house still exists, now called the Wonderbrook Center. The restaurant located below the room where my mother was born is now a favorite luncheon spot.

My mother graduated from Kennebunk High School in 1922 and from Gray's Business School in Portland. She became the executive secretary for the two brothers, Sam and Myer Sax, who managed Kesslen Shoe Company, Kennebunk's biggest employer.

My mother's KHS portrait, 1922

She had four siblings: Earl, Harold, Doris and Donald. Harold died of complications from the German measles at age 17. I knew Aunt Doris and her family. We visited with them many times over the years. But I remember visiting Uncle Earl's home in Arundel only once and Uncle Donald's home in Kennebunk only twice.

Our Family

My father met my mother when he worked with the road crew paving Route 1 in Kennebunk. As the paving proceeded north of town, they passed by the dairy farm owned by my mother's father. A courtship developed and they married in 1923. She, age 20. He, age 21. My father went to work for my grandfather delivering milk, cutting and delivering ice, and helping him manage the farm.

My parents were married 19-½ years before they had any children. My sister Barbara was born in 1943. Me, 16 months later. World War II raged around the world and my parents had moved to Kittery. There my father got a job as a machinist working on submarines at the Portsmouth Naval Shipyard.

Both of our birth certificates say we were born in Portsmouth, New Hampshire. In spite of the New Hampshire birth certificate I claim to be a Maine native. In Maine, it doesn't matter how long you've lived in the state, to be a native you have to be born in the state. I remember my mother telling me I was born in the Portsmouth Naval Shipyard Hospital.

Maine and New Hampshire had been fighting for two centuries over which state owns Seavey Island, the location of the Portsmouth Naval Shipyard and Hospital. In 2001, the Supreme Court barred New Hampshire from claiming hundreds of valuable acres and wide expanses of harbor waters from Maine. This decision keeps Seavey Island and the Navy yard in Maine. As a result of that decision, Maine got to collect $5 million to $6 million a year in income taxes from nonresident Navy yard workers. I'm proud to say the case also makes me a Maine native.

Early Entrepreneurs

My father always worked hard and had a variety of jobs over the years. He worked for a newspaper and the railroad. But by the mid-1920s, my father worked for himself. My parents owned Wonderbrook Filling Station which included a way-side stand in a building that used to be the farm's creamery. Their business card read, "Pan-AM Oil and Gas: ice cream, drinks, and light lunches." It was the first gas station in Kennebunk and the only gas station on Route 1 between the New Hampshire border and Portland for some time, so business was very good.

Wonderbrook Wayside Stand and Filling Station about 1928

During prohibition Maine made an excellent entry point for smuggled booze because of the state's many isolated coves and inlets. One prominent Kennebunk family made their fortune bootlegging. Many bootleggers transported their illegal cargo down Route 1 and out of state by car.

My father told us about the time a large, black car pulled into the station. Two suspicious looking men got out and proceeded to take the car apart as my parents watched from inside the building. They unloaded boxes of booze, took the Coke out of the big, red cooler outside the building, put the booze in the cooler and covered it with the Coke. Then they put the car back together.

A short time later a police car pulled in and two policemen got out. They took the bootlegger's car apart looking for the booze. When they didn't find anything, the policemen left. After the police disappeared down the road, the bootleggers reloaded the car with the booze and put the Coke back in the cooler. After they left, my father found a $20 bill—almost two weeks' pay—on top of the Coke in the cooler.

In 1928, the station achieved so much success Pan-AM Oil and Gas convinced them to take out a mortgage to expand the station. A short time later disaster struck. The stock market crashed in 1929. No one traveled, so no one bought gas. They lost the business and filed for bankruptcy. They never recovered their financial independence.

Tough Times

When times were tough—and they were until I was 12—I heard my father complain about the burden of having two children. It didn't help that, by the time I was four, I had grown as big as my sister, so I couldn't wear hand-me-downs. I remember it being a financial crisis whenever my parents needed to buy us new winter coats and boots.

My sister Barbara and me, 1948

My father always said he wanted a boy, but he got me instead. My parents named me Paula after him. I felt like an unwanted burden. He told me this story of my introduction to my sister more than once: When my mother came home from the hospital and entered the room carrying me, my sister Barbara, who had not yet walked unaided, got up from the floor and walked away from my mother and me and over to him. I guess she didn't want me either. Years later when my daughter Beth looked through my old photos, she remarked, "You weren't smiling in any of the pictures!"

I replied, "I didn't have much to smile about."

After the Japanese bombed Pearl Harbor on December 7, 1941, my father volunteered for the army. He was 38, the oldest age for the military service. The Navy yard called the draft board and asked them not to take him because they needed skilled machinists. So the army didn't induct him.

After the war ended, the work at the Navy yard dried up, and my father lost his job. Congress passed veterans' preference legislation, so he got passed over by veterans when jobs became available at the Navy yard again.

My father faced two major disadvantages whenever he applied for a job—his lack of a high school education and age. Many companies practiced age discrimination back then. Even though he had an excellent work record, when he applied for construction work on the expansion of the Kennebunk schools, he couldn't get the job. At the time, he didn't have enough money to join the labor union. He took what jobs he could find, including menial jobs. He bagged groceries at the local IGA or was unemployed. He depleted his pension savings from the Navy yard to pay our living expenses.

Once, we depended on general assistance from the town for our food and utilities. People called us "being on the town." More than once the electricity company turned off our power for nonpayment. One time my sister and I paid the bill with our meager savings, mostly in change. After the water company installed a meter requiring quarters to keep the water running, my father got in trouble for using a slug when the meter stopped working.

By the time my father went back to work regularly as a machinist at the Navy yard in 1951, he was heavily in debt to a finance company. Following his layoff in 1955, he finally found work again in 1956 at Pratt & Whitney in Connecticut. He lived in a boarding house and commuted home with fellow workers on weekends. His employer provided training classes for new employees. He wrote in a post card, "I got a 100 in math last night...and was the only one that got a 100." At 54 he was second oldest in the class.

My father returned to work as a machinist at the Portsmouth Naval Shipyard in 1957. At age 56, he needed to read the blueprints for the submarines to keep his job, so I taught him algebra. With his quick mind, he picked up the concepts with ease.

After he took the shipyard required physical, which included an X-ray, the doctor advised him to visit his family doctor. The X-ray showed he had a shadow on his lung. He didn't have a family doctor and couldn't afford to stay out of work, so he never got the check-up.

When he was 58, management moved him to a lower paying janitor's job. Showing his spunk and determination, he filed a complaint with the Labor Relations Board. The board decided in his favor, and he got his machinist job back.

In 1963, the nuclear submarine Thresher left the Portsmouth Naval Yard on sea trials. The submarine and all 129 seamen aboard were lost, a disaster that still remains a mystery. After the tragedy the yard downsized and my father lost his job again. He was 62 and eligible for a small Social Security benefit. By then he also suffered from lung cancer. To get money to pay living expenses, my mother went to work at the local dry cleaners and sold my father's tools.

My father died less than a year later. He left my mother at 61 with little income and no assets and with no family who could help. It was just my mother, my sister and me. Barbara was married, pregnant and living out of state. I was a full-time student in my junior year at the University of Maine in Orono and married to my first husband, Wayne, also a full-time student. We both lived on student aid.

After my father's funeral on a Saturday, my mother told me, "I don't have the $50 for next month's rent." It was due on Monday. I spoke with Wayne and he agreed she could come to live with us. We had a three-room apartment in Orono. We sold, stored, threw out or gave away the furniture and remaining possessions.

My mother stayed with Wayne's family for a month then packed her clothes and the few things she would bring to Orono.

This became the uncertain start of a new phase of her life living with us.

CHAPTER 5

Growing Up In Kennebunk:
The Only Village in the World So Named

Poverty makes you sad as well as wise.

– Bertolt Brecht

I had the good fortune to grow up in Kennebunk, Maine. We moved to Kennebunk in 1947 when I was three and my sister Barbara was four. Kennebunk was a solid middleclass town with many wealthy benefactors. Prominent families like the Parsons, Lords and Bournes made their fortunes as ship builders and business men involved with international trade. Their generosity gave the town the library, the Park Street School (the original high school), a playground, public access to Parsons Beach and even a museum.

As you enter Kennebunk, you can see a wooden sign with the inscription "Welcome to Kennebunk, the only village in the world so named." Kennebunk became incorporated in 1820, the same year Maine became the 23rd state as part of the Missouri Compromise.

Two rivers play an important part of Kennebunk's history. The Mousam River passes through the center of town and once served as the source of power for a manufacturing plant that employed hundreds of workers. The Kennebunk River separates Kennebunk and

Kennebunkport. Along its banks, from the Landing to the river's mouth, are the remnants of the many boat yards where sea merchants built more than 200 ships during the heyday when square riggers and schooners sailed the world.

One of the most photographed buildings in the county, "The Wedding Cake House," has become a popular tourist attraction of Kennebunk. Captain George W. Bourne built the house in 1825 in the classic Federal design. He added a lattice canopy and supporting buttresses that gave the building an impression of a wedding cake. While the inspiration for the building's intricate decoration came from Bourne's fascination with Gothic Revival Cathedrals in Europe, another more romantic legend persists. The often repeated story has a sea captain leaving his bride on their wedding night to go off to sea. On his return, to make amends for leaving his bride, he created the house in the style of a wedding cake. This legend has no basis in fact, but it's a better story.

The Week Maine Burned

While the history of Kennebunk is rich in tradition and folklore, my first memory of Kennebunk isn't a good one. It became known as the "Great Fires of 1947."

After a severe drought through that summer, the Maine Forest Service reported scattered fires in October. The dry conditions helped the fire spread until it destroyed more than 200,000 acres of land and hundreds of homes. Much of York County and—farther up the coast—all of Bar Harbor burned down.

At the time, we lived in Garrett's Cabins on Route 1 just south of town. Officials told us to be ready to evacuate as the fire approached. My father worked at the water pumping station in Biddeford and couldn't leave his post. He had to keep the water flowing.

Barbara and I prepared to walk out with our mother, our clothes and dolls packed in our two little blue doll carriages.

I remember seeing cars and trucks crammed with passengers and pets, their belongings strapped to the roof, escaping from neighboring towns. Thick black smoke filled the air. I started to have trouble breathing and became very ill. To this day I am sensitive to smoke. We were lucky because the fire stopped before it reached Kennebunk. But the fire burned down parts of Cape Porpoise and Goose Rocks Beach in neighboring Kennebunkport to the east, plus much of Biddeford and towns inland.

Men and young boys fought the fires with water pumped by hand from fire trucks or heavy metal tanks strapped onto their backs. Thousands lost everything but their lives. Lyman, the town where I now live, burned down. A dairy farm on our road lost 200 cows along with all the buildings. Only a few buildings in the town survived. By some miracle, the fire spared a huge apple tree on our property, although it has a burned out cavity big enough for a man to stand in as a reminder of the catastrophe.

The harrowing stories of the fires and those who fought and survived them are recounted in the book *Wildfire Loose, The Week Maine Burned* by local historian Joyce Butler.

We Didn't Have Much

Most Kennebunk residents owned their own homes, but we never did. By the time I left for college in 1962, we had lived in eight different apartments or cabins in Kennebunk. Most had no central heating. We had a big black Glenwood stove in the kitchen for heat. We shut off the living room, when we had one, to save heat during the winter.

I had lived in six places in other towns before 1947 and in three more towns when I lived away from Kennebunk with Wayne, my first husband. By 1976, when I married my second husband, Gary Singer, and we moved to Cumberland, I had lived in 14 different places in Kennebunk. Years later when I took a neuro-linguistics course, the instructor gave me the task to describe the front door of the home where I grew up. I couldn't.

We had a car until I was five—a Studebaker. I remember riding in it and falling asleep leaning up against my father. But my most vivid memory of that car was the day two men arrived at our door to repossess it. I stood in the screen door and watched them drive away with our car. My parents never had enough money to buy another car, or to pay for other modern conveniences such as a telephone. We got a telephone when my sister joined the Navy after high school.

I remember my mother's response if I whined, "It just isn't fair!" when I couldn't go somewhere because I didn't have a ride.

"Whoever told you this life was going to be fair?" she said. Regardless of the hardships my mother faced, I never heard her complain. I learned to stop complaining from her example. And I stopped saying "can't," too. Whenever I said "can't," she reminded me what her mother told her whenever she said "can't." "Can't is an animal in South America."

What I Couldn't Do

Most of my memories of the years before I reached 12 came under the heading "what I couldn't do." I also remember how I found creative ways to adjust and compensate for these shortcomings.

I couldn't play a musical instrument. My parents couldn't afford to buy one. But when I was in seventh grade, the school band needed trombone and horn players so they offered to loan instruments to students who got the highest score on a music test. Based on the results, I got to play the mellophone. When I got to high school, I changed to a French horn. I loved playing in the school band, marching in the parades and performing at the football games. Going with the band for exchange concerts was the most fun I ever had. We traveled as far away as Caribou, more than 300 miles to the top of the state. We'd take the trip in two yellow school buses with all of us singing most of the way.

I couldn't go to Girl Scout summer camp. My parents didn't have the $32 for the camp fee. But when I reached 12, the Baptist Church sent me to church camp in New York. In my senior year of high school, I received the annual scholarship for a week at the Summer Youth Music Camp at the University of New Hampshire. I also was chosen that year as one of three Kennebunk representatives to Girls' State held at Colby College.

As a youngster, I couldn't go to the beach. It was five miles away and the town had no public transportation. My sister and I went to the summer program for children at the Park Street Playground. They took us all on a school bus to the beach once each summer. I remember going to the beach only once or twice with friends. As a result, I didn't learn to swim, and, on one of these outings, I got caught in the undertow and almost drowned. No one saw me. I saved myself by paddling parallel to the beach. The water still frightens me to this day.

At 13, I got a job as a live-in babysitter at Kennebunk Beach and went to the beach every day. I worked there during summers at many different jobs throughout high school. The movie musical *Grease*, starring John Travolta and Olivia Newton-John, about high school teenagers who meet on the beach and fall in love, always reminds me of the happy days I spent at the beach.

• • •

Olivia Newton-John (1948 –) Singer, songwriter, actress and businesswomen, Olivia Newton-John is a breast cancer survivor and environmental and animal rights activist. She was born in England, grew up in Australia and relocated to the United States at the urging of expatriate Australian singer Helen Reddy. She won four Grammy awards, starred in the popular movie *Grease* and became one of the highest selling music artists of all time.

• • •

I couldn't wear nice new clothes. When we were little, my sister and I each had three dresses—one on, one clean and one in the wash. We didn't have Sunday clothes. So our parents decided to send us to the Baptist Church instead of the Congregational Church where my mother's relatives were members. We didn't need Sunday clothes to go to the Baptist church. When I turned 12, I began making my clothes after my father bought us a sewing machine on credit. And I borrowed gowns from friends to wear to the high school proms.

I couldn't eat fresh foods. Fresh food was too expensive. At home, I ate mostly eggs, peanut butter and jelly sandwiches, spaghetti, potatoes, canned vegetables, hot dogs and beans. I still like them all. My diet improved beginning in the third grade and into high school when I worked in the school cafeteria for free lunches. I went to work summers at the beach and began to eat all kinds of new foods to me—fresh fish, shrimp, lobster, fresh fruit and vegetables.

I couldn't go out to eat or even buy a soda with classmates after school. When I did go, one classmate, whose parents were well off, always bought me a soda. I remember going to a restaurant only once before high school. But when I began dating and working at the beach, I went out to restaurants, a real treat.

I couldn't watch television. We didn't have one until I was 12. Once in a while my sister and I would watch Howdy Doody, and later American Bandstand, at a friend's house. But even after my parents bought a television set I continued to read books most of the time.

I also couldn't go to doctors because we owed all three doctors in Kennebunk for prior visits. Visits cost $26 each. As a result, chronic problems such as my periodic ear infections went untreated. According to my doctor, it's the reason for my hearing problems today. But I went to the Kennebunk free clinic for vaccinations required for school. And when I got to college and had medical coverage, I received treatment for my chronic pain problems.

Although I wouldn't compare the hardships I worked through as a youngster with the tragic early life of Dr. Maya Angelou, I admired the courage she had to rise to greatness. Her ability to overcome her difficult childhood has served as an inspiration to many women.

• • •

Dr. Maya Angelou (1928 – 2014) Overcoming being raped at age eight, Dr. Maya Angelou rose to become an admired writer, poet and singer, as well as an actress, director and producer. Defying social convention and the law she entered an interracial marriage in 1951. She worked in the civil rights movement with Martin Luther King Jr. and Malcolm X. In 1993, she recited her poem, *On the Pulse of Morning*, at President William Clinton's inauguration.

• • •

What I Could Do

But there was a lot I could do because I lived in Kennebunk.

I could take books out of the library to read—it was free.

I could walk to town and look in the store windows—it was a beautiful town and still is.

I could go to the movies at the Anchor Theater on weekends—it only cost 10 cents.

I could buy a little toy at the 5 and 10 Cent Store on Fridays—it only cost a nickel.

I could have a cat but not a dog—the landlords didn't allow dogs.

I could play in the snow—we had lots of it.

I could ride my bike in our neighborhoods—our streets were safe.

I could play cards and board games with my sister and friends—we had lots of time with no television.

I could draw and paint—art supplies didn't cost much.

And best of all, I could attend public schools and be taught by wonderful teachers who changed my life.

CHAPTER 6

A Great Public School Teacher

A good teacher can inspire hope, ignite the imagination, and instill a love of learning.

– Brad Henry

My parents moved to Kennebunk so my sister and I could attend the town's public schools. Kennebunk had a great public school system—still does. In a recent survey of public school systems it ranked among the top 10 in Maine, one of the two top-rated states along with California.

I graduated from Kennebunk High School in class of 1962, 40 years after my mother. What makes a school great isn't its facilities—Kennebunk's were old. And it wasn't the class size either—we had two classes, each with 34 students. It's the teachers, and my teachers were the greatest.

I remember in particular our English teachers Miss Dwelley and Mr. Anagnostis—Mr. A for short—and our history teacher Mr. Merrow. It's thanks to Miss Dwelley and Mr. A that I became a good writer. They not only taught us grammar but also how to write. Every Friday we had to write an essay in Mr. A's class. I remember the day he stopped at my desk, picked up my essay and read it aloud in class. He didn't take a breath until he got to a period and then he took several loud breaths. I said, "It's grammatically correct isn't it?" He said, "Yes, but who cares. You have to shorten your sentences." I remember his admonition every time I sit down to write.

But Mr. Merrow did even more for me.

Mr. Merrow—My Inspiration

When my class gets together for reunions, we swap stories about our teachers. One of our reunion stories was about Mr. Merrow. We recalled the time he monitored our study hall in the school's auditorium. He had a regular routine. He would walk out onto the stage, take a folding chair and say, "Achtung peasants! Time to get to work!"

Then he'd open up the chair, sit down, spread open his newspaper and begin to read. One day a couple of the boys positioned a collapsible folding chair for him to take. When he opened it and sat down, his legs went up and his seat went down. We all had a good laugh, even Mr. Merrow. He got up with a smile, said, "OK, peasants, back to work." He found another chair, opened it, picked up his newspaper, sat down and began reading. And we all got back to work.

My class expressed our appreciation for Mr. Merrow by our dedication to him in our high school year book: "To Mr. Merrow ... With sincere esteem for your discerning mind, your ardent enthusiasm, your clever presentation of ideas and your ready wit."

Mr. Merrow had a great sense of humor. Often times, he would start the class with a joke or humorous story that led into the subject he taught that day. He knew it would get our attention and inspire us to become interested in our studies.

He made me laugh in class, but he was concerned I didn't smile much outside of class. He said, "You know, if you smile at people, they'll smile back at you."

Mr. Merrow and the other teachers stood outside their classrooms between classes to monitor the students. When Mr. Merrow saw me coming down the hall he'd get my attention and say, "Smile!" After a while I began to smile in anticipation of seeing him in the corridor. I can thank Mr. Merrow for teaching me how to smile. This was just one way Mr. Merrow changed my life for the better.

The Help I Needed To Go To College

I set my sights on going to college, even though I knew my parents couldn't help me financially. By my senior year, my father had a good income as a machinist at the Portsmouth Naval Shipyard. But he was laid off two years later at age 62 with a small pension. Before I benefited from government programs, the meager funds my father got from Social Security helped to keep him and my mother going. Today, it's difficult to imagine how controversial Social Security was when President Franklin Delano Roosevelt got it passed during the Great Depression. His wife, Eleanor Roosevelt, provided great support for him and, after he died, continued as a powerful champion for minorities and women's causes.

• • •

Eleanor Roosevelt (1884 – 1962) The widow of four-term President Franklin Delano Roosevelt, Eleanor Roosevelt ignored criticism for her support of human rights, children's causes and women's rights. Challenging the traditional passive role of "first lady," she wrote a newspaper column, gave press interviews and traveled the world as an ambassador of good will. She also served as a delegate to the United Nations' General Assembly where she helped write the Universal Declaration of Human Rights.

• • •

My parents never told me I couldn't go to college; they just said they didn't know how I would pay for it. After my 13th birthday, I began to save money for college. My high school math teacher, Mr. Clark, hired me to be his family's live-in babysitter. The Clarks owned the Sundial Hotel on Kennebunk's Middle Beach. By the time I reached 17, I had held almost every job at the hotel—hostess, waitress, chambermaid, laundress, cook's assistant and night clerk. The Clarks even left me in charge of the hotel one weekend when they had to be away on personal business.

I also waited on tables at conferences at the Colony Hotel in Kennebunkport and the Atlantis Hotel in Kennebunk Beach. Mr. Merrow owned the Atlantis with his brother. By my senior year, I had accumulated about $500 dollars in savings, a substantial amount in 1962.

Most of my teachers knew my family was poor. My grade-school teacher, Mrs. Cameron, once gave me some of her daughter's clothes when I was 12. They also knew I wanted to go to college and encouraged me, telling me that, if I studied hard and got good grades, I would get scholarships. I did study hard and got mostly straight A's and lots of honors. I received a $100 scholarship at graduation and a $250 scholarship for each of my first two years from the AAUW.

College recruiters met with the top students to introduce them to their private schools. But my guidance counselor cautioned me I wouldn't be able to afford those schools. She told me the only possible college I would be able to attend would be the University of

Maine in Orono—UMO now UMaine. Several of my classmates planned to go there. The cost for tuition, room and board, books and fees totaled about $1,400. I applied to UMO and sent in my application for student aid.

A Timely Pep Talk

The Saturday morning before I would travel to Boston with Mr. Merrow and two other students for a symposium at Tufts University, I received a letter from UMO. I ripped it open. It had news about my student aid. I didn't receive a scholarship, just a $200 National Defense Education Act (NDEA) loan. I was devastated. When I got in the car for the trip, Mr. Merrow saw how upset I looked and asked what was wrong. I told him, "I can't go to college. I don't have enough money in student aid and savings to make it through my freshman year."

He asked me, "Do you have enough for your first semester?"

I said, "Yes, I do."

He proceeded to give me a pep talk all the way to Boston about what I had to do to get through school. I had to do what he had done. Take it a semester at a time. Work to get the money for the next semester while keeping up with my studies. As I got out of the car at the end of the trip home, Mr. Merrow leaned over to me and said, "I never want to hear that you didn't go to college because you didn't have the money."

Reminiscing

Many years later when my husband, Gary, and I visited friends in Kennebunk, they told us about the ceremony they had attended earlier that week. It recognized Peter Hoff, a Kennebunk High graduate, as Teacher of the Year for Maine. When he accepted the award, Peter told a story about a trip to Boston with Mr. Merrow and two other students. He told about the pep talk Mr. Merrow had given to one of the students during the trip about how to get through college with little or no money.

I said, "That student was me!"

Mr. Merrow's pep talk that day had changed Peter's life too, inspiring him to become a great teacher.

At our 40th class reunion, a group of us, including Peter, reminisced about Mr. Merrow. Peter and I recounted the impact Mr. Merrow's pep talk during that trip to Boston had on both our lives. Another classmate, Eddie Fairfield, who had worked his way through college to become an engineer, said Mr. Merrow had influenced his life too. He and his wife named their twin sons Wesley and Scott for Wescott Merrow.

Mr. Merrow left public school teaching for a position at a small college for better pay a few years after we graduated. When he was our teacher, he received less pay than the head custodian. He had to help his own children get through college too.

I will always be grateful for Mr. Merrow's thoughtful encouragement. Together with my father's example of hard work and my mother's instructions not to complain about life being unfair, I found ways to overcome the many obstacles I encountered. As a determined woman entering the male-dominated business world, they taught me when I needed to tack and when to row.

CHAPTER 7

Being Smart—A Curse or Blessing

*It is not enough to have a good mind;
the main thing is to use it well.*

— Rene Descartes

My battle with the sexes started when I was in grade school in Kennebunk, Maine. I got along with most of the boys in my class, but two older boys bullied me. The best insults they could hurl at me was "Smarty pants," and "You think you're so smart." I didn't want to stoop to their level, so I just bit my lip and walked away. One stopped bullying me when we moved some short distance away.

In our new neighborhood, the second bully took up where the first left off. But I stopped him. As part of his taunting, he chased me down the street. I started to run, but slowed down long enough to grab a rock. I spun around and threw the rock at him. It caught him right in the mouth. He started crying and yelled as he ran away, "I'm going to tell my mother." He never bothered me again.

A Fight Won and Lost

Another incident had a long term effect on me. While in line at the movie theater on Main Street another bully pushed me from behind. I turned around and tackled him. As we fell to the ground in a heap, I sprained my ankle. I felt so much pain my father had to come get me and take me home in a taxi. Years later after a fall, I began to have occasional sharp prolonged pain in my ankle. My doctor had it X-rayed but found nothing wrong. After eight years of recurring pain, my ankle became unstable. I knew I had to get it fixed or I would have more falls.

I changed to a female doctor closer to home in 2005. She sent me right away to a specialist at Brigham and Women's Hospital in Boston. After months of tests—X-rays, CT scans and MRIs—the specialist found I had two holes in my ankle with a very thin bone between my foot and ankle. He said it would break eventually with excruciating pain, and my foot and ankle would fuse together leaving me with a limp. He said he could fix it with a bone transplant.

They gave me both a local and twilight anesthetic, so I was somewhat awake during the surgery. I was surrounded by new resident doctors in training. While I didn't feel any pain, it was a bit unnerving because I heard the doctor sawing my ankle. He transplanted a section of bone and cartilage and secured it with two pins. I couldn't put my weight on it for six weeks. I walked in cast for another six weeks and a space boot for stability for two months. Until then I couldn't drive. Five years later he took the pins out.

What Was All the Fuss About?

I took pride in my high grades and didn't get into trouble at school. So it came as a complete surprise when my parents got a note from my grade school principal. He wanted to speak to them about the results of my IQ test. The week before, the school had given IQ tests to all the students in my class. I couldn't imagine why they wanted to talk to my parents about it. I answered all the questions and thought I had done well.

When my parents got home from the meeting, I expected the worst. My mother smiled, but all she said was, "Nothing wrong. It was just about the results of your IQ test." My parents never told me about the results. They just left me to wonder what the fuss was all about. Over time I figured out my score must be quite high. I can't really take any credit for it. It's a gift I was born with.

Another natural gift I couldn't take credit for was my looks. The picture in my college year book caught a very flattering image.

My college portrait, 1965

So I had compliments on both my appearance and being smart. Women were thought to be either smart or pretty but not both. But some like Hedy Lamarr were both.

• • •

Hedy Lamarr (1914 – 2000) Actress Hedy Lamarr proved women can be both beautiful and bright. From the 1930s to the 1950s she played opposite many Hollywood greats, including Clark Gable, James Stewart and Spencer Tracey. She also co-invented an anti-jamming device for use in radio-controlled torpedoes. The technology is in use today in the U.S. defense satellite system, faxes, cell phones and Wi-Fi. In recognition of her scientific contribution, in 2014 she was posthumously inducted into the *National Inventors Hall of Fame.*

• • •

I never took the Mensa test to find out my IQ score. Mensa International is the organization open to people who score in the 98th percentile or higher on a supervised intelligence test. Even without knowing my IQ score I realized I had an extraordinary ability to solve difficult problems and unravel complex puzzles.

Years later, just for fun, a business colleague sent me a puzzle that involved a few different facts about a row of houses and several people. He asked me to solve the puzzle by answering who owned which house. He also wanted me to tell him how much time it took. I called him when I completed the puzzle and said, "Two and one half minutes. What does it usually take someone?"

He said, "Ten minutes or so if you're good at solving puzzles."

Schools in the 50s Had No Gifted Programs

Since there were no "gifted" programs in school my teachers created special projects to keep me challenged beyond the normal classroom lessons. In one task I handled the banking for the students at my grammar school. Each month, as I sat at a card table, the students lined up, passing me their coins and passbooks as they filed by. I recorded their deposits in the passbooks and a ledger. When I finished, I walked across town to the other grammar school and handled their students' banking as well. I gave all the money and records to a teacher for safe keeping.

I had no trouble earning mostly straight-A grades all through school—except for the B+ in solid geometry my senior year of high school. Researchers say women are not as good as men at spacial concepts. They're right. I defer to men on that skill. I had to work hard for that B+.

I graduated from Kennebunk High School in 1962, first in a class of 81 students. I delivered the valedictory address. I remember how my father beamed with pride in the audience surrounded by the other parents. Some Kennebunk residents looked down on him as a "renter." They said he didn't contribute to the town because he didn't pay property taxes. Well, he showed them. He had the smartest kid in the class. I almost felt guilty, because it seemed so easy.

One of the down sides of being so smart was the boys in my class seemed intimidated by me. Years later at a high school reunion, a group of them gathered around me, and one of them asked why I never dated any of them. I said, "I would have dated you, but none of you ever asked me out." My dates usually were boys from a nearby towns or private schools in Massachusetts.

Where Was the Competition?

When I started at the University of Maine in the fall of 1962, I expected to face stiffer competition. But in my freshman year, my logic teacher stopped me after class and asked, "Did you study set theory in high school?"

I said, "Yes."

He said, "As you know, we grade on a scale, where the highest score gets an 'A' and the lowest fails. You're creating a problem for the rest of my students. I've got to drop you from the grading scale in order to pass the other students."

I had a similar situation with the professor who taught the history survey course, two classes of 60 students each. He gave me the only 'A'. I heard he got in trouble with the administration and had to change the scale to give out higher grades to more students.

Even though I took an overload of credits while working 20 hours a week, I still received the highest grade point average my junior year, a 4.0 for each semester. Two other students got the same high grade. We split a $60 merit scholarship. It had been established at the turn of the century and was the only merit scholarship I ever received. I got the $20 check four months after I graduated. I used it to buy a sweater.

While I enjoyed writing for class work and had been an editor of my high school yearbook, I lacked time to write for the college newspaper or yearbook. If a law practice had not been my overriding goal, I might have followed a career more open to women such as writing or journalism. Many barriers for women had already been broken by female authors and journalists such as Martha Gelhorn.

• • •

Martha Gelhorn (1908 – 1998) Considered the best war correspondent of the 20th century, Martha Gelhorn reported on conflicts around the world in her 60-year career. In 1936, she met Ernest Hemingway and travelled with him to cover the Spanish Civil War. Their turbulent relationship is recounted in the 2012 movie *Gelhorn and Hemingway*. She was the only female correspondent to land at Normandy on D-Day, June 6, 1944. Lacking press credentials because she was a woman, she hid in a hospital ship bathroom. Upon landing she pretended to be a stretcher bearer.

• • •

I graduated from the University of Maine in January 1966, a semester early. I traveled back to the campus in the spring for my initiation into Phi Beta Kappa, the nation's oldest academic honor society.

I thought I would face even more competition in law school. But nine years later when I took the law school aptitude test (LSAT), I had time to go through each section a second time to check my answers—except for the section on three-dimensional graphs. My personal challenge with spacial concepts again. Most other test takers only had time to go through each section once. Not all could finish every section.

As an undergraduate, I had asked Professor Mawhinney, the pre-law advisor, about getting into law school. He advised me, "If they let you in, they won't give you any student aid." He knew about the restrictions for women applicants. Few women were accepted by law schools back then, and those who were didn't need financial aid. So I had to put off law school.

In 1974, when I took the LSAT exam, it was after Congress had passed Title IX opening up financial aid for women at professional schools. I wrote to Professor Mawhinney for advice again about law schools. He wrote back, "With your LSAT score of 681 and a grade point average of 3.8 you're in an enviable application position!" He went on to say, "The fall LSAT in October for some reason hit our students very hard. Students taking the examination the second time tumbled heavily in their scores. First-time takers did not come off well for the most part."

I felt elated. I knew they had to let me in. I applied to the University of Maine School of Law and got accepted.

Another example of my gift for analytical thinking occurred during law school in 1975. At orientation, the professor told our class, "The law program here is very demanding. Be prepared to spend at least three hours of study for each hour of class."

A few weeks later during a break with my classmates, I asked them, "When are they going to give us all the work they told us to expect? So far it only takes me 45 minutes for each class, not three hours."

An annoyed classmate piped up, "Well, maybe it only takes *you* 45 minutes, but it takes the rest of us three hours."

I had been dealing with complex analyses as a computer programmer and systems analyst for 10 years. I was like a trained athlete but with my mind, not my body. By our last year, my classmates had honed their analytical skills but still couldn't work as fast as I could.

It seemed like history repeating itself when I took the bar exam in Maine. I finished each morning and afternoon sessions—essay one day and multistate questions the next—one-half to an hour early. Others struggled through to the end.

Six of my male classmates and I arranged to take the bar in Massachusetts as well. We traveled to Boston right after the multistate exam, staying together in an apartment in Cambridge. We studied Massachusetts law late into the night. During the morning essay session of the bar, even though a bit bleary-eyed from the late-night studying, I finished 45 minutes early. I and one male lawyer exited the room where hundreds of lawyers still slaved over the essays. I wondered, "Where is all the Ivy League competition?"

I soon discovered the Ivy League competition didn't come from *doing* the job; it came from *getting* the job.

CHAPTER 8

More Exceptional Gifts

"Toto, I've a feeling we're not in Kansas anymore."

– Dorothy in The Wizard of Oz

I discovered a second gift while still in middle school—a photographic memory. My teacher assigned, as homework, the task of memorizing the "Friends, Romans, Countrymen, lend me your ears" speech from Shakespeare's *Julius Caesar*. I placed the speech beside my plate at supper and had it memorized when I finished eating.

When I entered college as a freshman, I became one of a group of about 40 students chosen at random to take a battery of tests for analytical skills and memory. The administration wanted to study the correlation between the skills students had when they first entered college and their educational outcomes. One test required us to memorize a list of 10 three-letter nonsensical words, memorize a second set of 10, and then recall the first set. I was the only one of the group who could accomplish this task.

Years later at a meeting with several accountants, we discussed the complex rules for payments to foreign nationals studying or working in the United States and the intricate tax implications they faced. After I walked them through the various tax rules and procedures, one of the accountants said, "You have a photographic memory don't you?"

I replied, "Yes."

She said, "That's why you can do this type of work and we can't. There are so many ins and outs of the rules and procedures to follow. We get lost in the analysis because we can't remember them all."

I said, "It's easy for me because I can visualize the flowcharts in my head and remember the path through them."

A Prodigious Memory Made Life Easier

Another time after I worked through a complex tax situation with a client and proposed a creative solution for his tax problem he said, "Did you know you're both left-and right-brained?" I didn't.

I didn't even know what it meant. I learned left-brained people are organized and systematic; right-brained people are creative and intuitive. I always follow my intuition, although my other gifts helped me when I needed to organize my thoughts.

Perhaps this explains another skill pointed out by a Windstar employee. While typing out a report, I answered a question she asked me. After a moment she said, "How do you do that?"

I said, "Do what?"

She said, "Type while you're talking to me."

Puzzled, but pleased she made me aware of my "multitasking trick," I said, "I don't know."

I also seem to have an eidetic memory—the ability to recall scenes, images and objects with precision. Although such a memory is said to be nonexistent in adults, the memories of the stories I tell in this memoir come back to me at the age of 70 as if they occurred yesterday. I remember most conversations verbatim. But like every other older person, my short-term memory can be embarrassing. I often wonder where I left my car keys or why I came into the room.

I know most people don't believe in astrology and numerology, but maybe there's something to it. An astrologist once gave me a Zodiac reading—I'm a double Leo. Both my sun and moon are in Leo. Once a numerologist, a person who studies numbers such as the figures in a birth date and their supposed influence on human affairs, determined my number was "1." He remarked, "You must be very powerful." Looking back at how I accomplished what I did, I guess I'd have to agree.

Extrasensory Perception a Plus

As if these incredible gifts weren't enough for one person, I learned the reason for another talent in an unusual way. After eight years of marriage to Wayne, I became unhappy and worse, depressed. I decided I needed help, so I visited a psychiatrist. At our initial meeting, I described the reasons for my unhappiness and my concerns for the future of my marriage. I was expecting the psychiatrist to ask me some questions, but his question surprised me. "Do you have déjà vu?"

I said, "Yes. Doesn't everyone?"

He said, "No, it's not that common." Déjà vu is a feeling that you are reliving a scene or conversation. He asked if he could give me a brain wave test. I became curious too, so I agreed. He had me sit in front of a disc with a spiral pattern. Then he attached some electrodes to my head, tuned on the machine and said, "Watch the spinning disc."

The disc started to spin and, before I knew it, I fell asleep. When I awoke he took 20 minutes to explain my brain waves weren't normal, but they weren't "abnormally abnormal." He said, "You have a brainwave pattern we just don't see very often."

My reaction was, "That must explain why I respond to some colleagues at work based on what they are thinking not what they are saying." The technical name for this is "extrasensory perception" or ESP.

Most people who haven't experienced ESP don't believe in it. Wayne was a skeptic. One day he took a card out of a deck of cards in front of several friends, held it up and told me to tell him what it was. I said, "The 10 of diamonds." He turned the card over. To everyone's amazement, it was the 10 of diamonds.

I told the psychiatrist about a conversation I had with a colleague at work. He had just received a software program from an outside consultant and said to me, "You'll never guess what I found."

I said, "Errors in the compile." This meant the program couldn't run without the consultant correcting it. I was right. I didn't realize it, but somehow I understood what he was thinking. And I had done this with him on more than one occasion.

Somewhat taken back, he said, "I know you know what I'm thinking, but I'd appreciate it if you'd not let me know when you know."

Whenever I dealt with him after that, I had to concentrate to make sure I responded to what he said and not what he was thinking.

When we got back to the purpose of my visit to the psychiatrist about the bleak prospects of my marriage, he said, "You don't need a psychiatrist, you need a marriage counselor."

A year later Wayne and I divorced after visiting a marriage counselor.

Good Work Skills Made a Difference

Perhaps all these extraordinary gifts—my high IQ, my photographic memory, my extrasensory perception—helped me become more sensitive to other people's feelings and the way they handle their work and personal concerns.

When I worked at Union Mutual Life Insurance Company, I had to deal with brilliant actuaries, visionary managers and a dedicated staff. Most worked hard and contributed to the growth of the company. They also had strong egos, personal agendas and territories to protect.

As in many other businesses, the bias against women in the workplace continued to frustrate many of my female colleagues. This unfair practice was commonplace in other fields as well, including politics, entertainment and sports. A wonderful example of someone who challenged this condition was sportswoman "Babe" Didrikson Zaharias. She excelled in many sports and earned recognition for her achievements.

• • •

> **"Babe" Didrikson Zaharias (1911 – 1956)** Babe Didrikson Zaharias got the name "Babe" hitting home runs playing in boy's high school baseball. By age 21, she had won Olympics gold medals in the javelin and the 80-meter hurdles. She introduced women into the male-dominated world of golf and won 82 golf tournaments. In 1949, she co-founded the Ladies Professional Golf Association (LPGA). In 1950, the Associated Press voted her Woman Athlete of the Half-Century.

• • •

I realized I needed to address these powerful forces with care if I wanted to advance my career.

I made it a point to use my gifts in a way that would complement the working styles of my co-workers, especially the men, without compromising my own abilities. I knew I had accomplished this well when one of my colleagues said, "working for you is just like working for a man." I took that as the ultimate compliment.

Dealing Well with Change

I also had one more advantage—I dealt with change well. Years later my boss at Arthur D. Little told me, "No one deals with change the way you do. Something new comes up and your reaction is 'let's get on with it.' No one else reacts that way. No one likes change. You have to understand how other people react if you're going to be successful."

So I learned to institute change without adverse reactions from those affected. I involved others early in the process. I explained the changes in ways they would understand. I used this skill throughout my many careers.

Change became a vital part of my own career path. Whenever my jobs turned into a routine, I looked for my next challenge. Sometimes that meant advancing to a new job level or taking on new responsibilities without additional pay. But the barriers to women for advancement remained in full force. I hit the glass ceiling several times before it had a name. So sometimes it meant finding a new career.

I progressed through my careers like the little white laboratory mouse running through the maze. After I hit my head on an immovable barrier, I changed directions.

CHAPTER 9

One College Semester at a Time

Education promotes equality and lifts people out of poverty.

– Ban Ki-moon

In September 1962, I had mixed feelings about starting my first semester at the University of Maine in Orono (UMO). I loved the idea of learning, but money, or more to the point, lack of it, worried me. Tuition and room and board cost $1,100. Books were an additional cost. I had been awarded a $250 American Association of University Women scholarship for each of two years and a $100 scholarship from my high school. With the $200 loan from student aid and what I had saved, I had just enough for my first semester and part of the second. My parents promised to mail me $5 a week for spending money, no doubt a hardship for them.

A month later it almost wouldn't matter if I went to school or not. The world came to the brink of war with the Cuban Missile Crisis. President John F. Kennedy announced a blockade on Cuba. He insisted the USSR remove the weapons from the nuclear missile bases they built on the island just 90 miles from Florida. I remember walking across campus that night wondering if our world was about to end. Everyone breathed a sigh of relief when the Russian's removed the missiles and war was averted.

When I got to college, I discovered it was very much a male-dominated world. The university president, top administrators, directors of schools and heads of departments were all male. The only exceptions were the directors of the schools of Nursing and Home Economics and the head of the women's division of Physical Education. I began to think my financial problems came from my not being male. It would be a decade before Dr. Gerda Lerner's work on women's contributions to history would affect academia.

• • •

Dr. Gerda Lerner (1920 – 2013) From the earliest times, history had been written about men by men. Dr. Gerda Lerner changed that by playing a central role in the establishment of women's history as an academic field. An early feminist, she was active in the Congress of American Women, a group concerned with social and economic issues in the 1940s. Her efforts contributed to the successes for gender equality in the United States as well as the spread of historical research to include women.

• • •

My Hardships Grew

My personal struggle at school continued. I found my first semester very tough—not the academics, but juggling ways to stretch my meager funds. To make matters worse, while I ate breakfast in the cafeteria one morning, someone stole some of my text books out of the cubbyhole outside the cafeteria. I couldn't replace them because more students had enrolled than expected and the university hadn't stocked enough books. I didn't have money to buy books again anyway. So I worked up the courage to ask some of the classmates I had just met if I could borrow their books. Several showed enough kindness to let me share their books for the rest of the year.

Adding to my financial predicament, I only had one winter wool coat. It was threadbare. I wore it for years and ruined it during a downpour while at a UMO football game. Desperate, I asked a classmate in the next dorm room who had a large wardrobe, "Can I buy one of your coats for $10?" She agreed and handed me a brown wool coat. So I had at least one good coat for my remaining years of college.

A few years ago, the woman at my dry cleaner asked me, "Why do you have so many winter coats?"

I replied, "Because getting a warm coat when I was young was a real hardship." Today I have 10 winter coats.

To get ready for life on the campus I corresponded with my assigned roommate during the summer. But she wrote back to tell me she decided to go to a private school instead. UMO had been her safety school. So I roomed alone for much of my freshman year. I missed the companionship of a roommate, but it was easier to study with the privacy.

My First Job—Unpaid

In the 60s, dorms were segregated by sex. School rules stated men could only visit the female dorms between certain hours, but they couldn't go beyond the reception area.

My dorm's house mother appointed me proctor for my floor. Even though I was the youngest student, she judged me as the most mature in the group. I assume she learned from my application I had lived on my own for four summers when I worked at Kennebunk Beach. While I didn't get paid as the floor proctor, I accepted the responsibility. My charge was to keep everyone out of trouble. Not an easy task for young women exploring their independence and freedom in new surroundings.

While I had to stay on top of my studies, I also had to keep a watchful eye on all the girls' activities. I guess you could say I took on the role of a "spy." Little did I know that the Central Intelligence Agency (CIA) would be interested in hiring me three years later. But I doubt I would have followed in the footsteps of a well-regarded female member of the CIA's predecessor agency, Julia Child. She could cook and I couldn't.

• • •

Julia Child (1912 – 2004) Best known for her television cooking shows, Julia Child introduced French cuisine to the United States with her co-authored cookbook *Mastering the Art of French Cooking*. She first tasted French cuisine when she moved to France with her husband Paul, a member of the United States Foreign Service. But she had a prior career. During and after World War II she worked for the Office of Strategic Services (OSS), the precursor for today's CIA.

• • •

On one occasion, I saved my two dorm mates next door from expulsion. Hearing a deep voice, I left my room, walked over to their door and knocked. They let me in and both made an effort to look casual and innocent. I could tell they were hiding something. I walked over to the closet, opened the door and said "Hello" to the surprised male student standing there in the tiny closet with no place to hide.

I knew if I reported my dorm mates had a man in their room they'd be expelled. Thinking fast, I covered him up in a long winter coat, hat and scarf and told him to roll up his pants and put on knee lengths. I took his elbow and snuck him down the back stairs. We were in luck. No one spotted us. I shoved him out the door and said, "Don't do this again or I'll turn you in!" He knew I meant it. The girls didn't give me any more trouble for the rest of the year.

In a noble effort to protect students from falling prey to temptations, the administration had even segregated the male and female dorms into quadrants. This meant the cafeterias were also segregated by sex. Everything changed my sophomore year. UMO integrated male and female dorms in the same quadrant, and the men and women began to enjoy each other's company in the school's cafeterias. But men still couldn't go beyond the reception area of the female dorms. While Betty Friedan's *The Feminine Mystique, NOW* and the pill appeared in the 60s, the sexual revolution hadn't started to heat up. It wasn't until the 70s that social attitudes underwent major changes.

My Financial Problems Kept Mounting

While I enjoyed my classroom work that first semester, my insufficient finances caused a lot of stress. When I recalled the advice of my high school teacher Mr. Merrow, it helped me deal with my concerns. He said, "Take one semester at a time. I'm sure you'll work it out."

I wanted to believe Mr. Merrow. But I had no idea from one semester to the next where the money would come from.

In the spring of my freshman year, I had a quarterly tuition bill coming due and no money to pay it. Desperate, I decided to find a job. I heard the school cafeteria needed workers. Many student workers quit to enjoy the spring weather. A luxury I couldn't afford.

I arranged an interview with Mrs. McCloud, head of the cafeteria system. I explained I would have to leave school if I couldn't come up with money to pay my final tuition bill.

Mrs. McCloud said, "I'd like to hire you, but I can't. You're a freshman, and freshmen aren't allowed to work."

I told her, "I have more experience than anyone you could possibly hire. I've worked in school cafeterias since I was eight and waitressed since I was thirteen. And besides, by the time the paperwork gets through the system, I won't be a freshman anymore."

To my delight she said, "You're right! You're hired." I worked the breakfast shift and waited on the head table for all of the conference dinners. I made 80 cents an hour and got a raise to 90 cents in my sophomore year.

During the first semester of my sophomore year, Wayne and I—by then we were engaged—talked about going home to live in Kennebunk. We'd transfer to the university's Portland campus and make the 25 mile commute. It would save us money by not living on the Orono campus.

At that point, I didn't have enough money to get through the whole year again. When I met with Dr. Alice Stewart, my history teacher and advisor, I told her about my plan to transfer to the Portland campus. She tried to talk me out of it. I told her, "I don't have enough money to pay for the next semester."

She wanted me to continue my classes at Orono. She asked, "Can't you get more student aid."

I said, "I've been trying, but I can't get any more. If you think you can do better than I can, you're welcome to try."

She stood up, said, "You wait right here" and stormed out the door. She was a big woman with a dominating personality. You didn't want to get in her way. After a suspenseful hour, she came back. To my relief, she got me the student aid I needed to remain at the Orono campus—a $300 NDEA loan. I never learned what she did to get me the funds.

President Kennedy Paid Us a Visit

The highlight of my sophomore year occurred when President Kennedy's visited the Orono campus on October 19, 1963. My father and mother came up from Kennebunk with Wayne's family for the event. The football field bleachers were packed on that sunny blustery day. The excitement built as we waited for his arrival. A helicopter came in sight and landed on the field. As President Kennedy deplaned, a crowd of 15,000 cheered him.

University of Maine President Elliott escorted President Kennedy, attired in a cap and gown, to the stage. Senator Edmund Muskie, Governor John Reed and other dignitaries greeted him. He spoke about foreign policy to a rapt audience. He stressed how basic American-Soviet differences "will give rise to further crises, large and small, in the months and years ahead."

President Elliott fitted President Kennedy with a symbolic hood as he received an honorary doctor of laws degree. We all rose and joined in singing the *Maine Stein Song.* Everyone knew the words. The singing bandleader Rudy Vallee wrote the lyrics and made it popular in the 30s. Valle attended UMO before transferring to Yale. In the height of irony, his recording of the *Stein Song* hit number one on the music charts for eight weeks in the midst of prohibition!

That November the tragic news reached us that President Kennedy had been shot. I was in anthropology class when someone came to the door and beckoned to Professor Emerick. He walked over, had a brief conversation, walked back to his desk and said, "None of this seems very important right now. Someone just shot President Kennedy."

We all filed out of the class in shock. I joined a group of teachers and students gathered around a radio, all of us in tears. We listened to the news report, fearing the worst. Then the announcement came President Kennedy had died. While the country and world mourned the charismatic president, we felt our world had changed forever.

Lyndon Johnson became the 36th president as life on campus struggled to adjust to some kind of normal pace. In spite of the distractions, I continued my studies. I worked hard and finished my sophomore year at Orono with excellent grades.

A Tragedy Strikes at Home

When I got home to Kennebunk for the summer, I had more personal sad news waiting for me. I learned my father had lung cancer. When Wayne and I met with the doctor, he said my father's condition had advanced too far for surgery. There was nothing anyone could do. The doctor advised us he would not last the year.

While we dealt with this upsetting news as best we could, we knew we had to find a way to carry on. With my father's blessing, Wayne and I decided to marry that September. Wayne had graduated that spring and stayed on to work on his Master's in English. Meanwhile, I finished my undergraduate degree.

Wayne had a scholarship and a good on-campus job, but I still needed student aid for tuition and books. I visited the student aid office before leaving in the spring and told them I would be married when I returned in the fall. I asked them to set up a new file under my new name. Wayne and I were married in his family's home in Arundel, the neighboring town to Kennebunk. The week of the wedding I still hadn't heard from student aid. So I called the student aid office. The officer said, "You said you were getting married."

I replied, "What does that have to do with anything? I told you I was coming back to school and needed student aid."

He asked, "Can't your father help you?"

Working hard to hold down my frustration, I said, "He's 62 years old and dying of cancer. How do you propose he do that?"

Sensing my dilemma, he said, "Come into the office when you get here and we'll see what we can do for you."

More loans! This time $900. But I did get a $400 university scholarship, too.

I did manage to have a bit of good luck. My advisor, Dr. Stewart, offered me a job working for her. She wanted me to identify and catalog books in the Folger Library with any connection to Canada. Later, Dr. Stewart had the books I identified moved to the new Canadian Studies Room in the Folger Library. The Canadian Studies Room grew over time to become the much acclaimed Canadian-American Center.

My job received funding under the legislation Congress had just passed for President Lyndon Johnson's War on Poverty. While there were harsh critics of Johnson's Great Society agenda, many like me benefited from its programs. A provision in the program set the minimum wage for work at $2.30 an hour. This made a huge increase over the $.90 an hour I made at the cafeteria.

But first I had to meet with the two government men who administered the program. After our meeting they assured me everything looked in order with my application. Then one asked, "What dorm should we send the paperwork to?"

"Dorm?" I said, "I don't live in a dorm. I'm married. I live off campus."

At which point, the other one said, "Oh, they didn't tell us what to do if a married *woman* applied under the program." They had to check back with Washington for instructions. I got word two weeks later I could keep the funding for the job. As a married woman, my funding received approval only because my husband also qualified under the program. Another example of the barriers faced by married women striving to be more than wives and mothers.

That winter, I became the only full-time married female student at UMO supporting a parent. Soon after my father died, my mother came to live with us in our three-room apartment in Orono. She helped with the cooking and housework. She also typed our school papers on our old Smith-Corona portable typewriter. Wayne completed his course work for his Masters. I had taken an overload of credits every semester and arranged to graduate a semester early.

CHAPTER 10

It Wasn't All Work

Just play. Have fun. Enjoy the game.

– Michael Jordan

Wayne worked in the pool hall in the Memorial Union, the students' activity center. I did most of my studying in the Bear's Den, the student cafeteria across the hall. I became a fixture. Friends joined me off and on during the day, each bringing me a cup of coffee. They knew I didn't have money to buy my own all day. One friend said my senior year, "They should put up a plaque on this booth: 'To the only student to make Phi Beta Kappa while studying in the Bear's Den.'"

Good Times at the Memorial Union

Most of our outside activities centered in the Memorial Union. I joined a candlepin bowling team. I wasn't very good. But, to my amazement, the first time I ever bowled 10 pin, I scored five strikes in a row. I have no idea how.

For entertainment, Wayne and I occasionally went to the movies. I remember the first James Bond picture *Dr. No.* Everyone's reaction was WOW! It was the first real action picture we had ever seen. I took my mother to the movies too, even foreign language flicks.

Wayne and I also played duplicate bridge at the Union. Years later we bumped into the student who ran the club when he organized a duplicate bridge club in Portland. He still runs it.

The Memorial Union also had a large room with a very small television screen. Our television didn't work and we couldn't afford to fix it. One Sunday night, the Ed Sullivan Show scheduled an appearance by the Beatles. I got there early. I pulled a big stuffed chair square in front of the television, sat down and waited.

Students wandered in and asked, "What's going on?"

I said, "You'll see." As the Beatles performed, the room began filling up. They were great! They performed the next Sunday, too. By then everyone was raving about the Beatles, as Beatlemania began to take over America. I had to get to the Union early the next Sunday to get a good seat.

When Wayne worked nights or weekends at the Union, I took my mother to the basketball and football games. I remember our excitement when the UMO Black Bears beat Youngstown University in football. We scored the winning touchdown late in the last quarter. The stadium went wild. My mother and I jumped up and down together. My mother called it "the year I went to college."

I Decided to Go to Graduate School

I spent the winter of my junior year and spring of my senior year wondering if I should continue my education or begin a career. I still cherished the idea of becoming a lawyer. But I knew I couldn't go to law school, my first choice. As a woman, I wouldn't be able to get student aid to attend a professional school.

I fell back on my second choice—the academic ranks. I took the Graduate Record Exam and began applying for fellowships for graduate school. My grade point average was 3.83 out of 4.0. I was also proficient in French and German, so I had good reason for optimism about getting a fellowship.

I felt proud as one of five students in Maine—four male students and me—nominated for a Danforth Graduate Fellowship. The fellowship covered tuition and fees plus a $1,800 living allowance. But I wasn't awarded one of the fellowships. I'm not sure if being a woman had anything to do with their decision. But, from bitter experience, I learned how the "system" works, so I thought "female" on the application didn't help. Even worse, I was married.

Ever optimistic, I applied for a Woodrow Wilson Fellowship. It would pay all expenses through a PhD. I made the first cut.

All interviews were scheduled in February at Tufts University in Medford, Massachusetts. In spite of a raging blizzard, Wayne and I began the trip in our VW Bug. The roads were treacherous. As we traveled on the Maine Turnpike, we skidded on some ice. Wayne lost control of the car. It rolled over onto its side and back upright again. Neither of us got injured since the VW had roll bars as standard equipment, and we wore seatbelts.

The woman in the car in front of us stopped. I got out and ran to her car and opened her passenger side door. She asked, "Can I help?"

I asked, "Are you going to Boston?"

She said. "Yes, do you need a ride?"

I replied "Yes." Ran back to the VW, grabbed my suitcase, forgetting my boots in the confusion, climbed into her car and we headed to Boston. Wayne stayed to deal with our car. She dropped me at the Parker House in Boston. I checked in, left my suitcase in the room and hurried back out to hail a cab to get to Tufts.

The storm got worse, and the snow reached several inches deep. The cabbie didn't know his way around the school, so he stopped in the middle of the campus and I got out. Without my winter boots, I had to trudge through knee-high drifts in my high heels. Soaked from the snow, I managed to find the right building and arrived just in time for my interview.

While my interview went well, I felt a bit embarrassed when I had to beg the panel of three surprised people to cash a check to pay for the cab back. Snow continued to pile up as the evening turned dark. A group of us got lucky and caught the last cab traveling to Boston.

After all I endured with the storm, I felt very disappointed when the committee did not award me a Woodrow Wilson Fellowship. It was small comfort that two UMO male classmates each got a fellowship. The one consolation to the experience came with the rejection letter which read, "Woodrow Wilson finalists usually receive graduate fellowships."

Encouraged that I might get the funds I needed, I applied for graduate study at Boston University and New York University. Good news/bad news—both accepted my application but rejected my request for student aid.

Dr. Stewart, my advisor, had urged me to apply to Radcliff College, Harvard's sister school. More disappointment came when they also rejected my application. She thought the problem came because I had changed my major from history to history & government so I would have sufficient credits in my major to graduate a semester early. I assumed they rejected me because I was married.

A Fulbright Award!

I applied for a government funded Fulbright Fellowship to study in West Germany for a year. At this time, the Cold War created great tensions between the West and East. The Berlin Wall became a symbol of the dramatic differences that separated our societies. It may not have been the opportue time to go to West Germany.

Yet, I felt it might provide an opportunity to travel and learn about another culture. This time I was awarded the fellowship. Probably the fact that I represented the only non-German major in the advanced German class helped. They assigned me to the University of Heidelberg, an American enclave in West Germany. I learned Germany required two years of study for a Masters. This meant, with only one year of study in Germany on the Fulbright, I couldn't earn a degree.

I wrote my proposal to study German society in the 1830's. This period gave rise to both Friedrich Nietzsche, the father of Fascism, and Karl Marx, the father of Communism. The awards package included specific instructions on how I should dress as a representative of the United States. I also learned for the first time I had to take a six-week course in German in New York City. Since I still wore some of my clothes from high school and couldn't afford to pay for the German language course, I had to make the difficult decision to decline the Fulbright Fellowship.

Later that year a Fulbright staff member tracked me down in Boston and called me at New England Mutual where I worked. She said the committee thought my proposal had great potential and asked me to reconsider taking the fellowship. She said they would pay for the language training and give me some additional spending money.

I explained, "I can't get a degree in only one year in Germany, and I won't get financial aid to attend graduate school after I return home. And I'm deeply in debt for my undergraduate education. What I need is a good job. I have one, and I'm going to keep it."

I never regretted turning down the Fulbright. But I felt bad for my male classmate who didn't get the award that year. I felt better when I learned a few years later that he had gone to Indonesia on a Fulbright award.

On-Campus Recruiting

Not knowing whether or not I would receive student aid for graduate school, I scheduled job interviews when recruiters came to campus. I even interviewed with the CIA. I was intrigued with the idea of becoming a spy. Perhaps they liked the idea of a husband and wife team, because they made an offer to hire both Wayne and me. But Wayne accepted a job with an investment firm in Boston instead. I guess it wasn't in the cards for me to become a spy.

The search went on.

In November, I interviewed with AT&T for their management training course. They offered me the job in their Boston program. It sounded promising, but it wouldn't begin until June. I told the recruiter, "I'll accept the offer if you can find me temporary work in the meantime." They said they would see what they could do. I told them I would continue to look for another job in Boston in the meantime. I received an offer by telegram for an interim job the day I had accepted another job in Boston.

I wondered what my career path might have been had I taken the AT&T job when I saw the smarmy comic phone operator Ernestine, played by Lily Tomlin on television's *Rowan and Martin's Laugh-In*.

• • •

Lily Tomlin (1939 –) In 1969 Lily Tomlin catapulted into fame in the *Rowan and Martin's Laugh-In* comedy show. Her character, Ernestine, the telephone operator, often asked, "Is this the person to whom I am speaking." Her hair net, snort and barbs with customers became her trade mark. AT&T offered Tomlin $500,000 to appear in a commercial, but she declined. Instead she appeared in a parody of a phone commercial on *Saturday Night Live* saying, "We don't care, we don't have to...we're the phone company."

• • •

I finished my graduation requirements in January 1966 and went to the dean's office to pick up my diploma. The dean said, "You should stay for the next semester and graduate with your class."

By now my problems with money had stretched my patience. I told the dean, "I need $500 to stay and I don't have it. What I need is a job, and I need my diploma to get one. So if you're not going to give me $500, you have to give me my diploma."

He chose to give me my diploma. A short time later we moved to Boston, and I began a serious search for a job.

CHAPTER 11

Who's Afraid of Computers?

The biggest failure you can have in life is making the mistake of never trying at all.

– Unknown

My summer jobs as chambermaid and waitress came to an end with the end of the Maine's tourist season in 1968. I needed to find something that paid better and used the skills I learned as a computer programmer.

My in-depth introduction to computers started at my previous job at the New England Mutual Life Insurance Company in Boston. When I took that job, I didn't know anything about computers.

Most history credits English mathematician Charles Babbage with designing the first digital computer in 1822. His design had more than 1,000 gears and levers and was so complex it was never built. The first working computer with complex gears and levers was designed by Allen Turing in Great Britain. He used it to break Germany's Enigma machine codes during WWII.

Although history credits the men, it was women who paved the way for the computer revolution that transformed how businesses and governments operate. In 1944, the six mathematicians who programmed the Electronic Numerical Integrator and Computer (ENIAC)—by plugging and unplugging cables and switches—and their teacher were all women.

One of those original programmers, Betty Holberton, was among the developers of one of the earliest "modern" computers, the UNIVAC.

• • •

Betty Holberton (1917 – 2001) In college, a professor told Betty Holberton she was wasting time with mathematics and should go home and raise children. Undaunted, she became the chief of the Programming Branch at the David Taylor Model Basin in 1959. There she helped develop the UNIVAC, the first commercial computer. She wrote the first statistical analysis program for the 1959 U.S. Census and worked with Admiral Grace Hopper to develop the programming standards for COBOL and FORTRAN. She was also responsible for the beige color of computers.

• • •

My First Computer—The Univac III

The first computer I worked on was a UNIVAC III, manufactured by Sperry Rand. While the UNIVAC III used compact transistors instead of the bulky vacuum tubes of previous models, it was still huge and required a large room. It also required specialized training to understand how it worked.

New England Mutual hired me as a COBOL programmer trainee along with several others. COBOL is the abbreviation for Common Business-Oriented Language. It was the first English-like programming language, and it made it easier to write, document and modify business application programs. COBOL remained the standard programming language for business applications for decades.

During the 60s in-house programmers and experts from the hardware manufacturer provided computer training. Our instructors started us with a programmed-instruction manual describing how computers work, with tests after each chapter to check our comprehension. The manual was filled with technical concepts and terms. In a brief period, we became immersed in computer jargon, such as batch and sequential processing, key punch cards, and internal and external data storage. We also had to learn about magnetic tapes, source codes, object code, FSEL (don't ask), programming logic, plus physical nomenclature and diagrams of processing called "flowcharts."

Wading through this labyrinth of hi-tech terminology, I quickly discovered I could handle computer complexity and even found the challenge fun. During this training I learned the earliest programs were written in "assembler," a low-level language of symbols, which is specific to a particular computer.

Some Strange "Bugs"

The new programs and systems were written in COBOL because it was easier for programmers to understand. In order to run on a computer a program—whether it was programmed in assembler language or COBOL—had to be translated into machine code. This was accomplished by a program provided by the computer hardware manufacturer called a "compiler." The first compiler was written by a woman—Admiral Grace Hopper.

• • •

WHEN THERE IS NO WIND, ROW

Admiral Grace Hopper (1906 – 1992) Known as "Amazing Grace" for her pioneering accomplishments in the computer field, Admiral Grace Hopper was the first woman to graduate from Yale with a PhD in mathematics. She was also the first woman to reach the rank of admiral in the U.S. Navy. The *USA Hopper*, a guided-missile destroyer is named in her honor as is the Hopper Supercomputer at the National Energy Research Scientific Computing Center at Lawrence Berkeley National Laboratory.

• • •

I didn't know how compilers worked. But I had some unusual experiences with them. I surprised my teacher with my first program compile. He said, "You didn't have any errors!"

I said, "It's not supposed to have errors, is it?"

He replied, "No, but it's unusual not to have errors in your first compile."

I didn't know they expected us to have errors. I was surprised and pleased I didn't. This experience helped build my confidence for the more difficult work ahead.

After the in-house training, we attended a one-week course in COBOL given by IBM. The teacher assumed we were all experienced programmers. We weren't. But our training up to that point helped us venture on to more demanding programs.

Those few intense weeks brought our formal training to an end. Everything else we learned on the job by trial and error with our programs. We also got considerable help about program design and techniques from discussions with our more experienced colleagues.

While programming in COBOL on the UNIVAC III, I discovered and documented two distinctive bugs. Most people know that a computer bug means something is preventing the computer from giving correct results. Usually bugs appear in the application programs. Programmers find and fix the program bugs with a process called "debugging." I debugged my COBOL program using deductive reasoning. An analytical mind made up the only debugging tool at the time.

Since new applications programs didn't have exhaustive testing, bugs showed up often. I became good at finding bugs and fixing them. But results of my tests to solve two very unusual bugs I had found made no sense. Researching the problems further, I found evidence the bugs causing the problem were in the compiler program supplied by Sperry Rand, not in the application program where bugs almost always occur.

I documented my analyses and reported these findings to my management. When they sent my documented compiler bugs to Sperry Rand, they responded, "No one else had even discovered one."

These made up the first of a long list of unusual problems with software and hardware I encountered over the next 35 plus years.

When I retired, one of my colleagues who worked with me for more than 15 years explained in her parting comments, "ANY electronic device that Paula even thinks of touching will without fail either already have gremlins pre-installed or develop them shortly after coming into her orbit. That's just the way it is."

I learned the origins of the term "bug" when Admiral Grace Hopper came to speak about her early experiences with computers at Union Mutual Life Insurance Company in Portland, Maine, the location of my next computer programming job.

Admiral Hopper became a pioneer and legend in the computer world and a powerful force for women's rights. She worked as one of the first computer programmers on the UNIVAC II, the first business computer, and was a co-developer of COBOL. She told us the story about the day, while searching to discover why a computer program broke down, she found a very large dead moth in the computer. From that day on, computer program problems have the term "bugs." This unfortunate moth gained such notoriety it can be seen on display at the Smithsonian Institution in Washington, D.C.

My First Programming Project

Once I got through the training program, my first project at New England Mutual proved a real challenge—my supervisor gave me the responsibility for the new malfunctioning Cash Accounting System. Without preparing me for the project, he stacked boxes of punch cards containing the program on my desk and said, "Fix it. It's wrapping core three times."

"Core" was the term for memory. The UNIVAC III's memory had 32,000 bytes, miniscule when compared to the gigabytes of memory available today. This malfunctioning program needed three times the existing memory to run. I needed to break it down into several sequential programs. It didn't help that the only documentation for the program was on a yellow sheet of paper on which my supervisor had scrawled the numbers of the accounts and their assignment in a table.

To resolve the memory problem, I had to rewrite the program into three interconnected programs. I also had to add editing to catch the errors made by data entry clerks or keypunchers.

Even though I felt confident with my solution, I believed it important to verify my test results. So I attempted to get a copy of the company's chart of accounts from my supervisor, from my user contact in the Accounting Department, even from the company's treasurer. But to no avail. Everyone thought a mere programmer like me didn't need that information.

In spite of my warnings, the programs went into production based on verifying accounts to the rudimentary specification provided by my supervisor. As I expected, the account table on the yellow specification sheet didn't reflect the current chart of accounts, which had changed since the original specification was written. So the system spread the amounts among the wrong accounts on its reports.

Time for the blame game. The users became upset with my supervisor, so my supervisor put the responsibility for the errors on me. When he confronted me about the incorrect reports, I took the yellow specification sheet out of my drawer. I handed it to him and said, "The system agrees with your specifications. If they're wrong, you'll have to correct the specs before I can fix the system."

He accepted the fact that I could only fix the problem if he gave me the chart of accounts. After he supplied me with the chart, I modified the program table to match the chart of accounts. With the correct information the system created accurate reports.

Working with COBOL convinced me computer technology would revolutionize the way companies conducted business. I also knew in order to compete with men I needed to match or better their skills and experience. So I made the decision to seek out companies that used computers as a key part of their operation.

My New Job in Maine

In December 1968, with my chambermaid and waitress jobs behind me, my search for computer work had succeeded. I joined the Programming Department of Union Mutual Life Insurance Company in Portland as a COBOL programmer. The manager of Programming was a woman, one of only two female department managers in the company.

When I joined Union Mutual, it was located in an office building in downtown Portland. Programming was in a small attached building with its own door to the back street, a short walk to the old warehouse area near Commercial Street. On my lunch breaks I walked down Exchange Street and watched as enterprising businessmen transformed derelict buildings used as warehouses into what became the now-famous Old Port Exchange.

Men who worked in insurance were conservative and staid—dark suits, white shirts and skinny ties. Not the programmers—first to sport colored shirts, light suits and sideburns. But the programmers worked hard. One afternoon a vice president rushed into the Programming Department to complain to our manager. He had just seen a programmer leaving work early. She explained to him, "He wasn't leaving early. He was leaving late. He just finished work from yesterday." After the very embarrassed vice president left the department, we all had a good laugh.

Programmers had fun at work too. When the company added partitions between desks, one brought in hay and placed it beside his "stall." Another tacked up a wall poster with a caricature of President Nixon in front of an old car with the caption, "Would you buy a used car from this man?" When a vice president visiting the department saw it, he made us take down all our posters, which included anti-war posters.

It was the height of the Vietnam War and war protests. The most notable war protester was Jane Fonda.

• • •

Jane Fonda (1937 –) Besides being an award winning actress, Jane Fonda is a model, writer, fitness guru, and political activist. As an actress, she starred with Dolly Paton and Lily Tomlin in the 1980 film *9 to 5* as office workers who take revenge on their sexist boss. As an active anti-war protestor during the Vietnam War, she endured vilifying attacks for the photograph taken of her sitting on a Vietnamese anti-aircraft battery during her non-sanctioned visit to Hanoi.

• • •

Many programmers were liberal in their politics and were against the war. A group of programmers went to the prayer vigil each day at the Henry Wordsworth Longfellow Mansion, where the FBI photographed them for their files.

I sympathized with them but protested in my own way by writing letters to people in government. Years later I was shocked to find out the FBI had a file on me too!

Working on IBM Computers

When I joined Union Mutual, the company was in the process of upgrading their computer programs from the outdated IBM 1401 to the new IBM 360 mainframe. Faster and able to handle large programs and more data, the IBM 360 used the COBOL programming language. With the knowledge I learned about COBOL at my previous job, I had no problem writing new programs in COBOL. My first programs for an actuary applied complex mathematical formulas to massive amounts of statistical data and historical records.

The programming language for the old IBM 1401 was Autocoder, an assembler language. When I didn't have enough work in COBOL to keep me busy, I decided to teach myself Autocoder.

As soon as my boss realized I had become sufficiently proficient in Autocoder, she made me responsible for maintaining the New Business System. This system processed new insurance policies before passing them on to the policy master file. In addition to ongoing maintenance, the system had lots of problems—programming errors, lack of documentation and New Business Department personnel needing to be trained. I tackled them all. I took great pride when my boss and the users expressed their approval with the improvements I made in the process.

Our test environment was the production system. I instructed the clerks on how to make sure my test records did not pass on to the policy master file. Years later when I was dating Gary Singer, he commented he had reconciled millions of records for an analysis he designed for management. But he had a handful of records for "Robert Testing" with no master record. We both had a good laugh when I said, "I used the name 'Robert Testing' for my records for New Business System testing. There's no such person. You can delete them."

While computer programs proved to be remarkable tools, the early programs also had serious limitations. In an effort to show the versatility and power of computers to upper management, the Programming Department had created a computer program for an important financial report needed monthly. Since the specifications for the report changed almost every month without notice to update the program, the program never created correct reports on the first run. Every time this happened, a programmer had to take time to update the program and run a revised report. As a result, the report for upper management always arrived late.

The member of upper management responsible for this report was Jack Ketchum. I knew Jack well. We both lived in Kennebunk and attended the same church. At times, we commuted to work together. We had learned to trust and respect each other.

After several months of frustrating report corrections, the manager of Programming called me into her office. Aware of my personal relationship with Jack, she asked me to speak to him about taking this report off the computer.

When I met with Jack, I said, "We can do almost anything on a computer, but this report should not be done on the computer. The specifications change too often. This requires us to make frequent program changes and delays delivery of the report. If you want it prepared right and on time, do the report yourself and have your secretary type it." He agreed with my suggestion. We took the problem program out of production.

They Thought I Was a Man

Until Union Mutual moved to its new building on the outskirts of Portland, our computer room was remote. We sent our projects on computer cards by courier to a location in a different building.

It was a long time before I met the computer operators who ran my jobs, which almost always processed without problems. A standard instruction form accompanied each job. The line for "Name" on the form wasn't long enough for my name, so I always wrote "P. Goodrich." (I was married to my first husband, Wayne Goodrich, at the time.) One day, my manager sent me to the remote computer room to resolve a production problem. When I walked in and introduced myself, the reaction was, "You're P. Goodrich?!" They expected a man.

CHAPTER 12

My Responsibilities Expand

Coming together is a beginning; keeping together is progress; working together is success.

– Henry Ford

My hard work at Union Mutual continued to gain the attention of upper management. In 1970, I received a promotion to Senior Programmer and became responsible for five programmers. When another senior programmer left, I became accountable for five more programmers. While I had no problem with the additional workload, I felt disappointed when they didn't increase my pay to reflect my increased responsibilities. I'm convinced such treatment would not have happened to a man.

A Missing Piece of Important Data

One of my programmers created an unusual and very serious problem. She made a modification to a program that produced the 1099 forms for reporting income to recipients and the IRS. Her modification caused the Social Security number not to print on the forms. Although the program's test results had been checked and signed off on by the user, they failed to see the error. Since it occurred on my watch, it became my job to fix it.

The completed Forms 1099 had multipart sheets with carbon copies. No supplier had enough forms left in stock for us to reprint the thousands of incorrect 1099s. Waiting for our supplier to print new blank forms would cause the company to miss the 1099 filing deadline. The IRS penalty would be huge, HUGE!

To solve the problem required a creative approach. I designed a program to compare the policy number on the 1099 print records with the policy number in the original source file, which had the policy holder's Social Security number. The new program printed the Social Security number and corresponding policy number on the already-printed 1099s. The computer operator stopped the printing periodically—printers didn't always use buffers back then—to verify the policy number corresponded with a printed report which included both the policy number and the Social Security number. The solution worked, and the 1099s were mailed out on time much to management's—and my—relief.

I Wanted To Be a Systems Analyst

By 1969, although my job title was Computer Programmer, I also took on the more difficult job of designing new systems. I became upset when I learned all the programmers transferred to positions in the new Systems Department were men. And worse, programmers weren't supposed to design systems anymore. But my manager continued to give me design projects.

When the new Systems Department posted their next job opening, I applied. I felt more than qualified to do the job of system analyst. I was the only one of the five applicants already designing systems for the company—and the only female.

When I went for my interview with the director of the Systems Department, I realized that, as a woman, I still had obstacles to overcome. He rummaged through his desk drawers, ignoring my responses to his questions. Needless to say he had a problem with women in upper level positions. I didn't get the job.

Although my official duties were supposed to be limited to programming, I continued to design systems and lead major projects for the Actuarial Department as a Senior Programmer.

While I had more responsibilities, I lacked the title, status and pay of a systems analyst. I got a boost to my sense of self-worth when one actuary refused to sign off on his projects with the Systems Department until I had reviewed and approved the test results.

My boss assigned me to the team for the conversion of the New Business System to COBOL and the IBM 360—but as a programmer, not as a systems analyst. After a few meetings with the analysts, I became frustrated by the process, so I assigned one of my programmers to take my place. I did not like the fact that the analysts ignored the functions of the old system as they designed the new system, but I couldn't do anything about it.

The new system went into production after considerable testing, but the analysts and programmers overlooked one important feature. I got a call in the middle of the night from a computer operator who said, "The checks created by the new system are printing without a magnetic strip."

I got up, dressed warmly—it was February—and drove the 25 miles from Kennebunk to the office in Portland. When I got there, I called the systems analyst in charge of the project to tell him about the problem and what I had to do to correct it. In an attempt to excuse his oversight, he admitted I was right and said. "It was Systems' fault for not checking it."

I said, "That's all well and good, but I'm the one here in the middle of the night fixing the problem." It turned out to be a complicated process. I had to determine the program steps from the old Autocoder program and code those program steps into the new COBOL program. After I tested the modified program, I gave it to the computer operator for the production run. He printed the checks with the magnetic strips. I drove home and went back to bed. I received several compliments when the checks were mailed out on schedule.

Actuarial Projects by the Numbers

The Actuarial Department plays a vital role in the success of the company. It uses formulas and historical data to determine the likelihood of future events. It also designs creative ways to reduce the likelihood of undesirable events to take place, plus decrease the impact of undesirable events should they occur. Once this data is analyzed, it establishes policy rates. Most actuaries and mathematicians were men. So were most programmers. But the mathematician who historians recognize as the first computer programmer was a woman—Ada Lovelace.

• • •

> **Ada Lovelace (1815 – 1852)** The daughter of romantic poet George Gordon, Lord Byron, Ada Lovelace's mother taught her mathematics and science, rather than poetry and literature. She demonstrated a genius for math while young and also learned music, art and French. In 1843, she wrote the first mathematical algorithm for a machine that was never built. By being the first person to envision machines would run codes without human calculation, Lovelace is considered to be the first computer programmer.

• • •

A mutual company shares its gain from operations—called "profits" in a stock company—with policy holders in the form of dividend payments. One of my periodic computer processing tasks included working with the Actuarial Department to update the dividend scale which determines dividend payments.

This process took over much of available computer time allocated to testing. At the beginning of each year, the Programming Department needed to know if there would be a new dividend scale. This way they could schedule their projects and computer time for testing.

One time we had been told there would be no new dividend scale. But I kept insisting in our staff meetings there *would be* a new dividend scale. My boss became so concerned by my insistence she checked with upper management. They assured her there wouldn't be any new dividend scale that year.

But in the fall, the head of the Actuarial Department came into the Programming Department and sat down at my desk. I could tell from his demeanor that he brought me a problem. He asked, "What will it take to create a new dividend scale by January?" Management had decided there would be a new dividend scale after all. So we had to accomplish in less than three months a task that usually took much longer. This delayed other projects because of the lack of test time. It was small comfort that my prediction about the dividend scale turned out to be accurate.

When the company began the complex design of its new individual long-term disability (LTD) products, I received an unexpected responsibility. Much to my surprise, I became a member of the design team which until then had only included Programming's manager. During planning meetings, she found she could not answer vital questions about necessary changes to the New Business System for the new individual LTD policies. Whenever a processing question came up, she responded, "I'll have to check with Paula."

The head of the team lost patience with her, and told her to go find me and bring me to the meeting. Since I had in depth knowledge of how the New Business programs worked, I had no trouble answering questions and offering solutions to the problems that came up. Rather than having a go-between, the team leader saw the wisdom of making me a member of the design team even though I was only a programmer.

No One Would Listen

After the design phase for the individual LTD products, I worked closely with the actuary responsible for automating the new policies. In working on the details of the policy, I once again discovered the unequal treatment of men and women in regard to business practices. The only policies available for women consisted of those designed for blue collar workers. Female doctors and lawyers were not eligible for the policies designed for professionals.

The decision resulted from an incorrect assumption drawn from valid facts. Actuaries assumed women went out on disability sooner and stayed out longer. But the correct assumption was that people in dull repetitive jobs—most often filled by women with fewer work opportunities—go out on disability sooner and stay out longer. Professionals—whether men or women—do neither.

I expressed my concern to my management but nothing happened. I told the actuary, "Two years from now I'll be back in this office working on system modifications for the changes to the policies for women."

As I had predicted, two years later I came back into his office to discuss how to modify the programs for policies for women based on the same criteria as for men—their job level. When we met to begin the task, I said, "Before we begin I'd like to remind you I said I'd be back in two years to do this job."

He had to admit I had been right.

I had the same frustrations within the Programming Department. One late Friday afternoon I worked with some male programmers to find a bug in a program needed to be resolved before the production run on the weekend. I went through the printed reports and was convinced the problem was in a basic assembler language (BAL) module linked to the program.

I wasn't a BAL programmer, so I couldn't identify the bug in the BAL logic. My three male colleagues working on the problem rejected my conclusion. They proceeded to run various test data through the application program to find the bug. When it got late with no solution in sight, I said, "I'm going to go take a nap on my boss's couch. When you find the bug, come get me." A little before 8:00 p.m. one of the programmers came in, woke me up and sheepishly admitted, "You were right. The bug was in the BAL module." I told them, "Next time please do me a favor; check out my theory first so we can get home in time for supper."

Being a senior programmer with management responsibly had its frustrations too. I supervised a young programmer who knew how to do the job but didn't do anything on time. It got so I had to do his job too when deadlines came up. I recommended he be given a three-month notice to improve or be terminated. I told him about my recommendation and why. I said, "You'll be happy and successful in a job you want. I can tell you don't want this job." My management didn't agree—he was the son of a senior executive. Six months later when they terminated him, he came over to me, thanked me and said, "You were the only person who was honest with me." I learned he found a job in theater, his passion, and was very happy.

An Unusual Event

I had never been the subject of sexual harassment at work. Perhaps because I appeared self-assured, I projected a somewhat intimidating personality. But one time I attended a quarterly social meeting with a female friend from Programming. The quarterly results exceeded expectations and everybody celebrated with alcoholic drinks. My friend and I sat at a table having a spirited chat with one of the top male managers. After he got up and left, my friend said, "Aren't you upset?"

I said, "About what?"

She replied, "He was hitting on you."

"He was?!!" I didn't catch the drift of his conversation. Perhaps the wine and joking blurred my awareness. First thing the next morning, he came into the Programming Department and spoke to our manager. Then he came over to my desk and, in a voice loud enough for the whole department to hear, apologized to me. I smiled at him and accepted his apology so all could hear. He left, and we all got back to work.

CHAPTER 13

More High-Tech and High Hopes

*Life that dares send a challenge to his end,
and when it comes, say, "Welcome friend."*

– Richard Crashaw

As a programmer, I continued to design applications systems but without the title and pay of a systems analyst. I still wanted the job of Systems Analyst but knew I couldn't go through the front door. I would have to find a more creative way to get where I wanted to go. That opening presented itself in 1971.

I Entered Systems through the Back Door

We had five major projects competing for computer testing time. The Systems Department held weekly meetings on Friday to allocate test time for the following week. I was the only programmer—and only woman—invited to the meetings. At the beginning of the first meeting, I said, "Of the five projects we're here to discuss today, I'm the analyst on four of them. Do you have anyone in the Systems Department who can do the jobs I'm doing?" I repeated my question at the next meeting.

Several of the analysts spoke to me after the meeting and said, "You should apply for a transfer to Systems."

I replied, "I did that once, and they ignored me because I'm a woman. I'm not going to be humiliated a second time."

At the end of the day, the manager of Systems came to my desk in Programming and asked me to see him Monday morning. Without my knowledge the analysts had pleaded my case to him. I felt humbled and touched by their support. I joined the Systems Department the following week. With a sense of satisfaction I became the company's first female systems analyst.

There were a lot of firsts for women in the 70s. The posters I decorated my home with had captions evoking how some women now "marched to a different drummer." My favorite poster was of Golda Meir, the first female prime minister of Israel. She is seated holding her pocket book above the caption, "But can she type?"

• • •

Golda Meir (1898 – 1978) Golda Meir became the first female prime minister of Israel in 1969. Former Prime Minister Ben-Gurion called her "the best man in the government." She grew up in Milwaukee, Wisconsin, and moved to a kibbutz in Palestine in 1921 with her husband. In 1948, she traveled to the United States to raise money to purchase weapons for the defense of the new state of Israel. She returned with $50 million.

• • •

When I moved into the Systems Department, I was assigned the only available desk, one designed for a secretary. I stood by the desk and said, "Is someone trying to tell me something?" The manager overheard my comment and hurried to correct the mix up. He had the desk swapped before I could put my stuff away. The new desk was designed for systems analysts and programmers who work on large computer printouts and need lots of desk space. It was the work space I needed for all the projects I'd have to tackle.

At my first meeting with a systems project team, we sat at a large rectangular table. The chairman passed a paper tablet to the man seated next to him. It passed from one male colleague to the next until it got to me. I knew, as the only woman present, they expected me to take notes. But I passed the tablet on to the male colleague on my left and said, "Either we should all take turns taking notes, or you should have a secretary come in to take them." The chairman accepted my point of view and got a secretary to come in to take the notes.

It wasn't unusual for a few of my colleagues to gather on occasion at my desk in conversation. When my manager commented to me about my distracting the men, I told him, "When they gather at my desk, we're discussing work-related matters. When they gather together without me, they're discussing sports." He never mentioned it again.

A Woman Commuting to New York Was a Novelty

I felt very reassured to have my colleagues recognize the contribution I made in the Systems Department. I started right in as a team member responsible for converting the computer data processing from Hamilton Life, an insurance company based in New York City, to the computer systems in Portland.

Union Mutual had just purchased Hamilton Life and didn't want to maintain multiple computer data processing systems for the same functions. As a result, the Hamilton policy records had to be converted to the codes used in our systems and added to the policy master file in Portland through new programs we designed. The job required me to travel to New York for three days each month for about a year. When my supervisor gave me the project, my reaction was "Is this some sort of a test?"

He said, "No. I think you're the best person to get the job done right."

Few women traveled on business in the early 70s. I was married and a mother. My daughter Beth was five. I had the good luck to have my mother living with us. She took care of Beth when I was at work and away on business trips.

The trips had many unexpected surprises. Hotel receptionists tried to register me as the wife of my business companion. The upside of the experience made me a seasoned traveler familiar with the bus routes and good restaurants. Broadway offered such great theater productions as *A Chorus Line, Chicago, Evita* and *Annie.* But our work schedule gave us so little free time the best show I managed to see was the dazzling lights of Times Square.

One of my tasks during my New York visits was to document the procedures for transactions in the New York office and how they affected the computer processing in Portland. At the end of the first year, we discovered a serious problem. The head of operations in New York had neglected to remove the deceased policy holders from the master file. This had the effect of overstating the policy reserves and reducing the gain from operations—the "profits." I wrote to him reiterating the procedures we had agreed on for removing these policies. The vice president of administration, Bob Cash, who had a copy of the memo said, "I think that's the nicest way anyone has ever told someone to shape up or ship out."

Following my success with this project, I received an unexpected compliment. It came from the director of Systems. He had ignored me in my interview for a transfer to his department a few years before because I was a woman. He admitted his attitude about women at work had undergone a significant adjustment. It gave me a sense of satisfaction to know I had contributed to his change of heart.

Standard Operating Procedure—No Documentation

The most challenging project I faced in 1974 came from Great Northern Paper, once the world's largest manufacturer of pulp and paper. It had mills in Maine, Georgia and Wisconsin. Great Northern wanted Union Mutual to manage their pension fund. But as part of the agreement, they stipulated we take and use Great Northern's computer system for processing their pensions.

When my supervisor gave me this project, much to my surprise, he also told me, "You're being promoted to Senior Systems Analyst." Promotions were always announced in the review process, so I asked "Why?" He explained they told management they were putting their best systems analyst on the project and management wouldn't believe that if I didn't have "Senior" in my title. I got a good raise too!

The first sign of trouble for the project began when the programs arrived with no documentation. There was no description of how the programs fit together for production runs or what each program did. I had to start by making a flowchart so the computer operators could run the production programs for the parallel test run. The parallel run allowed a comparison of output to the last system run at Great Northern. Everything tested out except for one individual's record. We learned the source of this problem when that individual came to work for Union Mutual months later. She had terminated employment at Great Northern. They must have forgotten to give us the computer input card indicating her termination.

Next I had to figure out what each of the programs did and document it. To add to the complexity of this task, Congress passed the landmark legislation, the Employment Retirement Income Security

Act (ERISA) while I was in the midst of documenting the system. ERISA sets minimum standards for pension plans in private industry to provide protection for individuals. After years of opposition by business and labor unions, Congress enacted the law. Passage of ERISA followed revelations of how employees lost large sums of their retirement savings due to misuse of company pension funds.

The manager of Group Pensions and I teamed up—he read the new Internal Revenue Code rules while I read the program code. We worked together to write specifications to modify the pension program processing to comply with ERISA's new rules.

Documentation—My Forté

Whenever we updated a system to a new computer language or improved processing system, the programmers documented the conversion process. But no one wrote a new procedures manual for the new system. Without a manual, because the systems had so many complex features, users and programmers alike had difficulty understanding how to solve operational problems when they occurred.

Department personnel who used the systems I had maintained knew I had the most knowledge about how the systems worked. So when problems came up, they looked to me to solve them. While it flattered me when they asked for my help, it put an extraordinary burden on my time. It became clear the problem stemmed from a lack of an updated user procedural manual. At the time there were no technical writers. Programmers and analysts didn't like to write manuals. And the users didn't have enough experience with the new systems to write an updated procedures manual.

We reached a crisis point when we converted a major system to COBOL. With no clear protocol to follow, users of the system began to call asking me to explain the undocumented procedures.

I met with Bob Cash about the problem. He agreed we needed an updated procedural manual and said the users should write it. He also said they had other priorities, so it would have to wait.

We faced an impasse. So I approached two well-placed and knowledgeable female colleagues, Dot Skillings, the manager of Policy Owner Services and Betty Rounds in the Actuarial Department. Even though it made extra work for them, they agreed to take on this project with me. My supervisor provided us with a typist. I wrote the initial manual. They reviewed and edited it, adding information from a user perspective.

As the project progressed, the documentation became voluminous and needed to be put into binders. I knew the executives and managers had extra binders with the system conversion documentation, so I made a brazen decision to collect them. I showed up at their door unannounced and explained, "I need your conversion binders." I ran my finger through the dust collected on the binders as a way to demonstrate their lack of use. Before they had time to react I said, "You don't need these," and grabbed the binders and left.

We distributed copies of the procedural manuals adding new content as we completed it. We had the manual about three quarters completed when we were in a meeting with Bob Cash in Dot's office discussing a needed change to the system. When Bob asked a question, Dot went to the manual, looked it up, answered him and put the manual back in the bookcase. After she did this for the third time, Bob said, "What's that?" She told him it was the procedures manual for the system.

He asked, "Where did that come from?" We told him about our informal collaboration. He said, "The users should be writing it."

We agreed. "But do they have the time?" I asked.

He said, "We'll find the time." And they did. They took over the project and completed the manual we started.

My reputation as a problem solver for complex issues got me more unassigned work. On one of my visits to the New Business

Department the clerks asked, "Can you please do something about these input forms?" As new projects came on line, they required new forms. To be efficient, they needed a form that included multiple types of transactions. But no new forms had been created. The clerks were using the conversion forms, each with multiple lines for the same transaction. The forms required additional time to work with multiple conversion forms for each new policy. In addition, the completed forms took up a lot of space in the policy file cabinets. I asked the New Business Supervisor to compile a list of the forms and the number used each month and told her, "I'll see what I can do."

At about the same time, a manager in the Supply Department asked me, "Can you do something about all these boxes?" They contained the conversion forms. I asked him for the number of boxes by type of form and the number of forms in each box.

I compiled the information and wrote a memo to Bob Cash. I pointed out the company had plans to construct a new building, in part for more storage space. I delivered the memo in person and he read it while I waited. When he got to the part, "Based on current use of the forms, we have a 50-year supply, and the system isn't projected to last that long." Bob looked up at me over his glasses and said, "We'll revise the forms." This meant fewer forms requiring less storage space, both in policy owner files and in the Supply Department. Everyone was happy when I relayed the results of our collaboration.

A Personal Bonus

My work at Union Mutual brought me in contact with many key professionals. One of the most prominent was Gary Singer.

Gary had designed and programmed a system in FORTRAN, a math-oriented computer language. He developed it to analyze the profitability of the company's group long term disability contracts. The results of his system helped Union Mutual become the dominate provider and very profitable in that line of business.

This success elevated Gary's standing in the company. He could pick the projects he wanted to work on. I first met Gary in a meeting where we discussed how to speed up the input/output processing for his FORTRAN system. A year later when the company became concerned Gary might leave, they gave me the job of following him around and documenting what he worked on. I was very impressed with his intelligence and liked his personal style and his sense of humor. He liked the ideas I suggested. I felt flattered when I discovered I was the only person in Data Processing he had agreed to work with on his projects.

It didn't take long for our conversation to shift from computers to more personal matters. We allowed our practical discussions to give way to our emotional feelings. We fell in love and got married in 1976. For years I said, "I can't believe I actually married Gary Singer!"

My Last Big Project

1974, the year I began my last major project at Union Mutual, was an eventful year in many ways. President Richard M. Nixon resigned as a result of his involvement in the Watergate scandal. 1974 was also the year Sandra Kurtzig—called the "first lady of computers"—founded ASK Computer Systems.

• • •

Sandra Kurtzig (1947 –) Sandra Kurtzig was one of Silicon Valley's first female entrepreneurs. She started ASK computer Systems in her bedroom with just $2,000 as a part-time venture to develop inventory control software, but it quickly grew to be a full-time vocation. Since there were no personal computers in 1972, she convinced Hewlett Packard to let her programmers use its mini-computers off hours. Then she convinced HP to bundle ASK with its hardware. In 1981, she became the first woman to take a company public when Ask became a public company.

• • •

My job was to write program specifications for a complex Reinsurance Division applications system. This division had the responsibility to buy and sell insurance to and from other companies as a form of risk management. I worked on the system specifications, 55 programs altogether, with Gary Singer, now the manager of Reinsurance Operations.

The vice president of Reinsurance wanted all the division's functions automated. I had misgivings about the idea, so I asked, "Are you sure you want everything computerized?"

He was adamant and said, "Yes."

Not long after we implemented the new system, upper management decided to stop selling new reinsurance policies and made plans for reassignments and layoffs.

Bob Cash called a meeting to discuss how the existing reinsurance business could be maintained. I explained, "The reinsurance clerk can provide the input; the computer system does the rest."

He said, "You mean we can run this business with one clerk?"

I replied, "Yes, along with someone in the Actuarial Department to oversee it." The reinsurance clerk kept her job, the division's vice president lost his and Gary joined the Systems Department.

Time for a Change

Union Mutual implemented an affirmative action program in 1973. I had worked as a computer programmer and systems analyst on systems for both life and health insurance and for both individual and group products. I was ready and eager for a change.

In 1974, the Personnel Department posted a management position in Policy Owner Services which tracked to the top position in the department. They called me and asked me to apply. Once again, sexual discrimination played a part in my not getting the job. Two men who reported to the position refused to work for a woman—especially a younger woman. I was 29.

It became clear opportunities for me at Union Mutual had reached their limits and I would have to change directions. I looked forward to my next career challenge.

CHAPTER 14

Trials of a Divorced Woman

*For of all sad words of tongue or pen,
The saddest are these: "It might have been."*

– John Greenleaf Whittier

In 1973, Wayne and I were both unhappy with our marriage, so we arranged to meet with a marriage counselor. Each of us met with him separately so he could get to know each of us. Wayne met with him first. At my meeting with him a few days later, I described how I liked family get-togethers, outings at the beach, a good book, activities at home such as sewing, knitting and gardening, along with my work as a systems analyst at Union Mutual.

Having heard Wayne's likes and dislikes, the counselor made an immediate assessment of our marriage and said, "You're an intelligent woman. You must have figured out a long time ago that you and your husband are very different people. In order for the two of you to get along, each of you has to make major changes which neither of you are willing to make. Why don't you admit you made a mistake? You don't need a marriage counselor; you need a lawyer." This was just the advice I needed.

Wayne and I divorced, and both went on to have long and happy second marriages.

Please Just Give Me the Divorce

Up until the 1970s, grounds for divorce were either adultery or extreme cruelty. Most marriages ended so one or both could marry someone else. But Wayne and I filed for divorce under Maine's new no-fault divorce law. We had sold our house and lived in an apartment. We had little to fight about. In the settlement I got custody of our daughter and what little furniture we had. Wayne was a commission-based stock broker. The brokerage business had begun to consolidate in the early 70s. He never knew which brokerage firm he would be affiliated with from one month to the next. We agreed on an amount for child support that our lawyer thought the court would accept.

In the divorce proceeding, the judge asked, "Is that enough?"

I said, "I work and have a good income."

He asked, "Who takes care of your daughter?"

"My mother," I said, "and I take care of her. We're going to be OK. Please, just give me the divorce."

He did.

Child Support Was Hard to Collect

In the 70s, only 15 percent of divorce awards included alimony. But divorce courts always awarded child support. Most child support went unpaid and was difficult if not impossible to collect. It required filing a civil complaint with a lawyer's assistance, a court hearing and collection proceeding after an award for arrearages, usually for less than the full amount owed.

A Department of Health and Human Services (HHS) survey found more than $1 billion due to women on welfare for outstanding child support payments. American taxpayers paid for the support of those children as Aid to Families with Dependent Children.

When HHS refused to make the survey results public, Margaret Heckler, a moderate Republican congressional representative from Massachusetts, did. She read the survey results into the public record on the floor of Congress.

• • •

Margaret Heckler (1931 –) In 1966 Margaret Hecker won election to the House of Representatives from Massachusetts by defeating a 42-year incumbent. In her 16 years in Congress, she supported moderate to liberal policies. In 1978, she became founder and member of the bipartisan Congressional Women's Caucus which focused on equality for women in Social Security and tax law. Following her stint at Health and Human Services, she became U.S. ambassador to Ireland.

• • •

As Secretary of HHS under President Ronald Reagan in the mid-1980s, Heckler worked to restructure the way child support was collected and delivered to custodial parents.

Finding the Right Man

I liked "talking shop." At a neighborhood cocktail party when I was 25, I was having a spirited discussion with a male friend when another man joined us. Men considered me good looking, so business might not have been on his mind. After a few minutes of conversation, he said, "You know, the average American man wouldn't be interested in a woman like you." I ignored him and continued talking shop. He said it a second time; I ignored him again. The third time he said it, I turned, looked him straight in the eye and said, "I wouldn't even be interested in the average American man."

He said, "You, know, you're right." And his attitude toward me changed.

Attitudes toward women became a ground breaking study by anthropologist Margaret Mead in the early 1900s. Her in-depth research helped expand the understanding on the impact of culture over heredity.

• • •

Margaret Mead (1901 – 1978) Revered as the most famous anthropologist in the world, Margaret Mead pioneered the idea that individual experience could be shaped by cultural demands and expectations. In her best-selling book *Coming of Age in Samoa,* Mead focused on the development of adolescent girls in American Samoa. Her reports detailing sex in the South Pacific influenced the 1960's sexual revolution. She insisted that human diversity is a resource not a handicap.

• • •

Although the divorce law changed, people hadn't changed their attitudes about divorce. Many still believed the reason for a divorce had to be to marry someone else. This attitude was typified by a bizarre conversation I had with the proprietor of a local store. I had known him since I was a kid.

"I hear you're getting married," he said.

I told him, "No, I'm getting divorced."

"But you're getting married."

"No, I'm getting divorced."

"But you like men don't you?"

"Yes, I do."

"You'll get married again won't you?"

"Yes, I will if I meet the right man. But right now I'm getting a divorce."

A divorced woman who was not actively looking for her next husband was a novelty in 1973. Friends even urged me to move to Boston where it would be easier for me to find a new husband. I told them, "I'm staying put. If he's out there, he's going to have to come to Maine to find me. And he's going to have to take the whole package—my daughter Beth, my mother and me."

Beth and my mother, 1974

In 1976, I married Gary Singer who had come to Maine from Boston to work at Union Mutual. He took the whole package. When we moved to Massachusetts three years later, his mother, Helen, became part of the total package when she also moved in with us. She had just been widowed for the second time.

Helen lived with us for 29 years, then moved to a retirement home. My mother lived with me and my family for 21 years. Both mothers lived together with us for seven years, until my mother entered a nursing home when she was 81 and suffering from dementia.

Beth attended public grade school in Norwood. She was a voracious reader and talented writer. In 6th grade she wrote, directed and narrated a play called "After Wonderland." My one regret as a working mother was a commitment at work kept me from attending her performance. Always a Mainer, when she was 14, Beth chose to move to Maine to live with her father and attend high school there.

You're Pregnant?!

In 1980, after a year establishing a new career at Arthur D. Little, Gary and I added to the family package when I got pregnant. At a project meeting when I was six months pregnant, a colleague started to schedule a follow-up meeting in three months. I said, "I won't be able to make it. My baby is due then."

He said, "You're pregnant?!"

I said, "Yes."

He said, "But you don't look pregnant."

"I don't usually show."

"You've done this before?!"

"Yes, my daughter Beth is 13."

When he got back to his office, he called me and said, "You'll have to forgive me. I've been operating under the obvious misconception that you were a much younger inexperienced woman."

I said, "Instead of an older more mature woman?" I was 36, but I looked 26.

He said, "Yes."

I felt confident enough to say, "You're forgiven."

It seems others had the same confused opinion about my being pregnant and my age because I had a similar conversation with another colleague a few days later.

By the time my second daughter, Samantha, was born in 1980, pregnant career women were not unusual. In the hospital, I shared a room with a doctor. It may have been the first time a doctor and a lawyer had shared a room in a maternity ward.

What's In a Name?

Throughout history women took their husband's name when they married. But in the 70s, married women began to keep their family name. Gary and I married just before my second year of law school. At the time, the wife of a Portland lawyer had sued for the right to revert to her family name after her application for a name change was denied. The court looked to Massachusetts law for a precedent because Maine was part of Massachusetts until 1820. Massachusetts law looked to English common law. In England, high-status women who married men of lesser status kept their family name.

The Maine court ruled a married woman could not be prevented from using her family name. My law school classmates wanted to know if I would change my name when I got married. I told them, "Since Goodrich is my first husband's name, I think I should change it to Singer, my new husband's name." And I did.

But, when my daughter Beth married in 2002, she didn't change her name. When Samantha married in 2013, she did take her husband's name. Go figure.

When I applied for admission to the Maine Bar, I had to explain my three different names, as well as the more than 20 places where I had lived. I received a call from a man at the Board of Bar Overseers with more questions about my application. I guess the Board of Bar Overseers considered me a novelty.

My male classmates also asked me, "Do you think women should be able to use 'esquire'?" The abbreviation "Esq." is used as a suffix in the United States to identify a lawyer. The term "esquire" was used in England to denote men of high social status. My answer was always, "I don't care what they call me as long as they pay me as much as they pay you." As women would discover, that still hadn't happened 40 years later.

CHAPTER 15

My Next Challenge: Law School

It's lack of faith that makes people afraid of meeting challenges, and I believed in myself.

– Muhammad Ali

I decided to become a lawyer at age 16. But my plan to enter law school after college got thwarted by lack of financial aid. That problem was resolved in 1972 when Congress passed Title IX of the Civil Rights Act. Title IX opened up student aid for women entering professional schools. This new law rekindled my interest in going to law school.

I got the push I needed from a friend, Roland Cole, who practiced law in Wells, the neighboring town to Kennebunk. I met Roland when I was in high school. When we were both students at the University of Maine, we worked together in the cafeteria. He was also a friend of Wayne's and had handled our no-fault divorce. Roland went on to become Chief Justice of the Maine Superior Court.

At a visit with Roland in his law office, as I sat opposite him at his desk, I perused the titles of the law books in the case behind him. I said, "This is what I've always wanted to do—practice law."

He looked up at me and said, "Well then, what are you doing just sitting there? If anyone can do it, you can." He proceeded to explain the steps I needed to take—the law school aptitude test (LSAT) and the application process—to be accepted at law school. When I told him I needed to take a course to get back into the swing of studying, he recommended a criminal justice course at the University of Maine. I began the class in the fall of 1974.

This was the same year the country felt a seismic eruption from President Richard Nixon's resignation following the Watergate scandal. Among the first to seek his removal was House of Representative Barbara Jordan an outspoken critic during the Watergate hearings on Capitol Hill.

• • •

Barbara Jordan (1936 – 1996) A graduate of Boston University Law School in 1956 when there were few black female law students, Barbara Jordan returned to Texas and became active in state and national politics. As the first African-American woman from Texas to serve in the House of Representatives, Jordan made national news during the Watergate hearings declaring, "I am not going to sit here and be an idle spectator to the diminution, the subversion, the destruction of the Constitution."

• • •

Back in the swing of studying, I entered the University of Maine School of Law in the fall of 1975.

I Needed a Job

In the two years following my decision to go to law school, everything changed for women at Union Mutual with the implementation of an affirmative action policy. A vice president told me, "You've been identified as one of the women eligible for promotion to upper management."

The job I wanted—working for senior management on planning for projects affecting computer systems—didn't exist when I made my decision. The company posted the job a month before I planned to leave work for law school. And word reached me that they wanted me to apply. It was too late. I had set a new course for my next career and I didn't turn back.

I notified my supervisor of my decision to go to law school, keeping him posted on my progress. I told him the date I would be leaving and asked him about a part-time job. He knew I supported my mother and daughter. He said, "I'll see what I can do." Even though management knew I would leave, the Personnel Department asked me to evaluate a public speaking course. During the course, each participant had to give a speech. Mine centered on my plan to go to law school and on hurdles I might face. I ended my speech with a poem by Edgar Albert Guest my wise mother had taught me:

> Somebody said that it couldn't be done
> But he with a chuckle replied
> That "maybe it couldn't," but he would be one
> Who wouldn't say so till he'd tried.
> So he buckled right in with the trace of a grin
> On his face, if he worried he hid it.
> He started to sing as he tackled the thing
> That couldn't be done, and he did it!

Weeks went by with no job in sight. I told my supervisor, "I'm leaving even if I don't have a job." I started to check the want ads. I felt sure I could find a job programming part-time somewhere.

On the afternoon of my last day at work, my supervisor walked into my office and said, "Take a couple of weeks off, get settled in law school and then come back. We'll work out a part-time schedule for you."

When I reported back for work, my boss said they'd reevaluated the systems jobs and asked if I'd return full-time for a 60 percent salary increase. I thanked him for the offer but told him, "No." I thought I must have been very underpaid for the offer to be so high. But a few months later when I learned they'd hired three people to replace me, I thought perhaps the offer represented belated recognition of my productivity. I never gave it another thought.

I spent the next two years writing new specifications for the company's old Autocoder programs. The IBM 1401 had been retired and the Autocoder programs ran with a simulator. Production runs were so slow one computer operator said they "brought the IBM 360 right down to its knees." By the time I left Union Mutual in 1976, they had replaced all 60 Autocoder programs.

I worked part-time all through law school, even after Gary and I married during the summer before my second year. As a result I had to schedule my time at school and at work with care. I studied at school between classes and went to work when I had large blocks of time between classes. I spent time on the weekends with my family and studying at home. One weekend in my second year, Gary and I went to the law school for a movie. My classmates razzed me about being at the school on a weekend. I asked, "What are you talking about?"

One replied, "Don't you know you're the only class member not here every weekend studying?" I didn't.

The Class of 1978

We had 100 students in the class of 1978. Three of us were in our 30s; three of us were mothers; 25 percent were women. At orientation, the professor told the men not to underestimate the women in the class. The statistics the professor quoted about the grade point averages and LSAT scores of the women applicants were impressive.

When the women students met with that professor the following week, I commented, "It's not possible to have only 25 percent women in the class based on the statistics you gave at orientation." He gave me a puzzled look. Many years later I learned no one outside of the dean's office knew about the quota.

The entering classes for the next two years only reached 25 percent female as well. After the school named a new dean in 1978, the class percentages for men and women were as random as would be expected for such a small number of students. Some years there were more women than men, and some years there were fewer.

I had done my homework about law school. I visited the law school the week before classes to get the reading assignments for the first week posted on the bulletin board. Many students didn't know to do this. They were shocked when the teacher called on them in class the first day to discuss a case.

Teachers taught us the law using the Socratic method—one student reviewed a case from our law book in class and the teacher queried the student and the class about the case. When the teachers asked questions about the first week's assignments in the first class, I raised my hand. Besides having read the assignments, I did not feel intimidated by teachers who were my contemporaries. I continued to raise my hand in classes for the next three years. Sometimes when professors didn't call on me, which was much of the time, I just spoke up.

One classmate told me, "You know, you intimidate the teachers." He pointed out how one teacher who asked questions of students by going row by row skipped over me. Years later a colleague told me that this teacher described me as one of his most notable students.

My Law School Courses

We took the traditional law school courses—Constitutional Law, Civil Procedure, Evidence, Property, Contracts and Criminal Law. Criminal Law classes focused on analyzing the new Maine Criminal Code. A friend who represented Kennebunk in the state legislature asked me to take notes on areas of the new law that might need to be amended. By the end of class, I had given him a report about issues with the code and possible solutions. You can imagine my surprise and delight when our teacher said for the class final we'd have to write about issues with the code and possible solutions. It was open book, and we could use our notes. No problem.

We also had courses on new legal topics—the Commercial Code and Intellectual Property. Stuart White, who wrote the first law book on the topic, taught Intellectual Property. He had represented the winning sides of two of the earliest cases in the field, the Beta Max case and Star War Dolls case. This class was the first law school class on this topic because Mr. White "just liked living in Portland."

A friend from Kennebunk, a vice president for a semiconductor company, worked on an invention in his off hours using his employer's facilities. He asked me to research the law on the issues raised by this situation. Mr. White pointed me to the leading cases in the area. Since intellectual property appeared as a new topic, the cases weren't indexed well. Back then we didn't have the internet or on-line services to search.

As a result of my research, I explained to my friend, "As the inventor you own the rights to your invention. But your employer has a royalty-free right to use the invention because you used the company's facilities."

When a case with these facts came up for discussion in the class, Mr. White had me give the analysis. To my pleasant surprise, an essay case on the Massachusetts Bar Exam had the same set of facts to analyze and discuss. No problem.

Two courses implicated taxes—Partnerships and Trusts and Estates. Another course was all about taxes—Federal Income Taxes. Unlike most of my classmates, I liked the tax classes. For me, reading the tax code was just like reading the logic of a COBOL program.

Although my fellow students had analytical minds, it became clear from their reactions when our teacher explained the tax law with examples, they didn't like numbers. I did. I had spent 10 years working with numbers in the insurance industry. I decided taxation might make a good career choice for me. The field had less competition and I might need that advantage.

By the mid-70s, some remarkable women became involved in business and government, paving the way for younger women to follow. One such woman was the future first female secretary of state Madeline Albright. She had become chief legislative assistant to Senator Ed Muskie of Maine in 1976.

• • •

Madeline Albright (1937 –) As a child refugee from Czechoslovakia, Madeline Albright grew up as a fierce advocate of civil and women's rights. Appointed the first female secretary of state by President William Clinton, she met on equal terms with the world's leaders—almost all men. When she heard Yasser Arafat had referred to her as a "snake," she wore a decorative snake pin on her lapel at their first meeting. From then on, when dressing for an important meeting, she chose an appropriate pin, which she describes in her book *Read My Pins*.

• • •

Our teachers introduced us to litigation and the courts with two projects. One, a trial played out before a real judge in which students played prosecutor, defense attorney and witnesses. I had fun portraying a witness who just kept talking and had to be reprimanded by the judge.

The second project involved a case in which the client had his driver's license revoked. We had to write a brief on the law and argue the case on appeal before a real judge. Thanks to my unusual memory, I recognized that a public benefit is property from *Goldberg v. Kelly,* a case described in our property book. I had my brief written before most of my classmates found the case. Some didn't find it because they didn't understand the facts presented dealt with the loss of property.

It Wasn't All Work

My fondest memories of law school are of the Christmas pageants. Every December, a group of students with unusual talents wrote, produced and acted in a parody about law school and our teachers. The students filled the large conference room. Our teachers filed in, standing at the back of the room, their apprehension obvious. One play had the title "The Wizard of Laws." Dorothy and her dog Toto searched for the way through Laws, meeting many characters parodying our teachers and administrators along the way. She discovered the way with "Gilberts," the Hornbook Series used by students to study law.

Another play depicted the Nativity. Our only female professor, Judy Potter, happened to be pregnant that year. A student parodying her came in riding on the back of one of our biggest male classmates playing the donkey. While leading the pregnant 'Judy' on the donkey, her husband Joseph read the tax code aloud, explaining how having the baby before the end of the year would result in tax savings from the additional tax deduction.

Every year, the law school invited Chief Joseph of the Penobscot tribe and Tom Tureen, lawyer for the Wabanaki Indians to give us an update on their lawsuit. The Indians had sued the state of Maine for breaching their treaties, taking their land and failing to pay them the income from natural resources they owned. I rooted for the Indians. My grandmother's Passamaquoddy tribe was also a plaintiff. The Indians won. The settlement required the pulp and paper companies to sell the land back to the Indians for $100 an acre, funded by the state.

At a neighborhood cocktail party, an executive of Great Northern Paper complained about the price the Indians would pay them for the land. I said, "I thought Great Northern made a tidy profit considering you paid the state two cents an acre for the land." In high school I read the book *Power and Paper*, about the questionable methods these businesses used to acquire Maine's resources.

Companies continued these questionable practices in the mid-70s. A law school classmate wrote an extensive article analyzing a proposed tax bill. He described how the bill disadvantaged the state and its taxpayers. Proponents of the bill tried to convince the university trustees to stop him from publishing the article, but they were unsuccessful. The *Maine Times* newspaper published his article. One of the lobbyists called and told him to "take a flying leap from the tallest pine tree" he could find in the state. He didn't.

Studying for the Bar

The graduation ceremony for the class of 1978 was held outside on a beautiful day in May.

With my mother and mother-in-law, Helen, on graduation day

But studying didn't end with graduation. We had to study next to pass the bar. The bar exam consisted of one day of essays and one day for the multiple-choice Multistate Exam. Most bar candidates in Maine signed up to take the bar review course. One of the courses covered common law crimes, a problem for my classmates. We had studied the Maine Criminal Code in law school but not the common law crimes. But I had studied common law crimes in my criminal justice course prior to law school. No problem.

In class I sat between two young men, one a Harvard Law graduate, and the other, a graduate of the University of Virginia Law School. From our conversations, they knew I was married, a mother and working. We had a friendly competition with the results of our practice exams. My grades were always higher. I told them "You should have gone to a good law school like mine." I never mentioned my unusual memory.

Gary, who originally came from Boston, told me, "If you're smart, you'll take the bar in Massachusetts as well as Maine." I did and passed the bar in both states.

My next job would turn out to be my biggest challenge—finding a job as a lawyer.

CHAPTER 16

I Wanted to Practice Law

*Have patience with all things,
but chiefly have patience with yourself.*

– Saint Frances de Sales

1978 was a landmark year for me. I received my Juris Doctor (JD) degree, my first step toward the practice of law. By that year, law firms in Maine had decided women could be lawyers—if they were both young and unmarried. I was neither, and I was a mother to boot.

1978 was a landmark year for women of color too. Harriet Tubman, an escaped slave and leader in the underground railroad during the Civil War, became the first black woman honored on a U.S. postage stamp. In 2020, she also becomes the first woman of any color to be on U.S. currency, the $20 bill. Her picture replaces that of President Andrew Jackson, a slave owner, who is relegated to the back of the bill.

Law students compete for internships at local law firms for their final year in school. The top law firms interviewed those of us in the top 25 percent of the class. I had interviews with six firms but only one second interview. That interview was with a prestigious Portland law firm whose senior partner, Sumner Bernstein, I knew well. Sumner and his wife were friends from the local duplicate bridge games and our partners when we played in Swiss team tournaments. I went through the grueling interview process with many members of the firm. But I knew my interview was a mere courtesy from Sumner. He was just being nice to me. No law firm wanted to be the first one to hire a new lawyer with my "credentials."

Sumner also served as the head of the Maine Board of Bar Overseers. He called me personally to tell me I had passed the bar.

Tax Law Provided an Opportunity

I decided to focus on an area with little competition from other law students—taxes. Accounting firms had just begun to hire female professionals and needed tax specialists regardless of gender for tax season.

But the legal profession moved very slowly to accept female lawyers as equals of male lawyers. In 1960, Supreme Court Justice Felix Frankfurter rejected Ruth Bader Ginsberg for a clerkship because of her gender, even though she came with a strong recommendation from the Dean of Harvard Law School.

• • •

> **Ruth Bader Ginsberg (1933 –)** The second female justice on the U.S. Supreme Court, Ruth Bader Ginsberg was an advocate for women's rights both before and after her appointment to the court by President Jimmy Carter in 1980. While a professor of law at Rutgers, she founded the first law school journal focused exclusively on women's rights—the Women's Rights Law Reporter. While teaching at Columbia Law School, she authored the first law school casebook on sex discrimination. Justice

Ginsberg is a strong advocate for the advancement of women's rights as a constitutional principle.

• • •

I interviewed with the senior partner of the Portland office of one of the major accounting firms, Peat Marwick Mitchell and Company. In the interview, he commented, "I heard the law firms think you're too old to begin practicing law." Then he asked, "How are you able to handle law school, a part-time job and responsibilities at home?"

I told him, "In the world of business, it's called good time management."

I joined Peat Marwick as an intern during my last year of law school and full time as a tax specialist after earning my JD. I became part of the first group of women hired by a major accounting firm in that capacity. My job responsibilities: prepare tax returns for individuals and pension plans, plus do tax research for clients.

After accepting the job at Peat Marwick, I was surprised to find out Union Mutual had an opening for a lawyer, and they were waiting for me to apply. I called and told them I had already accepted a position with Peat Marwick. I also told them who among the applicants from my class I thought they should hire—another older female. They hired her.

While the work seemed to go well, I was reminded of long established prejudices against women at a social event. Peat Marwick had its annual get-together for professional employees at the Portland Club, a men-only club. Before the meeting took place, our manager told us, "We're pleased you ladies will join the party, but you'll have to enter the club through the back door."

At first we couldn't believe what he said. Then we all rebelled and refused to attend the meeting. Our manager explained the dilemma to the Portland Club, which decided to change its policy. We went to the meeting and entered through the front door with the men.

While at Peat Marwick, I dealt with my first IRS audit. It challenged my first joint tax return with my husband, Gary. The audit focused on a deduction for a large lump-sum alimony payment Gary paid to his first wife. The court had accepted the end of Gary's alimony obligation with the payment of this lump-sum amount. At our meeting with the IRS, the auditor claimed we could not deduct the amount because it was not a periodic payment.

At the meeting, I played the dutiful wife while Gary dealt with the auditor. As we left the meeting, I introduced myself to him as a tax specialist at Peat Marwick and said I would appeal his decision. When I drew the toughest IRS Appeals Officer, everyone at Peat said, "You're going to lose."

I said, "No, I won't, because the law's on my side." A payment that doesn't survive the death of an ex-spouse is alimony, not a property settlement.

I spent more than three hours with the appeals officer going over the case law on alimony. He pulled out the relevant Bureau of National Affairs (BNA) portfolio and began to read the sections about alimony. When a case appeared to support the IRS's position, he paused for me to comment. I then explained why the case didn't apply. I thought I had lost the argument when he read a legal conclusion stated in BNA based on a case. He found the case in his library, and we read the case together. I said, "You can't draw that conclusion from the facts in this case." It was backwards logic. Although all tigers are cats, not all cats are tigers. He agreed. He ended the meeting and said he would send us his decision.

A few weeks later as I walked to my car after work, he drove by, rolled down his window and shouted out to me, "Mrs. Singer, I agree with you. I'll send you my decision." When I recounted this to my colleagues at Peat, they remarked this was "so out of character" for him.

When we received the tax refund on our return, we had put it in the bank in anticipation of an audit. After we received the IRS's decision we spent it on a much needed vacation.

That fall Gary got a new job in Boston. He commuted each week from Maine while I worked through tax season. I declined Peat Marwick's offer to transfer to their Boston office when I learned they wanted me to become a bank auditor. That didn't qualify for my to-do list. When I informed my manager, he asked me what I would do. I answered, "I don't know, but I'll do something."

He commented, "I don't worry about you. You're one of life's survivors."

At the end of tax season, we bought a house in Norwood, Massachusetts. Gary, my daughter Beth, my mother and I moved in. And Gary's mother joined us, too.

A Promising New Field—Intellectual Property

I decided to combine my computer background with law. Intellectual property law emerged as an evolving field and the Boston area grew as the center of the developing computer industry. Wang, Digital Equipment Company and Prime Computer had all established their companies there.

While at Peat Marwick, I traveled to Washington D.C. to attend the first conference ever on computer-generated evidence and how lawyers could use it in a court room. I was among the first to write about this topic. My law school thesis, published by *Rutgers Journal of Computers, Technology and the Law* in 1979, had the title "Proposed Changes to the Federal Rules of Evidence as Applied to Computer-Generated Evidence."

I wanted to meet two of the conference presenters, Roy Freed and Bob Bigelow, both from Boston. They had achieved recognition as the two foremost computer lawyers at the time. When I spoke to each of them separately about how I might combine my computer background with law in Boston, they each told me the same thing. "You can do it in New York, Chicago, San Francisco, LA, even Atlanta. But not in Boston."

Bob Bigelow did arrange for me to interview with the president of his former employer, John Hancock, but it didn't result in a job offer. I met Roy Freed at a conference many years later and reminded him of his advice about not being able to combine my computer background and the law in Boston. I said, "You were right." But years later I did practice intellectual property law—dealing with the contracts, licenses and agreements for the software company, Windstar Technologies, Inc., that my husband, Gary, and I founded in 1994.

Law Firm Recruiting

I began my search for a position in a Boston law firm with a legal recruiter. At our meeting, he told me, "I won't be able to get you any interviews." He was right. I sent my resume to 50 law firms and didn't get an interview or a call back. I assumed my public school education didn't play well in Boston. But it was also 1979 and the middle of a recession. Even lawyers from Ivy League law schools had a hard time finding jobs.

It would be a few more years before the legal field became open to hiring women with unusual experience. In 1981, President Ronald Reagan helped pave the way when he appointed Sandra Day O'Connor as the first female Supreme Court justice.

• • •

Sandra Day O'Connor (1930 –) Although Sandra Day O'Connor graduated high in her class at Stanford Law School, more than 40 firms refused to hire her because she was a woman. She got her first legal job, a deputy county attorney in California, only after agreeing to work for nothing and to share space with the secretary. In 1981, President Ronald Reagan appointed Sandra Day O'Connor as first woman Supreme Court Justice. She received many honors, the most unusual being induction into the *Cowgirl Hall of Fame*.

• • •

I met with that same legal recruiter five years later, and he told me again, "I won't be able to get you any interviews." In 1984, Boston law firms didn't hire lawyers with prior careers. But he added, "In 10 years, you'll be able to write your own ticket and go anywhere you want." He was right again.

By 1994 when I was 50, Boston law firms wanted to increase their number of female lawyers and recognized they needed international tax expertise as well. Beginning in 1986, I had received an AV—Preeminent rating—the highest grade by Martindale Hubbell's Peer Review Ratings, a rating that continued for the next 25 years. Recruiters began to call, and I received requests to interview with Boston law firms. But 1994 was the year my husband and I founded our software company. I explained to the recruiters I was personally liable on two office leases, two large term notes and two large credit lines—unusual for lawyers in large firms but not for owners of small businesses.

Besides, I felt very satisfied with my firm and practice. I declined, telling them, "I prefer being a big fish in a little pond to being a little fish in a big pond." Years later I discovered my partner Maureen Mayotte had been telling the same thing to recruiters who contacted her.

But in 1979, I had only one interview for the position of lawyer —in the Legal Department of Sun Life Insurance Company. They showed a good deal of interest in me because, as well as being a licensed attorney in Massachusetts, I had experience with all types of insurance—life, disability, health and group pensions. But the position would not be funded in the budget for another five months. I told the director of Personnel I would continue to look for a job in the interim.

A New Direction

At the beginning of my job search, I told Gary I would look for a job in the computer field if, after three months, I didn't have any success finding a legal position. At the end of the three months, I picked up the *Boston Sunday Globe* and looked through the classified ads. Arthur D. Little, Inc. had an ad for a computer specialist to head up the conversion of their payroll, personnel and benefits systems.

All I knew about Arthur D. Little (ADL) was its IBM 360 mainframe computer served as the backup computer for Union Mutual. When our mainframe broke down, we loaded the computer tapes and boxes of computer cards into a station wagon and sent our computer operators on their way to ADL on Route 2 in Cambridge. Gary explained ADL was an international consulting firm. I soon discovered that, for many decades, ADL had achieved recognition as the most prestigious consulting firm in the country.

I made an appointment with a recruiter in the Personnel Department at ADL and contacted a data processing recruiting firm to line up more interviews. But, before I did this, I called the director of Personnel at Sun Life for an update on the status of the job. He had left for a vacation, so the operator put me through to their general counsel. I asked about the status of the job and told him I was going to interview in the computer field. All he would say was he wasn't ready to fill the job because of the budget. He knew the legal field was a buyer's market, so he could wait. But what he didn't know was the computer field was a seller's market, so I didn't have to wait. I had so many interview opportunities, the recruiting firm had a hard time scheduling them all.

Before going to my ADL interview, I tossed away the second page of my resume describing my experience as a tax specialist. I replaced it with a hand-written page about my experience designing and implementing computer systems. I had designed a payroll system and been responsible for major software application conversions. When I walked down the hall in the Personnel Department, I had the feeling this was where I belonged.

During my interview for the computer position, the recruiter asked me to describe my experience at Peat Marwick as a tax specialist. Then she asked if I would also interview for a job in the Personnel Department dealing with the tax and immigration issues for consultants who relocate internationally. So I interviewed for that job as well. That week I also had interviews for several computer-related jobs including first and second interviews with Prime Computer.

After I completed my second interview at ADL for each job, the recruiter asked me when I wanted to begin work. I said, "I've been out of work for three months, the longest I've ever been out of work. I want to go to work right away, and I know I'm getting at least one good offer tomorrow." This would be from Prime Computer.

ADL offered me both jobs. I took the position in Personnel, even though it paid less, because it involved both law and tax. I later discovered the hiring process at ADL usually took two to three months, not two to three days!

As with my earlier experience with AT&T after college, the day I signed my contract with ADL, I got a call from the director of Personnel at Sun Life to set up my final interview. I told him, "I just accepted a position with ADL. I spoke to the general counsel while you were away and told him I was interviewing in the computer field." I took it as a major compliment when the general counsel had one of their lawyers call to convince me to change my mind. I didn't.

I had set my course for a new career, and I didn't turn back.

CHAPTER 17

How to Make a Silk Purse from a Sow's Ear

*Don't worry about failures,
worry about the chances you miss when you don't even try.*

– Jack Canfield

During the time I worked at Union Mutual, a vice president once told me, "If you ever move to Boston, you should go to work at Arthur D. Little. You'd fit in well there." When I moved to Boston, I took his advice and did just that.

Entrepreneur Arthur D. Little started the international consulting company bearing his name in 1886. Over the years the company established an extraordinary reputation for innovation and pioneering discoveries.

An Incredible Company

I joined Arthur D. Little—known as ADL—in the summer of 1979. I came to appreciate the company's motto: "Hardly anything is none of our business." It wasn't far from the truth. They invented fiberglass, made early contributions to cancer research, taught the Saudi's how to price oil and developed Cream of Wheat. They even designed the back office trading system for the New York Stock Exchange.

ADL had European offices in London, Paris, Wiesbaden and Brussels, plus offices in Tokyo, Japan and Sao Paulo, Brazil. Their clients included businesses around the world, government agencies and even entire countries.

Soon after I started working, I learned two stories about the company that convinced me I had found my place among kindred spirits.

Both stories illustrated that old accepted notions, no matter how ingrained into our belief system, could be disproved.

The first story dealt with the well-known expression, "You can't make a silk purse from a sow's ear." In 1921, the company challenged its chemists to refute this statement. The chemists studied how silk worms produced silk thread then analyzed pork products. After sufficient experiments and tests on the chemical makeup of both, they did indeed produce two silk purses from the pork by-products, not very practical silk purses and too expensive to develop. But they had proved that with sufficient motivation, skill and resources "anything is possible."

The company wrote a report about the experiment. It concluded, "The only way to get ahead is to dig in, to study, to find out, to reason out theories, to test them...."

The company's memorabilia including one of the two silk purses is now on display in the *Arthur D. Little, Inc. Archives* at the Massachusetts Institute of Technology in Cambridge. The other silk purse is in the Smithsonian in Washington, D.C.

The second story had a similar theme of disproving an often repeated adage: "You can't fly a lead balloon." In 1977, the company formed three teams to see which one could make a lead balloon that could fly. Using the similar ingenuity and experimentation, each team made a different model. One worked better than the other two.

By accident, during the test flight, the superior model broke away from its tether and went flying off. It headed toward Boston's Logan Airport, where amused control tower personnel treated it as an unidentified flying object (UFO). It was last seen heading toward Europe.

A Campus in Cambridge

ADL was located in Cambridge in a setting of numbered, multiple-storied brick buildings, much like a college campus. I soon learned the organization ran much like a college as well. When I arrived on time for my first meeting, held in another building, the room was empty. I walked back to my office to check the location. It was correct. By the time I got back to the meeting, everyone had arrived. I was the last to show up. After that I got to meetings a few minutes late like everyone else.

The Personnel Department was located on the second floor of Building 35 and took up one corridor of offices. The vice president of Personnel, Lew Rambo, had a corner office as did my supervisor Ron Williams, who was in charge of International Personnel.

Lew was a handsome, light-skinned African-American. There were few African-American professionals in the company at the time. During the 1970s and 80s, the country still held onto prejudices against ethnic groups as well as women in the workplace. So in many ways, I could identify with Lew's challenging journey.

Ron Williams was a silver-haired gentleman who had lived in Brussels. There, he had established the personnel policies for ADL's European operations. Ron stored his historical files in my office, one of the same-sized cinderblock offices along the corridor.

Lew told me. "If you need anything, it's in the files." Ron added, "But if it's not in the files, it's out there somewhere, and it's your job to find it." I became very adept at finding what I needed to do my job.

The Personnel Department included several personnel officers and support staff. Not long after I joined ADL, one personnel officer came down with a mysterious illness. He died the following year. I later learned he had died of acquired immune deficiency syndrome (AIDS). Not much was known by the public about AIDS until the famous movie actress Elizabeth Taylor took up the cause.

• • •

> **Elizabeth Taylor (1932 – 2011)** British-American Elizabeth Taylor was one of the most gorgeous and well-known actresses of the 50s and 60s. In her first starring role in *National Velvet* at the age of 12, she played Velvet Brown who wins the Grand National steeplechase race even though women were barred from being jockeys. In 1985, at a time when few acknowledged the disease, Taylor raised awareness about AIDS. She founded the National AIDS Research Foundation, and devoted much of her time and efforts to AIDS activism and fundraising.

• • •

A Job with a "World" of Possibilities

As a company with business operations in different countries around the world, ADL had hundreds of employees in foreign locations. At the time I joined the company, they also had project locations in less developed countries with rotating personnel. It became my job to deal with issues for U.S. citizens and lawful permanent residents who were assigned to the foreign offices. Lawful permanent residents, known as "green card holders," got the name from the color of the original cards the government issued them. I also handled tax matters for foreign project employees on temporary foreign assignment with their families. We called them "expatriates"—"expats" for short.

My first expat task was "tax equalization receivables." This meant that I became ADL's bill collector for amounts former expats owed the company. As you can imagine, it took a lot to sort out all the complex facts. After considerable research I managed to collect most of the money the expats owed ADL, and, as it turned out, pay the money ADL owed some expats.

I also had the responsibility for all U.S. immigration matters for ADL's foreign national employees. For all of this I had a nondescript job title—Project Associate. My salary started at $23,000. I learned much later that my salary was far less than rates for those with similar responsibilities in the Boston area.

Most of the consultants I dealt with were men because most college graduates in science, technology, engineering and math—now called STEM—were men. In a dramatic glimmer of hope for change, outer space became another frontier conquered by a woman when Dr. Sally Ride became the first female U.S. astronaut.

• • •

Dr. Sally Ride (1951 – 2012) American women rose to new heights—in a literal and figurative sense—in 1983 when Sally Ride became the first American woman astronaut in space. Ride graduated from Stanford where she went on to earn her Master's and PhD in physics. She joined NASA in 1978 after being chosen from among 8,000 applicants. As revealed in her obituary, she is also now the first known LGBT astronaut.

• • •

Her selection showcased an encouraging shift in attitudes about women filling occupations most often held by men. But we still had "a long, long way to go."

Solving Immigration Problems

One of my most vexing priorities dealt with the immigration status of ADL's foreign employees working in the United States. Since the process involved complicated procedures, Lew sent me to a Practicing Law Institute course on U.S. immigration law and procedure, held in New York City. He wanted me to get a handle on all the forms and procedures involved with foreign national employees.

Immigration documents got scattered among files in the Personnel Department and consulting sections. For all its achievements, ADL suffered from a territorial protection syndrome often found in academia. Managers guarded their turf like department deans.

It took a while, but I managed to retrieve all the pertinent documents. I moved them into my office and created an immigration file for each employee. I learned two startling facts after reviewing the immigration documents and talking with ADL's outside immigration counsel. First, the company faced a risk of losing several top consultants in their Energy Economics Section that would jeopardize vital projects in progress. These consultants were approaching the end of the seven-year maximum authorized period of employment under their intracompany transferee immigration status. Second, as a result of the course and all my research, I realized I now knew more about immigration law and procedure than ADL's outside immigration counsel.

I felt I knew Lew well enough to describe this harsh fact in a unique way. I told him, "If I can't get green cards for these consultants so they can continue to work in the United States, Energy Economics will have to be run on a barge beyond the 200-mile limit."

This situation got worse as time went on. I needed advice from an expert immigration lawyer. I wrote a recommendation to Lew to replace our outside counsel with a well-regarded immigration lawyer in Boston. This became a little touchy since our outside counsel happened to be a friend of ADL's general counsel Dick Murphy.

Undaunted, I walked into Lew's office and handed him my recommendation. He read it and agreed I needed expert guidance. But he felt reluctant to create a scene with a request to Dick Murphy to dismiss his old friend. We both knew that, without help from someone with greater knowledge on immigration matters, we'd have serious problems. Dejected, I walked back to my office.

A few days later Lew fielded a call from the Immigration and Naturalization Service (INS) but couldn't answer their questions about an immigration petition for a valued consultant. He called me in, but I didn't have the answers either. After he hung up, I refused to leave his office until he made the call to Dick Murphy saying, "I need expert advice and I need it now!" Without answers, this consultant couldn't continue to work in the United States.

Later Lew described this encounter to colleagues, "Paula came into my office with her hip boots and whip and made me call Dick Murphy." It boosted my ego to know that our relationship could handle such joking.

When I discussed the problems with our new immigration lawyer, to my surprise, I discovered he already knew the facts. He'd had previous discussions about our immigration situations with our original outside counsel. When I got the information the new lawyer provided, I moved forward and obtained green cards for all the consultants.

More than Just Paperwork

On another assignment, I had to untangle more convoluted immigration-related problems for some of our consultants in specialty worker status—known as "H-1B" for the immigration law section defining its terms and conditions. It once took me two days to convince the U.S. consular officer in Montreal to give an H-1B's wife and two-year old child a visa to reenter the United States. The consultant called me from Spain, where he was on business, and explained that his wife had changed her status to J-1 exchange visitor issued by a local university. J-1 regulations allow exchange for educational and other purposes. She had gone to Canada with their child to get a new U.S. visa stamp in her passport.

The consular officer reviewed her application and her husband's H-1B history. When I called the consular officer, he said, "He's been in the States more than 10 years. He's just not temporary anymore."

I explained, "He'll be leaving for assignment in Spain within three months. You can see it would be a hardship to prevent his family from returning to their home in the States."

This seemed to satisfy the consular officer. He issued the worker's family the nonimmigrant visas needed for reentry.

I helped another H-1B experiencing a unique international complication. He was being transferred to work for an ADL project in Saudi Arabia. The Saudi government required him to obtain the visa he needed to enter Saudi Arabia from their embassy in the country of his citizenship, Lebanon. The government had approved his visa. It waited for him at the Saudi Arabian embassy in Beirut. So far so good.

Unfortunately, the Israeli army had Beirut surrounded, so he couldn't get to the Saudi embassy to pick up his visa. Worse, his H-1B status in the United States would expire in two days. He couldn't work or obtain an extension after the expiration date. Working around the clock to beat the deadline, I completed the paperwork and submitted it to INS in time for the extension. When the siege of Beirut lifted, he got his Saudi visa and relocated to Saudi Arabia.

Another H-1B posed a special problem for me. His H-1B status would expire in another year and couldn't be renewed again. He needed to have U.S. lawful permanent resident status—a green card—in order to work here indefinitely. Before the green card could be issued, ADL had to prove no U.S. worker met the requirements for this particular job. Since the project he would work on required very specialized skills, we felt sure there would not be any available applicants with the required skills.

To satisfy Department of Labor requirements, we had to advertise the position. While commuting to work, I heard the job described on a local radio station's "Job of the Week." Applicants inundated ADL with resumes. I took them to the section manager who had posted the job and asked him to review the resumes using the chart I had made of the required attributes that needed to be documented.

The manager said, "I'm leaving tomorrow on a trip."

I said, "What are you doing tonight?"

He replied, "I guess I'm reviewing these resumes." The next morning, before he left on his trip, he gave me the completed chart and resumes. None of the applicants met the job requirements. This allowed us to get the labor certification and move forward with the green card processing for our H-1B worker.

My most perplexing problem involved a U.S. consultant leaving on a business trip to Angola. His secretary called me in tears after he kept insisting she obtain his new U.S. passport right away. His current passport would expire while he traveled in Angola. I called the consultant and said, "Under U.S. government rules, only *you* can renew your own passport. If you don't, and you are in Angola when your passport expires, it will be impossible for you to renew it. The

United States doesn't have diplomatic relations with Angola, so there is no U.S. embassy."

I conferred with my outside immigration counsel about what to do. He told me the complicated steps required to resolve his problem. Armed with this information, I called the consultant and told him, "Travel to New York City before you leave. You can renew your passport through the expedited process at the passport office there. Take both your old and new passports with you. Plan a stopover in Lisbon. Deplane. Go to the Angolan Embassy there and have them transfer the visa from your old passport to your new passport. Then you can continue your trip to Angola."

To make sure he understood the importance of this procedure, I told him, "If you don't follow these steps and get stuck in Angola with an expired passport, don't call me. I can't help you." I called his secretary and recounted my conversation. I could tell she was relieved by the way she laughed.

Some Successful Lobbying

In 1986, President Ronald Reagan signed the Simpson-Rizzoli Act—known as The Immigration Reform and Control Act (IRCA)—into law. IRCA imposed penalties on employers who knowingly recruit or hire illegal immigrants. It also gave amnesty to about three million illegal immigrants in the United States who met certain requirements. But, before this bill became law, another Simpson-Rizzoli bill was up for discussion.

The original Simpson-Rizzoli bill had two provisions problematic for ADL. The first: Foreign students could not change status after graduation to a status authorizing employment. The second: Labor certifications needed for green card applicants had to be based on labor market data showing a need for workers in that field. Most of the students in advanced degree programs in science and engineering, the targets of ADL recruitment, were foreign students. And ADL's labor certifications focused on work in emerging fields that wouldn't even be addressed by current labor market data.

The labor certification I worked on for a green card petition for an ADL employee who was in H-1B status was typical. He was a physicist with a PhD in molecular beam epitaxy (MBE), important to new developments in communications. During the labor certification process I had identified all PhDs in MBE, 15 in all, many of whom were foreign. ADL's labor certification was approved and I proceeded with the petition for his green card.

I pointed out to ADL management how the Simpson-Rizzoli bill would inhibit ADL's ability to recruit top-credentialed students in the sciences and engineering and would prevent ADL from petitioning for green cards for foreign workers in emerging new technologies. The general counsel asked me to draft a letter to ADL's congressmen about these problems to be signed by ADL's president, John Magee. I did.

At a symposium about the bill given at a Boston area university, Senator Simpson, the bill's co-sponsor, commented he was "surprised at the outpouring of letters" about the provision preventing foreign students from remaining to work in the United States following graduation. I raised my hand and asked, "Was it a surprise how dependent U.S. businesses had become on foreign workers because of the few Americans in advanced degree programs in the sciences and engineering?" At the time, most of the students in MIT's advanced electrical engineering program were foreign students.

He replied, "Yes, it was."

I asked, "Well, what are our leaders going to do about that?"

He said something about providing more funds for American students for advanced education in these fields. But, based on the huge and ever-increasing number of American students dependent on loans, that didn't happen.

The problematic provisions were not included in IRCA. The labor certification process remained unchanged. And U.S. businesses continued to recruit foreign students.

CHAPTER 18

Exploring Big Worlds at Arthur D. Little

*Man cannot discover new oceans
unless he has the courage to lose sight of the shore.*

– Andre Gide

While my immigration responsibilities gave me my biggest challenge, I spent most of my time in support of Arthur D. Little's U.S. expats on temporary work assignment abroad. I didn't know why, but the one document I had saved from working at Peat Marwick was their booklet on the tax rules and procedures for U.S. expats. I studied it the weekend before I started work.

During my first week at work, I met with ADL's outside tax advisor, Ken Vacovec. He gave me a brief overview of the tax laws and procedures that apply to U.S. expats. He also explained the income breakdowns he needed in order to prepare their U.S. tax returns and compute their tax reimbursements each year.

PAULA N. SINGER

Supporting ADL's Expats

I had to begin by learning the contract terms for each of ADL's employees on assignment abroad. It's fortunate I love a challenge. The memoranda of understanding describing their transfer provisions—for those who had one—and copies of related communications were not all in one place. The more I searched for meaningful documents, the more frustrated I got. But I managed to put together a transfer file for each of these employees on assignment abroad and kept them in my office.

Figuring out the W-2 income breakdown for ADL's expats became an arduous task. While most U.S. workers receive all of their wages through payroll, most expats do not. That's because their "wages" include the cost of housing provided in the assignment location, education expenses for their children, trips for home leave—plus R&R trips for those on assignment in the Middle East—and sundry other payments not made through payroll.

To complete this task for each ADL expat, I had to figure out what types of payments and benefits-in-kind each expat received and where to find the costs. The records were scattered among three departments—Payroll, Accounts Payable and Subsidiary Accounting—or the costs were in the overseas projects' records. It was September and the extension for their 1979 tax returns ended in October. I had to hit the pavement running. I designed a chart with items of income down the left side and location of payment across the top. I completed one for each expat to identify where to track down the income item.

Once I found it all, I compiled a breakdown for Ken and also gave it to Payroll, so they could issue a W-2C for each expat to report the additional income amounts. To make this process more efficient, I asked the computer staff to include new accounts for these types of income. By the time I left ADL in 1985, they collected and compiled 80 percent of this data automatically—many years before other companies automated this process.

I also had to estimate the value of this additional income and the resulting tax reimbursements needed to keep the expat whole as compared to U.S. counterparts. Contracting used these cost estimates for their contract proposals. To accomplish this task, I found a good resource in London that collected this type of data and provided it for a fee.

One of the consultants putting together a proposal didn't want to pay for the data, so I told him to collect the information from local sources when he traveled to the project location. He arrived back in my office a week later and asked for the resident assignment cost estimates. I asked him for the local costs so I could compute the estimates. He didn't have them, so I said, "Well, pick a number. You're as good at that as I am." He agreed to pay the fee for me to purchase the data. I managed to compute the cost estimates in time for him to get his proposal in under the deadline a week later.

Many Contracting Department proposals received funds from the U.S. Agency for International Development (USAID). The government had a rule that contractors couldn't be reimbursed for U.S. taxes. This rule posed a major problem when ADL began to bid on a contract for consulting on a new telephone system in Cairo, Egypt. Congress had changed the U.S. tax rules for expats so, instead of having little or no U.S. taxes while on overseas assignment because of income exclusions, expats had to pay U.S. income taxes. The additional taxes caused by the expat's housing and other benefits became substantial because of the high cost of housing in the Middle East—$20,000 to $30,000 a year. No employee would go on an overseas assignment if their net pay after taxes would be less than if they remained working in the United States.

I computed the tax reimbursement costs for the temporary assignments of 12 consultants and their families to be about $600,000. To convince USAID this was a necessary cost, I had to educate

ADL's and USAID's negotiators in Cairo about the U.S. tax rules—all by telex. I think if I hadn't been able to communicate so well by telex, I might have been sent to Cairo to teach them in person instead. Later I did take one trip to educate USAID personnel on expatriate taxation; Ken and I flew to Washington, D.C. to give a seminar to 18 of USAID's top managers.

Contracting had to convince USAID that this "special area allowance" became necessary because of the change in U.S. tax law. ADL's contract negotiator called me from Cairo and said, "What USAID is saying is, in effect, they have to pay $600,000 to another U.S. government agency."

I said, "That's right. Tell them if they don't like it, they can lobby Congress to change the tax law. They have more influence than we do." USAID lobbied Congress, and the onerous tax law was repealed retroactively.

When I first began this task, my only tools amounted to a pencil, ledger paper and a calculator. But when IBM introduced their new personal computer (PC), I managed to snag the second PC in the company. I did that by signing up for a course in BASIC, the PC's computer language, when I heard ADL's president, John Magee, would be in the class. It became obvious from my comments in class I knew a lot about computers and programming. John and I would chat during the break. We had something in common—he got his master's degree at the University of Maine in Orono. During one chat I told him I was creating International Personnel's reports on the Atari computer in my bedroom. Within the week, Lew told me management had approved an IBM PC for me.

My husband, Gary, transferred the company files through a network he created between the Atari and our personal IBM PC—perhaps one of the earliest home networks. I took the transferred files to work on a floppy disc. Gary was an expert in networks. When he worked at Hood in the early 80s, he had a terminal so he could dial into their mainframe computer from home. When he worked at Howard Johnson's, he was responsible for moving their reservation system from an outside vendor to their in-house computer center—a feat detailed in a March 1984 article in *Computerworld*, the leading computer newspaper at the time.

I set up a computer process for estimating resident assignment costs using the first spreadsheet program, VisiCalc. When the Lotus 1-2-3 spreadsheet came out, I converted this process to the improved spreadsheet program. I learned ADL continued to use this spreadsheet program for 10 years after I left the company.

While I felt good about all I accomplished, I couldn't resolve the benefit issues for the U.S. citizens on overseas assignment. The Benefits Department had the responsibility to administer benefit policies, and they didn't like anyone moving into their territory. All I could do was document the variety of issues, the most contentious—the number of days off for vacation and holiday. The number of days per year for U.S. vacations and holidays was much less than the days provided by other countries' official policies—a situation that remains unchanged to this day. I documented the benefit issues in a memo to Lew who passed it along to Benefits. Lew said, "Benefits wants to have a meeting about the policy." I knew "policy" meant they intended to dump the problem back in Personnel's lap. I remembered seeing a memorandum about benefits for expats when I reviewed the historic files in my office. I found it, made copies and left with Lew for the meeting.

The vice president of Benefits opened the meeting with, "What we need is a benefits policy for these situations."

Before anyone could say anything, I said, "We already have one," and handed each person a copy of the memorandum. It was signed by a consultant, John Magee, who was now ADL's president. The discussion changed to how the Benefits Department would administer the policy for expats.

As we left the meeting, Lew asked, "Where do you find this stuff?"

I answered, "You told me my first week of work everything was in the files. It was in the files."

Games Mother Never Taught You

ADL had a long history as a very male-dominated company. They experienced more than one sex discrimination claim brought against them. As a new member of Personnel, an administrative function in a consulting firm, I wound up low [wo]man on the totem pole.

The facilities for both consulting and administrative staff consisted of the same-size cinderblock offices on ADL's campus in Cambridge. The facilities became constrained as the company grew. I had my own office, but when Lew hired a young summer intern I had to share it with the intern. It became an awkward arrangement. He had to leave the office every time I met with a consultant or manager on a confidential matter.

As my knowledge, expertise and responsibilities grew, I gained respect for my accomplishments. But few knew I was a lawyer, even though my Massachusetts license hung on my office wall. More than one manager became upset with me when I offered a problem solution outside of my area of responsibility. The general counsel knew I was a lawyer but criticized one of my proposed problem solutions because I wasn't a member of the Legal Department. I told him, "Just because I'm a lawyer doesn't mean every opinion I give is a legal opinion." Rather it was a common-sense solution based on my skills as a systems analyst.

I discovered the solution when I read the popular book *Games Mother Never Taught You* by Betty Lehan Harragan. She explained how your office is furnished and the placement of the furnishings makes a difference in the way you are perceived by others. She explained having people sit opposite your desk gives you an air of authority. What you put on your walls matters too. Clutter is a no-no.

Pictures and documents should appear in plain view to catch the visitor's eye.

• • •

Betty Lehan Harragan A writer, consultant and advocate of women's issues Betty Lehan Harragan's book *Games Mother Never Taught You* sold millions of copies and became an important resource in college and business schools. The book described many unfair practices facing women in the workplace. Her articles about problems facing women appeared in major magazines such as *Working Woman, Woman's Day, Mademoiselle* and *Savy.*

• • •

I became inspired. I put together an office plan and presented it to Lew. He liked it. But we were in the midst of a recession, and he said it would have to wait. The company had put a freeze on employee salaries and expenses.

I found my own solution. I called the head of the Facilities Department and said, "I don't have a budget, but I have some furniture to trade." She came right over with some men to help out. They repositioned my desk and file cabinets, swapped my excess furniture for more functional pieces and moved my bookshelves to the side wall. They even put up a new curtain.

I hung two photographs of Egypt—the pyramids and hieroglyphics, gifts from an expat—on the wall behind my desk and hung my Massachusetts license where visitors could see it.

It transformed the entire office. When Lew walked by my door after the transformation and glanced in, he did a double take. He came in, looked around and said in amazement, "Singer, how did you do all this?!"

I said, "I did some horse trading."

Two Unresolved Problems

I had two problems I couldn't resolve—my noncompetitive salary and nondescript title. Based on a survey of my peers in Greater Boston, my salary fell lower than the lowest range of all but two companies, even though I had more responsibilities such as dealing with U.S. immigration matters. According to a national survey, my salary was below the 10th percentile! I still have those surveys.

I presented the salary surveys to Lew, but he couldn't solve the problem. Contracting, Accounting and the sections all benefitted from my work. They were not willing to support my salary with funds from their budgets. Personnel's primary benefit from my services—my work prevented personnel problems from developing. I told Lew, "I'd be better paid if I got a commission on what I saved the company."

When I received a 12 percent raise, Lew said, "You got the highest percentage given." But I began with a low salary, so the amount of increase was low relative to someone with a higher salary. One reason women's salaries remain low compared to salaries of their male colleagues.

Lew told me, "The way to get a good increase is to come in with a big offer from another company and negotiate." Men did this but I didn't. When I left Union Mutual for law school, they offered me a 60 percent raise to return. I didn't.

My husband, Gary, told me, "The reason your salary remains low is because you're working for a consulting company, but you're not a consultant." I knew some members of the Personnel Department consulted on contracts. I reasoned if I consulted too, my salary might improve. I had begun to receive calls from individuals in other companies seeking advice on international personnel matters. Most of the calls were from colleagues in the Boston area. But some were from companies in other parts of the country. I wondered why they seemed puzzled when I answered their questions for free and pointed them to other resources. I learned why when I called Contracting and asked whom they referred the potential international personnel leads to. Much to my surprise, the answer was "You."

There was a market for what I knew, so I presented Lew with a plan for me to consult on international personnel matters. But I needed some support staff assistance and time away from my assigned duties. Personnel didn't have the budget for me to do this, so I didn't become a consultant.

Lew did arrange for me to take a business trip to Europe as a bonus. I flew to London to meet with the director of Personnel for European operations. He took me to lunch at a British club. It had impressive dark wood paneling and a double staircase leading up to the dining room with a huge picture of Queen Elizabeth on the landing.

I chuckled to myself as I recalled Ron's story about his first trip to London, his visit to the club and its effect on him. He described how, as he walked with a colleague toward the stairs, they were approached by a dignified gentleman. His colleague said, "Neal!" Ron thought he said "Kneel" and went down on his knee. Then his colleague introduced him to Neal.

Gary was the director of Data Processing for Howard Johnson's, by then a British-owned company. He arranged a business trip to London to coincide with my trip. An ADL colleague recommended we eat at the Goring Hotel. We didn't realize how this hotel and its restaurant ranked among the most impressive in London. Years later Kate Middleton and her family stayed at the Goring Hotel during their stay in London for her wedding with Prince William.

We arrived at the hotel at 6:00 p.m. without a reservation. We didn't know people dined much later in Europe or that high end restaurants required reservations. The maître d' showed his annoyance. He asked us to wait while he went to see if he could find an available table. He came back, said he located an empty table and led us into a huge empty dining room.

I never used my nondescript job title, Project Associate, outside the office. I gave Lew a comparison of titles gleaned from a national directory of international personnel jobs. Men were manager, director, or vice president; women were associate or assistant, even when they had responsibilities similar to the men's. When ADL revised its job titles, my job title didn't change.

In spite of its frustrations, I had fun working at ADL, and the experience I gained on the job would prove invaluable for my future careers.

A Systems Analyst Again

It used to take me longer to identify the internal organization at ADL than it took me to get around the internal organization at Union Mutual. That's because ADL was run more like a university. Section managers controlled their area of business much like college deans. Consultants moved from one project to another including across section lines. As ADL became more international, consultants could be employed by one legal company, provide services for another legal entity and report to a section manager who might be of a different entity, even in a different country. The overseas projects had their own organizations with employees on assignment from any number of ADL offices and sections.

I became familiar with both the internal and external organization of companies because of my job and legal experience. Also, because of my specific duties, I knew benefits were tied to an employee's legal employer not their section. But I seemed to be the only one who understood that. ADL hired a president for the Canadian subsidiary and tried to include him in the U.S. qualified pension plan. A brouhaha broke out when top management read my memo explaining why it wouldn't work. They wanted to "shoot the messenger." But they did adopt my proposed solution.

My first interview at ADL was for project leader of the team assigned to convert the company's personnel, payroll and benefits processing to a new system. I kept in contact with the project team over the years. By the fourth year, they had been unable to convert to the chosen system provided by Management Science America (MSA). No one in management understood why. I did. MSA's system was designed for the traditional organization in which employees worked for and reported to managers in the same company.

At the outset of the project, I had explained in a memo to Lew why the conversion wouldn't work. He said, "No one will listen to Personnel." When management put together meetings to review progress and decide what to do, Lew asked me to attend the meetings with him because of my systems analysis background.

For the first meeting, I prepared a graph illustrating ADL's internal organization across the top and the legal companies down the left side and then plotted where employee's intersected on the graph. Seeing the chart, everyone understood why they couldn't convert to MSA. They decided the graph should be designed and enlarged by the Graphics Department. They also assigned me the job of presenting the graph with a memo explaining to top management why the system wouldn't work for ADL. By the time I gave my presentation, management had already heard about my graph and agreed to stop implementation of the MSA system.

The author of *The Problem Solvers* (a book about ADL) said, when a consultant tried to describe the organization, *he* created a graph that looked like "a map of the Paris subway system."

After my presentation I gave a copy of my original memo for Lew to ADL's Treasurer. He read it in disbelief. I said, "If only management listened to Personnel, the company could have saved a bundle."

No One Would Listen

Management didn't listen to Personnel about anything except personnel matters. And I was a female in Personnel who didn't have the title of Personnel Officer. People in and out of personnel ignored my advice. It didn't matter that I was a lawyer and knew how to avoid problems before they occur.

ADL management didn't like to put things in writing. Our expats did sign a memorandum of understanding laying out the terms and conditions of their overseas resident assignments. But ADL had no written policy for short-term assignments. I knew the government wanted everything in writing. So I volunteered to put the policy in writing, but management told me not to. USAID disallowed $17,000 of short-term assignment expenses in an audit because the company lacked a written short-term assignment policy.

After that, I implemented "Paula's personnel policy." If the company had provided the same benefits or expense reimbursements for three or more assignments, it qualified as company policy. Without telling Lew, I documented the overseas assignment policies in handouts that I gave to consultants identified for overseas assignment. I also wrote a document describing how tax reimbursements were calculated. The document illustrated typical assignment costs, including unusual housing costs in less developed countries such as in the Middle East.

While I was out on vacation, a Saudi senior vice president of Petromin, a long-standing ADL client in Riyadh, Saudi Arabia, visited the ADL campus. He wanted management to explain to him why the assignment costs were so high. Lew asked my assistant what they could do. She volunteered to meet with the executive and walk him through the assignment policies and related costs using my handouts. "What handouts?" Lew asked.

My assistant said, "The ones Paula developed for explaining everything to potential expats." The meeting went well; the vice president went away happy. And Lew was happy too.

When ADL hired a consultant who had worked the first phase of the project through a "body shop," I alerted everyone that the recruiter might sue for their commission. They did.

Time for the blame game. But I had raised the issue with Lew and documented it in my status report. Lew had raised the issue with Contracting. They passed it along to Legal. At the meeting of all staff involved including me, ADL's general counsel understood that he had to take responsibility for not preventing the problem. And he did.

When ADL made plans for transferring a consultant to Indonesia, I researched how tax reimbursement costs could be minimized legally by using dual contracts. One contract covered services in country. The other one covered out-of-country services. When the tax lawyer from Indonesia visited, I met with him to discuss the procedures we needed to follow for salary and benefits under these two contracts. I explained to Accounting and Payroll how these payments needed to be handled separately for each employment contract. But they decided that wasn't necessary and ran all of the consultant's compensation and benefits-in-kind through the U.S. payroll together. A year later Accounting asked me to help them split a year's worth of payroll records between the two contracts. They also wanted me to help put in place procedures for future payments under the dual contracts.

That was the last straw. When Ken Vacovec called me on another matter that week, I vented my frustration. Ken invited me to lunch that Friday. Both Ken and Lew knew I had begun looking for a new job and why. Before going to lunch, Ken told me about a conversation he'd had with Lew the prior week when I was out. Lew told Ken, "We both know Paula is going to leave ADL. The only way we can both keep her is if she works for you at your law firm."

Ken laid out an opportunity for me with his firm. That weekend I discussed it with Gary who said, "Do it. It's what you've always wanted to do." I gave my notice to Lew Monday morning.

More than one person at my going away party said, "A lawyer! Maybe now they'll listen to you."

I knew I'd be missed when one consultant asked, "Have they done an analysis on what your leaving will do to the profitability of the company?"

CHAPTER 19

International Taxes—Learning an Exotic Language

The hardest thing in the world is to understand the income tax.

– Albert Einstein

I left Arthur D. Little to join Ken Vacovec's tax law firm in early February 1985, just in time for tax season. Ken and I decided I should concentrate my practice on international tax matters. My announcement said, "Concentrating in Tax Law and International Relocations." After a short time my practice had expanded to cover cross-border taxation of individuals, payments, trusts and estates, and small businesses including the effects of international treaties.

Few lawyers had the perspective I had gained working at ADL. And because the laws and regulations were so complex, and few resources addressed these international tax rules and treaties, I knew I could become an expert with little competition.

My practice attracted individuals with tax issues in other countries as well as the United States. I knew I needed tax experts in other countries to assist these clients with the other countries' tax laws. So in 1987, I joined the International Fiscal Association (IFA), the only non-governmental and non-sectarian international organization dealing with fiscal matters. I knew I could find my needed contacts at IFA meetings as well as increase my knowledge of cross-border taxation.

It came as no surprise that the ingrained tradition favoring men over women continued across international boundaries.

This became evident on my first IFA meeting, the Global Congress in Amsterdam, where I was one of only 15 female participants out of 1,500. The fact that only a few women participated in IFA was highlighted at the conference in a unique way. By mistake, I wondered into a luncheon meeting for organization leaders from each country. Unaware of my blunder, I mingled with the leaders over pre-luncheon cocktails and chatted with the top tax professionals in the world. When one asked, "What is your office?"

I responded, "Oh, this is my very first IFA meeting!"

When we sat down at our lunch tables, IFA's president, who was also president of IFA USA that year, took the podium. He began by saying, "Gentlemen." He paused and added, "I think we're all gentlemen here." That's when I figured out my mistake.

I raised my hand and said, "Oh no, I'm here." He looked at me a bit flummoxed as heads turned to see where the feminine voice came from. The man sitting next to me said, "I'm in the wrong luncheon too."

I replied, "But you're not as conspicuous as I am." I was the only woman in the room. I stayed for the luncheon and chuckled as I got to know my table mates.

For relief from the days of meetings, IFA planned a day with a choice of sightseeing trips. I chose to tour The Hague, as did many other participants from the United States. One of the tourist attractions included the home of the famous 17th century artist Rembrandt van Rijn. During the tour the guide pointed out a huge painting of a voluptuous nude female. He said, "Rembrandt was criticized for this portrait because she could have been a washer woman."

I commented to the man beside me, "Realistically, it's hard to tell a person's station in life without their clothes on."

He said, "You mean naked we're all equal?"

"Well, no," I said, "Naked some are more equal than others." He started laughing and laughed whenever he saw me at meetings the next day. I saw him again in 2001 at the annual meeting of IFA's USA branch in Boston. He had become a high-level leader of the organization by then. As I reminded him of where we had met, he started to laugh again. I had discovered long ago, as did one of my favorite comedians Carol Burnett, that humor is a wonderful tool to help open doors for women.

• • •

Carol Burnett (1933 –) Multi-talented Carol Burnett started out in New York City night clubs and television shows. Her fame grew when she starred on Broadway in *Once Upon a Mattress*. In 1959, she joined the *Garry Moore Show* creating memorable characters like the little-old cleaning lady. In 1967, she began *The Carol Burnett Show* on CBS. Although management doubted a woman could head a variety show, a clause in her contract forced them to give her the opportunity. Her show ran for eleven years, winning 25 Emmy Awards.

• • •

Few Tax Rules and Regulations

When I began to work on taxes for international clients, I soon discovered the lack of specific tax rules for many international transactions and the dearth of IRS interpretive regulations and rulings—called "IRS published guidance"—when there were specific tax rules. The IRS also didn't have forms and instructions for many of the international transactions I encountered. A colleague asked, "How can you practice in an area where there are no rules?"

I said, "Easy. I make up the rules as I go along. I use general tax principles and take them to their logical conclusion." I also designed forms to attach to individual tax returns for procedures without forms.

Even when rules existed, I had trouble finding them. I had to become a super sleuth to locate them because most of the manuals I found didn't include indices for international topics. Automated content and indices would come many years later.

One day I sent an associate to our library on an important task. I wanted him to find the new IRS ruling that explained how to allocate stock option income for nonresident alien recipients between U.S. and foreign sources. Only the U.S. source portion was taxable. After a couple of hours I went to the library to help. He said, "I can't find it." I took the book he was researching, opened up to the index and pointed to the reference for the ruling. "There it is," I said. I guess it was just luck.

Primary Resources

My first education about federal taxes came during law school. The original tax code written by Congress in 1913 consisted of just 27 pages. Today, the combined code, IRS interpretive regulations and rulings, legislative history and case references comprise over 74,000 pages of CCH's *Standard Tax Reporter*. I learned the basic rules and how to research the code and regulations in my federal income tax course in law school. I also figured out how to apply them to two specific areas in my partnership and estate and gift tax courses.

The primary resources for my questions included the IRS personnel who wrote the regulations and rulings. When a ruling affected foreign students and scholars, I got on the phone to the drafter to get information not explained in the ruling.

Sometimes well intended and thought-out published guidance had devastating unintended consequences. One lawyer working for the IRS wrote a revenue ruling without realizing it obligated U.S. payers to withhold 30 percent on taxable scholarships and fellowship grants to nonresident aliens studying outside the United States.

I couldn't hide my annoyance when I called her, "Do you have any idea what you've done?" She didn't.

A firestorm of letters from colleges and universities about the problem ensued. It took the IRS three years to modify the burdensome ruling with a new regulation. A few years later I met the former IRS lawyer who wrote that original ruling. By then she had entered private practice. I hoped she didn't remember my phone calls. If she did, she never said so.

Tax Treaties

The United States has income tax treaties with more than 60 foreign countries. These treaties take precedent over U.S. tax laws and IRS regulations. Even now, few tax professionals understand how tax treaties work.

The purpose of tax treaties is to avoid double taxation when both countries tax the same income. This occurs when one treaty country imposes a withholding tax on income paid to a nonresident recipient and the treaty partner imposes its tax on the worldwide income of the recipient who is its tax resident.

Income tax treaties avoid such double taxation by reducing withholding taxes or eliminating taxes on specified types of income—called a "treaty benefit." They may also mandate tax credits to avoid double taxation. The country of source gets to tax the income and the residence country must give the tax credit. Some treaties also encourage cultural exchange by providing limited treaty benefits for students and scholars.

The application of treaty provisions is complex. Dealing with tax treaties is doubly difficult because tax treaty provisions vary with each country. And there is little IRS interpretive guidance for treaties. The few IRS treaty rulings for students and scholars pre-date 1990.

When I started to handle issues involving tax treaties, I had copies of all the treaties through a tax service that was updated for new and amended treaties. But I couldn't find a single source that included the technical explanations that told how the IRS interpreted the treaty provisions for U.S. tax purposes. I found a reference listing where to find the original publication of each tax treaty with its technical explanation and sent an associate to Boston University's law library with instruction to find and copy all the technical explanations. I created my own thick binder of technical explanations for easy reference a decade before the tax services published them. But today these explanations aren't much help because a Department of Treasury official said the explanations are only for purposes of negotiating the tax treaty.

The first time I couldn't find an answer for one of my foreign clients about how a tax treaty provision applied to that client's transaction, I called the IRS. They connected me to the personnel who negotiated the tax treaties. A few years and many phone calls and many clients later, I had gathered a sizeable amount of information about the tax treaties. More important, I understood how they worked. One of the negotiators told me, "We're more familiar with how treaties apply to U.S. outbound transactions. We wish we could refer some of the questions we get about how treaties apply to individuals in the United States to you." I felt flattered they recognized my growing expertise.

The United States also has estate tax treaties, but with far fewer countries. These treaties are either based on the domicile of the decedent or the location of the estate assets. My first client who received help from an estate tax treaty was the spouse of a decedent who lived in and was a citizen of the Netherlands. She explained her husband had a U.S. brokerage account. The brokerage firm wouldn't release the assets until the U.S. estate tax was paid. Under U.S. tax estate tax rules, U.S. brokerage accounts of foreign national decedents domiciled outside the United States on date of death are subject to U.S. estate tax. Only the first $60,000 of assets of such foreign decedents is exempt from estate tax. For estates of U.S. citizens, the amount was much larger—now more than $5 million—while the amount for foreign decedents remains unchanged. When my client asked me what to do, I gave her a copy of the estate tax treaty with the Netherlands and pointed out the provision exempting such U.S. assets from estate tax. I said, "Give a copy to the IRS and point out this provision. They will release the hold on the funds." She called me a few weeks later to tell me my advice worked.

My most complicated estate tax transaction involved the estate of a U.S. citizen domiciled in Canada. Estates of U.S. citizens are subject to U.S. estate tax regardless of where the decedent was domiciled on date of death. At that time, only the first $675,000 was exempt from U.S. estate tax. Because he was domiciled in Canada, his estate was also subject to Canada's deemed distribution tax computed on the unrealized gain in the assets—an income tax, not an estate tax. The decedent had died shortly after a unique amendment was added to the income tax treaty with Canada. Under this provision, I claimed a foreign tax credit on the U.S. estate tax return for the Canadian income tax on the assets. It might have been the first estate tax return submitted that used this new treaty provision to avoid the double tax.

Social Security Agreements

Like international tax treaties, the United States has special, but far fewer, agreements for Social Security taxes with foreign counties. The agreements and helpful booklets were available from the Social Security Administration (SSA). Many years passed before this information became available from the tax publications.

The Social Security agreements—except for the first agreement with Italy—have fewer differences from one to another than tax treaties. The purpose of Social Security agreements is two-fold. First, the agreements avoid double social welfare coverage and taxes. This occurs when U.S. citizens work abroad for a U.S. employer and are subject to both U.S. Social Security taxes and foreign social welfare taxes. The tax reimbursement cost to keep them whole would be huge. And second, they provide a formula—called "totalization"—so individuals who work in more than one country may consolidate coverage credits for future benefits.

When I worked at Arthur D. Little, I needed information about the new Social Security agreement with Germany, only the second U.S. agreement. ADL had a highly-paid U.S. citizen working in Germany, and I needed to find out if the new agreement eliminated the requirement for Social Security taxes in one of the countries, and if so, which one. I called SSA headquarters in Baltimore and spoke to the person who had negotiated the agreement. After some discussion of the facts, I was happy to learn the ADL worker was exempt from U.S. Social Security taxes.

When I asked this person, "How do I administer the exemption?"

He replied, "Oh, we didn't think about that."

This was the first of many situations I encountered that showed how government employees—and members of Congress!—lack understanding about how the rules they create affect taxpayers.

The good news came when my phone call prompted the SSA to negotiate a second agreement on how to administer the agreement with Germany. I wrote a memo to my supervisor at ADL explaining this solution and how to implement it to avoid both the double taxes and a huge tax reimbursement. But he delayed its implementation until the company received the same advice from a major law firm.

Before the United States had Social Security agreements, companies entered into agreements with the IRS called "3121(l) agreements" for the applicable section of the Internal Revenue Code. These agreements extended U.S. Social Security coverage—and taxes—to U.S. citizens working in foreign affiliates. ADL paid both the employee's and employer's share of taxes. So, whenever the United States entered a new agreement, I notified Legal to terminate ADL's 3121(l) agreement. Other companies must have been doing the same because the IRS began to expand the period between termination notice and expiration of the tax obligation. First 30 days. Then one year. Then three years. Then eight years. Then the IRS announced the agreements could no longer be terminated. I guess the government needed the tax revenue.

Years later I received a call from a tax accountant with a major accounting firm whose client wanted to terminate their agreements. He had discovered their client couldn't terminate them and asked me if I had a solution. I told him the only solution I could suggest was to wind down the affiliate and establish a new company. Not a very practical solution for any business.

Tax Returns

I learned to prepare tax returns without a computer for individuals, partnerships, trusts and pensions when I worked at Peat Marwick in the late 70s. When I went into private practice in 1985, I learned to use tax preparation software provided by Commerce Clearing House

(CCH). They did tax return preparation remotely on a mainframe computer system. Couriers picked up completed input forms and dropped off completed tax returns. When CCH replaced its mainframe system with a new PC-based system, I contacted them to find out how sophisticated the processing was for tax returns of U.S. expats. I knew from my discussion with a CCH programmer that they didn't understand the U.S. foreign tax credit rules. The programmer asked me questions about how the rules worked!

We began to use the CLR Accounting Go System which already included sophisticated processing for tax returns for U.S. expats. Each tax season I met with the CLR representative to describe the international tax forms they needed to add to their system. I learned Thomson—now Thomson Reuters—acquired this company. Years later they would acquire my software company, Windstar Technologies, too.

To learn the tax return rules for nonresident aliens, I studied the Form 1040NR tax return and its instructions. I stopped reading it when the instructions got to be 75 pages long. The most helpful publication for dealing with tax returns for foreign nationals was, and remains, IRS Publication 519, *U.S. Tax Guide for Aliens*. The IRS also issued a publication about the tax rules and procedures for foreign students and scholars, but discontinued it in 1987. I still have a copy. For sentimental reasons, I suppose.

Years later I would use my expertise with tax return processing to create an on-line tax return preparation system for foreign students and scholars.

CHAPTER 20

An Unconventional Law Practice

*Forget all the reasons it won't work and
believe the one reason that it will.*

– *Unknown*

When I joined Ken Vacovec's firm, an international tax practice was unusual—all the more so because the firm didn't have a downtown Boston location. Our office was in the suburbs of Boston, on Beacon Street in Brookline and later in Newton Corner.

And the firm was small—8 to 12 attorneys. Most people thought lawyers in the suburbs had a "suburban" practice—real estate, contracts and small businesses matters. A Boston lawyer remarked once, "I wouldn't expect there to be enough international tax work in Newton to keep you busy."

When I saw him next I told him, "I checked my client list. I have only one international client who lives in Newton, and he's from Hungary." My clients came from all around the world. They didn't care where my office was located. They just wanted to know they could reach me when they needed me.

Tax Return Preparation

We also had an unusual tax practice. We had a tax return preparation season just like an accounting firm. Ken told me when I joined, "These tax returns bring the clients into the firm every year. When they have other tax work, they bring it to us." We prepared more than 1,000 tax returns each year. On Patriots Day, during tax season, we hung out the windows of our office in Brookline watching the Boston Marathon runners in their final stretch.

Our clients included multinational U.S. companies with U.S. employees on temporary assignment abroad. My former employer Arthur D. Little, Inc. came on board as Ken's first major client when he started his private practice. My first client was Prime Computer. I had helped their international personnel specialist with a problem when I worked at ADL. I felt overjoyed at such an unexpected pay off for my free advice.

Our expatriate tax practice became very successful. Our clients included computer hardware manufacturers and emerging software companies. In addition to Prime, they included Stratus Computer, Thinking Machines, Lotus, McCormack & Dodge, Telex Computer Products and many others.

I enjoyed preparing tax returns. They had a beginning and an end, which satisfied my logical mind. The returns for expats gave me a real challenge. But the 1985 tax return filing season turned out to be the worst ever. The IRS was so understaffed that the Philadelphia Service Center, responsible for expatriate and nonresident tax returns, lost huge numbers of returns. Many clients received an IRS letter saying the IRS had a record of receiving their tax return but didn't have it, so please send a replacement. We had new tax returns printed by our outside tax return processor and sent them to our local and overseas clients to sign and send back. It became time-consuming for us and costly for the clients.

A colleague at the IRS told me years later they discovered the lost returns when they moved the Philadelphia office. Overworked international tax return processors had stuffed them behind file cabinets and above the ceiling tiles.

A Most Unusual Gift

When our clients' expats were in the Boston area, they stopped in to go over their tax returns and tax reimbursement computations. One expat based in Germany brought a heavy briefcase with him to our meeting. He told me this story about its contents:

While on a business trip to Berlin and sound asleep in his hotel, he awoke to a commotion outside around midnight. He got up, dressed, went outside and walked in the direction of the commotion—toward the Berlin Wall. When he got there, he saw people streaming through a breach in the wall and others sitting on top of it, everyone singing and cheering. The Berlin Wall had finally come down on November 7, 1989.

I remembered when the wall went up—overnight on August 13, 1961—first only barbed wire, then followed by concrete blocks over six feet high topped by barbed wire. The world reacted in shock. I wrote an essay about it in my high school English class. The day before the wall went up, 2,400 East Germans had emigrated to the West via West Berlin. In the 28 years after the wall went up, only 5,000 escaped from East Berlin to the West over the wall. About 200 lost their lives in the process.

When he finished his story, he offered me my pick of the colorful graffiti covered chunks of the Berlin Wall in his briefcase. I picked a small one and thanked him. I had it mounted and put it on display on my office wall.

Our International Scope

Dealing internationally proved more difficult in the 80s. We didn't have e-mail or fax. We used telex. The only international package carrier was DHL, and it could take 10 minutes for an international call to get through. I always hoped the person answering the phone spoke English.

I did a tax free like-kind exchange of an apartment in Boston with an apartment in London, all by telexed instructions and documents exchanged by DHL. Congress later closed this tax loophole that allowed the gain to escape U.S. taxes by disallowing tax-free exchanges with foreign property.

To provide services for relocating individuals, we needed tax advisors in other countries. I met many of our foreign advisors at the International Fiscal Association Annual Congress in Amsterdam. I worked with many other contacts in major accounting firms, back then called "the Big 8." Advisors we knew referred other advisors. I found our first advisor in China through a contact at the Sheraton Hotel, who referred me to a lawyer in Hong Kong, who then referred me to a lawyer in Beijing.

The Hong Kong lawyer told me when he first looked for a lawyer in China, his client, a local businessman, drove him to a cemetery and said, "That's where all the tax lawyers are."

The Orient had changed much since Pearl Buck described China in her book *The Good Earth*.

• • •

Pearl Buck (1892 – 1973) Pearl Buck was an American writer and teacher, and the first American woman to be awarded the Nobel Prize for Literature. Buck spent her early life in China where her parents were missionaries. She described peasant life in China in her best seller *The Good Earth,* which won the Pulitzer Prize in 1932. She became a champion of multiracial adoptions of the thousands of children of Asian women and American soldiers who left them behind when they returned to the United States.

• • •

I dealt with tax lawyers and accountants in more than 60 locations around the world. One of my foreign advisors went on to become his country's finance minister. I dealt with my chartered accountant in Toronto on cross-border matters with Canada for more than 15 years. Some of these firms came to rely on us for U.S. matters. My Hong Kong lawyer contacted me about a new client of their firm, a Boston-based financial institution. He asked me if the client was creditworthy. He said, "We've heard of Vacovec, Mayotte & Singer, but we've never heard of State Street Bank." I assured him State Street Bank, a major U.S. financial institution, was creditworthy.

In my correspondence with our foreign advisors, I always used my full name. But it wasn't unusual for them to refer to me as "Paul," not Paula, in their return correspondence. They weren't used to dealing with female professionals. Or they recognized the name Paul, but not Paula. But it also happened when I corresponded with U.S. lawyers and accountants. Even now, I'm sometimes referred to as Paul on return emails even though my name is clear on my sent email.

My law firm portrait

Our client base continued to grow with businesses sending U.S. employees to work abroad for the first time. One new expat said his manager asked him, "Which country do you want to pay your taxes to?" His manager thought the location of Payroll determined the country to which the taxes are owed. It doesn't always. It depends on the location of the company which benefits from, and pays for, the services. Sometimes it is more than one country, as when the hire/fire authority for an employee on loan to a foreign affiliate remains with the U.S. employer. The payroll function for these situations can be a real challenge.

One of our attorneys, John Ganick, had a saying, "Most businesses want to go international in the worst way—and they usually do."

These problems weren't new. Wang, a hugely successful company known for its word processing machine—this happened long before the introduction of word processing software—went international in the 70s. After setting up their U.S. sales force in several countries, they discovered not only were their employees taxable on their benefits-in-kind such as housing, education for children, cost of living allowance, home leave, etc., but they also had to pay income and payroll taxes in their countries of residence. Wang brought their sales force home and started all over again.

When it became known we dealt with cross-border matters, we began to get cross-border issues from businesses too. My first business client was a software company. They designed and distributed a computer system to manage transportation services. They had just made their first international sale to a Canadian railroad for $120,000. Their accountant called me after their client said they would withhold Canadian taxes on the payment. Countries collect taxes from nonresident businesses by requiring those making income payments to them to withhold taxes at a fixed rate. The accountant asked me if they had to pay it. I told him they would have to pay some Canadian taxes but not as much as the withholding. I asked him for a description of what the client was paying for so I could review the matter with Canadian counsel. The amount consisted of a license fee—a royalty for intangible property used in Canada—and fees for installation services performed in Canada. It also included technical services and support performed in the United States.

As it turned out, the royalty was exempt from Canadian tax and withholding under the tax treaty with Canada. The amount for services performed in Canada was subject to 15 percent withholding, and the amount for U.S. services wasn't subject to Canadian tax or withholding. The company could claim a foreign tax credit on their

U.S. return for the greater of their U.S. tax on their foreign income or the Canadian taxes withheld. It turned out as a good tax result but required collaboration between Canadian counsel me and to get there. My client was happy; our fees amounted to less than the taxes they saved—by a lot.

I began to describe the fees for my services to clients with cross-border transactions as "the price you pay me to figure out which tax is owed to which country."

An ADL Project

Our firm prepared the tax returns and tax reimbursements for ADL's expatriates. Before leaving ADL, I wrote a transition report, compiled a large binder of documentation and held recorded meetings so everyone understood the responsibilities I would leave behind. I learned they referred to the recordings for the next 10 years. They transferred my duties to three departments: Contracting, Legal and Accounting. They also gave the immigration work to ADL's outside immigration lawyer, even though his annual fees would exceed my annual salary. But they never assigned anyone to handle my personnel duties—*preventing* personnel problems.

Two years later at a meeting of ADL alumni, Lew told me, "We're beginning to figure out just what it was you did for us." I knew that because of the problems that had arisen since I left. One involved an expat who was covered by U.S. Social Security under the Social Security agreement with Belgium. He had been covered for the maximum period of five years. The period could have been extended before the five years expired but it wasn't. No one in Personnel tracked these expiration dates. The resulting Belgium social welfare tax and tax reimbursement cost was huge.

A problem Ken and I had tried to prevent while I worked at ADL arose soon after I joined the firm. ADL had hired an outside consultant for a temporary assignment in Thailand. But the contract was with his company, not with him. I knew this could become a problem. It smacked of foreign tax evasion. Ken and I had several meetings about the matter with Personnel, Contracting and ADL's controller. No one considered this a problem.

Lew called the firm and asked Ken and me to attend a meeting at ADL about this situation. The consultant had been stopped at the airport in Thailand and told he would go to jail if he didn't pay his tax bill. He had signature authority on ADL's bank account and wrote a check for $25,000. When we got to the meeting, everyone was seated around the large conference table including the tax lawyer from Thailand.

The Thai tax authorities knew about the individual because ADL International had sponsored him as their employee for a Thai visa so he could work on the project. It wasn't unusual for a U.S. company to treat an individual one way for tax purposes and another way for immigration purposes. The U.S. Immigration and Naturalization Service never shared information with the IRS. But other countries began sharing immigration information with their tax agencies for compliance purposes decades ago.

When we entered the room, the section manager said, "We know you tried to get us to do this the right way. Now can you help us fix it?" We could. The Thai tax lawyer provided the consultant's Thai tax returns. We amended his U.S. tax returns claiming tax refunds resulting from the foreign tax credits. The consultant repaid ADL from the U.S. tax refunds.

Law Firm Marketing

The Code of Ethics for lawyers didn't allow media advertising and marketing. To sidestep this restriction, lawyers networked with members of organizations and each other as a way to receive valuable referrals. To publicize our expertise, we also gave tax seminars through trade groups.

Ken and I joined many of the growing number of trade organizations representing foreign countries. We went to meetings two or three times a week to network with individuals who might send us business.

When the British trade group celebrated its first 10 years, its long-standing members included our firm, Vacovec, Mayotte & Singer, along with major companies like British Air. Ken later joined the group's board and became their president.

We gave tax seminars at the trade association meetings on the U.S. taxation of foreign nationals and estate planning for non-citizen spouses. We sometimes learned about individuals who attended a seminar who chose to engage a major firm for their tax matters instead of ours.

I heard about a Scandinavian woman who had attended my estate planning seminar with her husband, a U.S. citizen. After he died, his estate had paid a huge sum in U.S. estate taxes. Non-citizen spouses weren't eligible for the unlimited marital deduction that avoids estate tax on assets passing to a surviving spouse. The lawyer who advised her must not have been aware of the IRS regulation that allowed estate administrators to establish a post-mortem qualified domestic trust (QDT) to defer estate taxes. Assets passing to a non-citizen spouse through a QDT aren't subject to the estate tax until distributed. I had used this procedural solution on an earlier estate matter and explained it in my seminar.

Women In World Trade Helps Women Get Respect

By 1985, I had witnessed so many examples of women passed over for promotions and unfair pay practices that I helped found Women In World Trade—Boston (WWT). The organization gave women an opportunity to network with other women for mutual support at monthly meetings. Along with making social connections, we'd hear speakers on topics to expand our knowledge of international business. I gave a number of seminars at these meeting about taxes. As I had hoped, guests who attended felt I had considerable expertise on the subject and brought their tax matters to me.

As a way to gain a high profile, WWT put on an annual Christmas-time program where we honored ambassadors and consuls stationed in the United States from countries around the world. We discovered similar organizations in other states and became part of a nationwide network, The Organization of Women in International Trade.

At a VIP event during World Trade Week in 1996, WWT received the first Export Achievement Award for "increasing and retaining jobs in Massachusetts through its effort and activities in support of international business."

ADL Alumni Stick Together

In 1985, I also helped start the Arthur D. Little Alumni Association. We began with a small group of former ADL employees who networked for business. Our membership grew over the years. I joined the board of directors and became the clerk, a position I held for 20 years.

Years later my former boss Lew called saying ADL wanted to use the ADL Alumni name for the alumni organization they were sponsoring. I called my intellectual property lawyer and asked what to do. She said "Nothing." We had used the name without permission for more than three years, so the equitable policy of laches applied. The legal term "laches" prevents recovery by a plaintiff because the plaintiff sat on their rights too long to be accorded relief.

She said, "Their lawyer is telling them the same thing. He won't call about it again." He didn't. It's a good thing to know the law.

When a potential buyer for Arthur D. Little, Inc. approached ADL management, board members met with ADL's president several times. He began the meetings, "Gentlemen, and, ah, Paula, ..." We pointed out to him former employees held the majority of ADL stock in their accounts in ADL's retirement plan. So they had to include us in the process.

The original ADL organization ceased to exist, but the ADL Alumni organization still exists. It has grown over the past 30 years, adding chapters in Europe and South America, and now includes about 600 members.

Organizing for International Business

In the 90s, I became active in organizations promoting international business. I didn't expect to benefit right away from these efforts. The satisfaction of being part of these initiatives was enough for me.

In the spring of 1993, I approached a colleague James Barron, a consultant on international business and founder of International Boston, and suggested he broaden his focus to include the other New England states. I contacted the dean of my law school about meeting with us to discuss how Jim and his organization might help Maine businesses enter emerging international markets. The dean travelled to Boston for lunch with Jim and me, liked what he heard and said he would set up a meeting with leading Maine businessmen where Jim could present his ideas.

During that meeting at the law school, Jim explained to the group of Maine businessmen how the Maine economy could benefit from public/private partnerships that encourage and support businesses entering international markets. When he finished his presentation, no one said anything. So I said, "What we have to do is figure out how to use Jim's knowledge and contacts to create jobs for Maine people." And everyone started throwing out ideas.

The group included the business editor for the *Portland Press Herald* who wrote a series of articles about the initiatives. Jim told me they raised a toast to me at the kickoff meeting in early April. I wasn't there. I was hard at work preparing tax returns at my law office. Organizations founded subsequently to support international trade in Maine were an outgrowth of this early initiative.

I also began to attend conferences sponsored by The New Hampshire Organization for International Trade, which actively supported and promoted international business for New Hampshire businesses. Their director was an alumna of the University of Maine in Orono. We joked about the irony of two women from Maine being more involved with international business than most men.

I offered to give tax seminars at their conferences. Even though I had been giving tax seminars about going international sponsored by the Massachusetts Partners for Trade for years, the board didn't accept my offer. The director told me the board preferred to use New Hampshire professionals. She also said residents of other New England states had a term for those of us from Massachusetts—Massholes. Years later a board member invited me to give a tax seminar, but I had to decline. By then my software company Windstar occupied my spare time.

In the 90s, I became a member of several ad hoc committees formed by organizations to address international matters: the Ad Hoc International Committee of the Boston Chamber of Commerce, the Ad Hoc International Tax Committee of the IRS, and the Ad Hoc Tax Committee of NAFSA: The Association of Foreign Student Advisors—now the Association of International Educators. The committees were ad hoc because these organizations' standing committees didn't address international matters. Years later when these organizations absorbed international matters into their standing committees, they all dissolved the ad hoc committees. Members of the ad hoc committees all went on to other endeavors, including me. But it would be years before the standing committees actually dealt with international matters.

I joined a new Massachusetts Bar Association committee of lawyers. Our task was to write articles about Massachusetts legal and tax considerations for foreign companies that wished to set up business in Massachusetts. These articles would be consolidated into chapters of a free book and content for a new website.

Each member of the committee had an area of expertise. Mine was taxes. We each lined up lawyers throughout Massachusetts to write articles within our area. My group met the deadline for submission of their articles. But no one else's did. I guess only tax lawyers know how to meet deadlines.

When we discontinued the project, one committee member commented, "At least we had some great Thai food." The best Thai restaurant in the Boston area was across the street from my law firm where we met each month.

CHAPTER 21

Spreading the World with Taxes

*If you change the way you look at things,
the things you look at change.*

— Wayne Dyer

To increase its profile in the Boston market, our law firm put together a network of lawyers with different kinds of legal practices. We called it the "Boston International Legal Group." We designed an effective brochure, but we attracted only a few common clients. We commented later, "We should have known something with the acronym BILG wasn't going to work."

Our British tax advisors began giving annual tax seminars in London and invited Ken to participate. The topic was my specialty—U.S. taxation of foreign nationals. They had neither met nor dealt with Ken at the time. When I asked Ken why he thought they invited him instead of me, he said, "I'm a named partner, I've been practicing longer and I'm not a woman." I said, "Take that last reason and put it on top." Ken tried his best to get me on a program in subsequent years. He seemed very surprised when they deflected his efforts. I wasn't.

International Seminars

Our firm began to sponsor seminars in the Boston area and invited our advisors from the U.K. and France to participate.

Ken Vacovec on left, attorney John Ganick on my left and advisors from France and the U.K.

    We also gave seminars about international topics sponsored by the Massachusetts Partners for Trade initiative. I gave a soup-to-nuts seminar about tax issues for U.S. companies going international including issues related to employing individuals in other countries. I felt flattered and pleased when I read one participant's comments. He said, "The topic looked boring. She looked like she was going to be boring. But she went on to give the most fascinating discussion about taxes I've ever heard."
    My opening discussion explained the difference between the common law and code law. United States tax laws, along with those

of Canada, Australia and New Zealand, derive from the common law, which came from England. Common law is based on the substance of a transaction as defined by its facts, not its form. Most other countries, as well as the province of Quebec, Canada, (and Louisiana) are code countries. Their laws are based on the Napoleonic Code because their settlers came from code countries—France, Spain and Portugal. Code law is based on the form as described by the legal code rather than the substance of the transaction.

Lack of understanding of the basic differences between common law and code countries' rules and procedures causes businesses to make simple but serious mistakes. One client planned to travel to Mexico as a tourist to negotiate business contracts rather than wait for his business visa to be issued by the Mexican embassy. I said, "You can negotiate the contracts on a tourist visa, but none of them will be enforceable." He waited for the business visa.

Massachusetts Governor William Weld asked us on short notice to put together a seminar for some visiting dignitaries from Mexico led by a consultant. After my tax seminar, the consultant was effusive with praise because I had explained the differences between common law and code law. Another presenter adopted my seminar introduction to help explain the considerable differences in trademark laws between common law and code countries.

By the mid-90s, Boston law firms began to sponsor international seminars as well. One seminar, focused on international franchising, was presented by a Belgium attorney. During the pre-seminar networking, a colleague introduced me to a group of Boston lawyers saying, "Everybody talks about international. Paula just does it." When I walked into the room full of lawyers, accountants and businessmen, the Belgian lawyer spotted me, rushed over and kissed me on both cheeks. He was one of my International Fiscal Association colleagues. I could see the puzzled look from some members of the audience—no doubt wondering, "Who is *she*?" In his opening remarks, the moderator acknowledged a few members of the audience including me. Like Amelia Earhart traveling around the world—without her unfortunate disappearance—my reputation had spread across international borders.

• • •

Amelia Earhart (1897 – 1937) The first woman to fly solo across the Atlantic Ocean, Amelia Earhart inspired a generation of female pilots and women in all fields. A tomboy as a young girl she saved newspaper stories of women who became successful in traditional male professions. Six months after she started flying lessons she became the first women to fly to a record altitude of 14,000 feet in her yellow bi-plane "The Canary." Her disappearance in the Pacific in an attempt to fly around the world remains a great mystery.

• • •

New International Work

Our international practice expanded beyond our expat business. It also included estate planning and estate administration for estates and trusts with beneficiaries and assets, or both, in other countries. The estate administration for U.S. citizen decedents who had lived abroad became problematic. Amounts owed often included income taxes, penalties and interest. Many had failed to report income from assets recorded on the estate tax return on their U.S. income tax returns. Or worse, the decedent hadn't filed any U.S tax returns at all. Both became frequent problems.

We rectified these problems by preparing and filing correct original or amended tax returns to add the unreported income. The executor had to pay the taxes owed plus penalties and interest from the estate.

We had some unique small business clients with international issues as well. The owner of a company putting up a planatarium for the World's Fair in Barcelona, Spain, called me. He said he had been referred to me by someone in the Commerce Department. Their client told him they would withhold taxes on his royalties. Countries enforce their taxes on nonresident businesses and individuals by requiring the payer to withhold the tax from income payments to nonresidents at a fixed rate.

I asked, "At the lower treaty rate?"

He said, "It took me three months to find out there was such a thing as a treaty." My client called later saying, "They withheld the taxes at the treaty rate. Now, how do I get my money back from Spain?"

I said, "You don't get it back from Spain. You get it back from the U.S. government with a foreign tax credit. And you do that on your personal income tax return because your company's an S Corp." Income, deductions and credits of S Corps flow through to the individual owner's tax returns. My client was very happy, but his accountant wasn't. He had no experience with computing foreign tax credits.

Another small business client hosted electronic bulletin boards for information sharing by the international community of researchers—this was long before email and the internet. The company, owned by a husband and wife, was incorporating an affiliated company in a foreign country. They said, "We want to be completely compliant with the U.S. tax rules for our business."

I told them, "The tax rules haven't even been written for your type of business." They still haven't.

We had a growing individual practice dealing with more than just tax returns. One client, for whom I had prepared amended tax returns at a deep discount, met with me years later. He told me the story about a close relative, the decedent of an estate involving land in a foreign country. She had moved abroad, married into his family and never relinquished her U.S. citizenship. My client wanted to resolve the estate tax issues to his satisfaction. Estates of U.S. citizens are subject to U.S. estate tax regardless of where the citizen resided at time of death. And beneficiaries who receive assets from U.S. estates can be liable for unpaid U.S. estate taxes.

The New York law firm handling the estate for the executor had to review each proposal for resolving the U.S. estate taxes with us. We vetoed a couple of proposals that exposed my client to unpaid estate taxes. We agreed to a third proposal, and so did the IRS. My client was happy—and much better off.

One potential client who called me said she wanted to deal only with a female lawyer. Then she asked, "Are you gay?" I was so flummoxed I didn't say anything. She said, "Obviously you are," and hung up. I recounted this episode to one of our attorneys who had a good sense of humor.

He said, "I can see the headline now: 'Attorney Paula Singer doesn't deny she's gay.'"

Another potential client, a businessman I had met at a networking meeting came in for an initial meeting and then kept calling and asking me out for a drink or dinner. I politely turned him down each time, explaining I had to go home to my husband and daughter after work. Everyone in the office had a good laugh when we discovered he was the landlord of one of our secretaries.

Carlos Quijano's Tax Problem

The longest client matter I had lasted seven years. It began with an amended Form 1040 with a refund request and ended when the Supreme Court denied our request for an appeal from an adverse holding by the First Circuit Court of Appeals. I stopped charging the client after the IRS administrative appeal.

The issue was unusual. So much so that I opened my appellate brief with a quote from Lewis Carroll's, "Through the Looking Glass, and What Alice Found There."

> "...[A]fter looking everywhere for the Queen...[Alice] thought she would try the plan, this time, of walking in the opposite direction.
>
> It succeeded beautifully. She had not been walking a minute before she found herself face to face with the Red Queen, and full in sight of the hill she had been so long aiming at."

My client Carlos Quijano had worked for 13 years for a bank in London dealing with currency exchange. He and his wife bought a house in London completely financed in pounds sterling (PS). They sold the house before returning home to Maine. They realized a real gain equivalent to about $200,000, but paid taxes on $300,000. The additional $100,000 resulted from applying the IRS currency translation rule. It required the original cost basis to be translated into dollars using the exchange rate on date of purchase and the sale price to be translated using the exchange rate on date of sale. So the gain for U.S. tax purposes always included an exchange gain or loss depending on those exchange rates. His gain would have been only the $200,000 if the gain had been computed in pounds sterling (PS) and then translated to U.S. dollars.

Because the Quijanos never converted U.S. dollars to PS for the purchase, they never had the economic benefit of the currency exchange on which they paid a capital gains tax. The Quijanos had a currency loss on their subsequently acquired mortgage. But, under an IRS ruling, such a loss is personal and may not be used to offset the currency gain on the sale. A major accounting firm prepared their tax return and couldn't ignore these rules.

I prepared an amended return, requesting a tax refund on the basis that the tax was unconstitutional since my clients had no economic gain on the currency exchange. The IRS denied the request and we appealed the finding with the IRS. The IRS Appeals Officer from Maine travelled to my office to review the case. During our meeting I said, "Did you go to the University of Maine School of Law?"

He said, "Yes."

"What year."

"1969."

"That would have been my class year if they had given financial aid to women. There weren't any women in the class, were there?"

He shook his head, "No."

It seemed like old home week. We figured out that we both served on the law school board that year but had not attended the same meetings. And when I asked if he knew Roland Cole, he said, "He's my best friend!" Roland had encouraged me to go to law school.

At the end of the meeting, he said, "The equities are on your side, but I have to deny the appeal based on the law." The Tax Reform Act of 1986 had addressed the issue of income from currency exchange for businesses but not for individuals. The 400-page report leading up to the rules for businesses didn't apply to individuals.

We filed a request for summary judgment with the First District Court of Maine, requesting they overrule the IRS finding. They denied our request without a written report. We filed an appeal from the First District with the First Circuit Court of Appeals. The IRS just wanted the case to go away. In the settlement conference calls with the judge, the IRS litigator made an offer. He said we could recalculate the basis of the house by applying the exchange rate rule to each of the 28 improvements made on the house. That would result in a tax refund.

I spoke with the IRS litigator's assistant later and said, "If you're making an offer, don't expect me to compute it. That's your job." The offer resulted in a refund of about $7,000, enough to pay my bill. I continued with the appeal pro bono just for the experience. While we waited to argue our case in court, Carlos explained to the IRS litigator that the government loses more revenue with this rule than they gain. I explained I taught all of my clients with assets denominated in foreign currency to sell when they had real appreciation and an offsetting exchange loss.

I consider it one of my most memorable experiences. How many tax lawyers got to argue a case against the IRS in the prestigious First Circuit? I don't remember much about my argument. I admit I felt much too nervous. Although we lost the appeal, the case gets cited by tax reformers pointing out one more reason why the United States should change from citizenship-based taxation to residency-based taxation, the norm for developed countries.

My Problem with the Billable Hour

Legal and tax services bill their clients based on the billable hour, thanks to the advent of computer time-keeping systems. Because of my unusual memory, I could answer clients' questions off the top of my head as well as advise clients on many topics without doing costly research. Many clients objected when I billed them for answering their questions. My typical bill for answering a question came to about $75 because I didn't need to do extensive research to answer it. My contact at an expat-program client company complained, "Why do you have to charge for answering my questions?"

I explained, "I have to bill for my time."

She asked, "Why can't you give us a flat rate for questions."

I replied, "OK, tell me how many questions you're going to ask so I can compute the fee."

She said, "How should I know?"

I said, "OK, $30,000." I was joking. When a large corporation bought this client, they transferred their tax business to a major accounting firm. I heard from my contact years later, "Every time I ask the accounting firm a question, it takes three months for them to reply and I get a bill for $250! We didn't know how well off we were."

When the billable hour became the norm, many clients didn't want to pay for more than one attorney's time, so firm attorneys wrote off my time for answering their client's questions. It resulted in good value for the clients and for the law firm, but not for me. The majority of my partnership allocation was based on time billed *and paid*.

It got worse with the advent of the internet. Everyone thought information should be free even if it came from a professional firm. I got bombarded with questions from non-clients wanting me to answer to their "quick question"—a euphemism for "I don't want to pay." I took the calls from foreign students and scholars; most couldn't afford to pay me. But other calls came from U.S. lawyers and foreign lawyers, CPAs from big firms and small firms, and from accountants and human resource personnel in large companies and consulting firms. None of them wanted to pay. I asked an accountant at a large company whose call I took, "Why don't you just call your major accounting firm?"

She replied, "I'd have to pay them."

At the beginning of 2003, I asked our receptionist to screen out the calls to me from non-clients seeking free advice. There were more than 300 such calls that year! It became clear I needed a different business model.

CHAPTER 22

A Maze of Tax Laws for My Foreign National Clients

The spirit of seeking understanding through personal contact with people of other nations and other cultures deserves the respect and support of all.

– Gerald Ford

I enjoyed meeting new people, in particular individuals from other countries. When I began my international tax practice in 1985, I had the opportunity to get to know many foreign nationals. They included professors and researchers, economists and authors, company executives and students from Europe, Asia and South America. After we finished discussing their tax matters, I always took some time to learn about them as individuals and about their activities in the United States.

Starting my tax practice in 1985 resulted in a surprising benefit. That year the new rules enacted by Congress to determine when a foreign national becomes a "resident alien," and subject to U.S. tax on worldwide income like a U.S. citizen, became effective. Foreign nationals who don't meet one of the two objective tests remain "nonresident aliens" subject to U.S. tax under on only U.S. source income under a different set of tax rules and procedures.

Resident Alien or Nonresident Alien?

At first blush, the rules appeared simple. Foreign nationals who hold green cards are resident aliens. Other foreign nationals are classified as resident aliens if the result of the three-calendar-year weighted average formula, when applied to their U.S. days, equals or exceeds 183 days.

The terms "resident alien" and "nonresident alien" have different meanings for immigration purposes. A foreign national in the United States in a temporary status is a nonresident alien but may be a resident alien for tax purposes. To avoid confusion, I like to use the terms "tax resident" and "tax nonresident" instead. At a 2007 meeting with international personnel at IRS headquarters, I suggested that the IRS do so as well. But, because the terminology they use for their rules, forms and instructions come from the tax laws, that change might take an act of Congress.

What makes the residency rules complicated comes from the exceptions. The exceptions tied to a foreign national's immigration status while in the United States cause the most confusion. While most foreign nationals must count all their U.S. days of physical presence, including partial days, those in certain immigration categories don't always count their U.S. days.

Diplomats and employees of international organizations such as the UN never count their days of physical presence in the United States. They remain tax nonresidents regardless of their duration of stay. Students don't count their U.S. days for five calendar years, provided they are studying in student status. Exchange visitors (other than those who are students) do not count their U.S. days for two out of the current seven calendar years. Under these rules, individuals remain tax nonresidents for several calendar years before becoming tax residents. These rules apply to accompanying dependents too, but based on the dependent's U.S. days and status if different.

These exceptions are simple to apply as long as the individual had never before been in the United States as a student or exchange visitor, or did not change to or from another immigration status while in the United States. If they had a prior visit or changed status, the analysis is anything but simple. Some years they may be tax nonresidents but then change tax status to tax residents during later years. Other years they may be tax residents and change tax status to tax nonresidents in later years. Some individuals' situations are so complex it takes a computer system just to figure out their U.S. tax status.

As a result of my knowledge of the immigration rules on which the new tax rules depend, and my study of the new laws and procedures, I became *the* expert in the field—known as "nonresident alien taxation"—for the next 20 years. Like Amelia Bloomer, the first woman to wear trousers in public, I became the lone woman in this complex field of tax-related immigration. It added to my standing in the legal community.

• • •

Amelia Bloomer (1818 – 1894) If you are female and wearing pants right now, you can thank Amelia Bloomer. A champion of women's rights, she popularized the new "bloomers" that freed women from restrictive corsets and petty coats. When they learned about them, women all over the country wanted to have patterns so they could make them. In 1849, she started a temperance publication, *The Lily,* which promoted women's issues.

• • •

In 1986, to generate business for my tax practice, I began giving pro bono seminars at Boston area colleges and universities for their foreign students and scholars. The first year I gave seminars at Harvard and the Massachusetts Institute of Technology (MIT). I gave the seminar at Harvard with their payroll manager for foreign nationals. He knew his stuff but retired soon afterwards. For the next 10 years, I gave seminars at MIT and two or three other schools each tax season. I volunteered to give them at Harvard too, but the new director of the International Office wanted experts from the IRS and Massachusetts Department of Revenue. The IRS called and asked if they could recommend me to Harvard. I said they could. But Harvard never called.

I knew the foreign nationals needed someone to explain how their immigration status affected their U.S income tax obligations. With all the variables involved, it became obvious most people attending my seminars needed a professional to prepare their tax returns, but the majority couldn't afford one.

To help, I invited the IRS's director of Taxpayer Education in Boston to assign IRS personnel to attend my seminars. Since the tax rules were so many and so complicated, I felt that even the IRS needed help to understand the laws. And they needed to understand the real life complications faced by foreign national taxpayers and their payers. My idea worked. With the information and understanding they gained from my seminars, the IRS participants began to give tax seminars for foreign nationals too. And over the next 10 years, they helped thousands of foreign students and scholars with their tax returns.

Wrestling with Tax Problems

Foreign nationals who could afford a professional became my clients. One of my first clients was a German national teaching at MIT.

He inquired about an exemption from income tax under the tax treaty with Germany. In the 70s and 80s, most tax treaties included provisions to promote international exchange. Many of these provisions were later removed as the United States amended or replaced the treaties.

After researching the treaty with Germany, I determined there existed a two-year exemption from tax applied to the salary for teachers and researchers who were in the United States for no longer than two years. This professor expected to meet this requirement. But he wasn't aware of another provision near the end of the treaty that took this benefit away if the individual becomes a U.S. tax resident. He had become one because of his H-1B status. There were no exceptions as there are now. He did not appreciate my advice because he had to pay U.S income tax on his salary.

This experience illustrated how important it was for me to understand the precise detail of all the various limitations of tax treaties. I recalled, when I attended law school, a law professor advised us to "always begin at the beginning and read to the end." So I took the treaties home to study—not very light reading. Tax treaties are very confusing because of the lack of consistency in benefits and their limitations from one treaty to another. The German treaty was not the only one to give a benefit but then take it away if facts changed.

A few years later a German researcher was incensed at my advice that he wasn't eligible a treaty benefit if he extended his stay beyond two years. Being physically present in the United States beyond the two years would disqualify him for the treaty benefit retroactively. I told him, "Don't complain to me. I can't change the treaty. If you want it changed, complain to your government." I guess he did because the next group of amendments to the U.S. treaty with Germany removed the retroactive loss effect of this provision.

My most satisfying matter related to Germany came from a client of my law partner Maureen Mayotte. He had received a letter accompanied with a form in German and asked what he should do. I told her to tell him, "Find a German translator, complete the form and send it to the address as instructed in the letter." A few months later he received several hundred thousand dollars from the German government, reparations for property confiscated from his family by the Nazis. That was the best free advice I ever gave anybody. And we gave him some more good news—the reparations weren't taxable.

Another client, a tax nonresident, felt he deserved a tax exemption because of his involvement in research. His educational institution refused to allow an exemption from withholding. He complained to me, "I'm so upset with Payroll I want to blow them up." He was a chemist and knew how to do it.

I checked the treaty and found the section that described how he qualified for the exemption. I wrote a letter for the school so that they understood the U.S. tax law required them to honor his exemption request. From that point on they adjusted the withholding on his wages for his exemption. An unexpected bonus came from this experience. A decade later this institution became the first client of the software company I founded with my husband, Gary, in 1994.

My law firm's expat clients began to transfer employees from their foreign affiliates to the United States. We called them "inpats" for short. Our long-standing client Prime Computer transferred a unique couple with their new baby to the United States. The husband was a foreign national transferee. The wife was a returning U.S. citizen. They named their new baby Patrick. I told them, "It's the first time I had an expat, an inpat and a little Pat on the same tax return."

My most unusual request for services also came from Prime Computer. They asked me to give a seminar to their foreign national employees about U.S. taxation—and would I "please come in a costume." The company planned a festive occasion to celebrate their foreign nationals' countries of origin. I gave my tax seminar dressed in a Japanese kimono.

Solving Tax Collection Problems

Foreign students and scholars with serious IRS collection problems also became my clients. Their difficulties often resulted from incorrect withholding and reporting by their institutions. A collections case I handled for a researcher from Venezuela was typical. On her previous visit to the United States, her employer failed to withhold federal income taxes, which they should have, and withheld Social Security taxes, which they shouldn't have. Her predicament worsened because no one had informed her that she needed to submit a U.S. tax return for the year she left the United States.

She came back a few years later to head up an important research project to eradicate a parasite in South America that caused blindness. She was shocked when she found herself dealing with IRS Collections for taxes owed from her earlier visit to the United States. The IRS garnished her wages and placed a lien on her bank account. I helped with her unfiled tax returns. Getting the penalties abated on the taxes she owed was another matter.

The IRS person I contacted asked me, "Why should the IRS abate the penalties?"

I lost my patience and raised my voice saying, "On the basis that her employer doesn't know the rules! Most tax preparers don't know the rules! And, worst of all, most IRS personnel don't know the rules! How then can the IRS expect a foreign national with English as a second language to know the rules?" Then I took a breath and apologized for raising my voice. The IRS saw the wisdom of my argument and abated the penalties.

I had two clients the IRS dunned for more than $20,000 in taxes, penalties and interest. One was a professor from Japan who had returned home after teaching for two years at a local university. A concerned colleague came to me seeking assistance. Based on the information he gave me, the professor was eligible for a treaty exemption under the U.S. tax treaty with Japan. His employer had not withheld income taxes on his salary as he had requested, but his employer had reported his income on the wrong form—a W-2 instead of a 1042-S. His employer also failed to tell the professor he needed to submit U.S. tax returns. The professor's colleague collected the information I needed to prepare the returns. I sent the returns to the client in Japan to sign and send back to me to submit to the IRS. After reviewing the returns with the treaty claim, the IRS sent a notice that he didn't owe any taxes.

The second case involved a tax nonresident student who had been fighting an IRS collection matter for two years. His name and Social Security number were included on his father's U.S. bank account. The IRS billed the student for the tax due on the interest earned on the account. The bank had reported the interest in the student's name. The student argued the money belonged to his father, not to him. But the bank account setup did not support this claim.

He asked, "Do you think you can convince the IRS the interest earned on this account belongs to my father?"

I said, "No, but I can convince the IRS that you don't owe the tax." The tax code includes a special rule treating interest on bank deposits of tax nonresidents as nontaxable. I called the IRS collections agent, explained this rule and the rules and facts supporting this foreign student's tax nonresident status. Then I mailed him the tax law and regulations. He called me after he received them and said, "I never would have believed it, but you're right." He cancelled the collection action.

An Unusual Round Robin

One foreign national client presented an unusual situation to my associate, Arthur Kerr. The client was on temporary leave from his foreign employer and had accepted a job for training in the United

States. Because his U.S. pay was low, his foreign employer had volunteered to continue to pay half of his salary. Arthur asked me if that raised any U.S. tax issues. I told him, "It does, because the pay is U.S. source income. His foreign employer will have to comply with U.S. payroll withholding and reporting."

When Arthur passed along this advice, the client questioned it. So Arthur suggested he could call and ask an international tax specialist at the IRS. When the client called back, he said, "I talked to someone at the IRS named Ben Gondek. He gave the same advice but suggested I might want to check with someone named Paula Singer. Do you know her?" Arthur said, "Yes, she's here in my office now. She's the one who gave me the advice to begin with." Ben and I were both panelists at an annual international tax conference held in Wisconsin.

In my law office, 2003

Citizenship Matters Too

In one memorable meeting with a high-level Prime Computer executive from the U.K., I learned the hard way to ask clients to identify their citizenships—some had more than one—at the outset of our meeting. I reviewed the U.S. tax residency rules, income issues and tax return procedures for foreign nationals with the executive. At the end of the meeting, he said, "I suppose I should have told you, I'm a U.S. citizen. I moved to England with my parents when I was 10." I reached over, took his notes and, with mine, ripped them up and began again.

He was not aware he should have been filing U.S. tax returns even though he lived and worked in the U.K. I explained what information we needed to prepare his U.S. returns for the past six years. As it turned out, he owed no U.S. taxes on these returns because his foreign income taxes had been much higher than his U.S. taxes. Foreign tax credits reduced his U.S. taxes to nothing. He had unused credits that we carried to other years' tax returns for more tax refunds. The credits offset the taxes on his wages paid for services performed while traveling on business outside the United States.

My most troubling problem came from a German exchange student. He was born in New York City and, as a child, moved with his parents to Germany, where he was also a citizen. While attending college he lived in the United States for two years and returned home for a visit. He went to the U.S. embassy to apply for a new student visa to reenter the United States because his studies had been extended. His old visa had expired. When the consular officer at the embassy noticed he was born in the United States, he told him that, as a U.S. citizen, he must enter the United States with a U.S. passport. The student told me the consular officer also advised, "You'd better get a good U.S. tax lawyer."

I prepared his Form 1040 tax returns and computed how much he had to pay with his amended returns. As a U.S. citizen he was not eligible for the tax treaty exemption from tax that he had claimed on his Form 1040NR, nonresident alien tax returns. The IRS called with questions about the amended returns. They didn't believe an individual wouldn't know he was a U.S. citizen. He became the first of several individuals I encountered with this situation. No doubt there are many thousands of unknowing dual citizens living abroad like him who have not met their U.S. tax filing obligations.

CHAPTER 23

Some Unconventional Tax Planning

If you're not confused, you're not paying attention.

– Tom Peters

Where an individual is physically located can affect their U.S. and foreign tax obligations. Many countries besides the United States use a 183-day presence test to determine tax residency. Residence in a country can matter for social welfare tax purposes as well. And many tax treaties have tax benefits limited by duration of physical presence.

As a result, much planning for my foreign national clients and U.S. expats was based on their physical presence in a country. That's why, when a client would call me, I asked, "Where are you?" Depending on the answer, I asked, "What are you doing there?" Sometimes my immediate response was "Leave now."

U.S. Presence Matters

One foreign national couple planned to relocate in the United States to set up a software company. The wife already lived here and was a tax resident. During our initial meeting, she said, "My husband is going to be joining me here."

I said, "No he isn't and I'll tell you why." Her husband had been traveling to the United States but not enough to become a tax resident. He had just sold a business in their home country where, under a grandfather rule, the gain was not taxed. If he became a U.S. tax resident, he would have to pay U.S. tax on his worldwide income including the untaxed capital gain from the sale of his business which occurred after his first visit to the United States. To spend time with her husband with that in mind, my client and their children flew to locations outside the United States for visits. He moved to the United States the following year. This simple plan saved them millions of dollars in unnecessary U.S. taxes.

My knowledge of nonresident alien taxation saved another foreign national client a huge sum of money. At our first meeting, he explained a U.S. company planned to buy the foreign technology company he owned using a tax-free plan. I asked him for the number of days he was present in the United States in the current calendar year and in each of the two previous years. From his answer I realized he was about three weeks away from becoming a tax resident. I explained the U.S. tax residency rules and told him, "If you are a resident alien when your company is purchased, you'll be subject to U.S. income tax on the gain you make rather than exempt from U.S. tax on the gain as a nonresident alien." When I spoke with him the following week, it was by phone. He called from an island in the Caribbean.

Some tax treaties allow a two-year exemption from tax for teaching or research. The exemption period begins with the date of arrival for the treaty purpose. A few treaties have a retroactive loss provision, which means that an individual who physically overstays the benefit period loses the two-year treaty exemption. Taxes exempted from withholding because of the treaty benefit must be paid with the individual's tax return. The individual should submit amended returns to pay the taxes owed for the prior tax years—but they rarely do.

I received a call from a researcher at a local university about preparing his tax return for the year. I said, "You have a British accent. Have you been claiming exemption from withholding under the U.K. tax treaty?"

He said "Yes." I asked for his U.S. days. He was close to the end of the two-year benefit period. I said, "Did anyone tell you the benefit is lost if you overstay the two years?"

He said, "No. What should I do?"

I said, "How fast can you pack?" He returned to the U.K. and I prepared his tax return long distance.

Social Security Tax Planning

It is not unusual for a U.S. employee seconded—meaning loaned—to an affiliated company abroad to be covered in both the U.S. system and the foreign system. Employees remain subject to U.S. Social Security if the U.S. employer has control over the individual's employment and assignment. Social welfare obligations arise in the country where the employee works. Double taxation is the result.

Social welfare taxes in foreign countries are much higher than U.S. Social Security taxes because they pay for a broader range of social benefits. Social security taxes in the United States are lower because the government designed the system to give, in the words of President Franklin D. Roosevelt, "some measure of protection" against poverty in old-age. When FDR introduced the Social Security legislation, the highest concentration of poverty was in the elderly population. Although history credits FDR with creating the Social Security system in 1933, it was a woman with deep roots in Maine, Frances Perkins, who really created Social Security.

• • •

> **Frances Perkins (1880 – 1965)** In 1933, President Roosevelt appointed Frances Perkins Secretary of Labor, making her the first woman to hold a cabinet position in the United States. It became her task to design the New Deal programs for worker protections from unemployment, child labor, and poverty in old age. She created the Social Security system using the two principles laid down by FDR. It had to be self-financing and the benefit had to be based on what a worker paid into the system. An early feminist, Perkins, although married, kept her given name and defended that right in court.

• • •

In 1979, the United States began entering into Social Security agreements with countries with large numbers of U.S. employees. Under these agreements, employees sent abroad on temporary assignments for five years or less—called "detached workers"— remain covered by their home country. These agreements save U.S. companies sending workers abroad huge amounts in tax reimbursements as well as foreign social welfare taxes.

Social Security planning involves a request for a certificate of coverage from the country of coverage as proof of exemption from the other country's social security coverage and tax—an administrative task. But the request for one client had many complications.

My client, a Canadian physician and independent contractor, lived in Canada. But he also held a U.S. green card and was required to submit a U.S. tax return as a tax resident. He needed a certificate of coverage from Canada to avoid having to pay self-employment tax with his U.S. return. This was yet another example of a client with peculiar requirements that cut across national boundaries. These situations never had a straightforward solution.

An individual in Revenue Canada called and asked, "Can you please explain for us in writing why a Canadian living in Canada needs a certificate of coverage from Canada? We'd like to be able to explain that to your government."

I sent a memorandum that explained to Revenue Canada the physician's U.S. tax residence status caused by his green card and his resulting U.S. tax obligations. This prompted a discussion between Revenue Canada and the International Policy Staff at the Social Security Administration (SSA). Together they worked out a special procedure for applying for a certificate of coverage for these unusual situations.

It was satisfying to see governments working together when they have a mutual agenda.

One Social Security matter involved a foreign national who had been working in the United States for more than 10 years, but without INS authorization. She now had legal status and had been issued a U.S. Social Security number. She explained she had come to the United States to work as an au pair for an American family when she was a teenager. Her employer had given her a number and told her it was her Social Security number. She inquired about what to do because she now had a different Social Security number. I asked her if she had copies of all her W-2 forms from her employment. She did.

I explained, "Take your W-2s to the local Social Security office and ask them to transfer your earnings to your new Social Security number." Congress had mandated that SSA clean up its "suspense account" of funds not allocated to valid Social Security numbers, so I knew they would.

She felt nervous and asked me to go with her. I explained, "If you go in with a lawyer, they will think you did something wrong.

All you have to do is tell them the truth, what you just told me. You did what your American employer told you to do. He knew employing you without authorization and giving you a fake Social Security number was breaking the law."

She called me after her meeting at Social Security office. She explained the representative questioned her about her situation, and she told him the truth. After that he was very helpful and transferred her earnings to her new Social Security number.

Immigration Planning Too

Sometimes a client's immigration status matters a lot. One client, a green card holder from Hong Kong, told me he was part owner of a building in Hong Kong about to be sold. He would have a huge U.S. capital gain tax on the appreciation in the building. Under U.S. tax rules, all appreciation is taxed including appreciation occurring before a foreign national comes to the United States. The client had come to the United States from Canada where he still had landed immigrant status. I advised him to return to Canada prior to the sale of the building, give up his U.S. green card and get his Canadian paperwork straightened out.

Foreign nationals entering Canada can declare the market value of assets as of the date they enter—several years before coming to the United States in the case of this client. When any of these assets are sold while Canadian residents, they are only taxed on the appreciation from that date of first entry. This plan with the Canadian stepped-up basis saved him a huge amount of tax. Canada only taxed him on the gain since he entered Canada the first time. He had no U.S. tax because he abandoned his green card before the sale. Canada's favorable tax rule, contrasted with the unfavorable U.S. tax rule, is the reason so many individuals emigrating from the Far East have chosen Canada over the United States as their destination.

Another client, a British businessman had come to the United States as an Alien of Distinguished Merit and Ability, a category identified as "O-1" for immigration purposes. He had entered into a joint venture with a U.S. company. After a year, he became upset with his U.S. tax lawyer's inadequate advice and math errors in their letters to him. He told both his U.S. employer and U.K. tax advisor, "Find someone who does this all the time." Both recommended me.

The businessman worked in the United States and the United Kingdom. I explained to him how to limit his time in the United States so he would remain a tax nonresident. Compensation for services performed abroad by a tax nonresident is not subject to U.S. income tax even if paid on a U.S. payroll. I allocated his pay between U.S. and foreign work days on his Form 1040NR tax return, and he received tax refunds for the wage withholding on pay for foreign work days. This procedure saved him a lot in U.S. taxes. His original U.S. advisors didn't prepare tax returns, so they were unaware of planning opportunities available when applying the tax rules on tax returns.

A few years later the businessman called to tell me he would be working for a second U.S. company too.

I asked, "Did the new company sponsor you for O-1 immigration status too?"

He said, "No."

I explained, "You can't work for the new company in O-1 status sponsored by your first employer. But you can have more than one O-1 job and status." I gave him the name of an experienced immigration lawyer to handle the O-1 petition for his second job. He could not work for this company while he was in the United States until INS approved the petition.

My most stressful immigration-related matter involved a family from China. They were a few weeks away from taking their oath as naturalized U.S. citizens at Boston's historic Faneuil Hall. INS wouldn't allow them to continue the naturalization process after they discovered the husband and wife had filed a nonresident U.S. tax return after they had obtained green card status. INS considers the filing of a nonresident U.S. tax return to be evidence of abandonment of U.S. green card status. Without valid green card status, they wouldn't be eligible to become naturalized U.S. citizens. Their immigration lawyer referred them to me to see if I could help them. There was no appeal if I couldn't get INS to change their determination.

I met with them and discovered the returns were filed, with the assistance of a friend, for the year they worked in Hong Kong. I determined from their income that, even if they had filed Form 1040 as tax residents, they would have owed no U.S. income tax because they qualified for the foreign earned income exclusions. The presumption of abandonment based on nonresident returns may be rebutted with sufficient facts. I told them I would write a memorandum explaining tax law and facts to INS. I sent the memorandum and waited for a response.

Time was short. The citizenship ceremony would take place in little over a week. Every morning when I came into the office the husband, wife and their two small children waited for me in the reception area. I explained to them, if INS didn't respond to my memorandum, the only way I could get INS to review their situation would be for me to disrupt the ceremony at Faneuil Hall—for which I knew I would be arrested. Fortunately for all of us, INS agreed to allow them to proceed with their naturalizations a few days before the ceremony.

I much preferred to deal with people's money rather than their lives. I knew I could help people to resolve their tax problems with the rational IRS rules. But I knew I couldn't always help people if their lives were upended by immigration rules.

There's Nothing Simple about U.S. Taxes

U.S. tax returns for foreign nationals transferred to the U.S. can be very complex. State income tax returns add to that complexity. One executive from Belgium planned to leave for a trip just as I had completed his tax returns. He had very complicated tax returns because he had dual status. He essentially had two U.S. tax returns—one for his nonresident period and one for his resident period—consolidated into one return. He asked me to fax a copy to him so he could read it on the plane. As I faxed him the copies, he called and said, "Stop! I'll have to read it when I get back." His federal and state returns, including supporting statements for income and expense allocations between periods, totaled more than 35 pages. He preferred his Belgian tax return. It had two pages.

Our firm also provided planning and tax return services for employees of foreign companies setting up companies in the United States. An employee of a German client came to my office for tax return preparation services. He had worked in the United States for several months before transferring to the U.S. payroll. As a result, he owed $15,000 in U.S. and Massachusetts taxes on his wages paid in Germany for work done in the United States.

He complained, "But I paid my taxes."

I said, "The problem is you paid them to the wrong government. You have to pay your U.S. taxes and get your taxes back from Germany." I wrote him a letter explaining the provision in the tax treaty with Germany for avoiding double taxation and suggested he give it to the German tax authority.

He called me a few months later and said he had received a letter from the German government saying, "We agree with Mrs. Singer." He received a refund from the German government based on a foreign tax credit for U.S. taxes paid.

A Kennebunk Connection

I got lots more German tax return clients when a German scientific equipment company entering the U.S. market for the first time bought one of my U.S. high-tech clients. I did the tax planning and prepared tax returns for all of their employees transferred to the U.S. from Germany.

When I met in my office with the president of the U.S. operation, he noticed my Maine bar license on my wall and remarked, "I was an exchange student and lived for a year in Kennebunk with a minister and his wife."

I said, "I'm from Kennebunk. Who did you live with, Fred and Carol Holmberg?"

He looked shocked and said, "How could you know that?"

I replied, "I knew the ministers in Kennebunk, and if anyone was going to have a German exchange student it was Fred and Carol."

What a small world it had become!

A Challenging Project

One of my most challenging projects was for a large technology university. It covered the special tax rules and procedures that apply to patent-related payments made to their foreign national researchers. Some of the researchers were tax residents and some were tax nonresidents. Some researchers were in the United States and were tax nonresidents under the special exception from counting U.S. days for J-1 exchange visitors. Tax nonresidents who had returned home abroad were nonresidents because they had lacked countable U.S. days.

The tax code includes special rules for payments for the sale or use of a patent. The payments get treated as long-term capital gains and taxed at a much lower tax rate than ordinary income. This tax rule doesn't differentiate between payments to tax residents and tax nonresidents, so it applies to both. A special capital gain rule exists for tax nonresidents. They aren't subject to tax on capital gains as long as they don't have 183 days of presence in the United States. This is a different 183-day rule than the 183-day residency rule. Tax nonresident researchers who reside in the United States can't meet this special 183-day requirement. As a result, they are subject to 30 percent tax on the gain, not the lower capital gain tax rate that applies to U.S. citizens and tax residents.

Before completing my memorandum, I followed the rule I had been taught in law school: "Begin at the beginning and read to the end." I sat down with the tax code and began reading the special tax laws that apply to various types of income of tax nonresidents. Lucky I did. I found a section that changed payments contingent on the use of a patent to royalties for tax purposes. Under this rule, only the sale proceeds are treated as long-term capital gain. Subsequent payments for use of the patent are subject to 30 percent withholding. The withholding rate may be reduced by a treaty if the recipient is tax resident in a treaty country. But if the recipient is a U.S. tax resident, the contingent payments remain long-term capital gains.

When I explained how these rules worked in practice on a conference call with lawyers in the university's patent office, there was dead silence at the end of the line. I said, "No one ever said taxes had to make sense."

CHAPTER 24

Computers and the Law Don't Always Compute

> *Computer science is no more about computers than astronomy is about telescopes.*
>
> – Edsger Dijkstra

When I began law school in 1975, computers were making their first impact on the law. It began when defendants introduced documents generated by computers as evidence in lawsuits. Since lawyers and judges had limited experience with computers, courts did not accept computer-generated records because the legal system considered such documents to be copies of the original. Only original documents were admissible. As computer-generated records proliferated, judges realized they had to accommodate them. But that change created a problem. Lawyers did not know how to establish a proper foundation for the accuracy of the records.

This problem presented an opportunity for me with far reaching implications.

My Law School Thesis

One of my law school classes dealt with evidence. My professor, Kinvin Wroth, was an expert in the rules of evidence. He had worked on the federal rules of evidence and the rules of evidence for several states. When Professor Wroth queried us about a case involving computer-generated evidence, I pointed out the dissenting opinion was correct. The majority opinion came to the wrong conclusion because they lacked an understanding of computer-generated records. I was the only one in class who understood this.

After class Professor Wroth questioned me about my knowledge of computers. When I convinced him I had considerable expertise with this new technology, he asked me to teach a class about computer-generated evidence.

This led me write a thesis that I needed to fulfill a graduation requirement. I titled my thesis "Proposed Changes to the Federal Rules of Evidence as Applied to Computer-Generated Evidence." It had two parts.

The first part explained how computers worked, including the equipment, processing and reliability factors of computers. This section had no footnotes. The second part proposed the changes to the rules. It had numerous footnotes.

Professor Wroth said, "You need to footnote the experts for the first part."

I replied, "I wrote this off the top of my head. I am the expert."

He commented, "Then you need to include a footnote of references at the beginning for those readers who lack your expertise." To accomplish this, I referenced the books I had used to learn about computers and programming.

When I completed my thesis, Professor Wroth seemed impressed. He said, "Your thesis will affect the rules of evidence."

He submitted my thesis to the law school for publication. The law review editor agreed to publish it, but without the section that described how computers work. Professor Wroth understood this explanation was a necessary part of my thesis. He suggested instead that I contact the *Rutgers Journal of Computers, Technology and the Law*, the first law review with a focus on technology. They published my thesis in their 1979 journal, after an arduous editing process by mail. It didn't help that the editors only had a smattering of knowledge about how computers work in a business.

A review of my article appeared in the April 1980 *Computer Reviews*. The reviewer said, "She is to be commended for her very effective explanation of the process for the practitioner with no previous knowledge of electronic data processing." He also commented that the article provides, "a multitude of articles, decisions and documents related to this problem." Other law review articles referenced my article in footnotes well into the 90s. But the article itself didn't get added to any on-line services because they began with articles published in 1980.

The IRS and Its Outmoded Computers

Because of my experience as a tax return preparer, I had a personal interest in the development of IRS's computer systems. Major organizations upgraded their computer systems and hardware as technology improved. But the IRS could not keep up with technology improvements because of budget limitations. One reason for their lack of funds began as political retaliation. It began with an IRS audit of President Richard Nixon's 1969 tax return. As a result of the audit, Nixon had to pay the government over $200,000 in back taxes, penalties and interest. He had taken a huge charitable deduction based on a document backdated to before the effective date of a law that made this tax deduction invalid. How ironic it was that it was based on a bill *Nixon* had signed into law. For his part in creating Nixon's fraudulent tax return, his accountant went to jail. A short time later Congress cancelled the IRS's capital improvement budget.

Congress continued this capital underfunding for the next 20 years. As a result, the IRS still used outmoded Sperry Rand mainframes from the 60s in the 80s. Congress finally voted funding to modernize IRS's hardware and software in the early 80s when taxpayers were becoming aware of what the new computers could do.

By that time, Congress also had begun making regular, complex changes to the tax code. The biggest changes were added by the Tax Reform Act of 1986. Processing tax returns became even more problematic when Congress made changes retroactive to the beginning of the tax year. No one knew what the tax law for the current year was until late in that year.

In 2004, former IRS Commissioner Charles Rossotti described this as "driving a race car around the race track while the pit crew is running around alongside trying to figure out how to change the engine without slowing down the car." Racing legend Pat Moss would appreciate the analogy.

• • •

Patricia "Pat" Moss-Carlsson (1934 – 2008) Patricia "Pat" Moss-Carlsson was one of the most successful female auto rally drivers of all time, achieving three outright wins and seven podium finishes in international rallies. She was crowned European Ladies' Rally Champion five times. She was the younger sister of Formula One Grand Prix star Sterling Moss and, from 1963 until her death, the wife and driving partner of Swedish rally driver Erik Carlsson. She is the author of a memoir, *The Story So Far* (1967) and, with her husband, co-author of *The Art and Technique of Driving* (1965).

• • •

Regardless of the modern computer technology used by tax practitioners and taxpayers, IRS's technology has remained stuck in the distant past. In 2014, IRS Commissioner John Koskinen described the IRS's "abysmal technology" in an interview as "a Model T with a great GPS and wonderful sound system." He added, "We rebuilt the engine, but it's still a Model T."

The Computer College

When I joined Ken Vacovec's firm in 1985, he asked me to join the Computer College of the Massachusetts Bar Association. Ken was a founder. The purpose of the College was to educate the legal community about how computers could be used to improve the practice of law.

One Computer College member showed more interest in computers than the law. I told him, "Instead of practicing law and using computers, why don't you make computers your career and find a way to apply them to the law?"

He took my advice and made a major contribution to a high profile water contamination case. He provided technical support for the organization of evidence for Jan Schlichtmann, who represented residents of Woburn, Massachusetts, against powerful business groups. Defendants included a tannery, a subsidiary of Beatrice Foods, the chemical company W. R. Grace and another chemical company. With the help of technically-organized evidence, Schlichtmann won the case. I lived in the contaminated area in the 60s, and a business acquaintance in the 80s was one of the plaintiffs. Her son had died of leukemia.

In 1996, the case served as the subject of the nonfiction book *A Civil Action*, which became a movie in 1998, starring John Travolta who portrayed Schlichtmann. Also featured in the film was Kathleen Quinlan, whose first film was *American Graffiti*.

• • •

Kathleen Quinlan (1954 –) When George Lucas visited a high school in 1973 looking for cast members for his film *American Graffiti*, Kathleen Quinlan got her big break as an actress. After several more acting roles she was nominated for an Oscar for her performance in *Apollo 13* in 1977. When she played in the television series *Family Law*, she arranged her contract to read that she could not work past 6:00 p.m. so she could be home with her family.

• • •

American Graffiti is one of my favorite films. It's about four teenagers on their last summer night before college. The teenagers were members of the graduating class of '62—my class. Besides Quinlan, the cast included an ensemble of actors and actresses who went on to become well known, including Harrison Ford, Richard Dreyfuss, Ron Howard, and Suzanne Somers. The sound track includes the most memorable rock 'n' roll hits of the era, played by the gravelley-voiced disc jockey Wolfman Jack.

New Computer Applications

Computer technology exploded in the 90s, creating opportunities for software developers. Most consisted of small software companies or sole proprietors. As bigger companies saw the potential, they purchased these small companies, often creating vast fortunes for their owners. In 2011, Thomson Reuters purchased the tax software company Gary and I founded, although in our case for a modest gain.

As lawyers discovered how computers could make an indispensable contribution to their practice, they wanted to use the applications themselves. It's ironic that most of the lawyers were men, and senior partners refused to let them type on computer keyboards. The old prejudice trumped efficiency. The partners considered typing a "demeaning" job, suitable only for women.

When one well-known intellectual property lawyer left a major firm because of the typing restriction, law firms recognized their narrow view and changed the policies about men typing.

In the early 90s, law firms became one of the last business targets for the computer industry. Apple contacted the Computer College and set up a meeting to learn more about the needs of law firms. I explained to an Apple marketer, "Law firms don't have systems analysts and programmers to design software for them. The software available for law firms has been designed for the IBM PC. If you want to get into this market, make your MAC computer IBM compatible."

Instead, Apple chose to focus on the arts, design and higher education markets and didn't break into the legal market. They donated Apple desktops to schools and organizations so students would prefer them when they began working.

In 1995, our company, Windstar, introduced colleges and universities to our tax software which we developed only for the IBM PC. The software provided the complex analyses educational institutions needed for correct withholding and reporting on payments to their foreign national students and scholars.

Since they used Apple computers, when Boston College first called to inquire about licensing our software, the first question was, "Will it run on a MAC?"

Gary said, "No, buy an IBM PC." They did and became Windstar's first client. Our tax software became the incentive many of our college and university clients needed to justify their request to purchase their first IBM PC.

The Y2K Problem

As a tax software company, Windstar had to deal with the Year 2000 problem known as "Y2K." Since early computers had limited memory capacity and file storage, programmers used only the last two digits to identify the year. Once the century changed, the programs wouldn't be able to tell the difference between 1900 and 2000. The problem escalated into a major panic for computer users, with exaggerated fears, such as planes falling from the sky at midnight of December 31, 1999.

All this uncertainty created an incentive for colleges and universities to implement enterprise software systems provided by companies such as Oracle and PeopleSoft. Windstar developed interfaces with these systems. Organizations licensing software, including our clients, required written certification that systems were "designed to be Year 2000 compliant."

I had a unique history with the Y2K problem. At the IFA tax conference in Amsterdam in 1988, the moderator of a panel on software amortization rules—who was also IBM's senior tax counsel—said, "All software is obsolete within five years." During the Q&A, I walked up onto the stage, took the microphone and told the 1,500 participants in the audience, "In America, we have a saying, 'If it ain't broke, don't fix it.'" I explained that, as a computer programmer, I had seen computer systems last longer than five, even 10 or more years.

The tax counsel was visibly annoyed with me. I saw him next at the annual IFA USA branch meeting in Boston in 2001. As I approached him, I could tell by his expression he knew I was going to say. "I told you so!"

That year, an article appeared in the *American Bar Association Journal* about a Y2K problem at UNUM—formerly Union Mutual. As I read it, I realized I was the one who had created the bug described in the article. In the early 70s, I needed to solve the problem of limited disc space for the policy master file. To do so, I added a routine to remove policy records with no activity, such as billing, in the past five years. This solution had been eliminating active policy records from the master file for six months before the company discovered the problem.

My Y2K bug had been lurking in the system waiting to wreak havoc for almost 30 years!

CHAPTER 25

Gary Has a Great Idea

*Build your own dreams,
or someone else will hire you to build theirs.*

– Farrah Gray

Beginning in 1986 and for the next 10 years, I gave tax seminars to foreign students and scholars at Boston area colleges and universities. Participants asked questions throughout the two-hour seminars. Whenever they asked why they had incorrect withholding or reporting, I always responded, "You need to talk to someone in Payroll."

At the end of one seminar, a participant came up to me and said, "I'm from Payroll. What am I supposed to do?"

Little did I know then, my husband, Gary, would provide the answer to that question.

WHEN THERE IS NO WIND, ROW

An Unusual Request

In the fall of 1993, the director of the International Office at a large Massachusetts hospital called me with a strange request. She wanted me to explain how the hospital could modify its computer systems to handle the special rules and procedures for payments to foreign nationals. She knew I had designed computer systems before becoming a tax lawyer, and I gave tax seminars each year for their foreign national employees. So she figured I could help.

I told her, "I can't tell you where you're going if I don't know where you are." I asked her to schedule a meeting with the personnel involved with the processes. I arrived at the meeting expecting two or three staff members. Eleven people filled the room, four of them were lawyers. We spent a few hours going over their current procedures and reports. It became clear they didn't collect the data needed to add these new procedures to their mainframe systems. At the end of the meeting, I said, "I need to think about how I can help you. I'll get back to you."

That night, I described the processing problem to Gary, "I used to be able to do any kind of processing on a mainframe, but I would never do this kind of analysis on a mainframe. The tax forms, procedures and treaties all change too frequently."

Gary said, "What you need is a PC-based tax system that pulls information from the mainframe, does the analysis, creates the forms and sends the results back to the mainframe."

I went back to the director, described my discussion with Gary and said, "What we need to do is clone me. But if we're going to clone me, we're going to own me." Over the next few months, I wrote the system overview specifications in my spare time. Then I needed to find a programmer.

I found my programmer at home. My husband, Gary, is the best programmer I had ever worked with. By this time, we had two big incomes and lived on one. I was a partner with Vacovec, Mayotte & Singer. Gary was the director of Data Processing for a Boston insurance company. He had been complaining for a couple of years about a boss who knew nothing about computers and systems but wanted to make all the decisions.

The next time Gary complained, I said, "Why don't you quit. I have a project I think you might enjoy doing."

He gave his notice the next Monday, explaining to the company's president, "You know my wife. She's a lawyer. We can live on her income. And I have a new project that's going to keep me busy."

I was 50 when Gary and I began working together on our computer system. It wasn't unusual for female entrepreneurs to be late bloomers. Mary Kay Ash was 45 when she launched Mary Kay Cosmetics, Inc. She revolutionized the way women bought cosmetics and rewarded high earners with a pink Cadillac.

• • •

Mary Kay Ash (1918 – 2001) In 1963 at age 45, Mary Kay Ash started Mary Kay Cosmetics, Inc. with $5,000. Following her Golden Rule to make people feel important, she created a company for women to achieve personal and financial success. Fortune Magazine included her company in its "100 best companies to work for in America," and one of the 10 best for women to work. She also founded the Mary Kay Ash Charitable Foundation to combat domestic violence and cancers affecting women.

• • •

Gary took a few months off. Then I gave him the system specifications and he got to work. We had two home offices, each with its own computer and printer. We worked out processing problems on weekends, over breakfast at the Town Diner in Norwood, scribbling logic on our place mats.

Gary Takes Charge

Gary told me I needed to create a treaty database for the treaty analysis. Where the treaty text read "contracting state" or "state," I needed to insert either "the United States" or the treaty country name to make the treaty easier to understand. Next I created a database of records with questions with coded yes/no answers for each treaty using Microsoft Access. Each treaty had records for multiple topics—student compensation, scholarships, teacher/researcher compensation, self-employment income and royalties. By the time I finished, each treaty had more than 500 questions and answers along with descriptive data elements.

To make it easier for me to work with the database, Gary designed screens to display the treaty attributes by topic. To add to the screens' graphics, he displayed the flag of the treaty country as well as its name. He liked the effect of the added flags so much that he woke me up in the middle of the night to show me his creative work.

When I gave a demo for an intellectual property lawyer, he said, "Software designers with new ideas come in and demo their systems for me all the time. Your system has the best designed graphics I've ever seen from a small developer."

Gary got to work programming the work flow. The processing was so complicated I decided not to give him all the flowcharting logic at once. In my classes, I always taught the logic for complex tax rules in layers: first the general rules, then the exceptions, and finally, the exceptions to the exceptions. That's how I taught the new lawyers at my firm too. My introduction for the next layer of complexity for Gary was always, "Oh, by the way ...."

One day Gary said, "Every time you say 'Oh by the way' I have to change hundreds of lines of code. If you say it one more time, I'm going to divorce you."

To make the results of the analyses easier for users to understand, Gary added reports illustrating the logic of the residency determination—called "the substantial presence test." He also created a process for storing copies of all forms and reports so they could be easily retrieved by users. One client referred to our system as "the institutional memory we lose every time someone leaves or retires."

When I told Gary, "We can't debug this with deductive reasoning alone," he added processing to create a log of the step-by-step decisions. Whenever a client asked why the system gave them a certain treaty result, the answer always was, "Did you read the log?" The answers to clients' questions were all in the log.

Next, Gary studied the IRS forms and specifications for reporting payments and withheld taxes made to tax nonresidents. Treaty-exempt wages had to be reported on a 1042-S instead of a W-2. Other income payments had to be reported on a 1042-S form instead of a 1099. The processing allowed clients to create their 1042-S information returns on paper for recipients and either on paper or electronically for their IRS submission. The module made it easy for clients to combine data from their paying systems with data about their recipients and payments stored in our system. He added batch processing so clients could perform necessary processing for the next calendar year at year end—the residency and treaty analyses and preparation of withholding certificates for recipients. This module updated all active records—thousands for some clients—for the next tax year with the click of two buttons.

Our Problematic Patent Process

By early 1995, we had a working system and hired a lawyer to apply for a patent. Our lawyer had a skill most patent lawyers lacked—a thorough understanding of computer software. She had experience as a COBOL programmer and knew how to describe computer systems for a patent application. And she had the grit and determination to persevere. She started her one-woman firm and built it into a successful practice in a field dominated by men.

Throughout history, fields dominated by men have had successful lone women. One woman who became very successful in an unusual male-dominated field was sharp shooter Annie Oakley. She became a star of Buffalo Bill's *Wild West Show*. My mother had seen Buffalo Bill's traveling show when she was a child—in a meadow on my grandfather's dairy farm.

• • •

Annie Oakley (1860 – 1926) Born Phoebe Ann Moses (or Mosey) took the name Annie Oakley and used her ability as a sharpshooter to become a star of Buffalo Bill's *Wild West Show*. As a teenager, she attended the Drake County Infirmary where she cared for orphans and received shooting instructions. She became so skilled she hunted game for a local store and earned enough money to pay her mother's mortgage. She toured the world, and her life became the subject of Irving Berlin's musical *Annie Get Your Gun*.

• • •

We applied for our patent in April 1995. In the process, the Patent and Trademark Office (PTO) lost our accompanying documentation twice. The PTO was a mess because of two court cases involving software, decided by the First Circuit Court of Appeals in Boston.

The first of these two cases denied copyright protection for software, but said it could be patented. In response, the PTO issued its software regulations in 1996. A flood of software patent applications followed.

In 1997, the PTO asked us to reapply for our patent. I guess they wanted our software application to comply with the new software guidelines. But they had already sent us a Notice of Allowance in June. They just hadn't issued the patent yet, so we refused to reapply. In 1998, the issuance of our patent got further delayed when the First Circuit decided in the second case that business processes could receive patents too. Companies overwhelmed the PTO again, this time with business process applications.

The PTO didn't issue our patent until February 6, 2001. To speed the process along, I told our patent lawyer to explain to the PTO, "Our client is an older, irrational woman who keeps insisting she's going to call Senator Kennedy." That worked, and at last we got our patent. The process had taken five years, nine months and 20 days.

Our First Demo Makes an Impression

Before marketing our software, we needed to be sure the IRS would look favorably on our computer system. It did something that computers had never done before: It analyzed tax treaties for benefits related to U.S. activities and completed the relevant withholding forms. I also needed answers to many unanswered questions. This area of tax law has little IRS published guidance because it affects so few taxpayers.

I wrote to IRS Assistant Commissioner, International, Deana Lenehan, describing our system. I explained, "A computer program is a series of questions, each with a 'yes' or 'no' answer, but I am coming up with a lot of 'maybes.'"

Commissioner Lenehan called me to introduce me to Carol Dorsey, a top manager in the International Division. Carol and I connected. We discovered we both battled with the IRS—she from the inside and me from the outside—on the same matters. These included foreign addresses not in the city/state/zip code format and the inadequate 10-day time limit for overseas taxpayers to respond to an IRS notice.

I invited Carol to a demo of our system at my law office. She brought with her Lowell Hancock. He had the responsibility to advise educational institutions about their obligations to comply with these special rules and procedures. Lowell had also been involved with the audits of educational institutions for their noncompliance, which had begun in the early 90s. Some of the assessments reached millions of dollars.

Carol, Lowell and I discussed the tax procedures while Gary processed sample records. He printed out the results of the analyses and handed the reports and completed forms to Carol and Lowell. They stopped talking in mid-sentence, looked at the printouts, looked at each other, looked back at the printouts and looked at each other again. Lowell said, "You can do all this with a computer?!"

They agreed our software could help educational institutions come into compliance. That was just what we needed to hear.

CHAPTER 26

Launching Our New Business: Windstar

*The only way to do great work is to love what you do
If you haven't found it yet, keep looking.*

– Steve Jobs

In September 1994, we incorporated our software computer company. We called it Windstar Technologies, Inc. We wanted to include the word "tax" or "soft" in our name, but our intellectual property lawyer said all the possibilities were taken. She suggested we pick a name with meaning only to us. I liked her suggestion.

In our search for a suitable business name, it didn't take long for us to decide on "Windstar." Gary and I loved to sail.

We had named one of our sailboats *Windstar*. It worked on two levels—for us as a metaphor for our company's forward movement and as an easy name for prospective clients to remember. Like Naomi James, who circumvented the globe alone in 1978, we were ready to find new worlds for our business. Sad to say, after we started the company we had no time for sailing.

• • •

Naomi James (1949 –) In an extraordinary accomplishment, 29 year old Naomi James became the first woman to circumnavigate the earth in 272 days. She landed her 53-foot yacht *Express Crusader* in 1978 after only six weeks of sailing experience. Her trip broke the record held by Sir Francis Chichester by two days. She was born on a sheep farm in New Zealand and did not learn to swim until she was 23 years old.

• • •

We continued the nautical theme with other names of our products. Our flagship product became the *International Tax Navigator*. We also worked a compass rose into the Windstar logo. We named the module that displayed the tax treaty provisions on easy-to-understand screens *Treaty Navigator*. *A View from the Crow's Nest: Windstar's Eye on the Horizon* worked well as the name of our e-newsletter. We titled our periodic newsletter about developments at Windstar *Trade Winds*. We referred to our employees as "the crew." Gary became our "captain." He touted his position on his coffee mug. It had the portrait of a pompous yacht captain with the caption, "Captain: Decorative dummy found on sailboats. See *figurehead*."

Starting Up

Gary spearheaded technology development. I handled the business formation, finances and taxes. I took courses at the Massachusetts Technology Development Center, which gave me more insight into current business practices. This helped with matters for my law firm's clients as well.

It became a family operation. Gary excelled as our first salesman. Our daughter Samantha and a friend stuffed envelopes for our initial mailing. We sent 8,000 promotional pieces to colleges and universities with large numbers of foreign students and scholars.

Samantha, on left, and friend stuffing envelopes

While the business had its serious side, Gary made use of his wry sense of humor. After we sent the mailing, I discovered he had named the student on the sample 1042-S form, "Lighter A. Zippo," after the popular Zippo lighter.

We identified prospects through an annual published survey called *Open Doors*. Our first client, Boston College (BC), resulted from that first mailing. BC invited Gary to their orientation for incoming foreign students. He helped them add their records to the *Tax Navigator* database and create their IRS forms for signature.

Many IRS actions had unintended consequences. One helped us find new customers. IRS audits of educational institutions had created a market for our *Tax Navigator*. The fact that we could save a sizable amount in potential IRS audit assessments for these schools motivated them to sign on with Windstar. As a result, we added about 50 new clients a year in the first few years.

The quickest sales occurred right after the IRS walked through the doors of a school for an audit. One agitated prospect called and asked, "How soon can we get the system?"

In his no-nonsense style, Gary replied, "How soon can you get me the purchase order?"

We designed our system so users could install it like any shrink-wrapped software. When one prospect complained to Gary about the price, Gary said, "So don't license it." They later realized the value we offered and called back a few months later to license *Tax Navigator*.

When Gary told me the news, I said, "No surprise. I just heard the IRS assessed them $5 million." Before closing an audit, the IRS required the institution to explain how they would comply with the rules and procedures going forward.

Since Boston had the largest population of foreign students and scholars in the United States, we expected most sales would come from the Boston area. That didn't happen. Instead, Gary flew around the country giving demos and selling the system. After one trip he said, "I'll go anywhere Southwest goes." Southwest changed the way airlines priced flights. They no longer required passengers to stay over a Saturday night to avoid the $1,700 price of a round trip ticket to Texas.

In September 1995, Gary demonstrated our *Tax Navigator* at Windstar's exhibit at the American Payroll Association's Educational Institute Payroll Conference in Seattle. As Gary began the demo, a huge group gathered at our trade booth, surprised at the system's flexibility and functionality. The University of Pennsylvania had licensed our software, and their controller delivered a check to Gary at that conference. They liked to say they were Windstar's first client because they paid us first.

As our client base grew, we added institutions from the Boston area including a large hospital. To get the hospital as an account gave a particular sense of satisfaction. My meeting at that hospital years before had inspired our product.

In 1995, we moved to our first office, a little house on Route 1 in Westwood. The next year we hired our first non-family employee, Connie Lizio, to assist with training and sales. In fact, Gary's mother became our first employee. But Gary eased her back into retirement after she interrupted a conference to tell him to stop the meeting and eat his lunch.

Connie had dealt with the immigration and tax issues for foreign students and scholars in her previous position. Gary and Connie gave training on how to use the software. For additional instructions, we sent a videotape of a training session to users. Our prospects and clients became our analysts. They told us what functions they needed. If two or more asked for the same function, Gary added it to the system.

Our First Big Year

1997 became a big year for Windstar. We launched our first website for marketing in January. The son of my law partner Maureen Mayotte designed our website. He had one of the earliest web design businesses. We also received the good news of a Notice of Allowance from the patent office. This meant we would get our patent. Gary contracted with Sylvia Reed to create a Quick Start Manual to ship to clients along with the training video. Business increased, and we needed additional staff.

Gary hired Sirisha Venigalla as a software developer. Sirisha had been educated in India, training that was not appreciated by most software companies at the time. Over time, Sirisha took over responsibility for developing *Tax Navigator*. Scott Annis, an independent contractor who had worked for Gary before, came on board to deal with the hardware and technical issues. Soon he joined Windstar as a full-time employee. Gary hired Billie Jo Adams as administrative assistant, and we implemented an employee health insurance plan. As the business grew, we needed more room and found new offices in Norwood, the town where we lived.

Throughout the year, we set up Windstar exhibits at shows sponsored by trade organizations all around the country—St. Louis, San Diego, Newport, Boston, Anchorage, New Orleans and Seattle. Gary gave demonstrations of *Tax Navigator* to participants at St. Norbert's International Tax Compliance Workshop for educational institutions in De Pere, Wisconsin, and at the annual conference of the National Association of College and University Business Offices (NACUBO) in Boston.

The trips Gary and I took together for business became our only "vacations." We stayed in nice hotels and ate out at some great restaurants—all tax deductible. Gary is a steak lover, so we always made a point to eat at Ruth's Chris Steak House.

• • •

Ruth Fertel (1927 – 2002) As a single mother desperate for a way to pay her son's college education, Ruth Fertel bought a steak house restaurant. Even though she had no experience running a restaurant she convinced a bank to loan her $22,000. Since the bank didn't like making loans to women, she put up her house as collateral. She renamed the restaurant Ruth's Chris Steak House and, in 1976, she began franchising. Today there are more than 120 of her restaurants worldwide.

• • •

Time to Hire More Crew

Our daughter Samantha became our first job recruiter. She started with her personal contacts, friends from the local boys' Catholic school, for our help desk. In turn, they helped us hire their friends and family members. We used outside consultants for administrative functions until we were big enough to hire employees for these positions. Our part-time bookkeeper, Janet Chatfield, became our accountant. Steve Ivanoski became our part-time chief financial officer. Every time Steve came to me with a good idea, I delegated the task to him. After a while he got the hint and took the initiative to get jobs done on his own.

Gary hired programmers and technicians though Monster.com, the internet website for hiring staff. Our banker asked, "How are you able to attract software developers as a small company?"

Never at a loss for words, Gary said, "We hire people with potential and train them."

One senior technician, Steve Bonda, joined us at age 17. He stayed with us while he attended Northeastern as a co-op student and continued to work his way through with us for his Master's degree. After graduation, he joined us full-time.

To add a homey quality to the office, the crew included several dogs. Our Golden Retriever, Lilly, grew up at the office. Our web designer, Tom, added his Bichon Frise, Louie, to the roster. One developer, Hongcheng, brought in her Pit Bull. Our administrator Jennifer came to the office with her Havanese, and Julie, who worked at our help desk, kept her new puppy nearby for comfort. Too bad dogs couldn't learn to how to code.

Customer Support

From the beginning our business model educated our users about the special withholding rules, treaty exemptions and immigration-related rules that our software handled. We also explained other concepts such as how to distinguish between a fellowship and wages. For the most part, our users came from higher education and research institutions and were not trained accountants or even experts in the field. They needed a high level of hand-holding and training from us.

We approached the training in a number of ways: first with extensive on-screen helps for *Tax Navigator* and *Treaty Navigator* to explain the rules, next with the training video and Quick Start Manual that included discussions about the rules. We added a help desk for technical questions.

In 1998, we began extensive training sessions and even provided laptops for hands-on training. I taught seminars on topics requested by our users. We expanded the training to four-day sessions, held three times a year, and awarded certified credits for certified public accountants and certified payroll professionals. We added a one-day year-end update as a pre-conference to the annual International Tax Compliance Workshop at St. Norbert College in De Pere, Wisconsin.

These classes grew in popularity as administrators learned our system's thoroughness and the ease with which it worked. We added more seminars and presenters with expertise in applying these rules to real-life situations. They included immigration lawyer Linda Dodd-Major, founder and former director of INS's Business Liaison Office; Terri Crowl, George Mason's NRA tax coordinator; plus experts in nonresident alien (NRA) taxation from the IRS including Lowell Hancock. We opened the training programs to non-clients for marketing purposes.

In 1998, we added a special service we called "the windstarusers listserv." It became very popular because it allowed users to ask questions by e-mail and obtain responses that could be viewed by all members of the listserv. We expected users to educate each other, but, for the most part, they didn't. I took on that task. In the beginning, I answered listserv questions from my law firm for a fee. When I arrived at Windstar later on the first day that I began answering questions, several employees who had seen my many answers surrounded me, surprised at all of my quick answers. One asked, "How can you answer all those questions so fast?"

I replied, "I have a very good memory, so I don't have to look up the answers. And I type fast."

We engaged Linda Dodd-Major and hired Terri Crowl to help with the listserv by answering questions in their respective areas of expertise. Linda's covered immigration law and procedure, Terri's the U.S. taxation of foreign students and scholars. Because so many questions showed up so often, we added another product for free, the *Windstar Users Website*. It featured informative questions with their answers indexed by topic and only available to clients. Terri and I saved our posts and used them as the basis for training materials, e-newsletter articles and user website Q&As.

During income tax filing season, clients sometimes needed additional hand-holding when creating 1042-S forms to submit to the IRS, due March 15 unless the client had an extension. Gary had given his cell phone number out to some clients and fielded calls from anxious clients at all hours. One March 15, when we were on our way to a restaurant, Gary got a call from a frantic client. She couldn't get her forms to print. He pulled the car over and, in a calm voice, began walking her through the things to check. Everything checked out. Then he asked, "Is your printer plugged in?" It wasn't. Overjoyed when the forms started to print, she quickly thanked him and hung up, and we proceeded on our way.

In 2004, we launched *The View from the Crow's Nest* e-newsletter and sent it to all *Tax Navigator* users. I wrote a short tax article for each edition. I got ideas for topics from users' questions.

One user remarked upon receiving the first edition, "Finally, something I can understand!" We posted archived copies of prior editions on Windstar's website where visitors could sign up to receive our e-newsletter and also view our on-line abbreviated versions of tax treaty texts. IRS tax return reviewers used these texts every tax season.

We had launched *Windstar* and it was sailing at full speed.

Gary at the helm of our sailboat, 1988

CHAPTER 27

Windstar Expands Its Product Line

A lawyer without history or literature is a mechanic...

– Sir Walter Scott

In the 1990s, most educational institutions replaced their database management systems with applications provided by Enterprise Resource Providers (ERPs) like Oracle, PeopleSoft and SCT. Gary began negotiations with the ERPs to build interfaces with our *Tax Navigator*. We entered into our first ERP alliance with Oracle but refused to pay the $10,000 business fee. Oracle wasn't used to dealing with small companies. Plus, as Gary explained, "You need us more than we need you."

In 2002, Oracle introduced its two-way interface with Windstar on *Yahoo Financial* and at Oracle's *APPs World* conference in New Orleans. When I met there with Oracle's marketers, one said, "We understand you have a product for educational institutions."

I said, "Hold it right there! Our first market is educational institutions, and we can help Oracle with that market. But we don't need Oracle to get that market. We already have it. We want all of your other markets, including corporations, pension administrators, financial institutions and casinos. They all will need our software services. They just don't know it yet."

Years later a large financial institution approached me about assisting them with the automation of the residency and treaty analyses for pension payments to tax nonresidents. They had already spent two years trying to automate the residency rules but "weren't there yet." I explained we already had the most sophisticated residency analysis, and I had already added coding for tax-treaty pension provisions to our treaty database. But they wanted me to work on their system. I declined, explaining, "I only work on systems Windstar owns."

When our Oracle contact offered to give us a copy of their massive system for testing, once again Gary displayed his satirical sense of humor. He declined the offer, saying "I like to go to the zoo to see the elephants, and I like to feed the elephants. But I don't want to take an elephant home with me."

Negotiations with other ERPs took longer. Some told their clients and prospects they didn't need our software. At one trade show, we overheard an ERP salesman answer "Yes" when a prospect asked if their system prepared Form 1042-S. I knew it didn't. After the prospect left, the salesman rushed over to our booth and asked "What's a 1042-S?"

After a few years, we at last had an opportunity to give a demo to PeopleSoft's product manager when we visited Vancouver, where she was based, for a trade show. After we returned, she called and told Gary "I discovered I should have collected the fees required by PeopleSoft policy for such meetings and demo." The fees totaled $52,000. Without skipping a beat, Gary said, "We just started our own alliance and the cost for ours is the same—$52,000. Would you like the checks to cross in the mail or shall we just do accounting adjustments." PeopleSoft waived the fees.

We Purchased Education Catalyst

In 1998, the country reeled with the salacious revelations of the President Bill Clinton and Monica Lewinsky scandal. But we had other priorities and kept our focus on growing our business. We bought Education Catalyst, a software program used to prepare immigration paperwork for foreign students and scholars entering the United States. More than 500 educational institutions used this program. Our upgraded *VisaManager* handled this processing and more. But after 9/11, as a result of its anti-terrorism fears—some of the terrorists had entered the United States as students—the government replaced most of this processing with a system, now named the Student and Exchange Visitor Information System (SEVIS). So, by 2002, we had installed *VisaManager* in only 65 institutions.

The developers of SEVIS learned much about the necessary functions by viewing our software at our clients' sites. This violated our clients' license, but it was hard for them to say "No" to the government. I pointed this out in an editorial letter sent out on an immigration listserv with more than 30,000 members. The next morning, my law firm received an email from a foreign student advisor in South Carolina. He said my editorial had "disparaged the integrity of our law firm." As my partner Ken Vacovec dropped a copy of the email on my desk, he said, "Who'd you tick off this time?" At any other law firm, this would have been a problem, but my partners just laughed when I told them what was going on. I knew the individual worked at a SEVIS beta site. Hardly impartial!

This wasn't the only setback for *VisaManager*. One organization expropriated the name for their website's domain name. We sued them, and they took the website down. But to own *VisaManager* as a domain name, we had to buy it from them. We applied for a federal trademark to protect the name *VisaManager* from future infringements only to be told by another company we couldn't use the name. We filed a law suit requesting summary judgement that we weren't infringing on their trademark. When they brought in a major Boston law firm, I told our lawyer, "Tell them that I write a lot, and I'm going to make a career out of writing about this case." We were able to move forward and get our trademark. I guess they must have Googled me and discovered I wasn't lying.

Our flagship program, *Tax Navigator,* used the immigration data from *VisaManager* to determine the tax status of foreign students and scholars. When Gary created an interface to obtain immigration data from clients' databases—mostly spreadsheets—he discovered he had to convert their country names and codes to the IRS-specified codes. One client had 11 spellings for Great Britain—GB, G.B., United Kingdom, U.K., UK, etc.—one was London!

We also added a valuable interface between *VisaManager* and SEVIS. This allowed clients to process their SEVIS submissions in large batch files. One client that brought in exchange visitors as summer camp counselors sent SEVIS batches of 10,000 records at a time. As thanks, the client sent us a bottle of Dom Pérignon champagne.

How We Outsmarted Our Competition

In the early years, we had no serious software competition for *Tax Navigator.* The only challenge came from major accounting firms. All of them tried to develop an automated system to compete with *Tax Navigator,* but none succeeded. A CPA who had worked on a product for one of them told me years later, "We designed the specs for an automated system like yours and projected we would have to license it for $20,000 to recover our costs. You licensed yours for $5,000. We just couldn't compete."

Gary priced our system like insurance—a first-year cost with a renewal fee each year. This meant we had a long recovery period for our development costs. We knew partners in personal service firms don't like to tie up their current profits on long-term projects. Our strategy worked. It would be years before we had software competition. By then we had more than 300 clients. Whenever someone asked Gary how he managed to develop a system that the major accounting firms couldn't, he replied with a glint in his eye, "What can I say? I sleep with a tax lawyer."

In 2003, Windstar added the *Foreign National Information System* (*FNIS*) to counter the challenge of a new web-based competitor. This program provided students and scholars a means to enter information for *Tax Navigator* via the web. Windstar gave other colleges and universities permission to use the original manual form we had designed with our first client for this process. Many posted it on their websites. I became more than a little bit perturbed when I heard one of the major accounting firms had the gall to charge their clients for that form!

Windstar Publishing Enters the Print World

In 2002, we incorporated Windstar Publishing, Inc. in order to offer the tax guidebooks I wrote for sale to the public. We sent two books out to each new client: *Tax Treaty Benefits for Foreign Nationals Performing U.S. Services* and *A Guide for Filing Forms 1042 and 1042-S*. Gary co-authored the 1042-S book with me. We based it on the year-end seminars he gave on the numerous procedural rules for these forms. We also gave these two books, or substitutes, to each participant at our training seminars. And each tax filing season, we sent two 1042-S books to the IRS Martinsburg Computing Center.

The publishing business early on had included many women. One of the most influential was Katherine Graham. As publisher of the *Washington Post*, Katherine Graham exhibited great courage during the Watergate scandal and changed U.S. history by printing the facts about the event.

• • •

Katherine Graham (1917 – 2001) A Year after graduating from college in 1938, Katherine Graham went to work at the *Washington Star* owned by her father. When he retired in 1946, he passed the reigns to Graham's husband Philip. She took over as president following his death by suicide in 1963. During the two decades she ran the newspaper, she published historic reporting, including the Pentagon Papers and the Watergate scandal. As a result of these newsbreaks, Graham was considered the most powerful woman in publishing.

• • •

Other tax guidebooks in the series were for specific categories of foreign nationals: foreign students, exchange visitors, specialty workers, intracompany transferees and business visitors. I felt honored when one book, *International Aspects of Individual U.S. Tax Returns*, won the Bronze Medal in the first annual Axiom Business Book Awards in the Tax/Accounting category in 2008. A colleague who reviewed the book said, "There's information in this book you can't find anywhere else!"

A second series, under the title *Cross-Winds*, included: *What You Need to Know about J-1 Exchange Visitors* and *U.S. Taxation of Scholarship and Fellowship Grants*. In 2011, Linda Dodd-Major and I co-authored the third book in this series, *Honorarium and Other Payments to Independent Contractors: A Guide to Immigration and Tax Administration*. In spite of the long titles, we sold a fair number of books through the Windstar website. The IRS ordered our guidebooks to train their auditors and tax return reviewers.

A New Product for Taxpayers

In 2007, Harvard called. They had an unusual request. They had engaged me to give a tax seminar to their foreign students and scholars during the two prior tax seasons. The International Office personnel invited me to lunch and asked, "Could you create a website to provide answers to questions posed by foreign students and scholars?" The school was inundated with tax questions every year and needed a solution.

I said, "Yes, I can."

They followed up with me late in the year and asked, "Can you create the website and have it up and working in early 2008 in time for tax season?"

This came as an opportunity to create a new product, so we got started on it right away. I wrote the content, Gary took care of the technical matters and Steve took care of the business matters. Even the IRS didn't have some of the information we provided, in particular, a handy chart: *Where to Record Items of Income on Form 1040NR and 1040NR-EZ*. We also included a pdf file for each treaty country giving all the tax-treaty benefits and their limitations by country for the typical payments made to foreign students and scholars. The IRS publication on U.S. tax treaties includes an overview chart of these treaty benefits, but it lacks information on many of the limitations.

We licensed the site, called the *Foreign National Tax Resource*, to Harvard and began marketing it to other institutions. For tax year 2010, we added our on-line Form 1040NR/EZ tax return preparation software to attract educational institutions that wanted a complete solution for their foreign national students and scholars. More than 35,000 tax nonresidents used our software to prepare their federal tax returns each year. Tens of thousands more used the website to gain an understanding of their U.S. tax obligations.

Withholding Taxes Present New Opportunities

Our client base for *Tax Navigator* expanded to other nonprofit organizations—research institutes, teaching hospitals, museums and even a prominent U.S. government agency. Other organizations remained unaware of these withholding and reporting rules, that is, until the IRS implemented a voluntary compliance program (VCP) in 2004. Under that program, if organizations paid back taxes and interest for a limited number of years, the IRS waived most penalties. They designed the program for financial institutions. Educational institutions were specifically excluded because they had been offered a separate program a few years before. The IRS seemed surprised when a third of the organizations entering the VCP were major multinational corporations and service providers.

At a meeting in Washington, D.C. in 2007, I discussed withholding compliance enforcement with the individual who had drafted the withholding regulations. He told me, "The IRS doesn't know why so many multinational companies entered the VCP."

I said, "I do." I told him the following story:

It began with the 2004 annual meeting of the USA branch of the International Fiscal Association. One of the workshops covered activities of foreign nationals in the United States on behalf of their foreign employers. At breaks, I kidded the presenters about the U.S. companies' noncompliance with U.S. immigration rules and the tax rules for payments to tax nonresidents.

The foreign nationals providing those services entered the country as business visitors in B-1 status. Business visitors are not authorized to do productive work in that status, whether they're paid or not. Those who pay these visitors must withhold 30 percent withholding in taxes and deposit the amounts with the IRS. The recipients cannot receive tax-treaty exemptions if the foreign company charges back the costs to a U.S. affiliate. They almost always do.

At the end of the conference, an IFA colleague on the program committee told me they would include a workshop on this topic at IFA's next annual USA branch meeting in February 2005. They asked my partner Ken Vacovec to give the workshop. I felt disappointed they didn't ask me, but was not surprised.

When Ken returned from the conference that year, he said, "The participants couldn't believe tax rules existed that they didn't know about." The corporate tax lawyers and accountants went back to their offices and looked for information about the rules. They found the voluntary compliance program, put together their data and entered the program.

At the end of my story, I said, "I think I deserve a commission." The IRS had collected millions, maybe billions, of dollars as a result of the businesses that entered the program. I heard one major accounting firm paid $3 million for their own noncompliance!

W-8 Compliance

In 2009, the manager of Accounts Payable at a major multinational company asked Windstar to submit a proposal. They wanted a system to solicit and verify the W-8 forms from their foreign vendors. To obtain data necessary to comply with their U.S. withholding and reporting obligations, payers request that their foreign vendors complete one of the IRS W-8 series withholding certificates. U.S. vendors are asked to supply a Form W-9.

We already had experience with the forms and rules for payments to foreign vendors. Terri Crowl and I had been explaining to our clients' how withholding applies to payments made by Accounts Payable for years. We won the contract and proceeded with the system design and programming.

Gary and I traveled to the company headquarters to review their existing systems and procedures. We also checked the W-8 forms they used to support the withheld taxes, or exemptions from withholding, on payments they made to their foreign vendors.

Gary designed the architecture and supervised the programming. I created a new tax treaty database to analyze the various types of payments they made. I also wrote the on-screen content about U.S. tax rules and IRS procedures to educate both payers and foreign vendors. We urged their upper management to become involved early in the process, but they had other priorities. In addition, they viewed this as a huge clerical effort that didn't require their involvement. They resisted until an IRS audit forced them to focus on the tax compliance required for these payments. Only then did management understand the value of our system and why they needed to be more involved.

Our Ship Comes In

My mother always said, "when my ship comes in," looking forward to when times would be better. The saying dates back to the days of the clipper ships. In the late 1800s, the shipyards in Kennebunk built more than 200 ships, many that sailed around the world. They would leave the Maine coast with fish and lumber and return with cargo to sell. When the ships came in, their owners made fortunes and local businesses prospered.

Gary and me at the end of a sail on the schooner, Amsterdam

It took until 2011 for our ship to come in.

You could say our ship left our port in 2009 when I began participating in annual seminars sponsored by Thomson Reuters. Companies became interested in complying with these rules because of IRS compliance enforcement. In 2010, Congress passed the Foreign Accounts Tax Compliance Act (FATCA), adding even more rules. Although these rules focused primarily on foreign financial institutions, they affected Accounts Payable in U.S. companies as well.

As we dealt with Thomas Reuters over the years, they saw the potential our products and services offered their clients. In the summer of 2011, they contacted us about buying our company. We were thrilled when they made us an offer we decided to accept. We closed the sale in October. Gary stayed on for eight months and then retired to our 12-acre farm in Maine.

I stayed with the company, traveling for two years to Massachusetts a few days a week to the Thomson Reuters office in Quincy and my law firm in Newton. I stayed with a friend in West Roxbury. I came close to losing this friend in the 2012 Boston marathon bombing. Her son ran in the marathon, and she watched the running in the area where one bomb exploded. Fortunately, she had left before the tragedy because her son crossed the finish line early. Lucky her son was a fast runner.

I heard about the bombing on the radio as I left Quincy for my law office in Newton. I changed my route to return to Maine instead. Watertown Square, where the police were searching for the second bomber and where shots were fired, was walking distance from my law office.

I telecommuted for Thomson Reuters until mid-2015, working in my home office. I could look out the window from my desk and see birds at the feeders and hummingbirds in the flowers. Sometimes a white-tailed deer wanders by.

Now, when I ask Gary to fix a technical problem with my computer, he likes to remind me, "I'm a farmer now." But then he sits down at my computer and fixes it.

CHAPTER 28

Our Creative Funding - When 2+2=22

*An entrepreneur without funding
is a musician without an instrument.*

– Robert A. Rice, Jr.

In 1994, I attended a seminar at the Suffolk University Business School about financing start-ups. The speaker listed funding options on the blackboard:

Friends and family
Angel investors
Venture capital firms
Royalty arrangements
Factoring
Targeted government programs
Bank credit lines
Term loans

After the seminar, I told the speaker, "You missed one. Credit cards!"

He said, "I doubt credit cards are a viable option for funding companies."

Sometime later *Inc. Magazine* headlined a story about entrepreneurs using credit cards to fund their start-ups. To dramatize the point, the cover of the magazine featured a young man sporting a jacket made of credit cards.

Credit cards would become an important funding source for Windstar. But our first real source of financial support came from us. Gary received no salary for several years, and I provided unpaid legal and financial services. We struggled at first, but we knew living on a tight budget would give us the resources and flexibility to build our business.

We also got funding from many other sources.

The Government

We had the Commonwealth of Massachusetts to thank for our first major outside funding. As a new start-up company in 1994, Windstar obtained a $20,000 Capital Access credit line guaranteed by the Commonwealth. We had that credit line for 17 years. We used it for equipment, supplies and marketing. The credit line passed from one bank to another as they consolidated or spun off branches.

When our bank asked us to close the line, I refused. I explained, "It's your fault that this loan is with another bank. You sold the branch." They didn't like my response. But they had to admit responsibility for the account being with a different bank.

The government also provided our second source of funding—through tax savings. We set up Windstar as an S corporation. All income, deductions and credits flowed through to our personal federal and state tax returns—very complicated returns.

For the first few years, Windstar's net losses reduced my taxable income from my law firm. One year the only tax we paid was the self-employment tax on my income.

Credit Cards

In the 1990s, credit card companies expanded to new markets. I accepted every credit card offered. Some I had issued in my name and some in Windstar's name, which I personally guaranteed. At one time, I had over $125,000 in debt on credit cards. For years, MBNA, a credit card company based in Maine, was our primary source of funding.

I spent a weekend every month managing credit card debt. I transferred the balance from one card to another card offering a lower interest rate. But I never transferred a debt just to pay a bill. Over a period of time, I reduced one credit card line of $75,000 to an interest rate lower than the interest rate on bank loans guaranteed by a lien on our house.

Bob Crowley, president of the Massachusetts Technology Development Corporation, knew my credit card story from when I applied for funding and was turned down. At a Small Business Association of New England (SBANE) CEO Round Table discussion, Bob got me to tell the harrowing story of the creative way we got the funding we needed. The CEO sitting next to me, impressed with my creativity, asked jokingly, "Do you consult?"

At the coffee break, another CEO walked over and said, "Everyone else in this room is risking someone else's money. But you and your husband have risked everything. You and your husband are the real entrepreneurs."

I was delighted with this compliment that acknowledged our risks and my ability to create unique financing options.

Banks

The two most important words for a small business are "cash flow." Because our software was tied to the tax year, our cash flow became seasonal. As we grew, we needed a bigger credit line. We had sufficient revenue in the tax season to pay down the borrowed funds every year. Banks would only give small businesses a credit line and term loan guaranteed by the Small Business Administration (SBA). We also guaranteed our loans by a lien on our house. But we soon discovered to increase our credit line required us to move our account from one bank to another.

As a software company, we had a serious disadvantage. When we met with our second bank's loan officer and asked for an increase in our credit line, he turned us down. His reason: We didn't have any physical assets like a manufacturer's equipment or a retail business's inventory.

Gary said, "You're telling us a manufacturer or retailer is more creditworthy than Windstar when all we have to do is send out invoices for the software renewal and wait for the cash to flow in?"

He said, "Well, we don't really understand software."

Even with the SBA guarantee, Windstar had to put up with the whims of our bank. When we met with our third bank's loan officer to request a credit line increase, he said the bank had closed our line. Since the dot.com bubble had burst that year, they were dumping all their software clients.

It took us two months and a three-inch binder of documentation to get our fourth banking relationship. When that bank's loan officer left, a new one did not get assigned to Windstar. Our banking relationship with our last bank turned out to be the best—probably because we had so much cash in the bank we didn't need their money.

In 1999, and off and on for a few years thereafter, I had spoken to representatives of Silicon Bank but was always brushed off. Their clients consisted of high-tech companies. At a high-tech conference, I sat across the table from a Silicon Bank executive and next to the president of a high-tech company I knew through my law firm. I told him how Windstar had grown each year in spite of our struggles to secure funding.

The company president said, "Silicon Bank would be a good fit for Windstar."

I said to the executive, "You know the banker and our story. Why don't you see if the bank would be interested in Windstar?"

Much to my colleague's surprise, and my disappointment, the banker showed no interest in Windstar. I assume this occurred because we didn't have venture capital funding that helped establish most high-tech start-ups.

In 2004, at an SBANE meeting, Massachusetts congressional representative Barney Frank raved about how the SBA helps small businesses. He was taken aback when I told him afterwards, "I own two small businesses, and, as far as I'm concerned, all banks suck."

Employees and Colleagues

When we needed cash the most, two long-standing Windstar employees came to our rescue and invested in the company.

An early mentor on starting a business, Dr. Ruth Clarke, director of Suffolk University's international MBA program, became a shareholder and joined Windstar's board.

Our part-time CFO, Steve Ivanoski, also became a shareholder when he became Windstar's president. He became very effective at preserving our cash flow with his "policy of 'No'."

Nontraditional Sources

We also had a less traditional source of funding. Under the tax rules, an employee may borrow up to $50,000 from his 401(k). We set up a 401(k) for Windstar employees. Gary rolled his 401(k) from his prior employer to Windstar's 401(k) and borrowed $50,000 two different times, paying it back each time with interest.

We each had multiple Individual Retirement Accounts (IRAs). I began consolidating the accounts by rolling each account to a new investment company. Instead of doing a trustee-to-trustee transfer, we took distributions without withholding, used the cash for almost 60 days and then deposited the funds into our new IRA accounts. Our accountant said, "Can you do that?"

I replied, "Yes, veeery carefully."

Had I failed to redeposit a distribution amount into a new IRA on time, the distribution would have been subject to income tax, plus a 10 percent penalty. As of 2015, you can't do this anymore because IRS rules, based on a new court case, allow only one such rollover per individual per tax year.

Our most peculiar funding came from a disaster. The water heater for the office above ours broke. It soaked one-third of our office. The heater was directly above laptops we had just leased for our hands-on training classes. Most had remained in unopened boxes. We hired an adjuster and received a $55,000 settlement.

After the salvager moved the boxes of laptops from the loading dock to his truck, Gary went out and said, "I'll give you $5,000 for those laptops." He assumed enough of the laptops would be viable for our training, and we could replace those that got damaged. The salvager agreed and moved the boxes back into the office. We continued to pay monthly on the lease for the laptops.

Furniture and Equipment Suppliers

In Windstar's early years, our expenses exceeded our income—by a lot! We had to find creative ways to preserve our meager capital. We bought unassembled furniture and IBM clone computers with credit cards. We bought used telephone systems from John Tracey who had worked for Gary at his previous employer, the insurance company. Tracey also installed them.

As we added employees, we leased new computers from Dell. We gave the latest versions to our developers and cascaded the old computers down to administrative personnel. After being in business for years, we learned an unfortunate downside to leasing. When we tried to purchase some equipment, we discovered we didn't have a Dun & Bradstreet credit rating. At that time, Dun & Bradstreet didn't collect information on leases, and many of the credit cards we used had my name on them.

In March 2001, the dot.com bubble burst. My law firm shared our floor with a start-up company developing a product for on-line estate planning. We could have told them it would never work. People don't like to think about their mortality. They need advisors coaxing them to plan for the inevitable.

The company went bankrupt, and an auction followed. I walked over to check out the furniture. I asked the auctioneer what a cubicle setup cost new. He said, "About $3,000 plus another $2,500 for the computer."

I said, "I own a software company and it costs us about $500 to furnish a cubicle, plus $500 for an IBM clone."

He said, "There's one difference between you and this company."

I asked, "What's that?"

He replied, "You're still in business and they're not."

When we added new employees, we bought furniture and movable partitions from Office Max to create additional cubicles. For each move, Gary configured the office space using CAD-CAM software and assembled the new furniture and partitions. We applied for leases through Office Max's designated leasing company to finance our most expensive purchases.

Once we purchased $11,000 of furniture and partitions, and to our surprise, we couldn't find anyone to pay. We had submitted an application for a lease with the company Office Max used at the time for buyers who finance a major purchase. A few months later our bookkeeper asked why we hadn't made any lease payments. We called the local Office Max. They said the sale had closed, so we didn't owe them. We called the leasing company and discovered they no longer worked as the leasing company for Office Max. Office Max had changed leasing companies while our lease application was in process. We followed up by letter to both companies but received no response. We never paid the $11,000, so we recorded the amount as income.

We got an even better deal from another furniture supplier. We sublet our fifth and final office space from a company that sold office furniture and used the space as a show room. The office space was beautiful. It included an eat-in kitchen and large storage room. The sublet rent was cheap. But the best part of the deal: The company sold us all the furniture for $1!

The furniture was new and must have been worth $20,000 to $30,000, maybe more. The day before we moved in, Gary and I allocated the furnishings for each office. It was Christmas in July!

No Outside Investors

Windstar didn't have outside investors, but not for lack of trying. I took every opportunity to talk about Windstar and its products to potential investors. In 1999, I gave a presentation about our business and software at the Massachusetts Software Council Equity Forum. The only person who spoke to me was a bank loan officer. She wondered if we needed bank resources. I told her we already had a banking relationship.

Business improved over the years. In 2000, Windstar competed against 54 companies vying for SBANE's Innovators' Award. We didn't make one of the five announced winners. But I was pleased to learn later from one of the judges we had been among the top 10.

In July 2002, I attended the Venture Capital Tune-Up, an educational program that introduced female entrepreneurs to potential resources for equity capital. The Center for Women and Entrepreneurship sponsored this event. It pleased me to see that, after some hard fought battles, women had earned a right to take up leadership roles in all types of business enterprises.

Before the huge growth of high-tech businesses in the 90s, most successful female entrepreneurs had focused on products for women—Coco Chanel's fashions, Elizabeth Arden's cosmetics and Diane Von Furstenberg's iconic cotton jersey wrap dress. Introduced in 1974, the jersey wrap remains popular today and is worn by women around the world.

• • •

Diane Von Furstenberg (1946 –) With the sale of more than a million of her cotton jersey wrap dresses introduced in the 1974, Belgium-born Diane Von Furstenberg became an emblem of both feminism and femininity. With the success of the wrap dress she appeared on the cover of Newsweek. She relaunched her fashion firm, DVF, with 85 stores worldwide and expanded into cosmetics, jewelry, luggage and home shopping. Many famous women, including first lady Michelle Obama, have been spotted wearing von Furstenberg's wrap dress.

• • •

In September 2002, I gave a presentation requesting funding at Springboard's New England Venture Capital Forum. Springboard provided women-led emerging growth businesses with access to investment capital and resources. I made it through the first round but didn't make the final cut. In the networking session, an investor suggested we use a major accounting firm to have better access to funding.

I said, "You mean I have to pay $30,000 for accounting services that now cost us only $7,000 just to get investors to talk to me?"

He replied, "Yes."

I thought, "No wonder so many small technology companies with outside funding don't make it."

In 2003, once again in search of investment, I gave a presentation to the Commonwealth Institute eMerging Women Entrepreneurs' Boot Camp. Once again, no results.

In 2004, appearing at Springboard for a second time, I made the cut to speak to potential investors. I explained in my presentation we needed funds for sales and marketing so we could expand beyond the higher education market. After my presentation, one investor asked, "So you need money for technicians?"

I replied, "We have all the technicians we need. We need funds for sales and marketing." No one offered to invest.

In April 2003, I received a frantic call from the director of the Massachusetts Software and Internet Council. She said, "Can you give a presentation about Windstar to our annual meeting today? No more than five minutes long."

She explained one of the three companies scheduled to present had just backed out. She went on to ask, "Could you be here in two hours?"

I said I could, pulled together a short presentation and left for Boston. The two other companies went first, taking more than their allotted time. I began my presentation, "When we started Windstar, I read an article quoting Ken Olson, the founder of Digital Equipment Corporation. He told new entrepreneurs to go into 'something that bores the rest of the world.' I think we've done it."

I gave them a quick overview of our tax software products and told them I was a tax lawyer. Then I reminded them of the date: April 15. I suggested "those of you who haven't completed your tax returns yet might want to leave now." I got lots of laughs, and a reporter for *Mass High Tech, the Journal of New England Technology* interviewed me for a feature article, "Taxing Technology."

The advice I received when I approached potential investors was almost laughable.

Most investors wanted to invest in new technology start-ups that promised huge short-term growth potential. They weren't interested in a company with proven revenue that had been in business for 10 years. One investor said he would be interested if we could get a corporate investor such as ADP, the large payroll company. I didn't tell him that, if we had ADP as an investor, we wouldn't need him.

Another investor commented about the software, "It's just not Boston." I guess she meant Boston investors like to invest in certain types of technology, application systems not being one of them.

Some investors suggested I reduce my law firm commitment by withdrawing from the partnership and becoming of counsel to the firm, a much less rewarding position. Other investors wanted to replace the management team—me in particular.

One potential CEO recommended by a venture capital firm suggested to Gary—after I had left the meeting—I should go back full time to the law firm and serve Windstar only as an outside advisor. This would be unpaid, of course.

One venture capitalist commented I should stay with Windstar because of my knowledge and contacts and suggested replacing Gary instead. I guess it didn't matter that Gary had designed all our products and was actively involved in improving them.

Other potential investors wanted to compensate Gary and me as one individual, ignoring that we had different high-level skills and responsibilities.

It seemed ironic that many of the individuals we met with had no experience running a business. Many were newly minted MBAs, who didn't even try to understand the business, but rather made their decisions based solely on the financial data.

After giving a presentation to an investment group focused on our need for funding for sales and marketing, one young MBA asked, "Now, you need the money to make payroll?"

I replied, "We've been making payroll since 1995. We need funds for sales and marketing to expand beyond higher education." It didn't seem to convince this MBA any more than the others.

We decided to stop seeking outside funding—as it happened, just as investors began showing some interest in Windstar. Steve Ivanoski, our part-time CFO, became our president and took over responsibility for day-to-day operations. Gary and I worked on improving our products, creating new products and training clients. To demonstrate our tax software, we traveled around the country to conferences and trade shows.

We had been in business for 17 years with no outside funding when Thomson Reuters bought Windstar in 2011. We had four software products, 450 clients, no debt and cash in the bank.

Life was good.

CHAPTER 29

David Slays Goliath, How Sweet It Is!

Success is the best revenge.

– Vanshika Anand

In 1979, when I began dealing with international tax matters, most such matters were handled by the only international law firm—more like a franchise—or one of the eight major accounting firms, known as "the Big 8." There were no national law firms. Big firms expected to get their work from big companies. Small firms were expected to get their work from individuals and small businesses.

I expected to be able to work with major firms on matters for common clients. We each had our areas of strengths that were compatible. I found out the hard way that big firms didn't like small firms encroaching on their territory, regardless of who had the expertise to handle the business. And some didn't think small businesses could do what big firms could do.

Lost Clients

It became a common practice to begin dealing with clients only to lose them to a major firm. My first such client was a professor from Oxford University in the U.K. I did tax planning for his first year in the United States. A colleague of mine from the U.K., Richard Hume-Rothery, happened to be in the office on the day of our meeting. I introduced them. My client said, "There's a Hume-Rothery building at Oxford."

Richard said, "Ah, yes, my grandfather."

After I completed the tax planning, the client didn't come back for me to prepare his tax returns. His employer had advised him he needed to go to a major accounting firm. He did.

One new client, a business from Switzerland, came to me for tax planning for its employees relocated to the United States. I met with the director of Human Resources (HR) and gave her an overview of the rules and information the company needed to collect to report employee income. I gave her a proposal to prepare their tax returns and calculate the tax reimbursements but received no response. I later learned they had engaged a major accounting firm instead.

Three years later I received a call from the same HR director asking about the new Social Security agreement with Switzerland. I asked, "Why are you calling me? Couldn't your accounting firm answer your question?"

Her answer, "No, they couldn't. Not without research."

A client couple who planned to relocate to the United States needed advice about a distribution from the husband's superannuation (retirement) plan in Australia. I referred them to our tax advisor in a major accounting firm in Sydney to deal with Australian tax issues related to the plan. I heard from my clients that this accountant had referred them to the major accounting firm's office in Washington, D.C. for U.S. tax advice about potential tax exemptions under the U.S. tax treaty with Australia. It was very inappropriate for my Australian advisor to refer my client to another U.S. advisor without contacting me first. I guess she expected I wouldn't understand anything about tax treaties because I was in a small law firm. I wrote a letter to her that began, "Let me reintroduce myself. Last month in Washington, D. C., a top IRS international manager, Carol Dorsey, introduced me to the IRS Assistant Commissioner for International, as *the guru* on tax treaties." My clients still chuckled about that letter years later.

Major Firm Consolidations

My law firm dealt with tax professionals in both law firms and accounting firms throughout the world for years. Some belonged to foreign offices of major foreign firms, others to foreign offices of U.S. firms and some were members of independent local firms. But as international business grew, law firms consolidated to create national and international firms. The "Big 8" merged with foreign networks to expand their international reach. They also consolidated becoming the "Big 4." I learned about some of these expanding firms the hard way.

I worked on an expat tax matter for one corporate client with a tax lawyer in Beijing who had been referred to me by a colleague at a law firm in Hong Kong. My client's expat hadn't been paying his income taxes in China. I received a call from a U.S. lawyer who started off by saying, "We had a hard time finding out where the referral came from."

I didn't know who he was or what he was talking about. I asked, "Who are you and why am I talking to you?" He explained the lawyer who handled my tax matter in Beijing was a member of his law firm.

Then he told me, "All work in China has to go through me." I later learned this lawyer was *the* U.S. expert on China. He required an agreement with my client in order for the work to proceed. I made arrangements with my client for him to deal with my client's general counsel, and they promptly cut me out of the loop. This was not a good situation since the expat's total taxes required coordinating both country's tax rules and procedures. The next time I needed a lawyer in that part of the world, I asked for a referral from the tax lawyer I dealt with in Canada. That was the last time I was cut out of the loop.

Outsourcing

In the 90s, the major accounting firms made a big push to convince companies to outsource their expat tax administration to them. The outsourced services would include preparation of tax returns and computations for the tax equalization program. This made sense for multinational companies with hundreds of expats. We lost business to these major firms whenever a large corporation acquired a corporate expat client. Big companies wanted to deal with one major firm for their expat matters. When Computervision acquired Prime Computer, Computervision became our client. When another company acquired Computervision, we lost them as a client.

But the major law and accounting firms went after all the business, not just from major companies, even when they couldn't provide as good service to smaller companies. One year, Ken Vacovec and I submitted proposals and had follow-up meetings with several companies only to learn from individuals outside the companies that we didn't get the engagements. I assumed the companies had just used our proposals to negotiate down the costs proposed by the major firms.

Nevertheless, our law firm managed to sustain a thriving expat business, and my practice on other international tax matters grew. Our tax services provided unique features: We not only dealt with U.S. tax law and procedures but also dealt directly with overseas experts on matters involving other countries' tax laws and procedures.

I knew my international tax expertise was finally being recognized and appreciated in the Boston area when a lawyer from a major law firm called to refer me a trust matter requiring coordination with U.K. counsel. He told me, "I wish I could do what you do."

Sometimes it took a major event for women finally to be recognized in a field dominated by men. Women began to receive more recognition for their prowess in tennis after Billie Jean King defeated male professional Bobby Riggs in the highly publicized "Battle of the Sexes."

• • •

> **Billie Jean King (1943 –)** After winning her first major singles championship at Wimbledon in 1966, King continued winning and turned professional in 1968. The first female athlete to win $100,000 in a single year, she led the formation of the Women's Tennis Association with the major goal to equalize prize money for women and men. King defeated her male opponent, tennis professional Bobby Riggs, in the "Battle of the Sexes" in the Houston Astrodome in 1973.

• • •

One potential new client wanted us to do all the same work as the major firms but be paid at our lower fees. They even wanted us to bill them the fees for our overseas counsels in U.S. dollars even though we paid these fees in foreign currency. We always had to deal with an exchange rate difference with the U.S. dollar—and the difference could be very large. We would win or lose depending on the difference between exchange rates on the date billed and the date paid. We were tax lawyers, not gamblers. I declined to submit a proposal and told him, "You'll have to engage a major accounting firm. They can afford to take the exchange rate risk."

Major accounting firms liked to point out that, by outsourcing their expat program administration to them, a business saved the head-count cost of in-house administrators. Our business model required client companies to have a knowledgeable in-house administrator. I served that role when I worked at Arthur D. Little.

One new client learned the value of an in-house administrator the hard way—in litigation. That client, a multinational bank, needed a tax equalization expert for a lawsuit in Hong Kong brought by a disgruntled expat employee. The bank's general counsel called me. The expat claimed the company owed him about $17,000, a refund of hypothetical Massachusetts income taxes. Under their tax policy, expats were only assessed hypothetical state income taxes if they were actually subject to the state taxes. Regardless of his repeated requests, no one at the bank or in the outsourced accounting firm told him when he would receive this refund. The expat's issues escalated beyond the tax refund, and he sued his employer.

The general counsel asked if I would serve as an expert witness. I asked, "Am I correct in assuming all of the big accounting firms have a conflict of interest, and that's why you called me?"

He replied, "Yes."

I agreed to take on the project, and he sent me the company's tax policy. I wrote an explanation for the court about our federal tax system and how tax reimbursements under the tax policy are computed. In order to compute how much the bank owed this now-former employee, or how much he owed them, I needed the tax returns and related tax equalization computations. The general counsel needed permission from the expat to release that information to me and requested it when I began the project in the summer. I called the bank many times over the next few months requesting the information. I wanted to complete the project before tax season began. The bank's counsel continued to follow up with the expat's counsel for the permission and requested information. Close to the court's deadline, and in the midst of a busy tax season, I received three large binders of information to read and analyze.

I assumed this six-month delay had been intentional. I called the general counsel and said, "If they think I can't get this done during tax season, they're wrong."

Nowhere in all the correspondence and computations provided by the client could I find any reconciliation of who paid what taxes, or who owed, or was owed, a refund under the tax policy. My firm always provided this type of analysis with the tax reimbursement computation for each expat covered by our clients' tax programs. I prepared an analysis of four years of tax returns, reimbursements and payments to determine the amounts owed to or from the bank.

Based on my computations, the expat owed the bank a net amount for the years at issue. In addition, I found two bank credit memos in the binders adding up to the $17,000 the expat said the bank owed him. But the bank needed to prove the expat had actually received the refund.

I asked the general counsel, "Didn't the expat bank with your bank?" He did. I asked him to have someone find and fax me the expat's bank statement for the month in which the two credit memos were issued. The statement arrived the next day. It included two deposits totaling the $17,000 refund the expat had insisted he never received. The bank's counsel was ecstatic. I helped him win this part of the case.

Windstar's Experience

When Gary and I founded Windstar, we had no software competition. We hoped to work with the major accounting firms—we would provide the software, they would provide the policies and procedures and consulting services. When we approached the major firms about working together, they brushed us off—except for Grant Thornton, which had a big practice with nonprofit organizations in the Boston area. We soon understood why—the major accounting firms were busy trying to develop competing software products. One enthusiastic prospective Windstar client in Boston discovered their institution was obligated by contract with a major accounting firm to give them the opportunity to provide needed software solutions. They licensed our software three years later.

After the accounting firms abandoned their software development efforts, we thought things might change. They didn't. The accounting firms wanted educational institutions to buy their services to provide the expensive case-by-case complex analyses. Windstar's *Tax Navigator* performed the same analyses with the click of a couple of buttons.

Competing with major accounting firms didn't get any easier. Some institutions engaged major accounting firms to identify software solutions for their nonresident alien tax compliance, but they didn't tell them about Windstar's software. More than one new client that had paid for this search was incensed when they learned about Windstar's software from one of our clients. We spoke with a member of one accounting firm about working together several times over the years. The response, "We can't recommend an unknown product from a small company." We accepted this excuse at first, but the response never changed. Mine did.

I said, "We have more than 300 clients, many who've used the system for years. Isn't it time you let your clients know about our software solution?"

Sometimes when an organization considered Windstar's solution, they engaged a major accounting firm to assist them with their evaluation of our software. We learned from more than one new client that a major accounting firm had advised them not to license our software. I observed, based on our new clients that said they had used these consulting services, male decision makers tended to follow that advice while female decision makers didn't and licensed our software.

One prestigious institution already used our software when they engaged a major accounting firm to review their NRA tax compliance procedures. The client didn't renew based on advice from the accounting firm. But they became a client again a few years later.

Another client didn't renew its license because the consultant for their PeopleSoft implementation said they didn't need our software—even though the PeopleSoft system did none of the analyses.

The accounting firms' aversion to Windstar became well known among our clients. When one new large university client entered into a contract with a major accounting firm for consulting services, they included a requirement that the process had to include Windstar's software.

We were almost completely shut out of California. The state of California had a contract with one of the major accounting firms to deal with NRA taxation matters. We tried for three years to give a demo of our system to the CalState system. We finally had success after I met two female controllers from CalState at a conference. They were surprised to learn about Windstar's software. When they got back to California, they arranged for two meetings for Windstar to demo its software—one in the north and one in the south. A few CalState campuses became our clients.

Five years later CalState's request for proposal specified all campuses would use the same software, even though the campus administrations were independent. After the contract was awarded to our competitor, I wrote to California's attorney general, asked the reasons and requested a copy of our competitor's proposal. Gary followed up with a letter detailing what had transpired over the years to keep us out of California. CalState decided each campus could choose which software to use. We kept our clients.

When the University of California System decided to implement a computer system for NRA tax compliance, our sales staff contacted them repeatedly. Windstar never had an opportunity to demo our system for them. At an APA Educational Institutions Payroll Conference in California, I explained to an IRS auditor how our software worked to help our clients stay in compliance with the complex NRA tax rules and procedures. He commented, "With such compliance tools available, we don't understand why California is so out of compliance compared to the other states." I told him the above story.

We were encouraged about working with the major firms some years later when we received an invitation from the office of one of the Big 4 accounting firms to demonstrate our software to their tax partners. The office had a contract with a sizable teaching hospital for NRA tax compliance. Gary and I flew to half-way across the country at Windstar's expense. When we arrived at their office, we were surprised to learn the partners scheduled to view the demo wouldn't be attending the meeting. The tax manager who had set up the meeting seemed very embarrassed. She scurried around to find a few staff members to view our demo. We assumed, since no one had called to cancel our meeting, the partners had made their decision not to attend our demo while we were in the air. We never heard from them again.

Years later I learned from a former employee of this particular accounting firm that they were very upset with Windstar because "we took a whole practice area away from them."

I filed this under, "If you can't join 'em, beat 'em."

Like David facing Goliath, we may have been small, but we out maneuvered our huge competitors.

CHAPTER 30

Courses, Seminars and Conferences Keep Me Current

To teach is to learn twice.

– Joseph Joubert

In 1986, Congress passed the Tax Reform Act (TRA '86). Contrary to popular belief, although it had been promoted as tax simplification, it wasn't. In fact, it was quite the opposite. A tax conference about TRA '86 for tax professionals given by the Federal Tax Institute in Boston required two full days.

In 2007, I attended a panel on tax reform at the American Bar Association's Taxation Section annual meeting. A panelist referred to TRA '86 as tax simplification. During the Q&A I walked up to the microphone and said, "I prepared tax returns before the '86 act and after the '86 act. I can assure you, it was anything but simplification." Two older gentlemen at the back of the room said, "Here! Here!"

Boston's Federal Tax Institute

For several decades, until its demise in the mid-2000s, Boston's Federal Tax Institute (FTI) held semi-annual all-day courses. Tax lawyers and accountants came from around New England to dive in depth into the law, regulations and procedures for the broad tax topic announced for each conference. The conferences always took place in the Dorothy Quincy Suite in the old John Hancock building. A high-level IRS or Treasury official spoke, so we got the "unofficial" scoop—they couldn't comment officially—about new laws and upcoming IRS guidance and compliance initiatives.

My partner Maureen Mayotte and I never missed an FTI conference. We were among the few professional women who specialized in tax law back then. We joked to each other it was the only time we didn't have to stand in line at the lady's room.

The course included panels of tax lawyers and accountants from major firms. Dean Edwin Griswold moderated the discussions. Dean Griswold had served as dean of Harvard Law School for 21 years before being appointed U.S. Solicitor General in 1967.

When panelists discussed the new depreciation rules designed for ever-increasing real estate values, Dean Griswold asked, "But what if values go down?" The panelists looked puzzled and had no response. Once again, an idea emerged that writers of the rules had never considered. Values did go down because the new rules put an end to the real estate tax shelter industry.

In 1992, Dean Griswold commented to an interviewer, "...the tax legislation of the 1980s has produced a monstrosity...I shudder at the thought of trying to teach a beginning tax course in law school today."

Taxation played a role in the founding of America. During the time leading up to the American Revolution, the colonists protested British "taxation without representation." After the Boston Tea Party, Penelope Barker convinced prominent women of North Carolina to boycott British products. Imagine what she would say now about the kind of taxation we have now *with* representation.

• • •

> **Penelope Barker (1728 – 1796)** A widow with five youngsters, Penelope Barker became a revered colonial patriot who protested British "taxation without representation" in 1774. Following the Boston Tea Party, Barker convinced prominent women of North Carolina to sign a declaration to boycott British products. Barker said, "We are signing our names to a document, not hiding ourselves behind costumes like the men in Boston did at their tea party." London papers ridiculed them, but colonial women followed their lead and boycotted British goods.

• • •

The FTI held no conferences about international taxation as it related to individuals until 2004. That year, the all-day seminar was all about international taxation and included a panel about individual taxation. By then I become well-known as an expert on handling complex international tax matters for individuals. The seminar committee asked me to be a panelist and to contribute two tax outlines: one about the taxation of U.S. citizens abroad and the other about the taxation of foreign nationals in the United States.

At the break, two female associates from a big law firm asked me about how to collect tax refunds from their clients' employees. Their clients had overpaid their employees for federal income taxes on their salaries and benefits-in-kind. But their employees received all of these taxes back as refunds after they filed their tax returns. I said, "Who would ever pay expats current tax reimbursements for federal income taxes? They don't owe the tax because of income exclusions or foreign tax credits. The reimbursement just adds to their taxable income." They reacted to my question with horrified expressions. Knowing the tax law isn't enough. The ins and outs of the procedures are important too. There are special payroll procedures so employers can avoid wage-withholding on their expats compensation. Tax lawyers who don't deal with payroll or prepare tax returns don't gain this experience.

National Tax Conferences

To keep current on international taxation I had to travel to New York City, Chicago and other major cities around the country. I attended many tax conferences at the World Trade Center given by professionals from major law and accounting firms.

While attending one of these conferences, we all watched in shock as a man in a Spiderman suit climbed the neighboring tower. When someone said he just heard on the radio he came from Maine, I knew it had to be Danny Goodwin. He came from Kennebunk, and I knew his family! As Spiderman made sensational headlines and a feature on the news, we bored through the new tax rules, procedures, forms and examples.

Most seminars targeted business taxation, but some of their topics applied to individuals as well. At one seminar about the international aspects of TRA '86, I asked the presenter whose topic focused on the new foreign tax credit (FTC) regime, "Do these new rules apply to individuals?" He looked puzzled and didn't answer.

I said, "Of course they do, because there's nothing in the tax code that says they don't."

In 1990, the United States launched the Hubble Space Telescope to get a better view of our universe. To help me get a better view of the rules and procedures for payments to foreign persons, I began attending the Bank Tax Institute conferences. When I walked into one conference the Boston-based organizer approached me and said, "Paula, you're at the wrong conference."

I replied, "I'm at the only conference that can help me. I have to figure out from these courses for financial institutions how the rules apply to my business clients who also pay foreign entities and individuals."

He later introduced me to the director of IRS's Martinsburg Computing Center as the person who "knows more about more things that no one wants to know anything about than anyone I know." I reminded him of that introduction a few years later at a conference where he was giving a seminar about one of my topics.

When I began my practice, there were no conferences addressing how income tax treaties and estate and gift tax treaties work. I had to learn about treaties the hard way—by reading and analyzing them. But, in the mid-90s, one tax publisher issued a new treatise every month about an area of international taxation; one covered income tax treaties. I subscribed to all of them as they came out. But getting new ones soon became a problem. A large publisher bought the company and changed how sales reps worked with prospective clients. Instead of a geographic sales territory, sales reps' territory became based on size of prospective clients. When I tried to order one of the treatises, I discovered our small firm rep didn't sell international publications!

Professional Organizations

I always joined organizations so I could meet and learn from other professionals. When I worked at Arthur D. Little, I joined the Greater Boston International Personnel Forum—later expanded and renamed the New England International Personnel Forum.

During one of their meetings at the Sheraton Hotel in Lexington on September 11, 2001, tragedy struck the United States. Someone ran in and said, "A plane just struck the World Trade Center!" We all ran down the hall to the restaurant and watched the events unfold on TV. Everyone was crying. When I got back to my office, I had an email from a concerned colleague in Switzerland who feared I might have been a passenger on one of the planes. I wasn't. But a former expat client and the sister-in-law of our receptionist were. We realized our safe world had changed forever. Yet, somehow we pressed on.

I traveled to New York City for meetings of the International Personnel Committee of the National Foreign Trade Council. As I learned more, I began to give seminars and write articles for professional journals to showcase my expertise in dealing with complex international tax matters. I knew other professionals would rather refer these matters to an expert. The learning curve is long, the transactions are few and individual clients are sensitive to the size of legal fees, making this tax practice area unattractive to most professionals.

In 1985, when I began private practice, I joined the Massachusetts and Boston Bar Associations (MBA and BBA) and joined their sections and committees focused on tax and immigration practice. I also applied to the MBA's Young Lawyers Section to learn the basics about the practice of law. Much to my surprise, the section rejected me because I didn't live up to their idea of a "young lawyer." They had a cutoff age of 35. I was 40. Many years later the section began accepting "old" lawyers who were new to law. Too late for me.

In 2012, when I became a Maine resident again, I discovered I didn't qualify as an "old lawyer" either. Maine residents must comply with Maine's continuing legal education requirement. But a waiver exists for lawyers age 65 or older with at least 40 years of legal experience. I reached age 65 in 2009, but I wouldn't meet the 40-year requirement until 2018 because of my delay in entering law school.

In 1985, the MBA gave no seminars focused on international taxes. I soon began giving seminars sponsored by the Immigration Section on the taxation of foreign nationals and wrote articles about taxes for the MBA's *Section Review*.

That year I also began attending the BBA's international tax committee's monthly meetings. At the end of one meeting, after I had suggested a unique solution to a problem presented for discussion, the chair asked, "How did you get this experience?"

I said, "I had the good fortune not to get a job as a lawyer after law school. I worked for the international consulting firm Arthur D. Little. You can't get the kind of experience I gained there in a law firm."

He said, "You're right."

The committee chair invited me to serve on an international taxation panel. My topic covered the "extra baggage" U.S. employees take with them when their employers transfer them abroad to work—their U.S. tax obligations. Before the program began, the moderator asked each panelist to state their name, firm, and undergraduate college and law school. As they went down the panel, each named their schools—Harvard, Yale, Princeton, Boston College, etc. When they got to me, the only female panelist, I said, "The University of Maine in Orono and the University of Maine School of Law." I felt I made a social statement just by being on the panel.

Organizations with a Special Focus

In 1985, I also joined the American Immigration Lawyers Association (AILA) and began giving tax seminars at local meetings. For several years, my Boston colleagues recommended that AILA invite me to give a seminar on taxes at their annual meeting. It was 1993 before they did. Few immigration lawyers outside of the Boston area understood the connection between immigration and tax rules and their effect on their clients' U.S. tax obligations.

I wrote extensive outlines for AILA's annual meeting handbook on "The U.S. Taxation of Foreign Nationals" and "The U.S. Taxation of Foreign Students and Scholars," as well as articles for AILA's *Immigration Law Today* journal. My outlines helped stem the tide of phone calls from immigration lawyers seeking answers to their clients' "quick" tax questions.

I answered tax questions for the Boston area immigration lawyers who referred tax work to me. But I began getting questions from immigration lawyers from all around the country too. To avoid the inevitable long answers to their quick questions I always asked, "Did you read my outline." If the answer was "Yes," and the answer was short, I answered their questions without billing them. If the answer was "No," I said, "Go read my outline and call me back if you don't find the answer." Most questions had answers in my outlines, so few called back.

AILA's tax program panelists had about 10 minutes each to discuss a tax topic. For the annual meeting in Boston, I prepared an outline with handouts on the "10 Rules of Taxation of Foreign Nationals." I was the final presenter. Since most of the other panelists took longer than their allotted time, I had less than five minutes to give the 10 rules. Most rules ended with "unless an exception applies." After the program immigration lawyers surrounded me saying they expected to hear the exceptions. I said, "I barely had time to give you the 10 rules!" My next outline and articles for AILA's journal gave the exceptions.

In 1991, the National Association of Foreign Student Advisors (NAFSA)—later renamed the Association of International Educators—asked me to give a seminar on the U.S. taxation of foreign nationals at their annual meeting in Boston. At the urging of the seminar's organizer, I joined NAFSA and began giving tax seminars at local, regional and national meetings.

With Lowell Hancock and John Eng-Wong of Brown University, 1995

NAFSA put together an Ad Hoc Tax Committee, and I took an active role in it for about 10 years before they rolled it into their Government Regulations Advisory Committee. I also contributed to NAFSA's publication, *Tax Returns for Foreign Nationals,* and wrote articles for its *Government Affairs Manual.* In 1995, I worked with NAFSA and the IRS on the design of Form 1040NR-EZ, a simpler tax return for tax nonresident students and scholars.

In 1996, I joined the American Payroll Association (APA) and began giving tax seminars at its semi-annual Global Payroll Conference. My first seminar in Honolulu focused on "U.S Tax Treaties: Compliance and Coordination with Payroll." I wrote an article about the seminar for publication in APA's *PayTech* magazine. In 1999, I began giving this seminar at their annual Educational Institutions Payroll Conference too and later added additional seminar topics. I also began giving annual tax seminars for the New England Payroll

Conference. After the APA rolled its Global Payroll Conference into its annual Congress, I gave seminars at that conference too. The APA was also an important distributor of my tax guidebooks. In 2002, they presented me with its Meritorious Service Award for educating its members on the payroll tax rules for foreign nationals. From 2012 through 2015, the APA published my series of articles about the new rules and forms for NRA withholding and reporting affecting Accounts Payable.

Learning by Reading Too

Keeping up with changes in tax field required reading the daily, weekly and monthly tax journals, specialized tax journals, and new treaties. The Bureau of National Affairs (BNA) published the most complete explanations of U.S. tax law and procedure. When they began issuing international portfolios, I took them with me on weekend visits to Sebago Lake. While sitting on the beach, I read them cover to cover. Not very light reading! The descriptions of U.S. tax rules had more twists and turns than an Agatha Christie who-done-it.

But most often I accomplished this reading in a roller rink—after our daughter Samantha took up roller skating. Roll-Land in Norwood hadn't changed since they built it in the 50s—walls had wood-paneling with lighted window boxes filled with trophies and pictures of skate champions and their instructors. It was the only roller rink in the country that still had a live organist. Generations of area residents skated there—some even met their spouses there. I spent many hours with Samantha at the rink with my piles of tax reading. I was known as a "rink mom."

Samantha has natural rhythm. She began dance lessons at age three, first ballet, then tap and modern dance. She began skate competition at age 13. I spent every long weekend with her at roller rinks around Massachusetts, and each Thanksgiving holiday at the rink in

Merrimack, New Hampshire. Unlike ice skating competition, everyone had to skate the same routine. Samantha came in second the first time she competed. In 1995, when she was 15, she made it all the way to the national competition in Fresno, California, and came in first in her class. Then she retired from skating and took up the performing arts, joining the New England Conservatory Choral and the casts of local musical productions.

I had the most fun being her mother, vicariously participating in all her activities, experiences I never had when I was young.

A New Focus

In 2003, I changed to a part-time arrangement with my law firm. I began traveling around the country giving tax seminars to organizations whose members worked for potential Windstar clients. I also gave seminars for Windstar users at three four-day conferences in the Boston area each year. I gave more than a dozen seminars each year by 2011 when we sold Windstar.

I had shared what I had learned with thousands of taxpayers, professionals, administrators and IRS personnel.

It was exhausting but also satisfying and fun.

CHAPTER 31

Teaching the IRS about International Taxation

*Don't be afraid to stand for what you believe in,
even if it means standing alone.*

– Unknown

When I began my tax law practice in 1985, women around the world had begun to make major breakthroughs. Margaret Thatcher—called "the Iron Lady" for her resolve in the face of adversity—had already served as Great Britain's prime minister since 1979.

But few people understood the globalization of the economy had already begun too. That sudden awakening came on Black Monday—October 19, 1987—sometimes called Black Tuesday because of the change in time zones. On that day, stock markets around the world crashed from Hong Kong to Europe, to the United States and on to Australia and New Zealand.

Few individuals or organizations recognized the internationalization of economies meant the internationalization of taxation too. As a result, the application of tax rules and procedures became so complex even IRS personnel had difficulty explaining them. This created an extraordinary opportunity for me.

I took the time to decipher the intricacies of the tax laws and enjoyed explaining their meaning to my law firm clients in ways they could understand.

I also found opportunities to engage with IRS personnel as well as with higher education payment administrators so I could explain the application of these rules and procedures to their constituencies as well. As a result, I earned the respect of the IRS and worked with of them on many different occasions.

My Comments Make Progress on Proposed Tax Regulations

In 1987, the IRS proposed regulations interpreting the tax law that defined when a foreign national becomes a resident alien for tax purposes. I prefer the less-confusing term, "tax resident." The regulations also explain how the tax law applies in various situations. Before any proposed regulations become final, the IRS invites comments on them from tax professionals and the public. I noted right away they failed to address exemptions from tax under tax treaties for foreign nationals who had become tax residents. Tax treaties do not allow exemptions from tax for U.S. citizens and tax resident. But there are exceptions for provisions related to studying, training, teaching or engaging in research for tax residents who are not green card holders. I submitted comments pointing out this lapse, as well as a number of other issues.

Years passed with no decision about the proposed regulations. By 1991, I became impatient, called the person who had drafted the regulations and asked him about their status. He said, "The regulations will be issued in final form within a month."

I asked, "How will they deal with treaty benefits for resident aliens?"

He responded, "Only nonresident aliens are eligible for treaty benefits."

I could tell by his response he didn't understand that tax residents could also be eligible for treaty benefits. I asked, "Didn't you read my comments about treaty exceptions that allow some resident aliens to keep certain treaty benefits?"

He replied, "Did you come to Washington and testify at the hearing?" I didn't know I needed to appear in person to get my view across.

I replied, "On my dime and my time? You don't actually think foreign students would pay me to do that do you?"

Sticking to his guns, he said, "Well, the final regs will be out in a month."

Sticking to my guns, I said, "You can't use a procedural rule to override treaties between countries. If you do, I'll have to sue." He had no response and hung up.

By coincidence, the next week a new client, a Canadian, visited my office. He would become a tax resident that year. He presented me with the pertinent facts I needed for the law suit against the IRS. Under the regulations as proposed, my client would lose treaty benefits related to his Canadian pension distributions.

I called the IRS drafter back, reminded him of our conversation and said, "The lawsuit just walked through my door." I gave him the facts, told him what action I would take, how the IRS would respond, how we would respond and how we would eventually win in court.

After a pregnant pause, he said, "I have to talk to my supervisor."

Two years passed before the IRS issued the final regulations. The IRS had paid attention to the revisions I had advocated.

I'm sure IRS regulations are very helpful for most people. But the IRS's habit of ignoring the effect of their regulations on foreign students and scholars continued. In 1996, I commented about proposed regulations for withholding and reporting on payments to tax nonresidents and foreign entities. Again, the rules didn't address the forms and procedures for tax residents who are eligible for treaty benefits. The IRS corrected this oversight with the final regulations. Several years later the IRS added instructions to their publication for foreign national taxpayers about how to claim tax treaty benefits on a Form 1040 tax return.

I had addressed this problem for the first time in 1987. Altogether, the process of educating the IRS about tax treaty benefits for tax residents had spanned 12 years.

Tax Return Issues Get More Complicated

The IRS began auditing educational institutions for payments to tax nonresidents in the early 1990s. As a result, many more foreign nationals began filing a Form 1040NR tax return. For someone with simple income, this four-page form created great confusion. To make tax filing easier, NAFSA approached the IRS about creating a simpler tax return for tax nonresidents. I worked with Carol Dorsey and Lowell Hancock and NAFSA's Ad Hoc Tax Committee on the design of Form 1040NR-EZ, introduced for tax year 1996.

My foreign clients experienced another tax filing problem when the IRS implemented a new requirement for these nonresident tax returns. They had to include a U.S. tax identification number (TIN) on a nonresident alien tax return. Only foreign nationals authorized to work under U.S. immigration law are eligible to obtain a Social Security number (SSN). The Social Security Administration had issued SSNs to others needing TINs but eliminated this option. As a result, many foreign nationals required to submit U.S. tax returns didn't have a U.S. TIN to record on their tax returns. The problem got worse when the IRS began requiring taxpayers to include the SSN of each individual claimed as a dependent on their tax returns.

In 1986, I wrote to IRS Commissioner Percy Woodward to explain the problems experienced by foreign nationals without TINs. The IRS would return completed tax returns to me when they didn't include a required SSN. I would send the returns back with the comment "This is your problem, not mine." I requested the IRS provide a new type of TIN for these situations. It would be 10 years before the IRS introduced the individual taxpayer identification number (ITIN) for foreign nationals who aren't eligible for an SSN. Within a few years of its introduction, the ITIN became the de facto identifying number for these foreign nationals.

A few years later, to combat the use of ITINs for purposes other than federal tax administration, the IRS added restrictions to the ITIN application process. When the IRS discovered that many foreign nationals used fraudulent documents to obtain ITINs, they made obtaining ITINs even more problematic. New rules required original documentation such as a foreign passport. But—Catch 22—immigration rules and some states' laws require foreign nationals to keep their original foreign documents on their persons.

This TIN process had gone full circle. It had become so difficult to obtain an ITIN that many foreign nationals couldn't comply with their U.S. tax filing obligations. New legislation effective in December 2015 may resolve some of the ITIN problems.

St. Norbert's International Tax Compliance Workshop

Women received a fair share of recognition in 1996. In the entertainment world Frances MacDormand won the best actress Oscar for her role in the film *Fargo*. She played a pregnant sheriff and caught the bad guys. In sports Martina Navratilova became the first tennis player to earn $10 million. In a rare event of recognition for her charitable works, Mother Teresa received honorary U.S. citizenship.

• • •

Mother Teresa (1910 – 1997) Born in Macedonia, Agnes Gonxha Bojaxhiu became a nun at age 18 and took the name Sister Mary Teresa. She traveled to Ireland and then to India where she taught girls from poor families. She founded the Missionaries of Charity, a Roman Catholic religious congregation, which run hospices and homes for people with HIV/AIDS, leprosy and tuberculosis, plus other charitable programs. For her dedication to helping the less fortunate she received the Nobel Prize in 1979 and the admiration of people around the world.

• • •

1996 was a year of important tax activity as well with the introduction of the Annual International Tax Compliance Workshop for educational institutions. Seminars explained in detail how tax, treaty and immigration-related rules applied to the types of payments made to foreign nationals—wages, scholarships, fellowships, awards, honoraria and income from performances. The IRS agreed to send its personnel to this conference each year as long as funds were available. The conference took place each November at St. Norbert College in De Pere, Wisconsin. Hundreds attended the conference in its early years.

De Pere is just outside of Green Bay. They always scheduled the conference for a week the Green Bay Packers didn't have a home game. We flew in and out of the tiny airport in Green Bay. After one conference I rode to the airport with a long-standing Windstar user. A young man at the ticket counter checked our bags. When we got to the gate, the same man took our boarding passes. As we waited at the gate, we saw him again, this time on the tarmac directing our plane to the gate with two hand-held signal lights. My companion turned to me and said, "If he's the pilot, I'm not going."

The conference moderator, Ron Calewarts, the IRS's expert on joint ventures, could have been a successful standup comedian. He opened each conference looking like a serious IRS employee. Then he threw off his suit jacket and began cracking jokes in his sequined vest. He made learning about taxes fun. He told us he once gave a seminar for IRS employees on the check-the-box rules for classifying businesses wearing a box.

Employees of the IRS, the Immigration and Naturalization Service (INS)—now the Department of Homeland Security (DHS)—and the Social Security Administration (SSA) served as presenters and panelists.

Presenters allowed participants to ask questions and answered them throughout seminars. In that way, IRS personnel attending the seminars could learn firsthand about problems being experienced by this community. One memorable interchange between panelists and a participant involved the payment of an honorarium to a visiting dignitary.

Although many believe an honorarium is a "gift," it is self-employment income for U.S. tax purposes. Under the B-honorarium exception of the immigration law, individuals in B visitor status are eligible to receive honoraria. Under U.S. tax law, self-employment income paid to a tax nonresident is subject to 30 percent withholding unless exempt from tax under a tax treaty. To claim exemption from withholding under a tax treaty, honorarium recipients must submit a withholding certificate that includes their U.S. taxpayer identification number. It was common practice for colleges and universities to pay an honorarium to a high-level speaker in a manner that netted the honorarium amount after U.S. taxes when a treaty-exemption from withholding was not available.

The visiting dignitary was British Prime Minister Tony Blair. He would be in Crawford, Texas, to meet with President George W. Bush. While in Texas, he would speak at this participant's university, and they planned to give him a generous honorarium. The interchange between the participant and the panelists went something like this:

"Can we give him an honorarium?"

"No. As a diplomat, his immigration status is A-1. A diplomat may only be paid by the foreign government that sponsored him. To receive an honorarium, he must be a B visitor. He can't be both at the same time."

"If we give him an honorarium anyway, do we have to withhold."

"Yes, because he's a nonresident alien. His U.S. days spent in A-1 status don't count for residency purposes."

"Can he request exemption under the U.K. treaty?"

"Yes, if he has a U.S. taxpayer identification number. But he probably doesn't."

"Can we pay the honorarium to the British government instead? If we can, do we have to withhold?"

"Yes and yes. Tax exemptions for payments to governments are limited to certain investment income under the tax code."

"Is it exempt under the treaty?"

"Yes, but to exempt it from withholding under the treaty, the British government has to have a U.S. EIN. They probably don't."

Years before I had asked an INS official what they did in situations in which diplomats violated their status by accepting honorarium payments.

The answer: "Nothing, under the policy 'Don't mess with the Indians if you don't want to get shot.'"

In 1997, I began attending the St. Norbert International Tax Compliance Workshop. I answered so many questions from the audience the IRS invited me to join the government panelists the following year. My first seminar focused on U.S. tax treaties. I had become *the* nationally recognized expert on treaties as they apply to individuals studying, working, or engaging in research in the United States. IRS International Tax Specialist Lowell Hancock and I joined forces and gave this seminar together at the annual conferences for many years.

Linda Dodd-Major, founder and director of INS's Business Liaison Office, covered immigration issues and continued as a presenter after she left INS for private practice. She and I began giving combined seminars at the St. Norbert conference and other conferences around the country.

With Linda Dodd-Major at the Windstar trade booth, 2003

U.S. tax and treaty rules for foreign nationals are intertwined with their U.S. immigration status. Early on, we discovered the terms "resident alien" and "nonresident alien" had different definitions for tax and immigration purposes. And honorarium activities are not considered "work" for immigration purposes. But honorarium payments result in self-employment income for tax purposes. Linda and I later wrote a book together describing these conflicting rules: *Hon-*

orarium and Other Payments to Independent Contractors published by Windstar Publishing in 2010.

Windstar added a one-day seminar on the Monday preceding the four-day St. Norbert conference for its many clients who attended and relied upon it. Gary demonstrated *Tax Navigator* processing, focusing on year-end procedures and the preparation of 1042-S information returns. During the 1999 seminar, Gary described electronic filing for 1042-S forms as "designed by Hitler and programmed by Mussolini" just as two older women walked in and stood at the back of the room. At the end of his seminar, Gary asked them to introduce themselves. One said, "I'm Hitler and she's Mussolini." Everyone had a good laugh including the two women.

That's how Gary began a long working professional relationship with IRS personnel at their Martinsburg Computing Center.

Budgetary issues forced a reduction in the number of IRS personnel attending the conference. Eventually, their participation was eliminated altogether due to IRS-imposed travel restrictions. St. Norbert continued the organizational responsibilities. Ron continued as moderator because his office was in nearby Milwaukee. Linda and I continued to give a variety of seminars. By the last two years of the conference, the two of us continued as the only presenters. 40 to 50 devoted administrators from educational institutions attended each year. Ron, Linda and I retired from giving the St. Norbert conferences after the 2008 conference. A great tradition had come to an end. Administrators still ask when there will be another St. Norbert conference.

Linda and I gave seminars together for other organizations too and became life-long friends. We had much in common. While relaxing after an APA conference in October, we discussed our upcoming family gatherings for Thanksgiving. Much to our surprise, we discovered both were being hosted by respective family members in Merrimack, New Hampshire. We had so many coincidences, I always say, "There's no such thing as a coincidence." The most bizarre coincidence occurred when Linda and her husband visited us in Maine. A researcher for a Paris journalist called Linda on her cell phone to request content for an upcoming article. He said he would be calling me next. She shocked him when she turned on her cellphone speaker and we talked to him together.

TaxTalkToday.tv

The IRS also invited me to serve on the panels as an outside expert for two of their TaxTalkToday.tv webcasts. The first, in 2002, covered "U.S. Withholding in the Global Business Environment." The second, in 2008, was on "Understanding Income Tax Treaties." My friend and IRS counterpart, Lowell Hancock, sat on both panels. Participants emailed in their questions. It became obvious from the many questions from U.S. employers and payers that they did not understand their withholding and reporting obligations for payments to foreign nationals.

During a rehearsal phone conference for the tax treaty webcast, one IRS treaty specialist said, "We don't know anyone else who understands tax treaties the way you do."

It became clear to me they didn't understand how the residency rules in tax treaties worked. I described how the residency tiebreaker rule worked and gave them examples. The IRS panelists were quick studies and gave an excellent explanation for how and when this rule applies during the webcast. We answered some of the emailed questions during the show and promised to post answers to the remaining questions on the TaxTalk.tv website.

The IRS panelists answered the few questions about treaty interpretation. Then they sent me the questions—more than 80—to answer those about tax returns and withholding and reporting procedures. It took me almost two days to write the responses.

As with all good things, TaxTalkToday.tv came to an end a few years ago when Congress reduced the IRS budget.

CHAPTER 32

The IRS, the Agency People Love to Hate

*Underfunding the Internal Revenue Service
in itself has an element of tax relief.*

– Terence Floyd Cuff

The IRS is the U.S. government agency everyone loves to hate. Their mission is so overwhelming it's difficult for them to do a good job. It's doubly difficult when Congress tries to "help" by reorganizing the whole agency structure. It's likewise doubly difficult for those who have no major lobby to speak out on their behalf.

Congress Reforms the IRS

In 1998, Congress passed the IRS Restructuring and Reform Act. To meet the legislative goal of providing better service to America's taxpayers, they reorganized the IRS into four major divisions. These divisions were based on the category of taxpayer—Wage and Investment (W&I), Large and Mid-Sized Business (LMSB), Tax-

Exempt/Government Entities (TE/GE) and Small Business and Self-Employed (SB/SE).

IRS Commissioner Charles Rossotti led the effort. Jerry Songy, a senior IRS official, and Professor Malcolm Sparrow of Harvard's John F. Kennedy School of Government worked with Rossotti. The international consulting firm Booz Allen & Hamilton received a $400 million consulting contract for their work on the reorganization. The new structure was intended by Congress to benefit domestic businesses and individual taxpayers as well as major multinational businesses.

But the structure caused more problems than it solved for taxpayers and trustees, executors and payment administrators who struggled with international taxation issues. Before the reorganization, the IRS had a central focus on international administration for taxpayers, not just multinational corporations. This organization, which worked well for everyone with international issues, had been recommended by an earlier report by Booz Allen. I guess they hadn't read their own report.

The reorganization caused problems for IRS domestic personnel who were thrust into situations involving international tax matters for which they had no training. Right after the reorganization, I found myself dealing on an IRS audit of a client's complex international transaction with an auditor who had no understanding of the U.S. tax rules or procedures related to the transaction. I provided the auditor with information about the relevant tax law, regulations and procedures during the audit.

Once I identified the problems the new restructure caused these taxpayers and administrators, I began to write letters to Commissioner Rossotti and other IRS officials. Like the patient Abigail Adams, who had a continuous correspondence with her often absent husband, John Adams, I became a frequent writer. My letters covered the subject of taxes and urged officials to remember its international constituents who were not major multinational companies.

Adams wrote about political, as well as personal, matters and urged her husband and the Continental Congress to "remember the ladies."

• • •

Abigail Adams (1744 – 1818) Abigail Adams was the wife of John Adams, the second president of the United States of America. During her husband's travels the pair kept in contact through letters which have shed much light on their time and relationship. An early advocate for women's rights, Adams admonished her husband and the Continental Congress, "If particular care and attention is not paid to the Ladies, we are determined to foment a Rebellion, and will not hold ourselves bound by any Laws in which we have no voice, or Representation." She was so politically active during her husband's tenure as president opponents referred to her as "Mrs. President."

• • •

I explained the myriad of problems encountered by IRS's international customers not served by LMSB, the only division with IRS personnel experienced with, and assigned to deal with, international tax matters. According to IRS colleagues, my letters traveled throughout the IRS. In 2001, I wrote to senior IRS official Jerry Songy too. He came to my law firm to thank me in person for describing problems "no one else was telling them about."

When I learned Professor Sparrow lived next-door to my partner Ken Vacovec, I gave Ken a package of my letters to deliver to him. Ken told me Professor Sparrow understood first-hand the tax problems foreign students faced. He had been a foreign student in the United States himself.

At international tax conferences, panelists solicited questions and comments about the new IRS structure. I always took the opportunity and walked up to the microphone to describe these problems in detail. Reaction from the group showed there remained a lot to correct.

The IRS had 26 overseas offices to serve the needs of an estimated three million—now closer to nine million—U.S. citizens living abroad. When they transferred the budget for these offices to LMSB, that division shut down all but three offices—London, Paris and Wiesbaden, Germany. When the IRS office in Ottawa, Ontario, Canada's capitol city, closed, it serviced the needs of 11,000 U.S. expats. Later the IRS relocated the office in Germany to Frankfurt. In 2015, because of more budget cuts, IRS closed its remaining overseas offices including the office in Beijing that they had opened in 2010.

To service the needs of U.S. expats, the IRS established a telephone call-in center in Puerto Rico, manned by some who had English as their second language. The call-center had very limited hours and was in a different time zone than most U.S. expats. And it didn't make things any easier for the callers that their international calls were not toll-free. This same call-in center also answered international questions from employers and payers. When one Windstar client asked a question about the 1042-S form, the response was "What's a 1042-S?"

The problem got worse.

The IRS transferred the budget for its taxpayer assistance centers (TACs) to the W&I division. But services provided by this division to taxpayers were limited to domestic tax matters for individuals. Since it had no responsibility for dealing with tax nonresidents, the Boston TAC stopped giving tax seminars to foreign students and scholars and no longer helped them with their U.S. tax returns. The IRS issued a redacted statement about how responsibility for helping foreign students and scholars would be transferred to colleges and universities. Some of these institutions established Volunteer Income Tax Assistance (VITA) programs to help foreign students and scholars prepare their tax returns. But most didn't.

The growing number of small businesses with international transactions also had no place to turn for international tax help from the IRS.

In December 1998, a Treasury official addressed Boston's Federal Tax Institute about help on international transactions. He said the tax practitioner community needed to become educated in international tax laws and procedures in order to provide international tax advice to small and medium-sized businesses and individuals. I explained to him at the break why that wouldn't happen any time soon. The high cost of resources and professionals' time far exceeded the fees professionals could charge for these infrequent tax matters.

In April 1999, the IRS reallocated its international personnel to domestic duties including Lowell Hancock and Ben Gondek, both frequent panelists at the St. Norbert conferences. I knew this was a mistake. Following their transfers, I began writing letters to Commissioner Rossotti and others including Senator Edward Kennedy. I encouraged Windstar's clients to do the same. Many did, as did the president of NAFSA.

At one international conference that year, a colleague introduced me to an IRS panelist. He responded, "Oh, I know who she is. She's the one who generated all those letters to Commissioner Rossotti that I had to answer!"

It worked. As a result of all the letters, Lowell and Ben got reassigned to their international duties. I met them at a conference later that year. Lowell said, "Of course we can't say anything about this."

Then Ben blurted out, "But we'd like to thank you for saving our jobs."

Advocating for Foreign Students and Scholars

By 2005, my letters and informal communications to the IRS had become less effective. No one at the IRS addressed the problems I wrote to them about. Most likely, the IRS lacked experienced personnel to assign to these matters. I decided to communicate problems encountered by foreign students and scholars to the IRS in published articles. I submitted articles to Tax Analysts, the longstanding publisher of *Tax Notes* and *Tax Notes International (TNI)* journals. My law firm was a very early subscriber to *TNI*. Also, I discovered much later that one of the tax treaty negotiators I had dealt with for years is married to their founder, Tom Field.

Tax Analysts journals, *Tax Notes* and *TNI* and their on-line *World Tax Daily* have wide distribution with IRS and Treasury officials, as well as with tax lawyers and accountants. Tax Analysts touts its authors as "the experts' experts."

My 2005 article, "In Search of Guidance on U.S. Taxation of Scholarship Grants for Foreign Nationals," described how tax nonresidents with treaty-exempt grants could not claim exemption from withholding. This occurred when the IRS tightened ITIN eligibility and application rules. This isn't a problem for U.S. citizens and tax residents. Their taxable scholarships aren't subject to withholding or reporting. As a result, most never get taxed.

A withholding certificate with a treaty claim for exemption from withholding now required a U.S. taxpayer identification number. But foreign student scholarship recipients were not eligible for a pre-tax return ITIN application. I had tried for five years without success to get this problem rectified, both through comments on new ITIN application procedures and through IRS taxpayer advocacy committees. Nothing worked.

When I attended a conference where the National Taxpayer Advocate, Nina Olsen, was the guest speaker, I gave her a copy of my article. A Windstar user happened to be with me at the time and gave her examples of the problems faced by the foreign students at his university. It worked. The IRS issued new procedures for foreign nationals who needed an ITIN for a treaty claim. When I met the head of IRS's ITIN Policy Unit at the St. Norbert conference later that year, she said, "Next time just call me directly."

I wrote a second article in 2005 titled "Special U.S. Payroll Tax Rules and Procedures Apply to Foreign Employees." It explained how wages of nonresident employees were subject to a mandatory withholding deduction. This deduction offset the standard deduction built into IRS's wage-withholding tables. Tax nonresidents are not eligible for the standard deduction. But most earn so little they owe no tax. This mandatory deduction caused these foreign students two problems. First, it reduced the income they had to live on. Second, it required them to file a U.S. tax return to get back the withheld tax.

Over many years, the educational community had exhausted every avenue to get this problem resolved. A member of an IRS committee representing educational institutions sent the problem to me with a plea to "solve this problem." I presented the problem to the Taxpayer Advocacy Panel in Boston. Although they addressed this problem with the IRS, they had no success. Lowell Hancock understood the problem and presented it to IRS's Office of Chief Counsel. He replied it would require a change in regulations. With all the other problems the IRS faced, the tax problems of foreign students and scholars did not receive a priority.

In this article, I described how employers had to first determine which foreign employees were tax nonresidents in order to apply the special rules and procedures. I also described how tax nonresidents couldn't find the information they needed, either on the IRS website or in IRS publications. As a result, they couldn't support their W-4 certification that their payroll deductions were correct. I received a phone call the next day from an IRS official charged with solving systemic problems. He told me they would be issuing a notice describing new rules to solve this problem. They did.

I followed up with another article, "New U.S. Rules for Withholding on Wages of Nonresident Employees."

An article I wrote in 2007 stopped Congress from making changes in Social Security coverage based on incomplete information. It was in response to testimony by an immigration specialist with the Social Security Administration (SSA) to the Senate Finance Committee. She testified that extending Social Security taxes to currently exempt aliens could increase payroll taxes. My article "Don't Extend Social Security Taxation to Currently Exempt Foreign Workers" explained how her testimony overstated the increase. I pointed out how most foreign students are exempt from Social Security taxes under a rule that applies to all students. I also discussed how including tax nonresident J-1 exchange visitors in the Social Security program would increase benefit payouts because of totalization formulas in Social Security agreements with their countries of residence. I mailed copies of that article to all members of the Senate Finance Committee. A Senate counsel called and asked for a pdf copy of my article so he could forward it to the SSA.

Altogether, I wrote more than 25 articles published by Tax Analysts about withholding, reporting and tax rules that affect U.S. citizens abroad and foreign nationals in the United States. Two of the articles, co-authored with Linda Dodd-Major, make up the only published articles on these topics. The first on the history of the development and use of taxpayer identification numbers. The second on "When Immigration and Tax Converge." Following this article's publication, I received an email from a tax practitioner: "Your article was great" with "great" spelled out multiple times.

America's Tax Collector—Payroll

Contrary to popular opinion, America's primary tax collector isn't the IRS. It's Payroll. Every year, the IRS Commissioner—or a high-level IRS official in his stead—speaks to the payroll administrators gathered for APA's annual Congress and explains, "You are America's tax collectors." He then praises them for doing such a good job.

Revenue collected through payroll as a percentage of revenue collected annually by the IRS is about 70 percent of collections. Payroll collections include wage-withholding, Social Security and Medicare taxes, and Social Security and unemployment excise taxes paid by employers.

The importance of cash flow from payroll tax collections became apparent on September 11, 2001, when the IRS assistant commissioner contacted the payroll company ADP, the nation's biggest "tax collector." He needed to make sure they could pay over the payroll deposits that came due that day. ADP could, and they did.

Many will argue that payroll deductions for Social Security are contributions to fund future benefits. They are. But, beginning in 1983, the government increased Social Security required contributions to keep Social Security solvent for generations. The contributions paid in which exceeded benefits paid out were credited to the Social Security trust fund. Since 1985, these excess contributions have been "borrowed" by the government and used for general revenue purposes. The Social Security trust fund—now about $2.6 trillion—is invested in special nonmarketable U.S. Treasury bonds. These bonds may only be bought by the U.S. government. As a result, the amount in the Social Security trust fund is actually a huge percentage of the federal deficit.

The baby boomers who paid those excess Social Security contributions since 1985 are now retiring. As of 2010, annual Social Security benefits paid out exceed annual Social Security taxes paid in. Cash to buy back those special U.S. bonds to meet growing benefit obligations must come from somewhere. If Democrats take back the House in 2016, speaker Nancy Pelosi will make sure America's workers and retired baby boomers won't be the ones whose taxes get increased or benefits cut to pay those borrowed contributions back to the trust fund.

Nancy Pelosi (1940 –) Nancy Pelosi, the 60th Speaker of the U.S. House of Representatives from 2007 to 2011, was the first woman, the first Californian and the first Italian-American to hold that position. She referred to her success as "breaking the marble ceiling." She was elected to the Democratic National Committee in 1976 and held the position for 10 years. In 2004, she was instrumental in defeating a bill to "privatize" Social Security. Now minority leader of the House, Pelosi is considered the most powerful woman in American politics.

• • •

IRS's Budget Takes a Big Hit

During the Great Recession of 2008, Congress cut administrative agency budgets by 10 percent under legislation called "sequestration." When they repealed that policy, Congress restored agency budgets—except for the IRS's budget. The only way to solve even the simplest IRS problem required involvement with the National Taxpayer Advocate. This created a difficult problem for U.S. taxpayers abroad. The IRS requires at least one taxpayer advocate per state. But none is required for estimated nine million U.S. citizen taxpayers who live abroad.

In 2015, the IRS had seven million more tax returns and additional responsibilities under the Affordable Care Act and the Foreign Accounts Tax Compliance Act. They had to handle this workload with 17,000 fewer employees. The IRS operating budget was less than its 2010 budget and Congress slashed its training budget 83 percent.

Commissioner Koskinen describes the current state of the IRS with his refrain that "IRS went from doing more with less to doing less with less." The IRS closed the civil side of their four remaining overseas offices and for a short time eliminated tax return preparation services provided by domestic offices. Taxpayer wait time on phone calls to the IRS exceeded 30 minutes. Only 50 percent of calls were even answered. The IRS hung up on 6.8 million taxpayers—described as a "courtesy disconnect." That's a telephone company term for an automatic disconnect that occurs when necessary to protect the phone system from an overload.

I pointed out the IRS underfunding problem in a *Christian Science Monitor* February 2014 op-ed article. Several months later editorials on the IRS underfunding also appeared in the *New York Times* and *Washington Post. The Kiplinger Tax Letter* also discussed the problem. And John Oliver, host of *Last Week Tonight* on HBO, even included a segment on this issue. He pointed out the IRS only *administers* the tax laws passed by Congress. He described the anger directed toward the IRS about taxes like being angry at the grocery store checkout clerk for the price of groceries.

One thing is clear. If Congress continues to dismantle the IRS with budget cuts, the only solution for U.S. taxpayers is a simpler tax code. What are the odds of that?

CHAPTER 33

Advocating for Tax Reform

*The nation should have a tax system
that looks like someone designed it on purpose.*

– William Simon

Writing about tax reform is my hobby ... PNS

2004 turned out as an eventful year. Americans were shocked and thrilled when the Red Sox beat the St. Louis Cardinals to win the World Series and brought an end to the "Curse of the Bambino!" Also in 2004, while less sensational for those who don't get excited about taxes, another event held the prospect of major importance to all Americans. President George W. Bush formed a Tax Advisory Panel on Federal Tax Reform. Its purpose: to determine ways to reform the much beleaguered federal tax system.

A Simpler Tax Collection System

Since I had devoted so much time and energy to fathom how our tax system worked—or didn't work—I wanted to contribute to the tax reform panel. So I wrote and self-published a book, *A Simple, More Efficient Tax Collection System for America.*

In the book I explained several vital aspects of our tax code:

- Tax Simplification—What It Isn't
  - the Tax Reform Act of 1986
- Tax Simplification—What It Is
  - less complex tax rules and fewer returns
- A U.S. Tax System for the Global Economy
  - the U.S. tax system needs to be more like its competitors
- It's Time for an American Value Added Tax
  - a primary revenue source for all other developed countries

I also pointed out reformers need to understand how the federal tax system interconnects with other tax systems, i.e. state, local and international. This would avoid unintended consequences such as incompatibilities with other tax systems resulting in increased taxes.

I sent a copy of my book to each member of Bush's Tax Reform Panel and all members of the House Ways and Means Committee and the Senate Finance Committee. To my surprise, I received some responses. In addition to responses from two panelists, responses came from Representative Paul Ryan of Wisconsin and then-Senator Barack Obama of Illinois. Who knew!

The only major tax reforms during President Bush's administration came in the form of tax cuts for wealthy individuals.

A Revenue Offset Causes Tax Problems for Expats

To offset revenue lost by Bush's "reform," Congress made changes in foreign earned income exclusions used by U.S. expatriates—U.S. citizens and foreign nationals who reside abroad. These exclusions allow expats to avoid double taxation on their worldwide income from labor—called "earned income." The changes caused expats' investment income and foreign pension plan distributions to be taxed by the United States at high rates.

The foreign earned income exclusion became a simple way of eliminating the double taxation—once by their country of residence and again by the United States based on their citizenship or green card status. The IRS even provides a simple 2555-EZ form for computing these income exclusions. Most U.S. expats switched from using the simple foreign earned income exclusions to using the much more complicated foreign tax credits to lower their U.S. taxes. As a result, much of the projected revenue increase never materialized.

Efforts at tax reform have gone on for centuries all over the world. Perhaps no example is more extraordinary and captivating than the spectacle made by Lady Godiva when she rode naked through the streets of an English town in the 11th century. Whether it's a true story or a fable, it captures our imagination at what lengths people would go to affect taxes.

• • •

Lady Godiva (1040 – 1067) During the 11th century in England, Lady Godiva married a powerful leader, the Earl of Coventry. He imposed oppressive taxes on the townspeople. When they pleaded for relief, Lady Godiva took up their cause. Her husband told her he would lower their taxes when she rode naked through the streets. She did, and the Earl lowered their taxes. While Lady Godiva and the Earl were real, the account first written in the 13th century may just be a fanciful story.

• • •

Also in 2004, the tax publisher Tax Analysts published my first article, "U.S. Tax Policy for Citizens and Immigrants Living Abroad Merits a Closer Look." I explained the mechanisms U.S. expats may use—section 911 exclusions and/or foreign tax credits—to avoid worldwide double taxation. In June 2006, my second article for Tax Analysts on this topic explained how other countries tax the worldwide income of their residents.

Worldwide income refers to the total income of an individual of whatever type and from whatever source. Income from foreign sources must be translated to U.S. dollars using U.S. tax principles and IRS currency exchange translation rules. The opposite of worldwide income, called "territorial income," is income earned within the country where the individual resides. Territorial income is a lower amount for tax purposes, in particular for individuals who invest outside their home country as wealthy individuals do.

In the second article, I discussed the common misconception that the United States is the only country that taxes worldwide income. I listed 48 countries that tax worldwide income of their resident individuals. I explained extending section 911 exclusions to investment income—called "unearned income"—as recommended by some reformers, would convert the U.S. income tax system for individuals to a territorial system. Such a change would set the United States apart from its trading partners because most tax their residents—as defined by their internal tax law—on their worldwide income. This method of taxing individuals is called "residence-based taxation."

The U.S. system of taxing foreign nationals who do not possess a green card is a residence-based system because it depends on their physical presence in the United States. U.S. tax residents are taxed on their worldwide income. When these foreign nationals move back home, they leave the U.S. tax system behind. Not so with U.S. citizens and green card holders. When they move abroad, they take the U.S. tax system with them.

U.S. citizens and green card holders remain subject to U.S. income tax obligations unless they lose their U.S. citizenship or green card status in a manner that satisfies U.S. federal tax requirements. And when these "expatriates" lose their status, they might have a U.S. expatriation tax obligation, depending on the value and type of their assets. The term "expatriates" is not to be confused with the term "expatriates"—or "expats"—for individuals who *retain* their status while they live abroad. But I don't know how anyone could not be confused with the multiple uses of this term.

While it is easy to determine the date a U.S. citizen renounces their U.S. citizenship, it is not easy to determine when a green card holder loses their green card status. Most return abroad with no advice about how to keep or give up their status. Many green card holders think their status expires with their physical green card. It doesn't. Congress never coordinated the rules for immigration and tax rules when they added green card holders to the expatriation tax. The coordination is murky, as Linda Dodd-Major points out in her 2012 *TNI* article "Who Is A Green Card Holder and Why Does It Matter for U.S. Taxation Purposes?"

I decided to write a law review article explaining how the United States could convert from citizenship-based taxation to residence-based taxation.

By coincidence, in 2007 I received an email from Professor Cynthia Blum of the Rutgers Law School. She asked me to review her law review article, which included immigration-related references. I noted her other articles covered tax topics I also felt were important and asked, "Would you like to write an article together sometime?"

She emailed back, "Yes. Do you have a topic?"

I did. We began collaborating on our article, "A Coherent Policy for U.S. Residence-Based Taxation of Individuals." We accomplished it all by email. The *Vanderbilt Journal of Transnational Law* published our article in May 2008. My article "Common-Sense Tax Reform for U.S. Citizens and Residents Abroad," published by Tax Analysts that year, discussed the recommendations for reform laid out in our law review article.

Professor Blum and I co-authored a second law review article, again all by e-mail. This article, "A Proposal for Taking the Complexities Out of Taxing U.S. Retirement Distributions to Foreign Nationals," was published in the *Florida Tax Review* in 2011.

Since our 2008 article was published, many more professionals have written in support of changing the U.S. tax system for individuals from citizenship-based to residence-based taxation. American Citizens Abroad and other organizations representing the estimated nine million U.S. citizens who reside abroad have become active and effective proponents for residence-based taxation. To convince members of Congress, they describe the unfair economic effect of U.S. citizenship-based taxation both on them as individuals and on the U.S. economy.

The tax problems faced by American citizens abroad became more evident as foreign financial institutions began to comply with the Foreign Account Tax Compliance Act (FATCA). The purpose of this law, enacted by Congress in 2010, is to identify resident U.S. citizens hiding income abroad in foreign financial institutions and foreign entities. But FATCA had an unintended consequence—many foreign banks began to eliminate services for U.S. citizens who reside abroad.

Senator, and then-presidential candidate, Rand Paul filed a lawsuit on July 14, 2015, challenging the constitutionality of both FATCA and the requirement to submit foreign bank account reports—called "FBARs"—that overly burden U.S. citizens who live abroad. The District Court dismissed the suit. Since 2011, Senator Paul had also stalled ratification of several new income tax treaties and amendments to existing treaties because he objects to the information exchange provisions in the treaties. This action suggests Paul's opposition to FATCA might be more about stopping the exchange of information between countries under FATCA's intergovernmental agreements than helping U.S. citizens and residents abroad.

Tax Reform When?

In 2009, President Barack Obama also formed a panel to study ways to reform the federal tax system. That year, Tax Analysts published, *Toward Tax Reform: Recommendations for President Obama's Task Force*, which featured ideas for reform from 32 expert contributors. I was one of only five female contributors. My contribution was "Individual Non-filers and the International Tax Gap."

I also joined 48 contributors for Tax Analyst's book, *Forty Years of Change, One Constant: Tax Analysts*, published in 2010. The contributors included former IRS commissioners and tax experts from national law firms, major accounting firms and prestigious academic institutions. Only three contributors were women: Lee Sheppard, a well-regarded writer on tax policy for Tax Analysts; Jane Gravelle, a senior economist with the Congressional Research Services; and me.

In January 2009, Tax Analysts featured my article, "Common-Sense Tax Reform" in its publication, *Tax Notes Year In Review*. The article incorporated many of the ideas from my book. To reach a broader audience, I began writing op-ed articles about taxes and tax reform for the *Christian Science Monitor Magazine* and their on-line journal in 2014. The subject of one article, a dividends paid deduction as a solution to the double taxation of corporate profits, became the subject of congressional consideration a year later.

If tax reform happens, it just might include tax reform for Americans abroad too. When I joined Ken Vacovec's firm in 1985, I bet him the United States would end citizenship-based taxation before I retired. The loser of the bet gets to take the winner out to dinner—in a city of the winner's choosing.

I retired from Thomson Reuters and Vacovec, Mayotte & Singer LLP. But I'm not retired yet. I still write articles and consult on international tax matters. So there's still time for me to win the bet.

CHAPTER 34

Born 10 Years Too Soon

Patience is the calm acceptance that things can happen in a different order than the one you have in mind.

– David G. Allen

In 2001, Regina Pisa was the featured speaker at the Women's Leadership Breakfast. Pisa was the first female managing partner of a Boston law firm, Goodwin Proctor. The Breakfast, sponsored by the United Way of Massachusetts, is an annual celebration of women in power. Their vision is "a future where all children, youth and families achieve all they can be regardless of their background or circumstances."

Pisa told her story about how she grew up poor in Somerville and wanted to go to Harvard. She explained: She applied to Harvard—she was accepted. She applied for various grants—they were all awarded to her. She applied to Georgetown University for law school—she was accepted. She even competed for the Betty Crocker award—she won. It was an inspiring speech for the many young women in the audience.

I turned to the woman sitting next to me and asked, "Do you know how old she is?"

She said, "Yes, she's a friend. She's 47."

I said, "Oh that explains it. I'm 57. I grew up poor too. I could have given that speech except for the Betty Crocker part—I'm not a good cook. But the difference is, I got turned down for just about everything I applied for that wasn't connected somehow to government."

She said, "Your problem was you were born 10 years too soon." And that has been the story of my life.

What I Couldn't Do and What I Did

My life contains a litany of things I couldn't do. But I have had a richer and more rewarding life because I couldn't do what I wanted to do when I wanted to do it.

I couldn't go to a private college or university. Student aid for women in the early 60s was meager because we were supposed to become wives and mothers. But I got a great education at a public university.

I couldn't go to graduate school and join the ranks of academia because I couldn't get fellowship grants. But I did become a recognized writer and teacher in the tax field.

I couldn't go to law school following graduation from college because financial aid didn't exist for women for professional schools. But I had an exciting and personally rewarding 10-year computer career in the insurance industry instead.

I couldn't join my employer's new Systems Department—even though I did the job—because I was a woman. But they invited me to join the department several years later. And as a systems analyst, I began a longstanding working and personal relationship with Gary Singer whom I later married.

I couldn't get an internship at a law firm during law school because law firms had only just begun to hire women—young women. But I got a job as a tax specialist at Peat Marwick, a major accounting firm—great training for my future career as a tax lawyer.

I couldn't combine my computer experience with the law in Boston—I could have anywhere else—because Boston firms didn't hire lawyers with prior careers. But 10 years later I did combine my computer experience with law dealing with the trademark, copyright and software licensing matters for Windstar.

I couldn't get interviews with Boston law firms after we moved to Massachusetts because Boston law firms didn't hire women with my "credentials." But I got a unique job at an incredible company, Arthur D. Little, Inc., and gained experience with the emerging global economy.

Even after I gained invaluable international experience, I couldn't get a job—or even interviews—with Boston law firms. But I got a job with a small unconventional law firm in the suburbs and built a rewarding career as an international tax lawyer.

I couldn't bill clients commensurate with my legal and tax expertise because clients expected to be billed based on time spent and I worked too fast. But I found another way to earn income for my expertise when Gary and I built my expertise into Windstar's software system and charged clients an annual license fee for its use.

I couldn't convince major accounting firms to cooperate with our software company and serve mutual clients because they wanted all the work. But our software company got the clients anyway, and the accounting firms lost out on potential business.

Throughout my careers, I couldn't convince my employers to pay me what I was worth because I was a woman. But I created a valuable asset with Gary that made it possible for us to retire back to Maine in comfort after we sold our software company.

It's My Mothers Fault

It's tempting to join in the blame game and say it's my mother's fault for all the barriers I faced because I was born 10 years too early. I suppose I'd have to include my father as well. But I couldn't have been born 10 years later because my parents followed life's natural order for them and had me after more than 20 years of marriage.

How could they have predicted the obstacles I would face? They did their best and I feel blessed by their example of hard work, perseverance and, most important, their love.

Of course, rather than find fault with their timing of my birth, I thank them for providing me with such the natural rare abilities that made it possible for me to accomplish so much.

My analytical abilities, prodigious memory and other unusual gifts made it easy for me to conquer complex subjects and become proficient in diverse fields of endeavor. My ability to deal with change in a positive manner helped me convince co-workers to embrace new ideas and benefit from them.

Where did all these abilities come from? All I can say is thanks to my parents, by some mysterious process, they showed up in me. I'm not sure if my mother had a full understanding of how remarkable their gifts were to me. I do know, in her gentle way, she believed in me and encouraged me to find my own path.

• • •

Grace Smith Noyes (1903 – 1993) Born in the early 1900s, Grace Smith Noyes saw huge transformations in America—from oil lamps to electricity, first in barns, then in homes; from horse and buggy to trolleys and motor cars; from live entertainment and barnstormers to phonographs and movies. Married at 20 to Paul Noyes, she worked for 20 years. Together they experienced the Great Depression when they lost their business to bankruptcy and World War II when my father helped build submarines. For the next 20 years, she was a wife and mother, hardworking because she lacked modern conveniences, but never one to complain. During the next 20 years, she was companion, helper and grandmother living with her daughter Paula and her family. At 80, as with too many people today, she slowly slipped into dementia, spending her last eight years in a nursing home.

• • •

In spite of dreams dashed at every turn, it just wasn't in my make-up to give up.

Watching my mother's devotion to my hard working father, I learned to overcome obstacles that I'm sure would have disillusioned others with less drive and determination.

Somehow I had the fortitude to take the heartbreak out of stormy seas, embark on courses filled with detours and overcome obstacles that seemed never to end.

Rather than become bitter or discouraged, I followed my parent's example to tough it out and create opportunities out of hardships. Without realizing it, I made my life a metaphor of Arthur D. Little's experiment to make a silk purse out of a pig's ear.

Looking back, each triumph over obstacles, both large and small, helped me hone proficiencies and lead to next steps that required all of them in ways I couldn't have predicted. And more, or most, important, I learned to rely upon myself.

A combination of self-assurance and strong foundation of personal and professional skills made it possible for Gary and me to create our high risk venture Windstar that succeeded against formidable completion.

Over the years, I have had many "thank yous" from my clients, and from Windstar's client institutions and their administrators. I felt honored to hear compliments from professional colleagues that included IRS experts. I even received an occasional gift from clients and even one from a caller whose question I answered without charge. And I received a personally rewarding gift from *Boston Magazine* when they included me in their first edition of *Super Lawyers*. I appreciated them all.

Perhaps the most gratifying came from the peace of mind I know I provided to the desperate foreign students and scholars, administrators at schools and organizations, even IRS personnel, with my otherwise unavailable assistance.

Thanks Mom and Dad

I believe my mother and father would be proud of how much I have accomplished in spite of never-ending obstacles. Because of my close relationship with my mother, I'm sure she would say, "I knew you could do it."

I may have been born 10 years too soon, but it never stopped me from achieving my dreams.

EPILOGUE

I will be telling this with a sigh
Somewhere ages and ages hence:
Two roads diverged in a wood, and I—
I took the road less traveled by,
And that has made all the difference.

– Robert Frost

A framed copy of Robert Frost's poem, "The Road Not Taken," has hung on the wall over the desk in my home office for more than 30 years. I took that less-traveled path. I think it has made all the difference—not only to me but also to those who followed.

Opportunities available to me would have been different if I'd been born male instead of female or if I'd grown up well off instead of poor. But I wasn't and I didn't.

For sure, opportunities for a young female from a poor family would have been much better had I been born 10 years later. But I wasn't.

But some of us have to be the ones to wear down the path to make the way easier for others to travel. Maybe that became my real job. If so, I think I did it well.

But I didn't travel that path alone. Along the way I received encouragement from family, teachers, friends and colleagues. I also received invaluable help from public sources—public school, college and law school. Government-funded work study and loans for college provided the money I needed at desperate times. Without guarantees by the federal government I'm not sure how we would have managed to start our company, Windstar, and continue in operation.

Triumphs of courageous pioneering women served as inspirations along the way.

Looking back, I never had the job I wanted when I wanted it. But I always had the opportunity for that job sometime later. In every case, I didn't turn back from my new course, and I'm glad I didn't.

And I'm glad I married, had my children, and opened my home to our mothers, too. My living with my extended family has provided me with a very rewarding life.

I am writing this memoir at the age of 70. I have just retired from my careers, but not from life. When friends ask me what I'm going to do, I give the same answer I gave when I was leaving Maine for Boston without a job 35 years ago, "I don't know what I'm going to do, but I'll do something."

I'll find new challenges, and if I have the wind in my sails, I'll get there faster. If I have headwinds, I'll tack to port or starboard. If there's no wind, I'll row.

APPENDICES

PAULA'S TIME LINE

1944

Born to Grace and Paul Noyes

1947

Moved to Kennebunk, Maine, mother's home town

1962

Graduated from Kennebunk High School, first in the class
Entered University of Maine, Orono, class of 1966

1964

Married Wayne Goodrich

1965

Father died
Mother came to live with us in Orono

1966

Graduated Phi Beta Kappa with a BA
in History & Government
Moved to Boston
Began first job as computer programmer trainee at New England Mutual

1967

Moved back to Kennebunk
Beth was born

1968

Worked at Sundial Hotel and Nunan's Lobster Hut
Attended state Republican convention as alternate
Began new job as COBOL programmer at Union Mutual

1969

Promoted to Senior Programmer

1971

Became first female member of Kennebunk's budget board
Became Union Mutual's first female systems analyst

1973

Divorced from Wayne Goodrich

1974

Promoted to Senior Systems Analyst

1975

Entered UMaine School of Law full-time
Worked part-time at Union Mutual

1976

Married Gary Singer
We moved to Cumberland Foreside, Maine
Began internship at Peat Marwick

1978

Graduated from UMaine Law with a JD
Passed Maine and Massachusetts bars exams
Joined Peat Marwick full-time as a tax specialist

1979

We all moved to Norwood, Massachusetts
Gary's mother moved in with us too
Became an international personnel specialist with Arthur D. Little, Inc.
Wrote law review article published by
Rutgers Journal of Computers, Technology and the Law

1980

Samantha was born

1985

First year for new tax law on residency of foreign nationals
Joined Ken Vacovec's tax law firm

Mother moved to a nursing home

1986

Began giving pro bono tax seminars to foreign students and scholars
Received Martindale-Hubbell's highest AV peer rating for lawyers

1988

Attended International Fiscal Association annual congress in Amsterdam

1989

Became partner in law firm later named Vacovec, Mayotte & Singer

1993

Mother died
Meeting with Boston area hospital about payments to foreign nationals
Gary's idea for new software system

1994

Wrote system overview
Gary quit job with Boston insurance company
We began system design and programming
Windstar Technologies, Inc. incorporated

1995

Moved to first office in Westwood
Gave demo to IRS
Applied for a patent
Sent 8,000 promotional mailing
Gary sold first system to Boston College

Gary assisted with BC orientation for foreign students
Sold second system to University of Pennsylvania

1996

Assisted IRS and NAFSA with development of Form 1040NR-EZ
First Form 1042-S information returns submission
Hired our first employee

1997

Launched Windstar's first website
Created training video
Began exhibiting at trade shows
Received Notice of Allowance on our patent
Began hiring more Windstar crew
Moved office to Norwood

1998

Gary began teaching hands-on training classes
Windstar launched windstarusers listserv to answer user questions
Windstar purchased Education Catalyst's immigration processing products
Joined the panelists at the St. Norbert International Tax Compliance Workshop and continued to give seminars through 2008

1999

Gary gave first annual one-day year end update course prior to the St. Norbert International Tax Compliance Workshop
Gary began working on Oracle interface
Windstar entered business alliance with Oracle

2000

|

Linda Dodd-Major and Terri Crowl began answering windstarusers questions
Began writing and selling books—*Tax Treaty Benefits for Foreign Nationals Providing U.S. Services* and *A Guide for Filing Forms 1042 and 1042-S* co-authored with Gary
Windstar Publishing, Inc. incorporated

|

2001

|

Patent for International Tax Navigator issued
Windstar introduced new upgraded product *VisaManager* for immigration processing
Introduced more tax guidebooks in the series
Tax Guides for Foreign Nationals and Those Who Pay Them

|

2002

|

Windstar introduced at Oracle APPs World, New Orleans and on Yahoo Financial
Windstar introduced an interface to the government's Student Exchange Visitor Information System (SEVIS)
Panelist on IRS's TaxTalkToday.tv
on *U.S. Withholding in the Global Business Environment*
Awarded American Payroll Association's Meritorious Service Award

|

2003

|

Windstar added *Foreign National Information System (FNIS)* for web-based data entry
Became part-time with Vacovec, Mayotte & Singer LLP

|

2004

First article published in *Tax Notes International*
Published *A Simple, More Efficient Tax Collection System for America*

2007

Panelist on IRS's TaxTalkToday.tv on *Understanding Income Tax Treaties*

2008

Windstar introduced *Foreign National Tax Resources (FNTR)* website
Law review article co-authored with Prof. Cynthia Blum, Rutgers Law School published by *Vanderbilt Transnational Journal*
Began giving seminars at Thomson Reuters' annual accounts payable conference

2009

Gary began design of *W-8 Compliance*
Gary's mother moved a to retirement community

2010

Windstar added on-line tax return preparation to FNTR for IRS Form 1040NR-EZ and Massachusetts returns

2011

Second law review article co-authored with Prof. Blum published by the *Florida Tax Review*
Windstar added more state processing to FNTR
Thomson Reuters purchased Windstar
Became a practice leader with Thomson Reuters

|
2012
|
Gary retired
We moved back to Maine
|
2015
|
Retired from Thomson Reuters
|
2016
|
Retired from Vacovec, Mayotte & Singer LLP

ARTICLES AND BOOKS AUTHORED BY PAULA N. SINGER

Tax Analysts

"In Search of Guidance for Treaty Benefits for U.S. Retirement Distributions," *Tax Notes International*, June 2016

"A Proposal for Fair U.S. Tax Treatment of Foreign Pensions," co-authored with Jacqueline Bugnion, *Tax Notes International*, May 30, 2016

"The Confusing Tax Filing Deadlines for Foreign Students and Scholars," *Tax Notes International*, February 29, 2016

"Tax Return Challenges for Foreign Students and Scholars," *Tax Notes International*, April 6, 2015

"A New Challenge for Accounts Payable—FATCA," *Tax Notes International*, October 27, 2014

"Withholding and Reporting on Payments to Foreign Persons," *Tax Notes International*, March 17, 2014

"When Immigration and Tax Converge," co-authored with Linda Dodd-Major, *Tax Notes International*, March 12, 2012

"Certain Nonresident Aliens Are Now Obligated for U.S. Self-Employment Tax," *Tax Notes International*, April 4, 2011

Contributor, untitled article on the impact of the 1998 IRS Reform and Restructuring Act on individual taxpayers with international issues, *Forty Years of Change, One Constant, Tax Analysts*, 2010

"Information Reporting on Form 1042-S: A New Challenge for Accounts Payable," *Tax Notes International*, November 22, 2010

"U.S. Tax Rules for Paying Foreign Employees," *Tax Notes International*, January 18, 2010

Contributor, "Individual Nonfilers and the International Tax Gap," *Toward Tax Reform: Recommendations for President Obama's Task Force*, 2009

"Tax Reform for Americans Abroad," *Tax Notes International*, May 25, 2009

"U.S. Tax Returns for Foreign Nationals," *Tax Notes International*, January 26, 2009

"Common-Sense Tax Reform (includes proposal for taxing U.S. citizens and residents abroad)," *Tax Notes Year in Review Edition, Special Report*, January 5, 2009

"A Common-Sense Solution for Taxing U.S. Citizens and Immigrants Abroad," *Tax Notes International*, November 17, 2008

"U.S. Tax Code and Treaty Solutions for Resident Aliens Working Abroad," *Tax Notes International*, May 5, 2008

"The 10 Rules of U.S. Taxation of Payments to Foreign Nationals," *Tax Notes International*, January 7, 2008

"Don't Extend U.S. Social Security Taxation to Currently Exempt Foreign Workers," *Tax Notes International*, August 13, 2007

"Top 10 U.S. Tax Return Errors by Foreign Nationals Tax Notes International," *Tax Notes International*, March 5, 2007

"U.S. Policy on Taxing U.S. Citizens and Residents Abroad: A Closer Look," *Tax Notes International*, June 19, 2006

"New U.S. Rules for Withholding on Wages of Nonresident Employees," *Tax Notes International*, February 6, 2006

"New U.S. Acceptance Agent Application Procedures for Nonresident Taxpayers," *Tax Notes International*, January 16, 2006

"B-1 Visitors: U.S. Tax Traps for the Unwary," *Tax Notes International*, September 12, 2005

"In Search of Guidance on U.S. Taxation of Scholarship Grants for Foreign Nationals," *Tax Notes International*, April 18, 2005

"Special U.S. Payroll Tax Rules and Procedures Apply to Foreign Employees, *Tax Notes International*, May 23, 2005

"Important Information for Those Considering Expatriation," On-line Services, January 6, 2005

"Identification Numbers and U.S. Government Compliance Initiatives," co-authored with Linda Dodd-Major, *Tax Notes*, September 20, 2004

"U.S. Tax Policy for Citizens and Immigrants Living Abroad Merits a Closer Look," *Tax Notes International*, July 19, 2004

Commerce Clearance House (CCH)

"U.S. Tax Returns for Foreign Nationals," *Corporate Business Taxation Monthly*, November 2009

"B-1 Visitors-U.S. Tax Traps for the Unwary" *Corporate Business Taxation Monthly*, March 2009

"Tax Treaty Benefits for Workers, Trainees, Students and Researchers," *Corporate Business Taxation Monthly*, September, 2008

"How Foreign Students Claim Treaty Benefits," *Corporate Business Taxation Monthly*, May 2008

"The U.S. Tax Obligations of Foreign Nationals: Debunking the Myths," *Corporate Business Taxation Monthly*, February, 2008

"The 10 Most Common Mistakes Made by Organizations Paying Foreign Nationals," *Corporate Business Taxation Monthly*, February, 2008

"U.S. Taxation of J-1 Exchange Visitors," *Corporate Business Taxation Monthly*, October 2007

"U.S. Taxation of Foreign Nationals," *Corporate Business Taxation Monthly*, 1996

"U.S. Taxation of U.S. Citizens and Residents Abroad," *Corporate Business Taxation Monthly*, 1996

American Payroll Association

"Withholding and Reporting on Payments to Foreign Persons Pose Challenges for Accounts Payable, Part III," *PAYTECH* and on-line journal, August/September 2015

"Withholding and Reporting on Payments to Foreign Persons Pose Challenges for Accounts Payable, Part II," *PAYTECH* and on-line journal, February 2015

"Reporting on Payments to Foreign Persons, Challenges for AP, Part I," *PAYTECH* and on-line journal, November 2014

"Reporting on Payments to Foreign Persons: Challenges for AP, Part I," American Accounts Payable Association on-line Journal, Spring 2013

"Organizations with Foreign Employees Face Compliance Challenges," *PAYTECH* and on-line journal, Nov/Dec 2011

"Paying Foreign Employees Requires Thorough Knowledge Base," *PAYTECH*, November 2009

"US Income Tax Treaties: Compliance and Coordination with Payroll," *PATECH*, Nov/Dec 1999

American Immigration Lawyers Association

"Enjoying Exemptions and Avoiding the Pitfalls of J-1 Exchange Visitor Tax Rules," *Immigration Law Today*, March/April 2008

"Agency Alert—Foreign Nationals Beware: Easy Steps to Avoid Tax Return Errors," *Immigration Law Today*, May/June 2007

"B-1 Visitors: U.S. Tax Traps for the Unwary," *2005-2006 Immigration and Naturalization Law Handbook*, Annual Meeting, 2005

"Identification Numbers and U.S. Government Compliance Initiatives," co-authored with Linda Dodd-Major, *2004-2005 Immigration and Naturalization Law Handbook*, Annual Meeting, 2004

"Agency Alert—IRS Tightens Controls on ITINs," *Immigration Law Today*, March/April 2004

"The Ten Rules of U.S. Taxation," *2002-2003 Immigration & Nationality Law Handbook—Volume 1*, Annual Meeting, 2002

"The U.S. Taxation Obligations of Foreign-Born Persons: Debunking the Myths—Part II," *Immigration Law Today*, April 2002

"The U.S. Taxation Obligations of Foreign-Born Persons: Debunking the Myths—Part I," *Immigration Law Today*, March 2002

"Special Tax Withholding Rules Apply to Income Payments to Foreign Nationals," *2001-2002 Immigration and Nationality Law Handbook*, 2001

"U.S. Taxation of Foreign Nationals," *1997-1998 Immigration and Nationality Law Handbook*, Annual Meeting, 1997

"New Law on Expatriation to Avoid Tax," *New Law Handbook*, November, 1996

"U.S. Taxation of Foreign Students and Scholars," *1996-1997 Immigration and Nationality Law Handbook*, Annual Meeting, 1996

"Update on U.S. Taxation of Foreign Nationals," *1995-1996 Immigration and Nationality Handbook*, Annual Meeting, 1995

"U.S. Taxation of Foreign Nationals," *1994-1995 Immigration and Nationality Law Handbook*, Annual Meeting 1994

"Immigration and Business Development: Practical Considerations for Business People and Entrepreneurs," co-author, *Creative Lawyering in the 90's and Beyond*, 1995

"U.S. Tax Consequences of Employing Foreign Nationals," *1990 Hiring Foreign Nationals*, 1989

Massachusetts Bar Association

"Ten Common Tax Return Errors Foreign Nationals Should Avoid," *Section Review, Taxation*, Vol. 9 No. 2, 2007

"What Payroll Administrators Need to Know About U.S. Income Tax Treaties," *Section Review, Taxation*, 2004

"New IRS Procedures for U.S. Income Payments to Foreign Persons," *Section Review, Taxation*, Spring 2002

"Estates Involving Foreign Nationals Present Challenges," *Section Review, Taxation*, March 1999

"U.S. Tax Rules Can Apply to Inheritances and Gifts from Abroad," co-author, *Section Review, Taxation*, December 1998

"Special Tax Rules Apply to U.S. Real Estate Transactions Involving Foreign Persons," co-author, *Section Review, Taxation*, December 1998

"IRS Restructuring & Reform Act Highlights," co-author, *Section Review, Taxation*, December 1998

"Massachusetts Broadens the Definition of Residency," *Section Review, Taxation*, June 1996

"U.S. Taxation of Foreign Nationals," *Representing the Foreign Business*, Massachusetts Continuing Legal Education, December 1994

Thomson Reuters Acquired Publishers

"J-1 Exchange Visitors—Tax Opportunities and Pitfalls," *International HR Journal*, West, February 2001

"IRS Issues New Regulations for Payments to Foreign Persons," *Immigration Law Report*, Clark, Boardman, Callaghan, February 1998

"U.S. Taxation of Foreign Students and Scholars," *Immigration Law Report*, Clark, Boardman, Callaghan, April 15, 1996

"Payments to Foreign Students and Scholars Involve Complex Withholding and Reporting Rules," *Journal of Taxation of Exempt Organizations*, RIA Group, Sept/Oct 1996 and RIA Group, *Taxation of International Transactions*, Fall 1996

"How Customs Valuations of Imported Goods Affect Related-Party Transactions," co-author, *Journal of Taxation*, WG &L, November 1987

National Association of Tax Professionals

"Foreign Vendors: Why the Nature and Source of Income Matters," *TAXPRO Journal*, National Association of Tax Professionals (NATP), Fall 2011

"U.S. Tax Returns for Foreign Nationals," *TAXPRO Journal*, NATP, Spring 2009

"Ten Common Tax Return Errors and the Foreign Nationals Who Make Them," *TAXPRO Journal*, NATP, Fall 2006

NAFSA: The Association of International Educators

"Payments to Foreign Nationals: Answers to Frequently Asked Social Security Questions," *Government Affairs Manual*, 1996

"U.S. Tax Rules Applicable to Foreign Nationals," *Government Affairs Manual*, 1992

"Tax Return Filing Dilemma for Indian Students," *Government Affairs Bulletin*, September 1992

Other Publishers

"Tax Code and Treaty Solutions for Expatriates Working Abroad," *Payroll Managers Report,* IOMA, November 2008

"Tax Treaty Benefits for Foreign Students," Epochtimes, (Eng) and Dajiyuan (Chinese), April 2005

"Tax Treaty Benefits for Foreign Students," *Current Accounts*, The Georgia Society of CPAs, January/February 2005

"Tax Residency Rules," *Current Accounts*, The Georgia Society of CPAs, July/August 2004

"U.S. Taxation of Foreign Nationals," *Federal Tax Institute (Boston)*, 2004

"U.S. Taxation of U.S. Citizens and Residents Abroad," *Federal Tax Institute (Boston)*, 2004

"Taxation in the United States," *International Taxation of Employment Manual*, co-author, F.T. Law and Tax (U.K.), 1995

"U.S. Tax Rules Applicable to Foreign Nationals," City of Boston, Immigrant Rights Unit, June 15, 1990

"Estate Planning for Non-Citizen Spouses," *Gult Och Blatt I* (Swedish), October 1989

"Choosing a Channel for International Distribution," co-authored with John Ganick, *MassHighTech*, February 1, 1988

"The Effect of the 1986 Tax Reform Act on U.S. Expatriates," co-authored with Kenneth Vacovec, 1987

Books Published by Windstar Publishing

Tax Treaty Benefits for Foreign Nationals Performing U.S. Services

A Guide to Filing IRS Forms 1042 and 1042-S, co-authored with Gary Singer

U.S. Taxation of B-1 Business Visitors

J-1 Exchange Visitors Performing U.S. Services

L-1 Intracompany Transferees on U.S. Assignment

U.S. Taxation of H-1B Specialty Workers

U.S. Taxation of Foreign Students

U.S. Taxation of Scholarship and Fellowship Grants

J-1 Exchange Visitors

Honorarium and Other Payments to Independent Contractors: A Guide to Immigration and Tax Administration, co-authored with Linda Dodd-Major

International Aspects of Individual Tax Returns

A Simple More Efficient Tax Collection System for America

Law Review Articles

"A Proposal for Taking the Complexities out of Tax U.S. Retirement Distributions of Foreign Nationals," co-authored with Prof. Cynthia Blum, Rutgers Law School, *Florida Tax Review*, Vol. II, Number 10, 2011

"A Coherent Policy for U.S. Residence-Based Taxation of Individuals," *Vanderbilt Journal of Transnational Law*, co-authored with Prof. Cynthia Blum, Rutgers Law School, Vol. 41, No. 3, May 2008

"Proposed Changes to the Federal Rules of Evidence as Applied to Computer-Generated Evidence," *Rutgers Journal of Computers, Technology and the Law*, Vol. 7, No. 1, 1979

E-Newsletter Articles

More than 50 articles published from 2004 to 2014 in Windstar's e-newsletter, *A View from the Crow's Nest: Windstar's Eye on the Horizon*

NOTES

President Nixon's Tax Problems: Edwin S. Cohen provides a thorough discussion of President Nixon's IRS troubles in Chapter 25, "Charitable Contribution Rules and President Nixon's 1969 Tax Return," of his 1994 memoir, *A Lawyer's Life: Deep in the Heart of Taxes*, published by Tax Analysts. Cohen was an outstanding tax lawyer, inspirational teacher and high-ranking Treasury official.

The IRS Restructuring: Former IRS Commissioner, Charles O. Rossotti, describes how he transformed the agency from an outdated bureaucracy into a 21st century business in his book, *Many Unhappy Returns: One Man's Quest to Turn Around the Most Unpopular Organization in America*, Harvard Business School Press, 2005. Rossotti, commissioner from 1997 to 2002, was the first businessman to lead the Internal Revenue Service. He had described the proposed IRS structure in a report co-authored with Jerry Songy of the IRS and Professor Malcom Sparrow referred to as "Rossotti's Book."

David Cay Johnston describes the consequences of the IRS restructuring—fewer audits and increased tax evasion by the wealthy—in *Perfectly Legal: The Covert Campaign to Rig our Tax System to Benefit the Super Rich—and Cheat Everybody Else*, published by Portfolio, the Penguin Group, 2003. See in particular Chapter 11, "Mr. Rossotti's Customers." Formerly a reporter on taxes for the New York Times, Johnston won the Pulitzer Prize for his reporting in 2001. He also authored *Free Lunch: How the Wealthiest Americans Enrich Themselves at Government Expense (and Stick You with the Bill)* published by Portfolio, the Penguin Group, 2007.

IRS Budget and Technology Problems: Details about the IRS's inadequate budget and antiquated technology are from written Testimony of John A. Koskinen, Commissioner, Internal Revenue Service, before the respective Senate and House Appropriations Committee: Subcommittee on Financial Services and General Government on the IRS Budget on March 3, 2015 and March 18, 2015. Details about how the IRS is "doing less with less" may be found in prepared remarks of John A. Koskinen, Commissioner, Internal Revenue Service, before the Tax Executives Institute 65th Mid-Year Conference, Washington, D.C., March 24, 2015.

Interview Quotes are from editions of the American Bar Association Taxation Section's *NewsQuarterly*.

ACKNOWLEDGEMENTS

Steve Hrehovcik, Editor

I first met Steve in a memoir class he taught at the Senior Center in Kennebunk. Although I have written hundreds of technical articles and reports, I knew writing a memoir required me to adopt a more personal style. From the first class with Steve it was clear he knew how to fashion a narrative with a human touch. He made important contributions with editing, focus and suggestions about content which I believe helped me tell a more compelling story. He has professional experience as a writer that includes features in newspapers, material for advertising and public relations, plus work in theater and film. He is also an established artist with commissions for portraits, pen and ink drawings of homes and buildings, illustrations for children's books and caricature drawings. And he is even an award-winning cartoonist. He lives in Kennebunk with his wife Carol of 50 plus years. He has three children and one grandson.

    I thank him for his insights, creativity and patience with the many alterations I made as the writing process continued. It has been a pleasure to collaborate with Steve.

Linda Dodd-Major, Editor

I also wish to thank Linda Dodd-Major, immigration attorney, and founder and former director of the Immigration and Naturalization Service's Business Liaison Office, and a good friend. Linda's edits and corrections especially of the technical explanations could only have been done by someone with her understanding of both immigration and tax law and procedure.

Reviewers

I wish to thank all those who reviewed the full memoir for their corrections and constructive comments—Gary Singer, Beth Goodrich, Kevan Whitten and Nelson Hill. I also wish to thank those who are mentioned in my memoir who reviewed relevant excerpts.

www.ingramcontent.com/pod-product-compliance
Lightning Source LLC
Chambersburg PA
CBHW071146300426
44113CB00009B/1107

COMMON GRACE IN KUYPER, SCHILDER, AND CALVIN

Exposition, Comparison, and Evaluation

Jochem Douma

Translated by
Albert H. Oosterhoff

Edited by
William Helder

COMMON GRACE IN KUYPER, SCHILDER, AND CALVIN: EXPOSITION, COMPARISON, AND EVALUATION

Translated from *Algemene genade: uiteenzetting, vergelijking en beoordeling van de opvattingen van A. Kuyper, K. Schilder en Joh. Calvijn over 'algemene genade'*, by J. Douma, 2nd impression with appendix (Goes, Neth.: Oosterbaan & Le Contre, 1974).

Copyright © 2017 by Publication Foundation of the Canadian Reformed Theological Seminary. All rights reserved. Except for brief quotations in critical publications or reviews, no part of this book may be reproduced in any manner without prior written permission from the Publication Foundation of the Canadian Reformed Theological Seminary.

Website: www.canadianreformedseminary.ca.

Lucerna CRTS Publications
110 West 27th Street
Hamilton, ON, Canada
L9C 2A1

ISBN 13: 978-0-9950659-2-5

Ebook: 978-0-9950659-3-2

Unless otherwise indicated, Scripture quotations are from The Holy Bible, English Standard Version® (ESV®), copyright © 2001 by Crossway, a publishing ministry of Good News Publishers. Used by permission. All rights reserved.

Library and Archives Canada Cataloguing in Publication

Douma, Jochem, 1931-
[Algemene genade. English]
Common grace in Kuyper, Schilder, and Calvin : exposition, comparison, and evaluation / Jochem Douma ; translated by Albert H. Oosterhoff ; edited by William Helder.

Translation of: Algemene genade.
Originally presented as the author's thesis.
Includes bibliographical references and index.
Issued in print and electronic formats.
ISBN 978-0-9950659-2-5 (softcover).–ISBN 978-0-9950659-3-2 (PDF)

1. Kuyper, Abraham, 1837-1920. 2. Schilder, K. (Klaas), 1890-1952. 3. Calvin, Jean, 1509-1564. 4. Grace (Theology)–History of doctrines. 5. Reformed Church–Doctrines–History. I. Helder, William, editor II. Title. III. Title: Algemene genade. English.

BT761.2.D6813 2017	234	C2017-907147-5
		C2017-907148-3

Contents

Author's Preface to the English Translation	ix
Translator's Preface	xv
Introduction	1
Chapter I. ABRAHAM KUYPER	3
A. Kuyper's Doctrine of Common Grace	3
§ 1. The necessity of this doctrine	3
§ 2. The term "common grace"	6
§ 3. Scriptural proof	8
§ 4. Appeal to the Confession	24
§ 5. Further definition	25
§ 6. Panorama of the history of culture	41
§ 7. The relationship between particular grace and common grace	61
B. Background	71
§ 8. The opinion of Arnold A. van Ruler	71
§ 9. Objections	83
§ 10. The opinion of Gerard Th. Rothuizen	99
§ 11. Objections	105
§ 12. Political background?	114
§ 13. Kuyper's own opinion	116
Chapter II. KLAAS SCHILDER	129
A. Schilder's Opposition to the Doctrine of Common Grace	129
Doctrinal-historical objections	129
§ 1. Use the word "grace" sparingly (Augustine and Dort)	129
§ 2. Improper appeal to Calvin	135
§ 3. Reformed reaction against Descartes ignored in part	136
§ 4. Common or general? The fathers and Kuyper	138
Doctrinal objections	139
§ 5. Is continuation of history after the Fall grace?	139
§ 6. Kuyper's use of Scripture rejected	150
§ 7. Rejection of the use of the confession	165
Schilder's own solution	172
§ 8. Back to before the Fall	172
§ 9. The covenant relationship	173
§ 10. Yet further back	178
§ 11. Christ and culture	186

B. Background	210
§ 12. Three periods	211
§ 13. From the first to the second period	223
§ 14. From the second to the third period	229

Chapter III. JOHN CALVIN — 233

§ 1. Is the world better than expected?	234
§ 2. Objections	238
§ 3. The explanation	243
§ 4. Calvin does recognize a general revelation	249
§ 5. No natural theology	255
§ 6. Why is grace shown toward Gentiles?	260
§ 7. Grace to the reprobate within the church	266
§ 8. Revelation also about wrath	272
§ 9. Grace and wrath toward the same persons	274
§ 10. Enjoyment on our pilgrim's journey	279

Chapter IV. COMPARISON — 285

§ 1. Double predestination	285
§ 2. Parallelism?	287
§ 3. The breadth of predestination	289
§ 4. The concept of development from bud to bloom	291
§ 5. The place of Christ	294
§ 6. General grace – orientation and end result	296
§ 7. General grace – a doctrine?	301
§ 8. God's wrath	303
§ 9. God's disposition	306
§ 10. Grace and necessity	309
§ 11. Culture and pilgrimage	312
§ 12. Summary	316

Chapter V. EVALUATION — 319

§ 1. Double predestination	319
§ 2. Non eodem modo [not in the same manner]	326
§ 3. The breadth of predestination	333
§ 4. Speculation in the concept of development from bud to bloom	336
§ 5. Christ and the covenant of grace	338
§ 6. Wrong focus of Kuyper's common grace	344
§ 7. Grace – also toward the reprobate	350
§ 8. Judgment and wrath of God	364
§ 9. God's disposition – grace and wrath	367

§ 10. Grace and necessity	375
§ 11. Culture and our being sojourners	379
§ 12. General grace?	390
Bibliography	393
Name Index	401
Appendix – Culture and Our Being Sojourners	405

AUTHOR'S PREFACE TO THE ENGLISH TRANSLATION

More than fifty years have already passed since the appearance of my study *Algemene Genade* as dissertation at the Theological University in Kampen, the Netherlands. The fact that this work has now been translated into English is to me a source of unexpected delight. Evidently there is still interest in the subject that once kept me very intensively occupied for a number of years. It was during the time when in the Netherlands attention for the theology of Abraham Kuyper (1837–1920) sharply declined, also in the ecclesiastical circles in which I had grown up. Partly because of a church schism, in which particularly the subject of infant baptism played an important role, criticism of Kuyper grew constantly louder. Klaas Schilder (1890–1952) contributed forcefully to this criticism, not only where it concerned Kuyper's view of the steadfast promises of God in baptism, but also with respect to Kuyper's doctrine of common grace.

Schilder's writings and theological instruction have made a profound impression on me. As student in Kampen I was very briefly taught by Schilder at the theological seminary which he, together with others, continued on behalf of the Reformed Churches (Liberated). But already during my studies in Kampen, questions arose in my mind concerning certain elements of Schilder's critique of Kuyper. My questions yet increased because of what I read of Calvin in his *Institutes*. But everything remained quite vague until, after entering upon the ministry in Rijnsburg, the Netherlands (1961), I received a study leave in order to write a dissertation about "common grace." From the outset it was already clear to me that I would be concentrating on the three mentioned theologians: Kuyper as the first, with his virtually all-embracing doctrine of common grace; Schilder as the second, with his deeply penetrating critique and ultimately total rejection of Kuyper's "doctrine"; Calvin as the third, in order, among other things, to give an answer to the question whether Schilder did not go too far in this rejection.

AUTHOR'S PREFACE TO THE ENGLISH TRANSLATION

Also the author of a dissertation experiences a development of his thinking. This is certainly the case when it involves a subject that has deservedly continued to engage many, including himself. How do I now view the treatment of the theme of common grace as I presented it over fifty years ago? Let me take a brief look at it in the light of the three components mentioned in the subtitle of my book: the (1) exposition, (2) comparison, and (3) evaluation of the opinions of Kuyper, Schilder, and Calvin about common grace.

As far as my *exposition* is concerned, I am still satisfied with the data about the three theologians as I have recorded them. I gained great admiration for Kuyper when during my studies I began to grasp the connection between what he wrote in his *De Gemeene Gratie* [*Common Grace*] and in *Pro Rege*. It became clear to me that for Kuyper the coming and the work of Jesus Christ played a decisive role in showing common grace to be what, according to him, it actually is. The culture of the pagan nations before Christ's coming, however admirable this culture may sometimes have been, nevertheless remained restricted to cut-off "pools" and "lakes." Compare this with the broad stream of common grace, "tripled in power" by the special impact of our preservation through Christ. The Christian culture of Western Europe benefited the entire world. I share the enthusiasm of A. A. van Ruler, who was very critical in judging Kuyper's view but who could also write: "What an exceptionally impressive apologetic for the absolute and universal significance of Christianity! What a profoundly subtle orientation of common grace in the totality of [God's] plan for the world! ... One *must* have admiration for the broad appeal, the great intellectual force, the intrepid boldness of this historical-philosophical construct.... It contains something uncommonly fascinating." (See p. 50 below.)

It was difficult for me to break free from this fascination. Kuyper's view was unique, also in comparison with the views of Schilder and Calvin. In my description of Schilder's opinions it struck me that the aspect of God's plan for the world—traced back by Kuyper to predestination—was not the topic of any discussion by Schilder. For that matter, neither was it discussed by Calvin, although that is more understandable, since he lived long before Kuyper.

In my *comparison* of the opinions of the three theologians I naturally aimed at clearly formulating the differences between them. But I also repeatedly sought to indicate what these three great scholars have in common as Reformed theologians.

How did I in my *evaluation*, the last section, make my own choice in judging between the three approaches to the theme of common grace? I opted for the sobriety of Calvin's view with its focus on culture and *"vreemdelingschap,"* our position as strangers and sojourners. I followed him in his untroubled acceptance of "common" grace alongside the particular grace apportioned only to the elect. I am convinced that the way the Bible speaks about grace is impoverished if we, together with Schilder (and Greijdanus), assert: "Only when something promotes eternal salvation can we truly speak of grace." In my dissertation (see pp. 352–53 below) I pointed out that Schilder expressed himself differently when the discussion was about the promise of God's grace in infant baptism. It is clear that also wrath and curse must be the subject of careful reflection. But that is not yet a reason for doing so in an equilibrium construct, as if the Bible demands equal attention for wrath and curse. Scripture is in summary about the *gospel* of Jesus Christ.

When I opted for the sobriety of Calvin's view, I also opted more for Schilder with his culture as "truncated pyramid" than for Kuyper's concept of development from bud to bloom, in which all the potentials of human beings as image of God will be exhausted. I referred to this as a concept that we do not find in the Bible and must regard as speculative.

Am I, half a century after this book first made its appearance, still completely sure about the choice that I made at the time? No, for today I am hesitant about one important point. Was it indeed correct, I wonder, to join Calvin in so decisively emphasizing that human beings are strangers and sojourners and that they, as they wander through this world, must be filled with a longing for heaven?

Here I am reminded of a remark by H. Bavinck in his booklet

De navolging van Christus en het moderne leven (1918). It is quite clear, he says, that the morality of the New Testament was presented from the standpoint of the oppressed and persecuted Christian community. But there are times in which there is less persecution and oppression. We do not have to end up with a negative and reserved attitude toward politics and culture in general. The martyr is no monk who withdraws himself from the world. It is precisely in the world that he confesses his faith, and *in that way* he becomes a martyr.

It also became clear to me that initially I had too easily placed our position as sojourners *over against* the cultural mandate (Kuyper and Schilder). Those who belong to Christ and let their lives be governed by the adage "Be holy, for I am holy" *are* or *become* strangers and sojourners. It is not: cultural mandate *or* our being sojourners, but: cultural mandate and *consequently* our being sojourners, because most people do not accept a Christian attitude to life.

If such is the case, we do not need to minimize the scope of Genesis 1:28 ("Fill the earth and subdue it"), as if it is enough only to provide for our food and drink en route to our heavenly destination. Why could focusing on and striving for the development of human capacities in the broadest sense not be in line with the mandate of Genesis 1, also in the New Testament era? Are we oblivious to heaven if we are intensively busy with the earth? We must seek the things that are above, not the things that are on earth (Col 3:2), but the continuation of this text points out that this seeking of things that are above leads to changes in our life here on earth. Through Christ, can (must) these changes not have an impact on our everyday life, our cultural engagement included?

At the same time I now wonder whether we must reject Kuyper's views on culture because he develops all sorts of thoughts that we do not encounter in the Bible. Was I in the past too quick in passing judgment? In our theological and philosophical reflections do we not more often use terms and concepts not found in the Bible? "Speculative" in the sense of "sinful" is what our argumentation becomes if we detract from God's glory and if our conclusions are not *in line* with Scripture but go against it.

AUTHOR'S PREFACE TO THE ENGLISH TRANSLATION

We are permitted to reflect on the meaning of history and on the significance of the two thousand years in which meanwhile Christ has not yet returned. Are we concerned here only with the attainment of the total number of the elect? Or also with the attainment of a fullness from the world, as fruit of our labor here on earth, to the glory of God? In Kuyper's exalted vision as well as in Schilder's more sober depiction of culture as a "truncated pyramid" this orientation toward the glory of God is evident.

I am grateful that my dissertation could be republished. The critical comments now supplied by the author to accompany his own book serve to underline that what he once offered as a *contribution* must clearly have as aim not to conclude the discussions but to continue them.

Jochem Douma
Hardenberg, The Netherlands
June 2017

TRANSLATOR'S PREFACE

The author, Dr. Jochem Douma, was ordained as a minister in the Reformed Churches in the Netherlands (Liberated) in 1961. The first impression of this work served as dissertation at the Theological Seminary of these churches in Kampen, where he was awarded the degree of Doctor of Theology "with highest honor" in 1966. In 1970 he was appointed Professor of Ethics at this Seminary (since 1986 the Theological University of the Reformed Churches), a position he held until his retirement in 1997. From 1993 until 1998 he was also Affiliate Professor of Medical Ethics at the Free University in Amsterdam. Dr. Douma has written extensively in the area of ethics. His book *De Tien Geboden: Handreiking voor het Christelijk leven* was translated into English by Nelson D. Kloosterman as *The Ten Commandments: Manual for the Christian Life* (Phillipsburg, NJ: P&R Publishing, 1996).

The original title of Dr. Douma's dissertation was *General Grace* [*Algemene Genade* in Dutch]: *Exposition, Comparison, and Evaluation of the Opinions of A. Kuyper, K. Schilder, and John Calvin about "General Grace."* The use of the term "general grace" was a deliberate choice to distinguish the author's views from those of Abraham Kuyper. He came to the conclusion that Kuyper's doctrine of common grace [*gemene gratie*] is untenable. However, he does support the idea of general grace, and in that he follows Calvin. Since in prevailing usage "general grace" is normally referred to as "common grace," this more familiar term is also employed in the title of this translation.

The dissertation provides a comprehensive review and discussion of the views of Abraham Kuyper, Klaas Schilder, and John Calvin on the topic of common or general grace in the first three chapters, followed by a chapter comparing these views and a final chapter evaluating them and stating the author's own position. Included in this translation is Dr. Douma's paper "Culture and Our Being Sojourners." It was written two years after the publication of his dissertation in response to criticisms he had received on it and was published as appendix to the second impression (1974).

In chapter II, references to and quotations from the first edition of Schilder's Lenten trilogy, *Christ in His Suffering*, have been taken from the 1938 English translation of this work. However, references to the second edition apply to the Dutch version, and quotations from this edition have been translated as necessary.

The author quoted extensively from the 1953 edition of Schilder's *Christus en cultuur*. In this book all quotations are taken from the new translation, *Christ and Culture* (Hamilton, ON: Lucerna CRTS Publications, 2016).

In the original version of chapter III, Calvin's views were conveyed in Dutch in the text and authenticated by means of extensive Latin quotations in the footnotes. These quotations have now been omitted from the notes. Presented in English translation only, they have instead been incorporated into the author's exposition in the text. Aside from this modification, the layout of this book closely resembles that of the original Dutch edition, a distinctive feature of which is the use of two font sizes. The main body of the text appears in the larger font; the smaller font is reserved for sections in which the author elaborates on what he has presented and engages in further discussion.

Acknowledgments are due to William Helder for his intensive involvement in correcting and editing the translated text as well as to Ryan J. Kampen for his meticulous attention to detail in preparing the manuscript for publication.

Albert H. Oosterhoff

INTRODUCTION

The topic discussed in this study has fascinated many since the publication of Abraham Kuyper's three-volume work *De Gemeene Gratie* [*Common Grace*]. Many have expressed their opinions, both pro and con, in the extensive literature on the topic. More than once this has resulted in fundamental controversies, which already leads one to surmise that the topic of "general grace" encompasses wide-reaching complications and consequences. In this study I have made an attempt to contribute to a better understanding of the questions that the topic of "general grace" gives rise to.

The *first* chapter provides an analysis of Kuyper's opinions. It seems to me that this is not redundant, even though others have undertaken a similar task before me. I have made grateful use of their publications, but it would appear to me that certain elements of Kuyper's views deserve more attention than they have received thus far. I think especially of the connection Kuyper drew between common grace and predestination.

In the second part of the first chapter I inquire about the background of Kuyper's doctrine of common grace. Several aspects of my analysis are there considered in greater detail.

The *second* chapter provides a survey of Klaas Schilder's criticism of the doctrine of common grace. This is territory that still lies almost completely fallow. The chapter is a first attempt to arrange systematically what Schilder wrote about and against "common grace."

Also in the second chapter it seemed desirable to me to inquire into the background. When and why did Schilder engage in his criticism?

The *third* chapter consists of an exposition of what Calvin wrote on the topic. Did he recognize a general grace? If so, how did he write about it?

The first three chapters provide sufficient material for the *fourth* chapter, in which I compare Kuyper, Schilder, and Calvin with one another. This comparison shows how, over against both Kuyper and Schilder, Calvin's position on the question of general grace" is unique.

In the *fifth* chapter I come to my evaluation. I realize that here on occasion I have to discuss fundamental questions. These warrant a broader discussion than is possible in this study. Nevertheless, I hope that I have succeeded in clearly enumerating the topics that will need to be dealt with in a further discussion of the subject of "general grace."

I

ABRAHAM KUYPER

A. Kuyper's Doctrine of Common Grace

§ 1. The necessity of this doctrine

Kuyper: The confession of the "deadly nature of sin" has to raise a question for all who refuse to close their eyes to the facts of reality. How can they on the one hand confess that human beings are by nature "totally unable to do *any* good and inclined to *all* evil" (Heidelberg Catechism, Lord's Day 2) and on the other hand accept a reality that seems not to agree with this confession?[1] "Are there not many acts of maliciousness and dishonesty as well as violations of justice against which the public conscience, also among non-believers rises in protest? And can we not recount many deeds of neighborly love and mercy that have been performed by unbelievers, sometimes putting believers to shame? When Pharaoh's daughter saved the child Moses from the Nile, did she do evil or good? And does this not clearly show that the total corruption of our nature caused by sin ... in many cases clashes with reality?"[2]

One could therefore follow one of two courses: *either* abandon the above-mentioned confession and consider fallen humanity as not to have fallen so deep (but that is Arminian) *or* deny the facts noted above (but that is Anabaptist).[3] However, when confronted with this dilemma, Reformed confessors have refused to follow either route: "We could not close our eyes to what is good and beautiful outside of the church, among unbelievers. Those good things exist and had to be acknowledged. But at the same time

---

1. This formulation is found in *De Gemeene Gratie* [*Common Grace*] I, 11, 252–53; II, 8ff., 53–54. For a more complete list of the works cited in this study, see the bibliography.
2. I, 252–53. Unless otherwise indicated, the quotations are from *De Gemeene Gratie*, sometimes identified as *G.G.*
3. I, 11.

the total depravity of our sinful nature is non-negotiable."[4] If we want to retain both and only speak of a seeming[5] discrepancy, we must conclude that there is a "third something."[6] We then come to a confession of God's general favor, which does not take away the deadly character of sin but "in many cases arrests" the progression of this sin.[7]

The above-mentioned "many deeds of neighborly love and of mercy" brought Kuyper to a confession of general favor or "common grace." But he added, "We reach the same conclusion by a different route as well. For, provided that you look at relationships in general rather than at isolated cases, the spiritual condition always lies at the root of the external condition of life. A generation, a family, or a tribe in which sin progresses recklessly and without restraint will also perish externally. Even nations that are internally disrupted soon succumb externally also. This is evident from Babel, Moab, Ammon, and imperial Rome. It appears that instead of perishing soon after Paradise, our human race has in fact survived all these centuries, and that, with ups and downs, there has actually been a continuing development. In consequence, we now stand on a much higher plane than the human race in the days of Nebuchadnezzar or Cyrus. If so, this proves that the spiritual collapse cannot have proceeded unhindered and unbridled. A humanity concerning which nothing else could be said than that it lay under the curse of being 'inclined to *all* evil and unable to do *any* good' could not have had such a history. The history of our human race through all these many centuries is therefore proof that on the one hand the appalling *law of sin* ruled, but also that on the other a *law of grace* broke that power of sin."[8]

On this point Kuyper wanted to follow in Calvin's footsteps, who "in his *Institutes* II, iii, 3, formulated the deep meaning of this 'common grace' most clearly"[9] when he was confronted with the question how to explain the virtues of pagans. According to Kuyper, Calvin thus opposed all those who regard these virtues as

4. Loc. cit.
5. Loc. cit.
6. II, 8–9.
7. I, 253
8. I, 253.
9. I, 10. See also *Loc. de Foedere*, 29.

evidence that our human nature is not inclined to all evil and totally unable to do any good. The explanation must be found in the fact that (and now Kuyper cites Calvin) "amidst the universal ruin a certain common grace or favor operates, which does not cleanse the depraved nature, but prevents its breaking forth from within." Or in the Latin text, which Kuyper reproduces in part: *gratia, non quae illam purget, sed intus cohibeat*. Calvin, so Kuyper continues, "repeats this even more strongly at the conclusion of section 3: 'God by his providence so bridles our perverse nature that it cannot break forth into action, but he does not cleanse it within.'"[10]

Thus for Kuyper the doctrine of common grace does not arise "from philosophical invention, but from the confession of the deadly character of sin."[11]

It is now no longer surprising that Kuyper, for whom the necessity of the doctrine of general favor or "common grace" is very clear, speaks of an "indispensable part of the Reformed confession"[12] that is "intended to solve" one of the greatest riddles of life.[13] Indeed, Kuyper speaks of a *doctrine*.[14]

It is, however, a doctrine without a rich history. Although Calvin "did at times direct the attention of Reformed theologians particularly to this extremely important topic," it was never discussed in a separate chapter.[15] Indeed, a decline in interest in common grace is observable in doctrinal history. In their first struggle against the Anabaptists, "our fathers very decisively introduced the confession of common grace."[16] But then the battle against Arminianism began. In opposing the Anabaptists they used the doctrine of common grace to ensure that the coherence between the new and the old life was maintained. But it is understandable that the fathers "in their second struggle—this time not against the Anabaptists but against the Arminians—kept silent about common grace and placed all the emphasis on maintaining

---

10. Loc. cit.
11. I, 10–11.
12. I, 11.
13. II, 43.
14. II, 7, 86; III, 11, 14; *Het Calvinisme*, 51, 104, 107, 111; *Loc. de Magistratu*, 3 dictation, presupposes that Kuyper wants to see common grace dealt with in a separate locus of dogmatics.
15. I, 9. Cf. II, 192: "Calvin led the way in confessing common grace as fact and in assigning its place in the outline of the building, but without developing it further."
16. II, 194.

the character of the new life as created by God without contribution from the old nature. And since the second struggle was the last, and in the course of it the doctrinal formulations were established, it is easy to appreciate how the Reformed, after first speaking boldly of their confession of common grace, almost let that important doctrine fall by the wayside in their later dogmatic development."[17]

Also in Herman Bavinck's "well-upholstered" address on *De Algemeene Genade* (1894) the topic was not yet treated with any degree of coherence and completeness.[18] Hence Kuyper's own attempt, "not at all with the pretension that this will once and for all complete this part of dogmatics; rather, since this subject so deeply affects our lives and our current struggles, it is our present aim to offer an initial attempt at dealing with it, in the hope that it can lead to a more detailed and more complete doctrinal treatment."[19]

Doctrine *and* an initial attempt at dealing with it: that is not necessarily inconsistent. Kuyper is convinced of the necessity of the confession of the doctrine of common grace, but on the other hand he regards its *development* as being still in the early stages. However, it is difficult to square his modesty in speaking of a first attempt with what the author then presents, on crucial points, as a "complete explanation" (II, 417), a "solved question" (II, 504), and an "all-round discussion" (III, 295, about art. 36 of the Belgic Confession). At one point the author concludes the discussion of a topic with the observation: "Not one question remains in this entire mystery. Truly no insignificant gain" (II, 658).

§ 2. The term "common grace"

To avoid misunderstanding and confusion Kuyper preferred to speak of "common grace" rather than "universal favor."[20]

In the first place, so he explains, "common" is better than "universal." For "our fathers spoke of *gratia communis*, and in our language the word *communis* means not 'universal' but 'common.' In Latin *communis* is the equivalent of *universalis* and so does mean 'universal.' It is true that both concepts usually mean practically the same thing, but there is a distinction between them and it is better

17. Loc. cit.
18. I, 9.
19. I, 9–10.
20. I, 8–9.

not to lose it."²¹ Kuyper distinguishes the two concepts as follows: "'Universal' refers to something that is found everywhere, that is valid in all cases, and that is applicable to everyone; *communis*, on the other hand, refers to something that is common to a particular group. In this context the group is humanity, our human race, and the grace is common to this group."²² It is common to both the elect and the non-elect.²³ It does not consist "of something that is found in each person by nature, but of a good given to the human race. Therefore our fathers quite properly did not speak of *gratia universalis* but of *gratia communis*. 'Universal favor' was a term preferred by their opponents."²⁴

In the second place, "grace" is a more correct term than "favor." For in popular [Dutch] usage "favor" [*genade*] is "so exclusively taken to mean 'saving' grace ... that a more general word seemed more appropriate in this context. The word 'grace' is still commonly used for a stay of execution; and since our expanded argument deals precisely with that grace which stayed the execution of Genesis 2:17, the term 'common grace' seemed not inaptly to express the very character of our topic."²⁵

When we orient ourselves on the basis of these data, we can say: common grace is that favor of God which as *common* grace is not universal and found in everyone by nature, but is a conferred good within the circle of humanity, common to elect and non-elect; and which as common *grace* is not salvific, but only arrests sin and its consequences (and therefore the execution of Gen 2:17).

"Within the circle of humanity," says Kuyper, but in I, 9, and also in *Loc. de Foedere* (119, dictation), we read that "to a certain extent animals also share in 'common grace.' You can see that in Gen 9:9 and 10" (I, 9). Kuyper mentions this to indicate strongly and sharply that common grace does not at all concern particular, personal grace. "In itself it does not carry within it any salvific seed and is therefore of a totally different nature than particular or covenant grace" (I, 9). Despite the fact that he distinguishes the term "common grace" from "general favor," Kuyper uses both terms indiscriminately in his work. Apparently the terminological issue was not of prime importance to him.

21. III, 146.
22. Loc. cit.
23. II, 223–24.
24. III, 146.
25. III, 147.

§ 3. *Scriptural proof*

In this study I shall not give a complete overview of all parts of the Bible that Kuyper discusses in his doctrine of common grace. That is not necessary either, as long as we pay attention to five passages that, for Kuyper, form the pillars on which the doctrine of common grace can rest. They are: (1) Gen 9; (2) Gen 2:17; (3) Gen 3; (4) John 1; and (5) Rom 1 and 2. Also important, especially for later discussions about Kuyper's doctrine, is Rev 21:26.

1. *Genesis 9 – The Noahic covenant.* Kuyper: "The fixed historical starting point for the doctrine of common grace lies in the fact that God entered into a covenant with Noah after the Flood. Not enough attention has been paid to this very significant and decisive event of late. People too quickly directed their attention to Abraham and the patriarchs, and as a result the great significance of the Noahic covenant slipped into the background and then was almost forgotten."[26] To understand its importance again, Kuyper points to two momentous changes that occurred in the earth's condition. The first came about right after the Fall. "The world as God had once created it had perished under the curse, and a totally different, sorrowful, somber form of that same earth had now appeared. This could have been brought about only through the powerful actions of the elements, and it may obviously be presumed that in the desolate scenes that nature still offers us today in many regions, we can see the results of what then took place."[27] The descendants of Adam to Noah lived in this "desperate and brutalized world." But until Noah, "everything fluctuated in continual unrest and was subjected to change."[28]

But then, in the Flood, came "a second powerful upheaval … which again tore, fractured, and totally changed the face of the then existing earth in a violent manner. It was on that twice-shattered and altered earth that the current development of our race had its beginning after the Flood."[29] Precisely in this fact lies the significance of the Noahic covenant: that after a period of unrest

26. I, 11.
27. I, 16.
28. I, 18.
29. I, 16.

(from Adam to Noah) it sealed a new order of things that will remain unchanged until the end of days.[30] Gen 8:22 attests to this: "While the earth remains, seedtime and harvest, cold and heat, summer and winter, day and night, shall not cease." This surely implies "that the course of life achieved a regulated, fixed order only after the Flood."[31] This "constancy of the now existing order of things as it affects our entire earth and human life on the earth" was thus sealed in the Noahic covenant.[32]

This covenant cannot possibly be particular. Gen 9:8–17 expressly shows us "up to six times that we are not concerned with a covenant of particular, but a covenant of common, grace."[33] For the entire human race, indeed, every living creature and the entire earth are included in this covenant. But then it is "almost inconceivable how people, in disagreement with and in disregard of this six-times repeated pronouncement, have explained away the *common* character of this covenant and have virtually denied it. Only false spirituality drove them to it."[34]

As further evidence of the non-particular character of the Noahic covenant, Kuyper adds two points: In Gen 9:1–17 the name "God" is used, not the covenant name "LORD" (which is used when the topic is the salvific covenant of particular grace in Gen 3 and also in Gen 9:26, when Shem receives the blessing of the Messiah).[35] And this clinches the argument: The promise of the Noahic covenant "contains nothing spiritual whatsoever. It concerns only this one thing: 'The waters shall never again become a flood to destroy all flesh.' Only that. Nothing else. There is no indication of anything other than that."[36]

What changes did the earth display after the Flood? In the first

30. I, 18.
31. I, 174. Cf. I, 12, 92.
32. I, 18.
33. I, 21–22. Kuyper lists the six indications of the Noahic covenant as a covenant of common grace as follows:
1. Gen 9:9: "with you and your offspring after you." "You" is plural. Thus, Japheth and Ham and their descendants are also included in this covenant.
2. Gen 9:10 and 12: "and every living creature."
3. Gen 9:13: "covenant between me and the earth."
4. Gen 9:15: "my covenant that is between me and you and every living creature of all flesh."
5. Gen 9:16: *idem*.
6. Gen 9:17: *idem*.
34. I, 22.
35. Loc. cit.
36. I, 23.

place, as we already saw, *changes in nature*. Pursuant to God's providential decree, the "natural relationships on this earth" received such an appearance and form that the execution of God's promise not to send another flood was ensured.[37] But that was not all. "God's graciously saving hand did not extend itself solely to the elements of nature, but also to human beings themselves. Remarkable changes occurred in human life."[38] Especially Gen 9:1–7 informs us about this. Four important matters require our attention:[39]

(a) Human beings received moral dominance over all animals (9:2). "The greatest problem that then came to the fore as a matter of course was how human society could protect itself and hold its own against the animal kingdom. With a view to the anxiety and fear that therefore caused the human heart to tremble, God reassured our human race in this regard immediately after the Flood."[40]

(b) Human beings were permitted to eat the flesh of animals (9:3). "The eating of flesh was formerly a common practice. However, the original creation ordinance that assigned the plant kingdom to humans for their consumption had never yet been supplemented or expanded. That only happened *after* the Flood."[41]

(c) Human beings were forbidden to eat raw meat with its blood (9:4). The eating of raw meat with its blood is acceptable for a beast of prey, but not for humans. "A beast of prey attacks its prey and digs its claws and teeth into it. So, too, dehumanized people who presume to have an inherent right to animals and thus attack, slay, and devour them. It is against such an unholy and brutish practice that God institutes a state of *order*."[42] The boundary between humans and animals may not be erased, and that would happen if people threw themselves on animal or human flesh (v. 5 also contemplates cannibalism) to devour it. "The profound difference between the human race and the animal kingdom must

---

37. I, 32.
38. Loc. cit.
39. I, 37.
40. I, 40.
41. I, 40.
42. I, 45.

be protected against weakening and blurring."[43] This divine order ensures "the human character of human society."[44]

(d) In the fourth place, the command of capital punishment instituted government (9:6). Human life is protected from death caused by animals. "The beast of prey has been driven back and destruction is its future"[45] (v. 5a). But "just as serious ... is the second danger that humankind can destroy itself by the murder of human beings"[46] (vv. 5b, 6). At some length Kuyper defends the position that verse 6 ("Whoever sheds the blood of man, by man shall his blood be shed") portrays for us the institution of governmental authority. The conclusion of his exegesis is "that the Christian church has always correctly regarded these words not as a prophecy but as a command, an ordinance, and that God charges humankind with the duty to impose a sentence of capital punishment on the murderer. That immediately raises the question *who* is charged with this obligation. The context makes it clear that it is not intended that *anyone who wants* to exact the punishment may do so, but that the appointment of the agent referred to must take place according to established rule and order. In this respect Luther was entirely right to say that here *lies the official institution of government*, as were the Annotators of the Dutch States Bible (1637) when they comment that this verse confirms the legitimacy of government."[47] Before the Flood there was "nothing but a paternal authority, and paternal authority does not include the right to kill one's child. Nor is it possible to deduce anything about government from paternal authority. But after the Flood that mandate of authority was given in the conferral of the right over life and death."[48] In addition to the provisions of Genesis 9:2–6, the "new circumstances" of human life after the Flood are also evident in another respect. For human life is altered markedly by a shorter life span. "While Noah reached an age of ten centuries, Shem's age was already reduced to six, Eber's to four, Serug's to two, and Abraham's to a life span not much different from ours. People also matured earlier, for while

43. I, 46–47.
44. Loc. cit.
45. I, 51.
46. I, 51.
47. I, 69–70.
48. I, 70.

before the Flood Methuselah was 187 years old when he fathered Lamech, Shem's son Arpachshad was born when Shem was 100 years old, and Arpachshad received his son Shelah when he was only 35. With Abraham the order of things had altered to such an extent that the birth of Isaac, which was regarded as miracle, occurred at an age at which Methuselah had to wait almost another century before he received his first child. To explain this as due to a slow degeneration of our race is absurd. In the two thousand years before the Fall, the life span of people stretched out over centuries. Adam lived to the age of 930, and Noah, who lived twenty centuries later, reached the age of 950 and thus lived twenty years longer. There was thus no trace of any gradual regression before the Flood. The decrease in people's life span after the Flood was sudden and occurred always in two-century decrements."[49] The explanation is apparent: the long life span of early times must have contributed significantly to the development of wickedness and unrighteousness. "Even now, old sinners are always the most dangerous. How severe must the outbreak of unrighteousness have been when such 'old sinners' had eight or more centuries ahead of them to complete their wickedness." The shorter life span is thus another factor that arrests unrighteousness.[50]

After this short summary of Kuyper's discussion of the Noahic covenant, the question remains: in what aspect does Kuyper see the *grace* character of this covenant? In this: "Once Noah and his family had left the ark, you hear only the language of encouragement and reassurance. There was reason for this. The entire human society existing at that time had been swallowed up and had disappeared, and Noah and his small family suddenly stood alone and forsaken on the denuded earth. It still showed all the signs of destruction and bore the dead bodies of people and cattle in large numbers. This must have been so incomparably poignant and heart-rending for Noah and his family that you could imagine how it might have driven all of them insane. If they were to regain their courage and energy to continue living, to begin a new human society after those appalling events, it was necessary for God to come to them

49. I, 90.
50. I, 91.

in grace and to support their tottering steps on this painful path. The appearance of the Lord after the Flood responds to this need completely. The rescued human race receives practically nothing but words of encouragement and comfort, and from this point on, common grace no longer functions as it had for centuries, but is now expressed and revealed *as grace*, as *favor*."[51] For Kuyper, this character of grace is already included in the definition of "covenant": "When God enters into a covenant with his creature, it is an act of favor, of condescending goodness, of grace."[52] Or: "Entering into covenant is an act of friendship."[53]

Kuyper elaborates on what he states here in summary in his discussion of the details of the Noahic covenant. Very clearly, and with a direct reference to the Scriptural text, he discusses the above-mentioned four provisions from Gen 9:2–6. For vv. 2–6 of Gen 9 are anchored by 9:1 and 9:7, in which the "address of God Almighty to the saved human race" begins and ends with a blessing.[54] Kuyper writes: "It does not say: 'And God spoke to Noah,' but explicitly: 'And God *blessed* Noah and his sons.' Thus one does not do justice to the meaning of the story if one searches for the nature of this grace as a blessing only in vv. 1 and 7 and excludes it from the verses they anchor. We should, of course, admit that in vv. 1 and 7 the nature of this blessing is more readily apparent." And so the "four provisions" can then be regarded as expressions of *grace*.[55] It is grace when, because of the new circumstances in nature, in the relationship of humans and animals, through government, and through the reduction in life span, the general brutalization of humanity before the Flood cannot return. Then it was the case (Genesis 6:5) "'that *every* intention of the thoughts of [man's] heart was only evil *continually*.' *After* the Flood, Genesis 8:21 restricts itself to the observation of the simple and much less sharply defined fact that 'the intention of man's heart is evil from his youth.'"[56]

For Kuyper the shorter life span after the Flood is thus evidence of God's grace. But although he states that common grace also affected the human

51. I, 290–91.
52. I, 291.
53. Loc. cit.
54. I, 36–37.
55. I, 37.
56. I, 275.

body immediately after Flood, he says: "The first humans were endowed not only with a prolongation of life, but even a centuries-long prolongation. That many have tried to ignore the long lives of the ancient patriarchs was because they failed to understand the enormous grace that the duration of the lives of these ancient ancestors was not just for their own benefit but for our whole race" (I, 263). Here the lengthening of the life span is called *grace*! Can that be reconciled? Are lengthening and shortening of life *both* grace? Kuyper does not clarify things for us when he says: "In this way all is harmonized. The longer life span of the body accompanied the *lesser* degree of 'common grace' before the Flood. Conversely, it was evidence of a *greater* grace that after the Flood the long life span was discontinued and the excessive bodily strength was diminished. In this there was a weakening of the *flesh* which, combined with a strengthening of the spirit, was directed toward the same goal from two sides. That goal was to create a condition of human life in which the dominion of the stronger spirit over the weaker flesh would call forth a less brutalized human life" (I, 279). Two questions arise here:

If a longer life span resulted in a more brutalized life, how can Kuyper (in the same context, just before the above-quoted passage) say that the common grace before the Flood had "a strong [! J.D.] effect on the bodily existence of humanity," and also that the common grace before Noah displayed "a *higher* exponent" in the longevity of the first generations (*Loc. de Foedere*, 118 dictation, 125)? Since Kuyper speaks of a greater grace (after Noah) and a lesser grace (before Noah), one might have expected that he would not have assigned to the common grace before Noah a stronger but, rather, a lesser effect on the bodily existence of humanity—lesser in the sense that the non-shortening of the life span caused sin to increase without restriction.

The second question is: If Kuyper wants to continue to regard the long life span as also evidence of God's grace (albeit lesser), how does it display its *grace* (the arresting of sin)? For by the long life span sin was not arrested but promoted.

To do Kuyper complete justice, we have to remember that he already regards the "sheer continuation of our race" as grace (II, 608). The recipients of (long) life have no right to this conferred good. That is why it is conferred grace. We must therefore have regard to the aspect of the *gift* and not of the *operation* if longevity is to retain its character of grace. But even then, questions remain. For if "the arresting of sin and of its consequences constitutes the real substance of common grace" (I, 246), how can one then in a case such as longevity leave action out of consideration? Even stronger, how can one conclude that the way longevity functions does not arrest sin but promotes it, and yet speak of common grace?

2. *Genesis 2:17* – *"For in the day that you eat of it you shall surely die."* However, the common grace which attained "its more fixed

appearance"[57] with the Noahic covenant already dated from Paradise. "It finds its origin not just in the time of the ark but in Paradise, and, to understand common grace in its real character and in its true nature, we therefore have to go back to Paradise."[58] There "you find a somewhat strange phenomenon when you read of something that does not happen. You read of human beings in a state of righteousness when they are told: 'In the day that you eat of it you shall surely die.' Well, they did eat of the tree, *but they did not die that day*. On the contrary, Adam lived an amazingly long time yet.... We are not saying that God's word was not fulfilled.... But it cannot be contradicted that it did not happen in the way that Adam and Eve must have understood it when it was spoken. Adam did not die on the day he sinned. That fact is certain. If we may put it this way, Adam received a very remarkable 'stay of execution'—not as a result of his own entreaty but as the free gift of God's will. And that gift of God's will, which brought about that Adam did *not* die that day but remained alive and continued to live for centuries, was none other, nor anything less, than a very powerful act of common grace affecting all human beings, ourselves included."[59] We must not disguise the contradiction that lies hidden in Gen 2:17. "What God says, he says with a total perspicuity and full knowledge of what will happen, and for that reason you lack the right either to get around the 'in the day,' or to restrict the absolute truth of death that is encompassed by the expression 'you shall surely die.'"[60] That expression encompasses everything: spiritual *and* bodily death, a total corruption.[61] And it did *not* just begin with the Fall. If you ask how this is compatible with God's word, the answer is that all difficulties will disappear if you regard the expression 'for in the day that you eat of it you shall surely die' not as a threat but solely as a prediction. Thus, in this sense: eating from that tree will cause you to fall into sin, and sin has *death* as necessary consequence, either immediate death or death continuing until the end. But you have to

---

57. I, 18.
58. I, 94.
59. I, 94. Also I, 228–29, 243; II, 86, 606.
60. I, 212.
61. I, 205–10. Death as dissolution of the bond (1) of the soul to God; (2) of the body to the soul; (3) of the person to the world; and (4) of one human being to another, is often found in Kuyper. Cf. *Loc. de Peccato*, 93ff.; *Werk van de Heilige Geest*, 359ff. [English title: *Work of the Holy Spirit*]; *E Voto* I, 435ff., 443ff.; II, 206ff.

understand also the unspoken: *unless I, your God, in my mercy, arrest the progressive consequences of sin.*"⁶²

The "contradiction" in Gen 2:17 that Kuyper posited so decisively above, he rejected equally firmly in other of his writings. See *Uit het Woord*, 2nd series II, 91; *Loc. de Peccato*, 97; *E Voto* I, 75. Not only before he wrote his *Gemeene Gratie*, but also afterwards, he disputed that the "in the day" did not have immediate effect. See S. J. Ridderbos, *De theologische cultuurbeschouwing van Abraham Kuyper*, 31, who cites from *De Heraut* of 28 Sept. 1913, *inter alia*, "that in the threat directed to the first two human beings in Paradise it says expressly that 'in the day,' that is, on the day that they sinned, they would die, so that, if understood in a physical sense, it would not apply at all to Adam, who lived almost another thousand years after his fall. This has been explained by saying that he received *grace* in his *extended* life, but the Bible does not say that."

We find the exegesis that Kuyper defends in *De Gemeene Gratie* also in *E Voto* II, 203ff.; and *Loc. de Foedere*, 122. (The pronouncement "you shall die internally and in nine hundred years also externally" is "exegetical chicanery"!). The idea that common grace only appeared after the Flood is also found in other of Kuyper's writings. See *A. R. Staatkunde* I, 216; II, 387, 433–34; *Voleinding* III, 78 ("There was no grace at all until the Fall.") See S. J. Ridderbos, op. cit., 36.

Kuyper impresses on us what would have happened if Genesis 2:17 had taken effect immediately. "Just imagine that Adam had actually died on the very day when he fell. Then the whole history of this world would have been cut off. No human race would have come into being. As the Bible recounts it, before the Fall Adam and Eve had no children yet. Thus suppose that the Lord's pronouncement, 'In the day that you eat of it you shall surely die,' had been literally fulfilled. Then with their death the entire root of our race would have died off and none of us would ever have been born on earth. If it is 'common grace' by which Adam's existence on earth was unexpectedly extended, then it follows that also your life, your birth, your existence as a human being, arises not merely from *creation* but is an act that is rooted in *grace*. The complete and direct consequence of sin, *had it not been arrested*, would then have destroyed the entire human race with one death sentence."⁶³

Without common grace there would be no history (II, 28); the number of those who were doomed would have been limited to two (I, 215); everything would

62. I, 213.
63. I, 95.

"as in one appalling thunderclap" have collapsed and sunk into hell (II, 61; cf. II, 398, 419, 611); "our entire human race, with all the hidden treasure of excellent qualities that God had apportioned in Adam, would suddenly have vanished" (I, 218). See also *Loc. de Foedere*, 118 dictation; *Loc. de Magistratu*, 22 dictation; *Tweeërlei Vaderland*, 10.

However, *De Gemeene Gratie* also contains expressions in which the absence of common grace does *not* display such sudden effects. What is one to think of I, 457: "If common grace had *not* intervened after the Fall in Paradise, would the development of our human life have amounted to *less than nothing* [italics supplied, J.D.]"? And what happens to the immediate sinking into hell when Kuyper writes: "If you imagine the total absence of 'common grace,' the whole of our human race would not only have become brutalized, but would have sunk into madness, suicide, and complete brutalization, already long before the Flood" (II, 119–20), so that "*in the end* [italics supplied, J.D.] nothing [would have] remained but one huge wilderness"? (I, 495). I ask the same question when I read that "without common grace the destruction of family life would have succeeded many centuries ago" (III, 300). K. Schilder drew attention to the following quotation: "If common grace had not intervened, the judgment in Paradise would have had immediate effect and Paradise would have sunk into hell to submerge us all immediately and forever in an eternal death" (II, 528). Schilder comments: "Notice ... the words '*us* all' in the quotation. Surely *they imply the natural evolution of the human race* from the fallen first human couple" (*Heidelbergsche Catechismus* III, 233). Indeed, it is difficult to see how the "us all" is compatible with the number of those who were doomed, which according to I, 215, supposedly was restricted to two. But apart from the incompatibility of I, 215, it is possible that Kuyper wanted to maintain the "us all." Thus, in a passage in *Uit het Woord*, 2nd series I, 284, Kuyper writes that God "would have been completely justified if he had let Adam descend into hell right away, *together with all the seeds of life that he carried in his loins*" [italics supplied, J.D.]. That would have included "us" too! This organic consideration of our inclusion in Adam's loins is found more often in Kuyper. See *Uit het Woord*, 2nd series I, 123–24, 284; II, 81, 102; *E Voto* I, 101; *Loc. de Deo* III, 241 ("the human race would have died out"). But this causes further questions to arise about Kuyper's creatianism [*sic*]. See *Gemeene Gratie* II, 390–91, 438; *E Voto* I, 49–50; *Loc. de Providentia*, 44–45; *Loc. de Homine*, 60 dictation, although this creatianism is *moderate*. See W. H. Velema, *De leer van de Heilige Geest bij Abraham Kuyper*, 89ff. Kuyper cannot be exonerated from contradicting himself on the point in question. However, the first series of pronouncements (regarding an immediate and final execution of the judgment) is expressed more strongly than the second series (in which some development or time length is presumed).

3. *Genesis 3*. If one sees in sin "a deadly fast-acting poison that, unless arrested, leads immediately to a spiritual, temporal, and

eternal death,"[64] common grace becomes immediately apparent. Kuyper draws attention to the following facts.

In the verdicts pronounced on the serpent, Eve, and Adam, *grace shines through despite the judgment*: particular grace in the verdict on the serpent, and common grace in the verdict on Adam and Eve.[65] For, although the woman will bring forth children in pain, the "womb of all human life" is unlocked. "If absolute death had set in, Eve's womb, from which the entire human race had to spring, would have been shut forever."[66] And although Adam is condemned to derive nourishment from a cursed ground by the sweat of his face, yet he may eat bread. Both the creation and the maintenance of life have become possible through common grace.[67]

Also the fact that God provides humans with clothing attests to common grace. "If you realize what it means when people in their natural state walk around virtually naked, while civilized people cover themselves even under a hot sun, you must recognize how already in this one fact of being clothed lies the beginning of a developing world, which still continues, though in sin, to unveil itself to us."[68]

The arresting of sin and its consequences is immediately apparent from the sense of shame that humans developed. "Imagine that Satan after his fall had tried to hide himself in shame in a similar manner. But no. A Satan is not ashamed of his audacious rebellion against God; instead, he prides himself on it and raises his proud head high against the Thrice Holy One, taunting God.... So, suppose for a moment that sin in Adam and Eve had continued to the end at once, as a fast-acting poison. Then their remorse, their shame, their hiding from each other and from God, would be completely inexplicable."[69] It was not a "remorse toward God ... a sorrow toward the Eternal One, or even a salvific unrest of conscience. Nothing of the sort is apparent. Their remorse reminds one rather of the remorse of an Esau. But do not forget that even

---

64. I, 252.
65. I, 233.
66. I, 230.
67. I, 230ff.; cf. *Loc. de Foedere*, 118 dictation.
68. I, 264; cf. II, 467–75.
69. I, 246–47.

in the remorse of an Esau and, indeed, of a Judas, there is *common grace*. Satan never has remorse and cannot have remorse."[70]

Even Adam and Eve's attempt to excuse themselves cannot be explained apart from common grace. "Satan would never excuse himself, but would insolently have emboldened himself for his evil." However, with Adam and Eve it is apparent from each word "that they would have given anything *not* to have eaten of the tree."[71]

Also the fact that God sought fallen humankind is not imaginable without common grace. "If sin had immediately had its full consequence in Adam and Eve and had *not* been arrested, then this seeking would not have been conceivable. God never searches for Satan, but always rejects Satan and positions him as opponent."[72]

4. *John 1.* Kuyper explains John 1:4, "In him was life, and the life was the light of men," as follows: "Human beings do not derive their light from elsewhere, nor from themselves, nor did they create it. They live by the eternal Word. The eternal Word that causes them to exist is their life. And that life brightens in their consciousness to light, to light in all directions—light in their understanding, light in the exercise of their will, light in their communal life, light in their moral existence, light in their art and science, light in the eye of their souls by which they see their God."[73] But now "breaks the mirror in which the eternal Word reflected himself. Sin enters."[74] However, that does not end the revelation of the eternal Word. After all, even hell exists through the eternal Word. "Only, everything has now become darkness. But here is where we see 'common grace': the eternal Light has not allowed the darkness to become the 'outermost' darkness. Had there been no separating, no restraining grace, nothing could have prevented the continually increasing darkness from turning into a pitch-dark night. But that restraining by common grace did happen."[75] This points to "an intentional act of the eternal Word. He [John] does not say that

---

70. I, 247.
71. I, 248.
72. I, 249.
73. I, 398.
74. I, 398–99.
75. I, 399. Cf. I, 409: Without common grace it would have become "an Egyptian darkness," but now it is tempered "to a darkening in heavy mists, but mists that nonetheless allow twilight to penetrate."

the Word *was* also in the darkness. That is understood. Rather, he says that the Word *shone* in the darkness—shone in such a way that the darkening could not progress further, that a twilight remained in the midst of the darkness. And that twilight in the midst of the darkness, those beams of light shining through the mists into the darkness—*that is common grace*."[76] The aspect of grace is accentuated by what John says as he continues: "And the light shineth in the darkness; *and the darkness comprehended it not*" (v. 5b, KJV). For that resistance allows us to see common grace "in a deeper sense as *grace*, compassionate grace, because the darkness fortified itself against this shining light, did not understand it, did not drink it in, and did not absorb it. Rather, to the extent possible, in self-delusion it tried to banish the light."[77]

Verse 9 ("The true light, which gives light to everyone, was coming into the world") also speaks clearly of common grace, according to Kuyper. "'Everyone' can only ... be understood through the beneficial effect that was given to all people by Christ,[78] head for head. And that effect is not a matter of particular grace, but can only be a matter of *common grace*. What applies to every person is not particular, but universal. And so we should not understand the words "coming into the world" as applying to the Light, but to each person. The light shines on all persons from the moment of their arrival on earth, that is, from their birth as human beings. This is something that the Annotators of the Dutch States Bible correctly explained as the light of reason 'that remained in fallen humanity in order to give them some knowledge of God's nature and service, but not extending to salvation.' Rather, it was 'common grace' that found expression in the fact that the eternal Word did not leave the world, but continued to shine his Light in it."[79]

5. *Romans 1 and 2*. In broad strokes Paul portrays "godlessness in *idolatry*, and unrighteousness in the most extreme immorality."[80] But one may not say that this world, over which God's wrath is

---

76. Loc. cit.
77. Loc. cit.
78. The name "Christ" can lead to confusion. But it seems clear that Kuyper did not contemplate an enlightenment only *after* Bethlehem; cf. I, 404.
79. I, 404–05.
80. I, 410.

revealed, has become a hell. Rom 1:32 ("Though they know God's righteous decree...") and Rom 2:14–15 ("when Gentiles, who do not have the law, by nature do what the law requires, they are a law to themselves, even though they do not have the law. They show that the work of the law is written on their hearts, while their conscience also bears witness, and their conflicting thoughts accuse or even excuse them") declare otherwise.[81]

Kuyper makes the following remarks about Rom 2:14 and 15:

The Gentiles still have something written in their hearts. God has not completely taken away his original spiritual work in humanity from fallen sinners, but has left "a certain divine handwriting in their hearts."[82] But it does not say that the Gentiles "still have *the law* itself written in their hearts, but only the 'work of the law,' as if to suggest a practical inclination rather than a pure knowledge. Whatever one may say to detract from this, it states clearly that in the hearts of fallen sinners there is always something left of the original divine handwriting."[83]

This remnant of the law in the heart of fallen sinners "is kept alive in them up to a certain point by divine grace. For it says further that 'their conscience also bears witness,' that is, it bears witness to this remnant of the law in their hearts and says Amen to it."[84]

When it says that "their conflicting thoughts accuse or even excuse them," i.e., declare them not guilty, this "private and public pronouncement of judgment on each other" points to the fact that God "maintained certain general concepts about justice and injustice, about good and evil, in human society by his common grace."[85] When the apostle says: "For when the Gentiles, who do not have the law [of Sinai], by nature do what the law requires," then they not only know the law, but do it also. If it is true that even children of God declare that they are 'unable to conceive of any good of themselves, let alone to do good,' then it must follow that also the Gentiles do good not of themselves or in their own

81. I, 411.
82. II, 17.
83. II, 18–19.
84. II, 19.
85. II, 20–21.

strength, but only because common grace drives them to do so and enables them."[86]

However, it is a fact that people resist common grace. "As John says that 'the darkness did not comprehend the light,' so Paul also declares that 'the truth' continues to shine in this unrighteous situation but that we in our 'unrighteousness suppress the truth.' Our vision may have become very dim, but with a certain effort we are able to discern some glimmering of the light. Only we do not *want* to see it and we deliberately close our eyes so that we cannot see it. No matter how heavy the mists may be, the light still breaks through, but we deliberately raise dust clouds in order to make the mists even heavier and more impenetrable. That is how it is when we do not call on, welcome, and attract the light that seeks us, the truth that urges itself on us, but banish, exclude, and suppress them in our unrighteousness. The doctrine of common grace is therefore made clear and obvious also here. The dullness did not increase, but was arrested. The light of truth definitely did not withdraw itself completely, but continued to shine. It is entirely our fault when the light does not penetrate to our soul's eye. There is common grace, but we reject it."[87]

There *is* common grace. That is evident even from idolatry. "All idolatry is evidence of an impulse to worship. An animal does not worship God, but it does not commit idolatry either. Those lost in hell do not worship the Eternal One, but they also do not commit idolatry. Suppose therefore that sin, unbridled and not arrested, had brought our human race immediately to a total and complete confusion and brutalization. Then idolatry could never have occurred. The fact that wherever humans lived, idolatry arose is thus proof that the human impulse to worship remained. That would not have been possible if common grace had not arrested and stopped the total brutalization of humanity."[88] The impulse to worship is therefore not a figment of one's imagination, but rests on "a work of God in the human heart and in the human world." For God is still revealed *in the sinner* (Rom 1:19: "For what can be known about God is plain to them, because God has shown it to them"),

86. II, 21.
87. I, 412.
88. I, 412–13.

and *in the world* (Rom 1:20: "For his invisible attributes, namely, his eternal power and divine nature, have been clearly perceived, ever since the creation of the world.")[89] The last text also tells us that common grace is nothing new. Kuyper states that "ever since the creation of the world" means the following: "Thus, there was not a *new* revelation; rather, the revelation which radiated in creation is preserved, continued, and maintained by common grace over against the destruction by curse and sin."[90] A "real possibility to know God," a knowledge "of God and of his justice," persisted.[91]

It is not possible to conceive of idolatry without common grace, says Kuyper. But why is idolatry then still possible when God withdraws his common grace from nations "in religious and moral domains," as Romans 1 shows, according to Kuyper? (I, 421, 422, 425, 429, 430). In fact, idolatry thrives when God has given the nations up "in the wrong sense" (Rom 1:24, 26, 28). This "giving up," according to Kuyper, coincides with the withdrawal of common grace!

6. *Revelation 21:24 and 26 – "And the kings of the earth will bring their glory into it."* Of these verses Kuyper says: "This is not about any period *preceding* the end, but rather about the final outcome itself as it will be displayed on the new earth and the new heaven, after the conclusion of the judgment, as the *abiding new situation.* Immediately after these words follows the *last* chapter of Revelation and the ceasing of every vision."[92] Further, it is not doubtful what is meant by the phrase "the glory and the honor of the nations." Kuyper explains that it refers to "the continuing communal development that our entire human life has attained and will still attain in the history of the nations. And of this gain, which is of course nothing else than the fruit of common grace, it is now said that it will not simply perish and be destroyed in the universal conflagration. Rather, this gain will have a continuing significance, also for the new Jerusalem, i.e., for the new earth, for this glory and honor that our human race will have attained will also be brought into the new Jerusalem."[93] We should not visualize this "bringing into" as a mechanical process. "No book, no work of art, no product

89. I, 413.
90. I, 414.
91. Loc. cit.
92. I, 463.
93. I, 464–65.

as such will be brought in. But while "all *forms* in which the fruit of common grace is currently displayed will be destroyed," the powerful *seed* which underlies all this" will not be destroyed. God will give this seed a new form that is in holy harmony with the glory of his kingdom."[94]

§ 4. Appeal to the Confession

In support of his doctrine of common grace, Kuyper appeals to the following passage in art. 14 of the Belgic Confession: "Since man became wicked and perverse, corrupt in all his ways, he has lost all his excellent gifts which he had once received from God. He has nothing left but some small traces,[95] which are sufficient to make man inexcusable."

According to Kuyper, these *rudera* (small remnants), or *scintillae* (little sparks) can only be explained on the basis of common grace. For sin, without being arrested by common grace, would have deprived people of everything. But "when we consider someone like Kant, for example, we cannot say that all his excellent gifts were taken away. For he possessed an outstanding intelligence. There is a great difference between Kant and one who is insane. When we enter a psychiatric institution we can see what becomes of human beings if they are deprived of their excellent gifts and clear consciousness. Then we appreciate that when we build up each other's knowledge, not all our excellent gifts are lost. Otherwise human consciousness would be complete derangement and insanity. Yet, in principle and in theory, sin has the intent and inclination to ruin the excellent gifts in human beings. Nevertheless, God has preserved these gifts through common grace, although not completely, as in the original human pair [before the Fall], but by way of *rudera*."[96]

Kuyper also appeals to the Canons of Dort, III/IV, 4. They also speak of what is left to a human being after the Fall, namely, "some light of nature, whereby he retains some notions about God, about

---

94. I, 465.
95. Cited thus far by Kuyper.
96. *Loc. de Magistratu*, 61–62.

natural things, and about the difference between what is honorable and shameful, and shows some regard for virtue and outward order." But the Canons continue: "so far is he from arriving at the saving knowledge of God and true conversion through this light of nature that he does not even use it properly in natural and civil matters. Rather, whatever this light may be, man wholly pollutes it in various ways and suppresses it by his wickedness. In doing so, he renders himself without excuse before God."

Kuyper quotes a portion of this passage in *De Gemeene Gratie*.[97]

Only a portion. In discussing art. 14 B.C. and C.D. III/IV, 4, in the context of the doctrine of common grace Kuyper nowhere quotes the last portion, which speaks of the fact that human beings are inexcusable because they (see C.D.) completely pollute and suppress the light of nature.

In addition it should be noted that Kuyper seldom appeals to the confessions and does not discuss the above-mentioned passages in greater detail.

More than once Kuyper equates the "light of nature," the *rudera* or *scintillae*, with common grace.

§ 5. Further definition

It is not possible in the context of this comparative study to give a complete account of everything Kuyper wrote about common grace. But there are some essential points that cannot be omitted in a survey such as this if we are to compare and judge them profitably.

1. *Common grace as divine act or disposition?* When you speak about grace, you can emphasize different aspects. You can discuss grace as undeserved favor, in which case the emphasis is on God's favorable disposition. But you can also demand full attention for grace as indicative of the act, the benefaction, that God (without obligation toward us) performs. It will become apparent that this distinction will play an important role in later discussions about common grace.

Not so in Kuyper's work. Nowhere in *De Gemeene Gratie* does he

---

97. II, 15.

provide a broader analysis of his concept of grace. However, on close reading, the following becomes clear.

Kuyper does not neglect to point to God's grace as disposition. For example, he speaks of compassionate grace[98] and of mercy.[99] Both civil good (common grace) and salvific good (particular grace) derive "from the compassion of our God."[100]

However, we must be careful not to draw far-reaching conclusions from such expressions, which appear only rarely in Kuyper's work. Those who are tempted to conclude that Kuyper is referring to the love of God for all his creatures are warned and corrected by later expressions of his. We think here particularly of what Kuyper says about God's patience: "Among the 'virtues of God' it is his 'patience' which, although not exhausted in 'common grace,' is glorified in a remarkable way. God's holiness and majesty reacts against all sin, not just in part, but completely in the most absolute sense. If this operation of God's holiness against sin were to occur immediately, without further ado, in all its dreadfulness, there would be no 'common grace.' But our God is not only holy, but in his holiness he is also patient, and it is in his patience that the divine forbearance of the Almighty endures sin temporarily. That is how 'common grace' was born."[101] If one wants to understand Kuyper's reference to God's mercy and compassion correctly, one must not forget that common grace only postpones God's wrath. "God's patience means that he postpones his wrath, that he delays the vengeance of his justice for a time and, consequently, makes room to allow common grace to operate."[102]

Even stronger: On the terrain of common grace God's "wrath always operates in and through all things, and common grace does not remove the wrath, but merely mitigates and alleviates it in its execution."[103] And: "Those who are not converted remain children of wrath." They find no rest, "because God's wrath does not cease."[104] For that reason Kuyper could state a little earlier: "Although

---

98. I, 399.
99. II, 466.
100. II, 52. Cf. I, 291; II, 506.
101. I, 10.
102. I, 243.
103. II, 420.
104. II, 420–21.

'common grace' tempers this wrath, it never has the consequence that there might be a neutral terrain on earth on which neither wrath nor common grace rests. The expression 'God is never neutral' applies here too. And whatever place, whatever circumstance you might conceive of, that circumstance is always the result either of God's wrath or of his operative grace. But in this you can distinguish particular grace and common grace: when particular grace operates, wrath disappears completely to allow only grace to rule ...; but on the terrain of common grace, wrath always operates in and through all things and common grace does not remove wrath."[105] In the absence of God's patience, "neither *saving* nor *common* grace would be conceivable. It is always this patience that forms the indispensable background to all saving grace.[106]

The above clearly demonstrates that this patience on the terrain of common grace cannot be equated with "mercy" or "compassion" by itself. To do justice to the way Kuyper represents God's disposition toward the non-elect, we must recognize that postponement of wrath, or even its being maintained, is in his view an indispensable aspect of common grace.

In most instances Kuyper speaks of common grace as an operation, an act that proceeds from God. Common grace then forms the composition of those factors that make world history possible and effectuate it, despite Adam's fall. A few citations will illustrate this: "With 'common grace' it is important to see clearly that this involves an act of God..., an act of God that extends to the entire earth and the whole of our human race."[107] Many times Kuyper speaks of the operation of common grace. Not only sin but also grace operates in the world.[108] Common grace "is a powerful act of God that governs all of human life" and that has arrested the operation of the poison of sin in a miraculous manner.[109]

Also in the absence of a focus on God's disposition, Kuyper

---

105. II, 420. Cf. *Loc. de Providentia*, 247, 245 dictation ("God is never neutral.")
106. I, 243.
107. I, 94.
108. II, 289.
109. I, 243.

speaks of grace here, because human beings did indeed receive a completely undeserved "stay of execution."[110]

2. *Frightful grace.* The extent to which Kuyper almost exclusively pays attention to common grace as an act of God is convincingly apparent in his speaking of "frightful grace."[111] Kuyper uses this term to describe the "ocean of human misery"[112] that came into existence at the same time as God's display of grace. For if Adam and Eve had suffered physical death immediately after their fall, "the number of those who were doomed would have been limited to two, and the curse over the earth would not have happened. Further, all the untold misery would have been avoided, which now, because of sin and as a consequence of sin, has been poured out as a stream century after century."[113] Already in Adam. "It is difficult for us now to conceive of the situation in which Adam spent his long existence of not less than nine centuries after the Fall. Undoubtedly our hearts would flinch if we were required to endure such an existence, even if it were only for a lifetime of fifty years."[114]

Kuyper does not take this lightly and returns to this question again and again. When he speaks about the increase in sin during the end time, he calls common grace the reason "why in the end time unrighteousness will be revealed in such a frightful way in the 'man of lawlessness,' the 'son of perdition.'"[115] Even if unrighteousness would always have appeared, either with or without common grace, "only common grace gives it this refined form."[116] The same common grace makes its weaponry available both to evil and to virtue.[117]

The manifestation of common grace has more shadow sides to it. Sinners say of themselves in self-deception—"in which sin, strongly muzzled by common grace, necessarily catches the sinner"—that they are not so bad after all.[118] Idolatry, which derives

---

110. I, 95.
111. Term found in I, 215.
112. I, 216.
113. I, 215.
114. II, 608.
115. I, 447.
116. Loc. cit. Cf. II, 625.
117. I, 448.
118. I, 277.

from the need to worship, presupposes common grace since it maintains in people the urge to worship.[119]

So it is completely understandable that Kuyper states, "Through the same operation by which a common *grace* becomes ours, a common *dis-grace* can become ours also, if we may phrase it that way."[120] Common grace "works by means of an instrument that can lead to good as well as to evil."[121]

Kuyper does not assert these things casually. They must be regarded as integral to his doctrine of common grace. Already before he in 1894 began his series of articles on common grace in *De Heraut*, he had pointed out "the antithesis between the positive and negative development of the *gratia communis*" in his *Encyclopaedie der Heilige Godgeleerdheid*, II, 253 (1st edition, 1894).

3. *Why then "grace"?* One can ask why Kuyper, who recognized both aspects of development (good and evil) in common grace, continued to speak of "grace" with respect to the "mixed existence"[122] after the Fall.

Kuyper recognized this difficulty and responded to it as follows: "If you ask whether the term 'common grace' does not contradict itself when it is called 'grace' but leads to the strongest manifestation of sin, then you will have to draw sharp distinctions at this point. The cross of Golgotha is and remains the zenith of particular grace, and yet it is on Golgotha that human wickedness reached its nadir. Is this a contradiction? You know better. Well, it is no different here. In the complete development to which, under the protection of 'common grace,' our human life and human power over nature gradually advance, God is glorified. It is his plan, his work, that is evident in it. *He* had sown all these powers in the human field. Without common grace, the seed that was buried in that field would never have germinated, never have flourished. Thanks to common grace, it sprouted, it burgeoned, it shot up high into the stalks, and will in due course come out in full bloom, to the praise, not of human beings, but of God, the heavenly farmer. The skillful work of God that Satan wanted to destroy will then be complete after all and will reach its fulfillment. The world, when it

119. I, 412–13; *Encyclopaedie* II, 254.
120. II, 224.
121. Loc. cit.
122. II, 413.

is fully completed, will glorify God as Master Builder and Supreme Artist. What was only in bud in Paradise will then be in full flower. Only, just as humans misused Paradise and therefore had to be driven out from it, so also the man of lawlessness will try turn this entire system against God, and will therefore be consumed by God through the breath of his mouth."[123]

4. *Some distinctions.* The great breadth of common grace as Kuyper described it above, already makes us surmise that common grace is more than just "the arresting of sin and its consequences."[124] Common grace retains this negative character only when one compares it to particular grace. For the latter has "a positive goal, namely, to awaken a new and higher existence, to maintain it and to complete it in those who lay dead in their sins. In contrast, common grace only has a negative goal, namely, to arrest the complete development of the poison of sin."[125]

However, within common grace, Kuyper also wants to distinguish between a negative operation that prevents the outbreak of sin, and a positive operation that promotes the development of our natural power despite sin.[126] Common grace is then "that negative and positive act of God by which he has negatively arrested the continuing influence of Satan, death, and sin, and has positively called into being an interim period for both the cosmos and our human race, so that sin could not bring about its τέλος [telos], even though in principle human beings were and remained deeply sinful.[127] Kuyper has also pointed out the connection between the negative and positive factors of common grace. Sin wants to let the creative powers that are at work in us function in the opposite direction from what they were originally intended for. However, this ninety-degree turn was not executed completely. "God comes between the two, and by his common grace he arrests the turn in part [negative, J.D.] and ensures thereby that the operation does have effect to a certain point, in conformity

---

123. I, 452.
124. I, 246.
125. II, 243.
126. II, 246.
127. *Encyclopaedie* II, 231.

with God's will [positive, J.D.]."¹²⁸ How? Kuyper illustrates this with a couple of images. "When the wind is from the south, a ship departing from the Netherlands can only travel northwards if left to its own devices. But if the ship is equipped with a rudder that is turned, it will not go north, but will land in England, despite the direction of the wind. And what the rudder does to the ship, common grace does to sinful human beings. Their sinful inclination would drive them straight to absolute sin, but common grace turns them sideways, and that is how they arrive at civil justice. And yet, what drives the ship to England is not the rudder-stock, but the south wind. And so also, what causes sinful human beings to end up at civil justice is not the force of common grace, but the life that is at work from within them. Only, just as the rudder blocks movement in the right direction and turns the ship sideways, so also common grace arrests the operative power that drives them in a wrong direction and turns it in accordance with God's ordinance. But it does so in such a way that it is solely thanks to the rudder that the ship arrives where it should, and it is solely thanks to common grace, and not to the sinner, that civil justice comes into being."¹²⁹ Another image: "A ferry that crosses water on a chain, also called a cable ferry," would be carried away by the water's current; "nonetheless, it is that same force of the water which, now broken sideways, brings the ferry to the other side." Kuyper concludes: "If we are not mistaken, this answers the very difficult question how common grace, which does nothing else than arrest sin, still leads to some positive good."¹³⁰

The negative–positive distinction is found often in Kuyper in the context of the conceptual pair *constant–progressive*. The constant operation of common grace "consists in this, that God, with all differences of degree, arrests and reins in the curse of nature and the sin of the heart. The progressive operation, on the other hand, is that other operation which, by an ongoing process, arms human life always more abundantly against suffering and brings the inner life to a richer and fuller development."¹³¹ In this way the

128. *Gemeene Gratie* II, 307.
129. Loc. cit.
130. Loc. cit.
131. II, 606.

maintenance (constant factor) and the governing (progressive factor) in God's providence run parallel.[132]

Further, the operation of common grace must be distinguished according to the terrain on which it is active: "on the one hand on the moral-religious, and on the other hand on the intellectual-artistic terrains of our human life."[133] Kuyper also speaks here of common grace that directs itself to the inward or the outward aspects of our human life. The first form of common grace "operates wherever civil justice, domestic sense, natural affection, practice of virtue, sharpening of the public conscience, honesty, fidelity among people, and piety permeate life."[134] In contrast, the operation of common grace in the outward aspects of our life reveals itself "when the power of human beings over nature increases, discovery after discovery enriches life, a sense of community among nations is more rapidly achieved, the arts flourish, the sciences increase our knowledge, the comforts and pleasures of life multiply—when all manifestations of life show their luster, codes of conduct refine themselves, and the overall image of life gains in attractiveness."[135] Kuyper needs this distinction to declare how, at the end of days, despite all godlessness, "Babylon" can display the highest development that human life is capable of. In our discussion of Romans 1 we already saw that Kuyper speaks of a withdrawal of common grace when the nations act in a godless manner, although this withdrawal bears a restricted character: impoverishment of the inner life can go hand in hand with enrichment of the outward life. And that is how it will happen at the end of human history: "The common grace that operates on the human heart, human relationships, and public customs will shrink and be reduced, and only that other operation of common grace which enriches and delights the human mind and the human senses will proceed to its fulfillment—a most beautifully whitewashed mausoleum, but for those who open it, full of dry and reeking dead bones. The most dazzling life on the outside, but death in its heart—such is the Babylon that will ripen for judgment.

132. II, 605.
133. I, 427.
134. I, 456
135. Loc. cit.

And when you compare the brilliance of human life at present with the dullness of life in the preceding century, you know what the outcome will be and what judgment you now already have to pronounce on that unprecedented rich development of our outward human life."[136]

Common grace can shrink, but it will nowhere and never withdraw itself completely before world history has come to an end.[137]

Kuyper recognizes one exception to this: "Only once was common grace completely withheld, namely in Judas, when Satan entered into his heart" (II, 428). W. H. Velema correctly observes in his *De leer van de Heilige Geest bij Kuyper*, 94, that it is impossible to justify this distinction. Besides, Kuyper contradicts himself when he posits (I, 247) that common grace even operated in Judas' remorse. See § 6, 4, for the distinction between *general* and *special* action within common grace.

5. *Triumph over Satan.* Those who read *De Gemeene Gratie* in such a way that they are able to distinguish main from side issues will quickly notice that Kuyper seldom directs his attention to God's disposition toward human beings (see points 1-3, *supra*), because he wants to place a much more important theme in the foreground, namely, God's honor, which God maintains by means of common grace (anchored in predestination) over against Satan: "What Satan intended in Paradise was to inflict the *coup de grâce* directly on the whole of God's creation and to administer the deadly stab to God's people." It was not merely about his "filching a couple of souls from God. No, it was a much bolder and broader attempt to frustrate and prevent construction when the first foundations of the building barely rose above the ground. This attempt was designed to ensure that the great Master Builder and Artist would be embarrassed by the failure of his own work. And this is what common grace turned around. The construction begun by God was *not* stopped and *not* frustrated."[138] What God had intended was fulfilled: "In a broad division into all kinds of peoples and nations, tongues and languages, with very different degrees of development, God was

---

136. I, 456.
137. I, 429-30.
138. II, 120-21. Cf. I, 354; *Loc. de Christo* III, 39.

able to bring forth all the treasures that he had hidden in our human race. Among those nations and peoples he raised geniuses and heroes, great philosophers and artists, who used what he gave them to uncover those treasures for the human race, so that century after century the spiritual possession of humanity would increase in meaning and value. Apart from those heroes and geniuses, he in the life of those nations has also elicited morals and regulations, customs and laws, that caused their bravery and courage, civil sense and moral seriousness, to develop. Out of this gold, God poured out all the ornaments that he intended and displayed them before the admiring eyes of humankind."[139]

Had the "all-important benefit" of the triumph over Satan not been at stake, "then casting Adam and Eve into eternal death and thereafter newly creating the elect would have had everything in its favor. Think only of what horrors of sin would have been curtailed thereby, what human suffering would have been prevented, and especially how in that way the wretches now consigned to eternal death would never have been born."[140] Frightful grace! But there was indeed an all-important benefit in not proceeding with a "new creation." "This could, of course, be an all-important benefit only to God, because for humankind it would have been much more pleasing if those wretches had never been born. The efficient cause [the agent that initiates the process of change] could therefore lie only in this, that such a new creation would have amounted to a failure of the first creation—a frustration of God's governance and work by Satan's governance and work—and that the honor, the majesty and exalted position, of our God demanded that Satan be denied this triumph over the Lord our God."[141]

6. *Predestination.* If we want to understand Kuyper's doctrine of common grace properly, we must appreciate how he regards common grace, by which God triumphs over Satan, as anchored in predestination. He is critical of our Reformed fathers,[142] because they understood predestination almost exclusively "as a decree of

---

139. II, 121.
140. I, 244.
141. Loc. cit.
142. Kuyper notes this error also in Thomas Aquinas, II, 104.

God concerning the eternal weal and woe of his rational creatures."[143] For that way the vision of God's broad work is restricted. "So long as in your thoughts you abandon the rest of God's creation, have regard only to humans and angels, and do not ask any other question than what the outcome will be for humans and angels, you operate in a vacuum and let go of the organic connection between rational creatures and God's creation as a whole. In such a representation the salvation of the elect becomes the main point. That is the goal on which everything is focused.... In such a line of reasoning the lot of the reprobate is a side issue insofar as, from their point of view, nothing happens than that the spiritual pestilence they suffer functions in them unto eternal death. Nothing further is to be said about them than that they are not saved, and for the rest they are just earmarked *pro memoria*."[144] In this way we isolate humankind from the rest of creation, and the unity, the coherence, of God's creation is broken.

However, in predestination God's attention is directed toward the entire creation. "This leads us to an entirely different representation, namely, that predestination has the goal of giving God the certainty that nothing of the complete self-glorification that he sought through and in his creative work will escape him, but that he will receive it unbroken and unhindered. Satan threatened to frustrate this goal of creation. Predestination is thus to be distinguished in this, and only in this, from the creation decree, that predestination points out and determines the means that will, with complete certainty, ensure that God, despite sin, will nonetheless eventually receive full self-glorification from his creation.... In this way, the decree of predestination encompasses the totality of history, the entire course that earth and heaven will run, and is directed toward the end, in order that from this entire creation and the entire cosmos God may receive the honor due to him."[145] In this way we do not reduce our attention to the operation of particular grace, but continue to focus our attention on "that completely different work of God in the realm of common grace. And that work of common grace encompasses all the life of the world—the

143. II, 95.
144. II, 95.
145. II, 108.

life of the Bantu peoples in Africa, of the Mongols in China and Japan, and of the Indians south of the Himalayas. In all previous centuries there was nothing among Egyptians and Greeks, in Babylon and Rome, and there is nothing today among the peoples of whatever continent, that was or is not needed, that does not all form an indispensable part of the great work that God is doing to bring the world's development to its consummation. And although much in all this we cannot connect with matters of the Kingdom or with the content of our faith, nevertheless it all has significance. None of it can be spared, because it pleases God, despite Satan's devices and human sin, to actualize what he had put into the world at the time of creation, to persevere in its realization, and to develop it so completely that the full sum of the vital energies of his creation will be disclosed at the consummation of the world."[146]

Kuyper develops this in particular with respect to human life on earth. "The long course of the ages and the rich development of the human race in that course [has] at the same time a goal in itself and further serves all kinds of other goals. It most certainly serves a purpose in arriving at the number of the elect. It most certainly serves to let us follow a process that has significance for eternity. But all this does not prevent it from being, at the same time, an *independent* goal, *so that all that was hidden as seeds in our race will be brought to light, to the glory and praise of God's name*. And only on that standpoint will our worldview attain rest" (II, 626). Only in that way can the immeasurable number of human beings be explained. For each human being displays something unique of the image of God that God has created in humankind. But this image is "a concept that is much too rich to be realized in one single human being" (II, 627). And, "our [human] race will only be complete when all possibilities of the reflection of God's image in our race will have been exhausted. Then it ends. Not before" (II, 629).

Kuyper's purpose here is to introduce a correction in Reformed theology with respect to the image of God. In his view this has always been seen as pertaining to the individual and was also developed exclusively from the perspective of salvation. There has been no awareness of the social aspect of humankind's being created in God's image, which, "of course, has no connection with salvation, nor with everyone's personal state before God. This social element means only that when God created human beings in his image, he placed an endless multitude of seeds in our nature, and that these cannot develop *except by way of the social relationships among people*. You will appreciate that, seen in this light, the broad subdivision of human development attains a

146. II, 623.

significance of its own, an independent goal, a reason for existence apart from the matter of salvation" (II, 629–30; cf. III, 493, 387–88).

This theory of Kuyper's about humanity as organism in which all persons have their own necessary and indispensable place ("Nothing about it has been purposeless or superfluous" [II, 623]) conflicts with Kuyper's definition of the organism of the elect as the new humanity in which "together, all data for our human life, all powers and talents that are conceivable among people, and all human types, variations, and possibilities are so completely present that they supplement each other mutually and together form the synthesis of the human race" (*Loc. de Deo*, III, 254 dictation). See also *Gemeene Gratie* II, 100–01. For when Kuyper explains this description he is forced to say that, "in accordance with creation, the human race was created in such a way *that it exists in a plenitude that is an excessive, superfluous lavishness*. But that superfluity disappears, while *the integral remains*" (*Loc. de Deo* III, 255–56). Cf. Noah's family as "the noblest shoot from the stem of the ancient human race" (*Loc. de Foedere*, 127).

This same contradiction is apparent in Bavinck, *Reformed Dogmatics* II, 577ff. He is more careful than Kuyper. While the latter asserted that the image of God will be exhausted in the entire human race (see above), Bavinck says: "It can only be *somewhat* unfolded in its depth and riches in a humanity counting billions of members" (577, italics supplied). Bavinck also maintains that, "much more than was the case in the past the subject of common grace must be given its due also in the doctrine of the counsel of God" (392).

7. *Soli Deo Gloria*. Kuyper wants to impress upon his readers the development of all of creation's potential as an independent aspect of God's predestination: "You cannot have a good Reformed stance in life, and you will again be plagued with monastic ideas and Anabaptist avoidance, if you are not convinced of this fundamental truth."[147] The course of history exists not only "so that the church of God could find a place for itself."[148] For those who argue in this way commit the error of "seeking their own salvation rather than the honor of God."[149] "It is principally about God—not about human beings. Just as the Lord God causes his flowers to bloom on mountains and in valleys where no person has ever set foot, and on a thousand hills has his cattle from which no one has ever benefited, so also God has worked the wonder of his common grace for himself among all peoples and nations, also where it had no direct connection to the salvation of the elect."[150] In "common grace

147. II, 632.
148. I, 90. Also I, 26, 223, 357, 377–78; II, 52.
149. I, 223.
150. I, 254.

the Lord God seeks above all the self-glorification of his name. In that common grace itself already lies God's triumph over Satan, regardless of any other motive."[151]

Every locus of Reformed dogmatics does mention a twofold goal, the *Gloria Dei* and the *salus hominum*. But the Reformed have always "definitely ... placed in the foreground that human beings are never the motive for God's actions (*Loc. de Ecclesia*, 30; cf. *Gemeene Gratie*, II, 106).

This *theocentric*, instead of *anthropocentric*, orientation helps us understand much better that Kuyper does not concentrate extensively on common grace as God's disposition toward humankind. At bottom, it is God's inexorably hostile disposition toward Satan that is accompanied in its consequences for human beings by grace, but also ... frightful grace. You cannot reverse the order. In first instance it is about God's honor (over against Satan), but it is then that we can also speak of mercy (toward human beings).

8. *The necessity of common grace.* In *De Gemeene Gratie* we come across some passages that are of paramount importance for the evaluation of what Kuyper teaches. I am referring to what he writes about the connection between curse and creation. When sin entered the world, the curse had to follow. God willed "that as soon as the train of life derailed from the track of his ordinance, its momentum was interrupted and destruction began. That was the track of the creation ordinance. To have permitted anything else would have amounted to a renunciation of his divine majesty and a surrender of his divine plan of action to Satan or to a now sinful humanity."[152] Continuing to use the image of the "train of life" derailed by the Fall, Kuyper writes: "Imagine what would have happened if the derailed train of life had been able to proceed safely. It would then have become an endless deviation from the divine track, a constantly stronger outbreak of iniquity, a restless further deviation from communion with our God; in short, it would have been a continuing triumph of sin and Satan. It would have resulted in a world, human life, a human heart, that would ultimately have been forever without God. Everything that God had created would have found itself in one hell; hell would have become the only existing thing. The will of God that all derailments should and must be avenged in self-destruction is at bottom nothing else than the

---
151. II, 120.
152. II, 497.

will of God to maintain *his* governance in *his* ordinances, and to be neither able nor willing to tolerate that another plan of action, based on different ordinances, forced itself into its place."[153] Kuyper dares to put it in these terms: "We do not recoil from the pronouncement that the endless love of God for his fallen world was powerless to prevent this frightful consequence [curse on creation, J.D.]—a love that had been intended to save and that would have saved the world from suffering, but at the same time would have robbed the world of its God. For a God who in this way nullified the original plan of action that flowed out of his being and wisdom, would have ceased to be God."[154]

But just as the curse had to set in if God wanted to be[155] and remain[156] God, so he could not desist from opposing the curse for the same reason. "The derailed train of life would have been set back on the rails of his divine ordinance, and that same power that was now corrupted, would again have become a power that would bring the train of life, along the route of vocation, to within the gates of the heavenly Jerusalem."[157] For the self-destruction through the curse cannot have been God's actual intention. God had to stem and nullify it, for "creation has a purpose, and because the self-destruction opposes that purpose, it opposes God."[158] For that reason "it becomes clear that common grace could not be omitted from God's Counsel; indeed, thanks to the motive of common grace, the history of humanity could be included in the Counsel of God."[159] For, if the Fall is included in God's Counsel (and it is), "then, in that same Counsel, after the Fall the subsidence of this world into eternal corruption would have followed if common grace had not prevented this sudden collapse of the cosmos. Common grace therefore set in immediately after the Fall. However, and note this carefully, it did so not as an arbitrarily inserted aid, but as demanded directly by the end goal of God's Counsel," namely, the self-glorification of the triune God.[160] Therefore, Kuyper concludes:

153. II, 500. For the image of the train, see also *Loc. de Deo* III, 21.
154. II, 497.
155. II, 497.
156. II, 500
157. II, 497.
158. II, 503.
159. II, 611.
160. II, 611.

"If the Fall is included in God's Counsel, then it must follow that immediately after it not only particular grace but also common grace, as powerful motive, must be included. For if the Fall had not been followed also by common grace, the entire continuation of the world would for all time have been withdrawn from God's self-glorification. That would be unthinkable in God's Counsel, since it was especially the intention of God to glorify himself that determined the whole of God's Counsel."[161]

That is how Kuyper speaks about the necessity of the maintenance of this world,[162] and about common grace as an "essential link" in predestination.[163]

> The necessity of common grace: that is something different than the "necessity of the *doctrine* of common grace," with which I began my exposition of Kuyper's doctrine (§ 1). The facts led Kuyper to the doctrine of common grace. Now his dogmatic considerations in *De Gemeene Gratie* II lead to the argument of the necessity of common grace itself: it is necessary because of the self-glorification of God.
>
> Necessary—and yet *grace*? This question will not be answered here; I will merely demonstrate its reasonableness. After all, if common grace is an "essential link" in predestination since God *had to* turn back the self-destruction by the curse (if God wanted to be and remain God), does speaking about grace not become dubious now that we have looked into predestination "behind the scenes"? For "grace" surely implies: it could have happened in another way. Necessity means: it could not have happened in another way. When Kuyper asks us to imagine what would have happened if common grace had not come about and argues from that hypothesis to a display of grace toward us (see, e.g., § 3 about Gen 2:17), does his argument not become insubstantial? It is then a matter of positing something that could simply never have occurred. Is the concept of grace then not devalued to an anthropomorphic expression, which we recognize in its infantile deficiency once we, together with Kuyper, have passed the naïve phase of his exegesis of Gen 2:17 and have reached the final phase of predestination with common-grace-as-necessity? A comparison with particular grace will clarify this. In the case of particular grace, speaking about grace remains perspicuous. For it is and remains incomprehensible why the one is elect and the other is not. But after § 5, 8, it is completely understandable why we all share in common grace. Over against Satan, God could not abandon any of the seeds that were hidden in the human race. We are alive, and that is

---

161. II, 611–12.
162. II, 631.
163. II, 118.

also necessary. But is it still grace? According to *E Voto* II, 186: "Grace, because it is grace, is free."

We shall encounter more such questions in this study. I hope to answer them in chapter V.

§ 6. Panorama of the history of culture

Kuyper does not only posit that God will methodically let the history of our human race run its course. He also gives us in *De Gemeene Gratie* an image of the manner in which the historical process will display "what the creation order hid in the bud."[164] Note the following:

1. *From Paradise to the Flood*. According to Kuyper, this period comprises some sixteen centuries. Approximately one third of human history took place during this time period. From the few Scripture passages about this time it becomes clear "that the contending of God's Spirit with the human spirit was much more intense and much less sparing in the first sixteen centuries, while in the period after Noah it assumed a much more moderate form and less vehement character."[165] Kuyper bases this on Gen 6:3: "My Spirit shall not always strive with man, for that he also is flesh" (KJV). Further, one can discern from Gen 8:22 that the course of life before the Flood was characterized by great instability.[166] Also, Gen 6:5, compared with Gen 9:21, indicates that "the severe contending of God's Spirit with the human spirit had hardened the human spirit and thus the fruit of common grace had become almost completely lost."[167] Of course, one cannot assume "that God had made a mistake—as if, after first subjecting humanity to a severe test, the Lord realized after the fact that this could not continue and that humankind had become unmanageable as a result, and that for this reason he then first eliminated the failed generation in order to try again in a more prudent and effective way with humanity after the Flood."[168] For this period from Paradise to the Flood is

164. II, 28.
165. I, 274.
166. I, 274–75.
167. I, 275.
168. I, 276.

characterized by its pedagogic significance. God caused common grace initially to operate less strongly in order to show humanity by the outcome "what would become of the human race if grace operated less strongly and differently."[169] Facts and experience from this period must make clear "how the fallen human race, when left to its own devices, can succeed only in completely destroying itself."[170] Expressed in another way: "That first period is παιδαγωγὸς [pedagogue] to what came in the Noahic covenant, as the Sinaitic law is παιδαγωγὸς εἰς Χριστόν [pedagogue unto Christ]."[171]

Further, the culture of that first period was "so highly developed that major inventions took place and gifts and talents shone, which Calvin rightly ascribed to the Holy Spirit."[172]

2. *From Noah to Abraham.* The most important event the Bible informs us about from this time period is the disruption of the building of the tower of Babel. Its construction comprised a world plan "that directly conflicted with God's plan for the world" and can be described as follows: "Not to multiply too much, not to spread out over the earth, not to populate the whole earth, but to limit ourselves to forming one single relatively small nation, and to leave the rest of the earth unused."[173] But the building of the tower was frustrated, for God had a different plan. "In God's plan all the powers and gifts with which he had endowed our race would gradually be brought to light to the glory of his name. But according to this selfish plan for building the tower at Babel, all this would have been smothered and destroyed."[174] "God would make a name for himself according to the counsel and plan of the LORD of hosts, and the entire history of our race would result in the glorification of that name of our God."[175]

3. *From Abraham to Christ.* Kuyper has a serious objection to the fact that "after a cursory overview of the first eleven chapters of Genesis" the entire teaching of the church "focuses for the most

---

169. I, 277.
170. *Loc. de Foedere*, 124.
171. Op. cit.
172. *Loc. de Foedere*, 125; *Gemeene Gratie* I, 284–85.
173. I, 306–07.
174. I, 307.
175. Loc. cit.

part on particular grace and is generally silent about common grace."¹⁷⁶ For then we forget that the end goal of particular grace lies in the preservation of "the world created by God, maintained by him, and never abandoned."¹⁷⁷ Holy Scripture makes this very clear. "The concluding words in God's calling of Abraham do not specify that some of the nations will be incorporated into his family, but rather that *all* the families of the earth (and all the families of the earth together surely constitute our human race) shall be blessed in him."¹⁷⁸ Thus "the point of departure in Abraham's call ... is immediately and in a high and full sense as universalistic as possible, and definitely encompasses not only the Jews but *all* the families of the earth.¹⁷⁹

We have neglected too much, says Kuyper, the fact that Genesis 12–26 literally says nothing about a strict segregation in Abraham's life. It cannot be denied "that not only in the wording of Abraham's call the emphasis falls on the blessing of 'the nations' as ultimate goal, but that in fact his entire journey to and his actions in Canaan, as well as his life as shepherd prince among the other princes of Palestine, involved seeking contact, establishing all kinds of connections, setting up all kinds of relationships, rather than his withdrawing and isolating himself."¹⁸⁰ The location of Canaan suggests the same thing. "God had planned and ordained that Palestine, being situated at the crossroads of the Middle East, would serve the coming of his kingdom. With Babylonia and Persia to the east, Egypt to the south, Greece to the north, and Rome to the west, Palestine formed the center of what would become 'the great world empire' in Jesus' day. In God's call to Abraham the emphasis falls much more on the land than on the people who lived there. Abraham had to go the 'the *land* that God would show him.' And the Scriptures speak often of Mount Zion as 'the *place* of rest' that God had chosen for himself."¹⁸¹ Had "Abraham remained in Ur of the Chaldeans, he would have stayed in contact only with his own people. And precisely through his transfer to Palestine, he

---

176. I, 318.
177. I, 319; cf. I, 357.
178. I, 322–23.
179. Loc. cit.
180. I, 325.
181. I, 326.

was brought into contact with all the leading nations of those days. It is indeed true that he did not[182] enter into kinship with alien nations.... It is also unquestionable that when the transition from patriarchal to national life took place, the separation between Israel and the surrounding nations was for some time made complete by erecting a high dividing wall, both through God's plan and through his laws. Nevertheless, that temporary national isolation did not begin until after in the history of the patriarchs and particularly in the life of Abraham the broad foundations were laid for a higher development that would include all the nations and encompass the entire life of the world."[183]

Kuyper believes that this is clearly described in "the main events that portray Abraham's relationship to the nations in the ... encounter between Abraham and Melchizedek."[184] The significance of this history is *"that particular revelation, and therefore also particular grace, has only an interpolated significance; thus not particular revelation but the creation ordinance is lasting and enduring."*[185] For Melchizedek appears in Genesis 14 as the superior of Abraham (Heb 7:7). That superiority becomes apparent when he is described in Hebrews 7 as "priest of the Most High God," as "king of peace," and as "king of righteousness." This shows that his was a kingship and a priesthood that did not depend on his father or mother, nor on his genealogy. It had neither beginning nor end. He, more than Abraham, Aaron, and David, was therefore like the Son of God and was thus also his exemplar and reflection. That kingship and priesthood conjoined in him did not arise from a particular act of salvation, but out of the original ordinance of God."[186] Melchizedek possessed his priestly dignity "not according to a particular revelation of salvation, but according to the original creation ordinance that called man as man to rule in the Lord's name as *king* over his creation, to bring him the sacrifice of love and praise as *priest*, and to declare his name as *prophet*."[187] In Melchizedek we see "a final glimmer of the

---

182. The word "not" was omitted in the original.
183. I, 343–44.
184. I, 331. Also 331–338; *Loc. de Christo* I, 104; III, 73 dictation, 89ff.
185. I, 333.
186. I, 336.
187. I, 337.

priesthood that God himself instituted in Paradise."[188] That "final glimmer" testifies in its superiority over Abraham "that in Christ, in his Gospel, and in his Kingdom we are to honor not a continuation of the temporary, temporal, and transient revelation of salvation in Israel, but on the contrary, a manifestation in glory of what was intended in God's creation ordinance but was destroyed by sin."[189]

In that way the isolation of Israel can only be an intermezzo.[190]

We must pay close attention here. The quotation reproduced in the text at footnote 185, could give the impression that particular revelation in its entirety (including particular grace) constitutes an intermezzo. The quotation presented in the text at footnote 189, already clarifies Kuyper's intention: particular grace in Christ joins the creation ordinance and thereby stamps particular revelation (particular grace), as it was given shape in Israel, as an intermezzo. Christ (particular grace) is concerned about the *world* (common grace). Particular grace has "no other import or purpose than to save both the world and our human nature entirely in a universalistic sense. Israel serves the nations, and the fruit of Israel's suffering is that the nations enter into God's kingdom" (I, 338).

Kuyper felt strongly about his exegesis of Gen 14 and Heb 6 and 7. "It was *De Heraut* that first felt bound on more than one occasion to draw the attention of Reformed Christianity again to what Paul called 'pressing on to perfection,' by stating that the summary content of this important matter is no less than that the doctrine that ..." (and then follows the quotation in the text at footnote 185).

4. *Christ and common grace.* This topic warrants discussion in much greater detail. What Kuyper said about the previous periods was prelude for the universal significance of Christ's work.

(a) *The fullness of time.* Through his common grace, God prepared the world for Christ's coming. Holy Scripture speaks of the "fullness of time, and this means that not all times are equal. There are times of preparation, times in which a particular process operates unnoticed, and then also times in which that process is complete and has borne fruit. And then a state begins that depends entirely upon what God had decided to bring into being in the 'fullness of time'"[191] This plan of God concerning the nations follows the route of common grace from beginning to end and was made

188. *Loc. de Christo* III, 92.
189. I, 338.
190. I, 338–45.
191. II, 173–74.

conceivable and possible only because of common grace. Thus "we do not exaggerate when we venerate *one* policy in the entire operation of common grace that ultimately converged all its rays in the work of Christ as in *one* focus. In that sense the cross of Golgotha is indeed the central point of world history, into which all streams flow as into an ocean and, conversely, from which, as from a fountain, all brooks of subsequent history flow."[192] That is how the world was made ready for the coming of Christ. What the worldwide church, upon entering the world, needed for making rapid progress was available: spiritual receptivity, historical maturity, and communion among the nations.[193]

(b) *The great mystery.* For a proper understanding of the various passages in the New Testament about the "great mystery" we must note "that on the one hand the mystery appears to be found simply in the incarnation of the Word, while on the other it is found in the inclusion of the nations. These two are always intertwined."[194] What Paul says can only be fathomed "when you understand that he presents you in your mind with these two—i.e., on the one hand the incarnation or coming of Christ, and on the other the calling of the Gentiles—as one and the same mystery, as entirely the same hidden thing. The meaning of this is: you do not understand the incarnation of the Word so long as you are unable to move beyond the fact that Jesus was born a Jew. This is an undeniable fact. For he himself said: 'Salvation is from the Jews.' But by itself you will not understand the incarnation. The Word did not become a Jew, but *flesh*."[195] All further specifics (that he was of Israel, of David, of Mary) are secondary. "The main point and goal remain that he assumed human nature, the flesh and blood of Adam, the nature of our human race, that by which throughout the entire world humans as human are distinguished from all creatures."[196]

The meaning of this is clear. Christ's incarnation would save the world. "Had his birth as Jew been the main or essential point, and had the Son of God assumed Jewish nature but not human nature, he would be the Savior of the Jews, but not the Savior of humanity

192. II, 174.
193. II, 174ff.
194. I, 348.
195. I, 348–49.
196. I, 340–50.

as such."[197] But Christ assumed not the Jewish but the universal human nature.[198] Holy Scripture mentions eighty-eight times that he is the Son of *man*.[199]

Kuyper from the start emphasized this idea of Christ's universal human nature, especially because of Christ's organic communion with humanity. See *Uit het Woord*, 2nd series I, 50–51, 122; *Loc. de Christo* II, 3 dictation, 8–9, 33; *E Voto* I, 323; II, 275; *Gemeene Gratie* II, 142ff. I shall not indicate here what further consequences flow from this idea in Kuyper's view. For our topic it is sufficient to establish, also here, that Kuyper describes the person and work of Christ as encompassing all of humanity and the world, and therefore he wants to give them pride of place in the work of common grace.

(c) *Christ and world history*. With the coming and work of Christ, "a golden cord" begins to run "through all of history since Golgotha."[200] Although "one can observe in a certain respect even a wondrous development of common grace in regions and countries that to this point remained outside the current of Christian influence," that development took place "outside the historical development of our human race as a whole, and it is not through these countries and these nations that the broad current of common grace propels itself toward fulfillment."[201] What we find in Mexico and Peru, in India, in China and Japan, and in the Muslim world does show that "the fruit of common grace among these nations was very abundant," but also "that this fruit was restricted to these nations and did not benefit our human race as such."[202] We see here an "isolated operation of common grace that, restricted by time and place, benefits a few population groups but has only a limited power of development. Once that limit is reached," this common grace either stops or recedes and petrifies.[203]

Apart from this kind of operation of common grace, "there is a totally different kind that supports the life of our race as race and helps our human life as such to move forward and bring us further. The fruit of this action of common grace is a human development

197. I, 350.
198. Loc. cit.
199. I, 352.
200. II, 177.
201. Loc. cit.
202. II, 180.
203. II, 181–82.

that does not attach itself to any one population group, but is intended as blessing for all nations. It is a development that is not tied to a particular era, but steadily advances throughout the course of all ages. It is a development that is not bound to a certain *limit* of progress, but always continues to stride along and in each new century takes giant steps forward, not only in one, but in all areas of human life."²⁰⁴ "What you observe in ancient America, in China, in Japan, and India, and in part also in the Islamic world," belongs to the first kind of operation of common grace as special action. We see the second kind of operation as general action of common grace in service of our human race in "the human development that began in Babylon and Egypt, then thrived for a time in Greece and Rome, next was taken up by Christianity, and since then has, under the auspices of the cross of Christ, propagated itself already for some eighteen centuries in Europe and America."²⁰⁵ There was no human development in this more general sense prior to Golgotha.²⁰⁶

Thus the special development of common grace occurs outside of the Christian religion, while "that general action of common grace was tied to the Christian religion and only through the Christian religion reached its powerful growth."²⁰⁷ Here we see the historical significance of Christ for the world. If we keep in mind that his work did not end with his ascension, but truly began only with his being seated at God's right hand, it becomes clear "that Christ was completely bound to the general line of common grace for this second work of his, if we may call it that, and how, conversely, this general action of common grace is entirely controlled by Christ."²⁰⁸ When Rome and Greece, after Babylon and Egypt, had come to ruin, the leadership of the nations was entrusted to the worldwide church of the New Testament and "from that moment on, common grace [walked in] those new rich paths that were opened to it under the Christian religion. What we currently call the Christian world in Europe and America, displays the highest form of development of our human race that has been

204. II, 182.
205. Loc. cit.
206. II, 246.
207. II, 182.
208. Loc. cit.

known so far in the course of the centuries, and everything suggests that this development is destined to progress further and further. It is not yet apparent whether the turning away from Christianity that has begun will continue and whether the appalling struggle that will mark the end of the current age is already approaching. If this is the case, then, of course, the turning point in the progress of our human development has already been reached. But our argument is not directed to this. For then we would be confronting the beginning of a catastrophe and history itself would be approaching its final milestone. But even without wanting to glimpse behind the curtain that obscures this future from us, in our opinion the result of history is certain, namely that the general action of common grace, as it arose in Babylon and Egypt, and in Greece and Rome, was taken up by Christianity and, under Christ's direction, reached that general human development of which one can say that history, not of the individual nations but of humanity, truly began then. And thus we may say that common grace was prepared by the Father for the Son, not only to make the incarnation possible, to allow him to live as 'Son of man' among us, to offer him the form and language of his Gospel, to establish his redeeming work by his death under Pontius Pilate, and to make possible the wondrous entry of the Christian church into the Roman empire. Rather, it served a greater purpose in addition, namely that this same common grace was prepared by the Father for the Son to make possible the general development of our human race, indeed, a history of humankind in the richest, deepest sense of the word, in and through Christ"[209]—a history that makes the triumph of Christian Europe over the world complete. "The Christian nations together form barely one-third of the earth's population. Yet everyone knows that when the Christian nations stand together, neither heathendom nor Islam can do anything."[210]

1. Those who read and admire the chapter "*Christus en de wereldhistorie*" [Christ and World History], (*Gemeene Gratie* II, 177ff.) will not be able to express their feelings better than Arnold A. van Ruler did: "One can undoubtedly criticize" Kuyper's construct, "including the idea of one stream over against many lakes

209. II, 183–84.
210. II, 247.

and pools, and also what he says concerning the dominating significance of Christianity in the European-American cultural sphere.... But that aside, what an exceptionally impressive apologetic for the absolute and universal significance of Christianity! What a profoundly subtle orientation of common grace in the totality of the plan for the world! What a brilliant solution to the relationship between common grace and particular grace! One *must* have admiration for the broad appeal, the great intellectual force, the intrepid boldness of this historical-philosophical construct in connection with the dogmatic and cultural-theoretical problems in the concept of Christian culture. It contains something uncommonly fascinating" (*Kuyper's idee eener Christelijke cultuur*, 40).

2. There is much difference of opinion about the connection between particular and common grace. I will return to that later. But we do *see* the connection before us here. Without Christ, the world does not reach its actual development and one cannot "speak of a human development in a general sense" (II, 246). In Christ the powers hidden in our humanness by God "will light up and display the radiance of his original plan of action" (II, 248). It is easy to identify dualism in Kuyper's comparison of particular grace and common grace, but to come to a fair assessment about it without having seen and admired the unity of both is impossible. The sixth of Kuyper's Stone Lectures provides indisputable evidence of how he was convinced of the coherence of common grace and particular grace, of which only the latter could truly cause the world to progress according to Calvinistic foundational principles ("*Calvinisme en de toekomst*," in *Het Calvinisme*, 156–83). Kuyper's important vision justifies the words of Th. L. Haitjema, that "behind Kuyper's founding a university glowed the powerful ideal of a re-Christianized European culture. In his daring dreams of the future in 1880, Kuyper envisioned the Free University as becoming the cradle of a new European cultural life in which God's Word would form that all-encompassing center" (*Onder eigen Vaandel*, vol. 6, 38). The conclusion of the sixth Stone Lecture attests to Kuyper's belief in a future that includes Calvinism: "Unless God send forth his Spirit, there will be no turn, and fearfully rapid will be the descent of the waters. But you remember the Aeolian Harp, which men were wont to place outside their casement, that the breeze might wake its music into life. Until the wind blew, the harp remained silent, while, again, even though the wind arose, if the harp did not lie in readiness, a rustling of the breeze might be heard, but not a single note of ethereal music delighted the ear. Now, let Calvinism be nothing but such an Aeolian Harp—absolutely powerless, as it is, without the quickening spirit of God—still we feel it our God-given duty to keep our harp, its strings tuned aright, ready in the window of God's Holy Sion, awaiting the breath of the Spirit" (*Calvinism: Six Lectures Delivered in the Theological Seminary at Princeton*, 274–75).

(d) *Christ's power over nature.* There are some expressions in *De Gemeene Gratie* that could easily escape our attention if we did not know from another work of Kuyper how far-reaching they are. One of these is his statement that "in the Christian regions of the world the dominion over nature, assigned to us in Paradise but lost subsequently, has been given back to us in such a remarkable fashion.... All this is the fruit of common grace, and we confess that this grace continues to work so wonderfully because the hidden power of the Christian religion strengthened and preserved it in order to free the human spirit more and more from the curse."[211] The extraordinary power that humanity gained over nature in the Christian regions of the world we owe to the "natural sciences, which blossomed not in China or Japan, not in India or in Turkey, but in Christian Europe and in Christian America. One can therefore say with certainty that also in the power of these natural sciences we can see a blessing of the Christian religion. From our point of view this is totally rational. In Paradise human beings were told that they would have dominion over nature. Adam did, indeed, have that dominion, but it eluded us through sin. But then common grace took over in order to retain what would be lost through sin and to give it back to us. That is what common grace does. The power and dominion over nature that has been exercised in China and India and also in Muslim regions far exceeds the impotence in which the African races lie and lay. But when in this common grace the exponent that originates in the Church of Christ and in particular grace begins to work, then this *common grace* is tripled in power, and then you see how especially in the Christian parts of the world the superior power of humanity over nature increases in such an incredible way. Then you thank God for it and applaud this liberation of humankind."[212]

This theme of the liberation of the human spirit, which Kuyper merely notes in *De Gemeene Gratie*, he developed in detail later in *Pro Rege*.[213] The following is a summary:

God has placed humankind in this world to have dominion over the entire earth. Small and insignificant human beings were able

211. II, 267.
212. II, 274–75.
213. *Pro Rege* I, 123–76.

to do this because in them the spiritual element is predominant. "Physically, too, they can exercise strength, but this is of minor significance. In fact, the higher human beings rise, the more they abandon their physical strength in order to concentrate all their power in their spirit. God's ordinance giving humanity dominion over the entire earth thus rested on the indisputable foundational idea comprised in the plan of creation that the spirit should rule over matter."[214]

This dominion of humanity "is inherent in our being created in the image of God," which is usually considered in a much too one-sided way in spiritual and religious contexts.[215] "Only in the sphere of the holy have people attempted to discover the image of God as expressed in reborn humanity. But this is not possible and is not permissible. Our confession of our God is first of all that we believe 'in God the Father almighty, Creator of heaven and earth.' His omnipotence, his sovereignty, is foremost. Those who lose sight of that end up in mysticism or lose themselves, before they realize it, in the unfathomable depths of pantheism. The Almighty is his name; the Most High is his honorary title; and that omnipotence is his dominion, his superiority over all creatures, his kingly sovereign majesty by which he subjects all creatures under his feet. How can you then imagine a creature that would be 'bearer of his image and likeness' if you omit the principal trait, the substance of the Divine being, from that creaturely image and withdraw yourself into a moral and religious domain?"[216] With the image of God all emphasis falls on our royal dominion over the entire earth.[217] However, through the Fall came the struggle "in which human beings, weakened by sin, found themselves drawn into nature that was strengthened by the curse."[218] Savage, powerful nature, which like a madman became almost ungovernable in strength, attacks people to destroy them, and so they become involved in a centuries-long struggle.[219] If you see this struggle, you will understand also how much there was a need for a miracle to

---

214. *Pro Rege* I, 127; cf. 135, 155, 414–24.
215. Op. cit., 132.
216. Op. cit., 132–33.
217. Op. cit., 133.
218. Op. cit., 143.
219. Op. cit., 145, 142.

happen. "[This need] arose from the contrast between weak human beings and nature that had become savage and thus became increasingly strong and destructive.... Who could oppose that nature? Who could contest it? Who could overpower and rule it?... That fearful consciousness which draws one away from all faith could be broken only by the miraculous. When God performed wonders and signs that brilliantly displayed his sovereignty over nature for all to see, then indeed, but then only for the first time, did the fear of nature lose its power and God become a refuge and a rock, a high tower for those who are his."[220] That is why the wonder of the exodus from Egypt "was placed at the beginning of Israel's history, so that once and for all times the superiority of Yahweh over nature and its power was laid as the foundation for the whole of Israel's religion."[221]

The wonder of the history of religion is thus not something incidental, it is not merely an "ornament of history," but "rather, the wonder is in the vanguard. Out of the wonder comes the revival and confirmation of faith, and it is still true that after having been allowed and enabled to believe in the living God for so many centuries, we owe this to the coming of that wonder at Israel's beginning and in Israel's history. You will not fathom or understand the meaning of this wonder unless you go back to the ordinance of God, given to humanity, that they must exercise dominion over all of nature and the whole earth and must subdue it."[222]

In the Old Covenant it is not only God who did wonders; he also caused them to be performed by his servants. "Besides the many wonders God performed directly, others were performed through the medium of God's servants, partly in order to legitimize these witnesses of God, but also prophetically to restore humanity, or if you prefer, the spirit of humanity, in its royal power over nature and the world of evil spirits. They were a prelude to the triumph that would eventually let humankind regain what it had lost."[223]

But what was a "momentary glimmer"[224] here and there in the Old Covenant, only reaches its "fulfillment in unbroken majesty"

220. Op. cit., 184.
221. Op. cit., 151.
222. Op. cit., 152.
223. Op. cit., 156–57.
224. Op. cit., 157.

in Christ, the Son of man.[225] "The wonders of the Old Covenant are connected with the appearance of the Messiah. They were a distant indication of what would happen in Christ; but they were no more than a prelude. They recalled the exalted position of humankind in Paradise, showed that restoration of the original power was possible, and prophesied that this power would return eventually. However, they could not reveal that power in its fullness. That could, must, and would only happen when Christ himself appeared as the Son of man, the man without sin. That is when humanity in its original, unbroken power appeared again."[226]

Kuyper says wittingly that in these wonders of Christ restored humanity appears. We should not "transform" Christ's wonders "into wonders of the *Son of God*."[227] If you do so, you lose the correct view of him who appeared "as man, in our nature, as the *Son of man*.... Christ did not rule as the Son of God while on earth ... but he appeared as man, as one of us, and did not reveal any other power than what could arise from his *humanness*."[228] It is true that the Holy Spirit was allotted to him, and not merely in small measure, "but it was and remained a spiritual power that worked in, from, and through him within the confines of our human nature, which was bound to the ordinances that God himself had laid in creation for our human nature."[229] And therefore, "in Jesus restored humanity appears before us, and in this humanity appears the highest expression of the power of which the human spirit is capable over against nature, matter, and demons once this power has reached its culmination. You are not permitted to say that Jesus was like Adam, for human development only began in Adam, while it appears in completed form in Jesus. He was not just a man, but the Son of man. The central man. Humanity in its completion, in the richest and highest stage of its power and ability. And also while Adam's power over creation gave way and succumbed at the very moment when the curse reduced the entire creation to

---

225. Op. cit., 157–58; cf. *Loc. de Christo* III, 185–86.
226. Op. cit., 158.
227. *Pro Rege* I, 158; cf. *E Voto* I, 474–75; *Loc. de Christo* I, 102–03. Contrarily: *Loc. de Christo* II, 37–38: "We many never say that human nature performed wonders." It must be kept in mind that these words were not dictated by Kuyper.
228. *Pro Rege* I, 159.
229. Op. cit., 159.

madness, as we said, the Son of man had the heightened human spirit that had been raised to its highest point, by which he was able to subdue nature that had been shattered by the curse."[230] In him, Psalm 8 about the dominion that God gave humanity over nature was fulfilled.[231] And then Kuyper takes the following important step. What Jesus did, did not end with him. His *immediate* power to perform wonders, which only "continued to blossom in his apostles," did come to an end. But his *mediate* power, which triumphs over nature "through the higher development of the spiritual aspects of our race," did not.[232] For this, Kuyper refers to John 14:12: "Truly, truly, I say to you, whoever believes in me will also do the works that I do; and *greater works than these will he do.*" The kingship of humankind that revived in Jesus as Son of man radiates from him to those who believe in him.[233] Indeed, they will be capable of "greater works." In what sense are the works that the believers will perform "greater"? Kuyper draws a distinction between "the instinctive, unconscious acts and the conscious acts that in our contact with the things of nature are produced through practice."[234] While earlier, through God's marvelous grace, human beings had been enabled through instinctive actions to achieve spectacular things,[235] "we would share in a much greater power over nature as soon as human beings penetrated the essence of nature itself with their research and reflection. Then they would learn to dissect the powers hidden in nature to make them serve its subjugation."[236] "Therefore we must not go back to the period of instinctive life, although it behooves us to honor its relative excellence. Our rational strength does not lie in the unconscious, but in the *conscious* life. Only those who apply their conscious knowledge to nature exercise authority over it, and that reminds us of our royal calling to subdue it. Compared to the past, there is indeed something *greater* in such conscious actions."[237]

Those who know their history are aware "that the liberation

230. Op. cit., 159–60. See also C. Veenhof, *Souvereiniteit in eigen kring*, 99–100.
231. Op. cit., 129ff.
232. Op. cit., 184–85.
233. Op. cit., 167–68.
234. Op. cit., 176.
235. Op. cit., 179.
236. Op. cit., 180.
237. Op. cit., 181.

and elevation of the spirit only occurred in Christian countries which, having applied themselves to research and knowledge of nature, have also elevated our power over nature in such a totally marvelous way.... If Jesus' had not made his appearance and Christianity had not come to Europe, we would, like the Chinese in the East, or the Indians in the South of Asia, still be as powerless over against nature as the ancients were. To assume that Jesus had not anticipated, guessed at, or known about this course of development, this coming process, would shortchange his majesty. He was to be our King; all power in heaven and on earth was given to him. Jesus says to his disciples that the leaven he came to hide in three measures of flour would in time raise our whole human life. This must have appeared to be already true when he prophesied to his disciples that, no matter how great *his* miracles were, the fruit of his entry into the world would cause a yet still *greater* and more miraculous work to result when the dominion over nature would begin—the dominion that we now enjoy through the unveiling of nature's secrets and of the knowledge of its latent powers."[238] Christ's gospel has called forth a totally different, much higher development of human spiritual life."[239] When we compare this to what Jesus did directly though his miraculous power, then there is indeed a "greater something" here. Not "a greater something in the sense that it revealed a higher power. Nothing exceeds the commanding of the wind and the storm on the Lake of Gennesaret, the multiplying of the loaves, and the raising of the dead. But this power now given to us is a 'greater something' when you pay attention to its extent, dimension, and permanence. What Jesus wrought by his miraculous power always applied to one specific case, one single sick person, one single instance of demonic possession, or was confined to one particular area. This second mediate power over nature that was given to us, however, applies the same action and influence among all countries and nations, century after century, and benefits simultaneously thousands who suffer from want or illness."[240] But how can we then explain that "the general human development has, as a rule, been carried out

238. Op. cit., 183–84.
239. Op. cit., 186.
240. *Pro Rege* I, 186–87.

more by unbelievers than by believers?"[241] This fact does not detract from the above argument. For the actual struggle for the liberation of the spirit takes place in the spiritual realm.[242] "A veil hangs before us, and behind that impenetrable veil a struggle of the spirits takes place. That struggle eludes us and we can only observe the results in our lives."[243] It is the struggle between Christ and Satan that was decisive here. By breaking the power of Satan, the ruler of the world,[244] Christ liberated the human spirit, and "then, in the hour of the outpouring of the Holy Spirit, that new power went out into the world through the congregation of the living God. It created an atmosphere in which human nature was again liberated and the freedom of God's children began to flourish. The free development of the human spirit dates from that moment. Gradually all superstition was driven back. Then people no longer reached for magic and sorcery, but through research, through studies in the sweat of their brow, they could prepare for themselves also the bread of science and thereby recover their power over the forces of nature."[245] After the outpouring of the Holy Spirit, the demonic atmosphere was pushed back by a holy spiritual atmosphere.[246] And these influences of the Holy Spirit have extended themselves also "outside the restricted sphere of his living community. They had an effect on the life of the nations, on public opinion, on the making of laws, and on morals and customs. And it was those influences of the Holy Spirit that threw up a dam against the demonic stream."[247] Sadly, the Christian world did not believe in the liberation of the spirits. "It was much too narrow-minded and bound itself to the direct spiritual power that operates by miracle. It closed its eyes too much to the development of another spiritual power that was given to humankind during a process of twenty centuries through ingenuity, application of talent, and utilization of serious research in nature."[248] The unbelievers then especially applied themselves to the terrain that was neglected by the Christian community. That

241. Op. cit., 188.
242. Op. cit., 195–226.
243. Op. cit., 214.
244. Op. cit., 210, 218, 227.
245. Op. cit., 215–16.
246. Op. cit., 218.
247. Op. cit., 225.
248. Op. cit., 229.

community withdrew itself in impotence. "It no longer possessed the might of miracles and it abandoned the power of knowledge to the unbelievers. Conversely, those possessing knowledge broke with their faith and erected their scientific knowledge as a human stronghold over against the kingship of Christ."[249]

Fortunately, this is now changing: "The guilt of the past is being recognized. A new light is dawning. Christians are now reaching for the power of science. They are beginning to appreciate that the power of Christ is at work also in the field of scientific studies, and they are getting themselves ready to glorify Christ as our king also there."[250]

Kuyper's conclusion is "that the new form in which the life of the world now operates is indebted to the rule of King Jesus to the extent that it contains good, precious elements and that King Jesus bridles and combats it to the extent that ungodly powers are at work in it."[251]

1. Kuyper speaks here constantly of the *spiritual* kingship of Christ. Governmental authority is not included in this kingship (*Pro Rege* I, 113–23). The government does not rule by "the grace of Christ," but "by the grace of God" (*Gemeene Gratie* III, 123). The conferral of authority on the government bears an *immediate* character, and therefore we cannot regard Christ as an intermediary (*Pro Rege* I, 114). Christ is not named in the context of Romans 13, and what Jesus says to Pilate (John 18:36) confirms that his kingship is distinguishable from that of the world (114–16). Those who think otherwise, depict "the Father as having abandoned the exercise of his divine dominion after Jesus' ascension—a non-activity of the majesty of God, if we may put it that way. Then all creatures in heaven and on earth, and thus also governments on this earth, would no longer have to account to the Eternal Being, to the triune God, until the day of judgment, but exclusively to the Christ. It is thus supposed that the Father has distanced himself from the order and rule over the church and also over the world, for the benefit of the Son of Man" (*Gemeene Gratie* III, 275). Kuyper wants nothing to do with such an "abdication" (*Pro Rege* I, 372). There is "a "principial difference between secular power, which exercises force, if necessary with the sword, and the spiritual nature of the kingdom of Christ that has no servants who defend it with the sword and that is not of the world and does not have an external countenance, but is within you" (*Pro Rege* I, 121). The kingdom of Christ also fights sin, but does not attack it externally

---

249. Loc. cit.
250. Op. cit., 229–30.
251. Op. cit., 276.

in the wildly growing shoots of transgression, but in the core and root. It does not prune the tree, but heals the cankering in the root" (122). Kuyper's doctrine of the 'liberation of the human spirit' is an excellent illustration of what he understands by the *spiritual* kingship of Christ. See also *Loc. de Christo* III, 181ff., 192–93, and Kuyper's battle against dispensationalism here.

But it is difficult for Kuyper to maintain that Christ's power is restricted to the spiritual sphere. This is apparent from numerous other parts of *Pro Rege*. When he discusses Scriptural expressions that indicate Jesus' royal power, he calls them "of such far-reaching significance that they include powers of decision over everything that will determine the lot of the nations and of humanity. We do not find any restrictions at all in any of those expressions. Nowhere is the description of his power restricted to the spiritual realm. The expressions are, from beginning to end, always universal and all-inclusive" (*Pro Rege* I, 359). S. J. Ridderbos, in his research on *Pro Rege* regarding this point (op. cit., 85), summarizes it as follows: "Christ is king of nature (*P.R.* I, 428, 430), of history (*P.R.* II, 313, 316; II, 335, 336, 341), and also of family life (II, 379–90, 396, 538–41, etc.). Since the exaltation of the Mediator, 'the kingship of Christ' interposes itself 'between the supreme kingship of the triune God and the vicegerentship of humankind (II, 380). Christ's kingship also extends to society (III, 5–11, 164, 165, 221–26), over political life (III, 272, 282, 293), over the nations (III, 311) ... and no less over the sciences (III, 355–57) and over the arts (III, 544–47)." Ridderbos continues: "In all this, Kuyper fights not only against a Methodistic neglect of Christ's kingship, but also against a tendency of the Reformation 'to explain the kingship of Christ in a one-sided way as a kingship only over the believers' (III, 582)." It is impossible to harmonize the two disparate expressions (that Christ's kingship is exclusively spiritual and that it comprehends all and is all-inclusive). But it is indeed remarkable that Kuyper so clearly contradicts himself in the same work. Is there an explanation to be found for this?

Kuyper himself conceded his difficulty with the doctrine of Christ's kingship: "The kingship of the Redeemer belongs to those complicated doctrines that have never yet been dissected adequately.... Every attempt that strives to clarify this complicated doctrine through careful study of Scripture and dogmatic synthesis is to be applauded" (*Gemeene Gratie* II, 280). Kuyper himself remained uncertain, and that caused contradictions, for he wanted to oppose two opinions:

(a) Over against "the supporters of art. 36 of the Belgic Confession in its unredacted form, he rejected ... with conviction the rule of earthly powers by the grace of Christ. However, Kuyper blamed not only the interference by the government in the church, but also the opposite evil, usurpation of power by ecclesiastical authorities over the secular government, on the doctrine that Christ's kingship extends over both church and world" (S. J. Ridderbos, op. cit., 86). That explains the passages in which he spoke about Christ's kingship as *limited*.

CHAPTER I. ABRAHAM KUYPER

(b) Over against Christ's exclusion, in the liberal and Anabaptist sense, from the territory of science, politics, society, etc., Kuyper posits that the reign of Christ is absolute and total. This explains the passages in which he speaks about Christ's rule as totalitarian. See, e.g., Kuyper's orations *Souvereiniteit in eigen kring*, *Niet de Vrijheidsboom*, *Maranatha*, *Het sociale vraagstuk*, *Christus en de sociale nooden*, and *IJzer en leem*.

2. The restoration in Christ of human dominion over nature, which first made culture in the full sense of the word possible, is, in my opinion, the most brilliant idea that Kuyper developed in *Pro Rege*. This dominion goes to work as an exponent in common grace, by which the latter is "tripled" in power (see quotation presented in the text at footnote 212). But just as many of Kuyper's writings have gathered dust, so also has *Pro Rege* I, 123–276—even among authorities on Kuyper. What to think when J. H. Langman labels as "original" the argument of H. van Riessen in his *De moderne cultuur en de christelijke school*, in which Van Riessen takes a clearly Kuyperian approach and bases the development of western culture on the work of Christ? (Review in *Trouw* of 2 February 1963). In this context it is appropriate to mention another interesting fact. Shortly after reading *Pro Rege*, I came across H. Berkhof's *De mens onderweg*, in which he at cardinal points returns to Kuyper's line of reasoning. One quotation will suffice: "Through and around Jesus happened also this unheard of thing, that obstinate and threatening nature allowed itself to be commanded by human beings and placed itself at the service of God's plan of salvation for those who are his. This aspect of Jesus' work has not received nearly enough attention. If these miracles are considered to be believable, people do not give them much thought. They are ascribed to Jesus' divine nature and are regarded as a great exception that does not affect us and our relationship to nature any further. But this view is not in harmony with what the New Testament itself tells us. Of course, these miracles are connected to Jesus' divine mystery, just like everything he does. But this mystery is never separate from his human mystery" (24–25). Upon inquiry, it appeared that Berkhof had written *De mens onderweg* without knowing about Kuyper's *Pro Rege*. When, shortly after we met, he had read the latter, he indicated that he was deeply impressed with the broad and modern way in which Kuyper already had been engaged with the connection between Christ's miraculous power and culture. I also note in passing that there was an indirect connection between Kuyper and Berkhof. For Berkhof was already captivated during his high school years by the idea of Christ's miraculous powers in which Jesus Christ acts as man. This idea was impressed upon him by his teacher of religion, the Rev. S. G. de Graaf, who had undoubtedly read *Pro Rege*.

§ 7. *The relationship between particular grace and common grace*

This significant aspect of Kuyper's teachings, already discussed above, calls for yet further clarification.

1. *One goal.* Particular grace and common grace are ultimately directed to one goal, namely, the triumph of God over Satan and, consequently, to the self-glorification of God's name.[252]

2. *Individual goal.* Particular grace has as its own goal the "realization of the kingdom of heaven."[253] It "serves to magnify the compassion and mercy of God in that he, after humanity had fallen in sin and curse, nevertheless guaranteed eternal bliss to a reborn humankind."[254]

Common grace is subordinated to particular grace in that it must make "the coming to salvation" possible for the elect.[255] "After all, for the elect to appear and be born, the human race first of all had to continue to exist. How else would they have been born?... In fact, without common grace there would be no place for Christ's church in our human race.[256]

But we must not forget that common grace itself also has a goal.[257] Kuyper describes this goal as follows: "to bring to light all that was hidden as seeds in our race, to the glory and praise of God's name."[258] In this work God realizes for himself "an all-encompassing idea ...: the summation of the whole creation in the humanity created in God's image."[259] In common grace, God "seeks his own glorification as the original Artist and Master Builder of the cosmos."[260]

Kuyper insists that these two kinds of grace must be distinguished clearly: "Besides the great work of God in particular grace, there is also that *totally different work* of God in the sphere

---

252. *Gemeene Gratie* II, 52, 117–18, 639. Cf. § 5, 6.
253. II, 639.
254. II, 654.
255. I, 223.
256. I, 254.
257. Loc. cit.
258. II, 626.
259. II, 631.
260. II, 639.

of common grace,"²⁶¹ with its "totally different goal."²⁶² He speaks of "two sharply distinguished spheres," between which "a fundamental difference exists that is undeniable."²⁶³ Between the two forms of grace, there is a gaping difference, he says elsewhere.²⁶⁴

3. *Their territories must not be separated.* Although particular grace and common grace must always be sharply distinguished, "temporal and eternal life, our life in the world and in the church, religion and civil life, may not be separated."²⁶⁵ For both are focused on the cosmos; also particular grace is directed toward the restoration of "the world created and maintained by God and never abandoned by him."²⁶⁶ That is why particular grace and common grace are concerned with each other:

(a) *Particular grace does not exist without common grace.* This point is not self-evident for Kuyper. "In itself the end goal of particular grace lies on the other side of the grave. Its goal lies in eternity and, viewed in isolation, it could, if necessary, occur completely apart from earthly life. All particular grace serves to magnify the compassions and mercies of God in that he, after humankind had fallen in sin and curse, nevertheless guaranteed eternal bliss to a reborn humanity. It must be admitted that this requires only one connection with earthly life, namely the birth of the elect. But once they are born, particular grace confines itself to imparting eternal salvation to them. Actually, this also takes place in the many elect who, shortly after their birth and regeneration, are called from this earth and translated to the heavenly realm. This does not therefore involve an imaginary concept, something that our thoughts have produced. It is the literal description of what regularly occurs in life. There are elect who are born, who are regenerated, and who, never having known anything of earthly life, depart from this life. We must therefore never lose sight of this point of departure. It is decisive and characteristic of the entire relationship that exists between particular grace and the common human life that is the

---

261. II, 623.
262. II, 246.
263. II, 639.
264. III, 202.
265. II, 638.
266. I, 319. Cf. I, 495–96; II, 183, 682ff.

territory of common grace."[267] If it is true that "the number of elect who die unconscious [of earthly life] and the number of the elect who die after their regeneration are approximately equal" (and Kuyper calculates this for us),[268] then "a systematic theology that does not take this into account but, in open conflict with the data of actual life, insists on conversion as the rule and looks down on the imparting of salvation outside of conversion as an exception that hardly counts ... can and may no longer be our guide."[269] It soon becomes clear what Kuyper intends: "Any representation" errs "that makes the salvation of the elect depend on a longer life, or looks for the real goal of this longer life of the elect in their adding something to eternal salvation."[270] And therefore: "The existence of those of the elect who live longer lives in this world must have *a totally different goal* than their contribution [to salvation] or their personal blessedness. That long life is not necessary for their personal contribution [think of the half of the elect that die early, J.D.]. To regard that longer life span with its definite demand of conversion and sanctification as something incidental, would be irreverent. Those who are given a longer life must come to faith and conversion, and to them as converted persons the imperative call to sanctification is addressed. But all this is a demand that *follows* from what they contribute, not the means to achieve eternal life. They receive eternal life purely out of grace and only through an act of God. And it is on this basis that we, as Reformed Christians, have to return to the first and foremost end goal of our calling, namely, *the glorification of God's name*."[271] How? "If they are to sanctify and glorify God's name, then there must be a territory in which they do this and there must be people for whom and among whom they do this. So they may not withdraw themselves from the world, because it is exactly for this world that they must be witnesses, in which they must confess, and in the life of which they must reveal, the power of the Kingdom. The destiny of their individual lives that is determined and granted by God then lies

---

267. II, 654.
268. II, 655. See also *E Voto* III, 414–15. Cf. *Loc. de Sacramentis*, 147 (which is more careful and speaks of "more than a third").
269. II, 656.
270. II, 657. Cf. *Loc. de Salute*, 155–56.
271. II, 657.

precisely *in the world*. And when in that world God comes to them with his common grace, it follows that the particular grace that was given to them comes into direct contact with that common grace. Indeed, neither can reach its ultimate goal without the operation of the other."[272]

1. We must be careful to keep this in mind. Particular grace does not reach its full development or its goal except on the terrain of common grace. Particular grace is concretized by Kuyper as the church, the preaching, conversion, sanctification, the sacraments, the communion of saints, and good works (II, 658–59). These "powers of the kingdom" (II, 660), which are therefore to be fully characterized as aspects of particular grace, have effect on the terrain of common grace. "For the entire revelation of what the triune God does *for* us, *apart from* us, and *in* us for our deliverance becomes a powerful factor in the same world in which common grace operates, a factor that has the farthest-reaching influence on the life of the world subject to this common grace" (II, 664).

2. Those who read this argument presented by Kuyper will recognize in the background his doctrine of *immediate regeneration*, which is then effected shortly before or after birth. Immediate regeneration: "It has ... nothing to do with all the acts of God whereby he works *mediately* in us, such as through the Word and the sacraments, through our life experiences, through all kinds of encounters, etc. There is no *mediate* action of any kind in regeneration" (*E Voto* III, 409–10). See also *E Voto* II, 189, IV, 351, 472; *Werk van den Heiligen Geest*, 429; *Revisie der Revisie-Legende*, 18; *Gemeene Gratie* II, 207ff.

"Effected shortly before or after birth": almost half of the elect die young and can therefore not have been called by the Word. "If you admit, as you must, that the Lord God completes this marvelous act of regeneration in the elect who die young, possibly still in the cradle, or perhaps already in their mother's womb, then there is no conceivable reason why this act of regeneration in the other elect who will live for many years on earth should happen later" (*E Voto* III, 419). See also *Uit het Woord*, 2nd series, III, 57, 64; *Werk van den Heiligen Geest*, 373, 382, 387; *E Voto* I, 133.

Here, too, Kuyper was not always consistent. He also taught a mediate regeneration (*Uit het Woord*, 1st series, I, 49, 87). And as regards the time of regeneration, he also pinpointed it as occurring later. See *Uit het Woord*, 1st series, I, 296; *E Voto* II, 99; III (! J.D.), 385–86, 431; *Encyclopaedie* II, 506; *Loc. de Peccato*, 73ff.

Whether earlier or later, what remains the same is that the goal of particular grace, namely the salvation of the elect, takes place principally in that one

---

272. II, 659.

moment of regeneration. And as for the rest of life? In Kuyper's view, particular grace must thrive in the soil of common grace.

(b) *Common grace languishes without particular grace.* As we saw, particular grace cannot exist without common grace. But the reverse is true also. The glory of common grace would "never have shone brightly in its springtime if particular grace had not brought it fully into bloom."[273] Kuyper does maintain that common grace can exist without particular grace. This was discussed already in § 6.4(c) under the heading *Christ and world history.* Kuyper referred to Mexico, Peru, India, China, Japan, and the Muslim world as regions where you see an "isolated operation of common grace that, restricted by time and place, benefits a few population groups but has only a limited power of development."[274] For "wherever common grace lacks the factor of particular grace, it languishes and leads to only a deficient outcome. But wherever the factor of particular grace operates on common grace ... the latter comes to its full and always richer development. In order to substantiate this, you only have to compare the operation of common grace in, e.g., China with that in a country such as ours. In China, common grace drove on its own power and was not made fertile and enriched by particular grace. In our nation the factor of particular grace has been operative for some eleven centuries. Consequently, the people of China had only common grace during these centuries, while we had common grace and particular grace. And the difference in result is that common grace did come to a formally rich development in China, but in practice it remained at a low level. In contrast, also the unbelieving segment of our society has adopted a human and moral position that is far superior to that of China."[275]

Only in the *general action* of common grace does our human race reach its highest development. "Our race is blessed with but one broad, refreshing stream of life." Outside of it the forms of life remind us of pools, swamps, or at most lakes.[276] "Outside of it"—i.e., outside of particular grace.

273. I, 220.
274. See footnote 203.
275. II, 664.
276. II, 670.

Kuyper knew his world—also the nascent imperialism of China and Japan. But they could not really share in the triumph of common grace. For there is "the remarkable phenomenon that Japan and China imitate us. It is amazing that they are able to imitate us and, up to a point, to do what we do. But this connection with our life remains totally external.... When you observe the most recent developments in Japan, you are struck by the strange fact that it remains basically a pagan society but one that has been given a European veneer. Thanks to common grace, their own progress did develop their skill and ingenuity and keep their spirit awake, if we may put it that way. In that sense it has prepared them for the adoption of an entirely different culture. But beyond that, everything that they owe to their own history is a garment that cannot be altered but must be cast off. There is no organic coherence between what they themselves have developed and what they have taken over from Christian Europe.... What they had should have been discarded and removed, and replaced by what they adopted from Europe" (II, 179). About the above-mentioned imitation, see also II, 246–47; *Pro Rege* III, 348 ("they copy us").

4. *Merger: Church as organism.* Kuyper distinguishes four terrains in the operation of particular grace and common grace:[277]

(a) The terrain of common grace that has not yet undergone the influence of particular grace (e.g., China, and in our country "the broadly developed area of sports that operates solely on the powers of common grace and does not take notice of any higher criterion").

(b) The terrain of the instituted church, which as such arises entirely and exclusively out of particular grace.

(c) The terrain of common grace that is illumined by the light of the candle stand of particular grace (Christian countries of Europe and America, "where all kinds of customs, usages, morals, and laws are in effect that clearly betray the influence of divine revelation, both in the home and in society, and that are followed and observed also by that broad class of persons who will have nothing to do with faith and repentance themselves").

(d) The terrain of particular grace that has made the data of common grace serviceable to itself. This terrain "is found wherever the church reveals itself as organism, that is, where those who confess Jesus let the life of common grace have dominion in their own sphere through the principles of divine revelation").

It is on this fourth terrain, the church as organism, that the "fully

---

277. II, 680.

developed particular grace"[278] *and the completed common grace*[279] *merge. The "leaven" of particular grace has leavened the "flour" of common grace.*[280]

1. The third and fourth terrains must not be confused. The difference is clear: "When the kingdom of heaven is compared to a mustard seed and, in due course, all kinds of birds nest in the tree's branches, all those birds take no part in the nature of the grown tree [third terrain, J.D.]. However, when the leaven has permeated the three measures of flour, that flour has changed in nature [fourth terrain, J.D.]. The first depends solely on external contact, the second on an internal relationship" (II, 681; about leaven, see also I, 468). Both terrains have in common that one can use the epithet "Christian" for them. But then the meaning differs. "If I speak of Christian nations, of Christian societies, etc., it is in contrast to pagan nations, pagan societies, Muslim states, or Muslim societies [third terrain, J.D.]. However, if I speak of the Christian press, the Christian school, Christian singers, etc., I am contrasting them with the liberal press, the public school, unbelieving singers, etc." [fourth terrain, J.D.] (II, 671–72).

2. *The church as organism.* This is where, in Kuyper's view, the tension between particular grace and common grace is resolved.

(a) The church as *organism.* "Not just a bouquet of elect persons will eventually spread its lovely aroma before God. Rather, the *plant* of redeemed *humanity* itself will eventually bloom before God in eternity" (II, 113). The world is being saved in Christ as Head of humanity (II, 111). "It follows from the fact that the actions of the church are not *aliquid separatum et transeuns* [something separate and transient] beside cosmic life, but form instead the core of humanity and of the entire life of the world, that the church completes a process of which the starting point and the *point d'arrivée* coincides fully with cosmic life" (*Loc. de Ecclesia,* 278).

Kuyper does not weary of describing the broad humanness of the church-as-organism. See, *inter alia, Uit het Woord,* 2nd series, II, 335; *Calvinisme,* 51, 56; *E Voto* II, 177; III, 276–77; *Encyclopaedie* II, 250–51; *Loc. de homine,* 53; *Pro Rege* III, 2, 14. The church of Jesus Christ is not an aggregate of persons, but the human race, "comparable to a tree that is cut down and now grows back in smaller form. The ruins of the *genus humanum* are not being restored in their entirety, but become an organism of smaller proportions in their reconstitution" (*Loc. de Ecclesia,* 36). Smaller, yes, "but the organism itself was not changed" (loc. cit.; see also *Loc. de Salute,* 35–36, dictation). It is not the lost but the elect that are separated (*Gemeene Gratie* II, 114); the wild branches are lost, not the tree (*Pro Rege* I, 333; *Loc. de Consummatione,* 260). And in that way, in Kuyper's view, common grace has obtained its lawful place (attention for God's *world*).

278. II, 672.
279. II, 675ff.
280. Kuyper's own image. See II, 681.

(b) The *church* as organism. It is necessary to shift the emphasis at this point. For common grace obtains its lawful place *within the church*. Kuyper spoke about the independent goal of common grace, but at the end of history it is particular grace that has absorbed common grace. Not the other way around. For "the end of the operation of common grace lies ... in the Day of Judgment. In contrast, particular grace recognizes no end, but will propagate itself in all eternity" (II, 679). For the end of common grace, see also I, 432–32, 497; II, 395; *Loc. de Foedere*, 131 dictation. When the Day of Judgment arrives, the re-creative power of particular grace claims also the entire terrain of common grace, both our bodies and the whole world" (II, 685).

3. We must keep the last point in mind when Kuyper occasionally speaks with approval about secularization. For in his line of reasoning the epithet "Christian" does not thereby lose its meaning. When Kuyper speaks of the secularization of state and society as "one of the deepest foundational ideas of Calvinism" (II, 279) and when he praises Calvinism elsewhere because it has promoted the secularization of the arts (*Encyclopaedie* III, 342), this secularization stands in contrast to all patronizing of society and the arts in the church-as-*institute*. *Those* ties must be broken. But where the church-as-institute withdraws, "the life of the world on each terrain" is "emancipated, not from God but from the rule of the church. This emancipation happens so that [the life of the world] will receive the antidote against its inherent decay solely from *the solid faith of God's children*" (*Calvinism*, 24; emphasis added). The arts must again receive their universal human character (*Encyclopaedie* III, 342); that is, they must be free of ecclesiastical and national shackles, so that they can nonetheless be "arts baptized by the Spirit of Christ" (*Gemeene Gratie* III, 571), for "the Spirit of Christ ennobles all of life" (loc. cit.; see also III, 535–36).

5. *Both have their root in Christ*. The relationship between particular grace and common grace is not simply that of "a commingling, an intertwining, and an interlacing. In each of these three methods of contact various materials or items are brought together externally and it is only in this way that they form a unity.... But it is different when two branches *of the same tree* intertwine. For those two branches have a common origin. They have one root."[281] This last comparison can be applied to the relationship between common grace and particular grace: "For did the holy apostle not write to the church at Colossae that one and the same Christ is both the root of created life and the root of re-created life? First it says that Christ is 'the firstborn of all creation. For by him all things were created, in heaven and on earth,' so that 'he is before all things, and in him

281. II, 645.

all things hold together.' It could not be expressed more clearly that Christ is the root of creation and therefore also of common grace, for common grace ensures that not everything is plunged into nothingness. For it also says that all things *hold together in him*. But immediately following this it says that this same Christ is also 'the *head of the body*' and 'the firstborn from the dead.' Thus he is at the same time the root of re-created life, or of particular grace. Indeed, both are expressed in terms that are reminiscent of the other: root of common grace, for he is *the firstborn of all creation*, and at the same time root of particular grace, for he is *the firstborn from the dead*. Thus there can be no doubt that common grace and particular grace have an intimate relationship by virtue of their origin, and that origin lies in *Christ*."[282]

But more has to be added. For the name "Christ" could lead to the supposition "that common grace and particular grace only find their point of association in the manger of Bethlehem."[283] But then common grace and particular grace would "really remain independent and would only come into a more or less accidental contact with each other by the Incarnation."[284] But such is not the case. "God knows everything *in his Counsel*, and in that Counsel the Son is both Mediator of creation and Mediator of redemption from 'before the foundation of the world.' Thus it is clear, according to Scripture, that the mediatorship of redemption certainly does not begin only in Bethlehem, but becomes operative immediately after the Fall."[285] And even though it only became operative after the Fall and the work of redemption could not begin so long as there were as yet no sinners ... Christ had been appointed long before as Mediator of redemption, that is, as *God's Anointed*, and the title was therefore justly his."[286] Thus the point of association does not lie "in Christ's birth in Bethlehem, but in his eternal existence as the *Eternal Word*"[287] and as the "eternal Son of God."[288] "The Eternal Word is *before* the Counsel, is *in* the Counsel, and in that Counsel

282. Loc. cit.
283. II, 647.
284. Loc. cit.
285. Loc. cit. Cf. *Loc. de Christo* I, 97ff.
286. II, 647.
287. II, 635.
288. II, 637.

maintains the unity of creation and redemption in *his own Person*, and that is precisely why that redemption work of particular grace *cannot* stand separate and apart from the life of the world; rather, they both, as they proceed from one Counsel and from the same "I" [first person singular] in the Son of God, at bottom are and remain *one*. They are *distinguishable*, just as the Son is distinguishable from the Father, but they are never separate, just as you may never separate Father and Son in God's triune being. It is one and the same "I" of whom it is written that through him all things were created and hold together and, as we read elsewhere, that through him as many as are called must be saved."[289]

1. *One and the same "I,"* but then distinguished as the second Person of the Divine being and as the Word that became flesh, as Mediator of creation and as Mediator of redemption. Does Kuyper manage to make sure that this distinction never becomes a *separation*?

We have already noted tensions when Kuyper speaks about the kingship of Christ. To put it briefly: does the government rule by "the grace of God" or by "the grace of Christ"? Kuyper's answer is "that the Son of God is Head of the *community*, and thus also of the instituted *churches*, in his official capacity as Messiah, i.e., as Prophet, Priest, and King, and thus as *Christ*. In contrast, this Christ rules in civil life not as Mediator of redemption, but as Mediator of creation and as Son of God. The holy apostle therefore does not call the government 'the servant of Christ,' but 'the servant of God.' We, too, do not say that the government rules by 'the grace of Christ,' but by 'the grace of God'" (III, 123).

I make the conclusion of S. J. Ridderbos mine: "Kuyper's explicit doctrine is that common grace operates through the Mediator of creation, not through the Mediator of redemption. But in another sequence of thought he assigns such an extensive meaning to mediatorship of redemption that the denial of the 'original connection' between Christ and common grace can no longer be maintained" (op. cit., 87). Thus, the connection between particular grace and common grace is not as simple as it would appear at first blush. Kuyper himself sensed this difficulty. He writes about the connection between the two as a "very complex and difficult issue," adding that the intertwining of the two "has given rise to almost unsolvable problems that have divided the Christian world already for eighteen centuries" (II, 634).

2. It is clear that Kuyper uses the name "Christ" sometimes in a broader and at other times in a narrower sense. When Kuyper says that particular grace and common grace both have their root in Christ, he is referring to the second

---

289. II, 638.

Person of the Trinity. But when Kuyper opposes the idea of the government's rule by the grace of Christ, he uses the same name in the narrower sense as designation for the man Jesus Christ who is enthroned at God's right hand.

B. Background

What was Kuyper's intention with his doctrine of common grace? What was the motive, the driving force, that made it necessary for Kuyper to develop a theory of common grace?

What follows is an inquiry into the background of the doctrine. It will become apparent from the literature about Kuyper that the answers to the questions I raise are not identical—also that the different answers are connected with the different interpretations of Kuyper's teachings.

I am aware that my exposition in Part A already includes an interpretation. I wish to defend it in this part and, as necessary, to clarify it.

What motivated Kuyper to develop his doctrine of common grace?

§ 8. The opinion of Arnold A. van Ruler

In his book *Kuyper's idee eener Christelijke cultuur*, Arnold A. van Ruler defended the proposition that Kuyper's doctrine of common grace can only be understood properly against the background of what Kuyper understood by particular grace. He argues as follows: Kuyper understands particular grace in a one-sided way as "primarily and centrally regeneration," whereas it is also realistically regarded otherwise as "conversion of the inmost essence of human beings."[290] Hence for Kuyper the "particular" in the grace is more a qualitative than a quantitative indicator, in consequence of which this qualitative-particularistic leads to the

---

290. *Kuyper's idee eener Christelijke cultuur*, 7. As proof Van Ruler cites *Gemeene Gratie* II, 352, 209, 216, 217; I, 255; II, 52, 204, 207, 212, 213, 217.

spiritualistic.[291] For "according to Kuyper's view, particular grace retreats into the more inner-spiritual-mystic life of the soul."[292] And from this flows automatically the *dualistic* pull in particular grace: "The life that came into being in the soul by regeneration is already a little bit of 'eternal life' that translates it in principle to the hereafter."[293]

Van Ruler supports this assertion with the following quotation from Kuyper: "In itself the end goal of particular grace lies on the other side of the grave. Its goal lies in eternity and, viewed in isolation, it could, if necessary, occur completely apart from earthly life (II, 654)."[294] Van Ruler thus considers Kuyper's particular grace to be spiritualistic. In addition he believes that Kuyper restricts particular grace to the category of regeneration: "Kuyper's only fully theological category is regeneration."[295] That is particular grace "in its purity and according to its inner substance."[296] True salvation, "namely, the truly Christian element [lies] only in regeneration."[297] In Kuyper's doctrine of particular grace, salvation is "stored up in the soul";[298] particular grace is "immediate regeneration."[299]

This depiction of Kuyper's particular grace as particularistic-spiritualistic-dualistic[300] therefore governs Van Ruler's entire vision of Kuyper's idea of a Christian culture and, consequently, of Kuyper's doctrine of common grace. That is not surprising. For if particular grace in its actual essence (as enclosed in the soul and in principle translated to the hereafter) is regarded as spiritualistic, then it seems that, as far as culture is concerned, "decisive positions have already been taken. For culture is never something solely personal, but always also communal.... Mysticism and culture have never been good bedfellows.... Culture after all is certainly not something that pertains to eternal life, but insofar as we have

---

291. Loc. cit.
292. Loc. cit. Proof: *Gemeene Gratie* III, 21; II, 684–85; 130, 338, 293ff.
293. Loc. cit.
294. Op. cit., 7–8. Also cited: II, 679; III, 105, 307–08, 341, 387–88.
295. *Kuyper's idee* 26. Cited: II, 660.
296. Op. cit., 94.
297. Op. cit., 111 (italics supplied).
298. Op. cit., 146.
299. Op. cit., 148.
300. From this point on we shall speak principally about the spiritualism that Van Ruler believes is contained in Kuyper's work.

knowledge of it and share in it, it is very specific to temporal life. If we transfer the essence, goal, and existence of grace to the other side of the grave, we sever the connection between grace and culture completely."[301] And in Kuyper's doctrine of particular grace that connection *is* indeed severed: "Properly regarded ... particular grace itself, at least in its purity and inner substance, is not developed in the temporal and visible world."[302]

But Kuyper was very much engaged with culture. That was possible because he discovered the "the *medium* between particular grace and culture in the doctrine of common grace."[303] Van Ruler expresses himself this way deliberately. He wanted to warn against "forcing a contrast between the doctrine of particular grace (or palingenesis) and the doctrine of common grace"[304] in order to prevent the impression that Kuyper's doctrine of common grace was intended to lead to an appreciation of universal human culture. Such an impression would be incorrect, according to Van Ruler. For "he certainly did not develop his doctrine of common grace for that purpose. His neutral appreciation of culture was merely one of the consequences, not a motive for the doctrine. Kuyper was certainly not interested in awakening his own spiritual sympathizers to a broad humanistic appreciation of culture as such. Instead, he wanted to awaken them to *Christian* action in all areas of life and he needed his doctrine of common grace for that."[305] This would not work with particular grace (spiritualistic!); hence the introduction of common grace. "In the doctrine of particular grace the connection with the general human, earthly, and temporal life has been severed, but in common grace this connection (*this connection, the connection of common grace with this life!*) is established again. The motive for the doctrine of common grace does not lie in appreciation of culture, but in cultural activity. Its purpose is to confer on reborn believers the possibility of existence, material to work with, and meaningful activity. Also when their lives are extended in time as regards the issue of election and of regeneration, although this is really a matter of eternity, they

---

301. Op. cit., 8–9.
302. Op. cit., 94.
303. Op. cit., 11.
304. Loc. cit.
305. Op. cit., 12.

do encounter grace from the same God who elected them and regenerated them—grace from the same God, albeit not the same grace."[306]

Thus Kuyper remains engaged with particular grace. "The proposition that grace is particular is not only Kuyper's theological tenet, but also the driving force of the system of his world and life view, including his theory of culture."[307] Kuyper is concerned with *Christian* culture and he wants to get there from the core of particular grace. But if one is to be culturally active as a Christian, the link of common grace is necessary. It serves as "medium"[308] or, as Van Ruler also refers to it on occasion, as "point of departure."[309]

But it is an important question whether particular grace through its spiritualistic character can really be connected to culture via common grace and thus reach the goal Kuyper intended for it. Van Ruler does not leave us guessing about the answer. At the end of his study he concludes that common grace in its role as preparation and execution of particular grace "fails as such. That is because of the inflexible nature of particular grace in its psychic isolation. When considered properly, common grace and particular grace fail to connect at any point. For the latter can neither be prepared [*immediate regeneration*!], nor executed [mysticism!]. The idea of a Christian culture has remained incomplete."[310] For the real issue inherent in particular grace,[311] in its spiritualizing,[312] does not brook a solution: "Particular grace has been too strongly identified with eternity to be clearly visible in the temporal world. Common grace has been too firmly attached to creation to permit it to bear the insertion of a material part of particular grace in such a way that the *breach* does not always remain visible."[313]

If you take all this into account, you will understand the far-reaching conclusions Van Ruler arrives at when he analyzes the tensions and points out the fault lines inherent in the system of Kuyper's doctrine. When in chapter 2 of his book he discusses Kuyper's view of the relationship between the church

---

306. Op. cit., 13.
307. Op. cit., 7. Cf. 147.
308. Op. cit., 11, 58.
309. Op. cit., 79, 147.
310. Op. cit., 148.
311. Op. cit., 79.
312. Op. cit., 145–46.
313. *Kuypers idee*, 98.

and culture and must then analyze the influence the church exercises over the terrain of common grace through what it radiates, Van Ruler asks: "Is that which results from this influence still particular grace, or still common grace? His answer, without reservation, is that the result is a form of common grace.... The same operations of the means of grace and of spiritual gifts bear the character of particular grace if they are shared by those who are or will become regenerated. But they do not go beyond the character of 'common grace' in the case of persons and groups who will die outside of Christ (II, 242). In this respect Holy Scripture, for example, can also be regarded as 'falling within the framework of common grace' (II, 243).... And the church of Christ is 'one of the most powerful means' 'by which it pleases God to lead common grace to its goal.' We may summarize as follows: The influences of particular grace on common grace, of the church on culture, serve to strengthen common grace, and thus they themselves become means and forms of common grace. The Scriptures and the church end up on the terrain of common grace!" (op. cit., 25-26). This conclusion is not at all surprising for Van Ruler, for the supposition that "the church in Kuyper's view is 'of course' institute of particular grace and not of common grace is not so certain. It is doubtful. Not only because of the consequences we just drew from the position of the church in culture (the church as instrument and form of common grace), but also because of the dogmatic foundation of the church. For Kuyper, the church remains principially outside the deepest essence of salvation" (26). For the deepest essence of salvation is, of course, regeneration, and it is *not* worked by Word and Sacraments and therefore by the ministry of the church, but immediately by the Spirit. And in that way the church is withdrawn from the nucleus of salvation and pushed to the boundary. It stands on the boundary between 'Christianity' and 'culture'" (26). The church is "instrument in the revelation process in which the life granted in regeneration achieves clarification, self-awareness, and (especially) communication with its surroundings. The last of these has nothing to do with eternal salvation, but only serves the glorification of God's name. It is therefore not surprising that Kuyper could so readily declare the church in its cultural significance as instrument and form, as exponent, of common grace" (27). Van Ruler thus believes that his thesis concerning Kuyper's doctrine of particular grace is confirmed (26).

Van Ruler develops this thesis more broadly and radically when he discusses Kuyper's twofold meaning of the word "Christian" in "Christian culture." I have already pointed out this distinction made by Kuyper (pp. 64ff. above). Van Ruler now asserts that in using the word "Christian" in the first sense of the word ("namely, that very general, as it were diluted, meaning which allows one to say that the countries of Europe and America are 'Christian' countries as distinct from the 'pagan' and Muslim" countries of other continents" [op. cit., 28]), i.e., as referring to "potentiated common grace" (30), Kuyper's concern is with the idea of a *Christian* culture. Even when Kuyper speaks of common grace in

CHAPTER I. ABRAHAM KUYPER

its *independent* role as developing the original creation forces, we should not speak of humanism (12–13, 46ff., 59–60, 77). Also in its "extremely daring turns" regarding the collective display of the image of God, "the doctrine of common grace does not become a license for cultural liberalism. In this operation it on the one hand retains its formal function of encouragement, terrain, and arsenal for Christian cultural activity, and on the other hand that of positing the necessity of the completion of common grace through the influence of particular grace" (77). It does not become clear what the impact of particular grace on common grace consists of (34ff., 42ff.). The *culture-driving force* of particular grace is not clearly pointed out (37).

What then is the case with "Christian culture" in the second meaning of the phrase? "Is it a culture that does not spring from common grace, but from particular grace, a culture of regeneration?" (81). Then it is not about the culture-*driving* force but about the culture-*forming* power of particular grace (loc. cit.). Van Ruler's exposition on this point has our particular interest; for "is this second, more specific, more principal form of Christian culture not characterized by the principle of the antithesis? And is speaking about a 'Christian' culture in the first meaning of the phrase not a rarefied mirage in comparison with the second form?" (loc. cit.). His answer is: Kuyper was not concerned with humanism, nor with the antithesis; rather, he was concerned "with Christian culture in the most universal and at the same time strictest sense of the phrase" (82). Christian culture in the narrower sense (particular grace which makes use of the data of common grace) lies in the perspective of Christian culture in the broader sense (common grace strengthened by particular grace). Van Ruler uses the image of two concentric circles to illustrate the point and then quotes Kuyper, who says that the "Christian character is only sound in the center and becomes weaker the further you move away (cf. the image of concentric circles, J.D.). The center for each nation lies in the Lord's elect. They are the ones who bear the holy vessels. It is in them that the powers of regeneration, of faith and of sanctification, are constantly fed anew from its fountain in God.... After that comes the circle of the visible church.... Then the broader circle of the so-called national church.... Next the people who uphold tradition.... Following them comes the circle of modern Christians.... Then ... those who are socially respectable but have become complete atheists.... And finally, in the farthest reaches you find that very broad circle of people who do *not* think about anything and do *not* care about anything, but who in effect are not subject to any influence from the life of the nation (II, 251–52)" (83–84). Kuyper's viewpoint on the concept of a Christian culture is not breached by the "Christian" culture concept in the narrower sense. The following quotation is long, but useful in order to understand Van Ruler's argument. He is of the opinion that Kuyper has clearly demonstrated that he does "not on the one hand more or less casually call the national culture, as subdivision of the European-American cultural circle, 'Christian,' to be appreciated and accepted as such, while on the other hand, more or less inconsistently, he demands and constructs an individual, separate, Christian culture in the strictest sense. He sees a connection between the two. He looks for and finds the essence of the Christian-national culture in the culture of the circle of the believers. Conversely, he finds nothing in the concentrated Christian culture, nothing at all, even in substantially diluted form, that is present in the general Christian culture. Common grace and particular grace exist in both. And both fall under the same point of view, namely, that common grace only comes to fulfillment under the influence of particular grace. Their interdependence consists in this, that concentrated Christian cultural activity is necessary for the benefit of general Christian culture. On the basis of these considerations, Kuyper. could rightly justify his opinion that his Free University had the honor of bearing a national character. From this perspective it is understandable that Ph. J. Hoedemaker accepted a professorship at this Christian-national institution. It was established as the center, focus, and starting point of a re-Christianization of European-American culture. This lofty vision was the actual driving force of this dogma, and in it common grace and particular grace harmonize in beautiful agreement. That is what it is all about, that common grace can truly reach its real, complete development and that the Christian religion can celebrate its highest triumphs in this" (85).

But now the difficulties arise! What exactly is specifically Christian in "Christian" in the second, narrower sense of the word? Van Ruler admits that Kuyper wants to maintain the distinction. "Kuyper values the distinction. He urges us to 'distinguish sharply (III, 311), sometimes 'simply rejects' the first interpretation of the word 'Christian' (III, 395), calls it dangerous to confuse the two meanings (II, 681), and draws the attention of his readers 'very specifically' to 'the vast distinction between the twofold meaning of the word 'Christian' (II, 673)" (88). Van Ruler says that one can indeed identify a "certain duality" in Kuyper. But we should not speak "of a contradiction. The perspectivistic correspondence remains; however, the individual distance in the perspective is more broadly determined" (89).

This is also readily apparent from Kuyper's use of the expression "church as organism." For, as Van Ruler says, he can use this expression for Christian culture in the first as well as in the second sense of the word (89–90). Sometimes "in this idea of the church as organism particular grace achieves a significant expansion in life, and the Christian nature of Christian culture consequently acquires an important depth in the direction of the essence of salvation. But at other times the voluntary Christian ghetto threatens to replace the organic national church" (90–91). Hence, "the twofold use of the technical term 'church as organism' renders this conclusion impossible" (91–92). Therefore, "you *cannot* interpret Kuyper in such a way that he wanted to posit a qualitative-principial difference between 'Christianized common grace' and 'fully developed particular grace.' *It is no more than a difference in degree.... Appreciation of culture never becomes humanism. The antithesis never becomes principial, but is always solely practically motivated. The ghetto retains a national significance and development*.... Thus it really no longer makes sense to inquire which meaning of the word 'Christian culture' Kuyper especially emphasized. When he is engaged with the one, he is by the same token busy with the other. Ostensible contradictions are caused by Kuyper's rhetorical writing style and the fragmentary nature of a long series of articles. In essence Kuyper always remains true to himself" (92, italics supplied). But this having been said, the question nonetheless "arises with redoubled force ... what the influence of the supernatural powers of particular grace on the natural powers of common grace consists of" (97). For in connection with "Christian culture" in the second sense of the phrase "these questions about the what and how of this influence have a more urgent character, because the word 'Christian' has acquired such a more stringent character" (loc. cit). The issue is not "why we want to have a Christian culture, but what we understand by it! In the answer to this question lie all the tensions of the foundational principles" (98). In Christian culture Kuyper *must* involve "in one way or another, the revelation of 'the powers of the kingdom' (II, 349, 660)" (101). But is that successful? Van Ruler discusses successively what Kuyper writes about Christian education, the Christian family, Christian marriage, Christian science, and Christian art (101–15). Because these remarks touch the heart of Kuyper's doctrine and life, let us yet consider what Van Ruler says about them.

    Regarding Kuyper's discussion about *the Christian school*, Van Ruler asks: "What have you left if in this view you continue to distinguish the Christian school clearly from catechism instruction? Here and there you have a retouching of the material that is being taught (national history), and otherwise—since instruction in the doctrine of the church must, of course, principially be excluded—Christianized common grace. Surely we cannot speak of 'fully developed particular grace' in those circumstances? In our activity with regard to the Christian school, are we truly active in the sphere of Christian culture in the second, more stringent, sense of the word, or are we still in the general Christian culture?" (102). Van Ruler intends his comment to be far-reaching: "Do not minimize the reach of this question. Practically speaking, this question asks no less than whether we are to regard the free Christian school as the norm, the ideal, or rather as [something necessitated by] an emergency situation. The direction in which Kuyper propelled Christian education in our nation rests on the optical illusion that it was really involved to the full in the breakthrough of the powers of particular grace in the visible present, in that higher form of human life which is a portent of the realm of glory that is to come.... Kuyper was very reserved in connecting this eschatological reality to the theoretical foundation of Christian culture. Now we see how in its practical execution he wants to make it appear as if this reality were sufficiently comprehensive to incorporate the school into it" (102). Although Kuyper was unsuccessful in his *theory*, he nonetheless wants to realize it in practice.

    It is not any better with regard to what Kuyper says about particular grace and the *Christian family*. Here, too, Van Ruler asks "whether this particular grace is in principle nothing else than a concentrated form of common grace. The church, the work of Christ, faith, and conversion are all suspect in this question. Only regeneration is not.... That which is distinctively Christian in the Christian family, also in the second sense of the word (i.e., in the family as house church), remains outside of the central essence of salvation" (105–06). In what follows it becomes clear how far-reaching Van Ruler's conclusions are: "Here we encounter the same problem as with the Christian school. In itself this is not so bad. If you can reduce all that is Christian in Christian culture to common grace, you must make your peace with this Christianity and you will also appreciate it differently and call things by a different name (cf. Ph. J. Hoedemaker's use of the terms "national church" and "covenant of baptism"). But regrettably the illusion then arises that in the Christian character of your Christian culture you have in reality attained the total newness of eternal life! Because of this illusion our nation will perish. The desire to realize Christianity in this world can be too great" (106).

What Kuyper writes about *Christian marriage* causes Van Ruler to ask: "Is this strengthened common grace, or fully developed particular grace? It seems to me that the answer to this question is not in doubt" (108).

It is more difficult with respect to Kuyper and *scientific studies* as *Christian*. For the connection between the Christian religion and science "is sought exclusively in the formation of an independent, Christian science in the strict sense of the word" (III, 487–528). Aristotle, Plato, Kant, and Darwin are appreciated, "but only as fruit of common grace (III, 492–95, 497–98)" (108). Furthermore, "everything is directed to portraying the necessity of the antithesis." Kuyper wants to have a "science of palingenesis" (109–10). But this will also fail. For "the meaning of regeneration ... [is] not sought by looking at the truth and reality of things themselves—whereby, more or less gnostically, subjectivism would be cosmologically deepened and broadened—but ... this meaning of regeneration [is] curtailed to the possibility of understanding Holy Scripture in order to receive enlightenment and certainty from Holy Scripture concerning the cardinal questions that control our entire worldview. Therefore, in the final analysis, we do not receive definitive answers concerning the origin, governance, and end goal of all things from the inner enlightenment in which we shared through regeneration, but only—and now keep in mind that, for Kuyper, Holy Scripture is in doctrinal respect considerably more distant from salvation than regeneration—from the light of revelation in Holy Scripture. Is it then really palingenesis that supports Christian science, or does palingenesis in the end hide in the mystical darkness of eternity, so that it is in fact Holy Scripture on which Christian science rests?" (110–11). But then, here too, "the strict Christian character of this little bit of Christian culture" becomes "dubious." "For in doctrinal respect actual salvation, and thus what is really Christian about it, lies solely in regeneration, namely in regeneration that, in principle, can manage by itself without Scripture" (111). And, "the more you draw back in this way, the more the antithesis loses its necessity" (loc. cit.). When Kuyper then also claims that the revelation concerning the most profound questions about life was, indeed, granted us in the way of particular grace—although it does not itself form part of that grace, and we thus are again dealing with strengthened *common* grace—"the expression 'science of palingenesis' ... [seems] rather too jaunty if it is no more than a form of potentiated common grace. The same despair, failure, and lack of substance that we encountered with respect to the Christian school and the Christian family, we discover also with respect to Christian science" (112).

Van Ruler notes this failure also in the discussion of *Christian art*. In this context Kuyper wants to define "Christian" in a narrower sense based on a "spirit from on high," a sense of being inspired that must characterize art in all its forms. He speaks of an "artistically expressed palingenesis of art," of "art baptized by Christ's Spirit." About this Van Ruler remarks: "Is this Christian spirit 'Christian' in the first or second sense of the word? To what extent can these two meanings be distinguished in this context? Can natural life ennobled by Christ's Spirit be seen in accordance with Kuyper's dogmatic suppositions as part of eternal life, or also as only in essence connected with it?" (114–15). Or does Kuyper speak this way again because of *practical utilitarian* motives? Van Rules names three such motives: 1. the idea of correction: if the development of common grace remains in the hands of unbelievers, it would be corrupted, especially in moral and religious respects; 2. the idea of the protection of Christians: one's faith is so readily offered up to one's scientific views, and our people must be protected from that; 3. the propaganda of religious conviction: otherwise one will not have any influence at all on the course of events (98–100).

Van Ruler's conclusion: "On the one hand, Kuyper initially hid particular grace essentially in the mystical life of the soul, whereas he later demonstrated its role as culture-forming factor on the terrain of history. On the other hand, he logically proclaimed common grace too positively as the explanation of God's governance over life outside of the church, whereas he later wanted to be able to get rid of it, or to reduce it to second place. He can never really fit particular grace into Christian culture, and he can never take common grace out of it adequately" (115). And as far as the antithesis is concerned, Van Ruler states: "But it is regrettable that in the *practice* of Kuyper's life's work everything finally led to the antithesis as the form in which Christian culture appears among us. That was not necessary. *And Kuyper did not intend this to happen.* But that is where things got bogged down. It is undeniable that Kuyper contributed to the problem. There are elements in his system that appear to promote the transition from a practical to a principial motivation of the antithesis. These elements affected practical life most strongly and—what is much more worrisome!— they are nowadays also accentuated principially by theorists in such a way that they threaten to become the only components of the concept of Christian culture" (116, italics supplied. As a symptom of what he is referring to in his last sentence, Van Ruler mentions the ideas of K. Schilder).

We must finally pay attention to one further point in Van Ruler's views. In the last chapter of his paper ("Prospects") he concludes that "eschatologically particular grace is deprived of "its particularistic-spiritualistic-dualistic character" (139). For in creation's consummation it appears that particular grace is directed to all of creation. He quotes Kuyper, who states "that the covenant of particular grace is, indeed, spiritual in point of departure and essence, but also includes just as much, if regarded as complete [here note the eschatological turn, away from the present, Van Ruler], the world of visible things (II, 682–83)" (137). In the regeneration of the world, "the re-creating power of particular grace "claims also the entire terrain of common grace for itself, including our bodies and this entire world (II, 683–85)" (138). The incarnation also functions in this view of Kuyper. Eschatologically only. For "in and before the present, the incarnation, together with the entire redemptive work of Christ, was only appreciated as revelation, external appearance of (the in itself mystical) particular grace" (140). But eschatologically the incarnation achieves its own substance and meaning. In Kuyper's words, "if you believe and confess that Christ is and remains the center of the kingdom of glory, and if you confess also that your Savior ascended into heaven *in his body*, also still lives in his *body*, and shall also triumph in *our human flesh* in the kingdom of glory, then this in itself already requires this kingdom of glory to take on also an *external* form (I, 485)" (140).

There is something else to be added. Also *protologically*, in the figure of Christ as the mediator of creation, there is, according to Van Ruler, a bond between Christ and the world. "In the center, grace is particular; no bond with the world exists there. But in the two extremities, at the beginning and at the end, this bond is established all the more emphatically. And then in such a way that this cosmic importance of Christ in the eschatological perspective is based on his mediatorship of creation" (140–41, citing I, 225–28). But Van Ruler sees difficulties here too: For "now it becomes apparent that this eschatological actualization of the dogma of the incarnation is not intended soteriologically. *Kuyper's viewpoint prevents him from accentuating the fact that the flesh was accepted as an act of compassion.*" The significance of Christ for the world in the eschatological perspective is thus not "found in the fact that he is the Word who became *flesh*, but rather in the fact that the Word who became flesh, notwithstanding the incarnation, always was and remains the eternal Word through whom the world was created" (142). Van Ruler even dares to ask the question: "Is it really particular grace if it appropriates the whole terrain of common grace in the kingdom of glory?... Does the eschatological-cosmic significance of Christ not rest in his mediatorship of creation? If so, in the consummation of all things, common grace would not transfer to or merge into particular grace. Rather, stripped of all its particulars and its separate-act-character, it would fall back into the mediatorship of creation, whence it came.

That would also explain why the universal significance of particular grace, which was posited so strongly in eschatological perspective, cannot at present be fully actualized. For this universal significance of particular grace would then in the eschatological perspective also be just a sham. In truth, the mediatorship of creation would have to stand in that place" (142–43). Van Ruler is careful here: "I can only draw this conclusion with great reservations" (143). But the assumption that it is a possible one, illustrates the persistence with which Van Ruler, from the beginning to the end of his paper (including also what he says about protology and eschatology in Kuyper) maintained his main thesis about the spiritualistic character of Kuyper's particular grace.

Van Ruler received much support for his argumentation about the spiritualism in Kuyper's view of particular grace and for his explanation of Kuyper's doctrine of common grace against *that background*. Thus J. Kamphuis wanted to supply Van Ruler's argument with a *historical* foundation. The first sentence of his address "De algemene genade van Dr. A. Kuyper"[314] can serve as catchphrase: "If you want to understand common grace, you need to go to Pietje Baltus."[315] This woman, who in Beesd [Kuyper's first congregation] "had a tremendous influence" on Kuyper, was greatly influenced by the spirit of the conventicle, in which the truth of God was overgrown with mysticism, fanaticism, and spiritualism.[316]

Kamphuis: "When Kuyper became a pupil of Pietje Baltus ... you must think of him as locked up in the bunker of mysticism, in the cell of mysticism. There is no route leading from particular grace to created reality, to Christian scholarship, to Christian politics, and in fact also no route to church reformation. So if we could say nothing more than 'pupil of Pietje Baltus,' spiritualist that [Kuyper] was, he would have remained locked up in that cell; he would have been a profusely blooming flower on the dungheap of the conventicle and nothing more than that."[317] But Kamphuis states that there is more to be said about Kuyper: "Although 'theoretically' he was locked up in that bunker of particular grace as understood in a mystical sense, [he] knew one thing: You do have to serve the Lord; and it is not acceptable, as Pietje Baltus and her group did, to let the church fend

---

314. "De algemene genade van Dr. A. Kuyper," in *Jeugd en Politiek* 1, No. 6. For Kamphuis' interpretation of Kuyper see also "Over 'de gemene gratie,'" *De Reformatie* 33, 30–40, 55, 63 (under the pseudonym Leo Dregt).
315. Op. cit., 1.
316. Op. cit., 4–6.
317. Op. cit., 9–10.

for itself and to let the world continue being this wicked world, and nothing else. Kuyper knew: there is a calling for the children of God in this world."[318] And he understood this calling in a time of secularization and emancipation.[319] But in order to put this calling on a proper theoretical foundation, he needed common grace as a complement to particular grace: as "the valve through which the compressed air can escape."[320] Thus Kamphuis followed Van Ruler (at least on this cardinal point) and called his work "a powerfully fascinating study."[321]

§ 9. *Objections*

Above I have presented an extensive review of Van Ruler's study. I owed this to him as the man who, as none other, has provided such a deeply penetrating analysis of *De Gemeene Gratie*. No one who is engaged with Kuyper's work can ignore this study. I am also of the opinion that Van Ruler's main thesis about the spiritualistic particular grace in Kuyper has never been the subject of a thorough examination. This thesis makes or breaks Van Ruler's position. And let me declare now already that I consider Van Ruler's main thesis to be unacceptable. Thus I believe that a more thorough investigation of all of Kuyper's *oeuvre* (to which Van Ruler's study motivated me) will justify a refutation.

For if Van Ruler is correct, I would not know what to do with the following themes in and related to Kuyper's theology:

1. *The church as organism.* If, for Kuyper, the church as organism forms the new humanity as "restoration of our shattered human race"[322] and the church can therefore never be something separate and transitory beside cosmic life,[323] how could he possibly have devised such a definition of the church with a spiritualistic vision on particular grace?

---

318. Op. cit., 10.
319. Op. cit., 10–13.
320. Op. cit., 13.
321. Op. cit., 9. With regard to Kuyper's view of particular grace and the conventicles, see also H. J. Langman, *Kuyper en de Volkskerk*, 163–64.
322. *Loc. de Ecclesia*, 102 dictation.
323. See p. 67 above.

CHAPTER I. ABRAHAM KUYPER

Spiritualism *isolates*. Kuyper's particular grace *restores* and it does so over the whole breadth of cosmic life. This restoration *is* not just a matter of eschatology. It is true that the church in its full essence will only come about in the *regnum gloriae*, but the essential character of the kingdom of heaven must also "already attempt to be revealed ... in the *ecclesia* that moves from the Fall into this *regnum gloriae*."[324] God's honor demands this, "because his justice, visibly violated, must also be visibly restored."[325] Not only in individual human beings, but also in human life:

Socially – "Social life came from God. Satan ruined that social life. It must be reborn in the home, in society, and in the state."

Ethically – "Ethical life came from God. Satan ruined that ethical life. It must be reborn."

Intellectually – "The world of ideas came from God. Satan ruined it. It must be reborn. Hence Christian science over against secular science. Our Free University owes its existence to the organic character of humanity that is also apparent in intellectual life. All of human life, also intellectual life, must be won for Christ."[326] Therefore we must reject spiritualism, Methodism, and Anabaptism, which fail to recognize the regeneration of organic life.[327] Can anyone perceive any difficulty that Kuyper with "his" spiritualistic particular grace supposedly had in this context?

For that matter, Kuyper's terminology also points in a totally different direction. If he had really thought in a spiritualistic way about particular grace, how could he countless times have used the image of grafting[328] for the influence of particular grace as the new life on the old ("the grafting of the wild tree," II, 292–99), or the image of yeast,[329] of warp and woof,[330] of the balm of Gilead,[331] of the bulb and the tulip?[332] How could he have spoken so naïvely

---

324. *Loc. de Ecclesia*, 102 dictation.
325. Loc. cit.
326. Op. cit., 47–48.
327. Op. cit., 48–49.
328. *Uit het Woord*, 2nd series I, 342; *Werk van den Heiligen Geest*, 399; *E Voto* I, 128; *Loc. de Christo* I, 105; *Loc. de Salute*, 36, 70 dictation (*de regeneratione!*); *Gemeene Gratie* II, 254–55.
329. *Gemeene Gratie* I, 468; III, 307; *Pro Rege* III, 320.
330. *Loc. de Christo* III, 195.
331. *Gemeene Gratie* I, 357, 378.
332. *Loc. de Ecclesia*, 46: "The actual emergence is not something that is incidental, but that proceeds from it by itself."

about a merging,[333] blending,[334] and influencing[335] of particular grace in common grace? He did *not* think that way, and that is why his opposition to the Anabaptists derived from his view of particular grace. *They* only wanted to recognize the hidden body of Christ in its spiritual character; *he* regarded the church as having been revealed also in the visible form of the life of this world.[336]

We must regard Kuyper's view of the church as organism to be fully "Christian" in the second, narrower sense of the word. I maintain this view over against Van Ruler (see above), S. J. Ridderbos, *Theologische cultuurbeschouwing van Abraham Kuyper*, 197, and W. H. Velema, *De leer der Heilige Geest bij Abraham Kuyper*, 194. They are of the opinion that the church as organism "also [includes] Christian culture in the broader sense that does not arise out of personal faith, but is the result of common grace strengthened by particular grace" (Ridderbos, 197). This seems strange to me. In *De Gemeene Gratie* II, 680–81, Kuyper defines the church as organism clearly as the terrain "where those who personally confess Jesus in their own sphere let the life of common grace be governed by the principles of divine revelation," and (figuratively) as "the three measures of flour that were completely leavened by the leaven of the gospel." For it is the terrain of particular grace that has made the data of common grace serviceable to it.

All passages in *De Gemeene Gratie* about the church as organism can be explained in the same way (I, 224; II, 253–60, 271[!], 274, 667, 680, 689; III, 37, 425, 419). Van Ruler *cum suis* appeal to one quotation that, read in isolation, might support their point of view: II, 272, about the church as organism "which can also reveal itself where all personal faith is absent, but where something of the golden glow of eternal life is nonetheless reflected on the plain façade of the large edifice of human life." But we must pay attention to the words "reveal" and "reflected." In the context we read about *"radiance."* How could Kuyper believe that the church as organism also includes unbelievers when just before the above quotation he stated: "For the church as organism exists before the church as institute does; it always lies behind the institute; it alone gives that institute its *essential* value. The church as organism has its center in heaven, in Christ; it encompasses all ages from the beginning of the world to its end in order to bring all eternity to fulfilment"? (op. cit., 272; italics supplied).

Church as organism is particular grace that is given shape and growth in the world of common grace. But then it is dangerous when Van Ruler compares Kuyper's Christian culture in a narrower and broader sense with two concentric circles. It is true that Kuyper also uses this image (II, 251–52). But whereas Kuyper distinguishes the two circles sharply, Van Ruler blurs the lines. That is

---

333. *Gemeene Gratie* I, 432, 503; II, 252.
334. II, 335.
335. II, 253; *Loc. de Christo* I, 99.
336. *Gemeene Gratie* II, 80.

clearly contrary to Kuyper's intention. Kuyper does believe that particular grace receives shape in this world and therefore presented a principial distinction between "Christian" in the first and second sense. Thus Kuyper did not cause everything to lead to antithesis in *practice*; he also gave it a *principial* foundation: church as organism, i.e., a fully-developed particular grace is accompanied by antithesis—which is anti-Anabaptist!

2. *Breadth of election.* I can be more brief here because the connection with the previous point is apparent. For election does not have individuals as object, but rather the new humanity. You have to think organically and not atomistically about election, says Kuyper.[337] He also states that with respect to election we have to pay attention not only to the elected individuals, but also to the organic connections "as the total of those who have been assembled, to the extent that they have been inspired by the Christian spirit," and that it is "so totally wrong to speak of the church of Christ (as organism) almost exclusively as consisting of the elect or those incorporated in it, while deliberately disregarding the ample number of assembled ones who actually connect the multiplicity of members with the unity of the Body."[338] In view of that, how can this particular grace (election is particular grace, is it not?), which operates to unite, nonetheless in a spiritualizing way cause rejection, or at least expose fault lines everywhere? Van Ruler did not clarify this for us.

3. *The kingdom of heaven.* As we saw, Kuyper described the goal of particular grace as the "realization of the kingdom of heaven."[339] Now he warns against thinking of the kingdom of heaven as an "intangible concept."[340] For it is "not in the least an expression that describes the dominion of the good, the true, and the noble, but without a trace of metaphor, it is a *kingdom* in the full, rich, and very specific sense of the word."[341] It is a kingdom with a King and encompasses "all things, visible and invisible."[342] Therefore, we should not "yearn for a purely mystical regimen" of God that

---

337. Cf. pp. 33–34 above. See also *Loc. de Deo* III, 223ff., dictation 253.
338. *Gemeene Gratie* II, 259.
339. See p. 61 above.
340. *E Voto* IV, 464.
341. Loc. cit. Cf. *Gemeene Gratie* I, 389ff.
342. Op. cit., 464–65.

governs our existence and our actions.³⁴³ "The kingdom of heaven is real; it is not that we shall be *saved*, but that we shall have dominion over nature in order to bring God a sacrifice of all things," says Kuyper when he speaks about the kingship of Christ in Zion, which lies on the terrain of particular grace.³⁴⁴ The kingdom of heaven is "the highest order to which created nature rises" and therefore it is a false spiritualism to maintain "that only souls are saved and at most only humanity as a race is saved also. The dominion of our King encompasses the whole of creation."³⁴⁵ It is all about "the restoration of what existed in Paradise."³⁴⁶ Thus the work of salvation goes back to the work of creation, and the bond that was established in creation but unraveled by sin returns in the kingdom of grace."³⁴⁷

How can anyone fit all this into a spiritualistic grace?

4. *Christ's Kingship*. The kingdom of heaven is not just an eschatological quantity. Of course, its full revelation will come later.³⁴⁸ But meanwhile the realization of this kingdom on earth has begun.³⁴⁹ It is involved in a process of maturation.³⁵⁰ "The real seed from which the unifying power of the kingdom as kingdom will proceed" has entered "into the reality of this life" by and through the incarnation. And since that moment "the great process has begun that will govern all of history and that serves first to allow the Child of Bethlehem, as King of kings, to establish a kingdom and to maintain and expand it; and second, once this great work has been fully completed, to present that kingdom to God the Father again after the day of judgment, so that, as it was from of old, God will be all and in all."³⁵¹

I have already outlined Kuyper's view of the influence that Christ has on this history.³⁵² Christ's dominion "is not at all restricted to dominion over the new life in the elect. By influencing

---

343. Op. cit., 474.
344. *Loc. de Christo* III, 182.
345. *Pro Rege* I, 437, 445.
346. *Loc. de Christo* III, 182.
347. *E Voto* I, 330. Cf. *Gemeene Gratie* II, 366, 681.
348. *Pro Rege* III, 437, 445.
349. Op. cit., 438; *E Voto* IV, 478.
350. *Pro Rege* I, 439, 444.
351. *E Voto* IV, 469.
352. See pp. 47–49, 51 above.

those who are his spiritually, he through them spiritually influences the entire conscious life of our human race. Those who are his are not taken *from* the world, but are preserved *in* the world."[353] If you have read *Pro Rege* I, 123-276, and realize that in those pages Kuyper basically gives an exegesis of a few passages in *De Gemeene Gratie* about the "liberation of the human spirit," you can surely no longer maintain that particular grace operates only *in* the soul and really has *nothing* to do with culture. Either that, or you must place Christ, whose power over nature was depicted by Kuyper as a power in accordance with his humanity (the Mediator of creation does not dominate), outside of particular grace. But surely no one will dare to do so. Thus in the kingship of Christ over the kingdom of universal grace, particular grace and common grace are interwoven "as warp and woof."[354] That is quite different from saying that they, "properly considered," have nothing to do with each other (Van Ruler)!

It is very much to be regretted that in his research Van Ruler considered only *De Gemeene Gratie* (and also briefly the *Encylopaedie*). Had he read *Pro Rege*, he would not have written the following: "Kuyper does not enlighten us doctrinally about the reason why common grace can only come to its full development and actual goal under the influence of particular grace; and the manner in which this influence takes place is barely mentioned" (op. cit., 35). That is indeed true of *De Gemeene Gratie*, but Kuyper wrote more than that, and it is surely difficult to posit such a far-reaching thesis as defended by Van Ruler without examining Kuyper's Christology. For further exegesis of Kuyper's opinion about the liberation of the human spirit, he should have consulted both *Locus de Christo* III, 176-96, and *Pro Rege*.

5. *Expansion of regeneration.* From the foregoing it will be clear that Van Ruler wrongly calls regeneration "the only complete theological category" in Kuyper's work. But apart from that, Kuyper also does not consider regeneration itself to be as restricted as Van Ruler does. It is not limited to the mystical aspect of its immediacy.[355] No one can claim that Kuyper did not teach immediate regeneration. But neither can anyone maintain that Kuyper confined himself to this in his depiction of regeneration.

353. *Pro Rege* I, 446.
354. *Loc. de Christo* III, 195.
355. Cf. also P. A. van Leeuwen, op. cit., 175-76.

When Kuyper calls regeneration the new seed of life, this seed demands the fully grown plant,[356] the *potentia* calls for its *actus*.[357] Then regeneration acquires its stages of growth; then we can speak of a process.[358] Regeneration can be understood in three ways: as the gift of new life, as the entrance of new life in the world, and as the completion thereof."[359] The process begins with the "radical transformation of the properties of our nature, comparable to the grafting of a domesticated branch into a wild tree,"[360] and it will end with the regeneration of the world.[361] In that way the deepest inner parts and the broadest outer parts are joined to each other; essence calls for existence. The flourishing of the new life is not impeded by its spirituality, but by the resistance of sin. Hence "the very first holy impulse does set out to penetrate our consciousness and our will, but it is certainly not always capable of conquering and overcoming the opposite action that from out of the past has a lasting effect on that consciousness and will."[362]

From beginning to end on this road, says Kuyper, there is much that "does not contribute anything to your eternal salvation"[363] (actually, to all that is revealed of the life of the elect after their regeneration in the narrower sense, as we have already seen). But it is important to interpret Kuyper fairly! Although much is not a *means* to salvation, it is a *consequence* of salvation.[364] It remains one plant "that consists of three parts: 1. the seed of life; 2. the roots that extend into the ground; and 3. the branches that spread out in the sky. When we apply this metaphor to humanity, the first, the seed of life, is the person's hidden "I"; the roots are the inner development of the person's being, through which one receives life-giving sap from God; and the branches are the life expressions by which the person emerges into the world. This seed is made *holy* in *regeneration*; the roots are extended in the coming *sanctification*, and the grafting of the branches is the person's *self-purification*."[365]

---

356. *Gemeene Gratie* II, 299, 314, 336; *Loc. de Salute*, 149.
357. *Loc. de Ecclesia*, 46–47; *Loc. de Salute*, 93 dictation; *E Voto* IV, 472; *Gemeene Grati*e II, 52.
358. *Loc. de Ecclesia*, 45–46.
359. *Loc. de Salute*, 70 dictation.
360. Loc. cit.
361. *Gemeene Gratie* II, 689.
362. II, 365.
363. II, 336.
364. II, 337.
365. II, 331.

And while this self-purification is not "solely" a matter of particular grace and, in fact, takes place largely on the terrain of common grace (growth and development of trunk and branch "are also dependent on the air, wind, rain, sunshine, harmful insects, and external damage caused by animals or humans; in short, on the *environment* in which the tree has been planted"),[366] here, too, there is a *blending* of particular grace and common grace.[367]

How could it be otherwise? "If grace were solely about forgiveness of sin and the salvation of the soul, you could consider *grace* to be something that exists outside of nature, that occurs apart from nature, and so is like a jar of oil that, poured out on the tossing waves, floats on the waters but remains separate from them."[368] But the metaphors for the true relationship between particular grace and common grace Kuyper derives from the vegetable kingdom, where the root fibers of grace "penetrate everywhere into the joints and cracks of the life of nature."[369] Although after the immediate regeneration almost everything in the Christian life is, according to Kuyper, annexed by common grace, the trunk and the branches continue to be connected to the seed of life and the roots. Thus, also in conversion and sanctification. "Conversion is the consequence of regeneration and is only possible and conceivable for one who is regenerated. But furthermore, the consequence of regeneration will never happen except through the influence of the Holy Spirit and, since its aim is eternal life, it belongs unquestionably to *particular grace*. It makes a huge difference for a plant in what kind of soil you plant it.... If the same seed of regeneration falls on one occasion in the well-prepared field of a high-minded person, while on another occasion it falls in the infertile soil of a base person, the difference in the development of the crops *must* be significant."[370] The question which part of this is particular grace and which common grace does not concern us here. It is important to establish (for the umpteenth time) how well particular grace can *flourish* in the soil of common grace. How can such expressions arise from a spiritualizing particular grace? "Regenerated"? Yes, "but you

366. II, 333.
367. II, 335.
368. I, 227.
369. I, 228.
370. II, 283.

are regenerated as a *human being*."³⁷¹ This is said by a man who had just opposed the Neo-Kohlbruggeans.³⁷²

1. I will admit that what Van Ruler unjustly claimed *in general* about Kuyper's spiritualism, may hold true *in particular* situations. Who can deny that Kuyper's doctrine of *immediate* regeneration displays a spiritualistic trait? The just-mentioned qualification applies whenever Spirit and Word do not go hand in hand in the genesis of new life. But that is not what the current issue is all about. "In Kuyper's doctrine of grace there is undoubtedly spiritualism, dualism, and particularism, but not in the way ... Van Ruler suggests," says P. A. van Leeuwen in *Het kerkbegrip in de theologie van Abraham Kuyper*, 175. We were confronted with the question whether regeneration, when acting immediately, shows development in this life. In Kuyper's work, does regeneration really cross the bridge that God has built in common grace, a bridge to the life of the world (cf. II, 78)? Van Ruler's interpretation answers this question in the negative. Our answer is positive.

Hence the quotations in which Van Ruler tries to support his position are no longer particularly relevant. See footnotes 290, 292, 294. When you look them up you will notice (re footnote 290) that they merely substantiate the above-mentioned spiritualistic trait in the doctrine of immediate regeneration and (re footnote 292) that especially II, 684–85 demonstrates so beautifully how the world's resistance impels particular grace to withdraw itself more into the spiritual. Particular grace has to fight a *battle* (II, 679; *Loc. de Foedere*, 141–42!). For it is a stumbling block to the Jews and foolishness to the Greeks (II, 343). Hence no principial isolation; just a temporary retreat. The "idea of Anabaptist avoidance aims to separate particular grace sharply from the terrain of common grace (II, 684)," but Kuyper speaks of an antithesis that is only temporary (op. cit., 685).

I must be a bit more thorough with regard to footnote 294. For here Van Ruler quotes II, 654, which is also used by other Kuyper exegetes (Ridderbos, op. cit., 133–34; Velema, op. cit., 124–25; S. U. Zuidema, "Gemene Gratie en Pro Rege in Dr. Abraham Kuyper" [24 *A.R. Staatkunde*, 9, (1954)]; J. Kamphuis, op. cit., 7; R. H. Bremmer, *De Reformatie* 25, 265). Let me quote the relevant passage once more: "In itself the end goal of particular grace lies on the other side of the grave. Its goal lies in eternity and, viewed in isolation, it could, if necessary, occur completely apart from earthly life." By way of explanation:

(a) It says "*if necessary.*" So one should not make a *rule* out of "if necessary." This is what Kamphuis does with his exegesis: "Particular grace, whose goal is the salvation of the elect, has no point of contact with the world at all" (apart from the birth of the elect) (op. cit., 8). Has no point of contact? That should be: *does not have to* have!

(b) Kuyper speaks of an "*end goal.*" That is something quite different from

---
371. II, 340.
372. II, 328; cf. *Loc. de Salute*, 142; *E Voto* IV, 289.

"the one and all." For specifically about the elect Kuyper says a little later: If their own contribution to eternal life cannot, in the final analysis, be the end goal of their long life on earth (think of the children who die young), then the end goal must be something else: the glorification of God's name. "And since God comes to them in that world with his common grace, it is a matter of course [! J.D.] that the *particular* grace that was given them comes into direct contact with that common grace; indeed, neither can reach its end goal without the operation of both" (II, 659, italics supplied). I think here also of *Locus de Ecclesia*, 48ff., where Kuyper follows a line of reasoning similar to what we find in the above quotation (starting with "In itself") and then says that all spheres must be *reborn* and won for Christ (op. cit., 48).

(c) Kuyper states that "viewed *in isolation*" the end goal of particular grace "could, if necessary, occur completely apart from earthly life." He is speaking in an abstract way. For what was possible did not become reality. The elect with their particular grace *were* not placed outside of this world: "an idea that was central to the doctrines of the original Anabaptists" (II, 659). We have to guard against the possibility, says Kuyper, "that particular grace is treated too much as standing by itself, in disregard of its *basis* in 'common grace' and of its end goal [! J.D.], i.e., the preservation of the *world* that was created, maintained, and never abandoned by God. This mistake has the sad consequence that 'particular grace' hovers in the air, severs the salvation of the soul from our position and our life in the world, ... and prevents our Christian nation from achieving a perfectly sound, truly Christian, faith-inspiring, and resilience-boosting life and worldview" (I, 319).

(d) If particular grace withdraws into the spiritual-mystical realm, then that is only *temporary* in nature. The *ecclesia triumphans* exists "for the time being only spiritually" in heaven; the *ecclesia militans* on earth exists both in internally spiritual as well as in externally perceptible form, while the *ecclesia gloriae* will be both invisible and visible, "but in such a way that its visible aspect will completely cover its invisible aspect" (*Loc. de Ecclesia*, 33 dictation).

(e) Even if I had been unable to defend this "dangerous quotation" (Ridderbos) to any extent (it is not possible to do so fully, for does Kuyper not regard *all* particular grace here within a range of vision that he restricts too much *elsewhere*?), I would still have said that I have gathered enough material from Kuyper's *oeuvre* to refute the charge of spiritualism.

It is true that there are contradictions in Kuyper's work. Also in *De Gemeene Gratie* there are statements that do not fit within my interpretation. For example, II, 137, (particular grace touches "the center of the inner life of the soul exclusively," while common grace extends to our entire human life in all its manifestations); III, 105, ("particular grace saves unto eternal life and is not directed to our present life"); III, 308 (but cf. 321!), 341. Ridderbos notes correctly (op. cit., 136–37) that we should not seek Kuyper's fundamental view in such assertions.

As explanation of such statements I should like to adduce that in *De Gemeene*

CHAPTER I. ABRAHAM KUYPER

Gratie Kuyper is concerned so extensively with common grace that he sometimes gives it too much attention and, accordingly, too little to particular grace—too little if the totality of his theology is taken into account.

2. Kuyper variously uses the adjectives "new," "supernatural," and "natural" in reference to particular grace. See Ridderbos, op. cit., 64–69, 132. The adjective "natural" does not fit Van Ruler's objections to Kuyper, but as characterization of particular grace, which is *re*-creation and thus rectifies "the elements that existed but became warped (II, 390)," it directly opposes Van Ruler's view. So, too, regeneration is not a particularistic-spiritualistic affair, but "a re-creation of our own being, in such a way that it will again result in its original plan and aptitude" (*E Voto* IV, 285). Cf. Ridderbos, 66–67.

3. My rejection of Van Ruler's interpretation also makes me skeptical of S. U. Zuidema's study "Gemeene Gratie en Pro Rege in Dr. Abraham Kuyper" (*A.R. Staatkunde* 24 [1954], 1–19 and 49–73), referred to earlier. He disputes Van Ruler, arguing that he "has taken inadequate or no account of Kuyper when he overcomes and disposes of the polar tension between particular grace and common grace in principle, specifically in his doctrine of particular grace [church as organism! J.D.]." According to Zuidema, "Kuyper does this when he *refuses* to regard the operation of particular grace in regeneration as a transformation of our being, but views it as a deeply religious transformation of the 'innermost axis' of our existence, by which is *rectified* what sin had transposed *into its opposite*, as he taught in *De Gemeene Gratie* (II, 298)" (op. cit., 12, 15, 56, 71). Zuidema here says much that is true. But first he fell on Van Ruler's sword by presupposing a polar dualism in Kuyper (4, 67, 69; dual-polar relationship, 12, 15, 56, 71; dialectic relationship, 4). Zuidema continues as follows: That particular grace and common grace belong together is implied in these characterizations. Polar dualism is not the same thing as antithetic dualism (16–17). The poles attract each other. But "polar" also implies *tension*. *Where does that tension come from?* "Particular grace is not really directed ... to action on the terrain of temporal life and in the territory of visible things" (9). "Van Ruler is partly correct when he draws attention to the fact that Kuyper's doctrine of common grace is also governed by what he believed about the particular grace of God ... in this life" (12). Zuidema concludes that if Van Ruler's Kuyper is "not the only Kuyper," he is nonetheless "Kuyper" (72).

Although Zuidema, when he takes all of Kuyper into account, thus rejects Van Ruler's position (and rightly so) and although he *eventually* arrives at an assessment to which I can subscribe, he reaches this end goal via the proposition that Kuyper *broke through* the polar-dualistic contrast between particular grace and common grace (67–68, 71–72). I admit of certain tensions between the operations of the two forms of grace in Kuyper, but I do not accept that there is a tension that led from a spiritualistic doctrine of particular grace to a dual-polar way of thinking "the intent and effect of which governed Kuyper and which he continued to follow for the most part" (71). Zuidema's claim "that Kuyper had to change his *initial* exclusively spiritualistic and eschatological view of particular grace" (67, italics supplied) is peculiar. The word "initial" appears three times (17, 62, 67), creating the impression that Zuidema is able to identify the time of the "breakthrough." And indeed, as Zuidema continues, "While Kuyper initially taught that when the Noahic covenant (of common grace) concludes, the kingdom of heaven begins [citing I, 432, J.D.], he now abandons that spiritualistic and eschatological point of view in the sense that he makes room for the idea of a revelation of the kingdom of heaven in the realm of common grace in this dispensation—a revelation and a taking shape" (citing II, 672, and other places). So Kuyper changed course, shall we say, between volumes I and II of *De Gemeene Gratie*? But to be able to concur with Zuidema one would have to excise large portions from volume I. See, *inter alia*, 26–27, 221–28, 328–90, 378(!): Jacob's people were created and enriched by God, says Kuyper, "to prepare the medicine of eternal life for the peoples of the earth. And the mystical aspect consists exclusively of this, that this 'balm of Gilead,' which was prepared in Palestine for the whole world, is not a medicine that is administered *externally*, but one that penetrates the root of life and only operates by means of *rebirth* and *faith*." And as far as that "eschatological kingdom of heaven is concerned," I have already demonstrated (quoting especially from publications that predated *De Gemeene Gratie* I) that in Kuyper this also has its initial realization in this dispensation. Immediately before the quotation (I, 378) Kuyper already spoke about the church as organism (I, 377). Zuidema's conclusions were too hasty.

One other matter: I fully accept Zuidema's observation that it is in *Pro Rege* and the antithesis on the visible-temporal terrain of common grace that Kuyper's heart beats (66). But Zuidema also hears Kuyper's heart beating in the "mysticism" and in the "pilgrimage" that particular grace independently brings along with it: "That is where his heart beats. First there. Always there" (4; cf. also 9, 17; re "pilgrim": 10, 11, 17, 64). I would prefer to say: Kuyper's heart is there *also*. For otherwise, if not the entire, but certainly the *real* Kuyper again becomes a spiritualist—despite the fact that he continuously states in *De Gemeene Gratie* that Scripture always points "first to God's glory and after that to the salvation of the elect" (I, 227).

6. *Historical arguments*. I also have historical arguments to contest Van Ruler's view. It was not until 1887 that Kuyper introduced common grace in outline in his *Tweeërlei Vaderland*. Before then and also afterwards until 1895, when he began his series of articles entitled *De Gemeene Gratie*, one cannot really claim that the doctrine of common grace played a central role in Kuyper's thought. Nonetheless, his great achievements in the realms of politics and scholarship date from before 1887. The Anti-Revolutionary Party

and the Free University came into existence. How did Kuyper, if he had been locked in the bunker of particular grace, escape from it without the doctrine of common grace? Surely one can hardly assume that this brilliant thinker operated until around 1890 without a principial foundation for his actions on the terrain of this world?

I believe that I have an answer to this question. Kuyper never knew of a spiritualizing grace; from the beginning he regarded regeneration as *organic* in nature. His *Dat de genade particulier is* was followed by *De Leer der Verbonden*. In his covenant doctrine the organism-idea received "a truly Reformed stamp."[373]

Through the organism-idea the way of the soul to the world became passable from within; from without, the "natural knowledge of God" (in Kuyper's first period) and "common grace" (in his second period) ensured that this path remained open.

Kuyper published *De Gemeene Gratie* as a series of articles *De Heraut* between September 1, 1895, and July 14, 1901. It is surprising to discover that he only began to speak about common grace relatively late in his life. His address *Tweeërlei Vaderland* (1887) began a new period. Before that, we come across the word "grace" occasionally, but used in a more general sense (S. J. Ridderbos, op. cit., 105, points to *Heraut*, December 8, 1878, but we can go further back to *Uit het Woord*, 1st series III, 19, dating from early 1874). However, there was no development of this concept of grace, let alone of a "doctrine." Kuyper's assertion that when he wrote *Dat de genade particulier is* the doctrine of the covenant and of common grace served as background right from the beginning (*Gemeene Gratie* I, 5, 9, i.e., "since 1878") must be incorrect as regards common grace (so also V. Hepp, *De Algemeene genade*, 7). Kuyper made mistakes in dates more often. See P. A. van Leeuwen, op. cit., 49; C. Veenhof, *Predik het Woord*, 243.

It is also clear from his *Dictaten Dogmatiek* that Kuyper only began to think about common grace in greater depth around 1887. In *Locus de Creaturis* (1884) and *Locus de Homine* (1885) there is no reference to common grace. Initially there is nothing in *Locus de Peccato* (1885–1886) in places where Kuyper would certainly have spoken of it later (3, 15–16, 43–44, 70–71, 82–83, 84ff.). But then suddenly common grace is mentioned (109, 120ff., 234–35, 139, 142, 144), although the discussion is still very incomplete. Also in *Het werk van den Heiligen Geest* (1883–1886) the odd reference already appears (40, 365[?], 435, 502[?], 785–86[!]). But in other passages that are relevant to its discussion, common grace is not mentioned (269ff., 343–44, 365, 743, 780–81). After *Locus de Peccato*, Kuyper wrote *Locus de Christo* (1886–1888), in which volumes I and II do not

373. P. A. van Leeuwen, op. cit., 156.

mention common grace even in places where one would have expected it (71: about the arresting of sin because of the gift of the Messiah; 97ff. about the mediatorship of creation and salvation[!]; II, 74, 84–85). But in the third volume, written at about the time of Kuyper's address *Tweeërlei Vaderland*, we can already see the contours of what would later be broadly developed (30–31, 72, 177ff.!).

Still, also after 1887, it appears that Kuyper did not develop a complete doctrine of common grace right away. In *E Voto* he rarely speaks of it (1886–1894). V. Hepp (*De Reformatie* 4, 153) argued that it did not contain the term "common grace" but that the matter itself was very much in evidence. The first assertion is incorrect: IV, 306, 308, 462, speak of "common grace"; I, 414, 421; III, 355–56; IV, 176, 308, 568, speak of "common favor"; I, 414, 421; II, 203ff., 373, 377; III, 382, 431, 433; IV, 22, 65, 81ff., 100–01, 126, 187, of "general favor"; and further, I, 56, of "arresting favor"; and I, 396–97 of "grace" without a qualifying epithet. Nonetheless, it is remarkable that at essential points common grace is not mentioned (I, 34, 46, 52–53, 54–55 [Lord's Day 3, Answer 8!], 77–78; III, 191–92, 512–13, 517–19, 556ff., 589–90, 593–94, 619; IV, 239, 334–35). The *gratia communis* very definitely has a place in Kuyper's *Encyclopaedie* (1894). We have already seen that there he also speaks of the frightful aspect of common grace (see pp. 28–29 above). It is noteworthy that Herman Bavinck had already read *Encyclopaedie* before he delivered his address *De Algemeene Genade* in December 1994 (op. cit., 44). I venture the supposition that Bavinck was especially stimulated by Kuyper's passages about *communis gratia* to give this address. Hence it is incorrect to say, as G. Th. Rothuizen does in *Primus usus legis*, 219, that Bavinck "for the first time again gave expression to" the idea of common grace. Zuidema was also incorrect in saying that Bavinck preceded Kuyper on this path (op. cit., 1). The reverse was the case. Kuyper had already introduced the material, both in 1887 and in 1894, and a discerning thinker such as Bavinck would have immediately recognized its explosive power.

But what was the situation before 1887? After his conversion in Beesd, Kuyper expanded his activities well beyond the boundaries of the instituted church and became well-known in political and scientific circles throughout the Netherlands. He did all this without any reference to the doctrine of common grace, which he only started to make use of "long after he heard the call to serve the LORD in all human relationships" (C. Veenhof, *De Reformatie* 31, 122). How does Kuyper with his spiritualistic particular grace fare without having the benefit of the necessary corrective action of a common grace? The answer is not difficult. Read the chapter entitled "Wedergeboorte en Bekeering" [Regeneration and Conversion] in *Uit het Woord*, 1st series III (written in 1874). There regeneration is *re*-generation: "Thus it is self-evident that neither our feelings, nor our thinking, nor our will, not even our character traits as the inclination of our being, could operate prior to regeneration otherwise than in confusion, misconception, and therefore destructively rather than constructively. Nonetheless, they existed and operated albeit in their unnatural way. With regeneration, these qualities were not taken from us and replaced by a new apparatus; rather, *they were put in their place*, driven in the direction where they belonged, stripped of obstacles and so enabled to operate harmoniously" (op. cit., 42; italics supplied). Through regeneration everything is rejuvenated, says Kuyper (43). What is this "everything?" "Regeneration does not only operate with respect to *humanity*, but to the entire *creation*. If you lose sight of that, you do not understand the mystery [! J.D.] of regeneration. Human beings are never presented in Scripture as creatures that were placed on this earth without their having any connection with the earth" (51). Thus in "the destiny of humanity" there will be "a change for the better," and then this favorable change must also have an effect on the destiny of creation" (52). It is one single life process and therefore there must be "a necessary connection between the regeneration of humanity and the regeneration of creation" (53). That connection, so Kuyper continues, lies in the man Jesus Christ, in his incarnation and resurrection, by which the destiny of creation was determined (53). "Our regeneration can only be finished, be completed, when we, together with everything that belongs to us, with our entire personality in spirit, soul, and body, and therefore also with the ambiance that must surround us in order to allow our human essence to reach its full development, to shine in the radiance of regenerated life" (55). We are now standing between its beginning and its end (loc. cit.).

This depiction of regeneration clearly cuts off the *particularism* that Van Ruler speaks of. An earlier publication of Kuyper also refutes it, namely *Ons Program*, in which a passage written in 1872 says that the church has the task of "winning society for Christ." For is Christ not the "Head of humanity?" (493). See further, *inter alia*, op. cit., 126ff. (1871) and 127–28 (1873).

We would not have expected otherwise. You can probably not find any of Kuyper's publications of some magnitude, from the first to the last, in which the word *organism* does not appear. In this concept of organism, which Kuyper most likely borrowed from the German philosophy of his days (especially from Schleiermacher and Rothe; see P. A. van Leeuwen, op. cit., 109–21), humanity is seen as a unity, as one body. But this organic humanity is also connected with the entire creation. Kuyper explains: "There is therefore a most intimate relationship between human beings and creation. Together they form a unity. Just as human beings are not complete without their actual bodies, they cannot be conceived of without that second body that we call the world. Each preceding act of creation has humanity as its goal. And in the one human body the result of all wonders that the Lord God wrought in the mineral, vegetable, and animal kingdoms is summed up. What preceded it was but the foundation upon which human beings, as image bearers of God, would be placed" (*Uit het Woord*, 1st series, III, 51; cf. *Loc. de Consummatione*, 296: "We have one soul and two bodies"). If humanity falls into sin, then creation *must* also fall into disarray because of humanity's organic unity with creation (*Loc. de Peccato*, 17 dictation,

26, 35–36, 50–51; *Uit het Woord*, 1st series III, 55). But when fortunes change, says Kuyper, then regeneration *must* also operate organically from the center to the outer circumference: You cannot explain this on the basis of the individual human person, but it is possible on the basis of the general human nature that Christ assumed, in which we and the whole renewed creation are included as a seed of life. About the incarnation and creation, cf. *Loc. de Christo* I, 102; II, 74–75; about us and the incarnation of Christ, *Uit het Woord*, 2nd series I, 120–25; *Loc. de Christo* I, 38–39, 72; II, 3 dictation 8–9, 33. That is how the new life is propelled out of Christ into us (*unio mystica*) toward the circumference. "It does begin with the palingenesis of the soul, but it is directed also to the palingenesis of the body. At the center it establishes the bond with Christ in the *unio mystica*, but in the circumference it extends itself to all powers and forms of the cosmic life of humanity. It is particularistic by virtue of election; but in such a way that it does not merely save some individuals, but reorganizes the whole organism of our human race" (*Loc. de Foedere*, 133 dictation).

In this connection Kuyper speaks of the *covenant of grace*. That is not surprising. For in the doctrine of the covenant he was able to give the organism-idea a Reformed shape. He states that ethical life does not exist atomistically and that there is therefore a place for the covenant (*Loc. de Foedere*, 5 dict., 51–52 dict., 96, 99, 133 dict.). When Kuyper arrived in Utrecht (1867) he learned about the covenant and, after researching it, became familiar with the concept again (*Loc. de Foedere*, 93–94): "Slowly the doctrine of the covenant has, thanks be to God, again arisen as a vital force," and it is "of utmost importance to set aside false inventions and to see the solid basis on which the doctrine of the covenant rests. For that purpose it is necessary for us to remember, as we always must with regard to everything that has to do with the *gratia particularis*, that we are always dealing with the human person as instrument. Use is made of human nature in the form in which it exists" (loc. cit.).

That is why it is almost self-evident that Kuyper's *Dat de genade particulier is* was followed by *De Leer der Verbonden*. For election (we have seen this already and it was Kuyper's opinion from the outset) "is connected with all things." Election implies church, and church implies the world. The Son of God assumed a human *nature*. "And since human nature is the communal property of our entire race, and all nations, peoples and families of our human race, being of one blood, are mutually connected and stand in a relationship with one another, it is self-evident [! J.D.] that the Mediator, through his incarnation, entered into a *real living connection* with all branches and twigs that sprouted from the tree of humanity. Therefore," so Kuyper concludes, "those who, on the basis of an incorrect understanding of particular grace, make it appear that people who do *not* come to eternal life have nothing whatsoever to do with the incarnation of the Word, are seriously mistaken" (*Dat de genade particulier is*, 121–22; *Uit het Woord*, 2nd series I). Hence Kuyper announces that he will discuss these matters more broadly in *De leer der Verbonden* (op. cit., 122).

Those looking for a doctrinal break with the spiritualism of the conventicle world of Beesd can find it *here*. The testimony of a younger contemporary of Kuyper, who attended the meetings of conventicles for many years, also confirms this. Concerning the appreciation for Kuyper in those circles he writes: "There also came a time when people no longer enjoyed reading his doctrinal lead articles. Not after the series *Dat de genade particulier is* was followed by *De leer der Verbonden* and when in *Het werk van den Heiligen Geest* sanctification was addressed after justification" (M. van den Berg, in H. S. S. Kuyper and J. H. Kuyper, eds., *Herinneringen van de oude garde*, 29–30).

"Anabaptists have no organic concept; their world and life view is entirely atomistic," we read in *Locus de Christo* I, 101. And when election is not regarded as organically included in Christ, then, of course, "any connection is missing and you can never proceed from your own 'I' to your country and people" (*Wortel in dorre aarde*, 14). *Here* we have the true anti-spiritualistic Kuyper with his view on regeneration, church, and world. The way from the soul to the world lies open, from the inside out.

But it is also necessary and real from the outside. I will not yet present here what I will say about this later. But I can already mention that before 1887 Kuyper had a kind of counterpart of his common grace doctrine in his doctrine of natural knowledge of God. When I say that the way is kept open also *from the outside*, I am not forgetting how, according to Kuyper, the natural knowledge of God and common grace are also *inner* matters. But I am now concerned with a global image: Christians with their particular grace do not remain hermits when it is *outside* that they meet their God, who calls them to their task not in foreign parts but in surroundings where they may feel at home. For their familiar surroundings are safeguarded by *grace*. That is where God meets them with his common grace. See also footnote 272.

Here I conclude my refutation of Van Ruler's position on Kuyper's spiritualism. It is impossible to maintain that position. I have come to know a Kuyper who did not use the word "organism" casually, but who let himself be governed by the concept in his discussion of election, Christ, the church, and regeneration. As he put it, particular grace has no problem operating in the world as though it were shy and timid. It seeks expansion. The desire to realize the Christian religion "follows naturally" (*Calvinisme en Revisie*, 14).

§ 10. The opinion of Gerard Th. Rothuizen

Thus far I have been concerned especially with *particular* grace in order to discover the motive, the background, of Kuyper's common grace. It stands to reason that there are interpreters who demand all attention (also) for *common* grace in order to discover the background of Kuyper's doctrine from that direction, either fully or partially. Did Kuyper not state unequivocally that common grace also has an independent goal, namely, "to disclose in its full breadth and length what God intended when he laid the seeds of higher development in our race, in spite of Satan's resistance and notwithstanding sin"?[374] And did Van Ruler not write that there are portions in *De Gemeene Gratie* "in which this independent goal of common grace is celebrated and has its praises sung in a manner that leaves you perplexed as you search for the function of particular grace"?[375]

I shall briefly mention here what Van Ruler searched for and believed he found. According to him, Kuyper achieved two things when he posited this independent goal of common grace:

1. "Had Kuyper not regarded the operation of common grace as independent, had he viewed it solely as preparation for and condition of particular grace, he would have been able to appreciate culture as the fruit of common grace only as the terrain on which there is a place for the church as institute of particular grace. But that is not what he wants! For him it is all about a culture occupying an independent position and having a significance of its own, namely, Christian culture" (op. cit., 48).

2. By regarding common grace as independent Kuyper avoids the Roman Catholic view of the relationship between church and culture, "in which culture is drawn into the church and something may only bear the name of Christian culture if bound to the church" (op. cit., 48). Kuyper does not want a culture that is an appendix to the life of the church (II, 635)" (op. cit., 49).

What drove Kuyper to defend common grace in its independence with respect to particular grace? Let us listen to the answer that Gerard Th. Rothuizen gave in his study *Primus usus legis*.

Kuyper's complete view of particular grace and common grace, according to Rothuizen, "carries traces of: (a) an isolation of the first; (b) a fertilization of the second; and finally (c) an independence of the second that is granted by the first."[376] His line of reasoning continues as follows: Kuyper's realm of thought "was adaptable enough to produce the necessary respect and thankfulness for what the world was able to present on its own to humanity."[377] One can

---

374. II, 630. See further pp. 33–34 and 61 above.
375. Van Ruler, op. cit., 33.
376. Rothuizen, op. cit., 132.
377. Loc. cit.

speak of secularization here. Kuyper himself did that too when he called secularization "one of the most profound foundational ideas of Calvinism."[378] "It is clear that this secularization means dechristianization in the first place, but it is no less clear that it involves more than that. It also means that Kuyper was exceptionally able to appreciate common grace, not only thanks to particular grace but also as existing independently alongside it."[379]

Rothuizen clarifies what is meant by that "more" involved in Kuyper's secularization: There is "a secularization not directly from out of faith, but yet *in bonam partem* [in a positive sense]" also in Kuyper.[380] It is a secularization that the world "itself has power do something about."[381] Rothuizen finds a message in this: "Christians will not always reach out to the world and be at peace with this, not only when that is not possible, but also because it is not always necessary. One can promote the secularization of life (interpreted *in bonam partem*) by promoting it, but *also* by letting it carry on to see what will develop, and *that* also might well present a breathtaking scene. Psalm 8 does not place everything under the feet of believers, but under the feet of human beings."[382] "In addition to aggression *against* and synthesis *with* that which is secular," so Rothuizen says, "Kuyper has from time to time felt satisfied with an analysis *of* what is secular: *in bonam partem*! Christianization is, indeed, aggression and synthesis: correction. But adherence to common grace is more than Christianization, and the church does not think only in terms of Christian organizations."[383] In this quotation we clearly recognize Rothuizen's above-mentioned tripartite division of Kuyper's doctrine.

Rothuizen's interpretation gains a wider import (not only in Van Ruler's theology, but also) when he draws attention to Kuyper's doctrine of a Messianic intermezzo. For this he quotes Kuyper, who states *"that particular revelation, and thus also particular grace, merely has an intervening significance and that what is permanent and lasting is not particular revelation but the creation ordinance,"* and also that "in

---

378. Op. cit., 237. Cf. *Gemeene Gratie* II, 279.
379. Rothuizen, op. cit., 237.
380. Op. cit., 133.
381. Op. cit., 134.
382. Op. cit., 130.
383. Op. cit., 251.

the *re-creation* of all things the original creation will triumph."[384] Rothuizen argues as follows: It is true that this intermezzo does not involve a "liquidation of the incarnation," as in Van Ruler. But although Christ remains,[385] the "Christian element" disappears. The last does not necessarily mean that the incarnation is liquidated. "We believe that it is quite defensible without the disappearance of the Savior, the monument of God's humanness. That the law is possible, indeed, desirable without the gospel and that the divine and the human will meet at some point on this basis, free and immediate and therefore outside of a specific Christian context, does not per se mean that people are only human without Christ. Similarly, the handing over of Christ and his kingdom to the Father, as we read about it in 1 Corinthians 15, does not per se mean the disappearance of Christ himself or his total merger again into the Trinity."[386] But though the Messiah remains, the Messianic aspect disappears, also in Kuyper.[387] In the language of Rothuizen's study: "The first use of the law remains and the other uses are absorbed in it."[388] The function of the law, its first use (political or civil), which causes "our *being human*" to emerge in "our being *peccator*," is what remains, while the elenctical or pedagogical use, "which convinces us of our being *peccator* in our being human, and the didactic or normative use, which demonstrates our being holy in our being *peccator*,"[389] disappear. The first use of the law—therewith Rothuizen characterizes Kuyper's *De Gemeene Gratie*.[390]

Yet another characterization presented by Rothuizen demands our attention. "It was Kuyper who testified, specifically with a view to the consummation: 'The realm of grace does not exist beside and is not separate from natural life, but must in fact display its nobility by its impact on natural life. *The medicine serves no purpose by itself*' [italics supplied by Rothuizen]. Anticipation is indeed what typifies

---

384. Rothuizen, op. cit., 216–17. Kuyper is quoted from, respectively, *Gemeene Gratie* I, 333, and I, 489.
385. Rothuizen, op. cit., 240, quotes *De Vleeswording des Woords*, 31 ("Christ became human, remains human, will eternally remain human. He does not lay down his human nature again") as decisive for his argument. Cf. also pp. 195–96 of the same work.
386. Rothuizen, op. cit., 241.
387. Op. cit., 241–42.
388. Op. cit., 220.
389. Op. cit., 23 (italics supplied). Cf. op. cit., 16.
390. Op. cit., 146.

Kuyper."[391] Van Ruler describes this well, according to Rothuizen, when the former says: "Kuyper finds 'an initial irruption of the powers of particular grace already in the visible things today,' and points out how consequently 'that higher form of human life becomes public and is a foreshadowing of the future realm of glory' (II, 689). Kuyper thus sees in this an anticipation of the eschatological 'appropriation' ... of the reality of visible things, that is, of the data of common grace through particular grace, in which the re-creative power of particular grace will also claim for itself the entire terrain of common grace (II, 684–85)."[392] The one grace cannot keep away from the other, the church not from the state, the other uses of the law not from the civil use. "What is this fear of separation, this Kuyperian aggressiveness? Antithesis? Undoubtedly. But why? Fear of the present world? Certainly. But also anticipation of the world of the future."[393] We must leave this complexity with Kuyper, says Rothuizen. "For him, eschatology meant antithesis, but no less, anticipation. Thus, one could experience it in heaven and on earth, in Christianization and in secularization, too much in the church as well as too much in the world— to the extent that one did not encounter it when moving from one to the other!"[394]

1. *Secularization* – attention for the human, the purely human, also independent of the "Christian" element: this serves to encapsulate Rothuizen's view of what Kuyper means by his doctrine of common grace (first use of the law). The difference between Rothuizen and Van Ruler is plain. Van Ruler says: Kuyper is concerned with *particular* grace. Rothuizen says: he is concerned with *common* grace, with moving from the church to the world. The "Christian" element so disappears, the human remains.

2. To avoid misunderstanding it should be mentioned that Rothuizen sees not only a secularization from out of the world (op. cit., 129–30), but also a secularization from out of faith (127–128): "If possible, particular revelation does something with general revelation and we are amazed at it" (130). Kuyper wanted to give this a particular form in the Free University. Rothuizen: "It is especially the Christian who is the promoter of the secularization in the sense of a (nonetheless remaining) development of the human race. That is how he

---

391. Op. cit., 224. Citation of Kuyper, *Voleinding* I, 285.
392. Op. cit., 224. Citation of Van Ruler, op. cit., 91.
393. Op. cit., 231.
394. Op. cit., 255.

sanctifies the world and how public life is stripped of its demonic power" (231). But it is also true that "at the end of the day we are not human beings in order to become Christians, but Christians in order to become human beings. The rebuilding of the world is not the consequence of the Christianization of the world—rather the reverse—but it is very much indebted to it" (212-13). And to the extent that Christianity already now truly makes its appearance as Christianity, it gives "the world the same opportunity ... to make its appearance as world" (213). Also this tendency of secularization as he interprets it is what Rothuizen finds in Kuyper (214).

3. This is also the place to draw attention to the background of the *cultural optimism* that many have detected in Kuyper. It is not surprising that this was attributed to him, considering that he ascribed an independent goal to common grace and described its result as follows: "The result therefore is that the human race succeeds, that it rises out of its sunken state, that it always climbs to a higher level, and the principial creation ordinance, which was given to humanity before the Fall and would allow human beings to attain dominion over all of nature, is, thanks to 'common grace,' also carried out after the Fall" (*Gemeene Gratie* II, 631). But while some applaud such statements of Kuyper (Rothuizen, op. cit., e.g. 231), others condemn it. Thus Th. L. Haitjema, who directs his criticism of the common grace doctrine especially against its *independent* goal, writes: "This new Calvinistic doctrine makes it very easy to regard oneself fully as a person of culture and to sing loud praises of science, as Kuyper does constantly, but at the same time it does great harm to the Christian idea of the cosmic significance of Christ, also as mediator of *re*-creation" ("De Cultuur-waardering van het Nieuw-Calvinisme," in *Onze Eeuw* [1919], 101). Whereas Haitjema says that it would require a "leap" to get from an argument about a regeneration of culture to the doctrine of common grace (op. cit., 103), Rothuizen clearly sees no inconsistency in Kuyper. And though Haitjema complains that the theologian Kuyper has been engulfed by cultural philosophy, Rothuizen welcomes the theologian Kuyper who has been engrossed in it (220). S. J. Ridderbos does not go quite as far as Haitjema, but he admits that Kuyper exaggerated the independent goal of common grace (op. cit., 273, 322). But while Ridderbos believes "that Kuyper has *on occasion* [italics supplied, J.D.] described the independent goal of common grace in such a lyrical way that there was a danger [! J.D.] that the necessity of palingenesis would fade into the background" (275), Rothuizen discovers the *real* Kuyper (at least there) with his "secularization starting from the world" and his "Messianic intermezzo." In my assessment of Rothuizen's view I will also discuss the issue of cultural optimism.

Although I have noted with approval Rothuizen's criticism of the assertion that there is spiritualism in Kuyper, I do not agree with his own interpretation and find it unacceptable also.

Rothuizen considers it "incomprehensible that Van Ruler wanted to accuse Kuyper of a primacy of the inner self and of a ghetto on every terrain of life" (op. cit., 244). Indeed! When Velema speaks about a "spiritualistic tendency" in Kuyper, Rothuizen accurately notes, "Especially the word 'tendency' is surely incorrect" (246). I share this criticism, but what does Rothuizen replace it with?

§ 11. Objections

These are my objections to Rothuizen's views:

1. *Particular grace remains.* Rothuizen is too bold when he claims to have discovered a "Messianic intermezzo" in Kuyper. Christ incarnate would remain, but the "Christian" element would disappear? How then are we to understand those pronouncements of Kuyper which say that common grace, not particular grace, will come to an end?[395] What are we to think of the following quotation about particular grace: "In this dispensation it does not yet achieve its ultimate form, but restores and elevates all potentialities in human beings. Accordingly, it will not come to naught in the final judgment. On the contrary, it is only through the crisis of the final spiritual and cosmic catastrophe that it will reach its full development"?[396]

Rothuizen knew, of course, that Kuyper spoke about the end of common grace, but according to him this means "that then it no longer makes sense to refer to it as 'common.' That which common grace 'maintains' will not disappear. On the contrary, 'the maintenance of the human aspect will then change into the *glorification* of all *human* life.'"[397] Admitted! But in Kuyper it is *particular* grace that claims the entire terrain of common grace for itself, both our bodies and the entire world.[398] Particular grace has made the data of common grace *serviceable* to itself and accordingly, within the *church* as organism, it knows of "no end, but continues throughout all eternity."[399]

To understand this we need to remember that Kuyper

---

395. *Gemeene Gratie* I, 431–32, 497; II, 395; *Loc. de Foedere*, 131 dictation. Cf. p. 67 above.
396. *Loc. de Foedere*, 131 dict.
397. Rothuizen, op. cit., 217. Citation of Kuyper, *Gemeene Gratie* I, 432.
398. *Gemeene Gratie* II, 685.
399. II, 679. Cf. the entire context.

considered re-creation to be something more than the restoration of the original creation. He regarded those who are saved as *new creatures in Christ*, a new humanity.[400] It is true, says Kuyper, that the creation ordinance is permanent and endures (see footnote 384). But this ordinance appears in an elevated, glorified condition. "Something much more glorious will come into being than what would have come about if the Fall had not occurred."[401] We shall receive the δόξα [glory] from Christ;[402] the world is moving toward its *glorificatio*.[403] And how will the parts of the body share in it except through the head of the mystical body, Christ?[404]

When you read these statements of Kuyper, you will have to object to Rothuizen's analysis. Is it true that according to Kuyper Christ will remain, although the "Christian" element will disappear?[405] But we saw that these two are so closely connected in Kuyper's thought that the new humanity *in its new humanness* cannot be thought of apart from its head, Jesus Christ. How then is it possible to imagine that on the new earth the "Christian" element will be absent? Kuyper did not promote a Messianic intermezzo.

1. Still, Kuyper is not crystal clear on this point. It is possible to read into I, 333, quoted above by Rothuizen, that particular grace will come to an end. In I, 505, Kuyper says that "both particular grace and common grace will have concluded their course." However, nowhere does it say that common grace will remain. Rothuizen does not assert this either, if I have understood him correctly. Common grace vanishes, but its fruits remain. That is a correct description. Only, the identification of common grace with the first use of the law (see above) must be ascribed to carelessness. For according to Rothuizen, the first use of the law does remain. When Kuyper speaks of the disappearance also of particular grace, we must interpret that to mean, as he himself says: "A saving, reconciling, and regenerating operation of grace is then completely inconceivable" (I, 496). For everything that needed to be saved, *has* been saved (I, 505). There is nothing left to be saved, just as there is nothing left to be arrested (end of common grace, I, 497). But "of course, Christ's reconciling merit is and remains through all eternity the foundation on which the building of our *salvation* rests; it is also self-evident that the redeemed will eternally thank God for his 'inexpressible gift,' knowing that they are saved only by grace

---

400. II, 614.
401. *Pro Rege* I, 480. Cf. op. cit., I, 443ff., 560, 565.
402. *Loc. de Consummatione*, 272–73, 278.
403. Op cit., 298.
404. *Pro Rege* I, 380; *Loc. de Christo* III, 196.
405. Rothuizen, op. cit., 241.

and enjoy bliss by mere grace" (I, 496; italics supplied). Having supplemented it with what I wrote above about the new, elevated, humanity, I believe I am entitled to maintain my description of Kuyper's position: Not only now but also later, our bond with Christ determines our humanity and its expression. Particular grace: deliverance *here* and salvation *there*. Christ and *Christianum* [the Christian element] are inseparable.

I also do not really understand why Rothuizen in his discussion of Kuyper speaks so freely of a Messianic intermezzo but is much more careful when he deals with Bavinck (op. cit., 218–19). This carefulness does him honor, but it would have become him also in his discussion of Kuyper.

2. In support of his proposition concerning the interim character of particular grace, Rothuizen also cites I, 166, where Kuyper calls the Christian order "mechanical" and the cross "*un*natural" (op. cit., 216). Such expressions would favor Rothuizen's argument if Kuyper had not said more than this. S. J. Ridderbos, op. cit., 64–69, has demonstrated clearly that there are two series of assertions: one which says that particular grace is *supernatural* and something entirely new; another which argues that particular grace does not add anything new to creation and bears an entirely *natural* character (re-creation, organism, etc.). At first blush these appear to be contradictory, but Ridderbos believes (and I agree with his solution) that "a reconciliation is entirely possible. When Kuyper emphasizes the *supernatural* and the *new* of particular grace, he means that they do not arise automatically from creation, but that this involves an immediate intervention by God in the natural course of things. He also uses these terms to convey the idea that particular grace does not stand over against the *original*, but certainly over against the *corrupted*, nature. He speaks of a *new* creation, not because the first will come to naught, but because the world *broken* by sin will be done away with. Over against this, the *natural* character of particular grace lies in its joining with the original creation, which it does not abolish but, on the contrary, restores" (67–68). With regard to this point Ridderbos sees no difference between particular and common grace, commenting that Kuyper also calls the latter both supernatural and natural, depending upon whether its origin or its connection with creation is being considered. He adds, "When Kuyper several times nonetheless expressly posits a difference between common grace and particular grace in this respect, he is unable to clarify the difference in his argument" (68).

2. *No secularization "from out of the world 'in bonam partem' [in a positive sense]."* While I could understand Rothuizen's argument concerning the Messianic intermezzo in Kuyper in some measure, I fail to understand how he could find in Kuyper's work a secularization in the sense discussed above. Rothuizen assigns to Kuyper a view that we find in Bonhoeffer and Gogarten, but which

he cannot possibly ascribe to Kuyper. No one can deny that Kuyper wrote about an independent goal of common grace. But while Kuyper simply wants to establish a *fact* (that God receives honor also where particular grace is inoperative), Rothuizen distills from this a *task* that Kuyper supposedly assigned to us: that Christians must not always stretch out their hands to the world; that one must *also* allow the world to go its own way. But this conclusion is contradicted by Kuyper's adage, "There is not a square inch in all of human life of which Christ, who is sovereign over all, does not say, 'It is mine!'"[406]

For Kuyper, secularization never meant dechristianization.

1. We cannot really deny that Kuyper also presents a *message* in the *fact* of the independent goal of common grace, namely, (a) the church must be modest (there are more human beings than just the elect, and that has a purpose); and (b) when God gives his attention to the whole wide world, we may not turn away from it.

The cardinal question is: *how* ought we to be engaged with the world? For Kuyper there is only one possible answer: we must win it for Christ (*Loc. de Ecclesia*, 47ff.).

May we also leave the world to its own devices? We shall let Kuyper himself speak to this in a quotation that Rothuizen uses to defend *his* position (op cit., 238): "Your approach to the world must not be like that of a school teacher to his pupils, or of a physician to patients in a hospital ward, but you must approach it as a world that is of one family, of one flesh and blood, of one race with you, a world ... of which you know that God so loved it that he gave it his only-begotten Son. That is how you also must love that world, love it in such a way that you give yourself to it" (II, 355–56). Interrupting the quotation briefly, I ask: what does Kuyper mean by that "give yourself"? Just before the above quotation he says: It is your task "constantly" to descend from the extraordinary [of the spiritual life, J.D.] "into the *ordinary* life, in order to demonstrate in that ordinary life your spiritual superiority [! J.D.], and to do this with a three-fold motive, always in the following order: *first* to glorify your God, *second* to be a blessing to the world [! J.D.], and *third* to strengthen yourself for the battle and harden yourself against Satan." Demonstrating our superiority in order to be a blessing for the world, without spiritual pride (355), since we have to do it in a world loved by God—what does this have to do with a secularization that leaves the world to its own devices? The quotation continues as follows: "And you have to do this [i.e., give yourself, J.D.] not as an artificial means of enticing the world, but because it is in keeping with your views and beliefs, with the way you feel your solidarity with that world, because you know of the prophecy of its

---

406. *Souvereiniteit in eigen kring*, 32. Cf. *Ons Program*, 1187–88.

CHAPTER I. ABRAHAM KUYPER

regeneration, and especially because the purpose of *all* work of grace is to wrest the world from Satan, in order that it may again receive *praise and honor before our God* who devised and created it and, despite its brutalization, maintained it. God still does the latter by his common grace." I have italicized "all" and briefly paraphrase the above as follows: you must go out into the world also with your *particular* grace. That this paraphrase is correct is apparent from the conclusion of the excerpt from Kuyper, which Rothuizen does not quote: "And only when particular grace motivates you to discover, honor, and thankfully accept this common grace in the world, you will have arrived at the harmony that your faith needs in order for you to take your place in the world as a "child of God'" (II, 356). It is impossible for us to recognize in this "a moving depiction of the motif of secularization that reminds one of Bonhoeffer" (Rothuizen, op cit., 238). What it is in fact all about, Kuyper described a few pages earlier as follows: "What we have constantly fought against and, while God gives us life, will continue to fight against is the inclination to think that particular grace will suffice and then to neglect completely the broad terrain of common grace where our association with the world must be maintained and where we, in our superior strength, must engage in competition with the world, and where we must win our laurels for the honor of Christ" (II, 348). *Competition, superior strength, winning* laurels for the honor of Christ—does anyone still hear Bonhoeffer speak here? He would surely have shaken his head.

2. How could Rothuizen, after reading Kuyper's *Bedoeld noch Gezegd* (cf. the bibliography included in his study), speak in this way about secularization in Kuyper? In this publication Kuyper makes mention of a debate that he conducted with J. H. Gunning at a meeting of the Free University in The Hague (1885). Gunning proposed that the statutes of the university should not to refer to "Reformed principles" (as the basis for instruction), but to "Gospel truth." Now we quote Kuyper: "He believed that then [i.e., with the formulation 'Gospel truth,' J.D.] we would be on the right path. He admitted that the leaven must be in the dough, and for him that leaven was what Groen van Prinsterer had also called 'Gospel truth.' For the *exact sciences* he wanted to see added something that he sought to justify on the meager basis of a quotation from one of my writings, namely, *the secularization of science*" (op cit., 39). Kuyper was in Switzerland when he wrote this and did not have ready access to the book from which Gunning quoted. But he did recall very clearly what he had written in 1878: "Then the issue was whether the ordinances of God are to be found *solely* in his Word, or whether they exist also *outside* of his Word in what was created. Of course I opted for the latter and showed that also a politician already discovers such ordinances in the life of peoples and nations" (op. cit., 39). Rothuizen might also say of this quotation what he says about similar expressions of Kuyper: "Also nature receives its place and authority here, does it not? But then we can also speak of 'Scripture' *and* 'nature'; note the well-known reformational 'and'" (*Primus usus legis*, 146). But does this lead

to secularization? Let us listen to Kuyper as he continues: "This has nothing to do with the secularization of science, since God's Word teaches us only that aspect of things *by which they are in direct contact with the eternal, infinite, and invisible,* and leaves all that is *not* so connected to be researched by the creature." No secularization, for secularization of science "*separates dough from leaven*" (*Bedoeld noch Gezegd,* 40). After Kuyper then relates how he explained to Gunning that it would be incorrect to propose secularization for each of the faculties, he writes: "And after having thus demonstrated from the facts (I think correctly) that this system of secularization is untenable, I ventured to take an additional step and explained encyclopedically why it is even an impossibility. To that end, I pointed out in succession that the *material* to be examined, the *subject* engaged in the research, and the greater or lesser seriousness of *the research itself* are governed at virtually every turn by spiritual influences that cannot be divorced from the confession of the Christ" (op cit., 41). That applies also to political life: "What unites the state is constitutional *law,* and depending upon whether one secularizes that constitutional *law* or claims it for Christ, the conclusions must differ" (op cit., 42). In short, Kuyper does indeed recognize two sources: both Scripture and nature. But you can assume only one position: *either* secularization *or* claiming the world for Christ. Particular grace and common grace are both indeed independent. That is a *fact.* But Christians always allow them to go hand in hand in the sciences and in their walk of life. That is their *task.*

Kuyper rejected *ungodly* secularization (*Scolastica* I, 17) on more than one occasion: "Secularization is the stamp that is being put on public life more and more, and secularization, derived from *saeculum,* i.e., age, means precisely that one wants to withdraw the nation as public institution from the service '*of the coming age*' in order to let it be swallowed up in '*this current age*'" (*Tweeërlei Vaderland,* 35. In opposition to this, Kuyper opts for a well-considered isolation: "When the nation as a whole can no longer be an institution relevant to your confession and walk of life, create for your Christian life its own institution, or as Groen van Prinsterer so appropriately called it, *a separately created terrain"* (op cit., 34), in order to "be a blessing to your *earthly* homeland" by means of your own organizations (op cit., 38). No secularization and no ghetto, but leaven for the whole nation! Read Kuyper's *Ons Program,* 157–67, which is directed against Rome (its ecclesiasticism) and against A. Pierson, who asserted: "The value of the humanistic ideal lies, if I may put it that way, in the secularization of humanity" (op cit., 165). Here Kuyper calls secularization "the magic spell of the forces that are inimical to Christ's kingdom" (op cit., 157).

Kuyper also recognized a praiseworthy concept of secularization. See p. 65 above. Van Ruler rightly noted that what Kuyper meant by this secularization is "not a dechristianization, but rather a secularization of human life in general" (op cit., 20). Anything more that Rothuizen makes of it is excessive.

3. *Limited and directed cultural optimism.* In Kuyper it is difficult to get via the independent goal of common grace to an independent ethic ('Christians must not always stretch out their hands to the world'). This is evident from the fact that the cultural optimism in Kuyper's doctrine of common grace is clearly limited. We must not forget that he also spoke of a "frightful" common grace and said that the inner operation of common grace would shrink and that only the external, intellectual-artistic operation would be included in a progressive flourishing.[407] "We must therefore distinguish two aspects in Kuyper's expectation of the future. He is pessimistic with respect to what may be called the "higher" culture, i.e., that culture in which the religious and moral state of the cultural subject plays a large role. On the other hand, he expresses great optimism with respect to the future of the more external culture. In his opinion humanity's power over nature (in a narrow sense) will constantly increase."[408]

According to Kuyper, all cultural optimism for Christians is clearly restricted also by the struggle that particular grace brings in its wake and by the nostalgia that causes them to shout "Maranatha." They are pilgrims, and this they must not forget. In this context Kuyper's calling grace spiritual acquires a deep meaning.

Besides, although Kuyper posits an independent *goal* for common grace, its *realization* remains dependent on particular grace. Only in the general operation of common grace, which is entirely controlled by Christ, does our human race reach its highest development.

Finally, those who speak of optimism in Kuyper must not forget that he harbored this view especially with respect to *Calvinistic* culture.

A few remarks.

1. Rothuizen neglects almost completely what Kuyper teaches about the shrinking of common grace. It is indeed not so easy to keep the "moral-religious" and the "intellectual-artistic" separate in Kuyper (Rothuizen, op cit., 230; cf. Ridderbos, op cit., 154). But Rothuizen has the tendency to overemphasize the "technical," "intellectual-artistic" considerably. How can he

---

407. See pp. 28–30 above.
408. S. J. Ridderbos, op. cit., 216.

CHAPTER I. ABRAHAM KUYPER

write (and where does it say this in Ridderbos on page 104?) that *moral* life, which Kuyper described as follows, is also part of it: "Moral life is the terrain of conscience; it determines the relationships and obligations that we have toward our friends and companions, our neighbors and governments, our enemies and subordinates; and in addition to our behavior, it governs our association and interaction with people"? (Rothuizen, op cit., 230). Does moral life for Kuyper suddenly *not* fall under the shrinking of common grace?

Rothuizen believes that Kuyper has not logically applied the distinction between intellectual-artistic and moral-religious. I do not believe so either. But we must be doubly careful that we do Kuyper justice and not add to the "lower" what Kuyper does not always include in the "higher."

2. Only up to a certain point can Christians feel at home in this world, according to Kuyper. For they are engaged in *battle*. The covenant of grace normally causes persecution in first instance: "Physically, it usually results in a worse condition. It culminates in Christ, who said, 'If they have persecuted me, they will also persecute you' .... The stronger the effect of palingenesis is, the more suffering there will be. And that will not end or get better; rather, persecution will increase" (*Loc. de Foedere*, 142). In the struggle and in addition to it, there is also nostalgia for the heavenly homeland: "The heart of God's faithful weeps and chafes with nostalgia for the homeland above. Oh, whom else would they love, whom would they love more than the One in whom is all the delight of their soul. They are pilgrims on earth, and if all is well with them, God's commandments are to them like songs in the land of their pilgrimage. The real pilgrims know but one refrain to their holiest songs: 'Come, Lord Jesus; come quickly!'" (*Tweeërlei Vaderland*, 27–28).

Pilgrims can be travelers "through a strange country that is of no interest to them" (*E Voto* II, 124). That would be wrong. For they are citizens of two countries. "They are pilgrims, not as if they traveled through a world that did not concern them, but pilgrims in the sense that at every point of the long road they have to reckon with the God, full of majesty, who awaits them at the end of the road" (*Calvinisme*, 60; cf. 116; *E Voto* II, 124–25). But they *remain* pilgrims. The Maranatha must not cease (*Pro Rege* I, 274); the goal of the journey must determine the road (*Maranatha*, 4). "Christ and all his benefits" is "the short, summary expression for an entire world of blessings" in the atmosphere of *this* world, which can weigh heavily on the pilgrim (*E Voto* II, 86–87). In *this* context Kuyper can refer to particular grace in the covenant of grace as spiritual (*Loc. de Foedere*, 141), namely, spiritual *in principle* (op cit., 151), that is, in its beginning [*in principio*]! For the covenant of grace "begins by giving only the psychical, which often leads to a physical deterioration, while the physical only arrives on the day of judgment" (op cit., 141). This is not a matter of spiritual dualism (op cit., 151), but a recognition of reality in the life of the Christian: struggle and persecution. Spiritualists isolate themselves; but "spiritual" also includes the idea that the *world* "shuts itself in and fences itself off" (cf. *Tweeërlei Vaderland*, 20, thereby denying us access.

3. I shall not yet express my opinion about the question of cultural optimism. At this point I am still engaged in looking for the correct rendition of Kuyper's doctrine of common grace. And therefore I must guard against every distortion of Kuyper's understanding of the independence of common grace. The general operation of common grace is governed by Christ. That is where one discovers true human culture. Without the influence of particular grace, common grace languishes. From the general operation of common grace Kuyper does derive a particular *orientation* for his optimism about a *Calvinistic* culture. I have already said something about this (cf. p. 50 above). But in connection with Kuyper and secularization it may useful to add something here. When the already mentioned J. H. Gunning proposed "Gospel truth" instead of "Reformed principles" as leaven for the disciplines that were not to be secularized, Kuyper replied "that we, being required to use leaven, ought to ensure that we are not offered flour and putty; and for that reason we have, in accordance with the wisdom of the ages, further defined *Gospel truth* as the purified, i.e., the *Reformed*, principles" (*Bedoeld noch Gezegd*, 40). But Kuyper applies this to *all* the faculties. If one still wants to speak of secularization here, it is secularization proceeding from faith, in accordance with Reformed principles. Neither humanism nor Rome but only Calvinism offers the firm foundation on which the future can be built (*Calvinisme*, 156–83).

4. *What does Rothuizen understand by anticipation?* I do not object to the characterization itself. Kuyper writes, "An initial breakthrough of the powers of particular grace into the visible things [occurs] already now,"[409] One can, indeed, call this anticipation. But then we must not alter what it says: "an initial breakthrough of the powers of *particular* grace." How can Rothuizen echo this while refusing to acknowledge Kuyper's view of particular grace and of the *Christianum* in the realm of glory? For is the passage quoted from Kuyper not about the church as organism (particular grace that has made common grace serviceable to it) with its "*foreshadowing* ... of the realm of glory that is to come?"[410] Here Rothuizen's incorrect interpretation of Kuyper is very much apparent.

Compare the following statements made by Rothuizen:
(a) "In this way *sanctification* has gone further in practice for Kuyper than

---

409. *Gemeene Gratie* II, 689. Rothuizen, op. cit., 224.
410. II, 689.

CHAPTER I. ABRAHAM KUYPER

in the vision of Van Ruler [in response to Van Ruler's statement: 'The Christianization of the state, society, and culture is in itself a *dream* that consumes the heart of all who know the Lord in love,' J.D.] *Anticipation* is after all more than prophecy" (Rothuizen, op. cit., 243; italics supplied). Here Rothuizen uses "anticipation" in the true Kuyperian sense.

(b) When the discussion is about the last days, about the antichrist and Babylon, there is no such thing as "a violent mob," but a highest development, said Kuyper (*De Gemeene Gratie* I, 455), and others have pointed out that the world will then experience "peace." Rothuizen comments: "This is all possible. But also in addition to it—*indeed, in it*—a highly significant *anticipation* of the new earth, a portrayal of Micah 4:3–4, is possible ('they shall beat their swords into plowshares,' etc.)" (Rothuizen, 257; italics supplied). Here *nothing* is left of the Kuyperian anticipation. For what does the antichrist have to do with particular grace?

If we again read Rothuizen's statement as quoted in the text at footnote 394, it is striking that he places antithesis and anticipation over against each other as Christianization and secularization. He does so despite the fact that anticipation, as the breakthrough of particular grace into the visible world, having received shape in the church as organism, in fact brings the antithesis with it! We must most certainly not replace the true Kuyper with the Kuyper-image created by Rothuizen.

§ 12. Political background?

There is probably no one who would claim that Kuyper developed his theory of common grace solely because he needed it for a particular practical goal in his life. Kuyper produced a large number of publications for special occasions and sometimes he presented theories matching such occasions. However, it is impossible to make that claim in the case of the series of articles entitled *De Gemeene Gratie*. Kuyper addressed this topic in *De Heraut* over a period of six years and there probed deeper into it than he did in other series (such as *Het Werk van de Heilige Geest, E Voto*, and *Pro Rege*). The topic captivated his thought greatly. In discussing it, he unfolded his life and *world* view in a grand manner and, in the course of his doing so, hardly any theme that he had dealt with at some point in his life remained unmentioned. Life, suffering and death, humans and animals, Hottentots, the Chinese, Rome and the Reformation, the lightning rod, vaccination against cowpox, and many other matters were considered by him. Such a truly wide-ranging approach does not permit the work to be relegated to one or another utilitarian motive.

Of course, *De Gemeene Gratie* does have a background in which Kuyper's *thought* was strongly motivated by his *action*. Exceptionally erudite scholar that he was, Kuyper wanted to serve his people and (who can possibly doubt it) his country. His study was his headquarters; his publications, his orders of the day.

It may therefore be useful to pay some attention to assertions that Kuyper's doctrine of common grace also explains the principial possibility of his coalition with Roman Catholics in politics—claims made along this line: "Kuyper's conception of common grace, which certainly shows points of congruence with the Roman Catholic doctrine of nature and grace, explains how he could so easily develop a close political cooperation with Roman Catholics."[411]

I believe that I must criticize this assertion. First, because the cooperation with Roman Catholics was not as *easy* for Kuyper as the above quotation suggests; and second, because Kuyper always regarded the coalition as founded in *particular* grace.

1. For a long time, Kuyper rejected and was wary of a coalition with Roman Catholics. That is clear from his articles in *Ons Program*, 1202–14, dating from 1872 and 1877; it can be read in his *Confidentie*, 6 (1873), and in *Rome en Dordt* (1876); and his advice before the elections of 1878 and 1881 tells the same story. The first coalition cabinet came about in 1888. Cf. P. Kasteel, *Abraham Kuyper*, 93, 114, 129, 137–38. But one also has to pay attention to critical remarks Kuyper made after that: "It is not possible to proceed as one with Rome. Our glorious history, the blood of the martyrs, the position of the Pope, and the issue of freedom of conscience forbid it" (*Maranatha*, 15 [1891]; he stated that coalition always causes problems (*Diensthuis*, 25–26, and *Meiboom*, 18 [1912 and 1913]); and he said it would please him to be able to engage in untrammelled action again. He hoped that he would live to experience it (*Meiboom*, 19).

2. But coalition was viewed as *necessary*. He presented the following arguments: We have to do it. It is impossible to achieve a majority on our own (*Volharden*, 7, and *Wij Calvinisten*, 8); there are not enough capable men among us (*Volharden*, 7); opposition to the revolutionary principle is pointless otherwise (*Volharden*, 15, and *Eer is teer*, 13); that way at least we can achieve something and resist much evil (*Wij Calvinisten*, 12–13). This coalition is also *possible*, according to Kuyper. For we have much in common: the Gospel is the point of departure

411. P. Jongeling, *Terwille van het Koninkrijk*, 119.

for both in politics (*Volharden*, 6); a higher unity in the kingship of Christ and a belief in God's special revelation unites us (*Wij Calvinisten*, 10, and *Gemeene Gratie* III, 194–95); Roman Catholics also confess the Maranatha (*Maranatha*, 14); "our mystical union" lies in the *Pro Rege* (*Diensthuis*, 26); both recognize that authority comes from God, although this position is developed differently (*Eer is teer*, 11). Kuyper was even able to write: "The more clearly you see the antithesis, the stronger the coalition" (*Wij Calvinisten*, 15; cf. *A.R. Staatkunde* I, 602–03). He called the antithesis the "cement of the coalition" (*Wij Calvinisten*, 18) and also stated that the Lord's Prayer could be called its cement (*Voor den Slag*, 3–4). It is clear that common grace was not part of this discussion at all.

§ 13. Kuyper's own opinion

We should not make it more difficult than necessary, and therefore we now turn to Kuyper himself for an answer to the question what drove him to develop the doctrine of common grace. Then the following picture comes into view:

1. *A gap filled*. Right from the start, Kuyper regarded the confession that grace is particular against a double background: "The children of God as *individuals* belong to the *communion* of saints, but that communion of saints consists also of the children of *humankind*."[412] Although it is not true, as we have already seen, that Kuyper did not call that second background common grace from the outset (as he himself maintains),[413] it is beyond doubt that from the beginning, together with the doctrine of election, he also had in mind the place of human beings in the covenant and in the world. His organism-idea, which already appears in his earliest publications, is sufficient proof of that.

It is therefore not unwarranted to suppose that before he began his first series[414] about particular grace, Kuyper had already planned to write three series. The second was published soon after the first;[415] the third series appeared much later. When it did appear, Kuyper was able to write: "Only if *particular grace, covenant grace,*

---

412. *Gemeene Gratie* I, 6.
413. I, 9.
414. "Dat de genade particulier is," in *Uit het Woord*, 2nd series I (*Heraut* articles of April 1879–June 1880).
415. "De Leer der Verbonden," in *Uit het Woord*, 2nd series II. (*Heraut* articles of August 1880–October 1881).

and *common grace* are understood in their essence, tenor, and coherence, your thoughts will find rest in their search for unity."[416]

This is my first conclusion: With *De Gemeene Gratie*, Kuyper filled a lacuna that was evident in his publications. And it was certainly a lacuna: nothing less than his *world*view was lacking.

1. Aside from all other motives that might have led Kuyper to write such a trilogy: his soaring spirit found rest in the monumental completion of the two series: "Only in this way [i.e., in recognizing the importance of the doctrine of common grace] you will have *unity* in your confession, *certainty* in your point of view, and *decisiveness* in your conviction" (I, 107). He declares that the confession of the Holy Spirit (election) and of the Son (covenant) must be traced back to the confession of God the Father and our creation (I, 5-6, 26, 107; II, 610-11) and states that in the search for unity in one's thinking it is all about the "full and unrumpled confession of the holy Trinity in the Divine being" (I, 26).

2. J. C. Rullmann goes too far when he applauds *De Gemeene Gratie* as follows: "We dare ... to claim without fear of contradiction that those who make this work their own will possess a life and world view that is not to be found in the entire history of philosophy" (*Kuyper-bibliografie* III, 255). Still, no one can truly read this work without being impressed with the brilliance of its conception. We already heard Van Ruler say this (see pp. 49-50 above). Also correct is the judgment of H. N. Ridderbos, who calls *De Gemeene Gratie* the work in which the special and brilliant aspects of Kuyper's theology most clearly come to the fore" ("Eerherstel voor cultuurtheologie," *Gereformeerd Weekblad*, 5 Sept., 1958). Kuyper knew what he intended with his series of *Heraut* articles. Even though it is obvious that they are written in the style of a journalist (cf. Haitjema, 16, *Onder eigen vaandel* [1941], 160) and frequently show internal contradictions (which Kuyper would not have overlooked in a thorough revision), the three-volume work has become more than a journalistic attempt to fill a weekly publication. It displays a system following a purposeful plan. When he began, Kuyper knew where he would end up. His thoughts about common grace matured over the years (certainly after 1887), and while writing about it he constantly reminded us of the importance of the work in which he is engaged.

3. Kuyper reasons as follows: "Our *worldview*" must find rest (II, 626; cf. I, 353). And for that we need to know that *all* things have a purpose. History certainly serves to complete the number of the elect. But there is more. They do not form an oasis in the desert, and also this: All that exists in the seed in our race must come into the light to the honor and praise of God's name (II, loc. cit.). In my opinion it is completely justified to call *De Gemeene Gratie* the expression of Kuyper's worldview, even though he does not explicitly characterize it as such.

---

416. *Gemeene Gratie* I, 8.

Its broad theme and design permit this characterization. See further chapter IV, § 3 and 4, and especially chapter V, § 4.

2. *Warning against Anabaptist avoidance.* I have already noted that the thinker and the commander-in-chief in Kuyper cannot be separated. The man who found rest for his thought in the doctrine of common grace saw in it also the principial foundation summoning Christians to engage in Christian activity in this world. The pronouncements in *De Gemeene Gratie* about the Anabaptist danger are sufficiently numerous to regard the warnings against it as a *second* motive for the writing of this work. But we must not regard the Anabaptist movement, which constantly had Kuyper's attention, as restricted to that part of the nation which sought peace of mind in the conventicles.

1. In the index to *De Gemeene Gratie*, s.v. Anabaptists, we can see how often Kuyper refers to them. See especially I, 244–45, II 69ff., 194–95, 288, 525; III, 19, 23, 303, 424, as proof that he regarded the Anabaptist heresy as a contemporary one.

2. Kuyper fought against the spirit of the conventicles. Bur he also discerned an Anabaptist attitude in the Réveil and among the Irenics. This becomes quite apparent in the fight against *politicophobia*, an evil which Kuyper opposed numerous times. In reference to the Réveil, Kuyper said: We became an anti-revolutionary party "in opposition to the politicophobia of Christian timidity" (*Niet de vrijheidsboom*, 16–17, 14; cf. *A.R. Staatkunde* I, 593ff.). This politicophobia, "at bottom nothing less than the old idea of the Anabaptists," is nowadays "embraced by the thousands" among all ranks and stations "and promoted by celebrated men" (*Uit het Woord*, 2nd series III, 190–91). Kuyper speaks of "the false passivity of the Irenics on the political and ecclesiastical terrains" (op. cit., 309, 314). He regards the politicophobia of A. W. Bronsveld as resting entirely on Anabaptist principles (*Loc. de Christo* I, 101). See further, e.g., *Christus en de sociale nooden*, 94; *Meiboom*, 14; *Ons Program* 1262–63.

One can readily believe that Bronsveld *cum suis* made things more difficult for Kuyper than the conventicles. The latter group (only "small parts of the church" [*Drie vossen*, 78–79]) did not have near the influence that the Irenics had in the press and through competent spokespersons. We may assume that Kuyper was impelled more by the latter than by the conventicles à la Beesd toward deep reflection that found its way into *De Gemeene Gratie*.

3. *Maintaining the depth of the Fall.* The above does not yet explain why Kuyper had to present his ideas in terms of common grace

and why he could only conceive of a Christian's being active in this world through the lens of common grace.

I do not assert anything new, but maintain the old interpretation that for Kuyper the doctrine of common grace necessarily flowed from the depravity of the human race. In his own words, the doctrine of common grace "did not arise from a philosophical invention, but from the confession of the mortal nature of sin."[417] On the one hand Kuyper denied that the world lies in sin; on the other hand he contested the idea that the Fall had left human nature unaffected or had at most weakened it. In order nevertheless to maintain the depth of the Fall (contra Arminians and Roman Catholics) and the calling of the Christian in this world (contra the Anabaptists), he deemed the doctrine of common grace to be necessary. For common grace allowed him to encounter in this world not only the devil but also God: the God of common grace, who "on the one hand restrained the power of evil and on the other emanated good influences and in that way caused our *blended* life in its varying gradations of moral condition to arise."[418] The dualism of the Anabaptists would be completely justified and "also be ... a matter of our duty, if the world not only in and of itself 'lay in sin' but also had been left in it by God."[419] Dualism is judged, so Kuyper continues, by the confession of common grace, "which teaches us how God in his mercy also raised his preserving hand over that sinful world, thereby arresting sin and curse, and how precisely thereby that world gives God's children the opportunity to serve their God, to his honor."[420]

1. I wanted to let Kuyper speak for himself. And an abundance of material shows that for Kuyper the Fall, taken seriously, raised questions about the calling in and appreciation for this world. It concerns "the solution to one of the biggest puzzles of life" and an explanation of "how in our society on the one hand there is, and necessarily must be, such deep corruption, and how on the other hand that same society is filled with things that fascinate us, that lift our hearts, and that let us taste human happiness. *Without* the confession of 'common grace' your relative happiness causes you to ignore sin, or blindfolds

---

417. *Gemeene Gratie* I, 11.
418. II, 413.
419. III, 19.
420. Loc. cit.

your sense of sin and misery to the joy of life. *With* that confession you possess the desire and the ability to recognize the full significance of *both*" (II, 43-44).

2. Kuyper also rejected "the Roman Catholic solution" (II, 44-53; cf. I, 131-41), reasoning as follows: Although Roman Catholics also teach that the Fall caused a weakening of human nature, they do not admit of "an actual corruption of that nature so that it can no longer produce anything good, also not in the context of civil righteousness. According to them, it never produces saving good, but certainly all kinds of civil good. And the contrast is then such that we say: the corruption in our nature not only eliminates all good, but has the effect that it can produce nothing but evil, and it is only the tempering power of common grace that arrests this corruption and makes room for civil righteousness. But over against this Roman Catholics maintain that human nature, despite the Fall, still has within it a certain power enabling it to achieve civil righteousness. It must be understood that the Church of Rome does not ascribe this to the *pura naturalia*
[properties of human nature per se] apart from God's help, but it does understand this divine help to mean nothing else than that general support on the part of God which is presumed to be necessary and indispensable in all areas of creation and which flows forth automatically from the dependency of the creature as such" (II, 50-51). Kuyper also judges the contradistinction *nature-grace* to be incorrect. As he explains, it gives "too much the wrong impression that *nature* is still the nature it was in its original state, as called into being in creation; thereby one lost sight of the fact that a curse was placed upon nature and that a *cursed nature* necessarily sinks into corruption unless grace comes to its support. Thus it was overlooked that nature as we know it now is itself *blessed*.... If we now, after the Fall, place *nature and grace* over against each other, our meaning must be that the *blessed* nature stands over against particular grace, which saves those appointed to eternal life" (II, 613). Therefore it is "clearer and more accurate" to speak of *creation and re-creation* (loc. cit.). Kuyper has strong objections to a dualism that is traced back to creation, which is what he sees in the Church of Rome: nature plus a "complement," the *donum superadditum*. If this *justitia originalis* ... was something to which our nature was *not* predisposed, something foreign and heterogeneous to it ... then human nature will continue to differ, also in disposition and variety, from that higher grace and cannot grow together with it organically. We are then left with a purely mechanical connection, and the dualism will continue into humanity's highest development" (II 50, 49). Cf. I, 131ff., on Bellarminus and his golden bridle, which must control the "horse" of nature.

3. As mentioned, the background of Kuyper's doctrine of common grace can be seen there where Kuyper himself directed us: the doctrine of common grace is necessary against the background of the doctrine of the total corruption of humanity in the Fall. See, e.g., also G. C. Berkouwer, *Conflict met Rome*, 140.

CHAPTER I. ABRAHAM KUYPER

Those who adopt this interpretation follow not an original but nonetheless a safe route. Those who do not adopt it, will easily find themselves on slippery paths. An example of this is W. H. Velema in his *De leer van de Heilige Geest bij Abraham Kuyper* and *De genadeleer in the theologie van Kuyper* (*Kerk en Theologie*, vol. 11, no. 4). According to Velema, Kuyper makes mention of an organic relationship between Creator and creature, a substantial analogy that is maintained in spite of sin (*Genadeleer*, 211): "Consequently, there are such basic divine features in the essence of human nature that the relationship can never be wholly negative. An ontic substrate remains which forms a basis and a point of departure for God's actions, quite apart from the fact that human beings are God's children!" (*Heilige Geest*, 87). But, says Velema, the concept of such an analogy *had* to result in the doctrine of common grace; he reasons as follows: "Such an analogy between God and humanity must remain in effect, despite sin. It seems to me that it is thanks to Kuyper's Reformed thought pattern that he spoke here of grace. It betrays insight into the corruption that is the result of sin" (op. cit., 226). The doctrine of the depravity of humankind after the Fall does play a role in Kuyper, also according to Velema, but it is the role, if I may put it this way, of a *Reformed corrective* on an idealistic view of a substantial analogy between God and humanity. With this correction, so Velema continues, "Kuyper definitely follows a different path than Thomas [Aquinas] and medieval scholasticism with its schema of nature and grace. In this correction Kuyper shows himself to be a spiritual heir of Calvin. Nonetheless, it remains difficult to determine what that which is 'new' in these salutary and gracious actions of God consists of. Kuyper's analogy prevented him from fully understanding the grace of common grace as the surprising and salutary intervention of God. He had linked it too closely to creation. Consequently, the relationship between particular grace and common grace is ultimately the same as that between nature and grace" (op. cit., 226). Velema also believes that this double grace corresponds with the two aspects of the image of God in Kuyper, so that the image of God in the broader sense, connected with the analogy between God and humanity in the ontic sphere, corresponds with common grace (op. cit., 224ff.). It is "through common grace that this analogy is maintained" (*Genadeleer*, 211).

My objection is that Velema construes too much here. Surely one is entitled to ask that for a construct such as Velema offers the evidence be provided. Although that evidence is not found explicitly in *De Gemeene Gratie*, Velema ought to have demonstrated that this "background" was implied in it. But what happens when Velema's view contradicts Kuyper's explicit language? I believe such is the case. We read in I, 134–35, that the human essence remained what it was despite sin and that it shall remain even if human nature descended into hell to stay there forever. "Also in Satan, the angelic essence remains unalterably the same." This quotation is already not encouraging for an opinion stating that Kuyper regards the analogy as remaining in effect through common grace. For this analogy is *essential* and will be maintained in hell, where there is no longer *any* common grace. A bit further down, Kuyper mentions that by the expression "created in the image of God" he means two things:

"First, that the essence of man is created according to the image of God; and second, that man stood in the likeness of God in the perfection of his nature." Fallen man "bears the image of God in his essence even as Adam did before the Fall.... But if you look at the second aspect ... then we must say that through sin man lost [that aspect of] the image of God, that only *through common grace* small remnants of it have been rescued" (I, 135; italics supplied). It is very clear that Kuyper here, in connection with the image of God in the first (i.e., broader) sense, does not even refer to common grace. And that is understandable! "Human beings *cannot* cease to exist." They are "imperishable," and that is "because they have been created in God's image" (I, 159). Everything that has *essence* remains in existence in heaven and hell, also without common grace. "The sinner also remained a human being and none of the basic traits of the human essence have been lost through the Fall; even in hell not one of them shall ever wear out," Kuyper states in writing about the image of God as it was in fact formed (*E Voto* I, 52). Also the correspondence of particular grace and common grace with, respectively, the image of God in the broader and narrower sense is thus indefensible. For the "small remnants" that are preserved by common grace (cf. also I, 247, 256; II, 15), mentioned in the above quotation, refer to the image of God in the *second* (i.e., narrower) sense!

However, I do not claim that Kuyper is perspicuous on this point. On the contrary. Where it says in I, 256, that it is "precisely common grace that maintains the human element in the sinner," one can also think here of the image of God in the broader sense. So what does really belong to it and what does not? Perhaps the "small remnants"? In *Loc. de Deo* I, 73, Kuyper speaks about the oath in the public prayers of municipal councils, which *people as human beings* can be led to participate in through their *sensus divinitatis*. But he on the same page refers to these matters as *rudera* [small remnants]. It is, however, clear that this vagueness in Kuyper is additional evidence proving how difficult it would have been for this question concerning the substantial analogy to have formed the background to his concept of common grace. We would then certainly have been left less befogged than we are now as a result of the above quotations.

4. *From the natural knowledge of God to common grace.* I have already stated that for Kuyper the way of the soul to the world is passable from within (contra Van Ruler). We have now also seen that despite the depth of the Fall that way has also remained open from without. While Kuyper spoke of common grace later on, earlier he perceived the point of attachment between church and world in *natural theology.* This shift from "natural knowledge of God" to "common grace" amounts to a shift in the sense that what was

CHAPTER I. ABRAHAM KUYPER

"natural" before is now in common grace accorded the character of grace. Kuyper must have experienced this as an improvement. "Common grace" is a better vehicle than *"natural* theology" to describe the demarcation over against the Roman Catholic dualism of nature and grace. So also, the concept of "natural *theology"* was too limited to encapsulate what Kuyper had in mind with his broad cultural views.

1. Around 1875, Kuyper wrote a series of articles in *De Heraut* entitled *"Natuurlijke Godskennis"* ["Natural Knowledge of God"], *Uit het Woord*, 1st series III, 167–225. The significance of this knowledge (I am constantly mindful of what he would later ascribe to common grace) he describes as follows: "By disregarding, neglecting, and abandoning the natural knowledge of God, people have caused the collapse of the bridge that had been built by our ancestors over the deep chasm separating the world from the church community. The breach that thereby arose between society and the church has now caused the total enmity that came into being between science and faith, in the unbearable contradistinction between education and nurture, in the sectarianism of confessors, and in the impossibility of regaining those who have strayed into modernism, because the point of contact is lost" (170). The heresy must be eradicated, root and branch, "as if the natural knowledge of God was not as indispensable as the revelation in Christ" (194). Cf. *Gemeene Gratie*, passim. Indeed, "the entire Scriptures rest on the natural knowledge of God. Job, Proverbs, Ecclesiastes, and the Song of Songs are concerned with it almost entirely" (195). Cf. *Gemeene Gratie* II, 361–66; III, 72–73.

Kuyper continues as follows: In addition to the *innate* and as yet subconscious knowledge of God (*sensus divinitatis, semen religionis, theologia innata*, 184; there are no atheists, 177; the *semen religionis* also explains idolatry, 178, 182; cf. *Gemeene Gratie* I, 413) there is also the *acquired* knowledge of God, which arises from the impact of nature, the human world, history, tradition, and personal life on the innate knowledge of God (185). Hence the church can, for example, in regard to physics, admonish its confessors not to turn their backs on nature because of a misunderstood love for their God. The separation between godliness and life is wrong. Calvin called Holy Scripture not the eye, but the glasses. "That eye exists, even though you have not yet been introduced to Scripture, and though the eye is still weak and is not yet competent to read well, yet it receives impressions, it perceives that something has been written; and that, precisely, is what our church wants with regard to the natural knowledge of God" (193).

When Paul speaks of the great mystery, it consists "precisely in the insight that the special revelation of Israel and the general Paradisal revelation for all nations are two streams of the same origin. For a time they flowed in their own channels, but they were intended to flow together again in Christ, the full revelation of God" (202). Cf. *Gemeene Gratie* I, 348ff. But the natural knowledge of God ends in "bankruptcy" (209). For it does not lead to a personal relationship with God (209ff.). You can only speak of regressing when you possess no more than a natural knowledge of God. Among other things, the fruits of the natural knowledge of God are that it *"provides evidence of the necessity and indispensability of special revelation"* (219). Cf. *Gemeene Gratie* I, 457–58. And also: *"Where special revelation appears, there the natural knowledge of God is not discarded, but only there it shows its full value.* A Christian is not a hermit living outside of the world. The Christian church is not a monastery that barricades itself from humanity and the human element'" (220). Cf. common grace as it is made fertile by particular grace.

From this short summary it has become clear that according to Kuyper natural theology and common grace function alike. But on one cardinal point the depiction of the natural knowledge of God contradicts that of common grace. Kuyper states that our nature has been corrupted by sin "so deeply ... that it cannot go any deeper.... One should not argue that something is lacking in the deep corruption of our nature, as though this corruption could have gone further, so that by penetrating deeper, the corruption would also have led to the loss of the natural knowledge of God" (173). In other words, unlike common grace the natural knowledge of God does *not* have the task of arresting sin and corruption, according to Kuyper. He continues: "A sense of the existence of God and of affiliation with God is the irremovable attribute of all rational beings. One cannot for a moment conceive of them without it. Their moral degeneration does change their relationship with God, but it does not remove the sense that they are dealing with God" (173). Even in their hatred toward God, human beings are not free of him. "The more fierce your hatred, the more restlessly the object of your hate will fill your thoughts.... If hating God is the most terrible and appalling form in which sin can manifest itself, and if hate against God is unthinkable unless the sinner is restlessly occupied with God's existence and his holiness, then consider how superficial the objection of those is who believe that by recognizing a natural knowledge of God also in the fallen sinner you fail to do justice to the depth of our corruption. Quite the contrary. If you imagine the sinner as being indifferent to God, you do not yet fathom the depth of sin by a long stretch" (174).

Especially in *Ons Program* Kuyper made use of the doctrine of the natural knowledge of God. Here too, the congruence with what was later ascribed to common grace is striking on all points.

2. Kuyper always continued to speak of a natural knowledge of God, but later he assigned it a place within common grace. One can read this in his *Encyclopaedie* II, 254–55, where Kuyper says of the *semen religionis* (and therefore also of natural theology) that "thanks to the *gratia communis* it also yet remains in the fallen sinner." Cf. also *Gemeene Gratie* I, 415. This shows clearly that Kuyper is now of opinion that without common grace no knowledge of God

would have been possible. So far as I know, he never accounted for the inaccuracy of the contrary opinion that he had defended in *Natuurlijke Godskennis*.

3. Once Kuyper made the switch to common grace, much of what he formerly called "natural" (and which was as such maintained automatically despite the Fall) lost this character. Thus in *Het Werk van den Heiligen Geest* and also in *E Voto* we find several sections in which Kuyper describes as "natural" something that he in *De Gemeene Gratie* characterizes as "grace." An example is *love*, which is described in *Het Werk van den Heiligen Geest*, 643-44, and *E Voto* I, 34, as a natural instinct, whereas it is called fruit of common grace in *De Gemeene Gratie* I, 252-53; II, 304ff.; and *Loc. de Magistratu*, 65. Similarly, *prayer* is called a natural form of expression in *Het Werk van den Heiligen Geest*, 780-81; and *E Voto* IV, 334-35, 374-75, but in *De Gemeene Gratie* I, 413, it is described as an urge that would not continue to exist without common grace. We may assume that with this change from "natural" to "gracious," Kuyper also thought he was in a stronger position over against Rome. To that extent, I consider the remarks made by Velema, discussed above, valuable when stripped of the specifics of the substantial analogy issue.

4. Kuyper typically uses the expressions "natural knowledge of God" and "*theologia naturalis*" indiscriminately. Thus, in the series of articles entitled *Natuurlijke Godskennis*, 184; *Ons Program*, 187; *Encyclopaedie* II, 253ff.; but also in *Loc. de Deo* I, 69ff., Kuyper says that the *theologia naturalis* should more properly be called *theologia revelata naturalis*. For the *theologia naturalis* does not exist apart from revelation. Its "origin is Christian. Those who knew God's word, i.e., Christians, have learned from Scripture the confession of that primordial truth as based in nature" (op. cit., 71). *By* the light of Scripture, though not from Scripture but from nature, comes "the clue that human beings, as human beings can indeed be led by the *sensus divinitatis* and what ἐκ τῶν ποιημάτων ἐστιν τοῦ θεοῦ [is from the things made by God] to the awareness and the understanding that they are required to honor God and can only live through him" (73). It is clear that Kuyper, in discussing natural theology here in *Loc. de Deo* (vol. I dates from 1894-95), regarded it especially as a *doctrine* that derived its substance solely from nature without reference to Scripture (70-71). But Kuyper does not want to think of a *theologia naturalis* in that way: "Human beings in their natural state have no awareness of God, save by most imperfect means, whereas the souls of converted human beings are adapted to such an extent that they see in the heavens, in the ποιήματα [the things that have been made], everything as it truly is" (71). Kuyper does continue to maintain a *cognitio Dei naturalis* (40ff.). Otherwise it is difficult to understand how in his *Encyclopaedie* (dating from the same time as *Loc. de Deo*!) he could place natural knowledge of God and *theologia naturalis* side by side. For here he is not considering natural theology in the special sense of a separate doctrine. All in

all, Kuyper interprets the concept "natural knowledge of God" in more than one sense, accepting the one and rejecting the other. It is understandable that such a concept could not easily encompass what Kuyper was able to accommodate in "common grace." Besides, the concept of *theologia naturalis* is also much too narrow for everything that *De Gemeene Gratie* contains. It concerns much more than knowledge of God. We will see later that it is actually about something else.

5. Calvinistic background. We must also remember that Kuyper, after both his series of articles on election and covenant and their particular grace and covenant grace, must have had, by way of parallel, little difficulty in his worldview to speak about *common* grace. He was very familiar with classic Calvinistic theology and had read about general grace there. The problem facing Kuyper (the combination of the deadly character of sin and the good in the world) was also a problem for Calvin himself. I will consider later whether and to what extent Kuyper followed his own path in the development of the concept of common grace.

The topic "Calvin and general grace" will be discussed later. But I do need to anticipate it in part at this point. For Kuyper repeatedly appealed to Calvin for his doctrine of common grace. Was that *post hoc*, or did Kuyper in *his formulation of the problem* face a difficulty (and propose a solution) that Calvin also faced? I assert the latter and will try to demonstrate it in chapters III and IV. For now it will suffice to note that for a well-founded assessment of Kuyper's doctrine, one must not lose sight of its Calvinistic background.

6. The political objective. Almost certainly Kuyper also wrote *De Gemeene Gratie* in order to pay special attention to the relationship between church and state. The literature of classic Calvinism motivated him "in *De Gemeene Gratie* to adapt the old Calvinistic politics again to our very different time period."[421] Kuyper discussed this political motive in his doctrine in great detail, first in *Locus de Magistratu* (1893) and later in the third volume of *De Gemeene Gratie*.

Already during his studies in preparation for the competition for a prize offered by the faculty of the University of Groningen, Kuyper became familiar with Calvin and, so he writes, "Since church and state were so closely connected in the sixteenth century, my studies already then tempted me to enter the political realm" (*A.R. Staatkunde*, Preface, viii). Kuyper came into contact with political life only later and discovered that theology and politics were inseparable. For

---

421. *A.R. Staatkunde*, Preface, x.

CHAPTER I. ABRAHAM KUYPER

this insight he felt indebted to the conventicles: It is "solely the contact with life, which already rustled in the so-called *Nachtschool*, that I recognized the infeasibility of, on the one hand, separation of theology and politics, and, on the other, of choosing 1789 instead of 1578 as the starting point for the historical-political line. It was not the inspirations of the Réveil, and also not the supranaturalistic discoveries that gave me this contact with historical life. That contact came from the remnant of the old conventicles with their many adherents. They still had their own literature in those Reformed circles, and that literature described theology and politics as an inseparable unity" (*A.R. Staatkunde*, Preface, viii). In 1873 Kuyper found and bought from an antiquarian in Leiden "a whole library ... from which the early Calvinism spoke to me as from the grave. That is how I discovered the old literature and, especially through Dibbets, the heirs of the spiritual estate. This motivated me then to adapt the old Calvinistic politics again to our changed time in *De Gemeene Gratie* (op. cit., Preface, x).

Kuyper had already done this in 1893 in a detailed discussion of the *Locus de Magistratu*. Already the independent and broad treatment of such a *locus*, which does not appear in the work of other Reformed systematic theologians, shows how important it was for Kuyper to provide a principial, theological foundation for dealing with political problems. He found this in common grace, which was discussed in detail for the first time in the above-mentioned *Locus* (§ 2, *De gratia communi*). According to Kuyper, the relationship between church and state can only be framed clearly with the help of this doctrine.

Kuyper concludes that although Calvinism began "to err in its first attempt at a formal dogmatics and to adopt the prevalent view of the Roman Catholics," nonetheless, "from the beginning there was *another seed* in Calvinism, albeit hidden, that led Calvinism to make its appearance not only as a theological persuasion or ecclesiastical manifestation, but as a *formative power* in social life and in the life of states and nations. That seed consisted in the fact that Calvin, right from the start, appreciated the distinction between *gratia communis* [common grace] and *gratia specialis* [special or particular grace] and expressed it, although imperfectly. In consequence, that seed continued to work effectively in Calvinistic life and bore fruit in America, the Netherlands, and England, in breaking with the state church and in the rich and full development of a *free church in a free state*" (*Loc. de Magistratu*, 21).

Considering the above, it is no wonder that it was to the question of "church and state" that Kuyper devoted half of the "practical part" of volume III of *De Gemeene Gratie*." R. H. Bremmer correctly concluded from this that Kuyper "developed his brilliant concept not least in order to be able to demarcate theoretically the relationship between church and state" (*De Reformatie* 25, 266).

II

KLAAS SCHILDER

A. Schilder's Opposition to the Doctrine of Common Grace

Klaas Schilder was also very much engaged with the doctrine of common grace. After 1932 he directed increasingly stronger criticism against Kuyper's views. The date shows that Schilder did not contest Kuyper's doctrine from the outset (he became a minister in 1914). Before 1932 he approved of the common grace doctrine. This will be addressed in Part B of this chapter in an attempt to find an answer there to the question why Schilder made the switch from pro to contra.

First I will convey Schilder's criticism. To do so in an orderly fashion and to gain an overview of the topic, I have divided the material into three parts:
1. Schilder's doctrinal-historical objections.
2. Schilder's doctrinal objections.
3. Schilder's own solution.

Strictly speaking, the third part does not belong under the heading "Opposition to the Doctrine of Common Grace," but Schilder's criticism will become much clearer in a discussion of his own solution, which was born out of his critical confrontation with Kuyper.

Doctrinal-historical objections

§ 1. Use the word "grace" sparingly (Augustine and Dort)

According to Schilder (whose line of thought is presented in what follows), Augustine already knew of the difference "between the sloppy, imprecise use of the word 'grace' and the scholarly, precise use of that word much loved by the church, 'grace.'"¹ Augustine had learned to see this difference in his dispute with Pelagius. He became concerned when Pelagius used the term "grace" "*also when the issue is not nature's restoration but its creation.*"² Pelagius' misuse of the word "grace" was an attempt to protect himself against the accusation that he denied grace. "Would Pelagius do injustice to God's grace? Of course not, so he parried: I find grace everywhere and in all things!"³ By proclaiming his belief in free will he certainly did not want to exclude grace. "For he acknowledged that the *possibility of willing and of working*, without which we would be unable to do any good, was given to us by the Creator. Well, *that was a* gratia, *a grace, that was common to Gentiles and Christians, the godless and the pious, believers and unbelievers*. Thus Pelagius already calls a 'possibility' conferred in *creation*, in *nature*, 'grace' as such."⁴ And he does so in order "to subvert *true* grace, to twist and destroy it."⁵ Those who first examined the teachings of Pelagius did not realize this initially. And they excused themselves later: could we "really have suspected that he was thinking of a grace *that we have in common with the ungodly?* Had they suspected it, they would indignantly have rejected his views at once. They cannot be faulted for having been momentarily confused; they were used to the language of the *Bible*. And, as we can clearly read, it uses the term "grace" for works of redemption."⁶

It is true, says Schilder, that besides scholarly language there is also colloquial speech. "Concerning this, Augustine happily admitted that *quadam non improbanda ratione* (in a certain manner that is not to be rejected) one can say that there is a grace by which we are created and distinguished from lifeless and irrational creatures: we have God to thank for that. But this concession to custom does not permit us to identify two 'lines of thought' in Augustine, according to one of which the term 'grace' *is not*, and according to another of which it *is*, strictly speaking, acceptable with regard to the gifts of creation (*dona creationis*). The *quadam*

---

1. *Heidelbergsche Catechismus* (abbreviated as *Heid. Cat.*) IV, 21–22.
2. Op. cit., IV, 34.
3. Op. cit., IV, 30.
4. Op. cit., IV, 32.
5. Op. cit., IV, 33.
6. Op. cit., IV, 34–35.

in *quadam non improbanda ratione* ... speaks volumes."[7] Also Suarez maintains, in agreement with Augustine, "that such a b*roader* use of the word *'gratia'* does not comply with Holy Scripture, with the language of the prophets, evangelists, and apostles."[8]

This lesson from the days of Augustine must not be forgotten, according to Schilder. But did Kuyper take it to heart? He too, alas, illegitimately characterizes "natural gifts" as gifts of grace. The "remnants" of the image of God he calls grace:[9] "It is sloppy when Kuyper in his popular articles, published later in book form, called 'nature' a 'gift' (or a collection of 'gifts') but then immediately proclaims: it was given, it was not something owed, and thus it is 'grace.' But let us then readily admit that Pelagius' use of the word is still very much alive!"[10]

The history of Pelagius' misuse of the word was repeated in the days of Dort. That was the explicit conclusion of the Frisian deputies to synod. Schilder quotes them: "Augustine states that he pronounced anathema over Pelagius, that is, he cursed those who feel or say that the grace of God, through which Christ came into the world to save sinners is not necessary, not in every hour and every moment, but also not in all our actions. Augustine says that God's servants, having heard this and being proponents of the general truth, can recognize no other grace of God than what they were accustomed to read about in God's books and which they preached to God's people. But he [Pelagius] accepted a different grace, namely, the grace described in Augustine's pastoral letter 106, one that is common to Gentiles and Christians, the ungodly, believers and unbelievers, which he regarded as that general grace that is the light of nature. Each of us must determine the extent to which the Remonstrants take a different view of this meaning of the word 'grace.' But we are not afraid to say that their views are more akin to those of Pelagius and his adherents than to what the Holy Spirit taught in Holy Scripture, when they confer the name 'grace' on the light of nature. For the Holy Spirit always understands grace to be either the fountain of all saving gifts, including the

---

7. Op. cit., IV, 35.
8. Op. cit., IV, 37.
9. Op. cit., IV, 20; citing *G.G.* I, 252–53.
10. Op. cit., IV, 66.

mercy of God, or the gracious and supernatural actions and the supernatural and spiritual gifts which are given us out of mere grace and mercy in Christ and through Jesus Christ our Mediator."[11] Schilder comments as follows: "According to this view, one may therefore not ascribe to the light of nature what only God's true grace is entitled to. The adjective 'true' or *'vera'* is conclusive here; the addition that it is 'through Jesus Christ' precludes all misunderstanding. Thus above all slogans about common grace this warning can be heard: remember, there is a 'true and a false grace.'"[12]

It is therefore not the Reformed but the Remonstrants who, according to Schilder (with a reference to the Canons of Dort, III/IV, Rejection of Errors 5), denoted the light of nature as "common grace."[13] In the only place where the term "common grace" appears in the Three Forms of Unity, the Remonstrants' appreciation for the light of nature, which they call common grace, is contested.[14]

But there is something else. When Dort speaks of the light of nature, it says at the same time that human beings do not use this light properly, but obscure, suppress, and wholly pollute it. "They not only resist the light of God's Word, but also the light of nature. By virtue of their corrupt nature they want to banish not only the clear lamp, but also the smallest light flickering from the candelabra."[15] But the Remonstrants have, to use an expression of Trigland, made "a big fire out of small sparks."[16]

This is readily apparent from the Remonstrant doctrine of the *docilitas*. For this Schilder quotes Ph. a Limborch. According to Limborch, we may "not maintain that all are by nature 'intractable' or wicked: for that 'intractability' does not arise from nature, nor is it innate, but it is [who is not reminded of Pelagius? K.S.] the result of *upbringing and bad habit*. If it were innate, it would be the same for all.... Whence, so asks Limborch, do human beings derive this docility, this restraint, this pliability, this receptiveness? His answer

---

11. Op. cit., IV, 31–32. We have corrected the spelling in accordance with the *Acta ofte Handelinghen des nationalen Synodi*, Canin, ed., shorter edition (Dordrecht, 1621), vol. III, 273.
12. Op. cit., IV, 32.
13. Op. cit., I, 71, 118, 365; IV, 20–21; *De Reformatie* (abbreviated throughout as "*Ref.*") 18, 211; 20, 253; 22, 266; *Congres van Gereformeerden (Verslag)*, 111; *Christ and Culture*, 142.
14. *Heid. Cat.* III, 236.
15. *Ref.* 19, 67.
16. Loc. cit.

is: *they derive it from the common and general grace* that God gives to all persons through the operation of creation and providence. This Remonstrant tenaciously maintains that this involves grace. God gave people the light of reason, but in addition he *calls* them to him by his creation and providential work, by which he stimulates their rational consciousness."[17] In contradistinction to what Dort teaches, human beings are indeed able through their *docilitas*, as gift of God's grace, to use the light of nature properly. In other words, light and application (*usus*) of the light, being taught and being tractable, then go hand in hand![18] They always disregard "the important point" "that between the natural gift ('light of nature') and its *use* there is an 'intermediate entity' [Schilder means the corrupt human heart, J.D.] which has a decisive influence on that 'use.'"[19] But Reformed theology confesses in the Heidelberg Catechism (Answer 5) that "pre-occupied" sinners, i.e., sinners who are already beforehand biased against God and their neighbor, and thus "pre-occupied to such an extent that they resist and force back the more positive conviction concerning their complete corruption. The delusion that 'human beings are characterized by *docilitas*,' which is so attractive to humanists, is in itself proof of the 'hate' referred to in Answer 5; for precisely by devising such delusions, those who are unspiritual play hide-and-seek with themselves, so that when they are presented with a mirror that shows them their 'natural,' their 'innate' face, they immediately forget what they were like (James 1:23). There you have the 'hate' in practice, the 'suppression' of all the light given to us. The common grace concepts of the Remonstrants may contradict the doctrine of total depravity, but in fact they confirm it: the cause of the impotence lies in the fundamental corruption, the corruption of the heart with its enmity, its obstinacy, that *hatred* which wants to cut off by the root and from its inception everything that summons to better insight."[20]

Schilder's warning to use the word "grace" sparingly is thus made very clear. The derailment of the Remonstrants is indeed

---

17. *Heid. Cat.* I, 160.
18. Op. cit., IV, 44–45.
19. Op. cit., IV, 45.
20. Op. cit., I, 169.

a warning. With "that word much loved by the church, 'grace,'"[21] they have blunted the sharp point of what the Catechism says about our inclination to hate God and our neighbor.[22] And although the Remonstrants try to distance themselves from Pelagius,[23] in practice they also declare nature to be fundamentally autarkic. The Canons of Dort are directly opposed to this with their "God-honoring thesis that there is a 'new creation,' a *nova creatio*—the 'fine point' of Dort. Neither the synergists nor the Remonstrants have been able to employ Augustine's concept of grace logically in their doctrine of common grace. Also terminologically, it is not possible to have it both ways, neither for the contemporaries of Dort nor for us."[24]

Schilder wants to learn something else from Dort, namely, what Paraeus asserted over against the Remonstrant doctrine of common grace. According to Paraeus (as summarized by Schilder), this doctrine amounts to the following: "A 'grace' that is 'general' and from God's side is displayed 'indifferently' (without his being concerned about what the result will be for the various parties involved) still has to be 'specified' (one person will accept it when it comes to that point, another will reject it; only then what was once indifferent becomes distinct). That is how things would be if one could really speak of an indifferent grace, as the Remonstrants maintain."[25] But Paraeus rejects this, because "if we ... of ourselves ... specify the indifferent [grace] ... then the idol of free will" is erected (and so grace, which is never indifferent and always works insuperably, is nullified).[26] This rejection also gets to the nucleus of the question of common grace. "For if it is indeed true that speaking of *indifferent* progressive or even only retarding *actions* of God [as Kuyper does, J.D.] is an *abstraction*, and that life in its fullness, reality, knows of the so-called indifference only in specification, then the theological proposition according to which cosmic therapy (and therefore also the proposition of the *possibility*

21. See footnote 1.
22. *Heid. Cat.* I, 165.
23. Op. cit., IV, 46.
24. Op. cit., IV, 47.
25. Op. cit., IV, 56. For the address delivered by Paraeus, see the *Acta ofte Handelinghen*, I, 288–326; for the citation, op. cit., 315. Because of his age, Paraeus was not at the Synod himself. His written argument was read in the 99th session.
26. *Heid. Cat.* IV, 57.

of history) is common grace after the Fall, is—apart from God's concrete disposition toward specific individuals—utterly demolished."[27] An indifference lacking specification "does not exist; neither does a non-individual communality. Communal nature and its employment can only justifiably be regarded as communal and function communally *in* and *through* the individual *use* of nature; the individual-human element never exists without the effectuation of God's predestination, which is never pallid, never colorless."[28]

Schilder's comments on Paraeus' exposition will only become perspicuous when one understands his doctrinal objections to the doctrine of common grace. I will discuss these later. But for the sake of completeness regarding "Schilder and Dort" I presented Paraeus' criticism of the Remonstrants here already, together with Schilder's exegesis of this criticism. In light of what follows later, what Schilder said above will be become understandable. Schilder does admit that some Reformed fathers also discussed common grace. Thus the doctrine of general (or common) grace was debated by the disciples of the authors of the Heidelberg Catechism (*Heid. Cat.* I, 12–13). Also, someone such as Trigland did not fully reject common grace, which he regarded as consisting of what is revealed to all people in the book of nature (*Heid. Cat.* I, 167–68).

§ 2. Improper appeal to Calvin

We have already seen that in support of his doctrine of common grace Kuyper appealed to Calvin, specifically to the *Institutes* II, iii, 3. Schilder contests this appeal: "Certainly, Calvin speaks—just as Augustine sometimes did, or at least permitted so long as it was not taken seriously (as in the case of Pelagius)—of a certain (*nonnulla*) room for a 'grace' that one can encounter in the corrupt nature of specific people presented as examples from the circle of unbelievers, people in whom sin is restrained not in its nature but in its 'outburst.' But is this common grace as it is generally known? No, for as regards the adjective 'common,' Calvin himself speaks of 'particular.' And as regards the noun 'grace': in the first place, Calvin does not make those 'specious' gifts into a universally valid category: they occur as additional gift (in addition to natural gifts);

27. Op. cit., IV, 57–58.
28. Op. cit., IV, 59.

and in the second place, the use of the plural (*gratias*) makes it especially clear that Calvin applies the word in a looser sense, not in the categorical sense in which Kuyper uses it."²⁹ Schilder refers to a quotation from Calvin in which he uses the word "grace" in a broader sense "that was more closely related to the French concept of (elegant) 'grace' than to the confessional concept of 'favor.'"³⁰ It is true that *gratias* in the *Institutes* II, iii, 4, means "something more than elegance, charm; but it surely does not have the meaning of 'grace' in the sense in which Kuyper wants it to be understood in the term 'common grace.' *That plural form points in the right direction.* 'A grace' (which one can pluralize) is something different than a favor that is common to all, understood categorically."³¹ Accordingly, Schilder regards Kuyper's appeal to Calvin as 'completely immaterial.' Calvin does speak in II, iii, 3, of a certain bridled grace, "but does that solve the problem? Not at all, says Calvin; that is why he goes further in II, iii, 4, and concludes that we must deny all worth to everything that seems commendable in the ungodly. Such 'virtues' may be praised in the marketplace and by the mass of people, but they have no value whatsoever before God's tribunal."³² That Schilder did not recognize any harmony between Kuyper and Calvin on the point of common grace is also evident in his assessment of the dissertation by H. Kuiper, *Calvin on Common Grace*, defended at the Free University: 'A possible dissertation at Kampen about common grace in Calvin ... will ... be quite different from the one in Amsterdam.'³³

§ 3. Reformed reaction against Descartes ignored in part

Schilder readily admits that "the fathers before Dort ... also spoke often of 'innate knowledge,' of *capita communissima*— i.e., very *general principal truths common to all people* (thus giving them their

---

29. Op. cit., IV, 138. Here Schilder analyzes *Institutes* II, iii, 4: "these are not common gifts of nature, but special graces of God."
30. Op. cit., IV, 22. The quotation, already referred to in Schilder's *Tussen 'Ja' en 'Neen,'* 289, is from Calvin's commentary on Heb 11:1: *Hic vero gratia caret antilogiae species*. In the French translation: *au reste l'apparence de contradiction en ce propos à grâce*.
31. Op. cit., IV, 139.
32. Op. cit., IV, 130.
33. *Ref.* 24, 407.

own content)—also concerning 'the highest authority.' Indeed, more than once they declared the 'innate' knowledge of God (*theologia insita*) to be identical to those *capita communissima*."[34] Many among them asserted that the contents of "the book of conscience" in natural theology essentially corresponded to the Ten Commandments.[35] Against, among others, the Socinians they even defended tooth and nail the doctrine of the existence of a natural theology.[36] They believed that the natural knowledge of God could get one quite far.[37] "To our shame" it must therefore be admitted that when "Descartes later ... fanned the spark of the *lumen naturale* [natural light], which was also carried along by a Reformed wind, into a huge and scorching fire, he ... was able to appeal to a theological wisdom that the Reformed abandoned only in reaction to *him*. Descartes' so-called excesses roused them from the slumber induced by their notions of what is 'communal.'"[38] By going much further than the Reformed, Descartes caused the latter to become so alarmed "that thereafter they took every opportunity to make it very clear that they with *their* doctrine of 'innate' impressions and of a 'natural' knowledge of God or a natural theology most certainly did not agree with Descartes."[39]

It is true that Kuyper abandoned natural theology,[40] but in finding fault with V. Hepp and P. Prins for having "in part ignored the lesson of history regarding the Reformed reaction to Descartes,"[41] Schilder directed his criticism also against Kuyper when the latter counts Rom 2:15 (where we read that the work of the law is written in the human heart) as one of the places in Scripture "elucidating the idea that with regard to the people of this world *things are not as bad as expected*."[42] Besides, Schilder does not at all doubt the close connection between the idea of common grace and that of natural theology. Earlier Reformed theologians still regularly coupled the matter of general (common) grace to

---

34. *Heid. Cat.* I, 183.
35. Op. cit., I, 182.
36. Op. cit., I, 91.
37. Op. cit., I, 90.
38. Op. cit., IV, 125. Cf. *Ref.* 22, 266.
39. *Heid. Cat.* I, 92.
40. Op. cit., III, 238.
41. Op. cit., I, 98.
42. Op. cit., I, 98.

that of natural theology and of innate ideas or knowledge of God (with a content of its own that was then general or common to all human beings).[43] "With a little thought, everyone can understand that the one is connected with the other. That God's common grace operates in natural (and cultural) life and that one can also enjoy real grace outside of the church and without Scripture—that is a doctrine connected very closely with that of so-called 'natural theology,' namely the doctrine that one can acquire real *knowledge of God* outside of the church and without Scripture, a knowledge that can supposedly more or less *be systematized*."[44] And therefore Schilder states: "Whoever objects critically to one aspect of these theories will also have more and more reservations concerning the second." In his view the Reformed fathers have let the doctrine of natural theology languish and that of general or common grace likewise.[45]

§ 4. Common or general? The fathers and Kuyper

Schilder repeatedly points out the terminological difference between Kuyper and the earlier Reformed writers. Kuyper recognizes two kinds of grace: general and particular. In addition to the term *"general* grace" he uses *"common* grace" as its synonym. But, according to Schilder, equating the two terms is *"in conflict what was said by earlier Reformed writers.* For more than one of them distinguished between *three* kinds of grace: *general* (or universal), *common* (or communal, i.e., shared within a defined group), and *particular* (or special). The difference is clear: having eyes, for example, is general; having brown eyes, on the other hand, is common (communal). "[46] "Common" can, of course, also apply to all human beings, but not necessarily. *"The general is always common. The common is not always general.* And is certain that one can clearly distinguish between 'common' and 'general.' It is therefore possible that the fathers assigned to 'common grace' something that those

---

43. Op. cit., III, 237.
44. *Ref.* 17, 380.
45. Loc. cit.
46. *Heid. Cat.* III, 238–39. Kuyper did account for the difference between *universalis* and *communis.* Cf. pp. 6–7 above.

same fathers would not want to classify under *our* 'common grace.' Conversely, we might classify under '*general*' grace something that they definitely did not count as 'general,' but rather as 'common.'"⁴⁷

Because of this terminological difference, an appeal to the fathers can be dangerous. For example, when L. Berkhof quotes Johannes a Marck to defend Kuyper's doctrine with an appeal to the fathers, Schilder calls this quotation misleading because both Marck himself and his commentator, B. de Moor, speak in the quotation in question about a *gratia communis* that is restricted to the *externe vocati*, i.e., to "those called externally" by God's Word.⁴⁸ In other words, *this* 'common grace' is restricted to the sphere of action of the church and is not at all general. And when according to De Moor it concerns the grace that is common (only among those who see the means of grace come to them) over against a salvific grace, "what does this have to do with Kuyper's broad epic? Very little," so Schilder concludes.⁴⁹

Also in *this* respect Kuyper cannot make an appeal to Calvin, says Schilder: "What is common grace according to Calvin? Well, certainly not a general grace that comes to all people, as Kuyper ... [contends], but common grace, i.e., *exclusively for the people of the church*, the grace that everyone *in the church* receives."⁵⁰

Doctrinal objections

§ 5. *Is continuation of history after the Fall grace?*

Kuyper answered this question affirmatively, as we saw in chapter I. For if common grace had not arisen, "everything" would have collapsed "as with one frightful thunderclap" and sunk into hell. But that did not happen. A deferment took place.⁵¹ And this "stay of execution," as a result of which Adam did *not* die that very day

47. Op. cit., III, 239.
48. Op. cit., IV, 64. Kuyper does draw a distinction between "natural-general" grace and "common" grace (the latter explained, *inter alia*, by reference to Heb 6:4ff.); but this distinction did not find a further place in his theology. Cf. *Loc. de Salute*, 89.
49. *Heid. Cat.* IV, 64. For the quotation from De Moor, see ibid., 63–64, note 23.
50. *Ref.* 24, 407.
51. See pp. 16ff. above.

but remained alive and continued to live for centuries, is nothing else and nothing less than a powerful act of common grace that concerns all people, also us personally." For without that continuation "no human race could have arisen."[52]

Schilder's criticism of Kuyper is directed especially against this argument. In his own words, his "deepest inclination ... has always been ... to show that also after the Fall the continued existence of nature and human beings should not be characterized 'in a one-sided way' as 'grace' (favor)."[53]

What were Schilder's objections to Kuyper's argument?

1. *No hypothetical-speculative reasoning.* Schilder: "Assume for a moment that there had been something like a 'world' if God had immediately caused the extreme effect of the punishment, the 'second death,' to occur. Would that give me the right to compare my world of today with the presumed world of that day, and to conclude that the world of today is 'not so bad,' and further to explain this 'not so bad' as based on a decision pursuant to God's will that I may call 'grace' or 'favor'? That is, if I am to be understood as speaking *strictly*? Oh no. For *if* I may compare the world of the here-and-now to a *presumed* 'world' of the 'yonder-and-later,' why would I then not rather, even much rather, compare the world in which I live with, for example, the new earth, in which righteousness dwells? Why would I then draw a comparison with a 'hell' that *would* have existed today, but not with a 'heaven' that will certainly exist later?"[54] For in the latter case, says Schilder, the world would not be better than expected, but would disappoint and I would be overcome with feelings of terror instead of relief. "The world of today would then be happy with that hypothetical hell (that would have existed). But it would not be pleased about the coming non-hypothetical realm of peace.... What is it to be? Sweet or bitter? Common grace or a common judgment? Retardation of the curse, or of the blessing?"[55] Schilder's objection is that Kuyper's comparison is arbitrary and that it can be formulated with as much,

---

52. *G.G.* I, 95.
53. *Ref.* 23, 159.
54. *Ref.* 17, 388.
55. Loc. cit.

indeed, with more justice (if one replaces the hypothetical "would" with the non-hypothetical "will").[56]

Schilder agrees with S. Greijdanus, who says that there is no place for any remaining hypothetical questions about "what *would* have happened if this had not or that *had* occurred, *if*, e.g., sin had not entered the world."[57] But Schilder wants to go further: "We also make bold to ask what *would* have happened *if* after the Fall the protoplasts [the persons formed first] had immediately descended to hell .... The place of outer darkness would then have admitted *two* human beings. *Already concerning this place* [then in any case destined for more than two, J.D.][58] God's *Counsel* (known to us from Scripture) would thereby be abrogated." Then "we," in Kuyper's words, would not have descended into hell!

Schilder adds another hypothesis: "If it had pleased God to open a hell solely for the Adamics, *even then*, in order to achieve this goal, it would have been *necessary* to have a prolongation of history, a married life with one's spouse, a prevailing equilibrium, a universal stability, societal and political organization, indeed, even what the Canons call 'some regard for virtue and outward order.'"[59] And that is why the "hell" that would have come into being if God had caused the second death to take effect immediately after the Fall "is nothing but a fiction, a working hypothesis of those who want to reach conclusions about the existence of common grace but who do so too hastily."[60] Kuyper's comparison is self-destructive: "Those who 'compare' today's world with the 'world' that *would* have been there, or with the hell that *would* then have come into existence, compare reality with a fiction, that which *had to* come with that which *could not* come according to God's Counsel.... Worlds can only be compared to worlds—and then only if one discovers a criterion of comparison not in those worlds but in the spoken Word of him who created and subsequently explained it."[61]

---

56. Loc. cit.
57. *Heid. Cat.* IV, 68. See S. Greijdanus, *Wezen van het Calvinisme*, 32–33; and *Twee bijdragen* (rectoral addresses of 1942 and 1946) in *Almanak F.Q.I* (1947), 91.
58. *Heid. Cat.* IV, 68–69.
59. Op. cit., IV, 69, citing Canons of Dort, III/IV, 4.
60. *Ref.* 17, 389.
61. Loc. cit.

CHAPTER II. KLAAS SCHILDER

1. It will be apparent to the reader that Schilder rejects Kuyper's hypothetical argument, but then formulates not one but two hypotheses himself. Does this not render him subject to the same evil of which he accused Kuyper? Berkouwer thought so and "perceived ... the attraction of a speculation that distances itself from Scripture, right after the theoretical rejection of speculation" (*De Voorzienigheid Gods*, 83).

However, Schilder replied that Berkouwer's view was incorrect: "*We do not speculate here, but are engaged in analysis*" (*Heid. Cat.* IV, 69). Kuyper speculated with his "if" argument, but what Schilder raises against it is "nothing more than: *what are you saying*, when you (the opponent) fantasize about an 'immediate descent into hell'? Those who *analyze* a speculative question do not speculate themselves but crystallize the speculation of the other person" (*Heid. Cat.* IV, loc. cit). Schilder therefore maintains his assertion that Kuyper engages in speculative reasoning with his "if" argument.

2. Schilder does not make it entirely clear whether *every* hypothetical argument (disregarding the illegitimacy of contesting one hypothesis with another) is speculative and therefore illegitimate. In *Ref.* 17, 388 (1937), Schilder says that he would not want to ban "all such arguments and conclusions about supposed consequences of supposed causes. In many instances one has sufficient grounds for such conditional sentences." Schilder said this in 1937. But in *Heid. Cat.* I, 347, he labels as "dangerous" and "*usually* impudent" [italics supplied] the argument "what *would* have happened, *if* ...." And in his rectoral address of 1942 Schilder with approval quotes Greijdanus (see above), who, it seems, rejects all hypothetical argumentation: "There is no longer room for the question what would have happened if this had not, or that had occurred, if, *for example*, sin had not entered the world." The phrase "for example" (which I have italicized, J.D.) constitutes a total rejection of all hypothetical arguments (Greijdanus, *Wezen van het Calvinisme*, 32–33). When Schilder in 1947 discusses the Roman Catholic speculation concerning a "pure state of nature" that has never existed in reality, he asks: "Who gives us the right to *speculate* about the reality that God made or will make, and to do this on the basis of our self-willed, fantastic theories about *possibilities* that have never existed?" (*Heid. Cat.* I, 447; also already in *Heid. Cat.*, II, 56, when first published as supplement to *De Reformatie*, 26 Jan. 1940). And further see *Heid. Cat.* IV, 101 (where he mentions "the dangerous talk about God in the *modus irrealis* [the subjunctive irrealis mood])." Do such remarks perhaps incorporate a general rejection of "if" arguments? Did Schilder thus correct his statement of 1937?

But that raises a question. Did Schilder not fall on his own sword in his *doctrine of a catastrophe* by which human beings "*also if the Fall had failed to occur*" [had to] pass on to that higher form of existence in which, *without* marriage and the reproductive drive ... and *without* metabolism they ... could serve God in a better manner of existence"? (*Heid. Cat.* III, 447–48). If you read again what Schilder quoted from Greijdanus and accept it, then it is difficult to find very convincing the statement that he uses to support his catastrophe idea ("also if the Fall had not occurred") as follows: "We are afraid of fantasy and of ideas that are rooted in fantasy. But on the other hand, we believe that everything that can be derived from Scripture as the contents of revelation about itself must therefore also be true in all its implications and gives us leave to consider these implications" (*Wat is de hemel?*, 51).

3. It is regrettable that Berkouwer was so quick in his criticism of Schilder *here*. For *elsewhere he*, too, analyzes a hypothetical-speculative argument: would the incarnation have occurred *without the Fall?* See his *Het Werk van Christus*, 19–33. In summary (in my words) it comes down to this:

Osiander et al.: Had there been no Fall, the son of God would still have become human.
Berkouwer et al.: (*Elaborating on this hypothesis and thus analyzing it.*) Then the Son of God would have come without the cross and atonement of rebellion and guilt. But the Bible does not teach such a Christ anywhere. Conclusion: the hypothesis is pure speculation.

And now Kuyper–Schilder:

Kuyper: If common grace had not entered the world, Adam and Eve would have descended into hell immediately.
Schilder: (*Elaborating on this hypothesis and thus analyzing it.*) Then hell would have had two occupants and heaven none. The Bible does not teach such a hell and heaven. Conclusion: the hypothesis is pure speculation.

At this point I wish to emphasize that I am not yet making a judgment about the matter at issue, namely, whether the continuation after the Fall is grace. It is *possible* to find Kuyper's argumentation speculative and yet not agree with Schilder about that question. I have merely shown how easy it is for one person to accuse another and then become guilty of the same offense. I ask: what real difference in *method* is there between the arguments of Berkouwer and of Schilder?

2. *No childlike argumentation.* According to Schilder, one can also say of the speculation regarding common grace that it "is characterized by the great danger of being 'childlike.'"[62] By that he means the following: "Its proponents, upon discovering that humanity is spared (also after the Fall), present an argument on that basis, as if everything revolves around humanity and as if the continued existence of fallen human beings is a demonstration of grace addressed to them. They forget that ... the preservation of

62. *Heid. Cat.* IV, 67.

humankind ... is also always an aspect of God's *rule*; that therefore human beings are not addressed in first instance as the recipients of God's 'gifts' ... but that they as regards the understanding of God's intention concerning the continuation of the cosmos and in it the existence of humanity ... are primarily 'material' ... kneadable in the hands of the great *Kerameus* [Potter]."[63] Thus, says Schilder, we ask about God's intentions with regard to that continuation and do not proceed on the basis of *our* impressions. "That after the Fall human beings were still alive and breathed, that the sun still shone, that the rivers still ran, this might have—perhaps, perhaps—amazed them, but the bare registering of an *impression* when 'waking from a dream' has never yet proved sufficient for a prophetic and at the same time infallible nomenclature; especially not when waking from the first *nightmare*."[64] But our childlike impression, our "experiential point of view," with its *Aha-Erlebnis* [eureka experience] is subjectivistic, aphoristic, and naïvely empirical.[65] It must make place for God's light of revelation. And when we then pay attention to his eternal decree,[66] to his "building plan" for this world,[67] and to his *governing*,[68] we receive a different perspective on the continuation after the Fall. For, so Schilder continues, "Already before the Fall it was firmly established that: (a) they [the Adamites, J.D.] *had to* come into existence; and (b) their coming could appear under a twofold aspect: under that of *blessing* and under that of *curse*."[69] And therefore: "Maintaining an *'obligation'* imposed on us is not grace; giving back a 'permission' that was granted us but was defiled by sin, is grace. An *obligation* to exist is not grace; one has to exist, to live, to 'be there,' also in order to be punished."[70] Prolongation by itself "is not *grace*. Nor is it judgment. But it is the substrate of both, the great and indispensable presupposition."[71]

I will consider these ideas of Schilder in greater detail later. For now, a few quotations may suffice to clarify what Schilder meant by

63. Loc. cit.
64. Op. cit., IV, 68.
65. Op. cit., IV, 97.
66. Op. cit., IV, 70–71.
67. Op. cit., IV, 74.
68. Op. cit., IV, 67.
69. Op. cit., IV, 71.
70. Op. cit., IV 73. Cf. *Schriftoverdenkingen* III, 572; Satan exists too, and one can surely not call that grace!
71. *Heid. Cat.* IV, 68.

the childlike nature of speculation regarding common grace. For it has become stuck in what we in our naïvety ascertain superficially: we still exist and thus God is gracious toward us—without inquiring about the backgrounds, about God's intentions.

Here I can also discuss several other concerns that Schilder had. He also calls Kuyper's argument *anthropocentric*:[72] One can easily say that the world is "not so bad" and that we are much better off than if God had immediately after the Fall condemned us to hellish punishment. But those who argue *theocentrically* take a different view. They understand that the light of God's self-revelation shone unhindered before the Fall, that it shines hindered now, and it will later shine unhindered again both in heaven and in hell. Considered that way, theocentrically, the world cannot be considered as "not so bad," even compared to hell![73] All that talk about what God "still" left us, without going back to *before* the Fall in order to understand God's intentions, is anthropocentric.[74]

Schilder's reasoning continues as follows: The naïvety in this speaking about common grace also becomes apparent when one sees how *anthropomorphically* it is formulated. It sounds plausible when it is said: "God was able as well as entitled to damn Adam and Eve immediately; he did not do so, but postponed judgment and thus displayed his grace. "One can put it this way when we, human beings, 'see' things from our point of view. But are we allowed to name God's actions confessionally and theologically according to our *point of view*? May we take our own impression as basis for *scholarly terminology*? We think not."[75] Schilder then points to God's regret, about which, in addition to *apperceptive language*, Scripture also contains "the revealed content of Hos 13:14; Ezek 24:14; Num 23:19; 1 Sam 15:29; Ps 110:4; Zech 8:14; and Heb 7:21, in order to cut off all anthropomorphic speech in the *final conclusion*."[76] Well then: "Is it, strictly speaking, true that God 'postponed' something? We say: no. God ... knows all his works from eternity. To *us* it looks like this: when a captain turns the rudder, we (who are standing on another ship) say: look, the man has regret; he is changing his

---

72. Cf. footnote 63.
73. *Ref.* 17, 389.
74. *Ref.* 23, 272.
75. *Heid. Cat.* IV, 99.
76. Loc. cit.

course. But what if it concerns a captain who knew *everything in advance*? Then our observational conclusion is invalid. The same thing happens here."[77] We can speak empirically,[78] we can rely on "apperceptive language," we can express ourselves anthropopatically, in the way that the Bible, dealing with little children in a childlike manner, repeatedly speaks;[79] but there is also a *theological* appreciation that uses scholarly terminology.[80]

It is not difficult for Schilder to choose between the two: "It is better to stick to the reality of the continuation of human life and of its rich variation in individuals, looked at from *a theological* perspective. The meaning and value of human existence, protracted also after the Fall, are too often determined by the *impression* we form of that existence. So long as it seems pleasant to us, we call it 'grace,' but when the reality of wrath and punishment occupy us we say: take it away, take it away, cursed be the day I was born. But neither the one nor the other impression is capable of expressing God's truth in and of itself. Those who let Scripture speak to them, know that it regards the continuation of human existence with its individual variability and variety as an indispensable condition *both* for the administration of the curse *and* for that of the blessing.[81]

It is clear that Schilder wants to transcend childlike anthropomorphic representation. Already in *Bij dichters en schriftgeleerden* he wrote, that "every anthropomorphism *is a goad to reach a higher standpoint*; that an anthropomorphism, each time, *is something that must be overcome*; that it propels upward; that it wants to push us toward a more spiritual vision" (404). It is also clear that Schilder, on his standpoint, considers this reaching such a higher standpoint to be possible. For, in his words, "*the Bible itself moves its anthropomorphisms out of the way*" (op. cit., 410). In Scripture itself there is thus a "higher" and "lower."

What is *not* clear is how Schilder can nonetheless agree with Bavinck that the Bible always speaks anthropomorphistically (*Ref.* 17, 421; *Wat is de hemel?*, 87–88). For if Scripture *always* speaks anthropomorphistically, how can one then ever rise above that?

---

77. Loc. cit.
78. Op. cit., IV, 100.
79. Op. cit., IV, 137.
80. Op. cit., IV, 100. Cf. *Ref.* 17, 421; 18, 187.
81. *Heid. Cat.* I, 432.

Schilder also characterizes the common grace argument as *infralapsarian*. He connects this qualification to Kuyper's reference to an "intermediate state" that is "slotted in" between the Fall and the parousia.[82] Of this he writes: "If we say that the idea that after the world was created and had fallen, God was really obliged to impose punishment but, in order to achieve his goal, slotted in an intermediate period, an intermediate state, then that is an *infra*lapsarian representation."[83] "Postponement," "slotting in," "establishing," are terms borrowed from the representational dictionary of the infralapsarians, according to Schilder. And although Kuyper warns against the misuse of the infralapsarian method of representation in connection with an intermediate state,[84] his entire view is strongly influenced by infralapsarianism. Indeed, all of Kuyper's description of the providence of God in connection with common grace, proceeds, *as he himself says*, from a subjective representation of providence. Schilder quotes, *inter alia*, the following passage of Kuyper's: "The representation of God's providence that we acquire from our own life experience really begins only when sin comes into the world and, in our understanding, comes to an end with the final judgment. *And this is the point where God's providence enters into a direct relationship with common grace and is not conceivable for one moment without that common grace*. That is not the case when you confess God's providence as an absolute, for then it continues straight through, also there where common grace will no longer be operative. But it is the case in your subjective representation."[85] About this, Schilder says: "If I am not mistaken, then this quoted paragraph is one of the weakest that Dr. Kuyper ever wrote."[86] He also calls it the Achilles heel of Kuyper's argumentation.[87]

Is Kuyper's infralapsarian argument totally incorrect, or is it merely inadequate according to Schilder? The difference is clear. If the argument is merely inadequate, it deserves supplementation; if it is totally incorrect, it can neither

---

82. *Ref.* 17, 396, 405, 413–14.
83. *Ref.* 17, 413.
84. Loc. cit., citing *G.G.* II, 611, where Kuyper says about the coming into being of common grace: "But, and take note, not as an arbitrary slotted-in aid, but as directly required for the end goal of God's decrees."
85. *Ref.* 17, 413. Cf. Kuyper, *G.G.* II, 395.
86. *Ref.* 17, 414.
87. Loc. cit.

be supplemented nor corrected. It is not easy to determine how far Schilder ventures in his criticism on this point. For in the articles published in 1937, mentioned above, Schilder also says: "There can be no sermon that does not speak infralapsarically, no discourse that does not make use of infralapsarian terms, no *theologian* who can avoid it." And "our confessions themselves ... regularly use infralapsarian terminology and hence are so intimately connected with the confessing church" (*Ref.* 17, 413; italics supplied).

But, one might say, why then identify Kuyper's infralapsarian view of the providence of God ("Achilles heel," "subjective representation"!) as a *weakness*? And that while Schilder himself contends that one can raise objections not only against infralapsarianism, but also against supralapsarianism. Cf. *Ref.* 17, 420–21; *Heid. Cat.* III, 470ff.; *Om Woord en Kerk* II, 107. Schilder's answer is as follows: "In addition to what we just mentioned, Scripture instructs us *also* that God knows all his works from eternity. It is for this reason that we must constantly guard ourselves against drawing conclusions based on *our* observation, which comes *after the fact*, about *God's decrees*, which preceded all things and all observation" (*Ref.* 17, 421). The "also," which I have italicized, points to the validity of the one and the other. Both appear in Scripture.

But it is remarkable in Schilder that, as soon as we begin to speak in a *scholarly* way, the first (infralapsarian) viewpoint no longer appears to be tenable. He can appreciate Kuyper's arguments "as a rousing voice driving God's people out into the broad life of the world," but "would rather not see all this regarded as *scholarly* terminology" (*Ref.*, loc. cit.). In the same context he notes that Kuyper speaks in a popular way about the patience of God, but states that this must be distinguished from theologically precise scholarly discourse about God (loc. cit.).

This clearly reveals a tension in Schilder. On the one hand, both points of view derive their substance from Holy Scripture; on the other hand, *as soon as we become engaged in scholarly activity*, the second view declares the first to be popular, childlike, anthropomorphic. This tension must therefore find expression in Scripture! And that brings us back to remarks I made earlier about Schilder and the anthropomorphism in Scripture that Scripture itself does away with.

3. *No one-sided argumentation.* We already saw that Schilder's deepest inclination "has always been ... to show that also after the Fall the continued existence of nature and human beings should not be characterized 'in a one-sided way' as 'grace' (favor), because the continuation of these two by God was already necessary so that he would have a substrate for both blessing *and* curse.[88] For the preservation of the world and the continuation of history are

---

88. *Ref.* 23, 159. Cf. footnote 53.

"indispensable, both for building the road to heaven and for traveling down the roads that lead to hell."[89]

Schilder mentions this idea repeatedly and just as often it is then implied that in addition to grace we must now also speak of curse. Through the continuation after the Fall, God prepares the way to heaven and to hell and thereby ensures that the number of the elect and of the reprobate can be reached.[90] Consequently it is incorrect to use only the word "grace" for the continuation of the world and of history. That continuation can also be terrifying. An accused person expects to be placed in front of the firing squad on Monday. He is served oatmeal and meat until Saturday and perhaps thinks: it is not so bad. "But it could also be that the judge condemned him not to a quick death by firing squad but to a gradual death. Is that oatmeal then 'grace'? Of course not; it 'spared' him for something much more terrifying."[91] Therefore Schilder warns against a "single-track theology,"[92] a theology that wants to travel on only one set of rails, namely, grace, and airbrushes the other, the curse. [93] He states that we have to use "*both* words."[94]

Schilder goes further by saying that, strictly speaking, we can never use those two words without quotation marks.[95] For *we* are speaking here about grace and judgment from *our* point of view: I make too big a leap "when on the basis of *my* uncertain *impression* I dare to draw the conclusion that God's disposition is *firm*. 'Grace' is such a fixed disposition."[96] The preservation of human nature is "actually not grace. Nor is it condemnation, strictly speaking. But it is the *condition* for both. God cannot provide people with either what is humanly desirable or what is humanly undesirable unless their original nature remains *their* nature."[97] Prolongation [of time] is the condition, the substrate for the administration of blessing and curse. Schilder never tires of repeating this.[98]

And thus we see once again that Schilder wants to distinguish

---

89. *Heid. Cat.* I, 373.
90. *Ref.* 23, 159; *Heid. Cat.* I, 433.
91. *Ref.* 17, 388.
92. *Ref.* 23, 272; *Christ and Culture*, 148.
93. *Ref.* 12, 86.
94. *Ref.* 25, 96, 129.
95. *Ref.* 17, 388; *Heid. Cat.* I, 433.
96. *Ref.* 17, 388. Cf. *Heid. Cat.* I, 432–33, 473; IV, 68, 115.
97. *Heid. Cat.* I, 116–17; *Christ and Culture*, 74, 91.
98. *Heid. Cat.* I, 24–41, 402, 429, 502; II, 91, 201, 380; III, 224, 446; IV, 68, 96.

the scholarly use of language from naïve and popular usage. One must speak of "both–and." Both grace *and* curse. But in the final analysis theologians can use neither the one nor the other, for both describe, in an infralapsarian way, a very uncertain observation that *we* make. Does one want to speak of "grace"? All right, but then "loosely,"[99] and in that "loose" usage also still together with "judgment": "Neither of these terms would have a scientific basis. At best they could be used in a non-scientific description of concrete reality, but then *alongside one another*."[100] But those who are precise in the way they speak, says Schilder, characterize the continuation as *substrate* for the administration of blessing and curse, grace and judgment.

§ 6. Kuyper's use of Scripture rejected

Schilder also concerned himself with the Scriptural evidence that Kuyper adduced in support of his doctrine of common grace. In this section I will consider Schilder's repudiation of that "evidence" and discuss the relevant texts in the order in which they appear in Scripture.

1. *Genesis 2:17* – *"In the day that you eat of it you shall surely die."* Schilder never carried out a detailed exegesis of this passage. However, in the only place in his *Heidelbergsche Catechismus* where he does discuss it, what he says about it is clear enough. He writes: "When the anti-Origenist Isidore of Pelusium, in a letter to Dorotheus, considers the threat of Gen 2:17, *he* points out that evildoers do indeed *die* when they commit their misdeed, even though they might seem to live, or think they do. And he recalls the word of Christ: let the dead bury their dead."[101] Schilder uses Isodore's exegesis to dispute Kuyper effectively.[102] Those who contend that the punishment did not happen as required by the threat, contend that God did not speak *seriously*. Similarly, it is

---

99. Op. cit., I, 118.
100. *Christ and Culture*, 88.
101. *Heid. Cat.* IV, 103.
102. Kuyper's name is mentioned, op. cit., IV, 101.

wrong to abstract the threatened death in Gen 2:17 "from *ethical or moral* capacities."[103]

It is remarkable that Schilder says so little about the exegesis of Gen 2:17, although that text plays such an important role in the doctrine of common grace. One could point out that Kuyper contradicted himself more than once with respect to Gen 2:17. But aside from the question whether Schilder was aware of these contradictions, he most certainly would have known that G. Ch. Aalders in the *Korte Verklaring* (widely known among Reformed people of Schilder's time and also often quoted respectfully by him) agreed with Kuyper. Aalders writes that it is difficult to deny "that the threat was not carried out, at least not in the way it was expressed. From this we can only conclude that God immediately extended *grace* to fallen humanity. Those who object to the use of this particular word, may replace it with a synonym, but the fact that God did not immediately carry out the threat of punishment in its full force is undeniable. And so God displays his undeserved favor toward the guilty" (op. cit., *Genesis* I, 140–41).

2. *Genesis 9 – The Noahic covenant.* It did, of course, not escape Schilder that Kuyper wanted "not only to confirm," his theory of common grace but also "to locate its point of departure in the Noahic covenant."[104] But when Kuyper sees it as a covenant of grace, says Schilder, he can maintain "this too cheerful optimism ... by representing that all ordinances given by God after the Flood on more than one 'terrain' were something new, and also by giving an image of the circumstances in the world before the Flood that often does not get beyond pure imagination."[105] *Is* the Noahic covenant really something new? According to Schilder, those who assert this have not benefited from the lesson of the doctrinal-historical development "among us," including the theological discussion about the *doctrine of the covenant*: "The earlier doctrine of the covenant represented the different covenant economies as circles with common segments, in consequence of which the one repetition of revelation data from the prior circle informed the next. But now that image of circles and the idea of *repetition* of revelatory content has yielded to that of continuing *patefaction* [disclosure] after the principial *addition* in the *proto-gospel* [the 'first'

---

103. Op. cit., IV, 102.
104. Op. cit., IV, 130.
105. Op. cit., IV, 131.

gospel, the mother promise, Gen 3:15, J.D.] of the *Christologic* chapter to what Adam already knew."[106] From this Schilder draws the following conclusion: "We believe that, just as the story of the creation of 'all things' is a *tendentious story* that leads to *humanity*, and *so* to Fall and proto-*gospel*, so also the story of the Flood and the subsequent establishing of the covenant is a *tendentious* story that does not lead to an *intervallum*, an intermediate time period, an interim, but to Shem, Abraham, Israel, Christ. In other words, *the so-called Noahic covenant continues history to Christ; that was already old*; the only thing that is new is the manner in which a new ancestor is obsignated and the opening up of additional eschatological perspectives—n*ot a new* but *a clearer* story, to be announced anew when there is a second patriarch."[107]

In Schilder's view, Kuyper regrettably allows himself to be "ensnared in the tiresome debate about the question whether the so-called Noahic covenant ... is particular or universal.... A dilemmatic choice prompted by the other question: is the Noahic covenant a phase of the covenant of grace, yes or no? If yes, surely it is entered into solely with the believers. If no, then it applies to all; but is that possible: to establish *such* a covenant with the universal human race?"[108] We have to get rid of this dilemma, says Schilder. For this you have to pay attention to the word "covenant." It can be used with all kinds of meanings, and the meaning "is often no more than 'arrangement,' 'regulation,' 'ordinance,' 'provision.'"[109] That is also the case in Gen 9:8–17. When all living creatures, the earth, all birds, all livestock, all animals, etc., are named, "it goes without saying that the word 'covenant' is repeatedly used for 'ordinance.'"[110] God's pledge that there will not be another flood *affects* all cosmic beings and, precisely for that reason "they are included in it, but, of course, 'according to their kind.' God addresses Noah, but the living creatures, etc., share in God's plan. He acts 'with them, about them, and without them.' *Without them*. But, of course, not so with

---

106. Op. cit., IV, 131.
107. Op. cit., IV, 132. Cf. *Wat is de hemel?*, 187; the covenant of nature as "phase of the covenant of grace."
108. *Heid. Cat.* IV, 132.
109. Op. cit., IV, 133, with references to Jer 33:20, 25, and Hos 2:17.
110. Loc. cit.

Noah."¹¹¹ He is able, having been appointed as God's fellow-knower and fellow-worker, to see the day of the Messiah "as already now prepared and established: no flood shall disturb the ground any more, but the struggle between the seed of the serpent and the seed of the woman will occur according to the established plan. The struggle continues."¹¹²

Schilder therefore rejects Kuyper's dilemma: particular versus universal. The word "covenant," as used in Genesis 9, cannot have been used for both Noah *cum suis* and all living creatures, etc., in the same sense. God acts *with* Noah (actively) and *without* them (passively). Therefore, the dilemma "particular or universal" is not valid. Moreover, the above shows at the same time that Schilder regarded the Noahic covenant as a phase, one of the economies of the covenant of *grace*.¹¹³

1. Although it has become clear that Schilder takes issue with Kuyper's doctrine of common *grace*, it is not clear whether we may characterize the Noahic covenant as a demonstration of God's (particular) *grace*, as it is conferred in the continuation of history "until Christ" by the Noahic covenant. For the evangelical-Christological *tendency* of this phase of the covenant of *grace* fades into the background when Schilder writes: "Day and night will continue and the seasons will follow each other with fixed regularity—what is this in the final analysis but the 'preservation' of the earth for the fire?" (*Heid. Cat.* IV, 141). And: "'Preserved' also means 'reserved'" for a second *fin-de-siècle* (op. cit., IV, 142). My question is: does it say this in Genesis 8:21-22? Or may we not characterize any covenant as covenant (for the demonstration) of grace and should we instead always say: covenant (for the demonstration) of grace *and* judgment, blessing *and* curse? Is Schilder's designation of the Noahic covenant as a phase of the covenant of *grace* not really a one-sided characterization? Grace without the counterpart of judgment? Besides, Schilder himself makes a distinction *in* this Noahic covenant. He writes: "Noah's *being* a federal *co-knower with God*—that is ... grace, a very particular grace. But the knowledge itself, the guaranteed projects of divine providence—those are not grace, but substrate for blessing and for curse" (op. cit., IV, 141). In other words, we may characterize the promise concerning Noah's position as grace, but not the stabilization of the natural order (Gen 8:22), which (as noted) is "included" in God's promise to Noah. Then we apparently have to speak of the "covenant of retardation and of a providentially guided equilibrium," which is then also "the substrate for the

---

111. Op. cit., IV, 134.
112. Op. cit., IV, 135-36.
113. Apparently Schilder quotes Vitringa with approval. The latter characterizes the Noahic covenant as illustration and obsignation of the old covenant of grace (op. cit., 131, note 4).

other covenant history in which human beings may be called partakers of God's grace.... The covenant history concerning the *first*, serves the covenant history of the *second* creature-*Gattung* [sort or type]" (op. cit., IV, 117). Just before the last quotation, Schilder explained what he meant by the two creature-*Gattungen*: "The divine Speaker of Genesis 9:10 entered into a 'covenant' (arrangement) with all mere officeless created things, also with 'nature,' including our own physical and psychical regularly ordered existence.... But that is the substrate for the other covenant history in which human beings may be called partakers of God's grace" (loc. cit.). But can the one characterization "covenant of *grace*" then still be maintained for Gen 9, which speaks of a covenant "with you and your offspring, and with every living creature," and "between me and the earth"? The covenant of grace (with Noah) is included in and is supported by the covenant of retardation, which is directed at *two* goals, the administration of grace and judgment!

2. We saw that in Schilder's opinion Kuyper could only maintain the Noahic covenant as a covenant of grace "also by giving an image of the circumstances in the world before the Flood that often does not get beyond pure imagination." Cf. footnote 105. However, according to Schilder, there is not, as Kuyper maintains, a "new state of affairs" after the Flood. Schilder points out that Kuyper first speaks of a "conjecture," but later transformed that "conjecture" into a definite assertion (op. cit., IV, 138). Cf. Kuyper, G.G. I, 16. He rejects Kuyper's hasty conclusion with an appeal to J. H. Heidegger: 'Not a new state, but the old order, that is what Gen 8:22 is all about" (loc. cit.).

3. Schilder also took issue with Kuyper's exegesis of Gen 6:5 and 8:21. Kuyper believed that the former confirmed his thesis that evil had led to a terrible outburst of wickedness ("*every* intention of the thoughts of his heart was *only* evil *continually*"), while the latter would result in a milder judgment ("the intention of man's heart is evil from his youth"). Cf. p. 13 above.

The problem is how one can harmonize the two texts. Schilder appeals to Aalders, who discusses the question how in Gen 6:5 the evil of human beings causes God to repent that he had made them, while the same evil in Gen 8:21 causes the Lord to say to himself that he will not curse the ground again because the intention of human beings is evil from their youth. Schilder quotes the following from Aalders: "The difficulty is thus insoluble. *But it is a difficulty that one creates for oneself by making the wrong connection.* The evil intention of the human heart is not mentioned here as the motive for the *non*-renewal of the all-destructive judgment, but as motive for the judgment *itself*" (op. cit., *Genesis* I, 226). Schilder then continues: "For the construction of the doctrine of common grace these matters remain significant. Kuyper (*G.G.* II, 51) reads in Gen 6:5 '*not* a *general* statement about our human condition for all ages, but a *particular* statement about the terrible outburst of evil before the Flood.' However, Aalders believes that in 8:21 God, '*referring back* to 6:5–7,' says: 'I have sent this terrible

Flood because the depravity of human nature is so great, but I will not again bring such a judgment upon the earth *for the same reason*'" (loc. cit.). And Schilder concludes: "Regarding the intention of 8:21, as well as the scope of 6:5 (although, in our opinion, the actual image of sin from before the Flood does not have be disregarded), we prefer Aalders' exegesis to Kuyper's. One of the exegetical grounds for Kuyper's radical construct is thereby rendered invalid" (*Heid. Cat.* I, 164–65). In his comparison between Gen 6:5 and 8:21, Kuyper suggests that human nature is given an *antidote* by common grace" (*Heid. Cat.* I, 368), but, Schilder continues, "To me it seems ... incorrect to read in Gen 8:21 (as A. Kuyper does) a softening of the disqualification of humanity provided in 6:5. Aalders specifically emphasizes that the first-mentioned text refers back to what was said in 6:5; the depravity that was then the reason for the judgment of the *Flood* will be reason for such judgment no longer" (op. cit., 371).

3. *John 1.* In the third volume of Schilder's *Heidelbergsche Catechismus* there is an extensive discussion of the Prologue to the Gospel of John (following the exegesis of S. Greijdanus) which is not, however, directly referred to in any discussion of common grace but which in the discussion of Lord's Day 9 touches on Christological issues.[114] But even without a direct confrontation with Kuyper, it is clear that Schilder rejects Kuyper's exegesis of that part of Scripture.

Their paths are not that far apart regarding verse 5. Schilder presents Greijdanus' view as follows: "The Logos *always* shines in the darkness, as he did before his incarnation and later during his presence on earth, and he does that *also as Logos*, as the Light. He does it *now* also as Christ; but he does it *not only as Christ*, but also *as Logos*, just as before his incarnation.... At all times the Logos caused his light to shine in the darkness and irradiated the darkness with his light in order to brighten the darkness. It is the light of all kinds of gifts, goods, and knowledge, of what provides enjoyment and help, of whatever freedom and development people on earth may still be able to share in.... It is divine light that emits its radiance into the dark world."[115] Kuyper on the one hand and Schilder and Greijdanus on the other do differ in that Kuyper points to this light as common grace, while Schilder and Greijdanus do not share this view.

114. *Heid. Cat.* III, 137–81.
115. Op. cit., III, 167. Greijdanus and Schilder are aware that they diverge from the ideas of Th. Zahn and R. Bultmann, who think exclusively of the incarnated Logos in this context.

CHAPTER II. KLAAS SCHILDER

In addition there is a profound difference in exegesis regarding verse 9: "The true light, which gives light to everyone, was coming into the world." We saw that Kuyper connects "coming into the world" with "everyone" and also that he identifies the light as the light of reason, by which all human beings are illumined from their birth in God's common grace.[116] Greijdanus and Schilder apply "coming into the world" to "the true light." And in answer to the question which coming of the light is intended, we read: "Usually this is understood as referring to the Lord's incarnation, i.e., to the Lord as he appeared in his human nature, in and after his birth, at the same time as John the Baptist.... But the evangelist only starts to speak about the incarnation in v. 14.... What v. 9 says of the true light applies also to the Son of God in the time of the 'old dispensation,' throughout all the centuries from the time of God's promise of salvation in Gen 3:15 until the Lord's actual birth in Bethlehem, as well as thereafter. According to this opinion, the coming of the Lord in the world begins already with the mother promise of Gen 3:15.... Thus throughout all the centuries before the incarnation of the Word, there was a *coming* of the Son of God that served the preparation of his final and actual coming in the flesh."[117] In answer to the question: "How can it be said that the light illumines *everyone*? For did he not come only to *Israel*?" Greijdanus replies that the proclamation of the coming and the salvation work of the Son already happened in Gen 3:15 and that this mother promise extended to the entire human race, and he adds: "If they did not keep it thereafter, but neglected it, that is their fault.... The people remembered the promise for a long time as part of tradition: Gen 4:26; 5:29; Num 24:17. 'Sinai' happened only centuries after the Fall." Besides, "much of what God later gave to Abraham and Israel and wrought for them became known not only to Israel ... but also the peoples around them.... Already the hatred of various nations in the course of the ages shows that they knew there was something special about Israel. And that which God gave to and wrought in Israel also called upon other peoples to turn themselves to Israel and to recognize Israel's God: Ps 117; 148; Isa 49:6. Hence it

---

116. See pp. 19–20 above.
117. *Heid. Cat.* III, 170–71.

is understandable that John 1:9 says that the true light, in or through its coming, enlightens or shines on every person and that it did this already before the incarnation of the Word. The *shining* does not imply that every person also really *sees*: the *universal* of John 8:12a does not take away the *particular* of John 8:12b [K.S.]. Note Rom 8:7; John 3:19; 8:47; 18:37, 41."[118]

It is clear that Schilder and Kuyper are directly opposed in their exegesis of verse 10. Kuyper speaks of the Logos and of common grace; Schilder (with Greijdanus) speaks of the "*Savior* promised by God who, already in the time before the incarnation, [performed] his *work of salvation*" particularly in Israel and, radiating from there (*gratia particularis*!), among the nations round about.[119]

4. *Romans 1 and 2.* In the context of common grace, Schilder paid particular attention to Rom 1:18-21, and 2:14 and 15, more so than any other texts.

He maintains (against the Socinians) that the reference to God's eternal power and divinity in Rom 1:20 "indeed refers in the first place to God's works *in creation, 'although his deeds in subsequent history are not excluded'* (Greijdanus)."[120] Kuyper and Schilder do not differ on that point. But this revelation of God is most certainly not proof of grace. For what was God's *goal* with this revelation? This: "*so that they* [the unbelievers, J.D] *are without excuse.*"[121] It is true that the Greek expression in Rom 1:20 (εἰς τὸ) can indicate either a goal or a consequence. Schilder quotes Greijdanus: "'The pointing to a consequence is undoubtedly what is intended here in first instance. *However, God also intended that consequence.*" Thus we have to "maintain the meanings of both '*so that*' and '*in order that*.'"[122] Meanwhile Schilder places all the emphasis on the *final* moment. And for him it is then impossible on the basis of Rom 1:19 and 20 to speak of grace: "God reveals himself with the special *goal* of denying all innocence to unbelievers in order that their *judgment* would be the heavier. Hence ... the giving of revelation is not yet

---

118. *Heid. Cat.* III, 172. Greijdanus writes that his view is "not shared by most," but that the context demands it. For it is not until v. 14 that the incarnated Word is spoken of (op. cit., III, 173).
119. Op. cit., III, 173 (italics supplied).
120. Op. cit., I, 94.
121. Op. cit., I, 161.
122. Op. cit., I, 168. The Greijdanus quotation is from his commentary on Romans.

evidence of a gracious *disposition* on God's part."[123] One should not make the final εἰς τό consecutive ("so that they..."), exclaims Schilder (in a passage directed against Barth), for that "evades what is the central question here: is God's wrath not free, *and sovereign*, and *iure suo* [in its own right] also in creating its own objects with regard to a will to reject?"[124] The εἶναι αὐτοὺς ἀναπολογήτους ["they are without excuse"] is not a *fate* that the eternal God comes upon, whether it concerns the predicate or the personal pronoun, but it is the *goal* that he *is pursuing*."[125] How can one speak of grace when God in his wrath (Rom 1:18) hands over entire nations to godless delusion (1:24)?[126]

There is more. God reveals himself to the ungodly; but is it true that Rom 1:20 says that from what he has created God's invisible power and divine nature are really understood and perceived by the ungodly? That is "the older view."[127] But Schilder again follows Greijdanus, who "takes a different view. The Greek has: νοούμενα καθορᾶται ['clearly seen, being understood']. *If* they (namely, the invisible things) are ... pondered, grasped with the spirit, the mind, then they are seen! It is a conditional seeing! Spiritual activity must continue; otherwise the seeing stops."[128] But unregenerate persons resist the practical acknowledgment of the condition, contradict it, and, according to the Canons of Dort (III/IV, 4), wholly pollute and suppress consciousness of it.[129] What Schilder means by "spiritual activity" that must continue if one wants to see, is apparent from the following quotation: "God's invisible attributes were seen from the beginning of creation and continue to be seen *if* they *are pondered, grasped on the basis of the Word* with the spirit, the mind."[130] And also: "Scripture says, 'We observe the wisdom of God in his creatures, but only if our eyes are opened to that wisdom by God's Word, *not otherwise*.'" The latter has to be added expressly. It was the reason why we repeatedly pointed out that Rom 1:20 does *not* ensure that God's invisible attributes ... in his creatures are *indeed*

123. Op. cit., I, 161.
124. Op. cit., III, 435.
125. Op. cit., IV, 130.
126. Op. cit., III, 437.
127. Op. cit., III, 241.
128. Op. cit., I, 92.
129. Op. cit., III, 241.
130. Op. cit., III, 257.

understood and perceived. It says only that they *can* be seen *if they are considered and pondered; if* the spirit is occupied with it, *then* they let themselves be perceived."[131]

In summary we can say that, in respect of Rom 1:19 and 20, Schilder speaks of a revelation of God's wrath (and not of his grace), and moreover that this revelation discloses only *darkness* in a human world that extinguishes the light.

Rom 2:14 and 15 also receive Schilder's full attention. He reminds us that earlier Reformed writers thought highly of natural theology on the basis of this text. Even Calvin gives an exegesis of these verses in which appears a remark that one "will probably no longer come across among our current exegetes."[132] For Calvin speaks of "certain concepts of justice and right" (*conceptiones*), or what the Greeks referred to as *prolepseis*. "That Greek term came from a suspect source. The Stoics understood such *prolepseis* or anticipations as 'general concepts'; you constantly find the same 'general concepts' in the debates by the fathers about 'natural theology.' They understood that to mean: the concepts, ideas, impressions, or the contents of knowledge that are common to all and that without any specific study of Scripture, but only with the aid of the two 'books' of nature and conscience, are said to be common to and innate in all human beings.... These 'general concepts' are sometimes also referred to as 'dark knowledge'; they are part of human nature and precede all specific forms of knowledge."[133] In this way "the doctrine of *natural law* understandably gained more and more acceptance, also among Reformed theologians."[134] And often the factual content of these general concepts was regarded as identical to the Ten Commandments. Thus in his dissertation, defended at the Free University in 1884, L. van Andel says on the basis of Rom 2:15: "Even though the nations do not have the letter of the Ten Commandments, they *do* have the *spirit* of these commandments, which is innate in them and is written in their hearts. That spirit thus is evident in what they in fact achieve for the maintenance of

---

131. Op. cit., III, 423–24.
132. Op. cit., I, 96.
133. Loc. cit.
134. Loc. cit.

the legal order in laws and regulations that they decree and for the transgression of which they determine the punishment."[135] Schilder adds: "One might therefore say: it is not so bad; this way of looking at things greatly honors those who in the days of the fathers spoke of *capita communissima*, i.e., the most general chapters of doctrine, the principal concepts of knowledge, *prolepseis*, general ideas, which are accepted at the same time by those who possess the written Word as well as by those who do without it or pass it by. Indeed, 'on the basis of this point of view it is not so bad'; that is why Dr. A. Kuyper (*G.G.* II, 18) counts Rom 2:14 as one of the places that 'elucidate the "it is not so bad" for the people of the world.'"[136]

In his own treatment of Rom 2:14–15, Schilder concludes first that it is not the *law* that has been written on the heart of human beings (for immediately before this text it says that they are *without* the law),[137] but the *work* of the law and says that we must not gloss over this distinction.[138] Schilder presents two interpretations that have been given. The first (and most accepted) interpretation is that it is "a human act that supposedly is carried out in harmony (more or less) with what the law commands. 'Work of the law' thus means something like: a work that the law demands and that is consonant with the law."[139] The second interpretation contemplates "a work that *the law itself* performs. Something that the law *itself* carries out. A *result* of the law. *Not what it commands, but what it does.*" In that case the expression could refer to the curse of the law; to "its punishment; the fact that it does not give the transgressor any peace, that it does not allow itself to be mocked" (examples: Cain, Saul, Judas).[140] Schilder is apparently captivated (understandably) by the second interpretation, but "the fact that some who take it into account but do not consistently follow it as the only correct interpretation calls for caution." Accordingly he believes the first interpretation to be most likely the correct one.[141] But even though "work of the law" thus speaks of human actions, it really involves no

---

135. Op. cit., I, 97.
136. Op. cit., I, 98.
137. Op. cit., I, 102.
138. Op. cit., I, 98.
139. Op. cit., I, 100.
140. Op. cit., I, 100–01.
141. Op. cit., I, 101.

more than "an externally observable action, and does *not* examine the *reasons*, the *principles*, the *motives*."[142] Schilder believes that this is expressed in the word *poiein*, used here for the "doing" of the works of the law. As he notes, it does not say *prassein*, as in vv. 2, 3, 25. In vv. 13 and 14 the word *poiein* is used. "When you compare these verses, what do you discover? This: *prassein* means a doing in which persons are engaged with their whole being, are fully involved in the work, give themselves to it, bring it 'into practice.' *Poiein* in contrast denotes an act without *paying particular attention* either to the *persons* who perform it, the *reasons* for it, or the regularity with which they do or do not perform the work."[143] Schilder gives a few examples: "One who uses a defective club and yet hits the intended object correctly, *performs* the correct action (*poiein*). An *enfant terrible* does too. *In vino veritas*. But that does not *make one an expert* in hitting objects correctly (*prassein*)." Another example: "The *work* of the law of woodcutting was written on the hearts of the prisoners of the Nazis and of the Russian Soviets. They included bankers, professors, priests, and generals. They did not cut wood on their own initiative, of their free will, wholeheartedly; they did *not* aspire to the '*prassein* of hewers of wood.' Had they been able, they would have thrown the axe to the ground. But the *work* of cutting wood was written in their hearts. It was on their mind when they awoke and when they went to sleep. Each day they delivered their quota: their *poiēma*, the result of their *poiein* (their producing) of things that belong to the law of woodcutters as it was issued for these wretches by the camp commander."[144]

Keeping this in mind, one does violence to the text by asserting that the law *has been written* on the hearts of the Gentiles: "No, only certain *works* of the law have been imprinted on them, have become flesh and blood for them. But that is as far from the law *itself* being written on their hearts as clinging to particular *customs*, adopting a fixed *rule of life*, or in a thousand-and-one cases rejecting *a living by that rule itself or the principle* from which the rule derived and which caused the drafter of the rule to enact it."[145]

142. Op. cit., I, 102.
143. Op. cit., I, 102–03.
144. Op. cit., I, 103–04. Schilder refers to Greijdanus' commentary on Romans also for the difference between *poiein* and *prassein*.
145. Op. cit., I, 105.

If this is clear, says Schilder, "the most dangerous speculation about Rom 2:14-15 is prevented. In the part of the text under discussion it does not say that God gives his general revelation in the human heart; it also does not say that God in his general revelation works from the internal to the external. For if Paul had said that here, he would have been obliged to say that the general revelation urges the Gentiles to the *poiein* (doing) of acts that correspond with the law externally. But Paul does not say that. He observes only that they come to that *poiein* 'by nature,' *phusei*, i.e., 'by virtue of their innate nature or existence, by their inner state.' That is something different from saying 'by general revelation.'"[146] Thus, so Schilder continues, one cannot derive a paean on general grace from our text. On the contrary: "If I, because I rather enjoy peace and quiet at night and suppose that my neighbors do also, keep the piano closed after eleven o'clock and avoid all noise that might disturb my neighbors, that is a work of the law 'written on my heart' after some ten or twenty years. It is not because I do not want the police to charge me with noise pollution. I am a law unto myself, and that is really not something to be proud of. It does not merit a paean on my being 'not so bad.' Because 'I am a law unto myself' I will be judged more severely when God eventually confronts me with the fifth commandment of the law (authority)."[147] Therefore, it is not general revelation but human nature that is the cause of the Gentiles' *poiein*. Schilder adds: "It is another question whether that nature is itself in part determined by what one understands by general revelation. But that is a different matter. They act through their nature. Not through revelation in a direct sense the way Rom 2:14 regards them."[148]

The evocative example of the woodcutters in the concentration camp should not tempt us to think of *poiein* as always involving a labor that is carried out with dislike. This is already apparent from what has been said above. If *poiein* were always an acting with dislike, Schilder could not really have said: "Their actions in this respect are for them [i.e., the Gentiles in general, J.D.] the 'most natural' thing in the world, they speak for themselves, and 'have become second nature' to them" (*Heid. Cat.* I, 102). Besides, Schilder describes their *poiein*-by-nature

---

146. Op. cit., I, 107.
147. Op. cit., I, 109.
148. Op. cit., I, 109-10.

as "by virtue of their own disposition, their own constitution." But the image of the woodcutters does not fit this description. When Schilder later speaks of the many *works* of the law that carnal human beings gladly do "on their own account, *from their own impulse* [italics supplied, J.D.], on the basis of their own deliberations" (*Heid. Cat.* I, 112), because God's law ("*the only garment that truly 'fits' the world*," op. cit., 113) is, "properly considered, always so '*advantageous*'" (op. cit., 112), I wonder whether such actions cannot almost be denoted as *prassein*, as defined above. Almost. For an important difference (at least for Schilder) between *poiein* and *prassein* remains the *principle* from which the act originates: "The profit of religion, the benefit, the fast-acting healing power, the 'suitability' of the law, our 'acceptance' of God's signature impressed on human life—all these unbelievers can acknowledge and publicly proclaim when it 'suits' them. *But they look at things from the wrong angle*" (op. cit., 114). *Prassein* is (and here Schilder quotes Greijdanus) "about abiding by the law in our work, inwardly and outwardly, completely" (op. cit., 105). But the Gentiles "do" (*poiein*) the works of the law, but they "do" (*prassein*) scandalous things (loc. cit.; cf. Rom 2:3).

In the evaluation presented later (in chapter V) I will not be able to reconsider many of the details that we have looked at in the first three chapters, such as the meaning of *phusei* in Rom 2:14. For that I refer to what is in my opinion a convincing translation proposed by D. Holwerda: *re vera* (in truth, in reality). See his *Commentario de vocis quae est 'phusis': VI atque usu praesertim in graecitate Aristotele anteriore*, 85–86.

5. Revelation 21:24 and 26 – "And the kings of the earth bring their glory and honor into it" [NKJV].

According to Schilder, the exegesis of this text "more or less crowns Dr. Kuyper's common grace epic." The glory of the nations, without distinction between belief or unbelief, supposedly would be brought into the new Jerusalem as an "enduring benefit."

Schilder does not accept this explanation. He again follows the exegete who had already provided him with more ammunition against Kuyper's explanations of various texts: "Dr. Greijdanus (*De Openbaring des Heeren aan Johannes*, 429) says in his exegesis of this text, according to which the kings of the earth bring their glory and honor into holy Jerusalem: '*That is happening now, in this age.*' It is true that this is the exegesis of verse 24, where [in the translation he quotes] the *present* tense is still used (they *bring*]. But in verse 26, in which the *future* tense is used (they *will* bring), it is no different, according to Greijdanus. 'They will bring into it the glory and honor of the nations,' so the translation goes; and this is the explanation: 'Meant are those who do this, i.e., who from among the nations become believers. Among them will also be those who are held in high regard, have various excellent attributes, exercise power *that they use for the benefit of the Lord's congregation.'* This therefore happens in the present age, although 'it is reflected in eternity,' according to our exegete (430). Although it will only be visible in all its clarity in eternity, it takes place in this age. 'In this earthly dispensation God also causes the conversion of kings and those who are powerful and prominent, people of note in all areas. And he also causes many of great influence and high position to collaborate in the *advancement* of his congregation and the *coming* of his Kingdom in glory' (429)."[149] Kuyper definitely does not see it that way ("This ... is not about any period *preceding* the end but certainly about the final outcome itself, as it will be displayed after the conclusion of the judgment in the form of the *abiding new situation* on the new earth and under the new heaven.")[150] But according to Greijdanus what is *also* presented is "what happens in this temporal dispensation."[151]

Schilder further pays attention to the "bringing" of glory into the new Jerusalem, as follows: "Who is doing the 'bringing'? God? But he is always referred to by name in the book of Revelation. One cannot include him under the personal pronoun 'they' or the possessive adjective 'their'.... The angels? But they are also always referred to expressly in John's Apocalypse and sometimes even counted one by one. The words 'they' and 'their' can only refer to *human beings*."[152] Schilder argues further that it is possible to speak of "bringing" [glory] into the church of today, "but the last day means the end of our actual 'bringing' .... On the boundary between time and eternity no one is actively involved in any transporting. One *is* only transported."[153] Moreover, Schilder wonders "what we could possibly 'bring' into the *new* Jerusalem, which is thought of in terms of our traversing a border." "Why would one want to have our cultural treasures in that new Jerusalem? Our bodies are radically different, so how relevant will our palaces be there? The process of becoming will have stopped, the womb stilled: Male and

149. *Wat is de hemel?*, 210–11.
150. Cf. *G.G.* I, 463.
151. *Wat is de hemel?*, 211.
152. Op. cit., 213.
153. Op. cit., 213–14.

female *as such* therefore will no longer have a reason for existence. What could we possibly do there with all the riches of our erotic culture?"[154]

Schilder also rejects Kuyper's idea that the *seed* of common grace, preserved in the fire, will blossom profusely on the new earth. "Seed and fruit both belong to the same world and world form, to the same dimensions, and lie on the same continuum. If one were to interfere with this fundamentally, then the 'seed' would no longer be the seed of what comes thereafter."[155]

§ 7. Rejection of the use of the confession

Schilder issues a strong warning against the danger of using the "small traces" mentioned in art. 14 of the Belgic Confession to make an image of God in a broader sense. In any event, the confession "does not say at all that human beings retained some small traces of the *image of God*; it says that they are left with some small traces of the excellent *gifts* that the Creator and covenant God had bestowed on them."[156]

What Schilder says about art. 14 he emphasizes more strongly when he discusses the Canons of Dort, III/IV, 3 and 4, and states that the small traces and the light of nature appear in a context that is intended to make clear that human beings have no excuse, because they suppress the light.[157] In other words, all optimism based on these statements in the confessions is unjustified. For the fathers of Dort applied "a brake to every fiery person who wants to use the light of nature as foundation to build on, a basis on which grand buildings of science and art can be erected, and so on."[158] One should "not transform a residue ... into a seminal thetic principle. Trigland already issued a warning against Uittenbogaert, who had lit 'a great fire' from those little sparks."[159] We may not tamper with

---

154. Op. cit., 214. Schilder still maintained this in the third edition of *De Openbaring van Johannes en het sociale leven* (1951), 311ff.: The Apocalypse sees "all cultural treasures of the unbelievers as trophies in the new Jerusalem, i.e., Christ's city, the city of *Christus Victor*," op. cit., 313.
155. *Wat is de hemel?*, 214.
156. *Heid. Cat.*, I, 295.
157. For Belgic Confession, art 14: *Heid. Cat.* I, 361–62, 364; IV, 27–28. For Canons of Dort, III/IV, 4: *Heid. Cat.* I, 85, 166, 365; II, 175, 380; IV, 45, 123.
158. *Ref.* 19, 67.
159. Loc. cit.

the Catechism's confession about human beings who are "totally unable to do *any* good and inclined to *all* evil" (Q. 8.). The Canons of Dort, III/IV, 3, do not do so either when they "seek to clarify and crystallize" the Heidelberg Catechism "a little" by speaking of being "incapable of any *saving* good (*bonum salutare*)."[160] This is not a change in substance and is elaborated in III/IV, 4 ("there is left in man after the fall some light of nature, whereby he retains some notions about God, about natural things, and about the difference between what is honorable and shameful, and shows some regard for virtue and outward order"). Behind the belief that there is a change lies "the unsubstantiated and incorrect hypothesis that the Belgic Confession [Schilder undoubtedly has art. 14 in mind, J.D.] failed to address these matters, or considered them in a principially different way."[161]

Here Schilder does not address the question that might be asked, *how* Canons of Dort, III/IV. "clarifies and crystallizes" Heidelberg Catechism, Q. 8. He insists that there is no substantial change. His reference to *Heid. Cat.* I, 158–59, where he, as he says, "spoke about this in another context" (op. cit., 364), does not help. At least, not with regard to the particular point that concerns us *here*. It does state clearly (and that is undoubtedly what Schilder is pointing to in his reference) that Dort, together with the Heidelberg Catechism, holds on to the principle that "I am inclined to *hate* God and my neighbor. So much so, that by nature I pollute, suppress, and act against not only the light of the gospel, but also the light of nature." And so Schilder concludes: "Now the Canons of Dort [contra the *docilitas* of the Remonstrants, J.D.] are restored to their place, and the Catechism also" (166). Dort did not permit "the sharp point of the Catechism's answer, that we are inclined to *hate* God and our neighbor, to be blunted" (165).

The "light of nature," so Schilder continues, "does not take possession of human beings. Does it occupy them? Not really, although, loosely speaking, they do occupy *themselves* with it: they are engaged with it. It is not really possible to maintain that the light of nature occupies (i.e., exercises control over) human beings if you accept that they 'suppress it'.... But what *pre*-occupies them is not that light of nature, but *hatred* against God and thus against all light, also the light of 'nature'.... That is why the light of nature is not

160. *Heid. Cat.* I, 364.
161. Loc. cit.

really capable of arresting the wickedness of the unregenerate, for they themselves most often 'arrest' and 'snuff out' the light. Even in natural and civil matters they do not use it properly; indeed, it is worse in that, 'whatever this light may be, man *wholly pollutes it in various ways and suppresses it in wickedness.*'"[162] The Canons of Dort show clearly that "the light of nature and its use or application are separate things."[163]

Thus Schilder wants to guard against any attempt to take the sting out of the doctrine of the depravity of human nature. That is a depravity in every respect. Human beings misuse even the little bit of light they receive.

Schilder tries to refute the appeal to Canons of Dort, III/IV, 4, in support of the doctrine of common grace in yet another way: "*If* ... the natural light *could* be called 'common grace,' as is done by the Remonstrants, and *if*, pursuant to the conception of many, God *had* intended this common grace as an *action* on his part that was to *arrest evil, then human beings would have been unable to 'suppress' the light of that grace, and would not have been able 'wholly to pollute' it.*"[164] To understand Schilder's conclusion here, you have to realize that he had just said of the 'actions' of God: "Every action that proceeds from God, and it does not matter which, [is] *always invincible*." This therefore applies also to that action by which he wants to arrest sin. For who "can checkmate God? Who breaks down as he builds, who presses on as he thwarts? Who places under the bushel something that he places on top of it?"[165]

The range of these remarks is far-reaching for our topic. If every action of God is insuperable, human beings cannot suppress the light of nature, assuming it was intended to arrest evil. Therefore: "The 'light of nature' is not a dam on which the waves of sin and enmity break."[166] Furthermore, since the light of nature can be suppressed, one cannot call it common grace, because "God's grace, so said the fathers, is always insuperable, invincible. There is no

---

162. Op. cit., I, 365. About occupation and pre-occupation, see also op. cit., I, 166, 169, 184.
163. Op. cit., IV, 45, 123; *Christ and Culture*, 142–43.
164. *Heid. Cat.* I, 365.
165. Loc. cit.
166. Op. cit., I, 366.

reason at all in our [i.e., Schilder's] view to make an exception to that rule. He is *always* and in everything insuperable."[167]

The last quotation continues as follows: "But *if* there is indeed a common grace that, with a will-to-progression, yields fruit by virtue of God's intervention, and *if* those fruits are the *imago Dei* that has been partially preserved (an image of remnants), *then* one can no longer say that the image is dominated by the original image, which is now totally darkened (the image as distorted by sin). For then God would *no longer be insuperable* with respect to that which people call 'grace'" (*Heid. Cat.* I, 290). Here Schilder opposes L. van der Zanden, who in his publication *De mensch als beeld Gods* spoke of an "image of remnants" (the remnants of the original goodness, which remained in people after the Fall); an image of remnants that would, however, be dominated by the image distorted by sin (the entirety of human beings as they were affected, in soul and body, by sin and its consequences) (Schilder, op. cit., 274–75, 289). Schilder rejects both the concept of an image of remnants and of a distorted image and, by reference to Kuyper's concept of common grace as a *"progressive* action," wants to point out the inconsistency in the concept when one does let the image of remnants be dominated by the image distorted by sin. For then God's common grace with its will-to-progression would *not* be insuperable. In my opinion it is clear that I have properly adduced this entire passage (including the first part of the quotation, presented in the text at footnote 167) to corroborate how Schilder considers Kuyper's appeal to the Canons of Dort to be impossible, on the basis of III/IV, 4, *and on the basis of* the proposition that all of God's grace (thus also a potential common grace) is insuperable in its operation. That which is suppressed cannot be called God's insuperable action and therefore cannot be characterized as grace.

Quite apart from all of Kuyper's appeals to the Canons of Dort, Schilder believes that the difficulty with the concept of "insuperability" emerges especially when one speaks about common *grace* as *disposition* of God. According to Schilder, that was done by the Synod of Kalamazoo and by S. J. Ridderbos, but also by Kuyper himself (*Heid. Cat.* IV, 66). For if God's disposition toward all is a gracious one (common grace), how then can it *by specification* (there are elect and reprobate) be gracious *and* wrathful? "Does wrath specify love?" (loc. cit.). For the concept of specification, see pp. 134–35 above.

God's grace is always insuperable, says Schilder, and thereby purports to follow the Reformed fathers. But that raises a question. In 1937 Valentijn Hepp challenged S. G. de Graaf, who had contended that the general goodness of God was a consequence of the particular grace in Christ. Hepp wrote: "But that is not possible. Grace, as it springs from the source, must have the same effect wherever it wends. Scripture teaches us that grace in Christ is always and

---

167. Op. cit., I, 290.

everywhere the same, without exception. For it renews the heart. It sanctifies and beatifies. It is *irresistible*" (*Ref.* 18, 93, cited by J. M. Spier; the quotation can be found in V. Hepp, *Common Grace*, 38). However, Spier challenged Hepp as follows: "It does *say* that the grace that is connected to Christ is irresistible, but it is not demonstrated. *Indeed, it cannot be demonstrated*, for Scripture does not teach it anywhere. God's Word certainly states *that* irresistible grace exists, but not that it *always* exists. On the contrary: covenant breakers have resisted God's grace, and that is why their judgment will be so heavy. Only one of the ten lepers who were healed *by the grace of Christ* came back" (*Ref.* 18, 93). Spier maintained his opinion after he was challenged about it. Among other things, he referred to Grosheide's *Korte Verklaring* of Heb 6:4ff.: "... Scripture teaches that there are heavenly gifts, i.e., gifts that do not originate in nature but that are connected with, and are the consequence of, the particular grace of God revealed in Christ. Such gifts are bestowed even where they are not accepted and where they serve to make the judgment heavier" (*Ref.* 18, 158–59). In support of Spier, Schilder also challenged Hepp. And although he does not share De Graaf's opinions about common grace, he states that one may "not reject an opinion such as that championed by the Rev. de Graaf with the ... unexplained adage 'grace is always irresistible,' for *that does not accord with the historical position*" (*Ref.* 18, 135). "One may not say of grace as such what is indeed true of *regenerating* grace, namely, that it is irresistible" (*Ref.* 18, 112). Trigland and also Paraeus (!) are cited to corroborate this thesis (*Ref.* 18, 135, 136 [note]). Cf. also *Ref.* 18, 66–67, where it is demonstrated that, according to Trigland, even the grace of the inward call is definitely not always "efficacious."

My question is whether what Schilder maintains here does not conflict with what he later writes about grace as such being invincible. The fact that Schilder then speaks of invincible (insuperable) grace, instead of a grace that is irresistible, is irrelevant to *my* question. This terminological matter is a question of preference. Schilder: "The Reformed *preferred* to speak of insuperable, rather than of irresistible, grace" (*Heid. Cat.* IV, 51; emphasis supplied). Cf. *Ref.* 18, 112, where Schilder quotes Bavinck: The Reformed did have "some objections [to the term "irresistible grace"] because it was absolutely not their intent to deny that grace is often and indeed always resisted by the unregenerate person and thus can be resisted. They therefore preferred to speak of the efficacy or of the insuperability of grace, or interpreted the term "irresistible" in the sense that grace is ultimately irresistible. Accordingly the point of disagreement was not whether humans continually resisted and could resist God's grace, but whether ultimately—at the specific moment in which God wanted to regenerate them and work with his efficacious grace in their heart— they could still reject that grace" (*Reformed Dogmatics* IV, 82). But now, disregarding the terminology, in 1937–38 Schilder still speaks (or lets Trigland speak, without offering any criticism) about certain operations of grace (!) that are resistible (*Ref.* 18, 159), referring among other things to Acts 7. Would he still have accepted that way of speaking a few years later? That is, a speaking of grace in general (and thus without any gradations) as being irresistible? Is it possible to call something grace if it is not (*finaliter* [ultimately], see Bavinck) irresistible? I am thinking here also of Schilder's agreement with the definition of grace provided by Greijdanus: "Only when something promotes eternal salvation can we truly speak of grace" (*Twee bijdragen*, 99; the Greijdanus quotation is from *Wezen van het Calvinisme*, 37).

Schilder: Did Kuyper's view actually not fail to do justice to the confession of Lord's Day 2, Answer 8 of the Heidelberg Catechism? Kuyper does not want to dispute "our confession concerning our being 'unable to do any good' and 'inclined to all evil.' On the contrary; that must be maintained.... However, he believes that 'in many instances' (many!) this total corruption conflicts with reality. Those who would ask him whether the *actual situation* of total corruption (confessed in the confession) clashes with the *actual* situation (in all those instances) will hear him respond: A human generation 'such as in the days of Nebuchadnezzar or Cyrus' *was relatively so highly advanced* that one would have to conclude: *something more* can be said of it than that it is 'unable to do any good and inclined to all evil.' 'Something *more*'—agreed. But does Kuyper perhaps *mean* 'something *different*'? He recognizes a *law* of grace, but also a *law* of (common) grace; *a poison, but also an antidote*. And according to Kuyper that antidote also truly lies 'in the human heart.' God dribbled it *into that heart*.... The question cannot be resisted: Kuyper does not *want* to dispute the confession, but *does* he perhaps do so in spite of himself?"[168] And is the restraint of sin, mentioned in artt. 13 and 36 of the Belgic Confession, "a diminution of *sin* and of *corruption* itself, or is it a restraint of their *coming out in force* and of their *consequences*?"[169] We must make a distinction between these two matters. When art. 13, which can point us in the right direction, speaks about God holding the devil and all our enemies in check, "no one will interpret this to mean that their *corruption* is mitigated, or reduced by some 'antidote,' i.e., neutralized in part. Here *there is no* 'more' or 'less.' Rather, their hands are held in check, their influence is curtailed, their power is coerced in advance. Evidently there is a difference between restraining *sin* on the one hand and restraining the *consequences* of

168. *Heid. Cat.* I, 368–69.
169. Op. cit., I, 369.

sin on the other. This difference can indeed go further than the recognition of a *distinction* between the two, for there is a separation between them. The one applies to devils, the other does not."[170] Art. 36 of the Belgic Confession also draws attention to this difference when it speaks of restraining human lawlessness. We find the first example of that in Cain. God put a mark on him "so that no savage anarchy would surround him to overpower him. On the contrary, anarchy would be suppressed and the law of the avenger would be restrained. But neither for Cain nor for his descendants did this suppression of the 'outpouring' or demonstration of lawlessness mitigate or curb the corruption as such. On the contrary, Cain's hubris now became truly apparent, and his followers 'fortified themselves' with and in him. Besides, also the Antichrist will impose discipline on his storm troops: and will it then not be imposed on virtually the entire world? And yet his hour will at the same time be the hour of the released Satan, the Satan who can *'no longer be resisted.'* It will also be the hour in which 'the natural light' will know how to invent among humankind the most brilliant way to exclude the spiritual light."[171] We should not speak of a restraint of corruption, so Schilder continues, but rather of a keeping in check of its "primary or extraordinary effects, or of its improvisations, its ferocity, its individualism, its audacity, its ataxy. But the confession does not speak of an administered 'antidote.'"[172] Scripture speaks of a "more" and "less," also of a going "from bad to worse," in the coming to light of corruption in certain sins. Thus Rom 1:24–28 speaks three times of "a successive *giving over* of the Gentiles by God; a 'giving over' from bad to worse. However, this 'giving over' is not a withdrawal of a moral 'antidote,' but the gradual withholding of the factors that restrained the poison of *sin* in its *progressive effect*. The 'poison' is given free rein, but that is something different from taking back the initial gift and administering an antidote. For abandoning persons who suffer from smallpox is different from draining the vaccine from their bodies."[173]

170. Loc. cit.
171. *Heid. Cat.* I, 370.
172. Loc. cit.
173. Op. cit., I, 370–71.

Our entire human nature is "poisoned,"[174] and so it was and is at all times. "Are Pss 14 and 53, and Rom 3 in any way milder, more forthcoming for actual humans than Gen 6:5? No one would dare to maintain that."[175]

No one, not even Kuyper? Does Schilder really take the consequences of Kuyper's exegesis of Gen 6:5 and 8:21 (see pp. 154–55 above) seriously? It seems to me that Kuyper does not in fact adopt these consequences and that Schilder has misunderstood him. For Kuyper also speaks in the same context from which Schilder quoted of a restraint of the "fatal *effect* of sin" (*G.G.* I, 252), of the "mortal *effect* of sin" (op. cit., 253; emphasis supplied). Does that differ from what Schilder has in mind?

It is another question whether the idea of a restraint of the effect of sin actually functions in Kuyper's opus. If not, then Kuyper may still have weakened the confession of Lord's Day 2, Answer 8. I will not answer this question yet. Now I will merely point out that the distinction between the corruption caused by sin (which we "must maintain at all costs," according to Kuyper) and the restraint of the effect of sin is not absent from Kuyper's *oeuvre*. Schilder gives the impression that this is the case. Cf. *Christ and Culture*, 87, where he speaks of common grace as merely involving "the restraining of sin."

Schilder's own solution

§ 8. Back to before the Fall

I will now discuss Schilder's own solution to the questions surrounding common grace in order to gain a better understanding of his criticism of what Kuyper taught. Schilder himself provides us with an indication how he structured his ideas. Confronted with the dilemma whether "to take into account only what happens to me after the Fall," or "also to take into account ... what was said about me before the Fall, and thereafter maintained," Schilder's choice is not difficult: "*I opt for the second position*; I do so in *all* my dogmatic work. I do so, for example, also when I speak about the church (then it becomes for me God's people); about the kingdom

---

174. Op. cit., I, 373. The original text of the Heidelberg Catechism states in Answer 7 that our nature is *poisoned* (op. cit., I, 329, 359).
175. Op. cit., I, 371.

of heaven; about Christ and the covenant, eternal joy; and about the possibility of human merit, yes or no. In all these questions I do not only take into account what God spoke to humankind *after* the Fall, but also what he told them *before* the Fall as he himself informed me about this in his Word."[176] Christ also spoke in that manner. In the Sermon on the Mount[177] and in Matt 19 (the dispute about marriage)[178] he confronted people with "how things were *in the beginning*, i.e., in the first, original relationship, *binding for all time and created as foundational*, between God and humankind.[179]

For all our problems, says Schilder, we must return to before the Fall, and thus also for common grace. When someone represented to Schilder that Kuyper had surely brought humanity's cultural mandate to the fore sufficiently, he replied: "Who denies that? But the question is whether he *'moved it to the back'* sufficiently, ... whether he adequately based it on God's words *in Paradise*."[180]

§ 9. *The covenant relationship*

The above means that, according to Schilder, Kuyper in his views about common grace did not take the doctrine of the covenant sufficiently into account.[181] About the covenant and Paradise he says the following: The relationship between God and humans has been determined from the beginning by the covenant that God entered into with them. This covenant was not something necessarily included in creation: "Human beings were created for a covenant relationship, but they were not automatically included in it. God announced the covenant *after* creation. The covenant does not stand analytically but synthetically with regard to creation, i.e., it *added* something to it that was not already included in the fact of creation. It was not merely something that made the relationship between the two *concrete*; it was also something that *enriched* it in such a way that they *became* parties. One can say that it was not

---

176. *Ref.* 19, 365. Cf. *Heid. Cat.* II, 15.
177. *Heid. Cat.* I, 73-74.
178. Op. cit, I, 146-47; *Schriftoverdenkingen* I, 159-60.
179. *Heid. Cat.* I, 73.
180. *Ref.* 23, 159, against S. J. Ridderbos.
181. *Heid. Cat.* IV, 90.

a matter of natural law, but of 'evangelical' or 'gospel' law. (The word 'gospel' means 'joyful good news' and can therefore be used also for God's good news given in Paradise. Today, *after the Fall*, 'gospel' means the good news of God's unimpeded grace, in Christ. But in Paradise the gospel was the good news of God's unimpeded *favor*, which is a *free* favor, a gift that did not '*of necessity*' flow from the simple fact that he created the world, including human beings.)"[182] Through this covenant relationship with God, human beings acquired a special position that differs from the position of all other creatures. It is true that all creatures have their *officium*, their task, as part of the created entirety of God's works, but for human beings (and also for the angels) the *officium* became an *office*. "To be qualified as office-bearer: that is what God had created [the first Adam] for, not merely to be one of the parts in the huge world-as-engine, but also as engine-driver appointed by God and responsible to him."[183]

Schilder continues: It is true that the two parties to the covenant are very unequal. The distinction between God and human beings is immeasurable.[184] "However, one may not, on the basis of that distinction, assert that therefore the covenant is actually not a true covenant but rather a mere arrangement that God made unilaterally with respect to human beings and without their input."[185] For although the covenant is monopleuric (one-sided) in its origin, it is dipleuric (two-sided) in its existence.[186] The Reformed fathers therefore regarded the dipleuric nature of the covenant as a matter of first importance, "because they wanted to draw a sharp distinction between, on the one hand, a one-sided covenant of God with the plants, the animals, the earth (the covenant of Genesis 9, that he would not destroy the earth again by water) and, on the other, a (two-sided) covenant of God uniquely with living human beings."[187] That is how the covenant is "*reality*; its promulgation was therefore much, much more than the introduction of a symbol,

---

182. Op. cit., I, 318. I, 390 also speaks of the "gospel" in Paradise.
183. *Christ and Culture*, 59.
184. *Heid. Cat.* I, 317.
185. Loc. cit.
186. *Wat is de hemel?*, 176. Cf. *Heid. Cat.* I, 326, 331, 382, 390, 396.
187. *Ref.* 18, 122.

an ideogram."[188] With complete seriousness we must maintain that the covenant is two-sided. For in the covenant human beings are addressed, and "note that they are addressed in it as a *responsible* party, and thus they were *made in order to be* and afterwards *treated as a true* party."[189] Human beings are not zeros, but truly count. Certainly, the parties are unequal, for *"human beings must 'look up' to God."* That is, "all renown, all pride, all glorying in self-efficacy, is excluded. But that same inequality must now also take into account the fact that *God 'looks down' on human beings.* And that means that all false quiescence, all lifeless resignation is excluded, all passivity is excluded, all merely mechanical dependence on laws of physics is excluded, also for human beings."[190] With respect to humans, Schilder even speaks of *autarky*, as follows: "God is autarkic in and of himself; human beings can only share in a *created* and *bestowed* autarky; and the covenant exists to develop and preserve *that* created autarky in its concrete existence."[191]

That is how, according to Schilder, *history* becomes possible. For the establishing of the covenant elevated the relationship between God and his people beyond the sphere of "fate" or of "natural inevitability," "in order to place it in a sphere of a mutual free relationship that must from now on operate on the basis of 'all or nothing.' An *eternal recurrence of things*—that means that what is called "divine" and what is called "human" are both included in a *'process'* about which neither can do anything. But the *covenant* permits them to 'proceed'.... Eternal recurrence means: everything is nothing and nothing is everything. *Covenant* means: everything or nothing; within it or without.... *Eternal recurrence: fate. Covenant: God.*"[192]

So also *evolutionism* is cut off as being "the killing of religion." For "the struggle is all about this: What stands at the beginning of history? Is it person against person, God over against human office-bearer, Covenant partner against covenant partner? And is that beginning of everything principally described as history controlled by words of address proceeding from God and is it therefore

---

188. *Heid. Cat.* I, 317. Cf. *Wat is de Hel?*, 187.
189. *Heid. Cat.* I, 321. Cf. II, 365–66.
190. Op. cit., I, 321–22.
191. Op. cit., I, 320. Cf. I, 66.
192. Op. cit., II, 275–76.

governed by his *covenant*? Or is it governed by 'winds' of fate that 'flutter' over the chaos and can only send out cosmic or terrestrial rays? Are human beings animals in origin, or are they in origin friends and children of God, the ones whom he addresses? "[193] The office of human beings cuts off all evolutionism. Adam was not a child, not a frolicsome simpleton, not the naïve protohuman;[194] rather, his office places him as *God's fellow worker* in a process of evolution of the world of the "alpha" to that of the "omega."[195]

It is also apparent from Schilder's discussion of the two parts of the covenant, promise and demand, that he finds the concept of the naïve paradisal human reprehensible: The *formula foederis* in this first phase of the history of the covenant is: "Do this": that is the law (demand). "And you will live": that is the promise. Adam did indeed know what the consequences would be if he broke the law (the test command).[196] To suppose that God did not tell humans or did not tell them adequately about the place of suffering in this world is a fictitious and false hypothesis. "Certainly, God did not reveal *everything*. But he did reveal what was fundamental, essential, and foundational.... Already in Paradise ... he spoke in advance about suffering and death as possibilities that, should they become reality, would be seen as the wages of sin: 'for in the day you eat of it you shall surely die' (Gen 2:17). Thus suffering and death were already made known in the very first phase of the history of revelation and of the covenant as God's covenant vengeance."[197] Adam received a promise as well as a threat.[198] There is much wisdom in the statement in the Canons of Dort: "grace is conferred through *admonitions*" (III/IV, 17). "What applies to the 'grace' after the Fall, was also valid for the 'favor' (before the Fall).”[199]

Schilder's line of reasoning continues as follows: Therefore, it is subjectivistic, aphoristic, and naïvely empiristic to assume an *Aha-Erlebnis* [eureka experience] on the part of humans: "it is not so bad after all."[200] One should "not be so quick let a prophetic-

---

193. Op. cit., III, 297.
194. *Christ and Culture*, 59; cf. *Heid. Cat.*, I, 69; *Tusschen "Ja" en "Neen"*, 135–36.
195. *Christ and Culture*, 74–76, 59–60. About being a fellow worker of God, cf. *Ref.* 18, 90ff.
196. *Heid. Cat.* I, 392. Cf. I, 388.
197. *Heid. Cat.* I, 192.
198. Op. cit., II, 363.
199. Op. cit., II, 367. Cf. I, 489; III, 350.
200. Op. cit., IV, 97.

perspectivistic act of qualifying—also of the potentially continuing cosmic arrangements as they were presumably in evidence in the competent spirit of Adam in the state of righteousness, the spirit of him who as public person was appointed to be consciously responsible for all generations—shrivel into a complete *nothing*. One should certainly not be quick to do so and then, in the effort of a *theological* appreciation of those preserved arrangements, conform oneself to the *supposedly* fallen Adam with the fictitious *Aha-Erlebnis* in his hypothetical, blank, still neutral *tabula rasa* spirit."[201] For in Paradise "obedient reason" strides "forward to a double syllogism: the one about heaven and the other about hell. Both were framed at the same time. That was the hour in which humans began to analyze the contents of God's 'word' in two directions: in the direction of the *created* connection between covenant faithfulness and covenant blessing, and subsequently to the connection between covenant breach and covenant wrath. And so they remained always inextricably connected to each other. They are as inseparable as 'promise' and 'demand,' for they made their debut together from the beginning in the charter of the covenant. They were announced in one revelatory dialogue in which God, referring to himself as 'I,' speaks to human beings, addressing them as 'you.' Those syllogisms about eternal life and eternal death are chained together with the same divine judiciousness as is evident in the way that the one law contains a *dual sanction*: a sanction that rewards obedience, but also a sanction that punishes disobedience."[202]

We have already seen that Schilder did not challenge Kuyper's explanation of Gen 2:17b ("In the day that you eat of it you shall surely die") in a separate detailed discussion. But what was quoted above from what he wrote about the covenant already shows how differently (and more completely) Adam must have understood this threat in Gen 2:17. And also how less surprised Adam was about the continuation of history after the Fall. God's charter of the covenant "told him *immediately* that continuation of time and history *could* be

---

201. Op. cit., IV, 98. In *Ref.* 17, 421 (1937), Schilder adds that the continuation of life and history was a surprise for Adam.
202. *Heid. Cat.* I, 193.

substrate, and eventually *had to* be substrate, of a propagation, an *extension* of the curse on Adam and his descendants."[203]

This receives a sharper emphasis when Schilder points to the distinction between existing and living: "Living" is: "existing in *peace* and in *harmony* with God as Father. But there is also an 'existing' in discord and in disharmony with God as Judge who refuses to be called our covenant Father. Such 'existing' is death."[204] Again, office is determinative: "Existence for human beings, just as for angels, is *substrate for 'life' and for 'death.'* For existence for creatures (angels and humans), who have been appointed to serve in office and are thus also equipped to that end, is closely connected with their *official* function. The manner of existence and the (natural) history of existence *to that end*, have been prescribed by the Creator according to his great wisdom."[205]

Focusing on Gen 2:17, we can render Schilder's position as follows: The surprise is not that history is being continued and that Adam does not disappear from the scene (Kuyper). Rather, the surprise is that he may return in the covenant of grace to a life in peace and harmony with God.

§ 10. Yet further back

The death with which human beings were threatened before the Fall was already included in *God's decree*. And thereby God had already executed the "separation" before sin began to operate against his will.[206] It is the separation between life and death, heaven and hell, elect and reprobate. For Schilder, the doctrine of God as Elector and as Reprobator governs the question of common grace.[207] We have already learned something of this, but in this section dealing with Schilder's own solution it calls for a fuller elaboration.

God is not only preparing "a heaven, but also a hell with an

---

203. Op. cit., IV, 96.
204. Op. cit., I, 391.
205. Op. cit., III, 446. Cf. III, 360–61; IV, 74ff.
206. Op. cit., III, 427.
207. Op. cit., I, 309.

'infinite' number of variations."[208] God is concerned about "a last day with two outcomes: self-glorification in a full adoption of children, and self-glorification in a complete subjection of rebels."[209] He preserves a "remnant" for himself, but he also prepares a "carnage" [as sacrificial feast] for himself.[210] In the progress of history, God maintains himself; he remains *true to himself* to carry out his Counsel concerning heaven and hell.[211]

Theology has posited that *all that is in God is God*[212] and we are not permitted to place greater emphasis on the one self-glorification of God than on the other. We ought to acknowledge "the *glory* of God regarding his own *justice* ... to be *exactly as great* as the glory of the same God regarding his own *mercy*."[213] No one has the right to attribute a 'pre' [before] to *mercy*. *If* there is a 'pre,' why then does *wrath* not take advantage of it?"[214] Schilder wants to be governed "by the revelatory datum, and later by faith's insight, that there is *equilibrium* in all God does." Although "it seems commonsensical," he 'did not want to close his eyes to the revealed future fact of the co-existence of blessing and curse, *in heaven and hell*, in the *'evenly balanced' cosmos* after Christ's last 'parousia.' Who on earth, especially as believer, would dare to do anything other than extol God's *evenly balanced actions*, first in time and thereafter ... also 'in eternity'?"[215]

But Schilder's opinion that not only God's love but also his wrath is from eternity is very closely connected with this equilibrium in God's actions. For God's wrath is not an "affect"[feeling or emotion]: God "is not moved, not 'affected,' as if he were one thing today and something else tomorrow, and as if something *that happens apart from him* could cause change in him. When Scripture speaks of God's wrath, it does not thereby indicate an 'affect,' according to Gomarus, but rather an 'effect.' For people, that effect of God's

---

208. Op. cit., I, 433.
209. Op. cit., III, 8.
210. Op. cit., II, 389.
211. Op. cit., I, 122, 381ff.; II, 259–60, 266–67.
212. Op. cit., III, 348.
213. Op. cit., III, 343.
214. Op. cit., III, 429.
215. Op. cit., IV, 172–73. See also IV, 143–44. About the equilibrium in God's attention see also IV, 143–44. Cf. further Schilder's interpretation of the designation "Zealot" for God as *vox media* [neutral expression]: God's taking delight in bringing ruin on someone (Deut 28:63; Isa 1:24), and "I have no pleasure in the death of the wicked" (Ezek 33:11), op. cit., I, 486. Cf. IV, 143–44, 195.

wrath is the punishment, and the punishment that God imposes on sin is also figuratively called wrath."[216] God's wrath is not fate "that he can do nothing about, a force that sweeps him along also, or, whether in first or second instance, restricts him in such a way that his absolute sovereignty, his good pleasure, his peace and delight, would be onerously affected by it."[217] No, God's wrath is from eternity, Schilder asserts. It "is *revealed* (Rom 1:18); revealed in its *effects*, and is thus distinguishable from them. It does not connote only a conflagration, but also a 'fire' burning in God himself'.... That wrath does not 'arise' only after sin, but is *eternal*. It is an eternal aversion to evil. This is also relevant to our confession. For if God's wrath would be 'aroused' by evil in its actuality once it comes into existence, then we would have to fall back on the doctrine of the wrath of God as *affect*. No, the wrath is from eternity. Hence, God's Counsel concerning sin and predestination, including reprobation, is in him not an exalted game with possibilities, like a purely cerebral game of an abstractive intellect. Rather, it is a fully engaged consulting of God with God, in self-love, self-preservation, and the will to self-glorification of the 'entire' God, who is simple in all his thought and will, in his turning toward and turning away. In wrath he calls into existence the non-existent vessels of wrath (cf. Rom 4:17)."[218] Hence Schilder can write that God's wrath is *unrestricted*, and *sovereign*, and "*iure suo* [in its own right] also in *creating its own objects*, in a will to reject."[219]

What Schilder writes about God's wrath, returns when he discusses God's hatred: "Although God's wrath often denotes an effect, an action of God, this can for that reason not be said, at least not always, of God's 'hate.' It is true that the word 'hatred' is often used in the Bible as an indication of what is in fact its effect, its operation.... But 'hating' can also signify a disposition. Christ says to the church at Ephesus in Rev 2:6 that he hates the works of the Nicolaitans. No one yet knows then whether he will later burst out in wrath. But the 'hatred' is already there, and he already lets it become known that it is real."[220] Although wrath and hatred

216. Op. cit., I, 483.
217. Loc. cit.
218. Op. cit., I, 483–84.
219. Op. cit., III, 435.
220. Op. cit., I, 487.

are not identical, they are both from eternity: "For God's hatred is actually a form of love—namely of the eternal love that God bears toward himself and that in his eternity sees all things temporally, while at the same time, over against this, it acknowledges, loves, and therefore maintains itself and his Counsel completely. This eternal self-love of God is also hatred from eternity. That is, it rejects from eternity to eternity everything that does not turn itself to him as the first and last goal. That hatred is the obverse of the 'self-love,' as we, involuntarily using a deficient metaphor, express this. Accordingly, that hatred 'does not need' an object outside of God, as if (only) by it, that is, by its historical existence and clarity, it is called into being, but it already exists for that purpose. He always precedes the object; he 'calls' it.... Just as that hatred is the obverse of God's eternal love toward God, so he can glorify himself, both in justice that rewards and in 'another' justice that punishes, or more clearly, in one and the same justice that both rewards and punishes. The love that God has for himself creates its objects; it creates objects of election and objects of reprobation. Actually, the hatred is not aroused by the creature, but the love of God toward God awakens the creature, also those who will later, as effect, become hated."[221]

When God, already before the Fall, proclaimed the vengeance of the covenant, "he did not just impact humans as Pedagogue and did not just address them with an expression coined for the occasion, but also then he spoke 'with all his heart,' and with all his 'soul,' and with all his strength. That word of threat also came out of the treasure of his heart. The 'Comfort for the Sick' [formerly included in the Dutch psalter, although it never received an ecclesiastical imprimatur] does not shrink back from quoting from the apocryphal book of Jesus Sirach: 'the covenant of eternity is this: you shall die'" (art. 2).[222] The threat comes not only with pedagogic intent, but it exists "also by virtue of the internal evidence of God's being, and of his taking counsel with himself from eternity, even concerning the 'vessels of wrath.' The doctrine of God's hatred includes not only that he is Judge in his thoughts from eternity, or that he knows himself to be Judge, but also that he infinitely loves

221. Op. cit., I, 488.
222. Op. cit., I, 489.

and desires himself as Judge, and also for that reason calls the world into existence (Rom 4:17)."[223]

Now it no longer surprises at all that Schilder does not want to characterize the continuation of history after the Fall as only grace. He reasons as follows: When love and hate, grace and wrath, and election and reprobation receive equal emphasis, we must use two words. Or more precisely, we must describe the continuation as substrate for the administration of blessing and curse. History has a double meaning. Also the reprobate "are propelled along from Genesis 1 to Revelation 22. But in their case, Revelation 22 must be regarded as the chapter not of the opened heaven, but of the opened hell. Is reality meaningful here too, or as many put it, is it relevant? We answer yes to that question."[224] Predestination, "in its dual content" governs history.[225] "The conservation of the world and the continuation of history, together with the possibility of culture and the ensuing culture as reality ... are all indispensable, both for building the road that leads to heaven and for traveling down the roads that lead to hell."[226]

Schilder believes that this parallelism agrees with Scripture: "Peter says in 1 Pet 1:4b-5a that God's utmost care and governing power become apparent in the fact that he preserved the inheritance and 'guards' the heirs. But a similar divine care also lies in the action that runs parallel: guarding the unrighteous day in, day out, 'until the day of judgment,'" as it says in 2 Pet 2:9.[227] So also the fact that the heavens and the earth that now exist are stored up for fire, of which 2 Pet 3:7 speaks, is programmed from the beginning: "Although the great fire will come only on the day of judgment, it clearly lay ready in the clouds and under the earth's crust, also when Paradise existed."[228] And just as the water of the Flood signified curse as well as blessing (1 Pet 3:20, 21), so also the fire will have the same double function: "It will destroy, but also

---

223. Loc. cit.
224. Op. cit., III, 252.
225. Op. cit., I, 372–73.
226. Op. cit., I, 373.
227. Op. cit., IV, 94. Schilder regularly cites 2 Pet 2:3, 4, 9, 17; 3:7; and Jude 6, 7, 13. Cf. I, 454; III, 219–20; IV, 84–85, 91, 173.
228. Op. cit., IV, 85.

save; it will take life and give it; it is instrument of a wrathful *and* of a favorable disposition."[229]

The same ambiguity is inherent in Schilder's concept of God's patience: "On the one hand, patience is: granting time for repentance. On the other hand it is: waiting until the measure is full in order to administer the punishment that has not been forgotten for an instant and that has not for an instant truly been postponed to a time when the verdict will become evident even to 'the blind.'"[230] For the Septuagint uses the word μακρόθυμος (and related forms) "for the Hebrew expression *he'erik 'ap*, that is, someone who 'lengthens his wrath' and so restrains its outburst."[231] Schilder continues: Alternatively, μακρόθυμος can be a rendering of the Hebrew *'erek 'appayim*, that is, "having lengthy nostrils." "For one who is full of wrath, livid, snorts with his nostrils, his breath is arrested, and that 'breath' betrays his 'spirit.' But that breath is not the hand: the breath can show displeasure, while the hand, although perhaps clenched, does not yet strike. Those who see only that breath say: it is burning wrath. Those who look only at the hand say: it is most certainly no wrath as yet; the wrath (outburst) is not yet revealed from heaven. But only a fool concludes from the fact that if there is no striking hand, then we have grace."[232] One cannot draw a conclusion about God's disposition from the facts.[233] God's disposition is "in a narrow sense expressed only in 'the books' that are above."[234]

Nevertheless, Schilder certainly understood that his interpretation of God's patience as *vox media* [neutral word] cannot be regarded as conclusive in the discussion. The evidence of the texts that point to the second meaning (with as background: waiting until the measure is full, restraining wrath) is much too weak. The use of μακρόθυμος as translation of *he'erik 'ap* appears in only one place, namely in the Apocrypha (2 Macc 6:14). This text reads: "In the case of the other nations, the Lord waits patiently to punish

---

229. Op. cit., I, 454. Cf. IV, 142: "conserved" means also "preserved."
230. Op. cit., IV, 114.
231. Op. cit., IV, 111, with reference to 2 Macc 6:14, which Schilder compares to Gen 15:15–16, op. cit., IV, 112.
232. Op. cit., IV, 116–17.
233. Op. cit., IV, 118.
234. Op. cit., IV, 117.

them until they have reached the full measure of their sins" (NRSV). It is understandable that in this connection Schilder refers to Gen 15:15–16 (according to which the iniquity of the Amorites must become complete before the judgment over them is executed).[235] We can also point to what Schilder writes about Rom 9:22. He prefers Greijdanus' translation, which reads that God with great patience bore (instead of endured) the vessels of wrath that were prepared for destruction. Why, Schilder asks, "does God bear those 'vessels of wrath'? Because it is his will to cause his wrath to become apparent and to make his power, that almighty power, his omnipotence, known, as Paul says."[236] For *'erek 'appayim* as *vox media*, Schilder refers only to Exod 15:8: "at the blast of your nostrils the waters piled up."[237]

No wonder that Schilder's real argument against the application of the concept of patience by defenders of common grace lies elsewhere. Here, too, Schilder wants to take into account that, in its speaking about God's patience, Scripture does not use a conceptual, scientific expression, but employs language of apperception and of an anthropopathic way of speaking. Then it appears as if God's patience leads to postponement, to retardation, of the curse. However, "that entire concept of retardation is nothing more than an ideogram that fits in with our naïve constructs and that is only, to the extent that it is Scriptural, pedagogic in intent."[238] For the concept of retardation, "insofar as it seeks apperceptive expression," is in fact rejected in 2 Pet 3:9 ("the Lord is not slow ... as some count slowness"!) over against the scoffers of 2 Pet 3, who asked: "Where is the day of his coming?"[239] When 2 Pet 3:9 speaks about both God's patience and of his not being slow, Schilder writes: "The expression 'patience' looks at God's actions from our perspective, and the apperceptive language chooses that expression. But the expression 'the Lord is not slow' harks back to the scientific discussions with false teachers. In that context (to speak conceptually now) it rejects the concept of retardation as such."[240]

235. Op. cit., IV, 112.
236. Op. cit., IV, 154.
237. Op. cit., IV, 116ff.
238. Op. cit., IV, 104.
239. Op. cit., IV, 105–06.
240. Op. cit., IV, 106.

And that has brought us back to Schilder's criticism of the theory of common grace. He rejects it as being childlike, anthropomorphic and, consequently, not theological.

In this section it should further be pointed out that Schilder does not accept a concept of God's providence that is not qualified. He says that one may not reproach him for that.[241] With Paraeus, he rejects the notion of any general or common grace that is unqualified. That is why he for the continuation of life rejects "especially the subjectivistic qualification that it is *only* grace": "The qualification is just as thousandfold as God's momentaneous ... act of governance is."[242] And that is true not only of the execution of his predestination, "as execution of the so-called double predestination, but also of the x^n deputations or predestinations of the x^n creatures."[243] Negation of an indifferent action of God *"compels one to admit that, with respect to each individual, God's disposition, also in granting what we in our apperceptive language refer to as manifold gifts, is determined by the individual's predestination."*[244] God regards every individual person very specifically before him "in a total disposition of love or of hate, for he is never neutral."[245] It also, in Schilder's view, conflicts with the doctrine of God's simplicity to suppose that there is a general and a particular disposition of God in regard to the same persons and individuals characterized as office-bearers.[246]

In this way history acquires an entirely different look. God is present in it, electing and reprobating, with love and hate, so that God's preservation, his continuing the world and history, is as "horrible" as his act of predestination.[247] The optimism inherent in Kuyper's concept of common grace is thereby invalidated.[248] "It will not do to call the decree horrible while essentially robbing the execution of the decree of this characterization by theorems with an optimistic signature and a common grace coloration."[249] God's

241. Op. cit., IV, 69–70. The reproach was expressed by G. C. Berkouwer, *De Voorzienigheid Gods*, 83.
242. *Heid. Cat.*, IV, 69–70.
243. Op. cit., IV, 205.
244. Op. cit., IV, 116.
245. *Ref.* 25, 86.
246. *Ref.* 22, 2.
247. *Heid. Cat.* IV, 91.
248. Op. cit., IV, 172, with a reference to Ursinus.
249. Op. cit., IV, 195.

action is never less horrible than his Counsel. And it "is, to put it bluntly, culpable poverty to isolate Calvin's well-known declaration that God's decree is "horrible" as a given by itself, in order to defend it as typically Calvinist and to present it as something that calls for veneration, while failing to consider God's action, his actual deed."[250] What one can say about predestination-as-decree must also apply to predestination-as-fact to which God is stimulated by all his virtues. "It is also true of God's actions that they are a deep abyss. We must not look into that abyss to say: 'All I smell here everywhere is grace (albeit common grace).' Nor to groan in the manner of G. H. Kersten's followers: 'I smell nothing but sulphur here.'"[251]

In one respect Schilder does speak of a general love of God. But it concerns creatureliness. Although God's wrath rests "for all time"[252] on the reprobate, "he loves in them their creatureliness, their personhood. But he does not love all persons. A divine φιλανθρωπία [love for humanity] can have the ἀνθρώπινον [what is human], the φύσις ἀνθρωπίνη [human species] as object, without recognizing the concrete ἄνθρωποι [people] as object of divine love." For "he always loves his own handiwork, also in Satan and in the Antichrist."[253]

This distinction in God's disposition toward his creatures and the creatureliness in them is something that Schilder constantly reiterates.[254]

§ 11. Christ and culture

In the previous chapter it was established that Kuyper developed his doctrine of common grace in part to summon Christians to become culturally active in this world. Schilder, too, understood this and therefore esteemed Kuyper's arguments "as exhortation to drive God's people out into the life of the world in all its breadth."[255]

---

250. Loc. cit.
251. Op. cit., IV, 93.
252. Op. cit., IV, 119.
253. Loc. cit.
254. Op. cit., I, 429, 492, 509; III, 227; IV, 49, 217. *Ref.* 19, 208; 20, 20–21.
255. *Ref.* 17, 421.

His rejection of common grace did not therefore mean that he distanced himself from the cultural question: "What I want in respect of common grace is not anti-Kuyperian. Rather, it is an attempt to get rid of some inconsistencies in what Kuyper truly wanted and what he also preached in so many words ... and, by lopping off the few flawed branches, to save the old tree of the real Kuyper."[256]

How then did Schilder speak about culture without basing it on the doctrine of common grace?

1. *The common mandate.* As we saw already, human beings were placed in Paradise as office-bearers. And to be able to serve as office-bearers, they were made by God, says Schilder, "not merely to be one part in the huge world-as-engine, but also as engine-driver appointed by God and responsible to him."[257] The idea of office thus has "direct and constitutive significance" also for the concept of culture.[258] The labor of human beings is included "in such a wide cosmic context that in the original world of paradisal purity this labor could immediately and always be called 'liturgy,' i.e., ministry in and for the kingdom. Which kingdom? The kingdom of which God is King, i.e., the kingdom of heaven, the subjects of which have been divided over two levels of the cosmos: an 'upper' level and a 'lower' level."[259] This liturgy is cultural service. "For the Creator himself is culturally interested. 'Culture,' after all, is a word derived from the Latin verb *colere*, which means 'to cultivate,' 'to care for.'"[260] We come across "'culture' ... on the first pages of the Bible: till the garden, fill the earth, be fruitful and multiply [Gen 2:15; 1:28]. The very first pages of the Bible are the pages of the ABC. They comprehend these three brief commandments within the description of the phase of what is there called the 'covenant of works' and thus they already fit into the uncorrupted world *which has not yet been completed*; that is, which is still in the process of being developed (by virtue of the plan for creation) in order to reach the end, the *teleōsis*, the entering into the state of being full-

---

256. *Ref.* 16, 259.
257. *Christ and Culture*, 59.
258. Op. cit., 58, 169–71.
259. Op. cit., 60.
260. Op. cit., 72.

grown. Therefore these first pages of the Bible, replete as they are with federal [covenantal] regulations, are also directly of cultural interest."[261] The world of Paradise was a beginning, in which (in principle) was given "everything that had to be there potentially in order to let it develop into a completed world of perfect order."[262] To that end a historical process of many centuries was required. In Paradise God declared "that he would work evolution on the foundation of creation."[263]

To that end, human beings serve as God's co-workers, so Schilder continues: "'We are God's fellow workers' [1 Cor 3:9]: this is not a soothing word of posthumous reassurance proclaimed by Paul to a seceded church somewhere in a secluded corner. No, this is a command that leads us back to the 'first principles of the world.' It is not only a suitable text for a minister's inaugural sermon, but also the day-text for any cultural worker, for a professor as well as for a street sweeper, for one who is busy in the kitchen as well as for a composer who has to write a Moonlight Sonata."[264]

We should not magically transform Paradise "into a secluded, solidly fenced-in spot where zephyrs blow and which only a popularly misunderstood romanticism seems best able to write about."[265] It is entirely different: "The garden is the beginning of *adama*, of the inhabited world. Hence it is also the beginning of the cultural world. The garden lies open."[266] People must "take out of the world all that it has in it."[267]

Schilder then gives the following definition of culture: "culture becomes the systematized striving for the sum-total of labor that in a gradual process is to be attained by the sum-total of humanity present at any historical moment—humanity as it belongs to God and as it evolves itself unto God in history with and for the cosmos. In this endeavor human beings set themselves the task of disclosing the potentialities latent in creation according to how these will successively become attainable to them within the framework of

---

261. Op. cit., 71–72.
262. Op. cit., 75.
263. Loc. cit.
264. Op. cit., 76.
265. Op. cit., 76–77.
266. Op. cit., 77.
267. Op. cit., 68.

the progression of world history, of developing these potentialities in compliance with their individual natures, and of making them subservient to their environs, from the nearest to the most distant, in accordance with their cosmic relationships and in submission to the norms of God's revealed truth. The aim of all this is to make the outcomes thus achieved fit for use by human beings as liturgical creatures, and, subsequently, to bring these, together with the thus increasingly well-equipped human beings themselves, before God and put them at his feet, in order that he may be all in all, and all work may praise its Master."[268] Schilder believes that in this extensive definition he has provided "the foundational culture-related elements of the biblical creation story." He then paraphrases it as follows: "*Till the garden*: this is the concrete cultural mandate to take out of the world what is in it. *Be fruitful and multiply*: an increasing sum total of humanity is to be subjected time and again to the cultural mandate, *the duty to engage in culture*, in every temporal phase and every area of geographic space. *Subdue the earth* and *have dominion*: when those who are products of God's creation work are engaged in culture, they are faced with their own order of rank, that of being God's vicegerents. *Humanity created in God's image*: cultural work must therefore be spontaneous (the attributes of human beings have been created in them with a view to their *munus*); it is a matter of serving God as representatives of his supreme authority and consequently a matter of discovering God and causing him to be found in the discovering of the future. God speaks *to and with human beings* because of their appointment as the chosen representatives of God's dominion over all other creatures, and within the communion of the covenant that God has made with them, God speaks *to* them and *with* them *about* the rest of the cosmos in spite of the fact that they themselves are a part of it—which means that self-distinction is thus awakened in them, and that they are made aware of self-cultivation as a duty, not as an end in itself but as a matter of mandate. And finally, they are given a *moral* commandment: together with all that belongs to them, in their cultural labor they are subject to their Creator. In determining their own goals with regard to created things they

---

268. Op. cit., 77.

are bound to what they have heard from God's mouth by Word-revelation concerning God's own purpose with respect to the cosmos. They are summoned to bow down, now and later, before their Maker in and together with a cosmos prepared by their own hand under God's providence, culturally engaged as they are in view of their own *sabbath*, but especially because of God's sabbath, into which they as human beings have to enter [see Heb 4]."[269]

Schilder continues as follows: Cultural labor is therefore religion. "More than incense," petroleum has been "an express theme in the Bible."[270] We may not separate culture from religion, for "religion is not a 'province' of life, not a separate function of or for the 'heart,' not an isolated activity of a devout conventicle of people during elevated fragmentary stages of human life."[271] Cultural labor is religion, as service to God. In Paradise "everything is included within cultivation: the ground that one treads upon as well as the heart in all its depth, vegetation as well as the meditative spirit. There undefiled hands as well as souls are washed in righteousness; the one thing cannot be separated from the other."[272]

History continues despite the Fall. God maintains himself and carries out his counsel.[273] What was discussed in § 10 also finds its place in Schilder's cultural arguments, but then especially in Christological form. I will discuss this later, but already now it should be pointed out that heaven and hell are included in the program of divine action. To reach both, extension of time is necessary, marriages must take place, an economic equilibrium is essential. And thus, "culture is the precondition for all the works of God, even with respect to hell."[274] God "does not permit the thermometers of culture to be broken to pieces by premature heat, also for this reason: that he is waiting for the last one of the elect, as well as for the latter's opposite, the last reprobate."[275] The cultural commandment remains in force for all. For that "*mandate* is general because God has not abolished any command that is original and

---

269. Op. cit., 78–79.
270. *Ref.* 16, 219; *Christ and Culture*, 135; *Ref.* 23, 136 (about the "song of labor").
271. *Christ and Culture*, 79.
272. Op. cit., 80.
273. Op. cit., 95.
274. Op. cit., 91.
275. Op. cit., 133.

permanent in character."²⁷⁶ The Heidelberg Catechism says it so correctly and radically in Answer 9: "that God does not do human beings an injustice when he requires of them what had already been imposed on them in Paradise, *even though they are no longer able to meet this requirement*."²⁷⁷ The commandment, the mandate, continues even though those who received it go on strike.²⁷⁸

Aside from his insurmountable objections to the term "common grace," which have already been mentioned, Schilder wants to abandon this concept because it leads to cultural accidents. For "'grace,' being undeserved, forfeited 'favor,' is then a word related to the idea of what is *permissible*, what is *allowed*. As a result many Christians have come to look upon the cultural problem as a question of what is and what is not permissible. Hence the numerous mishaps. In my opinion—and my whole argument confirms it—our cultural mandate must be seen primarily as a matter of a 'common command,' a 'common calling,' a 'common mandate.' Here our *may* does not stand detached from our *must*. The standpoint I [i.e., Schilder] have taken above shows the cultural question to be, already before the Fall, a question of assigned duty, of creation mandate, or creaturely service to God."²⁷⁹ God maintains his demands after the Fall. The Heidelberg Catechism (Lord's Day 4, Q. 9) strongly condemns "those who let their theory of 'common grace' speak only and exclusively about what by God's charter has still been left to us as being *permissible*."²⁸⁰ However, the doctrine of common grace falls into error because in formulating the problem it takes as point of departure that which after the Fall was still left to us. Schilder points out three errors:

(a) "Without neglecting what happened after the Fall," the doctrine of common grace "has to go back to what happened before the Fall in order to understand God's intention."

(b) "It keeps talking about what has yet been left to us human

---

276. Op. cit., 110 (emphasis added).
277. Op. cit., 145. Cf. *Ref.* 13, 139; *Heid. Cat.* I, 381ff.
278. *Ref.* 18, 11.
279. *Christ and Culture*, 144–45. Cf. *Ref.* 13, 139. Schilder speaks of a *common* mandate and then undoubtedly regards "common" as the equivalent of "general." The parallel with "common grace" caused him to use the adjective "common," although, strictly speaking, he did not regard it to be synonymous with "general." For this, see pp. 138–39 above. Sometimes Schilder does speak also of a general mandate; see, e.g., *Ref.* 18, 26.
280. *Christ and Culture*, 146.

beings, as if it is all about us (people) instead of about God. This doctrine is more anthropocentric than theological." And, connected with (b):

(c) "In a culpable way it starts to broadcast culturally optimistic sounds. For 'nature' (as the material that is to be fashioned or developed) has never been given to us, but it has been put at our disposal .... Culture, then, is a question of *must*."[281]

2. *Renewal in Christ.* Schilder: The creation mandate was maintained after the Fall. But can it also still be fulfilled? This question was answered by Jesus Christ at the midpoint of history. As the second Adam, as office-bearer, he harked back to the beginning and to the ordinances then given. "By performing his office (an office fundamentally identical to that of humanity) before God's countenance, he takes upon himself the great reformational task of returning to the ABC of the order for life and for the world."[282] For also with regard to Christ, Schilder places all emphasis on his office. For, "to put it strongly, if nothing more is added to it, 'Jesus' is of no use to us in dealing with our problem."[283] The gospels do not provide us with a "biography of Christ" from which one can derive what he signified and still signifies for, among other things, culture.[284] "If one conceives of the man Jesus—he who without any sin always lived before the face of God—as the chief prophet and teacher also as far as artists are concerned, then his stance in this respect will be all the more disappointing, at least for anyone who would like to hear from the mouth of "Jesus" a more or less developed cultural ethics or aesthetics."[285] But "it is impossible to characterize the work of 'Jesus' correctly as long as it has not become clear from the Scriptures as a whole what Jesus came to accomplish as the Christ and thus what he, as God's office-bearer par excellence, has to accomplish in and for and also with the cosmos."[286]

However, in this office he is completely unique with his

281. Op. cit., 145–46.
282. Op. cit., 60.
283. Op. cit., 26. Cf. 26–48.
284. Op. cit., 29.
285. Op. cit., 45.
286. Op. cit., 30–31.

"exhaustive, definitive, and pleromatic anointing."[287] Hence, "one cannot copy him without misunderstanding him. There are thousands of soldiers, but there is only one supreme commander. Whoever wants to see the latter's uniqueness imitated paralyzes the whole army. The supreme commander is closely connected with all the soldiers, and prescribes for each one the regulation uniform that is be worn, but he himself is beyond such regulation."[288] It is apparent how he cannot serve as cultural model, among other reasons, because he was unmarried. "For he is not ashamed to call himself the brother of us all. That is his office. But he would indeed have been ashamed to be called the (physical) father of some of us. *For that is not his office.* His unmarried state is not a pattern for us; nor is it a humiliatingly 'high' ideal for one who lacks the charisma of abstinence. His *office* is so very different."[289] The office-bearer Christ, as we saw, took upon himself the great reformational task of a return to the ABC of the order that governs life and the world. "To make it again possible for human beings to fulfill this original service of God and, by rights as well as in fact, to give back to God his world and his work-community, Christ comes to do two things."[290] First, he comes to reconcile God's wrath. That is a judicial struggle. "With the ransom of his blood he purchases the right to the renewal of those who are now called God's 'new' humanity. It is now called his redeemed Christian congregation, which through him and together with him is heir to eternal life."[291] He sets the foundations of the world firm again. But second, since eternal life already begins here, he comes with his power struggle, a dynamic struggle that again brings "to God's newly purchased work-community—the new humanity, which in its basic features is nevertheless 'the old humanity'—rich powers of the outpouring of the Spirit, powers of sanctification, of church conquest, of world maturation, of cultural action."[292] This power struggle has a dual aspect. Here we encounter in Christological attire what was presented in § 10: Christ administers eternal death *and* he

287. Op. cit., 52.
288. Op. cit., 53.
289. Op. cit., 54.
290. Op. cit., 62.
291. Op. cit., 63.
292. Op. cit., 64.

administers eternal life. "Consequently through his Holy Spirit (who actively propels the 'middle of history' toward the 'end') he is coming to do two things. On the one hand, he will in the culture world cause the grapes of the earth to ripen fully in order to be trodden in the winepress of the administration of God's wrath. On the other hand, he is coming, through the same Holy Spirit, 'in' whom he himself 'completes' the 'thousand years' of his dominion of peace, to *equip* the 'work community' and 'office community' of God, which he himself has purchased, for the work and service of God, in order that all its living members may enter into the city of perfected glory."[293] That is what is already very well known to us as "and–and." The continuation of the world is necessary because of the blessing *and* the curse. Christologically interpreted, that must then imply: "for the sake of his double significance as Savior-Redeemer and Savior-Judge."[294]

That is how, according to Schilder, history receives its Christological meaning. Christ appeared "in order to put in place the work and ministry of grace in this world, and to mark off the ground (not of election and reprobation, for which only God's good pleasure is the ground, but) of salvation and of condemnation as the ground further determined through *his* work. The ground of salvation would be: Christ's merit. And the ground of condemnation would be: human guilt, which after the Fall showed itself to be determined by the presence of Christ's work. The guilt resulted from rejecting Christ. Thus Christ took action as the Savior-Redeemer and as the Savior-Avenger. The constitutive element in both functions is his evangelical work of redemption, which is never satisfied with being a negligible quantity. Because in this spirit and with this double intention, Christ, before the countenance of God, thus took upon himself the burden of the world, he became the Redeemer of the world, culture included. At the same time he gave (from that point on, Christologically determined) meaning to all cultural activity. This Christologically determined sense—*that* is what is universal or general. The grace in this is not universal, but it is indeed common."[295]

293. Loc. cit.
294. Op. cit., 95.
295. Op. cit., 94–95.

What change is brought about in the world by the dual performance of office of Christ? By it, "this corrupt world experiences once again the miracle of the appearance of the flawless, unblemished, original, or, if you will, 'ideal' human being."[296] That flawlessness was visible during Christ's humiliation only in concealed form; later, in his glorification comes "its reward, a reward which glorifies Christ also externally."[297] But not only he himself is flawless. "He creates (also by the almighty power of the Spirit given to him) human beings who in principle are flawless again, as a fruit of creative regeneration."[298] In principle, for it counts only for Christ who, as "the sinless one, is the only one who has acted and is acting upon culture in a completely faultless manner—at any rate, the only one among humanity after the Fall. Who can comprehend the fullness of the thoughts, also the culture-related thoughts, that are included in the dogma of the church when it sees and preaches Christ as man without sin? As the sinless one he responds, in words and deeds, always entirely to the point in every situation into which the Spirit thrusts him, in order that he should show himself to be the second Adam, and to do so in a world far removed in cultural respects from that of the first Adam. What is a more direct cultural act than to react to cultural situations and complications fully and purely and fundamentally and according to the original rule?"[299] But by virtue of his redeeming power he "makes people again what they were 'in the beginning': God's people."[300] They are office-bearers in accordance with Lord's Day 12 of the Heidelberg Catechism, which in Answer 32 describes the Christian as prophet, priest, and king so broadly and comprehensively that the question of Christ and culture immediately comes up for discussion.[301] "In the midst of a 'crooked and twisted generation,'" Christ again "sets up types of the humanity that is in principle *unblemished*. They are not yet perfect, but in principle they *are* there again."[302]

---

296. Op. cit., 65.
297. Loc. cit.
298. Op. cit., 66.
299. Loc. cit.
300. Op. cit., 67.
301. Op. cit., 2, 171; *Ref.* 13, 138.
302. Op. cit., 67.

CHAPTER II. KLAAS SCHILDER

In the administration of Christ's own office and in the formation of those who were anointed with him ("Christians"), a divine action now takes place "to conquer the world for God, by the Christ of God. 'The earth is the Lord's and the fullness thereof' [Ps 24:1]. This conquest is a re-conquest: the property is, to the extent that it has been destined thereto from eternity, brought back to its Owner in its proper relation to him."[303] Now the alpha is joined to the omega; the talents handed out by God to his laborers in the early morning of creation were by evening to have earned a profit equal to the number distributed at daybreak.[304] The order of the day in Paradise so gripped and governed Christ "that, just to give an example, he told the parable of the talents [Matt 25:14–30], where this ABC is taught again—for 'to reform' means 'to teach the people the ABC again'—as the last parable (according to the synoptic Gospels) before he, in accordance with his office, took the path of his suffering and resurrection. It was the last parable he told them before his 'millennium' broke through. It had so gripped him that in his last great prayer for the church, offered up in the days of his humiliation, he told the Father: 'I do not ask that you take them out of the world, but that you keep them from the evil one' [John 17:15], that you may keep them *there*, not in their cloister, which becomes a refuge of self-willed obstinacy, a refectory [place of healing and refreshing] for the tired and weary, at least if it has no window and no door open to the world."[305]

In response to this prayer, Christ's servants enter the world. That is how Paul entered Rome. "An unblemished human being, a man of God, entered the flaccid and corrupt city of Rome, a maker of tents and a philosopher, a theologian and a missionary; someone who dared to look the emperor in the eye, even when the latter would no longer dare to do the same to him. A man who caused his fellow prisoners to see a great light and who made a rented house in Rome [Acts 28:30] the forecourt of an academy of philosophy."[306] By the grace of God that was given to him, Paul was "the epitome of soundness, also cultural soundness." The Sermon on the Mount

303. Loc. cit.
304. Op. cit., 68–69.
305. Op. cit., 69–70.
306. Op. cit., 97–98.

and the seven letters in Revelation are also monuments of cultural history. "For in the Sermon on the Mount, Jesus Christ teaches here on earth, and in these seven epistles the same Jesus Christ teaches from heaven, how at the trough, and at the office, and in the temple, and in the factory, and in the academy, and in the artist's studio, people must again realize that their starting-point, purpose, and direction are determined by God, that they must fill their 'yes' and 'no' with the strength of an oath [Matt 5:33–37], and that under the tension of living between primeval and eschatological history they must therefore do their work as *kohanim*, that is, as priests who stand and perform their service before God." That is how Christ "again connects 'religion' with 'culture', thus making cultural activity a concrete service of God, and, when it comes to the point, denies anything that is not from God the name and honor of 'positive culture building'"[307]

"As it was in the days when Paul stumbled into the city of Rome, so it has always been in the world since then. Every reformation that, driven by the Spirit of Christ, returns to Scripture, to the Word of God, is at the same time a healing of culture. Luther with his round head, when he at last married a woman, and could laugh again in a wholesome way, was worth a hundred ducats as a healing and direction-giving producer of culture in contrast with the entire entourage of papal and imperial courts, which was hardly worth a single ducat, even from a cultural perspective."[308] Calvin's position is even stronger than Luther's, and the Calvinist countries subsequently "manifested a cultural structure that thetically and antithetically was far stronger and produced far greater strength than was the case in Lutheran countries. The cultural chaos that Adolf Hitler left behind—because he had first brought it with him—could arise in Lutheran countries also with the support of orthodox Lutherans but met with positive and unbreakable resistance among Calvinist communities."[309] In Geneva and Strasbourg a Christian culture was created "which had been freed from the secularist-imperialist aspirations that still corrupt Rome's imagination, inspired as they are by the same false distinction

307. Op. cit., 99–100.
308. Op. cit., 101.
309. Op. cit., 101–02.

between 'nature' and 'grace' that played tricks on Martin Luther"[310] Calvin "preached and gave depth to office-consciousness and taught us to understand again how in culture the struggle of sin and grace, of obedience and disobedience, is of supreme and all-embracing importance."[311]

Prophecy that is true to the Word is always a great cultural force. Thus Schilder writes, very antithetically, that "a church magazine that weeds out what is wrong and keeps principles pure" means a hundred times more for culture building than "a gilded stage"; that "one good study outline means more than seven, even good, dramas inasmuch as the power of God's Word is greater than that of the image, and doctrine is more than sign. A Christian family that understands what it means to live according to its own distinctive style is for cultural life, in whatever complications it may be placed, another manifestation of the wholesome power for which one looks in vain in Hollywood.... A Christian worker daring to be himself as Christian is again an epitome of wholesomeness.... He is worth more in potential force than a complete academy of science that has not seen God."[312] And also: "Blessed is my wise ward elder who does his home-visiting well. He is a cultural force, although he is probably not aware of it. Let them mock him: they do not know what they are doing, those cultural good-for-nothings on the other side!"[313]

Soon the conclusion will come in the new Jerusalem "that pure and perfect cultural-city-at-rest." But this city does not come into being along gradual lines. Its presentation depends upon the catastrophe of the last day. "But let us not forget that at the very moment when this catastrophe takes place, whether 'in heaven above' or 'in the earth beneath' or 'in the waters under the earth,' all necessary spiritual and material potentialities are already present to put this city in place 'materially' or to restore it.... This catastrophe itself will not create chaos, nor will it destroy or trample upon any seed. On the contrary, it will function in a refining and cleansing

---

310. Op. cit., 102.
311. Op. cit., 171.
312. Op. cit., 104–05.
313. Op. cit., 174.

way in order to purge this cosmos of every culture-destroying element, of everything conducive to cultural disintegration."[314]

Schilder is fully aware that his opinion about what may truly bear the name culture "has been called impertinent."[315] For he limited culture, "strictly speaking," to culture that, "as concrete service of God," has sprung from Jesus Christ as its source,[316] and he considered the designation "positive cultural activity" to be appropriate only "wherever people build and labor according to God's will."[317] Schilder did not regard anyone or any community competent to "engage in a homogeneous and continuous *colere*, in the actual eschatologically determined sense of the word, unless they live and work in faithfulness to God."[318] For *colere* "is always constructive, but sin is destructive.[319] Those who called this point of view impertinent "do not share our creed. They do not know a Word of God that effectually enters into history in a historical way, that is, in continuously producing fruit from its own seed. The 'Word of God' as they view it is not the 'seed of regeneration.' In their opinion, no 'chain of salvation' is forged here, under the clouds of heaven. According to their way of thinking, that which produces fruit, thirty-, sixty-, and a hundredfold here below, can never have been seed from above."[320]

However, the pro and con of this standpoint is not determined in a dispute over arguments. "For at bottom we are faced here with a decision of faith. Either Scripture as it presents itself to us is acknowledged as the Word of God, or it is not acknowledged as such. I know full well that if I were to be deprived of the Scriptures, it would at once be no longer possible to adduce any evidence to show that my standpoint is correct; the same applies to the other standpoint. But I do not wish to present anything but a statement of faith, also this time. Not only matters concerning the church and the forgiveness of sins are matters of faith, but of all things it must be said that they are known only through faith, not by 'experience.'

314. Op. cit., 105–06.
315. Op. cit., 127.
316. Op. cit., 100, 127.
317. Op. cit., 108.
318. Op. cit., 122–23.
319. Op. cit., 101.
320. Op. cit., 127. Schilder is referring here to the followers of Karl Barth.

CHAPTER II. KLAAS SCHILDER

Even questions about what culture consists of and how it manifests itself are answered by faith only."[321]

When referring to those who called his opinion on culture impertinent, Schilder undoubtedly also had O. Noordmans and A. A. van Ruler in mind. In *De Reformatie* 16. 115–16 and 123–24, Noordmans, having been invited for that purpose by Schilder, discussed Schilder's view of culture and rejected it sharply. He believed that such a view precluded the way to reunion of the Reformed and the *Hervormd* [those belonging to the state church]. Indeed, he regarded Schilder's view as a counterpart of what the *Deutsche Christen* believed. [The so-called *Deutsche Christen* were (the majority of the) Lutheran Christians in Germany, who saw the hand of God in Adolf Hitler's National Socialist revolution and thus offered no resistance to it.] For politics and culture then gain the upper hand over the preaching and faith life; Christians are called the true human race; culture is being absolutized, and the absoluteness of the categories that have their place on the terrain of particular grace are being introduced into the terrain of common grace. According to Noordmans, Schilder's work reveals a worldly radicalism that, if it were adopted, would pervert the character of the church, even more so than the biological gospel of the *Deutsche Christen*. (And this was directed at the man who a few years later would write his *Geen duimbreed* [Not an Inch] against membership in the N.S.B. [the Dutch Nazi party] and as no other in the Netherlands would expose the false [Nazi] ideology of race, blood, and soil, J.D.). While Schilder unites faith and culture, Noordmans desires a diastasis between the two: "Culture and faith remain two different things" (124).

In his *Kuyper's idee over een Christelijke cultuur* [Kuyper's Idea about a Christian Culture] A. A. van Ruler also confronted Schilder. What he thought of the latter's views on culture becomes apparent from the following comparison: "Dialectical theology places grace in heaven; in reaction to this, Schilder places it in history; but Kuyper placed it in the soul!" (118). If Kuyper's point of view (i.e., according to Van Ruler's explanation) already amounts to an "an excess of particular grace in time," because it is "no longer stored in heaven" (146), and in that respect already betrays "an unoriginal Christian overconfidence" (124), what should the verdict on Schilder be? "The complete uniqueness, ... the presumptuousness, in short, the absolutizing of Christian culture is being posited here without any hesitation" (122).

The comparison drawn by Noordmans and by Van Ruler between Schilder and Kuyper will be discussed later.

From his "Scriptural" point of view Schilder draws certain

---

321. Op. cit., 127–28.

consequences from which he does not recoil.[322] For our purpose it suffices to mention the following:

(a) Strictly speaking, there is no such thing as culture in general, culture as such. For there is no "unity of cultural endeavor." The world may dream of a tower of Babel, but it remains "fragments, torsos, exponents of diverging aspirations and orientations that are not from God and contradict each other, cancel each other out, and can never consolidate themselves to form a unity. For the imposed unity of the totalitarian antichristian state will be of short duration. If it were not imposed, this sham unity would fall to pieces."[323]

But also, the culture of believers will not be finished. That is because of our sin and "our being plundered by 'the world' that ousts us from the areas still to be cultivated."[324]

(b) Abstaining from culture in the form of going on strike is sin. "Now that Christ has comprised in himself all the real treasures of 'culture,' that is, of 'grace,' abstention for the sake of abstention is nothing but a denial of Christ, self-imposed poverty, and guilt before God."[325] But abstention from cultural participation is "justified and mandatory if it is imposed as a measure arising from urgent necessity. For there will indeed be such a necessity until the end of time. And it is growing, gradually becoming greater, for it is war time." Thus, because of the struggle, "there is nowhere a possibility of a simultaneously harmonious and centrally guided development of all cultural forces."[326] Because only a portion of humanity begins to do its duty, that portion is burdened with a much heavier load than would be the case if all people feared and served God. "The Christian laborer who toils to save a quarter and on Sunday puts it in the collection for mission work is also engaged in 'culture,' be it indirectly. Half of this amount would have been enough for him to give if the idlers who spend their two quarters in the movie theatre had been able to find the dividing line between entertainment and labor, creative effort and recreation.... The son

---

322. Op. cit., 128.
323. Op. cit., 130–31.
324. Op. cit., 131.
325. Op. cit., 136.
326. Op. cit., 137.

who works in his Father's vineyard is overburdened because his brother who does not do any work is unfaithful to the Father."[327]

(c) "Deep reverence ... also from a cultural perspective, may be demanded for the church. As Head of the church, Christ is the King of the whole world also, the one who in history brings nature to its completion.... He is God's Ambassador, who wants to lay down at God's feet all the results of the cosmic process of development and recruitment; and consequently he is also the Governor of culture, and the Judge and Redeemer of its agencies and institutions. In him (Eph 1:10) God will one day 'recapitulate' all things."[328] "There is one single history only, and this history is 'Christian,' that is, governed by Jesus Christ."[329] But now he has been given to the congregation as Head, and to it only. "In the Head of the church the sum of all things is drawn up. This statement does away with the theory according to which the church itself is as such a cultural state or is permitted to become one. No encouragement is here given to any suggestion that the church is in any direct and practical sense engaged in the business of culture, let alone that it is an exponent of culture, for the church is always, as institute, to be instituted, and therefore never gives away the name 'church' to that which—sometimes in order to characterize Christian cooperation in education, family relationships, social and political contexts, etc.—is incorrectly called "the church as organism." The sort of church concept in which the church is a directly active participant in, or exponent of, culture would murder her, violate her."[330] The sermon during a church service is not a cultural lecture that the church gives. But that church service does subject all of life to promises and norms. Regeneration happens in the church. "It is in this way that the church can, must, and is permitted to be the fiery hearth where God's people are from on high 'charged' with power from on high.... Take the church away, and the kingdom of God becomes a nebulous affair. Put the kingdom of God in the fog, and the Christ is denied in matters of culture.... Only the church, as the 'mother' of believers [Gal 4:26], gives birth to the 'new' humanity, those

---

327. Op. cit., 138.
328. Op. cit., 149–50. For the exegesis of Eph 1:10, see op. cit., 150–56.
329. Op. cit., 157.
330. Op. cit., 158.

people who, also as far as culture is concerned, bear the burdens of the whole world."³³¹ Take away the church, "and the essentially human element will disappear, while a humanism that boasts about its ruins will come back."³³² The church is not permitted to be even "the smallest and least significant center of culture in any direct sense, but as indirect cultural force she *must* be the very greatest."³³³

3. *The possibility of a non-Christian culture.* Although only Christian culture qualifies as true culture, Schilder does not deny that outside of the church "there is 'as yet' the possibility of a wide scope of development in science and art, in trade and industry, in national and international communication, in technology or whatever else," and he admits that all of this is culture up to a point.³³⁴ One can therefore speak of cultural tendencies.³³⁵ And although, according to the book of Revelation, only the number 7 and also the number 1,000 befit the work of God, while the Antichrist gets no further than the number 3½, so that "the cultural structure characterizing the last days is only a truncated pyramid," Schilder does speak of "culture" (the quotation marks are in the original!) in this context.³³⁶

How is this cultural activity and productivity possible if we want to hold on to the confession of the deep corruption caused by the Fall? Kuyper introduced the doctrine of common grace, but what explanation does Schilder give? In his *Heidelbergsche Catechismus* Schilder points to three factors "that can explain the fact that also Gentiles, although they lack the light of revelation, nonetheless often perform actions that agree externally with the law of God."³³⁷ These factors are also taken into consideration in answer to the question that occupies us now with respect to culture. Schilder provides the following summary:

"First, there is their *sinful nature*. I can, motivated by self-interest, and thus pursuant to my sin, decide to perform a particular work of law since it seems advantageous to me. Second, there are the *remnants* of the original gifts. And third, there is also yet the

331. Op. cit., 159.
332. Op. cit., 160.
333. Op. cit., 161–62.
334. Op. cit., 115.
335. Op. cit., 118.
336. Op. cit., 122.
337. *Heid. Cat.* I, 110.

preservation of the world and humanity in the way that God's providence desires and for the particular goal that God wishes to achieve."[338] I will add a fourth factor that is closely connected with the third, namely the factor of *restraint*. Schilder discussed this factor in more detail in *Christ and Culture*. I will say a bit more about each of these four factors:

Re 1. When Paul says that Gentiles do the things of the law "by nature," it means, says Schilder, that "they do it by themselves, out of their own impulse, on the basis of their own considerations."[339] Fear of punishment, escape from unpleasantness, gaining honor from others, reaping thanks, improving one's position, being rewarded, etc., can be the motive.[340] In this, one readily copies the law, since God's law, "properly considered, is always so 'advantageous.' God's law does cut through the heart, does crush, does pierce to the 'division of soul and spirit, of joints and marrow'; it does bring the sword. In short, it does all that God's Word also does, the Word of which it is itself a part. But nonetheless it gives the true medicine to the world."[341] Consequently, "the protective band with which it surrounds human life can only benefit that life." Non-Christians can also often notice that benefit. Schilder points to the day of rest every seven days, and also to the display of obedience in civil, political, and social contexts. The law does desire this, but it is also "the safest way in which the power of the state can operate." In other words, "God's law is the only garment that truly 'fits' the world."[342] One can speak of the profit of religion, although this way of speaking at the same time discloses that things are then viewed from the wrong angle. "The flesh can assent that the law's effects, acknowledged by the flesh, are praiseworthy, but it assents to this in its own manner, and that is its judgment."[343]

Re 2. Schilder: Although it is true that unbelievers do not use the light of nature properly, but pollute it and suppress it by wickedness (Canons of Dort, III/IV, 4), the confession does make it clear "that

338. Op. cit., I, 110–11 (italics supplied).
339. Op. cit., I, 112.
340. Op. cit., I, 367, where Schilder agrees with Trigland.
341. Op. cit., I, 112.
342. Op. cit., I, 113.
343. Op. cit., I, 114. See further Schilder's exegesis of Rom 2:14–15 on pp. 159–62 above.

there are such residues of the original gifts."³⁴⁴ Human beings retained their human character, endowed with understanding and will, and they retain a sense of accountability. That is how they are constantly prevented from actually becoming brutish beasts."³⁴⁵ Human understanding "can never consider hell, as what it actually is, to be attractive or desirable. Even if they want to wade through 'a hell,' they do want to reach 'a heaven' eventually. Any period of deformation that can be mentioned also proposes utopias.... For false testimony can also not for a moment divorce itself from the problem posed by the true testimony." Satan and his minions, to whom understanding and will were also left, cannot fall into the heresy of polytheism (Jas 2:19). Human nature is "bound to the law of motion and the will to self-preservation. By virtue of the first, it can never remain idle; it must act. By virtue of the second, it must constantly reach for what, at bottom, protects it, no matter how much sin blinds people and makes them foolish, and causes them to do what is contrary to their own welfare. Nothing is safe, unless it is guided by God's commandments."³⁴⁶ To the extent that "culture is not driven by faith and is not in accordance with God's law and to his honor, it operates with corrupt 'remnants,' that is with mere 'leftovers.' The material (of Genesis 1, cosmic nature) has remained. And there are still remnants, residues, of the original gifts."³⁴⁷

One should not conceive of these remnants only in a quantitative way. They are also called *vestigia*, i.e., traces that have been left behind. "*Vestigia* is not a quantitative concept, for footprints left in the snow by a dog's paw or a man's shoe are not remnants of this paw or this shoe."³⁴⁸ But it is wrong to exaggerate here: "Acknowledging the double fact that there will always be remnants of the original gifts ... but that they will become smaller and smaller and the 'light of nature' more and more suppressed (Canons of Dort, III/IV, 4), and that thus, even when these remnants are smaller, there will always remain (for believing observers, in accordance with the strength and acuity of their faith's understanding) clear *vestigia* in this intoxicated world—vestiges of

344. Op. cit., I, 115.
345. Op. cit., I, 116.
346. Op. cit., I, 117.
347. *Christ and Culture*, 115.
348. Loc. cit.

the paradisal gifts (even in the midst of antichristian cultural infatuation)—we nevertheless speak, in this sense and with these reservations, of remnants and *vestigia*. In conclusion, culture is then the tragic business of being stuck with remainders only; it is never more than merely an *attempt* to achieve something. God has indeed left things behind in fallen humanity. But these are only 'small remnants' of the gifts originally granted, about which remnants the Calvinist confession speaks in such a brilliantly dangerous way."[349]

One must not make these "remnants" into new creations of God's Spirit and hence conclude that that there is "an intentional act of God demonstrating that he is well-disposed toward us." For as "the rain showers that make also the fields of the impious fruitful are an inheritance of the creation results recounted in Genesis 1, as is the sunshine that alternates with the showers, so it is no different with the 'light of nature'" (*Heid. Cat.* I, 118).

Nor must the light of nature be called general revelation. For "revelation" gives the impression of an action of God that is new, beyond those creatures, at least beyond this (natural, J.D.) light—a separate action that emanates from God and goes beyond his action of maintaining and governing. The light of nature would then be a *donum superadditum* given as an addition to his revelation. This raises problems" (loc. cit.).

One must also not make more of conscience than what Scripture permits. P. Prins does this, for example. He argues that that Holy Scripture "operates *a priori* with respect to the highest authority," and calls the action of this operation of the Spirit irresistible and irrevocable (op. cit., 120). Schilder follows Greijdanus, who understands συνείδησις [conscience] to mean "a co-knowledge with oneself." "Nature has been preserved; so have understanding and will, and hence so has 'a co-knowledge with oneself' (similar to 'taking counsel with oneself'). It has all been left to human beings" (loc. cit.). It is true that those who have become a law unto themselves "will, in many respects, praise what should be condemned and disapprove of what is praiseworthy. The judgment of their consciences is not at all sound. But taking counsel with oneself is something that remains, for it is a remnant of the original gifts.... The functioning of the law, the establishing of tribunals, the taking counsel with oneself—these are things that cannot be obliterated from the world" (op. cit., 121). However, there will be no unanimity among people "about the primary questions." Cf. Rom 2, 15, loc. cit.

Re 3. Schilder: God preserves and continues creation according to its "nature," For his own sake. "Certainly not especially 'for the sake of the elect.' No, for his sake. To demonstrate his righteousness in

---

349. Op. cit., 115–16.

the coming salvation and in the approaching administration of the curse." For God remains true to himself. But for that purpose he does "not just let history continue, which he needed to do in order to reach the total of his predestined children of Adam, with the preservation of their Adamic nature, but he also preserves nature itself for and until the destined time and according to the order appointed for each creature."[350] The connections, as ordinances, remain, although the concrete connections are constantly broken again by human beings. The constitution is never abrogated. "Within the framework of the dilemmas, of the concrete yeses and nos by which it teaches us God's will, there must necessarily be movement toward either obedience or disobedience; toward not only reformation, but also revolution; toward the Spirit, but also the beast." History has constantly tried to erase the boundaries between God and human beings, but it is only an attempt. "And the concepts of 'mine and thine' have never left off being foundational concepts for an unbelieving legal theory, sociology or political science. The concept of guilt and sin may have been contested, invalidated, and emptied, but the titanic struggle that is required for this will always demonstrate that humanity is caught, again and again, in the pitfalls and traps of the law." It always comes back to the two tables of the law, to the double-sidedness of the religious relationship.[351]

Re 4. Human sin has been arrested in its course. Christ has bound Satan (Rev 20), so that the progression of sin and curse has been tempered.[352] According to Schilder, one should not only call this grace, for "this restraining of the Antichrist corresponds to the self-restraint of Christ Triumphant.... In this world, judgment is held back, but so is grace."[353]

However, in addition to this restraining by Christ, Schilder realizes that there is also another restraining of a more general nature, namely, a restraining that is characteristic of time.[354] "Where nothing is any longer 'restrained,' there is either a *possessio tota simul* (a possession of life in which the fullness of this possession

---

350. *Heid. Cat.* I, 122.
351. Op. cit., 123.
352. *Christ and Culture*, 111, 132–33.
353. Op. cit., 111.
354. Op. cit., 88.

is always simultaneously available in full measure) or a *privatio tota simul* (a state of being robbed, of deprivation, and then again in such a way that the fullness of this deprivation is total, in full measure at every moment). That is to say, wherever there is no restraining, temporal existence is no longer possible; there eternity is found. For even in Paradise there was a restraining. If the Spirit of God had been given to Adam without any restraining, then he would have been excluded from the possibility of falling into sin. Development—or alternatively corruption—is a feature peculiar to time. Development and corruption belong to time. The state of having been developed and of having been corrupted (both pleromatically, according to the subject's nature and capacity) belong to eternity."[355]

The consequences of this opinion are clear: Development is characteristic of time. "As long as time exists, mobility, pregnancy and birth, begetting and conceiving, belong to nature." The fact that the gifts of creation develop is not grace, but nature. Untenable is therefore the argument of those who view nature as "dead capital" and who draw the conclusion from this view that, because human beings can still use nature after the Fall and that the dead capital still delivers profit, that is grace. "The terminology 'dead capital' is here too playful and too frivolous because it is not applicable to nature-in-time."[356]

Schilder considers this view of time so important that he writes: "The problem under consideration, then, is fundamentally the problem of the assessment of 'time.'"[357]

Schilder also combines the restraining that is characteristic of time and the restraining of Rev 20 and 2 Thess 2 under the concept of *tempering*. He distinguishes that word from *temperance*. "Temperance is a matter of governing (something that will always remain, also in heaven and hell, through all ages), and tempering is a particular manner of governing (which manner may change)."[358] This tempering will "never be lacking completely in this world; it will be completely absent in heaven and in hell. But within the

355. Op. cit., 88–89.
356. Op. cit., 90.
357. Loc. cit.
358. Op. cit., 113.

duration of time it will not be constant in measure.... In the last days this tempering will then decrease to a minimum."³⁵⁹

Schilder follows Boethius in his description of God's eternity as *interminabilis vitae tota simul ac perfecta possessio*: "God's eternity is a perfect and always complete possession of an interminable life" (*Heid. Cat.* III, 116). For human beings, however, life "is always terminable (i.e., limited by their nature as creatures). Temporally they do not "possess" a perfect life and their possession is not *tota simul*. In eternity (by the measure of the terminable) it is perfect (in its own way) and also *tota simul* (in its own way), for then it is no longer capable of growth" (*Christ and Culture*, 88, note 101).

4. *Koinōnia – Sunousia.* As we saw, positive development of culture is, strictly speaking, restricted to Christian culture alone. But here a possible misunderstanding must be prevented. God did not "after the Fall ... split up the world into two halves; even less did he draw sharp lines of demarcation between these two halves in such a way that the one half would only perform cultural service according to God's commandment, while the other would be a wilderness or chaos containing only ruins and caricatures. The mere thought is already foolish. It not only clashes with the tangible facts obvious to everyone, but it also trifles with all preconditions of cultural action."³⁶⁰

Indeed, a true *koinōnia*, a communion, exists only "wherever the same nature is directed toward a common goal by virtue of love for the same motivating principles and wherever the similar interests are promoted in common faith and hope and love." Cultural *koinōnia* is therefore at bottom a matter of communion in faith. ³⁶¹

But besides *koinōnia* Schilder also speaks of *sunousia*. *Koinōnia* unites a portion of humanity. *Sunousia* exists among all people. *Sunousia* means "a being together."³⁶² This *sunousia* is imposed on all people. "Wheat and chaff have not been finally separated. One day even this *sunousia* will be taken away from them; however, things have not yet reached that point. To all those people placed next to one another in *sunousia* comes the command to engage in cultural labor (which mandate is general because God has not abolished

---
359. Loc. cit.
360. Op. cit., 108–09.
361. Op. cit., 109.
362. Loc. cit.

any command that is original and permanent in character) just as also in everyone the impetus to engage in cultural labor is innate. Besides, the given material to be fashioned is the world inhabited by us (and who can say if regions not yet inhabited by us will not become part of our area of endeavor?). For that reason there cannot be the cultural activity of the one without that of the other. The *koinōnia* is given us by Christ; the *sunousia* comes from God the Creator. There is only one nature, but a twofold use of nature; one material, but a twofold fashioning of it; one area of endeavor, but a twofold development of it; one cultural urge, but a twofold cultural striving. And since all fashioning of material, for good as well as evil purposes, is bound to the nature, the structure, and the laws of the material, the products of the believer's labor and the unbeliever's will always show great similarity."[363]

That is how cooperation is possible. "In this mixed and restrained world it is still possible to do constructive work, also where the constructors do not belong to God's people. No ark was ever built by only Noah's family. The candidates for death, too, always make their various contributions."[364]

B. Background

Already at the beginning of this chapter about Schilder I mentioned that he only began to criticize Kuyper's doctrine of common grace during a later stage of his writing. Initially, he adopted and defended this doctrine. It now remains for me to ascertain when and especially why Schilder changed his view.

Moreover, in Schilder's criticism of common grace a clear development can be detected. Is it possible to show the background of this development?

---

363. Op. cit., 109–10.
364. Op. cit., 112.

§ 12. Three periods

It is not difficult to divide all that Schilder wrote about common grace into three periods.

1. *The first period (to 1932)*. Schilder does not appear to have had significant concerns about the doctrine of common grace before 1932. The statements cited below bear this out:

> The Indian poet Rabindranath Tagore is called "one of the best students in the school of common grace" (*Om Woord en Kerk* II, 208 ([1920])). It is thanks to common grace that people have a will to fathom problems (*Schriftoverdenkingen* I, 25 [1923]). Not for nothing did Kuyper promote common grace in the arts (*Om Woord en Kerk* IV, 143 [1921]). Particular grace makes use, also in matters of linguistics, of the gifts of common grace (op. cit., III, 207 [1923]). They know nothing about common grace in Old Reformed [i.e., pietistic] circles. "If you were to speak in those circles about 'common grace,' the response would be: 'Not weighty enough, man, far too lightweight.' Should you whisper the words 'little sparks" in their ears, they will, unless they remember in time that those words are in the confession, respond with: 'heresy!'" (op. cit., IV, 198 [1924]]).
>
> The "enlightenment" of which Heb 6:4–8 speaks is "of course the fruit of common grace" (op. cit., I, 218 [1924]).
>
> Healing the sick is making use of common grace (*Schriftoverdenkingen* I, 156 [1924]).
>
> Without faith, we live by common grace (op. cit., I, 269 [1928)]). There is a connection between common grace and caricature (*De Kerk* I, 51 [1928]).
>
> So far as I could determine, Schilder wrote more extensively about common grace on only one occasion. That was to defend the doctrine against Th. L. Haitjema's reproaching it with secularization. See "Gemeene Gratie en verwereldjking" in *Gereformeerde Kerkbode van Delft*, 14 and 21 February 1925. However, in other respects, neither article discusses the doctrine of common grace and thus they are not relevant to our topic.

The first period concludes with the appearance of Schilder's Lenten trilogy, *Christus in Zijn lijden* (1930) [English translation: *Christ in His Suffering, Christ on Trial*, and *Christ Crucified*]. In it, Schilder still speaks quite candidly about common grace. But the trilogy also announces a new period. For it speaks not only of "common grace" but also of "common judgment." Thereby, Schilder's open-minded agreement with the doctrine of common grace comes to an end.

CHAPTER II. KLAAS SCHILDER

1. Schilder: Christ's action of washing the disciples' feet reveals Christ's love toward the disciples, a love that comes from above. This love is no sublimation of "a love which is solely the product of *common* grace," of a love that "is included in that eternal rotation of our natural life" (*Christ in His Suffering*, 219). In that washing, Christ also reveals himself as King in a relationship of authority that differs from what develops merely from *common* grace (219–20). There is no breakthrough, no decisive victory in the authority over natural life on the terrain of common grace. "If Christ's superiority were based on common grace alone, He would be a mere man among men" (221). But in fact the relationship of authority "of the natural life of common grace" is now being "sanctified by and put in the service of the Gospel of special grace" (223). In the healing of Malchus' ear the law of Cain's mark (the mark of protection) is fulfilled (423). Cain's generation is protected against all swords, also against those of fiery Peters. And although Christ, as the great Abel, was completely forsaken by God, "He will nevertheless continue extending to 'Cain' every cup of cold water as long as God himself includes that 'Cain' within the pale of the law of common grace" (423). The mark of Cain "proclaims God's long-suffering to the world, a long-suffering which spares Cain throughout the days in order that he may be preserved (this is a biblical idea) until the day of the great retribution of the greater Abel himself. The sign set upon the ear of Malchus proclaimed the law of *common* grace which meted out to Malchus and his company the full measure, renewing his power, regulating his pulse, until *the day of Jesus Christ* (423–24). More than once Schilder speaks of Ecclesiastes and its theme of the vicious circle. It demonstrates how deficient "common grace is *when it is independent of special grace*" (*Christ on Trial*, 59). "Nature and ... the busy and multiple historical life of man. These are the two domains of general revelation and of common grace. And these two are a part of that deterministic cycle which we have called the vicious circle, *unless*.... Unless? Yes, unless the domain of general grace is governed by a living and quickening power derived from special grace and unless the domain of general revelation is illumined by the special revelation of God which intervenes from above" (59). When Pilate officially and definitively declares Christ an outlaw (who despite lack of evidence is chastised), Christ's enduring the curse was worse than it was for Adam. "For when the first man was driven from Paradise, he was still lighted on his way by the sun of God's mercy. He entered into the wide world, but before him lay the expansive history of many centuries, in which he would, of course, have to suffer the curse of sin, but in which common grace would temper that curse, and would give him a life which would be made bearable by law and order" (421). Even Cain was allowed to enjoy the fruits of this hour of Christ, when he was given the assurance that he would never become an outlaw (422).

Schilder compares the scourging administered to Christ, which caused his blood to flow, to the death of Adam and Eve. "When man had sinned God told him that he should surely die. In other words, God announced that separation would come between the soul and the body. Thus bodily death was instituted. Even in this, however, God's evangelical will unto grace was operative, for God introduced physical death into humanity: that is, God interposed physical death between the first sin and the punishment accruing to that sin, in order that in this way he might make room for a history lasting many epochs, a history consisting of cyclical movements, of the vacillations of life, of the circular course of blood and of those who bleed" (514). And a little further on: "It was God's gracious will that the blood of Adam and Eve would not immediately be parched by the firebrand of the punishment of hell, but that it should be limited to that circular course, to that 'vicious circle'" (515). Adam and Eve deserved a complete death. And that "would have annihilated the world, and that catastrophically and at once, if God had not introduced a hiatus, a moratorium, by which the curse was tempered, and a state was introduced in which God—according to the plan he had conceived before—made it possible for a new life-principle to flourish, a principle known as re-creation" (*Christ Crucified*, 116). (See also *Schriftoverdenkingen* I, 216, on the postponement of death in Gen 3.) Thus, Kuyper's "unless" argument with respect to Gen 2:17 is found also in Schilder!

2. However, now there appears a broader view in Schilder's thoughts about suffering. A broader view, not a different one. The polemics for that are still absent at this point. And therefore Schilder does not yet expressly place "common judgment" next to "common grace" as an essential correlative. I am referring to the following passages:

The circular course of which the Preacher speaks has a dual function: "On the one hand it is a hindrance to the curse which came upon the world for the sake of sin, a hindrance to keep it from conducting the life of the world straight down to eternal death. In this sense, therefore, the crooked line is a postponement and a moratorium of the death sentence which would have thrust a cursed world into the depth of hell by the straight route of death itself. In this sense, too, we can accordingly speak of the circle of common grace, regarding it negatively as restraining the full power of curse and death. On the other hand, however, that crooked line is also a postponement of the true and boundless life which would soar straight up to God and to full and unrestrained blessedness. For the cycles of our temporal life have by God's redemptive will been inserted between the first sin and the final penalty. These consequently are a moratorium; they represent a postponement of the punishment, in order that by means of it he might cancel the penalty and prepare the way for a breaking through of grace in Christ. These cycles will therefore continue until the process of redemption, of the most special actiivity of the special revelation of history, the continuous Christological work of the 'day of the Lord' shall be complete. Thereafter that 'great day of the Lord' will see the new life, which cannot yet fully unfold its capacity for blessedness and glory, nor triumph or soar directly to perfect blessedness. *Only then; not before*" (*Christ on Trial*,

151–52). That is how the circular course of our lives is "a postponement of heaven but also of hell. It represents a delay (by virtue of the 'common grace' and the 'common judgment') for eternal death as well as for eternal life" (152). The postponement of eternal youth and of complete salvation means that the "circulation of the blood [contains] all the sorrow of the vicious circle." But it also "contains the *joy* and the *grace* of the vicious circle. It represents the removal of perfect death and of existence in hell" (515).

The waves of God's wrath are arrested by "*the atmosphere of common grace*." Although they will pierce that atmosphere, they are being tempered by it. Hence the difference between earth and hell. But the rays of sunshine of God's love are also being tempered by it (*Christ Crucified*, 19).

As soon as the procession of the circular course of time "will be broken, ... this disruption will be the conclusive triumph of the newly created life, a life which transcends the restraint and tempering of common grace and the common judgment. But over against this triumph of the new life there is the equally conclusive and catastrophic breaking through of the forces of perdition which are to annihilate the world" (118).

In the chapter "Christ Disrobed" Schilder says about clothing that it is "on the one hand a restriction upon life and blessing; a hindrance to the perfect expression of beauty." For God would not have covered the most beautiful of his creatures with a garment if there had been no sin. But on the other hand clothing is "part of the activity of God's *grace*," because it impedes and arrests sin. In that way clothing is fruit of common grace "in order that the retrogression which sin introduced into the human body also, might be retarded and thwarted in its curse-laden, fatal work" (171.

2. *The second period (1932–1938)* is introduced by the essay *Jezus Christus en het cultuurleven* (1932).[365] In it Schilder considers the concept of office (of Christ, Adam, and Christians) as constitutive for carrying on true culture. Up to a point culture is possible for unbelievers because Christ's power of grace and Satan's power of corruption (common grace and common judgment) are being restrained. Schilder also states that characterizing the issue of Christ and culture as an issue of common *grace* is one-sided. Supplementation and correction are needed. The doctrine of common grace must also be regarded as the doctrine of the common command, calling, and the *common mandate*. Using "grace" in the sense of "favor," which is related to the concept of what is permissible, what is allowed, turns the cultural issue into a question

---

365. Included in H. L. Both et. al., *Jezus Christus en het menschenleven* (Culemborg, 1932), 226–85.

of what is permissible and what is not. But what is permissible and what is not permissible cannot be separated from each other.

1. Everything of importance in connection with office and culture in *Jezus Christus en het cultuurleven* has already been discussed above on pp. 172-74 and 186ff.

2. We have already come across the concept of restraint in *Christus in Zijn lijden* [*Christ in His Suffering*]. It "is the mystery of common grace (and of 'common judgment') in the question of culture. Life has not yet been separated into heaven and hell forms" (*Jezus Christus en het cultuurleven*, 265). Under the law of such a governing by God we can recognize culture "up to a point" even among unbelievers (266). The small remnants, of which our Calvinistic confession speaks "in such a brilliant but dangerous way," can "create new cultural products by virtue of the scheme of development and restraint that God in Christ maintains in the Christological process of history so long as he pleases. However, the possibility of these products was already given in Paradise, and they are only possible because Christ is pursuing his goal with the world and still saves it" (267).

It is clear that this concept of restraint places dynamite under the doctrine of common grace. The concept was not yet implicated directly in the question of culture in *Christus in Zijn lijden,* nor in the third edition of *Wat is de hel?*, 92-93, which was published shortly before the essay mentioned above. But it is now. "The restraint of the curse now receives its complement in the restraint of the blessing. The restraining of the Antichrist now corresponds with ... a self-restraint of the *Christus Triumphator*. He also does not yet give himself free rein, for he does not yet allow this world ... a view of the full extent of his exalted power. The brakes on all the chariots are still set, all the horses are still being kept in check. Judgment is still being held back in this world, but grace too" (*Jezus Christus en het cultuurleven*, 265).

3. The following quotation is typical of Schilder's second period: "No, we do not want to criticize this doctrine now, although we are of opinion that it needs to be supplemented and, in the form in which it is often presented, in part corrected" (277). The criticism is still presented circumspectly, but from the outset it is radical. *Beside the correlatives common grace–common judgment, we now have those of common grace and common mandate.* The Heidelberg Catechism states correctly "that God does not do people an injustice by requiring of them what was already imposed on them in Paradise, even though they can no longer do it." But then this answer [Lord's Day 4, A. 9] "turns its sharp goad against those who regard the doctrine of 'common grace' as a theory *only* about what God in his proclamation *has left* us in the form of permissions, of what we may do" (277-78). See further pp. 187ff. above.

In *Wat is de hemel?* (1935) the criticism of 1932 comes to the fore again. But now it is broader[366] and more penetrating. Nonetheless, the criticism remains limited. In the context of his book Schilder is particularly interested in "this one point, that every argument about culture and about the value, goal, boundaries, and tendencies of culture must be constructed not on the basis of the concept of 'grace' as the dominant factor in formulating the problem, but rather on the basis of the revealed reality of God's institution of *office-bearers* and of his giving them his mandate."[367]

Moreover, Schilder challenges Kuyper's exegesis of Rev 21:24, 26, about the kings bringing their glory and the honor into the new Jerusalem.

1. This criticism is more penetrating. "Instead of the 'Christian' gourmand who also managed to get his hands on the knucklebone of rich cultural treasure, we now see the Christian *office-bearer who draws eschatological lines* to the new Jerusalem and *does not dare to speak of 'common grace' without its correlative, the 'common curse'*" (*Wat is de hemel?*, 2nd edition, 207). Had he included the idea of office, Kuyper's theory could have been "so much broader, more cosmic, still more compelling" (210). Regarding this "broader," Schilder writes in a note: "On the basis of his [Kuyper's] point of view, there is a place for the church on earth thanks to common grace.... If we choose the other point of departure, then 'the world' is given a chance of survival so long as God is busy restoring the earth into a completely level site for the church. Of course, Dr. Kuyper also accepted this idea ... but here, too, is missing the structuring of an argument strictly on the basis of *one* fundamental principle" (210).

2. See pp. 163–65 above for the exegesis of Rev 21:24, 26.

In a series of articles *De vergelijking in de gemeene-gratie-leer* (Aug.–Sept. 1937)[368] the criticism becomes more fundamental. The "unless" argument of Kuyper is now out of favor. Further, the terms "common grace" and "common judgment" are now placed in quotation marks, because, says Schilder, we may not draw a conclusion about God's disposition from a very uncertain (anthropocentric, anthropomorphic, infralapsaric) impression on our part. Consequently, in scholarly discourse different, namely theocentric, terminology is employed.

366. *Wat is de hemel?*, 204–10, 220.
367. Op. cit., 213.
368. *Ref.* 17, 380–81.

Further, the term "'common mandate,' although not made into a unifying term,"[369] becomes the only correct term to use for those who go back to the origin of all things.

1. This criticism is significant. In the preceding years, Schilder's objections were largely restricted to an egocentric concept of culture (cf. *Wat is de hemel?*, 206). Now he also objects to the *anthropo*centric dogmatic method: "Not as we 'see' the earth, but as God sees, knows, assesses it and rightly determines it to be, that is what it is really like. Human 'seeing' is more vain than vanity itself" (*Ref.* 17, 389).

In the above-mentioned series of articles everything that Schilder would develop in the writings of his third period is already included in a nutshell. *In reality Schilder has here already taken leave of the doctrine of common grace.* See further pp. 147–48 above.

2. In addition, the term "common mandate" appears no longer to stand in correlation with the term "common grace." We can use the first but not the second when we go back to Paradise, says Schilder. Further, the concept "common mandate" does not make a choice between supra- and infralapsarism, because it is "not derived from our representation of things [cf. common grace, J.D.], but from God's revelation" (*Ref.* 17, 421). See also *Ref.* 18, 3, 10.

This second period, which I believe ran until 1938, is characterized by criticism that does not yet (at least not expressly) abandon the doctrine of common grace. It is a time when Schilder still speaks of necessary *correction*.

In his 1932 essay *Jezus Christus en het cultuurleven*, Schilder did not yet want to give an evaluation or condemnation of the doctrine of common grace: "One can regard a doctrine as good in itself, but at the same time believe that in the discussion of a specific question the point of departure must be found not in that particular doctrine but in another" (*Ref.* 13, 13, where the above-mentioned publication is discussed). In *Wat is de hemel?* Schilder calls the difference between Kuyper's views and his "more a matter of word choice and especially of method ... than of content" (213). He tells Noordmans that he only wants to strip of "some inconsistencies" what Kuyper "at bottom wanted and also preached in great detail in many ways" so that by lopping off the few flawed branches "the old tree of the real Kuyper" can be maintained. Kuyper is not a scapegoat for Schilder (*Ref.* 16, 259). Rather, he wants to make the grounds of Kuyper's foundational ideas "theoretically more secure" than Kuyper did (*Ref.* 16, 274). Schilder does not think his opposing Kuyper's "unless" argument has done

---

369. *Ref.* 17, 421.

away with the "foundation of the popular common grace theorem," but believes that this argument largely dominates the common grace constructs that are in circulation (*Ref.* 17, 388).

Even at the end of 1938, Rev. D. Zwier writes about Schilder's views: "It is clear to us that Dr. Schilder does not at all deny common grace ... but that he seeks for this doctrine a broader foundation, one that is more purely in conformity with Holy Scripture" (*Ref.* 19, 109).

3. *The third period (1938–1953)* is characterized by Schilder's breach with Kuyper's doctrine of common grace. Now that Schilder gives his own explanation of the "good things" found among unbelievers, he no longer needs the answer that Kuyper sought for this conundrum in common grace.

This period begins with the first edition of Schilder's *Heidelbergsche Catechismus* (1938–1940). It finds further expression in two rectoral lectures (1942 and 1946), in the second edition of the *Heidelbergsche Catechismus* (1947–1953), in Schilder's address *De Gemeene Gratie* to the Amersfoort Congress (1948), in *Christus en cultuur* (1948), and in the second edition of *Christus in Zijn lijden* (1949–1952).

Schilder states that we must abandon the term "grace" to designate God's favorable disposition toward unbelievers. For the continuation of history provides the *substrate* for both the administration of God's blessing and his curse. The double aspect of predestination receives a dominant place in Schilder's critical and thetical views.

1. The first publication of Schilder's *Heidelbergsche Catechismus*, in the form of weekly supplements in *De Reformatie* (discontinued when the German invader forbade the publication of this weekly), already displays all the elements that characterize the third period.

Common grace as an explanation of the many "good things" found among unbelievers despite the being "unable to do any good and inclined to all evil" of Lord's Day 2, Answer 8, of the Heidelberg Catechism, is replaced by another explanation (op. cit., I, 89ff.). This new point of view, which later appeared also in the second edition, has been described above on pp. 203ff. *It marks the beginning of Schilder's definitive abandonment of the doctrine of common grace.* Later he would say it explicitly: The thesis of common grace "conflicts with Scripture and the confession, and must therefore be abandoned" (*Congres van gereformeerden*, Report, 100). The criticism, expressed already during the second period, now becomes more sharp-edged. In the second period Schilder still said that Kuyper did not ignore the danger of secularization and did not give it a foothold. However, in *Ref.* 18, 10, Schilder now posits that Kuyper's constant references only to grace have led to a dangerous cultural optimism" (*Ref.* 23, 159).

2. The tone in Schilder's *Heidelbergsche Catechismus* (1st edition) remains mild. However, in the two rectoral lectures of 1942 and 1946, "*Twee bijdragen tot de bespreking der 'Gemeene-gratie-idee'*" (*Almanak F.Q.I.* 1947), he on the basis of the history of doctrine (Augustine, Dort) put "a knife to the throat of all common grace theorists" (87). The substrate idea now becomes very apparent (90ff.). The criticism of the doctrine of common grace, especially of the word "grace," is no longer (as in the second period) specifically directed against a misuse of the term that in practice creeps in so easily in arguments about what is and what is not allowed. Rather, the criticism is directed against the misuse of the term itself as being indefensible in a scholarly context since the aspect of the curse, of judgment, finds no place in it. "The prolongation of natural existence after the Fall in itself, and consequently also of history, is not *grace*. Nor is it judgment. But both are the substrate, the great indispensable presupposition" (90). Schilder's greatest objection to Kuyper's book on common grace concerns its *title* (92). In his opinion we must keep in mind both aspects of predestination. "To call *retardation* 'grace' is already for that reason incorrect and unscriptural, because it is not curse, nor blessing, nor communal curse, nor communal blessing, nor a mixture of both, but only the *substrate* of curse and blessing. According to God's original Counsel, these are governed from beginning to end as components of history and of the propulsion of the world that is coming into existence, *to* the world in reality" (113).

3. The dominance of the substrate idea in Schilder's thought is clear from the fact that in his second period he still spoke of common grace in the Kuyperian sense, in addition to "common judgment," whereas in the third period he assigns different meanings to these terms. "Common grace" is common only among believers, while "common curse" and "common judgment" are common among all other people (*Christ and Culture*, 92–93, 111). The difference is clear: the word "common" is now used in a more restricted sense than how it was used by Kuyper, while "grace" and "judgment" are not the portion, respectively, of unbelievers and believers (as stated in his second period), but of believers and unbelievers. That which is general (continuation as substrate) is now intensified for everyone in grace or judgment, which are but general (common to more than one).

4. The best way to illustrate the development in Schilder's thought is to compare the earlier and later versions of his publications. I will demonstrate how significant predestination with its double aspect became for Schilder by reference to the following quotations from the second edition of the trilogy *Christus in Zijn lijden*, passages corresponding to the quotations from the first

edition that were discussed above. Italics have generally been supplied to identify the basic changes.

The mark of Cain is no longer called a "mark of protection," but "a sign of the prolongation of his temporal existence, so that it would be imposed on Cain 'as treasure' until the day of God's dreadful wrath. He must still generate his offspring: God in his Counsel has rejected them, and therefore wants to generate them from Cain's loins" (I, 2nd ed., 499).

In the first edition Cain "was included in the procession of the law of common grace." But now it has become "in the procession of the times" (I, 2nd ed., 500). The mark of Cain does proclaim God's patience in this world (1st ed.). However, "it makes it immediately clear to us that the word 'patience' is derived from the *anthropopathic dictionary*, for it does bear with Cain all his days, but that is merely to preserve him (a Scriptural image) for the day of the great retribution by the greater Abel. The sign of Malchus' ear announced the law of the *common temperance* which meted out to Malchus and those accompanying him the full measure, renewing his strength and regulating his pulse until the day of Christ's return. It is *substrate of the service of blessing or of the service of curse*, depending upon whether the answer will point to the *cura medicinalis*, the act of healing by the Man with the soft hands, but who also holds the iron rod of world government in those hands" (I, 2nd ed., 500).

We constantly meet the double aspect of the application of blessing and curse, *also in Christ's work*, in Schilder's third period. In the second period the emphasis was still on the administering of *salvation*. We will see this in the following quotations:

In the first edition, with reference to Christ's washing the feet of his disciples, Schilder still speaks of love that grew out of common grace, in contrast to the love that comes from above. However, in the second edition the natural pull in the *sunousia* stands over against the true fellowship of love in the *koinōnia* (I, 2nd ed., 201). Similarly, there is no longer a power relationship that grows out of common grace, but out of the gifts of creation (I, 2nd ed., 204–05).

Schilder continues to be fascinated by the vicious circle of the Preacher, but he no longer speaks of common grace in this connection. He still mentions "nature and the varied and bustling historical life of humankind," but the corresponding "common revelation and grace" have disappeared (II, 2nd ed., 53).

In the passage in which Christ is declared an outlaw by Pilate, we no longer read about a curse that is tempered by common grace and that makes Adam's life bearable (II, 2nd ed., 468). So also Cain, who was "permitted to pluck fruit," has become a Cain who lets his birds "nest in the foliage of the tree of the legal order instituted when Christ appeared, a legal order that holds all flesh in the *tempered* balance of powers" (II, 2nd ed., 469).

About death, which was instituted for humankind after the Fall, the first edition says that God's evangelical will was operative in it. But the second edition says: "It is true that God's evangelical will of grace was *also* operative here already. But also his holy wrath, which wanted to punish under an aspect of grace, to punish those who would reject the grace revealed to all people in Christ. He instituted a death that is thrust in. That is, God "inserted" [note the quotation marks, J.D.] it, as it were, between the first sin and the completion of the punishment that was deserved, in order to obtain room for the *history of all time*, a history with sin and grace as justification, a history *as substrate for the administration of grace as well as of curse, the curse on account of the rejection of grace*" (II, 2nd ed., 543–44).

God did not demand Adam and Eve's blood immediately. That was because of his gracious will, according to the first edition. The second edition says that it was because of his will to administer grace and his will to administer judgment (II, 2nd ed., 545).

While the first edition, II, 136, speaks of the "postponement, the stay of judgment that would send a cursed world into *hell*," Schilder now calls this an "*impression* of a certain postponement" (II, 2nd ed., 168). "In reality, looking at it from God's perspective, the matters are the exact reverse: because God does not yet want to fix an end to time, he lets the circular course of historical life, which is constrained by natural rules, remain (insofar as he is observable in it) until the 'world's grapes are fully ripened'" (II, 2nd ed., 168).

In history with its circular course, God "makes room for Christ and for salvation history," says the first edition, and adds, "observed from God's point of view, these crooked lines are luminous. God's will to grace projected them in order to save the world through the peace of Christ" (*Christ on Trial*, 153). But the second edition states: "But observed from God's point of view, also those crooked lines are luminous: God's will to glorify himself in Christ *in or for precisely the number of people* that he will call into being, that will has created and preserved them" (II, 2nd ed., 170). The differences are apparent. The expression "*salvation* history" is no longer used in this context. Instead of speaking about the preservation of this world, Schilder speaks of God who glorifies himself in Christ in the election and reprobation of individuals. And third, God's will is (obviously) no longer characterized as (only) a gracious will.

The course of our temporal life is no longer inserted, as the first edition said (II, 1st ed., 136), but only *appears* to be (II, 2nd ed., 169). Similarly, heaven and hell are not postponed, but only give us that *impression* (loc. cit.).

According to the first edition, there is also joy and grace in the vicious circular course "because it is a postponement of the final death and hellish existence (II, 1st ed., 493–94). But the second edition restricts that joy and grace *to what appears to be postponement to those who are in Christ* (II, 2nd ed., 545–46).

It is a pity that Schilder was unable to publish a second edition of volume III of his *magnum opus*. Consequently, we cannot compare the passages quoted from this volume with those he might have corrected.

5. I will deal more briefly with the changes made in *Christus en cultuur* [*Christ and Culture*] (1948) as compared to the publication that laid the basis for it, *Jezus*

Christus en het cultuurleven (1932). In the former we read of the restraint that is inherent in time (*Christ and Culture*, 88); about the continuation of the substrate for the administration of blessing and curse (89–91); about *sunousia* and *koinōnia* (109–10); and about temperance and tempering (113–14). These concepts did not yet appear in 1932 publication.

What interests us particularly in this comparison is the different depiction that is given of Christ's work. In the 1932 version it says that "through his Holy Spirit" Christ wants "to prepare God's work community and office community for the work and service of God" (250). In *Christ and Culture* that preparation acquires a dual aspect: Christ administers eternal death as "his sentence of condemnation to those who have alienated themselves in their historical existence from his judicial decision (to which they were also 'destined')," *and* he administers eternal life "as Christ's verdict of acquittal to those who in their historical existence trustingly surrender themselves to his judicial decision (to which they were also 'destined')" 63–64. Thus the Holy Spirit comes to do two things: in the world of culture "he will cause the grapes of the earth to ripen fully in order to be trodden in the winepress of the administration of God's wrath," *and* (cf. 1932) he equips God's work community and office community, "both of which he has himself purchased, for the work and service of God" (63–64). While in 1932 "a history of many centuries was inserted," in which God made room "for Christ's work of salvation" (*Jezus Christus en het cultuurleven*, 259), now we meet Christ "as Savior-Redeemer and as Savior-Avenger." A history is "inserted" (note the quotation marks, J.D.) for his sake. But that can no longer mean: *only* for the sake of his redemptive work (or *only* for the sake of the elect). It *must* mean: for the sake of his double significance as Savior-Redeemer and as Savior-Judge" (95). Also in his Christology, Schilder emphasized double predestination.

6. Schilder was not given opportunity to correct the first edition of *Wat is de hemel?* completely. He was able only to make corrections to the first and part of the second chapter, neither of which are relevant to our topic. So we have no materials for comparison. But the difference between Schilder's second and third period can be clearly demonstrated by comparing a quotation from this book with what he in his third period wrote in *De Heidelbergsche Catechismus* (2nd edition) about the Noahic covenant. See pp. 151–53 above. In *Wat is de hemel?* we read that the covenant with nature became a phase of the covenant of grace: "This was universal; it was concerned with humanity as the assembly of all who are truly alive. And in the covenant with nature God makes *everything subordinate* to the work of those gathered together; all of 'nature' is involved in the growth and development of the new Jerusalem designed by God. *It becomes God's shop floor, so that he can in due course lay down his church floor*" (187–88, italics supplied). Here Schilder speaks only of the salvific aspect. In the third period the aspect of doom is necessarily added, even though the identification of the Noahic covenant as a phase of the covenant of grace is maintained, as we saw.

7. It stands to reason that for the explanation of Schilder's ideas in chapter II A, I drew primarily on his publications from the third period, especially on the second edition of his *Heidelbergsche Catechismus*. There is a demonstrably clear development as well as a clear difference between the periods. This clarity makes it easy for us to say of chapter II A: that is how Schilder speaks; and of II B: that is how he spoke.

It does happen in the third period that Schilder still speaks of grace in a general sense, which one would not have expected. C. P. Plooy correctly pointed to a passage in *De openbaring van Johannes en het sociale leven* where he does this (3rd ed. [1951], 305). There he states that the disintegration of life in Babylon "was restrained at first by the *grace* of God, even though Babylon cursed him" (emphasis mine). Evidently this reference escaped Schilder's eye, which is what Plooy also assumed.

§ 13. From the first to the second period

Schilder: "So long as we (leaders in politics and in society included) do not return to supporting the absolute word, our labor is in the process of secularizing. Then we will not get Christian works, permeated with yeast, but works by Christians. And the consequence will be a Christianity that will find it strange when such a morning song is sung. It will be a sound from a world foreign to them."[370]

"The absolute word" – necessary in a situation of secularization. How can anyone who reads this quotation from Schilder's work in 1929 still be amazed that a few years later, having traveled from Erlangen to Rotterdam to dictate the manuscript of *Jezus Christus en het cultuurleven* to a stenographer,[371] he spoke about this topic in truly absolute terms? In a time when the "Reformed garment" was being eaten by moths?[372]

The absolute word. – That is why the approach to questions of culture must be different from the approach to the doctrine of common grace: the *mandate* and the *dreadfulness* of the question of culture demand our attention.

In a situation of secularization. – In this situation we must, "for the sake of Christian culture, i.e., of true culture, work with all our

---

370. *De Kerk* I, 97, from *Ref.* 10, 45 (1929).
371. *Ref.* 23, 353.
372. *De Kerk* I, 111, from *Ref.* 11, 338 (1931).

strength for the *church*, for the body of Christ,"[373] in order to retain what is truly human.

1. Shortly after the publication of *Jezus Christus en het cultuurleven*, Schilder wrote an article entitled "*De 'aanpak' van de cultuurvragen bij de 'gemeene-gratie-leer'*" (*Ref.* 13, 138–39) to explain the background of his essay. In my opinion this is the most beautiful article that he ever wrote about this material. From this fascinating article we come to know not only a brilliant writer, but above all a *prophet* who had a message for his time—a message that could not be a repetition of the doctrine of common grace. All the criticism that he would later level at this doctrine, and that so strongly bears the mark of a learned *theologian*, springs from the message of this penetrating *prophet*. A prophet who himself did not suspect how explosive the essay would become in the ecclesiastical situation of his time. Much later he once wrote that he had discussed the theme of Christ and culture in all innocence (*Ref.* 23, 353). But it is the innocence of the man who (according to a well-known image) *had to* sound the alarm and then became frightened by the noise he had caused.

"*Had to* sound the alarm." For, according to Schilder, things will not go well if Kuyper's doctrine is applied in the question of culture. "In our circles," he states, the argument often runs thus: "God has still ... left us so many good things. 'Still.' He has still not given the world over to corruption. 'Still.' He has still restrained sin and the curse. 'Still.' He has still kept Satan bound. 'Still.' Thus we may still enjoy many good things. 'Still.' We still have the arts and sciences, we still have business and recreation, we may still travel, we still have a broad terrain over which the world can accompany us and we can accompany it for quite a distance. 'Still,' and 'still' again" (13 *Ref.* 138–39). But those who argue like this easily fall into casuistry ("how far we can 'still' go, what is 'still' permissible, even if only just"). However, so Schilder continues, if we know ourselves to be placed by God "before his never-to-be completed work, then the matter is quite different. Then we shall have plenty to do. Instead of the 'still' at the foot of the mountain of sleeping Pharisees [with their casuistry, J.D.], we get the bewildering and striking 'not yet' of Christ, who climbs the mountain and from it teaches people about the kingdom of heaven." He "blew away that entire 'still' casuistry in his Sermon on the Mount. The scribes knew precisely what was 'still' permissible. And so a marriage breakdown could 'still' not quite be called adultery, and the formula for an oath would 'still' be lawful. However, Christ placed all those 'still' tacticians under the pressure of the absolute [! J.D.]. Looking at a woman with *lustful intent* already was adultery. Consequently, there was no longer anyone who had already arrived; everyone now had to say 'not yet.' And those who swore oaths suddenly learned that anything more than 'yes' and 'no' was wrong, in other words, that the ordinary 'yes' and 'no' were just as weighty before God as the extraordinary oaths they reserved for special

---

373. *Jezus Christus en het cultuurleven*, 280.

occasions. Thus, the ordinary and the extraordinary ought to be precisely the same and there are no lighter and weightier cases that can be weighed against each other. Everyone now says: I am 'not yet' there" (op. cit., 139).

The significance of these words for culture is readily apparent: "Meanwhile it is never again a question of whether something is 'still' possible (that is the question the Pharisees ask too). Rather, the issue has become: How much have I already seen of this culture, how much have I done in and for it as servant of God? The spiritual gourmet method lets all persons crawl into a corner with a couple of knucklebones of the rich cultural treasure between their teeth, i.e., fragments of a life of enjoyment. In contrast, the office-bearer sketches out the entire project before he begins; he does not view fragments of life, but life itself, and then, with a sigh of 'I am not yet there,' he begins to work methodically toward his goal, because he has surveyed the whole with the rules of office before him" (loc. cit.). The 'still' argument is one of reaction (reminiscences of Paradise), while all permits and orders are dated, and "therefore we must work with the possibilities currently present in the world in order to reach the great future of Christ." Human beings were already *"pilgrims"* in Paradise. "There, too, there was no enjoyment of yesterday's inheritance, but there was a simultaneous enjoying and working in and of everything that must be carried from yesterday, through today, to tomorrow, because God is served by it and in his joy the people of culture may rejoice" (loc. cit.). That paradisal dating has remained. For God has, "oh grace, oh terror, still left history. He prevented the world from breaking apart following the first sin. Thus he left us our existence, for we have to do his work." The cultural question is always posed as "what is permissible and what is not." But we may not and must not separate them. "And that is why common grace cannot be our starting point, for the word 'grace,' even apart from the misconceptions about it, is too one-sided. At bottom it only means 'favor.' And Paradise is not a matter of favor only. It is also a matter of mandate, order, and command" (loc. cit.).

But if God's assignment, his *mandate*, is maintained, then, so Schilder continues, the *"terrifying* nature of the cultural question calls for our attention at the same time. It always amazes me that people are so pleased with culture, regarding it as something we (may!) possess and enjoy. Is it such a good thing? Engaging in culture appears to be a heavy burden once people have finished a good feed of their knucklebones.... Is there a greater burden than to engage in culture?" (loc. cit., emphasis supplied). God does not do us an injustice by demanding of us what we can no longer do. Only, "we no longer hear the deep sob that comes to the fore in that question of the Catechism.... God is not unjust when he 'still' requires it of us. 'Still'! The office is 'still' there. Grace is diminished, but the office remained *undiminished*. 'Still'—that only begins to make sense now. If you want to use the word 'still,' do it properly: the office was not diminished, but grace was" (loc. cit.).

It makes sense, says Schilder, that, in addition to the word "grace," the adjective "common" in the phrase "common grace" is now also under attack.

CHAPTER II. KLAAS SCHILDER

"As soon as culture is no longer called 'grace,' but becomes *service* again, then the fairy tale of a common-grace culture has disappeared. Then we do not have a 'common' culture, but we get what we should have: a Christian culture over against the cultural corruption that is in the world." It is impossible to speak of a kind of neutral terrain between the two, where we can pause and rest from time to time (loc. cit.). Cf. also *Wat is de hemel?*, 206–08.

2. Absolute words for culture: "mandate" instead of "grace"; the "not yet" and the frightfulness of the cultural question instead of the "still just" of egoistic casuistry; a Christian instead of a "common" culture—this strong language will amaze no one who *circa* 1932 heard Schilder speak about the *church*. Schilder did not look for the connection between church and culture then, but he clearly put it in place. "Take away the church and God's kingdom is shrouded in mist. Place God's kingdom in the mist, and Christ is forsaken in culture." Only the church joins all believers "into an unbreakable community and teaches the norms for all relationships in life, also those outside of the church" (*Jezus Christus en het cultuurleven*, 279). Take away the church, "and the essentially human element will disappear, while a humanism that boasts about its ruins returns" (op. cit., 280).

No wonder, for the church is *the new humanity* (*De Kerk* I, 375ff.; *Schriftoverdenkingen* II, 117–18). In it alone all the riches of natural aptitudes can and will be developed (*Schriftoverdenkingen* I, 446).

In this way, Schilder's church struggle becomes striking. He fights for the good confession about the church, so that the church will remain the "fiery hearth": it is from out of the church "that the fiery hearth of obedience, its pure cultural glow included, must blaze forth throughout the world" (*Jezus Christus en het cultuurleven*, 279). Hence Schilder's sharp attack on those who would prefer to see the church disappear into an alley. "Where the heavy traffic rages—*there* the people appear who worry about the question how they are to *live*. In the cul-de-sac, together with the secluded courtyard—*there* those people sit and crouch who are getting ready to *die*" (*De Kerk* I, 142). However, the church is no *Heils-anstalt* [institute for salvation] about which one can reason as follows: "For the making of our sermons we retain Calvinist doctrines. Nice work, is it not? But in addition we also recognize other terrains, such as the political, esthetic, scientific, and social terrains, where we maintain a strict neutrality. Leave it to the 'churches' to tell their respective members how those members can discover the sure marks of spiritual life within themselves" (op. cit., 143–44).

However, says Schilder, we may not operate in discrete sectors. The church is not a boarding school whose rules do not apply to the outside world (145, 147). In God's name its windows must be opened and its voice must be directed powerfully to those political, esthetic, scientific, and societal neighbors! (145). "Why are you hiding in the dark, O *church*? Why do you let humanists and sectarians fool you into believing that the church can be a club, something in the world's cul-de-sac, not at all human, not humane, not at all broad in its

CHAPTER II. KLAAS SCHILDER

mission and outlook?" (160). Everything is at stake: "For God's sake, do not let your church concept slip into the mist, for then everything, everything is lost. Also in God's kingdom" (196).

The striking conformity between Schilder's struggle for a *Christian* culture and his struggle for the *true* church is evident from the fact that he attacks "the fatal word 'still'" in both contexts. Some time before his article "*De 'aanpak' van cultuurvragen bij de 'gemeene-gratie-leer,'*" Schilder wrote "*De vergelijkende methode: het funeste woordje 'nog,'*" which deals with the church (*Ref.* 13, 18–19). See *De Kerk* I, 202–10. How does one recognize the church? People look around "in their neighborhood. Here there is the church to which they themselves belong; yonder there is an institute that looks much like it. Then they start to *compare*. Christ is 'still' being preached over there. They still use the right formulation for baptism. The Holy Spirit apparently 'still' does his work of conversion there.... There they 'still' many good ministers who faithfully proclaim the gospel. The conclusion is: "Wherever that word 'still' is 'still' apt, let us 'still' refer to the institute as 'church'" (*De Kerk* I, 204).

Here, too, Schilder rejects this "still" argument (cf. what was said above about this argument in connection with common grace): "*One may not isolate the 'marks' of the church* (statistical data o*nce they are identified) from the living, existing, actual,* coming down from heaven to the earth, daily renewing dynamic *act* of the glorified Christ" (op. cit., 205). The church is not a static entity, but travels along with the living Christ. And where one no longer experiences this movement, one can only speak of a wave in a can: "If I put a wave in a can and so isolate it, and if I then put the wave down somewhere in a place where it does not belong, is it no longer a wave? Everyone will realize that this is a silly question. The wave already stopped being a wave when it was put in the can and isolated." That is how "the living water from the channel dug by Christ ends up in a small canal." It remains water, "but the dynamic power of Christ, the Living One, who gathers according to his will and not according to the will of Thomas [Aquinas], Luther, Calvin, De Cock, Kuyper, and Van Lingen, is also autonomous *and never allows itself to be pushed into a side road*" (206–07). One may not give his "blessing" to all available institutes on the basis of "the 'marks' that 'still' remain, despite the constant diluting of those 'marks.' For one can dilute the wine in the cask, but not the wine in the grape, for it is full of life" (209–10).

3. An assessment of Schilder's concept of the church lies beyond the scope of our discussion. But I do have to point out the background of his resistance to the doctrine of common grace. And that leads us inevitably to his confession about the church. It can be put this way: When one takes a wrong approach to particular grace (cf. the church in a cul-de-sac, pluriformity), there is no future for culture that is classified under common grace. "Common grace is less than particular grace. It is frightfully superficial for persons who do not question whether they, in their most *special* convictions about life, receive God's blessing but are content to conclude that they share in a *common* blessing with

others. For it is a rule of life that stronger and more personalized lives also *particularize* themselves more and more, and become unique. The *life of grace* also enriches this law of life. Hence, returning to things held in common and seeing a blessing in them amounts to spiritual poverty and is culpable and irreligious. Both Jacob and Esau received the promise of the 'fatness of the earth' and of increase and great numbers. Woe then to Jacob if he were to say: together with Esau I have the fat of the land, the wine, and a large family; hence I have the blessing: *te Deum laudamus*. No! Jacob received the *blessing of Jacob*; he needs God's blessing and must believe in his supremely special calling, namely, to be Israel" (op. cit., I, 78–79).

The terminology will change somewhat later from what we find in this quotation dating from 1929, but the substance remains: " Let all personally receive in the church, from God's particular grace, their strength for life, their call to awaken to a new life, the renewal of their hearts. And let them then go out from there into the broad terrain of the kingdom of heaven. The doors of the church are wide open on all four sides, open to the kingdom of heaven. But the church differs from that kingdom and none will be able effectively ... to serve that kingdom unless they have understood and grasped what God has given them and charged them with in the church" (op. cit., I, 196). Schilder concludes that many "shrug their shoulders and ignore all those who keep talking about the church concept and its absolute significance. They regard it as nonsensical and singularly 'ineffective.' But we believe that it is impossible for people to be 'effective' in in the kingdom of heaven unless they have had their batteries charged in the church by God-Yahweh" (loc. cit.). These were not trifles about which Schilder polemicized in *De Rotterdammer* (*De Kerk* I, 61–100) with W. J. Kooiman about the Deventer inter-church evangelism committee (op. cit., 161–79); with the *Christelijk Gereformeerden* [cf. the Free Reformed in North America] about their right to exist after 1892 (op. cit., *passim*); with Hepp about pluriformity (op. cit., 303–59); and with the *Hervormden* [people of the state church] about the Secession of 1834 (*Ons aller moeder anno Domini 1935*). He fought for reformation in the church, so that the "*Vocativus* [word of direct address] of the Reformation" from Micah 6:8 would be heard: 'He has told you, O man, what is good....' When Micah thereby "calls people to reformation, he does not say: listen, you Israelites, you children of David, you seed of Abraham. Of course, he could have done that too. But all those vocatives go back to that single 'O man'" (*De Kerk* I, 376). Schilder explains this more fully as follows: "*Ultimately*, in *the final instance*, it is not about matters that are Israel-specific: sacrifices, temple, shadows. For although at that moment it did indeed concern those things, that was only so because in all those things God asks pure *humanness* of you" (op. cit., 377). *Schilder struggled for what was particular in order to preserve the general.* In the context of our topic: he defended the *church* for the sake of true *culture*. Those two are bound together by an indissoluble tie. They also show the right direction: *from* the church *to* culture. And the obvious consequence is that it is not common grace but particular grace that determines the direction of the cultural question. *Jezus Christus en het cultuurleven* [Jesus Christ and Cultural Life]— the title of Schilder's essay was a direct hit.

§ 14. From the second to the third period

In the third period, Schilder defended the proposition that God's wrath should be given the same theological emphasis as God's grace. This theological formulation, in which God's grace and wrath receive identical emphasis, is not found in Schilder's earlier period. But there is indeed a connection between the earlier and later periods. Right from the start Schilder pointed to the *reality* and the seriousness of God's wrath: "O God, you are a fearful God!"[374] He is the author of *Wat is de hemel?* [What Is Heaven?] but also of *Wat is de hel?* [What Is Hell?]. About the wrath and the curse of God in the suffering of Christ he wrote as no other.

Here, too, Schilder's prophetic warning against "our current enfeebled Christianity"[375] forms the background to what he places thetically over against common grace in the third period. If the criticism of Schilder as *theologian* is to be fair, one may not disregard what Schilder said as *pastor and prophet*.

I cannot accept the verdict of G. C. Berkouwer that "in his argumentation" Schilder "was virtually dependent completely on H. Hoeksema's lengthy polemics since 1924."[376] Although Schilder was certainly influenced by Hoeksema, he was not dependent on him. When we understand the continuity in Schilder's thought, we cannot reduce this great theologian in his critique of common grace to a second-rank figure.

1. One should read Schilder's discussion of the Christian feasts to understand how incisively he constantly pointed to God's wrath. Pentecost and world judgment are *one*. "God's wrath is always a great wrath. Who dares to speak in this context of a *more* or *less* when we are talking about a measureless God who shows his wrath every day? Thus today it is a day of God's great wrath; but then that day is also the great day of the Lord, the great day of his great burning wrath!" (*Preken* I, 368 [1923]). Cf. *Licht in de Rook*, 117–18. The Holy Spirit does not come only with his flame of love, but also with the fire of his wrath (374).

374. *Om Woord en Kerk* I, 251 (1927).
375. *Schriftoverdenkingen* I, 359.
376. G. C. Berkouwer, *De Voorzienigheid Gods*, 93.

CHAPTER II. KLAAS SCHILDER

Christmas "with all its mild-mannered friendliness, and its edifying packaging, is generally not sufficiently charged with matters pertaining to eternity. We do not have to be preachers of 'tension,' of 'paradox,' or of 'crisis' to confront the question whether ... our celebration of the feast ... and our enjoyment of Christmas ... do not become bare and shabby once we deduct from it such a percentage of domesticity, such a percentage of esthetic enjoyment, or custom, or suggestion, or whatever else." For we then forget that we are eating at God's table and that it is very difficult "to be his guest. For we must break with our normal assessment of things. We must understand that with him who 'feels indignation every day' (Ps 7:11) and whose 'mercies (like his wrath) ... are new every morning' (Lam 3:23) the everyday things of life are the wonder" (*Om Woord en Kerk* I, 248 [1927]).

The secularization "of our Christian era does not begin at the theatre, or at the cinema; rather, it begins with the devotional times in which we place the emphases there where God does not." People speak of "the beautiful star, and the manger, and the sheep and the shepherds, and they [in Dutch] use the jolly, agreeable Christmas diminutives, ah yes. But the music of war, and the thunder of revelation, and the multitude of the heavenly host (a war-related term!), they are there first of all...." (249). What our piety needs is "a spoilsport, so that we may learn to play before *God's* countenance" (250). An ecclesiastical feast is not a moratorium in the war. "Precisely the religious events are the great moments in the holy war that God will wage in this world until the day when he will establish the kingdom of peace and will invite the conquerors to the feast where they will shout hallelujah over an eternal schism" (*Om Woord en Kerk* II, 126 [1927]).

A few years later Schilder wrote a meditation about the concluding verse of Isaiah (66:24): "And they shall be an abhorrence to all flesh." He comments that we must not moderate this expression. That is what the synagogue did of old by rereading verse 23, which sounds more cheerful, after verse 24. "Our modern-day enfeebled Christianity is heading in the direction of the old synagogue. They want to remove the rough edges" (*Schriftoverdenkingen* I, 359 [1931]). But Isaiah knows "that if it pleases God, love and wrath, atonement and punishment, heaven and hell, conversion and hardening, election and reprobation must stand beside each other and must be preached, and the one may not cancel out the other. And hence any questioning of the appropriateness of the 'last' word, that 'concluding word' [of Isaiah] is actually utter nonsense. We human beings think about things serially, one after the other, even though they exist simultaneously. But for God, his decisions are one and undivided: election and reprobation, heaven and hell, beauty and hideousness are all present at the same time as ultimate data in the depth of his being, as his thoughts, as reality that he has 'seen,' i.e., has put in place" (359). Those who "wish to speak about the most supreme beauty out of which a radiant God arises, must also have the courage, the honesty, the beginning of

God's truth, to hear simultaneously about hell and horror, and not allow the one to be ousted by the other. For the 'one' and the 'other' belong together" (360).

2. It is clear from the above quotations that Schilder did not just reflect on God's wrath, but that he preached it. He deemed it necessary, for he saw the wrath of God blow upon and through the churches in his time. Already in a 1918 sermon he demanded attention for a forgotten doctrine, the doctrine of the common disgrace (disfavor), the common judgment," when he preached about 1 Pet 4:17a: "For it is time for judgment to begin at the household of God" (*Preken* I, 179). He did not want "to speak eschatologically at large" about this judgment and about the Day of the Lord that will come as a thief in the night (*Schriftoverdenkingen* I, 377 [1931]). Instead, he wanted to draw attention to the energy of ecclesiastical deviation as God's punishment. "That we, for example, do not weep about our errors, but ignore or denigrate those who ask ... whether there is perhaps the beginning of error among us, which is a much worse portent than an earthquake, and than the gold of England, whether or not it is connected with Transvaal" (377). "The energy of error, O God, that is punishment. Punishment. Retribution. Editors of church papers who are dozing, churches that acclaim diplomats, principles that are wearing out.... We must see our deviation as preparation for the last day. And we see so little of that, as little as the sick person notices of the foul air in the room" (378). Schilder preached the wrath of God already long before he began to give it a dominant place in his systematic theology in 1938 and thereafter to combat the doctrine of common grace. This theological style remains to be assessed in a later chapter. But I can already posit now that Schilder saw it as a compelling necessity to speak not only of God's grace, but at the same time of his wrath. This was born out of his calling as preacher.

3. Those who recognize the unity of thought in Schilder's *oeuvre* will be unable to accept Berkouwer's assessment of the relationship between Schilder and Hoeksema. It is certainly true that Hoeksema influenced Schilder. When Schilder made his first trip to America (at the end of 1938), he had, in his own words, "after studying the problem of common grace, drawn close to his [Hoeksema's] insights on the cardinal issue [the designation 'common grace'] (*Ref.* 22, 402). The decisions of the Synod of Kalamazoo (1924) about common grace elicited "some criticism" from Schilder before his trip to America (*Ref.* 18, 127; *Ref.* 19, 212, 364). Later he rejected these decisions entirely (*Ref.* 22, 402; *Ref.* 24, 145, 394, 401; *Ref.* 25, 96, 177).

But his being influenced does not necessarily imply that Schilder was dependent on Hoeksema with regard to the cardinal issues. All of the building materials for the more systematic discussion opposing common grace, as found in his *Heidelbergsche Catechismus*, were present already before Schilder's first American trip. What especially comes to mind in this respect is the already mentioned series of articles in 1937 entitled *De vergelijking in de gemeene-gratie-*

leer, for which see p. 216 above. I have already stated that in this series, which Schilder would develop in his third period, everything was included in a nutshell. And there the name Hoeksema is not mentioned anywhere. If the latter had influenced Schilder as much as Berkouwer suggests, I would undoubtedly have come across his name. Also conversely, I have not discovered anything in Hoeksema's publications that suggests a significant dependence on Schilder. It makes much more sense to speak of a striking similarity of thought and to add that each of the two theologians reached his conclusions in his own way.

"Each ... in his own way." For if we read again what was quoted from Schilder's 1931 meditation about Isa 66:24, it will be evident that it is not such a large step from this meditation to his *Heidelbergsche Catechismus*.

"Each ... in his own way." Surprisingly, Schilder already in 1928 commented that besides common grace we must speak about a "'common judgment' as a necessary complement of common grace" (*Ref.* 8, 360). And in this same meditation about Ps 7:12 (a text also mentioned above), Schilder says a bit later: "Heaven and hell—in them can history find rest. Hell the way God sees it. Heaven as he wants it" (op. cit., 368). Cf. *Schriftoverdenkingen* I, 464–72.

I will take yet a further step back to before the sermon of 1918. According to his own words, Schilder was captivated by the parallelism between 1 Pet 1 (the preservation of the inheritance of the believers) and 2 Pet 2 (the preservation of the unbelievers until the day of judgment) already since his student days: "Since the time when I was a student, that parallelism has remained with me" (*Heid. Cat.* IV, 94).

Heaven and hell, election and reprobation, grace and wrath, also in their interconnections, engaged Schilder already from the beginning.

III

JOHN CALVIN

We have come across the name of John Calvin a few times in the previous chapters. This should come as no surprise since Kuyper and Schilder are Reformed theologians. For them it was important to be of one mind with the father of Reformed theology.[1] But it is significant that Kuyper appeals to Calvin in support of his doctrine of common grace, while Schilder disputes that appeal. Hence this third chapter is devoted to an examination of what Calvin thought about our topic.

I have used Calvin's *Institutes* as foundation for my research. We are dealing with a doctrinal topic and, if one wants to know what the reformer thought about the topic, the *Institutes* (which were prepared so carefully by Calvin) should have the final say.[2]

Nonetheless, I have also made grateful use of Calvin's exegetical work. In his dissertation *Calvin and Common Grace*, H. Kuiper has conveniently arranged the material relevant to our topic and I am pleased to have been able to make use of it.[3] The impression that the material was not only conveniently arranged by Kuiper but also amounted to a complete compilation proved to be correct. This is affirmed by Werner Krusche, an expert on Calvin, who highly

---

1. Kuyper, writing to J. H. Gunning, Jr.: "... I am not presenting original material; I am only a copyist. What I envision in the realm of theology, church polity, and politics is nothing else than to present a pure copy of what Calvin and his followers envisioned" (*Bedoeld noch gezegd*, 46).
With respect to Schilder, his struggle against dialectical theology is particularly important, "In a time in which so many appeal to Calvin, although they pay little or no attention to him, the question what Calvin intends is significant for the history of doctrine" (*Tusschen 'Ja' en 'Neen,'* 237).
2. I believe that this comment is not superfluous. It is easy to lift a number of passages about our topic from Calvin's commentaries and, on that basis, say: that is how Calvin speaks about common grace. However, in that way the image is mutilated, for then only one facet is illuminated at the cost of other aspects. Thus one disturbs the balanced discussion of our topic that Calvin presents in the *Institutes*. In that work he summarizes what he found in Scripture.
3. Defended at the Free University in 1928.

praises Kuiper's dissertation.⁴ I have also made grateful use of the studies by Krusche, P. Barth, Niesel, Berger, and others.

For the quotations from and references to Calvin's exegetical works and his *Institutes* extensive use has been made of English-language editions of these works.⁵

§ 1. *Is the world better than expected?*

It does not seem difficult to answer this question when we read what Calvin presents in the following.

1. *All have knowledge of God.* "There is within the human mind, and indeed by natural instinct an awareness of divinity."⁶ There is, as Cicero rightly said, "no nation so barbaric, no people so savage, that they do not have a deep-seated conviction that there is a God."⁷ "So thoroughly does this common conviction occupy the minds of all, so tenaciously does in inhere in the hearts of all" that one has to speak of "a certain seed of religion."⁸ "A sense of deity is inscribed on everyone's heart. Even idolatry is ample evidence of this conception. For we know people do not willingly lower themselves so as to set other creatures above them. Therefore, when they choose to worship wood and stone rather than be thought as having no God, it is evident how very strong this impression of a Deity must be."⁹ "All were born subject to the condition that they would know God.... This was not unknown to the philosophers. Plato taught repeatedly that the soul's highest good is likeness to God, i.e., when the soul, having grasped the

---

4. Werner Krusche, *Das Wirken des Heiligen Geistes nach Calvin*, 98: "In his dissertation dealing with Calvin's doctrine of common grace H. Kuiper has given a good description and evaluation of this doctrine, first organizing his material according to Calvin's books and writings in 170 pages and then, but without systematic criteria, expanding on it in about 70 pages." See also 101, 249. Further see V. Hepp: "Kuiper accomplished this work in a manner that has earned the highest praise" (*De algemeene genade*, 58).
5. The main, but not exclusive, sources of quotations from Calvin are the *Institutes* as translated by Ford Lewis Battles and edited by John T. McNeill (1960) and the commentaries as translated by John King et al. (1847–1850). References to the *Institutes* are given in the standard form: book, chapter, and section. References to the exegetical works are to the Scripture passages being discussed. Some translations have been adapted. All italics in translated texts have been supplied.
6. *Inst.* I, iii, 1. Cf. *Comm.* John 19:8 and *Comm.* Acts 17:28.
7. Ibid.
8. Ibid. Also *Inst.* I, iv, 1: "God has sown a seed of religion in all people"; I, iv, 4: "Yet that seed remains which can in no way be uprooted: that there is some sort of divinity."
9. *Inst.* I, iii, 1.

CHAPTER III. JOHN CALVIN

knowledge of God, is completely transformed into his likeness."[10] "In the same manner Gryllus, in the writings of Plutarch, reasons very skillfully when he affirms that, if once religion is banished from their lives, humans are ... in many respects more wretched than brute beasts.... Therefore it is the worship of God alone that makes them superior to those beasts, and through it alone they aspire to immortality."[11]

However, God "not only placed a seed of religion in human minds; ... he also revealed himself in the entire structure of the universe ... so that we cannot open our eyes without being compelled to behold him."[12] Creation declares the glory of God; its "language is understood by all peoples [Ps 19: 2–3].... The apostle Paul, stating this more clearly, says: What human beings need to know concerning God has been disclosed to them ... for everyone without exception perceives his invisible attributes, which have been clearly perceived since the creation of the world, even his eternal power and divine nature [Rom 1:19–20]."[13]

"Humanity itself is a rare example of God's power, goodness, and wisdom; some philosophers have rightly called a human being a microcosm." Aratus already said that "we are God's offspring [Acts 17:28] ... and, as it were, at the dictation of experience heathen poets called him the Father of humankind."[14]

In the second book of the *Institutes* Calvin discusses in detail what human reason, apart from revelation in Christ, can still achieve.[15] "The human intellect is not so dull that it cannot experience a small portion of the higher things."[16] "The Lord gave philosophers a slight taste of his divinity."[17]

A remarkable pronouncement is found in the sixth chapter of book II, where Calvin speaks about the necessity of being delivered by Christ: "In all times and among all peoples it has been the common opinion that those who are estranged from God and are

---

10. *Inst.* I, iii, 3. See also *Inst.* III, 25, 2. Regarding Plato, cf. also *Comm.* Ps 104:29, and *Comm.* John 4, 36.
11. Ibid. See also *Inst.* IV, xx, 9, where Calvin points to the connection that Gentile writers made between government and religion.
12. *Inst.* I, v, 1.
13. Ibid.
14. *Inst.* I, v, 3.
15. *Inst.* II, ii, 12ff.
16. *Inst.* II, ii, 13.
17. *Inst.* II, ii, 18.

called accursed and children of wrath cannot please God unless they are reconciled to him."[18]

2. *Achievements and virtues are not absent.* In this context Calvin pays attention to the conduct of Gentiles in "government, household management, all mechanical skills, and the liberal arts,"[19] and also to their "knowledge of the works of justice."[20]

Regarding governance and household management: "Human beings seek communal relationships by nature and, thus, they are by natural instinct inclined to the maintenance and preservation of those relationships. We observe that in the hearts of all people there are universal impressions of a certain civil virtue and order. That is why everyone understands that all forms of community must be held together by laws and that all comprehend the principles of those laws. Consequently, there is agreement among all nations and human beings individually with regard to laws, for the seeds of those laws are implanted in all of them."[21] Thus "a certain seed of civil order has been scattered on all people. This demonstrates very clearly that in the organization of this life no human being is deprived of the light of reason."[22]

Regarding the arts and sciences: Here, too, we must recognize "a common capacity," "rudiments that are inborn in human nature," "a universal apprehension of reason and understanding naturally implanted."[23] Calvin certainly appreciates the pagan writers: "Read Demosthenes or Cicero; read Plato, Aristotle, and others of that tribe. They will, I admit, allure you, delight you, move you, enrapture you in wonderful measure."[24] And in a broader context: "Shall we deny that the truth shone upon the ancient jurists who established civic order and discipline with such great equity? Shall we say that the philosophers were blind in their careful observation and artful description of nature? Shall we say that those were devoid of understanding who conceived the art of disputation and taught us to speak reasonably? Shall we say that they are insane who

18. *Inst.* II, vi, 1.
19. *Inst.* II, ii, 13.
20. *Inst.* II, ii, 22.
21. *Inst.* II, ii, 13.
22. Ibid.
23. *Inst.* II, ii, 14.
24. *Inst.* I, viii, 1.

developed medicine, devoting their labor to our benefit? What shall we say of all the mathematical sciences? Shall we consider them the ravings of madmen? No, we cannot read the writings of the ancients on these subjects without great admiration. We marvel at them because we are compelled to recognize how pre-eminent they are. But shall we count anything praiseworthy or noble without recognizing at the same time that it comes from God? Let us be ashamed of such ingratitude, into which not even the pagan poets fell, for they confessed that the gods had invented philosophy, laws, and all useful arts. Those whom Scripture [1 Cor. 2:14] calls 'natural' were, indeed, sharp and penetrating in their investigation of inferior things. Let us, accordingly, learn by their example how many gifts the Lord left to human nature even after it was despoiled of its true good."[25]

Gentiles also have "knowledge of the works of righteousness" (Rom 2:14) and therefore "we may certainly not say that they were completely blind in their way of life." They "by nature have the righteousness of the law engraved on their hearts."[26] And even stronger: it is especially the things that we must learn from the two tablets of the law, which are "in a certain sense commanded us by the inner law that has been written in the hearts of all and has been imprinted in them, as it were." Our conscience testifies in our hearts and reminds us of that which we owe to God; "it confronts us with the difference between good and evil."[27] "People have somewhat more understanding of the commandments of the second tablet [compared to the first tablet, J.D.], because these have a greater bearing on the preservation of civil society among them."[28]

The question about virtuousness among the Gentiles is raised again in II, iii, 3. "In every age there have been persons who, with nature as their guide, were all their lives devoted to virtue. Although there may have been many lapses in their moral conduct, in their striving for virtue they have shown that there was some purity

---

25. *Inst.* II, ii, 15. See also *Comm.* Titus 1, 12, where Calvin rejects all fear of quoting the ancient writers: "Since all truth is from God, if wicked persons said anything that is true and just, we ought not to reject it, for it has come from God."
26. *Inst.* II, ii, 22. Cf. *Inst.* III, xiv, 2: "The Lord ... has engraved a distinction between honorable and shameful deeds in individual minds."
27. *Inst.* II, 8, 1. See also *Inst.* II, ii, 22: "The sinner tries to evade his innate power to judge between good and evil."
28. *Inst.* II, ii, 24.

in their nature."[29] "We must not regard Camillus as the equal of Catiline."[30] Later, Calvin again draws our attention to differences among the Gentiles. He does not wish to claim "that there is no difference between the justice, moderation, and equity of Titus and Trajan and the madness, intemperance and savagery of Caligula, Nero, or Domitian; between the obscene lusts of Tiberius and the (in this respect) moderate lifestyle of Vespasian; and ... between the maintenance of justice and law and of the contempt of them."[31] There are also differences among the philosophers. Calvin says that of all of them, "Plato is the most religious and sensible."[32]

§ 2. Objections

Is the world better than expected, according to Calvin? One could assume so, on the basis of the above quotations. But I will now hasten to place them in their context and show how the author intended them to function there.

1. *A continuous restriction.* "The conviction that there is a God is indeed by nature inborn in all, but ... to the extent that it can, the world attempts to ban all knowledge of God and by every means to corrupt the worship of him."[33] "It is in vain that so many bright lamps shine for us in the workmanship of the universe to show forth the glory of its Maker."[34] "Reason, by which human beings distinguish between good and evil, ... [is] the light that still shines in the darkness [John 1:5].... Yet ... this light is extinguished by the great density of ignorance."[35]

Thus, Calvin presents us with a depressing conclusion. I will now discuss this in greater detail and in doing so will follow § 1 step by step.

29. *Inst.* II, iii, 3. In *Inst.* III, xxiv, 10, Calvin refers to the integrity of Aristides, Socrates, Xenocrates, Scipio, Curius, Camillus, and others and states that one cannot conclude from their uprightness "that all who are forsaken in the darkness of idolatry were earnest seekers of holiness [!] and purity."
30. *Inst.* II, iii, 4.
31. *Inst.* III, xiv, 2.
32. *Inst.* I, v, 14.
33. *Inst.* I, iii, 3.
34. *Inst.* I, v, 14.
35. *Inst.* II, ii, 12.

CHAPTER III. JOHN CALVIN

"God has placed a seed of religion in all people, but one can scarcely find one in a hundred who cherishes this received seed in his heart and none in whom it matures, much less that it shows fruit in season."[36] Idolatry is perfect proof that an awareness of divinity is inscribed in the hearts of all people. It is so difficult to erase that it would be "easier to change a person's natural disposition."[37] But the latter does happen "when human beings voluntarily descend from their natural hubris into the lowest depths in order to honor God."[38] Pagans such as Plato and Gryllus could reason very intelligently, and by nature we and they, too, "are sometimes driven by the progression and direction of things to a contemplation of God.... Yet we immediately fall back into the ravings or evil imaginings of our flesh, and corrupt by our vanity the pure truth of God. We differ from each other in this respect, that we each privately accept our own particular error. But we are very much alike in that we all without exception forsake the only true God for unnatural drivel. Not only are common folk and dull minds enmeshed this way, but also the most excellent persons who are in other respects endowed with exceptionally keen discernment. How profusely have the entire tribe of philosophers betrayed their stupidity and foolishness in this respect!"[39] Plato can assert that the highest good for humanity consists of their union with God, but "he was unable to grasp even dimly how this union is achieved."[40] The uniqueness of God may have been "inscribed in the hearts of all,"[41] but even "the Turks, although they loudly proclaim that the Creator of heaven and earth is God, still, while repudiating Christ, substitute an idol in place of the true God."[42] Pagan poets have also called God the Father of humankind, but "the foul ingratitude of human beings becomes apparent. Within themselves they have a workplace graced with countless works of God and, the same time, a storehouse overflowing with inestimable riches. Consequently they ought to

---

36. *Inst.* I, iv, 1. Calvin repeats this ratio once again in *Inst.* I, v, 8: "And certainly however much the glory of God shines forth, scarcely one person in a hundred is a true spectator of it." Cf. *Comm.* Rom 1:21: "Their unrighteousness was this: they quickly choked by their own depravity the seed of right knowledge before it grew up to ripeness."
37. Cf. text at footnote 9.
38. *Inst.* I, iii, 1.
39. *Inst.* I, v, 11.
40. *Inst.* III, xxv, 2.
41. *Inst.* I, x, 3.
42. *Inst.* II, vi, 4.

break forth into praises of God, but instead they are puffed up and swollen with all the more hubris."[43] For "human beings, finding God a hundred times in their body and soul ... have drawn the curtain of nature, which is for them the maker of all things, before God, and that is how they eliminate God."[44] That happened in the pigsty of the Epicureans, but also with Aristotle.[45] One does not have to "deny that among the philosophers incisive and apt statements about God can be found here and there, but these are nonetheless such that they testify to a dizzying imagination." "The greatest geniuses are blinder than moles" with regard to the knowledge of God and in particular of his Fatherly favor toward us, in which our salvation consists.[46] They see,[47] but they are "like a traveler passing through a field at night who in a momentary lighting flash sees far and wide, but the sight vanishes so swiftly that he is plunged again into the darkness of the night before he can take even a step—let alone be directed on his way by its help."[48]

The "capacity to understand, with the understanding that follows it, is an unstable and transitory thing in God's sight when a solid foundation of truth does not underlie it." Even the natural gifts that remain are corrupt. "Not that the gifts could become defiled by themselves, since they came from God. But to defiled human beings these gifts ceased to be pure. Hence, they cannot derive praise from them."[49]

Similarly, the universal judgment that enables human beings to distinguish between good and evil is also "not always sound and flawless."[50] "There is an inward law that is inscribed in the hearts of all, but because they are enveloped by such a darkness of errors, they hardly begin to grasp through this natural law what worship is acceptable to God."[51] Human beings do not understand the most important parts of the first table of the law, and their reason sometimes causes them to fail with respect to the

---

43. *Inst.* I, v, 4.
44. Ibid.
45. *Inst.* I, v, 5.
46. *Inst.* II, ii, 18.
47. Cf. text at footnote 13: "everyone without exception *perceives*."
48. *Inst.* II, ii, 18.
49. *Inst.* II, ii, 16.
50. *Inst.* II, ii, 24.
51. *Inst.* II, viii, 1.

commandments of the second table.⁵² Especially "those endowed with the most brilliant talents find it most absurd to bear an unjust and excessively imperious domination if they can shake it off in one way or another." Also, "the philosophers do not consider avenging injuries to be a vice." Moreover, "those who are unspiritual refuse to be led to recognize the diseases of their lusts. The light of nature is extinguished before they even enter upon this abyss."⁵³

We can observe virtuous life among heathens, but "those among the philosophers who at any time maintained most strenuously that virtue should be pursued for its own sake were puffed up by such great arrogance as to show that they sought after virtue for no other reason than to have something in which to take pride.... They have received their reward in the world, and prostitutes and tax collectors are closer to the kingdom of heaven than they."⁵⁴ Calvin concludes: "Therefore, let us hold on to this undoubted truth that no cunning arguments can shake: the human mind is so completely estranged from God's righteousness that it does not conceive, desire, or undertake anything that is not irreligious, perverted, tainted, besmirched, and shameful; and the heart is so steeped in the poison of sin that it can breathe out nothing but a loathsome stench."⁵⁵

Is the world better than expected? A second objection to this argument will now receive our attention.

2. *Deceptive masks.* "As long as we do not look beyond the earth, we are quite satisfied with our own righteousness, wisdom, and power, but ... what wonderfully impressed us under the name of wisdom will stink in its utter foolishness; what wore the face of power will prove itself to be the most miserable weakness. That is, what in us *seems* perfection itself corresponds ill to the purity of God." Among the philosophers, "as each was endowed with higher wit, graced with art and knowledge, so the more *specious* was the coloring he gave his opinions; yet if you look more closely upon all these, you will discover that they are all *painted face masks that quickly vanish*."⁵⁶

52. *Inst.* II, ii, 24.
53. Ibid.
54. *Inst.* III, vii, 2.
55. *Inst.* II, v, 19.
56. *Inst.* I, I, 2; I, v, 12.

"In the knowledge of the works of righteousness ... the human mind *seems* to be somewhat more acute than in the knowledge of God and his Fatherly favor."[57] "The excellent gifts of Camillus "*seem* rightly praiseworthy if judged in themselves."[58] "What power for good will you attribute to human nature in this respect," Calvin exclaims, "if in the loftiest appearance of integrity, it is always found to be impelled toward corruption? Therefore, just as you will not praise people for their virtue when their vices deceive you with the *semblance* of virtue, so you will not ascribe to the human will the capability of seeking after the right so long as the will remains riveted to its own perversity."[59] "The more people have excelled, the more they are driven by their own ambition (a blemish by which all virtues are so defiled that before God they lose all favor). That is why anything in the ungodly that *appears* praiseworthy must be considered worthless."[60] "As for the virtues that deceive us with their vain *show*, they shall have their praise in the political assembly and in the talk of the masses. But before the heavenly judgment seat they will have no value in obtaining righteousness."[61] "If some occasionally *seem* to display any good, their minds nevertheless remain wrapped in hypocrisy and deceitful equivocation, and their hearts remain bound to an inner perversity."[62] "Where the service of God as principle and foundation of righteousness has been taken away, everything people practice among themselves in the form of righteousness, purity, and moderation is vanity and insignificant before God."[63] Virtue is practiced, but "some are restrained by shame, others by fear for the law.... Still others, because they consider a respectable lifestyle profitable, in some measure aspire to it; others rise above the common lot in order by their dignity to keep others obedient to them."[64] Thus it matters from what inclination of the heart the works arise! Titus and Trajan are better than Caligula, Nero, or Domitian; and Vespasian lived modestly compared with Tiberius. But what Calvin adds to this is not

57. *Inst.* II, ii, 22.
58. *Inst.* II, iii, 4.
59. Ibid.
60. Ibid.
61. Ibid.
62. *Inst.* II, v, 19.
63. *Inst.* II, viii, 11.
64. *Inst.* II, iii, 3.

flattering: "There is such a great distinction between justice and injustice that it is even apparent in *the dead image of it*."[65] Virtues? No, rather "a *semblance of virtues*"![66] The Fabriciuses, the Scipios, and the Catos "did not direct their deeds toward the goal to which they ought to have directed them. Therefore there was no true righteousness in them, because duties are not measured by deeds but by intentions."[67]

Deceptive masks – The virtues of the pagans are "deceptive masks. Curius and Fabricius were renowned for courage, Cato for temperance, Scipio for kindness and generosity, Fabius for patience; but it was only in the sight of human beings and only in the appraisal of civil society that they were so distinguished. In the sight of God nothing is pure but what proceeds from the fountain of all purity" (*Comm.* Gal 5:22).

The world is *not* better than expected. Both Camillus and Catiline "are included under the universal condition of human depravity."[68] And yet there are differences. "We are not afraid, in common parlance, to call one a person of good character and another a rogue." We do not regard Camillus as equal to Catiline. But how can that be explained, since it is also true of Camillus that, as a natural human being, he was wicked and crooked?[69] Whence then the difference?

§ 3. *The explanation*

"The surest and easiest solution to the above question is that those endowments of Camillus are not common gifts of nature, but God's *special gifts of grace*, which he bestows variously and in a specific measure on people who are otherwise ungodly."[70]

1. *Grace.* "The Lord has bestowed a special grace on the one, while not deigning to bestow it on the other."[71] Calvin does not just use

---

65. *Inst.* III, xiv, 2.
66. Ibid. Cf. *Inst.* II, iii, 4.
67. *Inst.* III, xiv, 3.
68. *Inst.* II, iii, 4.
69. Ibid.
70. Ibid.
71. Ibid.

the word "grace" occasionally; he uses it in a general sense,[72] consciously[73] and continually. To following quotations from the *Institutes* will serve to demonstrate this:

"Paul, having pointed out that the blind can also feel their way toward God, adds immediately that one does not have to search far off [Acts 17:27], since all undoubtedly feel within themselves [in this passage Calvin discusses the person as a microcosm, J.D.] the heavenly *grace* that inspires them."[74] We" feel his power and grace in ourselves and in the great benefits he has conferred on us."[75] Although philosophers and human reason "subscribe to the words of Paul that in God we live and move and have our being [Acts 17:28], yet they are far removed from a sound understanding of the *grace* that he commends; for they do not at all taste God's special care [Calvin speaks here of God's providence that is special for each creature, J.D.], by which alone his Fatherly favor is truly known."[76] "In the law and the prophets God says on a number of occasions that as often as he waters the earth with dew and rain, he testifies to his *grace*."[77] "Although humans have been given the power to bring forth children, God wants it to be regarded as evidence of his special *grace* that he leaves some childless while he deems others worthy of offspring."[78] "By nature humans have an inborn understanding of reason and knowledge; yet, this good is but general in the sense that everyone must recognize in it a special *grace* of God. And the Creator of nature abundantly awakens thankfulness in us in that he creates persons who are challenged intellectually. In them he demonstrates the endowments in which the human soul would excel unpervaded by his light. That light is present as a natural light in all, in this sense that it is entirely a gift of *grace*, a gift of his benevolence toward each person individually."[79]

72. As grace shown to Gentiles; hence more general than God's demonstration of grace to the church.
73. By demarcating this grace from the grace that is conferred in regeneration. Cf. *Inst.* II, v, 15: "God's grace, as this word in understood in discussing regeneration." And II, ii, 6: "special grace, which only the elect receive through regeneration." See also *Comm.* Gen 4:20: "But, while we may admire the riches of his grace which he has bestowed on them [i.e., on the family of Cain], let us still value far more highly the grace of regeneration." See further *Lectures* Isa 44:3.
74. *Inst.* I, v, 3.
75. *Inst.* I, xiv, 22.
76. *Inst.* I, xvi, 1.
77. *Inst.* I, vii, 5.
78. *Inst.* I, xvi, 7.
79. *Inst.* II, ii, 14.

CHAPTER III. JOHN CALVIN

"Even though some are born as imbeciles or fools, that deficiency does not cloud God's general *grace*; on the contrary, by observing it, we are reminded that what was left to us is truly to be ascribed to God's indulgence. For if he had not spared us, the Fall would have dragged the ruin of the whole of human nature with it. Some excel in discernment, while others are superior in judgment, and yet others have a quicker understanding to learn this or that skill. In this diversity God shows us his *grace*, lest people should claim as their own what flows from the sheer bounty of God. For why does one person surpass another? Is it not to display in common nature God's special *grace*, which, in passing many by, declares itself bound to none?"[80]

Human nature is wholly corrupted and if "some people have ... excelled not only in outstanding deeds but have also conducted themselves honorably throughout their entire lives ... we should realize there is still some room for God's grace amid the corruption of nature, not such a *grace* as to cleanse it, but to restrain it inwardly. For if the Lord had given loose rein to the minds of all to run riot in their lusts, there would doubtless be no one who would not show that, in fact, every evil thing for which Paul condemns all nature is most truly to be met in him."[81] We should also not simply give free choice to people for those actions that are not in themselves righteous or sinful, but that pertain more to the physical life than the spiritual. For we know that "as often as we are prompted to choose something to our advantage, as often as the will inclines to this, or conversely as often as our mind and heart shun anything that would otherwise be harmful—this is of the Lord's special *grace*."[82]

Calvin's commentaries confirm that he did indeed not just sporadically characterize God's gifts to the Gentiles as "grace." Note the following instances (all to be found in H. Kuiper, *Calvin on Common Grace*):

The descendants of Cain excelled in the arts and sciences. "We admire what God has bestowed on them as riches of his *grace*" (*Comm.* Gen 4:20).

The uniform language before the confusion of tongues indicates "the special

---

80. *Inst.* II, ii, 17.
81. *Inst.* II, iii, 3.
82. *Inst.* II, iv, 6.

grace of God" for the maintenance of "the sacred bond of society among the people" (*Comm.* Gen 11:1).

Also the dispersion of the people, which had already occurred before the confusion of tongues, "ought not to be regarded as a punishment, since it rather flowed from the blessing and *grace* of God" (*Comm.* Gen 11:8).

"Fecundity is a special gift of God.... the *grace* of obtaining offspring was poured out over the entire human race" (*Comm.* Gen 25:21).

So also, "it is of God's special *grace* that some surpass others in eloquence" (*Comm.* Exod 4:11).

Moses' prayer after the rebellion of Korah, Dathan, and Abiram is a plea asking God to preserve his own work in creation. Moses does not mention the special grace with which God had embraced his people, but he speaks in a broader context of the "general *grace* of creation" (Num 16:22). Cf. *Comm.* Isa 44:3: "The prophet ... alludes to the universal *grace* which is spread over all creatures."

Even "honorable, serious, and moderate men," such as Aristides, "relying on their own virtue, despised the *grace* of God's with the arrogance of impiety" (*Comm.* Ps 86:2).

More than once, Psalm 104 says that God provides people with food. This repetition serves "to commend the grace received from God, who raises people with tenderness and generosity the way a very indulgent father raises his children" (*Comm.* Ps 104:15). Psalm 145:16 also attests to the "sheer *grace* and kindness" of God, who feeds all living creatures (*Comm.* Ps 145:16). On the same topic Calvin is able speak of God's "*grace* and of his fatherly love of the human race" (*Comm.* Ps 147:7).

The human race had to be protected from annihilation by powerful wild animals.

"This instance of *grace* the prophet commends the more on account of its necessity; ... in this is to be seen the unparalleled goodness of God, who in so fatherly a manner has provided for human well-being" (*Comm.* Ps 104:22).

Also Psalm 107 testifies more than once to the *grace* that God grants to believers and unbelievers when he saves them from various dangers (*Comm.* Ps 107:10, 17, 23, 39; cf. Pss 32, 139; and *Comm.* Ps 104:20). "Everything that we find profitable for the support of life [and is found among the nations] flows from the sheer *grace* of God" (*Comm.* Isa 3:2).

The restoration of Tyre "is rightly ascribed to God's *grace*," a grace demonstrated toward the wicked. Regarding wickedness the following is added: "Though the Lord is a severe judge toward the wicked, yet he leaves room for the exercise of his compassion" (*Comm.* Isa 23:17).

If there were no authorities, people's passions would have free and unbridled rein. "But God's *grace* shines forth in all governments" (*Lectures*, Dan 4:10).

Just as God led Israel out of Egypt, so also he led the Philistines out of Caphtor and the Syrians out of Kir. For all these nations this deliverance was grace: "All had been alike redeemed by the Lord, and this *grace* was common to all" (*Lectures*, Amos 9:7).

Although God revealed his special grace to Judah, "the signs of God's *grace* shone forth everywhere" (*Lectures*, Mal 1:2).

"What can they bring of their own, who, being destitute of all good things, owe everything to God's *gracious* beneficence? Indeed, they are nothing but by his mere *grace*" (*Comm.* Acts 17:25).

2. *Other indications.* Calvin also uses other terms to express what he describes above as "grace" [*gratia*]. Thus he speaks of God's goodness,[83] mercy,[84] love,[85] indulgence,[86] favor,[87] clemency,[88] blessing,[89] liberality,[90] benevolence,[91] graciousness,[92] and beneficence.[93] And the list is still incomplete. It is easy to verify from the "grace" quotations that Calvin does not at all limit the meaning of these terms with respect to "grace." And that will also show that Calvin does not regard grace as just "deed" and "gift," but also highlights it as God's gracious disposition.

It is unnecessary to quote from Calvin's commentaries on this point. All the above variants gathered from the *Institutes* can be found in H. Kuiper's dissertation *Calvin on Common Grace.* Calvin uses these variants indiscriminately also in his commentaries. See, for example, his explanations regarding "blessing" and "grace" in *Comm.* Gen 11:8; "grace" and "liberality" in *Comm.* Ps 145:16; "grace" and "love" in *Comm.* Ps 147:7; and "mercy" and "grace" in *Comm.* Isa 23:17.

3. *Grace also before the Fall and toward other creatures.* We have seen that Calvin uses the word grace in a broad sense. It is important to note that Calvin also used a yet broader application. Not only after the Fall, but also before God displayed his grace to (sinless) humankind. That is already implied in Calvin's exegesis of John 1:4, in which he calls life "a special grace of God that makes humans

---

83. *Inst.* I, ii, 1; I, v, 6; I, x, 1; I, xvi, 3.
84. *Inst.* I, ii, 1; I, v, 6. Cf. *Comm.* Rom 1:21.
85. *Inst.* I, v, 3.
86. *Inst.* II, ii, 17. Or also "gentleness," *Inst.* III, xx, 15.
87. *Inst.* I, xvi, 2; I, xvi, 5.
88. *Inst.* I, v, 8.
89. *Inst.* I, xvi, 8; III, 9, 3; III, ix, 3; III, xiv, 2; III, xxv, 9.
90. *Inst.* I, v, 4; II, ii, 17; III, xxv, 9.
91. *Inst.* II, ii, 18.
92. *Inst.* I, v, 7; I, v, 14; III, x, 2; IV, xx, 1. Also "favor," *Inst.* III, xx, 15.
93. *Inst.* I, v, 7; I, x, 1; II, ii, 14.

surpass the other living creatures."[94] And he says this clearly when he compares the current situation of humankind with that before the Fall: "For what remains then for human beings but that they, having been denuded and robbed of all glory, acknowledge God, for whose beneficence they were not able to give thanks when they overflowed with the riches of his grace?"[95] "Augustine is completely correct in teaching that ... the gifts of grace were withdrawn from humanity after the Fall."[96]

Calvin's use of the word "grace" here is well-considered. There is now "a chasm between our uncleanness and the God's perfect purity. But even if human beings had remained free of all stain, their original state, their condition would have been too lowly for them to reach God without a Mediator."[97] To be able to remain standing in the light of God's majesty—that was grace also in Paradise for weak (though sinless) humankind.[98]

In his commentary on Col 1:20, Calvin declares that according to Job 4:18 even the greatest purity among the angels is filthy compared to the righteousness of God. They also need the grace (of Christ): "And this beyond all doubt is what is meant by that statement in Job 4:18, 'He will find iniquity in his angels.' ... The Spirit declares there that the greatest purity is vile if it is brought into comparison with the righteousness of God. We must therefore conclude that there is not on the part of angels so much of righteousness as would suffice for their being fully joined with God. They therefore have need of a peacemaker through whose *grace* they may wholly cleave to God." Thus what we read in the *Institutes* about human beings before the Fall also applies to the angels.

The following passages show how broadly Calvin uses the word "grace." They speak of grace even toward animals and mountains:

"The prophet spoke in this manner for the purpose of magnifying the *grace* of God, because God considers brute beasts to be worthy of his care.... The wild animals enjoy some blessing of God" (*Comm.* Ps 104:11).

"The Prophet intimates that the mountains cannot remain standing in their own strength, except as far as they are supported beneath by the *grace* of God.... the world cannot for a moment remain standing, except as far as it is sustained by the *grace* and goodness of God" (*Lectures*, Nah 1:5).

---

94. *Inst.* I, xv, 4.
95. *Inst.* II, ii, 1.
96. *Inst.* II, ii, 16.
97. *Inst.* II, xii, 1.
98. About the weakness of human beings in Paradise, see *Inst.* I, xv, 8. And see also III, xii, 1: "[Job] sees that not even the holiness of angels can please God it he should weigh their works in his heavenly scales."

Two important conclusions can be drawn from what in the *Institutes* has had our attention up to this point: § 4. Calvin does recognize a general revelation, but § 5. He does not recognize a natural theology.

§ 4. Calvin does recognize a general revelation

1. *General revelation.* "God has implanted in all persons a certain awareness of his divinity, but he also constantly renews the memory of that awareness."[99] "He not only placed the seed of religion in human hearts but also revealed himself and daily discloses himself in the whole workmanship of the world, As a consequence people cannot open their eyes without being compelled to behold him."[100] "Nature and in particular the agile motions, the excellent faculties, and the rare gifts of the soul clearly display a divinity that does not readily allow itself to be hidden."[101] "This way of seeking God is common both to strangers and to those of his household, if they trace the outlines that above and below in nature sketch a living likeness of him."[102]

Also in his "works outside the ordinary course of nature ... God by open and daily indications declares his clemency to the pious and his severity to the impious and wicked."[103] In hopeless circumstances, such as those described in Ps 107, God "suddenly and wonderfully and beyond all hope" proclaims his "fatherly mercy."[104] We must "contemplate God in his works by which he renders himself near and familiar to us and, in a certain sense, communicates himself to us."[105] "The Lord does not want for testimony while he pleasantly attracts people to the knowledge of himself by his abundant and varied benevolence."[106] The evidence of the knowledge of God is "general."[107] "Isaiah rightly charges the worshipers of false gods with obtuseness because they failed to

---

99. *Inst.* I, iii, 1.
100. *Inst.* I, v, 1.
101. *Inst.* I, v, 4.
102. *Inst.* I, v, 6.
103. *Inst.* I, v, 7.
104. *Inst.* I, v, 8.
105. *Inst.* I, v, 9.
106. *Inst.* I, v, 14.
107. *Inst.* I, vi, 1.

learn from the foundations of the world and the circuit of the heavens who is the true God."[108] "God's inestimable wisdom, might, righteousness, and goodness shine forth in the composition of the universe."[109] Indeed, "the wisdom, might, and goodness of the Creator present themselves of their own accord and even force themselves on those who are unwilling" to take notice of them.[110]

The distribution of gifts is the work of "God's Spirit, the only source of truth"; therefore we may not disparage the Spirit's gifts, for then "we would disdain and revile the Spirit himself."[111] "The light of nature is present in all, but only in the sense that it is entirely a gift of grace of God's mercy to each person individually."[112] "God fills, moves, and invigorates everything by the power of his Spirit."[113]

"Although sinners try to evade their innate power to judge between good and evil, they are again and again dragged back to it."[114] "The Lord has not only engraved the distinction between honorable and wicked deeds in the minds of individuals but often confirms it also by the dispensation of his providence."[115]

Thus, in addition to God's special mode of communication that "enlightens the souls of the pious into the knowledge of God" (*special* revelation), there is also a general mode of communication that "is spread out over heaven and earth and all the creatures of the world" (*general* revelation).[116]

It should not escape the reader how topical, dynamic, and personal Calvin's view of general revelation is. God reveals himself *constantly, daily, suddenly, to each person individually, again and again,* etc. See above. This revelation thus does not at all amount to a certain law of nature. On the contrary, *general* revelation for Calvin always has a special character. If it is not posited this way, Calvin sees the threatening danger that God's grace and wrath in everyday life are ignored. The following passages are instructive:

"Suppose we grant that the beginning of motion rests on God's power, but that all things either by themselves or by chance, are borne whither inclination

---

108. *Inst.* I, xiv, 1.
109. *Inst.* I, xiv, 21.
110. *Inst.* I, xvi, 1.
111. *Inst.* II, ii, 15.
112. *Inst.* II, ii, 14.
113. *Inst.* II, ii, 16.
114. *Inst.* II, ii, 22.
115. *Inst.* III, xiv, 2.
116. *Inst.* II, x, 7.

CHAPTER III. JOHN CALVIN

of nature impels them. Then the alternation of days and nights and also of winter and summer will be God's work, insofar as he prescribed a fixed law for them by assigning to each its own role; that is, if the days that follow the nights, the months that follow the months, and the years that follow the years always maintain the same course in the same measure. But that sometimes intemperate heat combined with drought, scorches all crops, or that unseasonable rains destroy what has been sown, that sudden calamity results from hail and thunderstorms—this will not be God's work, unless, perhaps because clouds or weather, heat or cold, derive their origin from the conjunction of the stars and other natural causes. *But*," continues Calvin, "*in that way no room is left for God's fatherly favor, nor for his judgments.* If they say that God is beneficent enough to humankind because he gives heaven and earth an ordinary power to supply food, then that is a very weak and ungodly fabrication, as if the fruitfulness of the one year were not a special blessing of God, and scarcity and famine of the other year were not his curse and punishment.... As often as he moistens the earth with dew and rain, he testifies to his grace. And it is a sign of his undoubted and special vengeance when, by his command, the heavens become hard like iron, the grainfields consumed by blight and other disasters, as often as the fields are struck with hail and storms" (*Inst.* I, xvi, 5). "That is how God regulates every single thing by a *special providence*" (*Inst.* I, xvi, 1).

Calvin will speak of a general providence if one admits "that the universe is ruled by God not only because he watches over the order of nature set by himself, but also because he exercises special care over each of his works" (*Inst.* I, xvi, 4). Moreover, "it is childish to restrict [the special providence] to particular acts ... for not even one sparrow, which has no value, falls to the ground without the Father's will" (*Inst.* I, xvi, 5).

Only in this way is it understandable when Calvin writes that God "with open and daily indications displays his mercy to the pious and his severity to the impious and wicked" (*Inst.* I, v, 7). That is the "unfailing rule [*perpetuam regulam*]," but "it ought not to be obscured by the fact that frequently he lets the impious and wicked exult for some time with impunity, while he permits the upright and innocent to be afflicted and oppressed by much adversity" (*Inst.* I, v, 7). The latter must "arouse and raise us up to the hope of the future life" (*Inst.* I, v, 10).

Even though there may be deviations, for Calvin they clearly do not detract from the rule that he rephrases later: "All prosperity is a blessing of God, while disaster and adversity are a curse" (*Inst.* I, xvi, 8).

Calvin does recognize a general revelation of God. Those who deny this will not know what to do with Calvin's statements about human beings not having an excuse. They are inexcusable precisely because God clearly revealed himself to all!

2. *Why human beings do not have an excuse.* "On each of his works God has engraved unmistakable signs of his glory. They are so clear and prominent that even unlettered and stupid folk cannot plead the excuse of ignorance."[117] "Human ingratitude is totally deprived of defenses by the radiance that all can see in heaven and on earth."[118] "It is a scandalous ignorance not to cling to the one God."[119] "It may seem preposterous that the Gentiles should perish without any preceding judgment. That is why Paul speaks of the conscience of human beings that is as a law to them and that is sufficient for their just condemnation. Consequently, the result of the law of nature is that humans are rendered inexcusable."[120] "Human beings always gladly desire to evade God's judgment. But, although that judgment has not yet been revealed, so alarmed are they by the testimony of the law and of their conscience that already now they betray in themselves what they have deserved."[121]

3. *Inexcusable, even though human beings hardly know God.* It is true that general revelation compels[122] human beings, "whether they want to or not," to know God.[123] And even though this knowledge is smothered and corrupted, it is *just enough* to make them inexcusable: "When Paul (Rom 1:19) teaches that what is to be known about God is made plain from the creation of the universe, he does not identify a manifestation that can be understood by human perspicacity. Rather, he shows that it goes *no further* than to render them inexcusable."[124] "Because all without exception have been dragged or have slipped into false inventions by their own vanity, and because their perceptions so vanished, all that they naturally sensed about the only God has *no value* beyond making them inexcusable."[125] "The Lord did allow philosophers to sense *something* of his divinity, so that they could not hide their impiety under a cloak ignorance."[126] "Human hearts are permeated with the

---

117. *Inst.* I, v, 1.
118. *Inst.* I, vi, 1.
119. *Inst.* I, xii, 1.
120. *Inst.* II, ii, 22.
121. *Inst.* II, vii, 9. Cf. II, viii, 1.
122. *Inst.* I, iii, 2. See also I, iv, 4; I, v, 6; II, iii, 22.
123. *Inst.* I, iv, 2. Cf. I, iv, 4; I, v, 6.
124. *Inst.* I, v, 14.
125. *Inst.* I, x, 3.
126. *Inst.* II, ii, 18.

ability to distinguish just from unjust, solely so that they should not pretend ignorance as an excuse. Hence it is not at all a necessary consequence that truth should be discerned in individual instances. It is more than enough if their understanding extends so far that evasion becomes impossible for them and they, convicted by the testimony of their own conscience, begin even now to tremble before God's judgment seat."[127]

4. *General revelation is insufficient.* Unspiritual people hardly know God. They know enough to make them inexcusable. But their knowledge is insufficient truly to know God as Creator, and therefore certainly not as Redeemer.

We can contemplate God "in his works, by which he places himself in a close and intimate relationship with us and [then follows the restriction, J.D.] *in a certain sense* communicates himself to us."[128] "There is indeed more than enough to withdraw all support for human ingratitude, but it is still necessary that another and better help be added to direct us in the right manner to the Creator of the world himself. It was not in vain, then, that he added the light of his Word, so that thereby he might become known unto salvation. And he deemed worthy of this privilege those whom he wanted to gather more closely and more intimately to himself."[129] "Just as older people, or those with an ocular disease and all who have poor eyesight, even when a very fine book is placed in front of them, though they perceive that it contains writing, are barely able to make out two words, but, when they put on their glasses, begin to read distinctly, so Scripture gathers up the otherwise confused knowledge of God in our minds, disperses the darkness, and clearly shows us the true God."[130] "God not merely uses mute teachers but also opens his own hallowed mouth."[131] "God wanted to preserve this treasury of knowledge for his children, and therefore it is no wonder or absurdity that among the great mass of people we see such a great ignorance and obtuseness."[132]

---

127. *Inst.* II, ii, 24.
128. *Inst.* I, v, 9.
129. *Inst.* I, vi, 1. Cf. I, x, 1: "more intimately and also more vividly." See also I, xiv, 1.
130. *Inst.* I, vi, 1. The image of glasses also appears in I, xiv, 1.
131. *Inst.* I, vi, 1.
132. *Inst.* I, vii, 5.

Humans not only have bad eyesight. Calvin puts it even stronger: they have no eyes. In the knowledge of God and especially of his Fatherly favor toward us, on which our salvation depends, "the greatest geniuses are *blinder than moles*."[133] "They have never smelled the certainty of God's beneficence toward us."[134] Those who are unspiritual understand nothing of the spiritual mysteries of God. "Why is this? Is it because they neglect them out of slothfulness? No, for even though they do their best, they can do nothing, for those mysteries can only be discerned spiritually."[135] "Therefore we need the Spirit of sanctification. And that is not the Spirit that we observe working by a general power, both in the human race and in the other living creatures, but the Spirit who is the root and the seed of heavenly life in us."[136]

Let us therefore make this distinction, says Calvin: "God's revelation, whereby he makes his glory known in his creation, is sufficiently clear as regards his light. However, it is not adequate in the same measure when we take our blindness into account. But we are not so blind that we can plead our ignorance as an excuse for our perverseness. We understand that there is a Deity and we then conclude that, whoever he may be, he ought to be worshiped. But this is where our understanding fails, because it cannot ascertain who or what sort of being God is" (*Comm.* Rom 1, 20).

Calvin's example of needing glasses to read God's revelation in his creation has been criticized a number of times. W. Krusche agrees with S. P. Dee when he comments: "If we are completely blind, glasses will not help us!" (Krusche, op. cit., 78). That is true. But Calvin states clearly that we need eyes (*Inst.* II, ii, 21).

However, it is not the entire truth. For even without new eyes there is "a knowledge of God that is confused in our minds" (*Inst.* I, vi, 1).

We do *not* see with our old eyes. That is why we are blinder than moles in regard to the knowledge of God.

We *do* see with our old eyes. Hence we have no excuse.

Cf. also Calvin's commentary on I Cor 1:21: "For notwithstanding that God shows himself openly, it is only with the eye of faith that we can behold him" (with new eyes): "save only that we receive a slight perception of his divinity, sufficient to render us inexcusable" (with old eyes).

---

133. See text at footnote 46. Cf. *Inst.* II, ii, 21; "until he ... gives eyes"; III, I, 4: "in vain would light be given to the blind unless ...."
134. *Inst.* II, ii, 18.
135. *Inst.* II, ii, 20.
136. *Inst.* III, I, 2.

§ 5. No natural theology

General revelation, no matter how clear in itself, does not lead those who receive it to a pure knowledge of God, because of their corruption. Stated positively: ignorance and malice lead to such a smothered and corrupted knowledge of God[137] that only a caricature of the pure knowledge of God[138] remains. That cannot be called theo*logy*,[139] let alone *theo*logy: "If people were taught only by nature, they would hold to nothing certain or solid or clear-cut but would be so tied to *confused* principles as to worship an *unknown* God."[140]

"We would be able to speak only of a primal and simple knowledge of God as our Creator [the second is the knowledge of God as Redeemer, J.D.] as pure knowledge, if Adam had remained in the state of righteousness."[141] But after the Fall the light of "so many burning lamps" is maliciously extinguished and they burn "in vain."[142]

Anyone who wants more quotations should reread § 2. One of Calvin's images is worth repeating because it is particularly instructive, namely the image of lightning. God reveals himself (light!), but people are "like a traveler passing through a field at night who in a momentary lighting flash sees far and wide, but the sight vanishes so swiftly that he is plunged again into the darkness of the night before he can take even a step—let alone be directed on his way by its help."[143]

The light of lightning is not that of a lodestar.

1. The material collected in §§ 1–5 makes it possible for us to assess the Barth–Brunner controversy, insofar as it is connected to their respective interpretations of Calvin.

---

137. Heading of *Inst.* I, iv: "This knowledge is either smothered or corrupted, partly by ignorance, partly by malice."
138. Calvin gives the following definition of the knowledge of God (*Inst.* I, ii, 1): "Now, the knowledge of God, as I understand it, is that by which we not only conceive that there is a God but also grasp what befits us and is proper to his glory, in fine, what is to our advantage to know of him."
139. See text at footnote 130! What human beings know has the character of vagueness and confusion. This cannot be "logical" in the sense of being "orderly."
140. *Inst.* I, v, 12.
141. *Inst.* I, ii, 1.
142. *Inst.* I, v, iv.
143. See text at footnote 48. Cf. *Comm.* Eph 4, 17: "The power of perception [of the light of human reason] is such that it avails no more than blindness: before it achieves results it is gone."

CHAPTER III. JOHN CALVIN

In this controversy Barth was particularly concerned with denying a natural theology, whereas Brunner wanted to maintain the reality of creation revelation (E. Brunner, *Dogmatik* I, 136).

With respect to Barth, it is to be noted that he completely and correctly denied the existence of a natural theology in Calvin's writings. But in his dispute with Brunner, he in my opinion failed in two respects:

(a) In his *Nein!*, he did not deny, but also did not honor, the fact that Calvin does indeed teach a general revelation of God. Because he failed to state clearly that both are true—that there is a general revelation and no natural theology—all discussion of this question remains unclear.

(b) Barth gives too simple a depiction of Calvin's thoughts when he maintains: "The possibility of a real knowledge of the true God from Creation for natural man is, according to Calvin, a principial possibility, but not an actual one, not one to be realized by us—one could also say: an objective possibility, existing from God, but not a subjective one, accessible to man. Between what is in principle and what is actually possible inexorably stands the Fall. So this whole possibility can only hypothetically be spoken of: *si integer stetisset Adam* ['if Adam had remained upright'] (*Inst.* I, ii, 1)" (*Nein!*, 42).

Everything that Barth says here is true if Barth understands the *actual* knowledge of the true God to be the *pure* knowledge of God as defined by Calvin (see footnote 138). Then one can only say of the knowledge of the Gentiles that their "vague and erroneous opinion of the divine " is nothing but "ignorance of God" (*Inst.* I, 4, 3). But before God's tribunal all Gentiles will be addressed on the basis of their *actual* knowledge of God. "Even unlettered and stupid folk cannot plead the excuse of ignorance" (*Inst.* I, v, 1) We are blind by nature, "but we are not so blind that we can plead our ignorance as an excuse for our perverseness.... We are prevented by our blindness from achieving a correct insight. But we do see well enough that we cannot pretend any excuse" (*Comm.* Rom 1:20). It concerns *two* matters. Hence, he speaks of ignorance and knowledge, of blindness and of still-not-being-so-blind. *The "knowledge" of the Gentiles is ambiguous.* Quotation marks are needed here.

But that is why Barth's criticism of Brunner is wide of the mark when the latter writes that human beings "in a certain sense" know God's will. Quite properly, Brunner says that this "in a certain sense" is "thoroughly appropriate in its vagueness." Cf. Brunner, *Natur und Gnade*, 12, 45–46, 56; Barth, *Nein!*, 17–18, 42. It is regrettable that W. Krusche's criticism of Brunner's "in a certain sense" is also not sufficiently nuanced (op. cit., 71–72).

With respect to Brunner, our criticism goes deeper. Brunner did see correctly that general revelation and natural theology are two different things. Further, it is to be appreciated that, following Barth's criticism, he dropped "natural theology" as a valid term (*Natur und Gnade*, V, 50; *Dogmatik* I, 136). However:

(a) If only Brunner had left the "in a certain sense" (*quodammodo*) in Calvin indeterminate! In connection with Calvin's remarks about the remnant of the image of God after the Fall, Brunner writes: "On this remnant of the *Imago Dei* Calvin lays great weight. One can say that it is virtually one of the bearing columns of his theology. For with it he identifies no less than the whole of humanity, rational nature, the immortal soul, cultural capacity, the conscience, accountability, the relationship with God also available in sin (even when it is not salvific), all of cultural life. And on this he builds essential pieces of his ethics" (*Natur und Gnade*, 28). Yes, "at first glance Calvin seems to have an ethics—one could say a pure ethics of humanity—built up entirely on the idea of the *imago* that is still present also in sinful human beings." And although there is no indication of a "pure ethics of humanity" in Calvin, nonetheless Brunner assigns an important place to a natural ethics in Calvin's theology: "The correct natural ethics is thus *perfected* ... only in Christ" (op. cit., 29, 30; emphasis supplied).

I am unable to share this opinion. For all discussion about a correct natural ethics in Calvin is a pure abstraction. For it abstracts all positive sounds (see § 1) from the always accompanying negative sounds: "but ..." (see § 2). Remnants of the image of God? Indeed. "But Calvin leaves no doubt about it that these remnants are not something like the result of a process of subtraction: *imago* minus sin equals the remnant of the *imago*. Also these remnants are horribly disfigured; they are wretched ruins (at any rate, to build on them is an extremely dubious enterprise). To describe these disfigured remnants as preserved remainders of the 'formal *imago*' and, with regard to these, to speak of the 'power of revelation,' 'receptiveness to the Word,' or 'responsiveness' [as Brunner does, J.D.] did not in any case cross Calvin's mind," states W. Krusche (op. cit., 63), citing *Inst*. I, xv, 4: "God's image was not totally annihilated and destroyed in him, yet it was so corrupted that whatever remains is frightful deformity." And also: "[the image of God] was "so vitiated and almost blotted out that nothing remains after the ruin except what is confused, mutilated, and disease-ridden." How is it possible to expect an ethics from Calvin that is built on these heaps of rubbish and only needs completion in Christ?

Calvin's positive statements about the Gentiles ("in a certain sense," *quodammodo*) serve to deprive them of all protestations of innocence, while the negative statements prevent us (or at least ought to prevent us) from looking in Calvin's *oeuvre* for the development of a natural religion or ethics. In this respect Barth's criticism found its mark when he reproved Brunner's abstraction and systematics (*Nein!*, 22, 39, 42–43, 44–45).

When Calvin in his works constantly points to the natural order, natural law, saying that "nature teaches," he always incorporates this and subsumes it under the wisdom that speaks from Scripture. It cannot operate independently or foundationally, but only affirmatively and illustratively. August Lang already saw this very clearly in his study *The Reformation and Natural Law*. This study has its flaws, as J. Bohatec has rightly pointed out in his *Calvin und das Recht*. But Lang clearly formulated the essence of the matter: In his *Institutes* Calvin never deviates from his method "based upon Scripture and the *analogia fidei*, or in this case also upon the revealed moral law *confirmed* by natural *aequalitas*. This method he does not sacrifice at a single point for the benefit of a general ratiocination, certainly not for natural law theories of any description" (71). Those searching for Calvin's ethics must read *Inst.* III, vi ff., about the Christian life, in which he presents only what it says in Holy Scripture. See also P. Barth, *Das Problem der natürlichen Theologie bei Calvin*, 38ff.

One must also not, as Brunner does, consider that which those who are unspiritual know "of God, of law, and their own suitability for God [*Gottgehörigkeit*]," to be a starting-point for divine grace (*Natur und Gnade*, 20). For if according to Calvin this "knowledge of God ... is nothing but a frightful source of idolatry and of all superstitions" (*Comm.* John 3:6), it is difficult to maintain that God's grace in Christ is connected to it. Here, too, Barth is correct when he does not want to speak of a connection, but of repulsion (*Nein!*, 43–44). As soon as we evaluate the knowledge of God among the Gentiles independently (i.e., apart from its function before God's tribunal to declare the Gentiles guilty) and then appreciate it, we interpret Calvin incorrectly. John writes that the light shines in the darkness, but this expression "is not at all intended for the commendation of depraved nature, but rather for taking away every excuse for ignorance" (*Comm.* John 1:5).

(b) Although Brunner rightly devotes himself to maintaining God's general revelation, I can agree with only part of what he means by that. For Brunner treats this revelation especially as a matter of human capabilities, of regulations and creation structures (*Natur und Gnade*, especially pp. 30ff.). He presents revelation as *static*, while Calvin, as we have seen, very clearly depicts it as *dynamic and actual*.

In addition, Brunner assigns no place to *God's wrath* in his general revelation. But the two are connected. Those who let general revelation be a matter of capabilities and structures fail to see God's concrete blessings and punishments, which are the overt and daily distinguishing marks of God's revelation.

Therefore, Brunner's term "*Schöpfungsoffenbarung*" [revelation in creation] is not really appropriate. See, e.g., *Dogmatik* I, 136. At least, this term is much too abstract and too general to apply to Calvin's lively and dynamic treatment of general revelation (which is always so "extraordinary").

See further § 8, *infra*, about God's wrath in general revelation.

2. The above will make it clear that I can also not adopt G. Th. Rothuizen's *Tweeërlei ethiek bij Calvijn?* According to Rothuizen, Calvin wanted to dissociate himself from secular ethics, but he also wanted to retain it (9). But I wonder how he can maintain that Calvin accepted a secular ethics beside a Christian ethics. It is not Calvin who is speaking here, but Rothuizen, who believes that Calvin supports his ideas of secularization and accountability (16). But one may well ask what would Calvin say about the following sentence: "Also when this accountability *coram hominibus* [before the face of humankind] is not at all the equivalent of an accountability *coram Deo* [before the face of God], we

CHAPTER III. JOHN CALVIN

may never play off a deficiency [! J.D.] in the latter against an excess in the former" (16). My response is a quotation from W. Krusche in which he discusses the sciences in Calvin but which can *mutatis mutandis* apply to everything that Rothuizen means by accountability: " Science is good per se, but where it wants to be per se, i.e., where it is not only handmaid but rather mistress, where it thus wants to be an end in itself and not only a serviceable end (preservation of life unto salvation), it is a perishable impediment. Therefore science is to be considered vain and void until it has completely submitted to the Word and the Spirit of God.... *Scientia* without *religio* (and *religio* is the fear of God and a high regard for his *Word*!) or, to be precise, without the knowledge of God, it more an empty semblance of science [*inanis scientiae opinio*] than true science" (op. cit., 106–07). Krusche points to Calvin's commentary on 2 Cor 3:19: "The liberal arts, and all the sciences by which wisdom is acquired, are gifts of God. They are confined, however, within their own limits; for into God's heavenly kingdom they cannot penetrate." Accountability within their boundaries? No, for note the following: "Hence they must occupy the place of handmaid, not of mistress; or rather, they must be looked upon as empty and worthless, until they have become entirely subject to the Word and Spirit of God. If, on the other hand, they set themselves in opposition to Christ, they must be looked upon as dangerous pests" (agreed, Rothuizen would say, but then:) "and, if they strive to accomplish anything of themselves, as the worst of all hindrances" (359–60). Calvin does indeed know of the distinction that is dear to Rothuizen: *coram Deo* and *coram hominibus* (*Tweeërlei ethiek*, 11, 16, 26, note 105). But one would have to look long and hard in Calvin for an *accountability* before the face of God [*coram hominibus*]. I have already referred to Calvin's interpretation of 1 Cor 1:19. But it is important to refer also to his interpretation of 1 Cor 1:20, particularly because Rothuizen works with this passage himself. Rothuizen quotes it (26, note 105). But only partly! He quotes the passage in which Calvin says that Paul does not simply condemn "either natural human perspicacity, or wisdom acquired from practice and experience, or cultivation of mind attained by learning," but does declare of all this that it has no value "for acquiring spiritual wisdom." But Calvin says more: "In *general* it *also* holds true that without Christ sciences in every department are vain, and that those who do not know God are vain, though they may be conversant with every branch of learning. *Rather*, we may affirm this, *too*, that these choice gifts of God—expertness of mind, acuteness of judgment, liberal sciences, and acquaintance with languages—are in a certain way profaned *in every instance in which they fall to the lot of wicked people*." For Calvin, to be "profaned" means something other than to become accountable. It is surely impossible to derive from such explanations that the "theocratic deficiency encountered by Calvin [! J.D.] ... does not always" appear to be "the same as an anthropological flaw" (op. cit., 11). Is it not an anthropological flaw when people do not know and acknowledge their God?

Who recognizes Calvin in what Rothuizen says in the following passage? There he states concerning the doctrine of the *corruptio totalis*: "One must look at this in a nuanced way, if only because that is what Calvin did, for human dejection at the foot of the cross, thus *coram Deo*, does not necessarily have to lead to a pessimistic view of life on their—also moral—achievements in general" (16). Here call to mind my remarks in § 2 and Calvin's commentary on Gal 5:22. Rothuizen knows also that in commenting on this Scripture passage Calvin calls the virtues of Gentiles deceptive masks. But he misrepresents Calvin's devastating sentence where he writes: "but this applies explicitly *apud Deum* [in the sight of God], and not *civili aestimatione* [in the appraisal of civil society]" (op. cit., note 105). For the criterion of civil righteousness is not sound: "but it was only in the sight of human beings and only in the appraisal of civil society [*civili aestimatione*] that they were so distinguished. In the sight of God [*apud Deum*] nothing is pure but what proceeds from the fountain of all purity"(*Comm.* Gal 5:22). *Apud Deum*? Yes, and that is why it is repeated by Calvin. For if in the sight of God [*apud Deum*] virtues lose all favor, "anything in ungodly people that appears praiseworthy must be considered worthless" (*Inst.* II, 3, 4). How can one really suggest that Calvin does *not* think pessimistically about a world without God? Cf. § 2, 2, about *semblance*.

Rothuizen has missed the depth of Calvin's assessment of total corruption. Unintentionally he provides evidence of this when he quotes the following passage from Calvin and translates it in part. Calvin says: "It is a diabolical science ... which fixes our contemplation on the works of nature and turns it away from God" (*Comm.* Ps 29:5). In Rothuizen's translation this science is described as retaining "*something* that is diabolical" (9 and note 81; italics supplied).

§ 6. Why is grace shown toward Gentiles?

We must now seek an answer to the question why God, according to Calvin, displays grace[144] to Gentiles. For this we point to the following motifs.

1. *Invitation*. "All human beings are born and live to the end that they may know God."[145] "It is beyond dispute that they were created for the contemplation of heavenly life."[146] "Lest anyone be excluded from access to happiness, God not only sowed the seed of religion in human minds, but he also revealed himself and daily discloses himself in the whole workmanship of the universe."[147] "He would

---

144. "Grace" is here taken to include all indications of God's display of grace, as mentioned in § 3, 2.
145. *Inst.* I, iii, 3.
146. *Inst.* I, xv, 6.
147. *Inst.* I, v, 1.

have us look unto him."[148] "We are *invited* to come to know him."[149] To put it even stronger: By God's virtues (shown in his creation) "the entire human race is *invited* and *enticed* to knowledge of him, and through this to true and complete happiness."[150] "By many and varied kindnesses he sweetly attracts people to knowledge of himself."[151] God is not "in conflict with himself when he universally invites all human beings to him" (Calvin says this in the section that deals with election!).[152]

Calvin lets this invitation motif come into view very clearly by speaking about God as the Father of humankind. "Secular poets ... called him the Father of the human race [Acts 17:28]. Indeed, none give themselves freely and willingly to God's service unless, having tasted his fatherly love, they are drawn to love and worship him in return."[153]

The invitation motif appears also in Calvin's commentaries. A telling example is this: "Although by that small measure of light [of understanding[that still remains in us, the Son of God has always invited human beings to himself, yet the Evangelist says that this was attended by no advantage, because seeing they did not see" (*Comm.* John 1:5). "Even God's punishments over the world are restrained, and in them God demonstrates that he invites people to repent" (*Lectures*, Hos 5:9).

In the commentaries we also often find references to God's Fatherhood in a general sense. See, e.g., *Lectures* Jer. 2:3: "For he is the Creator of all: thereupon he showed himself to all as Father and Provider of nourishment." See also *Lectures*, Amos 3:1. About Acts 14:17, Calvin writes: "Yet the fatherly love of God breaks through even to the unworthy. Especially the generality of humankind testifies that the benefits of God never cease, in which he appears to us as our Father." And about Acts 17:26: "They have all one Maker and Father, who must be sought of all with one consent."

2. *Critical motif.* According to Calvin, what is revealed in Rom 1:19 cannot be understood by human discernment. On the contrary, Paul "shows that it goes no further than render them inexcusable."[154] God extends grace *with the goal* of making humans inexcusable.

148. *Inst.*, I, v, 6.
149. *Inst.* I, v, 9.
150. *Inst.* I, v, 10.
151. *Inst.* I, v, 14.
152. *Inst.* III, xxii, 10.
153. *Inst.* I, v, 3. See also I, v, 8: "proofs ... of fatherly kindness"; I, xvii, 1: "fatherly favor and beneficence." And further I, xvi, 5, and II, vi, 1.
154. See text at footnote 124.

We may call this second motif the *critical motif*: human beings receive grace for their judgment (crisis). *In order that* no one can take refuge in the pretense of ignorance, God has implanted in all people a certain understanding of his divinity. Ever renewing its memory, he repeatedly provides new impressions, *so that* all without exception will see that there is a God and that he is their Creator. Hence they will be judged by their own testimony."[155] To what end is knowledge of the law given to people? "The purpose of natural law is to render people inexcusable." Natural law is "an insight of conscience depriving people of the excuse of ignorance."[156] To put it more strongly: Their "hearts are permeated with the ability to distinguish between just and unjust only *for this purpose*, that they would not pretend ignorance as an excuse."[157] Even the wicked share in the gift of Matt 5:45 ("the sun rises on the evil and on the good") "*to render* them all the more inexcusable. The wicked often experience God's kindness by remarkable proofs so as sometimes to obscure all the blessings of the pious, yet these lead to their great damnation."[158]

H. Kuiper's dissertation demonstrates clearly that the critical motif is also mentioned very frequently in Calvin's exegetical works (208–09). Calvin uses strong expressions in this context. Thus, in reference to Ps 17:14: "As [the godless] are not among the number of the children of God ... it follows that when they are ... fattened, it is for the day of slaughter ... since they have so long abused his indulgence." See also *Comm.* Deut 28:12, and *Comm.* Acts 12:20.

The extent to which the first and second motifs are interwoven in Calvin is apparent from the following:

God invites both the elect and the reprobate "to come to repentance, and by his invitation he makes the latter inexcusable" (*Comm.* Gen 6:13). God "also condescends to bless even the reprobate, in order to invite them kindly and to entice them to repent and thereby to make them the more inexcusable" (*Comm.* Gen 39:1, about Potiphar).

To King Sihon and his people God shows that he "stimulates the reprobate to repent and invites them to the hope of salvation for no other reason than that they, by the unmasking of their godlessness, may be rendered inexcusable" (*Comm.* Num 21:21).

The invitation is the means whereby the critical motif can be realized.

155. *Inst.* I, iii, 1.
156. *Inst.* II, ii, 22.
157. *Inst.* II, ii, 24.
158. *Inst.* III, xxv, 9.

However, it is important to note that the invitation, as Calvin speaks of it, must be taken seriously, i.e., it must be maintained as *independent motif* when one quotes Calvin. For the invitation to all people remains a well-meant offer (as is evident from the above passages quoted from the commentaries), even though, in addition to the invitation, mention is made of reprobation and the use of the invitation as means to make people inexcusable.

Apart from the other motifs that will be discussed below, the following quotation is too strong in stating that "all assertions about the meaning of God's general revelation" end up at "the one intention ... to make mankind inexcusable" (W. Krusche, op. cit., 84). Calvin's discussion of general revelation is more varied than that. In fact, this becomes apparent in Krusche's work a bit later (84–85, 88, 104).

3. *Restraint*. God's indulgence has left us much after the Fall. "For if he had not spared us, the Fall would have caused the ruin of all of nature."[159] "There is still some room for God's grace amid the corruption of nature, not such a grace as to cleanse it, but to *restrain it* inwardly. For if the Lord had given loose rein to the minds of all to run riot in their lusts, there would doubtless be no one who would not show that, in fact, every evil thing for which Paul condemns all nature is most truly to be met in him."[160] "God heals these illnesses in his elect; he *restrains* them in others and keeps them in check only so that they may not break loose, inasmuch as he foresees their control to be expedient to preserve all that is.[161] "Thus by his providence God *bridles* the perversity of nature, that it may not break forth into action. But he does not cleanse it within."[162]

This shows that the restraint serves the preservation of the totality of all things. Calvin says this more often. People are "God's instruments for the preservation of human society in righteousness, continence, friendship, temperance, fortitude, and prudence."[163] Also to be mentioned in this context are the magistrates: "We see that they are ordained protectors and vindicators of public innocence, morality, virtue, and tranquillity, and that their sole endeavor should be to provide for the common safety and peace of all."[164] "The magistrate's office is a very precious

---

159. *Inst.* II, ii, 17.
160. See text at footnote 81.
161. *Inst.* II, iii, 3.
162. Ibid. For restraint, see also II, vii, 10, and II, vii, 11.
163. *Inst.* III, xiv, 3.
164. *Inst.* IV, xx, 9.

gift of God's beneficence for the preservation of society's well-being."[165] "Those who would rob people of the resources of government, rob them of their very humanity."[166] "Some form of organization is necessary in all human society to foster communal peace and maintain concord. And in all kinds of transactions some procedure is always in effect, which is to be respected in the interests of public decency, and even of humanity itself."[167] "Barbaric and crude laws such as gave honor to thieves, permitted promiscuous intercourse, as well as others more scandalous and absurd, are not to be regarded as laws, for they are abhorrent not only to all justice, but also to all humanity and gentleness."[168]

Restraint therefore makes *human* society possible.

Under this motif of restraint one can classify all that Calvin says in general about God's gifts for the *well-being* of humanity (Kuiper, op. cit., 206) and also what he mentions concerning God's gifts of grace in the arts and sciences in terms of their *usefulness* to humanity. See Krusche, 104: "Science has nothing to do with salvation, but rather with well-being.... Where this limited purpose is forgotten, there science becomes superstition and art idolatry."

4. *Help for the church.* The revelation of God's grace outside of the church also serves to benefit Christians. "If the Lord wants *us* to be helped by the effort and service of the godless in the natural sciences, logic, mathematics, and other like disciplines, we ought to make use of them, so that, when we neglect God's gifts that are offered to us by specialists in those fields, we are not rightly punished for our sluggishness."[169] "God demonstrates that the entire human race is an object of his care, but *principally* he watches over the government of the church, which he deems worthy of his special regard."[170] "God chose the church as his dwelling, and thus it cannot be doubted that he shows by singular proofs his fatherly care in ruling it."[171] "Thus it is his care to govern all creatures for their own good and safety."[172] "God's servant ... will thus reason in

165. *Inst.* IV, xx, 25.
166. *Inst.* IV, xx, 2.
167. *Inst.* IV, x, 27.
168. *Inst.* IV, xx, 15.
169. *Inst.* II, ii, 16.
170. *Inst.* I, xvii, 1.
171. *Inst.* I, xvii, 6.
172. *Inst.* I, xvii, 7.

his mind: surely it is the Lord who has inclined their hearts to me and has bound them to me so that they may be instruments of his kindness toward me."[173]

That is why it is so understandable that in Calvin's view civil government "does not exist "merely to see to it ... that people may breathe, eat, drink, and be kept warm (although it surely embraces all these activities when it provides for their living together) ... but also that idolatry, sacrilege against God's name, blasphemies against his truth, and other public offenses against religion may be prevented from arising and spreading among the people; that the public may not be disturbed; that people may keep their possessions safe and sound; that in their transactions with each other they may be unharmed; and that virtue and modesty may continue to be respected among them—in short, that *a public manifestation of religion* may exist among Christians, and that humanity may be maintained among people."[174] Religion and humanity go together.

"It is a Jewish vanity to seek and enclose Christ's kingdom within the elements of this world,"[175] but we must also "know that they are not at variance." For this kingdom "is indeed already initiating in us upon earth beginnings of the heavenly kingdom, and in this mortal and transitory life affords a certain forecast of an immortal and imperishable blessedness. Yet civil government has the task, so long as we live in society, to *support and protect the outward worship of God*, to defend the sound doctrine of piety and the position of the church, to adjust our life for human society, to shape our social behavior for civil justice, to bring us together, and to promote general peace and tranquillity."[176]

We are pilgrims and have not yet reached our true country. Until we do, we still need resources (government, etc.). That is why "those who rob people of these resources deprive them of their humanity."[177]

---

173. Ibid.
174. *Inst.* IV, xx, 3.
175. *Inst.* IV, xx, 1.
176. *Inst.* IV, xx, 2.
177. Ibid.

"In the whole arrangement of the world, the object which God had in view was to provide for his elect people: for, although his bounty extended to all, still he had such regard for his own, that, chiefly on their account, his care also extended to others" (*Comm.* Deut 32:7). King Cyrus receives his conquests "for the sake of the church" (*Comm.* Isa 45:5). "God so highly values the well-being of the church since he not only prefers it to the whole world, but even shows that the stability of the world depends upon it" (*Comm.* Isa 51:16). "God created all things for the sake of those who are his, since he exercises a special care over them" (*Comm.* Isa 60:19). And see also *Comm.* 1 Tim 4:3: "Strictly speaking, God has appointed to his children alone the whole world and all that is in the world."

§ 7. Grace to the reprobate within the church

Thus far we have been concerned with Calvin's depiction of the grace that God (also) displays to the Gentiles. But in addition, Calvin demands our attention for God's display of grace within the (sphere of influence of the) church toward those who are not elect. Both operations (toward the Gentiles and the unbelievers) have in common that they do not lead to salvation.

1. *Well-meant offer.* "The generous favor that God denied others shone in the adoption of Abraham's line."[178] But where God "invites a particular people to himself, a special mode of election is employed for a part of them, so that he does not with indiscriminate grace effectually elect all."[179] There is also an "external change, without the operation of inner grace, which might have availed to keep them in the covenant, something that is intermediate between the rejection of the human race and the election of a small number of the godly."[180] This intermediate state is due to God's *"general election,"*[181] which is distinguishable from the particular election to salvation. In this situation he still displays grace to the reprobate. "God illumines their minds enough for them to recognize his grace."[182] "He illumines wicked persons with some rays of his grace."[183] His "outward call," which they hear but do

---

178. *Inst.* III, xxi, 7.
179. Ibid.
180. Ibid.
181. Ibid.
182. *Inst.* III, ii, 11.
183. *Inst.* III, ii, 12.

not obey, "is rightly considered evidence of God's grace, by which he reconciles people to himself."[184]

In using the word "rightly" Calvin is entirely serious, and that is why he says more than once that God does not treat people deceitfully. Although God reveals to these reprobate only his immediate grace[185] and they receive a light that is later quenched,[186] yet "the Spirit is not deceitful when he does not give life to the seed that he sows in their hearts to keep it ever incorruptible as in the elect."[187] "When the Lord invites people by his promises, not only so that they will receive the fruits of his beneficence, but also so that they will reflect on it, he also displays his love at the same time. Therefore we must again confirm that every promise is a declaration of God's love for us."[188] "And although experience teaches that it is his will for those whom he calls to him that he does not touch the hearts of all, yet one may not therefore say that he acts deceitfully."[189] The hypocrites discredit his kind invitation.[190] "God's mercy is offered to both the godly and the wicked. The wicked cannot claim that they lack a refuge to which they can retreat from the bondage of sin, inasmuch as they out of their own ungratefulness reject it when offered."[191]

Calvin makes that very clear when he discusses the offer of God's grace in the sacraments. It is incorrect to maintain, he says, "that the sacraments are not testimonies of God's grace because they are also offered to the wicked.... For by the same argument, because the gospel is heard but rejected by many, and Christ was seen and recognized by many but very few accepted him, neither gospel nor Christ would be a testimony of God's grace."[192] "It is ... certain that the Lord offers us mercy and the pledge of his grace both in his Sacred Word and in his sacraments. But it is understood only by those who take Word and sacraments with sure faith, just as Christ is offered and held forth by the Father to all unto salvation, yet

---

184. *Inst.* III, xxiv, 15.
185. *Inst.* III, ii, 11.
186. See text at footnote 183.
187. *Inst.* III, ii, 12.
188. *Inst.* III, ii, 32.
189. *Inst.* III, xxiv, 15.
190. *Inst.* III, xx, 13.
191. *Inst.* III, xxiv, 17.
192. *Inst.* IV, xiv, 7.

not all acknowledge and receive him."[193] "Yet it is one thing to be offered, another to be received."[194] "God wants his truthfulness to be acknowledged, not in the reception itself but in the constancy of his goodness, in that he is prepared to give to the unworthy what they reject, indeed, offers it freely. This is the *integrity of the sacrament*, which the whole world cannot violate: that the flesh and blood of Christ are no less truly given to the unworthy as to God's elect believers. But at the same time it is true that, just as rain falling on a hard rock flows away because it has no opportunity to penetrate it, so also the godless by their hardness of heart repel God's grace so that it does not penetrate them."[195]

2. *This grace makes the godless inexcusable*. Obviously what was presented in §§ 4, 2, and 6, 2, with regard to what Calvin taught about the inexcusability of the Gentiles, returns here with emphasis. God's display of grace is deeper in the church and therefore the responsibility of its members is the greater. The godless may taste something of the heavenly gifts and a temporary faith "so that they will be the more convinced of their guilt and the less excusable."[196] "They are plied with the great and repeated benefits of God's generosity and therefore bring a correspondingly heavier judgment on themselves."[197] "The haughtiness of those who impudently kick against the goads will be the more seriously condemned."[198] "A heavier judgment remains on the wicked because they reject the testimony of God's love."[199] "Their transgression is doubled because they do not respond to God's great kindness and goodness."[200]

3. *This grace is insufficient inasmuch as it is not efficacious*. Also § 4, 4, is again relevant here. Just as a different and better resource than the contemplation of God's works is necessary to make God known as Creator and Redeemer, so also grace poured out within the sphere

---

193. Ibid.
194. *Inst.* IV, xvii, 33.
195. Ibid. For the integrity of the sacraments, see to C. Veenhof, *De volkomenheid der sacramenten*.
196. *Inst.* III, ii, 11.
197. *Inst.* III, ii, 32.
198. *Inst.* III, iii, 25.
199. *Inst.* III, xxiv, 2.
200. *Inst.* III, xxiv, 15.

of the church leads to salvation only when it is efficacious and penetrates and transforms the heart. Without the inner efficacy of grace, the godless will not remain in the covenant.[201] The opinion that the doctrine of salvation is presented to all so that it will be effective for their benefit is false.[202] "The proclamation of the gospel does spring from the well of election, but because such proclamation is shared also with the reprobate, it cannot of itself be reliable evidence of election. But God efficaciously instructs his elect in order to lead them to faith."[203] Of the pious and impious "only the former experience the efficaciousness of the gospel, while the latter receive no profit from it."[204] The wicked "can recognize God's grace, but God so distinguishes that awareness from the special testimony he gives to his elect that they do not attain the full effect and fruition thereof."[205] "God does not convert the obstinate, because he does not manifest that more powerful grace, which is not lacking if he should please to offer it."[206]

4. *Why this grace?* A few motifs from § 6 are relevant here too—especially the invitation and critical motifs. We do not need further citations since they can be found under points 1 and 2 of that section. However, the emphases are stronger here. The invitation is richer. The addressees are invited to the salvation of God in Jesus Christ. The judgment is heavier. Their rejection of his invitation gives God the more reason for their condemnation.

The restraining motif is also present. Relevant in this respect is Calvin's explanation of the second[207] use of the law: "at least by fear of punishment to restrain certain persons who are untouched by any care for what is just and right unless compelled by hearing the dire threats of the law. They are restrained not because their inner mind is stirred or affected, but because, being bridled, so to speak, they keep their hands from outward activity and hold inside the

---

201. See text at footnote 180.
202. *Inst.* III, xxii, 10.
203. *Inst.* III, xxiv, 1.
204. *Inst.* III, xxiv, 17.
205. *Inst.* III, ii, 11.
206. *Inst.* III, xxiii, 1.
207. The first use of the law, according to Calvin, is that it "warns, informs, convicts, and lastly condemns all people of their own unrighteousness" (*Inst.* II, vii, 6). "This first function of the law is exercised also in the reprobate" (*Inst.* II, vii, 9).

depravity that they would otherwise brazenly have indulged in.... This constrained and forced righteousness is necessary for human society."[208] The operation of this motif is stronger than that stated in § 6, 3. Those who are unspiritual do have the inward law engraved upon their hearts, but they are "so shrouded in the darkness of errors that they hardly begin to grasp through this natural law what worship is acceptable to God.... Accordingly the Lord has provided us with a *written law* to give us a clearer witness of what was too obscure in the natural law, shake off our listlessness, and strike more vigorously our mind and memory."[209]

Obviously the fourth motif (help for the church) is not relevant in this context.

"A gracious invitation to salvation was first in order ... because vengeance was ripe after grace had been rejected" (*Comm.* 2 Thess 2:6). With these words Calvin succinctly expresses what we constantly find in his commentaries. God's grace is offered to all by the proclamation of the gospel, and in that way people's godlessness becomes the more apparent. ("I seem ... to hear Paul discoursing as to the universal call of the Gentiles—that the grace of God must be offered to all—that Christ must enlighten the whole world by his gospel, in order that the impiety of humankind might be the more fully attested and demonstrated" (*Comm.* 2 Thess 2:6). Eternal salvation was offered to all the descendants of Abraham, "for the promise by which the Lord had adopted them all as children was common to all; and it cannot be denied that in that promise eternal salvation was offered to all.... All without exception are in this respects accounted children; the name of the church is jointly applicable to them all; but in the innermost sanctuary of God no others are reckoned the sons of God than they in whom the promise is ratified by faith" (*Comm.* Gen 17:7). See also *Comm.* Gen 25:23: "God embraced, by the grace of his adoption, all the sons of Abraham, because he made a covenant with all; and it was not in vain that he appointed the promise of salvation to be offered promiscuously to all.... God therefore chose the whole seed of Jacob without exception ... because he has conferred on all alike the same testimonies of his grace, namely, in the Word and sacraments. But another and peculiar election has always flourished...." And see further, for example, *Lectures,* Jer 7:12; *Lectures,* Ezek 2:4; *Lectures* Ezek 16:61; *Lectures,* Ezek 18:23; *Lectures,* Hos 9:7; *Lectures,* Am 5:4; *Comm.* Rom 1:16; *Comm.* Rom 5:18; *Comm.* Rom 9:6; *Comm.* Heb 6:4.

The invitation, the offer of grace to all the descendants of Abraham, is a well-meant offer. What the *Institutes* already taught us is confirmed by the commentaries. "God attempted to draw the Jews to himself by mild and gentle

208. *Inst.* II, vii, 10.
209. *Inst.* II, viii, 1.

methods..... [They] treated with disdain invitations so gentle and proceeding from more than maternal kindness. It is an amazing and unparalleled instance of love that he did not disdain to stoop to blandishments by which he might tame rebels into subjection" (*Comm.* Matt 23:37).

It is remarkable how carefully Calvin chooses his words to express the divine emotion: "So often and so kindly we are invited" (*Lectures*, Isa 42:24). Those who despise God in this, show contempt for "so great a benevolence" (*Lectures*, Ezek 2:4). That is why God cannot tolerate the unthankfulness of his people: "As the Lord had treated his redeemed people so kindly and so humanely, yes, with so much indulgence, how great and how intolerable was their ingratitude" (*Lectures*, Mic 6:4).

For this grace of God, which the elect *and* the reprobate among his people have in common, is richer than the grace shown to the Gentiles. And thus Calvin speaks of *steps in election* (Cf. *Lectures* Mal 1:2–6). There are four steps:
1. People are created as human beings, in God's image, and not as donkeys and dogs.
2. Only the people of Abraham have God as Father and Savior, although the entire world is under his authority.
3. Jacob's descendants, and not those of Esau, share in a special grace.
4. Also among Jacob's family there are elect (from eternity), while others are reprobate. See also *Lectures*, Mal 1:2–6.

It is obvious that the scorning of God's grace in the second and third steps of election is more serious than in the first. *Comm.* Isa 42:20: "The heathen nations will indeed be without excuse; but the Jews and others to whom the Lord revealed himself in so many ways will deserve double condemnation for having refused to see or hear God." *Comm.* Matt 11:21: "If he withholds his word from some and allows them to perish while, in order to render others more inexcusable, he entreats and exhorts them in a variety of ways to repentance, who shall on this account charge him with injustice?"

The invitation and critical motifs come back here with increased force. In the proclamation of his Word, God truly offers *grace*. Calvin makes that clear in his description of God's Word as being *per se* and by nature *salutary*. *Comm.* Matt 23:34: "The word of God indeed *in itself and by its own nature brings salvation* and invites all indiscriminately to the hope of eternal life."

Does the Word not also speak of *judgment*, and is it not, besides being an aroma that brings life, also an aroma that brings death? However, Calvin does not regard this orientation to life and to death as being equivalent. The *essence* of the gospel, its *opus proprium* [proper work], is the proclamation leading to salvation, while all judgment is an *accidental* accompaniment of the gospel. *Comm.* 2 Cor 2:15: "We must therefore always distinguish between the *proper* office of the Gospel and the *accidental* one (so to speak) which must be imputed to the depravity of humankind, to which it is owing, that life to them is turned into death." Life is being offered, but it can be changed into death. The essential can be changed into the accidental.

This idea is also present in the *Institutes*. "Christ came *properly* not for the destruction of the world but for its salvation" (*Inst.* III, xxv, 9).

C. Veenhof has demonstrated with a selection of citations that the distinction between essential and accidental is a vital element in Calvin's views concerning the Word of God and Christ's office. See *Ref.* 30, 289ff. The following are some other quotations, which can also be found in Veenhof's article: "Now this ought to be understood as referring to the office which *properly* and naturally belongs to Christ; for that unbelievers are not more severely *condemned* on account of the Gospel is *accidental*, and does not arise from its nature, as we have said several times before" (*Comm.* John 12:47). "The doctrine is not, *in a proper sense*, or by itself, or in its own nature, but by accident, the cause of blindness" (*Comm.* Mark 4:12). About the "binding" in Matt 16:19, Calvin says: "It must be observed, however, that this is *accidental* to the Gospel and, as it were, beyond nature." "When Christ says in other passages that *he had come to judgment*, ... when he is called *a stone of offense*, ... when he is said to be *set for the destruction of many*, ... this may be regarded as *accidental*, or, so to speak, as arising from a different cause; for they who reject the grace offered in him deserve to find him the Judge and Avenger of contempt so unworthy and base" (*Comm.* John 3:17). God punishes, but he does not do so gladly. Cf. *Lectures*, Lam 3:33, and *Comm.* Deut 28:63.

It has been mentioned in passing that, in addition to grace, Calvin also speaks of God's wrath in his general revelation. I will deal with this expressly in the following section.

§ 8. Revelation also about wrath

God "bears with the human race in his mercy, and watches over it by his protection" but he also "governs it with his justice and judgment."[210] Gaius Caligula "erupted in an audacious and unbridled contempt of deity, yet no one trembled more miserably than he did when any sign of divine wrath manifested itself. Thus he shuddered before God against his will. The more audacious people are in their contempt for God, the more they are disturbed even by the rustling of a falling leaf. How does this happen except by the wrath of God's majesty, which strikes their consciences all the more violently the more they try to flee from it."[211] Diagoras may mock and Dionysius may sneer at the heavenly judgment, but "it is a bitter laugh. For inwardly the worm of conscience, which

---

210. *Inst.* I, ii, 1.
211. *Inst.* I, iii, 2.

is more fierce than all branding irons, eats away at them."[212] God can surrender people to their own lusts, even to such an extent that "all who extinguish the fear of heavenly judgment and heedlessly indulge in their own lusts deny that there is a God. And it is God's just punishment of the wicked that fatness envelops their hearts, so that after they have closed their eyes, in seeing they do not see."[213] But even after that it happens that God sometimes "pulls them back to his judgment seat."[214]

God glorifies himself in this wrath. He "created all things for his own sake, also the wicked for the day of trouble [Prov 16:4].... Thus among humankind some are born destined for certain death from the womb, who God's name by their own destruction."[215] The Lord "has his judgments against the reprobate, whereby he carries out his plan for them: ... those whom he created for dishonor in life and destruction in death to become *instruments of his wrath* and examples of his severity. That they may reach their destiny, he sometimes *deprives* them of the opportunity to hear his Word and at other times makes them even more blind and foolish by the proclamation of that Word."[216]

God glorifies himself also in the revelation of his wrath. I propose to call this the *glorification motif* (cf. footnote 215). But I will already now point out that this motif cannot be added to the motifs listed in § 6, for it would not have belonged under the heading "Why is grace shown toward Gentiles?" In the glorification motif, God does not confer grace. Instead, he deprives unspiritual and wicked people of grace.

Now we have to answer an important question: How does Calvin explain that God is both gracious (§§ 3 and 6) and wrathful (§ 8) toward the same persons? For it concerns the same people. Calvin says that "the wrath and curse of God *always* rests on sinners so long as they have not been delivered of their guilt."[217] "All those who belong to the number of the reprobate are vessels made for dishonor and therefore they do not cease to provoke God's wrath

---

212. *Inst.* I, iii, 3.
213. *Inst.* I, iv, 3. Cf. II, iv, 3.
214. *Inst.* I, iv, 2.
215. *Inst.* III, xxiii, 6. See also III, xxiv, 14.
216. *Inst.* III, xxiv, 12.
217. *Inst.* II, 16, 1.

against them by continual shameful acts."[218] But all persons also share, in a greater or lesser measure, in the demonstration of God's grace. How can these two go hand in hand?

§ 9. Grace and wrath toward the same persons

Calvin's answer to the question just posed above is nuanced. Taking all data into consideration, I believe he calls our attention to three things.

1. *Let both expressions stand side by side.* One might think that God has a twofold will. But that is not Calvin's opinion. "Although *to our perception* God's will is manifold, he does not will this *and* that in himself, but according to his diversely manifold wisdom, as Paul calls it [Eph 3:10], he strikes dumb our senses until it is given to us to recognize how wonderfully he wills what at the moment seems to be against his will."[219] That is how God can be the Father of all and at the same time reject people. Thus he "lets the sun rise over the evil and the good," but "the inheritance is kept in store only for the few.... God does not hate any of the things he has created," while the fact remains that "the reprobate are hateful to God."[220]

Strictly speaking, the answer Calvin gives is not a clarification of the problem. Reverently he lets the one stand next to the other. The unity of both grace and wrath does exist, but because our understanding is feeble, we do not grasp it.

No manifold will, but God does assume a twofold role. For this, one may read Calvin's explanation of Ezek 18:32 and C. Veenhof's rendering of it: "Calvin rejects as strongly as possible that God himself is twofold! But with the same emphasis he maintains that, for our sake, God does assume a twofold persona" (*Ref.* 30, 321). "Persona" is used here in the sense of "role" or "appearance." But we must remember that it is true, correct, and reliable to speak of God in both "roles" (see Veenhof's article). It matters little that in his discussion of Ezek 18:32 Calvin does not concern himself with God's grace and wrath toward the Gentiles but with God's revealed will of salvation and his hidden decree

---

218. *Inst.* III, xxiii, 12.
219. *Inst.* III, xxiv, 17. The same solution is found in I, xviii, 3.
220. Ibid.

of reprobation, both of which apply to the wicked among Israel. The problem presented here is the topic under discussion in this section.

2. *In a certain* sense.... Calvin is placed before the question how the fact that God comes to us with his mercy is compatible with the fact that he was our enemy until he was reconciled to us in Christ. For how did he give us a special pledge of his love in his only-begotten Son if he had not already before embraced us with undeserved grace? Calvin wants to untangle this knot.[221] How is the fact that God is *favorably inclined* toward us from eternity compatible with the fact that he was hostile toward us until we were reconciled to him in Christ ? It is clear that the answer to this question (which is focused on God's love and his wrath toward the elect) is also of great significance for the concurrence of God's wrath and grace toward the reprobate. What is Calvin's answer?

He says that expressions such as those in Rom 5:10, Gal 3:10, and Col 1:21, 22 (about the elect, on whom formerly the curse and wrath of God rested) "have been accommodated to our understanding, so that we may better understand how wretched and disastrous our state would be apart from Christ. For if it had not been clearly stated that the wrath and vengeance of God and eternal death pressed down upon us, we would scarcely have *recognized* how wretched we would have been without God's mercy and we would have underestimated the benefit of redemption."[222] Calvin gives an example of this: "Suppose someone is told: '*If* God had hated you while you were still a sinner and had rejected you, as you deserved, a terrible destruction would have awaited you. But because he kept you in grace voluntarily, and of his own free favor, and did not allow you to be estranged from him, he thus delivered you from that peril.' This person then will surely be moved and will feel something of what he owes to God's mercy. On the other hand, suppose he learns, as Scripture teaches, that he was estranged from God through sin, is an heir of wrath, subject to the curse of eternal death, excluded from all hope of salvation, beyond every blessing of God, the slave of Satan, captive under the yoke of sin, destined finally for a dreadful destruction and already involved in it; and that

---

221. *Inst.* II, xvi, 2.
222. Ibid.

at this point Christ interceded as his advocate, took upon himself and suffered the punishment that, from God's righteous judgment, threatened all sinners; that he purged with his blood those evils which had rendered sinners hateful to God; that by his expiation he made satisfaction and sacrifice duly to God the Father; that as intercessor he has appeased God's wrath.... Will he then not be even more moved by all these things that so *vividly portray* the greatness of the calamity from which he has been rescued? In short, since our hearts cannot, in God's mercy, either seize upon life ardently enough or accept it with the thankfulness we owe, unless our minds are first struck and overwhelmed by fear of God's wrath and by dread of eternal death, we are taught by Scripture to perceive that apart from Christ, God is *in a certain sense* [*quodammodo*] hostile to us and his hand is armed for our destruction; to embrace his benevolence and Fatherly love in Christ alone."[223]

I have italicized a few words in this quotation. What is said about God's wrath toward the elect before the reconciliation by Christ has a *pedagogic* intent. Without such references we would not receive God's mercy with sufficient thankfulness. It has to be portrayed to us in such a vivid way in order that we can rightly appreciate God's love. But as far as the reality of God's wrath itself is concerned, God, without Christ, is *in a certain sense* hostile toward his elect.

We also find expressions in the *Institutes* that suggest the opposite with respect to the reprobate. All the emphasis is then on God's wrath, while the description of what the elect receive by way of grace is qualified by the words "in a certain sense." Note the following passages:

"If God does *truly* shows his grace [to his elect], this remains fixed for all eternity. For nothing prevents God from enlightening some with a temporary *sense* of grace, which afterward vanishes."[224] "The reprobate are sometimes touched by a *sense* of God's grace,[225] just as God's children sometimes experience his anger "not because he is disposed of himself to hate them, but because he wants to frighten them with the *sense* of his wrath."[226]

223. Ibid.
224. *Inst.* III, ii, 11.
225. *Inst.* III, ii, 12.
226. Ibid.

Calvin immediately adds the following to the passage just quoted: "For that reason they [the children of God] become aware that he is at the same time angry and merciful toward them, or toward their sins. For they unfeigned pray that his wrath be averted while with quiet confidence they nevertheless flee to him for refuge" (*Inst.* III, ii, 12). But is the reality of wrath and grace in the lives of the elect and the reprobate, respectively, not weakened when Calvin speaks here about a *sense* of wrath and grace? A critical assessment of what Calvin has said about this topic will be given later. But it is important already now to note that §§ 9, 1, and 9, 2, are clearly different.

In § 9, 1, we saw how Calvin allowed two things to stand side by side although they seem contradictory. He provides no explanation for this.

In § 9, 2, Calvin goes further. He does give an explanation in which he places certain emphases: the love of God toward the elect is real and so is the wrath toward the reprobate. It is necessary, he says, to speak differently about the wrath of God toward the former and about grace toward the latter. But he qualifies both with "in a certain sense"!

The commentaries also contain expressions that should make us careful in speaking simply of grace when it concerns the wicked. Thus in the explanation of Jer 33:8 we read that "whatever God grants and bestows on the *wicked* cannot, *strictly speaking*, be regarded as evidence of his favor and grace." God is not favorably disposed toward the wicked. Why not? He is only favorably disposed toward us when he does not attribute our sins to us because we are reconciled to God: "We must now see how God becomes propitious to us. He becomes so when he imputes not our sins to us.... We are therefore always accursed before God until he buries our sins. Hence I have said that the first fountain of all the good things that are to be hoped for is here briefly made known to the Jews, even the gratuitous favor of God in reconciling them to himself" (loc. cit.). "Strictly speaking"! Grace is *actually* a matter of reconciliation and is for those who are reconciled. Beyond that, misery and curse remain. "All happiness is ruinous if it does not flow from the fountain of God's gracious love; ... if God is not our Father, the more we abound in all kinds of blessings, the deeper we sink in all kinds of miseries " (*Lectures*, Zech 1:15).

3. *Sinners, but creatures nonetheless.* Under point 2, *Inst.* II, xvi, 2, was cited. But Calvin went further. In II, xvi, 3, he argues that God's wrath, even though Scripture speaks about it in accordance with the weakness of our understanding, is a real wrath. "For we all have *something in us* that deserves God's wrath. With regard to our corrupt nature as well as our evil life, all of us surely displease God, are guilty in his sight, and are born for damnation in hell.[227] But something must be added to this. "Because the Lord does not

---

227. *Inst.* II, xvi, 3.

want to do away with what *is his in us*, out of his kindness he still finds something to love. For although we are *sinners* by our own fault, we nevertheless remain his *creatures*. But because there is a perpetual and irreconcilable disagreement between righteousness and unrighteousness, he cannot *completely* receive us so long as we remain sinners."[228] To speak with Augustine: "God hated us insofar as we were not as he made us, but because our unrighteousness had not destroyed his work in all respects, he at the same time hated in each of us what we had done while he loved what he had made."[229] "God is enraged at the corruption of his work rather than at the work itself," says Calvin elsewhere.[230]

When we read this, it will not surprise us that Calvin makes a similar argument about the reprobate. God hates them, but he is also able to love them in that they are his creation. We hardly find this argument explicitly in the *Institutes*, but it does appear in the commentaries.

Thus "God loved Aristides and Fabricius, and also hated them; for, in so far as he had bestowed on them outward righteousness, and that for the general advantage, he loved his own work in them; but as their heart was impure, the outward semblance of righteousness was of no avail for obtaining righteousness.... For it is not inconsistent that the good seed that God has implanted in some natures shall be loved by him, and yet that he should reject their persons and works on account of corruption" (*Comm.* Mark 10:21). "Apart from Christ, God is always angry with us.... For God does not hate in us his own workmanship in that we were created as human beings, but he hates our uncleanness" (*Comm.* Rom 3:25).

"God declares implacable war on all malefactors, but insofar as humans are his creation he embraces them with his Fatherly love" (*Comm.* Ps 92:10). "Corrupted by original sin, we are detestable to God, but insofar as we are humans he can do no other than love us, and also our welfare is dear to him" (*Lectures*, Ezek 18:1).

The last-quoted words are typical of Calvin. Because God loves human beings as his creation, he seeks their well-being or salvation, even though this is a salvation limited in scope. Jonah is therefore called inhumane in his attitude toward the Ninevites. "God does not create human beings in vain; it is then no wonder that he wishes them to be saved.... Jonah was not unsuitably taught ... how inhumanely he conducted himself toward the Ninevites.... For although the

---

228. Ibid.
229. *Inst.* II, xvi, 4.
230. *Inst.* II, i, 11.

Ninevites were alienated from God, yet since they were human beings, God, as he is the Father of the whole human race, acknowledged them as his own, at least to such an extent as to give them the common light of day and other good things of earthly life.... [God said:] "Should not I ... whose prerogative and whose constant practice it is mercifully to bear with humankind—should not I spare them, though they are worthy of destruction?" (*Lectures*, Jonah 4:10).

Hate *and* love. And his love toward human beings impels God to show them his beneficence and clemency.

An assessment of what Calvin says will be given later. At this point I am still making an inventory of his thoughts. And the picture is not fully complete without a final section discussing the question how Christians must appraise what God's grace offers them in this life. We already heard Calvin say that the gifts of the Spirit are not regarded as small without disdaining and reviling the Spirit himself. A discussion of *Inst*. III, vi-x, (about the Christian life) will help us obtain a more complete picture.

§ 10. Enjoyment on our pilgrim's journey

"When the philosophers exhort us to virtue, they announce merely that we must live in accordance with nature."[231] But Scripture teaches "that Christ ... has been set before us as an example whose pattern we ought to express in our lives."[232] We will not reach perfection "in this earthly prison of the body."[233] Nonetheless, "we must look toward our goal in sincere simplicity and aspire to the end goal, not fondly flattering ourselves, nor giving in to our shortcomings, but in a continuous striving we must devote ourselves to becoming better than we are, until we have attained to goodness itself."[234]

The Christian must follow three steps on the way to perfection. The *first* is that of self-denial. Calvin cries out: "O what progress have they made who have learned that they are not their own and have taken away dominion and governance of themselves from

---

231. *Inst*. III, vi, 3.
232. Ibid.
233. *Inst*. III, vi, 5.
234. Ibid.

their reason, that they may attribute it to God!"[235] But they must rise yet higher with a pious heart. The *second* step is to bear the cross.[236] But even so, the depiction of the Christian life is incomplete. "We rightly receive the benefit of the discipline of the cross only when we learn that this life, when judged in itself, is restless, confused, unhappy in countless ways, and in no respect blissful."[237] That is why a *third step is necessary*, namely the *contemplation of the life to come with contempt for the present life*. "No matter what kind of oppression we face, we must always look toward this goal: to accustom ourselves to contempt for this present life and to be aroused thereby to meditate on the life to come. For since God knows very well how much we are inclined by nature to a brutish love of this world, he uses very fitting means to draw us back and to shake off our sluggishness, lest we cling too tenaciously to that love."[238] "To combat this evil the Lord teaches those who are his concerning the vanity of this life by continual proof of its misery."[239] Calvin is very definite here: "We must look at it this way: that our heart will never be raised up to a longing for eternal life and to contemplation of it unless it has previously been filled with contempt for the present life."[240] There is no middle way. The earth must either become worthless to us or hold us bound by intemperate love of it."[241]

But this contempt of the present life has limits. It must "generate no hatred of it and no ungratefulness toward God. Indeed, this life, however filled with innumerable miseries it may be, is still rightly to be counted among those blessings of God that are not to be spurned. Hence, if we recognize in it no divine benefit, we are already guilty of a considerable ingratitude toward God himself."[242] Especially believers should regard it as evidence of God's benevolence.... For before he shows us openly the inheritance of eternal glory, God wills by lesser proofs to show himself to be our Father.... Since, therefore, this life serves us in understanding God's

---

235. *Inst.* III, vii, 1.
236. *Inst.* III,, vii, heading.
237. *Inst.* III, ix, 1.
238. Ibid.
239. Ibid.
240. Ibid.
241. *Inst.* III, ix, 2.
242. *Inst.* III, ix, 3.

goodness, should we despise it as though it contained no grain of good in itself?[243]

However, "when it comes to a *comparison with the life to come*, present life cannot only be safely disregarded but, compared the former, must be utterly despised and loathed. For if heaven is our country, what is the earth other than a place of exile? If departure from the world is the entrance into life, what is the world other than a grave? And what does it mean to remain in the world other than to be immersed in death? If to be freed from the body is to be released into total freedom, what is the body other than a prison?"[244]

But "although we may long for its end, we must be prepared to remain in this life at the Lord's pleasure. For life is like a *sentry post* at which the Lord has posted us and which we must hold until he recalls us."[245] "We must leave the borderline between our death and our life for God to determine, but in such a way" (and now the theme reappears, J.D.) "that we may burn with zeal for death and be constant in meditating on it. We must despise this life in comparison with the immortality to come and, because of the bondage of sin, long to renounce it whenever it shall please the Lord."[246] "Indeed, let us consider this as established: that no one has made progress in the school of Christ who does not joyfully await the day of death and final resurrection!"[247]

Can we then still truly enjoy the things of the earth? Calvin again first places a check on the argument. "If we must simply pass through this world [as pilgrims! J.D.], there is no doubt we ought to use its good things in so far as they help rather than hinder our course."[248] "There were some who ... allowed people to use material things to the extent required by necessity.... but they were far too severe. For they bound the consciences with tighter bonds than those that God's Word binds them with—which is a very dangerous thing."[249] "Crates the Theban went so far as to cast his treasures into the sea, because he believed that, unless they were destroyed, they

---

243. Ibid.
244. *Inst.* III, ix, 4. For the body as prison, see also *Inst.* I, xv, 2; III, iii, 20; III, vi, 5.
245. *Inst.* III, ix, 4.
246. Ibid.
247. *Inst.* III, ix, 5.
248. *Inst.* III, x, 1.
249. Ibid.

would destroy him."²⁵⁰ The right approach is to use God's gifts "for the purpose for which the Giver himself created and destined them for us, since he *created them for our good, not for our destruction.*"²⁵¹ Hence "God created food ... not only to provide for necessity but also for enjoyment and happiness. Thus the purpose of clothing, apart from necessity, was for adornment and decency. In plants, trees, and the fruits of the field, apart from their various uses, there is beauty of appearance and pleasantness of odor.... Has the Lord clothed the flowers with the great beauty that greets our eyes, the sweetness of smell is wafted upon our nostrils, and will it be unlawful our eyes to be drawn to that beauty and our noses to the sweetness of that odor? What? Did he not so distinguish colors as to make some more pleasing than others? Did he not endow gold and silver, ivory and marble, with a beauty that makes them more precious than other metals or stones? In short, did he not render many things attractive to us apart from their necessary use?"²⁵² "It is an inhumane philosophy that permits only the necessary use of created things, for it deprives people of all their senses and turns them into blocks of wood."²⁵³

However, Calvin immediately follows the foregoing with a warning against the lust of the flesh. For acknowledgment of God and thankfulness toward him is so often lacking. "The pleasant smell of the kitchen or the sweetness of its odors can so blunt the senses that some no longer smell anything spiritual."²⁵⁴ And again Calvin returns to the principal idea: "There is no surer or more direct course than that which we receive from contempt of the present life and meditation on heavenly immortality. For from this two rules follow: those who use this world should be so affected as if they did not use it; those who marry, as if they did not marry; those who buy, as if they did not buy, as Paul teaches [1 Cor 7:29–31]. The other rule is that they should know how to bear poverty with composure and patience, as well as to bear abundance with moderation."²⁵⁵ "Besides, Scripture has a third rule with which

250. Ibid.
251. *Inst.* III, x, 2.
252. Ibid.
253. *Inst.* III, x, 3.
254. Ibid.
255. *Inst.* III, x, 4.

to regulate the use of earthly things.... It declares that they have all been given to us by the kindness of God, and so appointed for our use, that they are, as it were, entrusted to us, and we must one day render account of them. We must therefore administer them so that this saying may continually resound in our ears: 'Give an account of your stewardship' [Luke16:2]. At the same time let us remember by whom such reckoning is required: namely, by him who has so highly commended abstinence, sobriety, frugality, and moderation and has also abominated extravagance, pride, ostentation, and vanity."[256]

Calvin concludes by pointing out that "the Lord's calling is in everything the beginning and foundation of well-doing."[257] "No task will be so sordid and base, provided that you obey your calling in it, that it will not shine and be considered very precious in God's sight."[258] We are standing at "a sort of sentry post assigned to us by the Lord," so that we "may not heedlessly wander about throughout life."[259]

To summarize it in two words: *pilgrimage* and *sentry post*. *Pilgrimage*: We are headed toward something better. That is why we must show contempt for our present life. *Sentry post*: We still have a task here. That is why we make use of this life and are even allowed to enjoy it. Pilgrimage and sentry post circumscribe the enjoyment and make it possible.

For the last section the commentaries offer an abundance of material, such as W. Kolfhaus' extensive study, *Vom christlichen Leben nach Johannes Calvin*.

One remark is not superfluous at this point. It is very easy to select passages from Calvin's work showing that he views culture either negatively or positively. But it is important to remember a remark made at the beginning of this chapter about Calvin: The *Institutes* should have the final say. That is where we find a systematic treatment of Calvin's doctrinal and also his ethical ideas. For our topic the commentaries can provide only illustrative material.

This means that every account of Calvin's ethics that does not let the eschatological element dominate misses the mark, just as much as any interpretation that simply portrays Calvin as one who holds the present life in contempt.

---

256. *Inst.* III, x, 5.
257. *Inst.* III, x, 6.
258. Ibid.
259. Ibid.

IV

COMPARISON

This chapter is devoted to a comparison of Kuyper, Schilder, and Calvin on the basis of the material collected in the previous chapters. Page references to what was discussed there have been inserted in parentheses. This comparison consists of twelve short sections that correspond to the same number of sections in chapter V, in which an assessment will be made.

§ 1. Double predestination

The treatment of our topic would have been unthinkable but for the fact that each of the three theologians accepts the doctrine of double predestination. A *Reformed* formulation of the problem forms the basis for postulating and challenging the idea of grace in a general sense.

Calvin, Kuyper, and Schilder taught a double predestination, "by which God adopts some to hope of life and sentences others to eternal death" (*Inst.* III, xxi, 5). There is no need to demonstrate this further, since no one doubts it. But some explanation is necessary. Among all three theologians there is a connection between this double predestination and our topic. This is very clear in Schilder's case. His criticism of common grace is to a large extent determined by the doctrine of double predestination (pp. 178–80 above). But we must also not miss this connection in Calvin and Kuyper, who accept grace in a more general sense. For they demarcate this grace from "particular" grace, which, as effective and insuperable grace, is extended only to the elect. For Calvin, see ch. III, footnote 73 (and also pp. 268–69 above), and for Kuyper, see *G.G.* I, 8: "That we ... avoided the term *general grace* and chose the title *common grace*, that is, *gratia communis*, for this series [of articles] is to prevent misunderstanding. For the impression could easily be given that in our view grace is extended to all and that accordingly we have abandoned the fixed foundation that grace is *particular*." To speak of common grace and particular grace is "a theological necessity for those who believe and confess the biblical doctrine of predestination, a predestination unto eternal life which does not include every member of fallen humanity" (A. C. de Jong, *The Well-Meant Gospel Offer*, 137).

CHAPTER IV. COMPARISON

The Reformed formulation of the problem in this demarcation, which is anchored in double predestination, becomes more clear when we realize that opponents of the Calvinistic doctrine of double predestination thus speak about common grace in an entirely different manner.

Here I am thinking of *Arminian* theology. "In it, common grace toward all people is the starting-point on the road on which God places *all* sinners, *so that they may reach salvation by that road*. Hence God's common grace toward all people is the ground and source of God's favorable and merciful *disposition* toward all sinners to bring them to salvation" (H. J. Meijerink, *Ref.* 24, 173; see also *Acta et Scripta synodalia Dordracena ministrorum Remonstrantium*, II, 302–03, 327ff., and further Canons of Dort III/IV, Rejection of Errors, 5). Such a universalistic doctrine of election does not permit a demarcation from particular grace in a Reformed sense.

It is no different in *Roman Catholic* theology. To quote from a recent publication: "When the Council [of Trent, J.D.] teaches that there exists a general salvific will of God toward *all* people, then also most Protestant Christians and theologians will nowadays admit that God's gratuitous and free grace, against which there is no appeal, cannot on that basis prove that he excludes some people from his grace even before they have rendered themselves guilty, but rather that he, because he is the Savior of all, also offers his grace to all" (Karl Rahner, *Brandpunten in de hedendaagse theologie*, 103). This "general grace" also rests on a doctrine of predestination (cf. Denzinger, *Enchiridion*, 31st ed., older pagination, *inter alia*, 160a and b, 794, 827, 1096, 1380, 1382). But it differs completely from that of Calvin and Kuyper.

I also want to refer to *Karl Barth* at this point. When this theologian posits in his doctrine of election that humanity in general, *all* people, church and world, Christian and non-Christian, are elected in Christ (cf. *Kirchliche Dogmatik*, II/2, 563; III/3, 246; IV/1, 1, 98ff., 135, 143; IV/3, 43, 61, 69ff., 129ff., 207, 240–41, 349ff., 420–21, and *passim*), there is no place here for particular grace in the Calvinistic sense. Particular grace has become general grace.

Karl Barth maintained this point of view from first to last. In the first edition of his *Römerbrief* [The Epistle to the Romans], Moses and Plato receive the same treatment (pp. 46, 60, 69, 73, 331, 420, and see also the second and subsequent editions, and cf. the 1933 edition, pp. 53, 118). In his *Kirchliche Dogmatik*, IV/3, 90, we read that "grace as such speaks and gives light," a speaking and a light that extends beyond church walls (122–23). Bible, church, *and* world can testify to the one and only Word of God in Christ Jesus (107–08, 123–24). Also with respect to "secular prophets and apostles of all kinds and at all levels" (107) this allows for no other explanation than that "thus the grace of God's true presence [*Realpräsenz*] would have been shown to these people. And by the power of that grace they would as human beings with their human words—truly beyond their own capacities—be accounted competent and in effect also authorized as speakers of true words" (124). Barth's emphases shifted over the years. The strong "no" [*Nein*] of his first period changed into the

CHAPTER IV. COMPARISON

"no" "that Jesus Christ has taken on for us human beings, so that it no longer affects us and so that we no longer want to place ourselves under it. What happens in God's humanness is, as it encloses this 'no' in itself, the affirmation of human beings" (*Die Menschlichkeit Gottes*, 22) The emphases shifted, but the word "all " ("*all* people"!) remained the same. All are included in the "no," and all are included under the "yes"—world and church, church and world. And it is precisely this word "all" that makes visible the chasm between Barth *cum suis* on the one hand and Calvin and his followers on the other—even when among the latter *general* grace is discussed. For then particular grace, the *numerus clausus* [fixed number], election *and* reprobation, is still confessed.

§ 2. Parallelism?

Calvin and Kuyper let double predestination remain in the background when they speak about grace in a more general sense, while Schilder places it in a dominant position in the foreground when he disputes such a grace. Election and reprobation, God's eternal love and eternal wrath, blessing and curse, heaven and hell, function in parallel in Schilder, but not in Calvin and Kuyper.

There is a clear difference in how the doctrine of double predestination functions. For Calvin and Kuyper, double predestination operates in the *demarcation* of grace in a more general sense, but it does not, or only barely, illuminate the *treatment* of this topic.

This is quite clear in Kuyper. We should not forget that in his explanation Kuyper does place predestination front and center (see §§ 3 and 4, below), but *double* predestination with its personal election and personal reprobation, the latter of which might have raised questions about the nature of grace in common grace, does not play a role. Reprobation only receives a brief role (but then only in the background) when Kuyper rejects the idea that "the lot of the reprobate is a side issue insofar as, from their point of view, nothing happens than that the spiritual pestilence they suffer functions in them unto eternal death" (p. 35 above). For more can be said about them. A doctrine of predestination that focuses exclusively on the salvation of the elect, does not give a perspective on the work of common grace, in which the reprobate also have a role. Kuyper broadens the narrower basis of the traditional doctrine of predestination. The organic aspect receives full attention, while the eternal decision about personal salvation and condemnation remains in the background. It is not constitutive for the domain of common grace.

Calvin also leaves double predestination out of consideration when he discusses grace in a general sense. At least normally. For there are a few exceptions. The exceptions state that God truly displays his grace to the elect,

CHAPTER IV. COMPARISON

but only enlightens the reprobate with a *sense* of his grace. And also that what God gives to the wicked can, strictly speaking, not be regarded as evidence of his favor and grace (pp. 276–77 above). But we can count such statements of Calvin on the fingers of one hand, in contrast to the many passages in which he speaks in an uninhibited manner about grace shown to those who are not elect. (For this, see H. Kuiper, *Calvin and Common Grace*, 219–22.) However, we must not read more into the "strictly speaking" than Calvin intends. "Calvin in this connection intimates that we can consider only those things to be blessing and tokens of God's favor and grace *in the fullest and deepest sense of those terms* in case they proceed from the fountain of God's revealing love and are subservient to the eternal salvation of men" (op. cit., 221; italics supplied). Calvin *continues* to speak of grace, and therefore Kuiper interprets him correctly when he states, "It need hardly be said that Calvin in this passage [with "strictly speaking," J.D.] places himself in irreconcilable opposition to what he says in other places when he affirms that the reprobate receive many temporal and earthly blessings which are *in a sense* tokens of God's beneficence toward them" (op. cit., 221; italics supplied).

Here, Schilder clearly stands in opposition to Calvin and Kuyper. For him the confession of God's reprobation does not tolerate speaking of grace toward the reprobate, for God's disposition, "also in granting what we in apperceptive language refer to as manifold gifts," is determined by his predestination. God regards each individual person very specifically "in a total disposition of love or of hate" (p. 185 above). God's wrath rests on the reprobate—at all times (*Heid. Cat.* IV, 119). Election and reprobation are decisive in determining whether it is grace or not.

The difference between Schilder and the two other theologians is even more clear when he speaks about election and reprobation *constantly as being in parallel*. No one "has the right to attribute a 'pre' [before] to *mercy*. *If* there is a 'pre,' why then does *wrath* not take advantage of it?" (p. 179 above). We must praise God's *balanced* actions (cf. pp. 178–86 above). God pays equal attention to election and reprobation, eternal love and eternal hate, blessing and curse, heaven and hell. Everything that is in God is God, and we are not permitted to emphasize one self-glorification of God over another (p. 179 above).

We would search in vain for a similar parallelism in Kuyper and Calvin. Kuyper depicts the relationship between election and reprobation as follows: "The decree of predestination is directed to the realization in the cosmos as one entity (and more particularly as an organic whole under Christ, as Head and epitome) of what God determined in order to attain his self-glorification. Consequently, in this predestination election does not have a different or greater significance than the determination of some persons who, together under Christ, will constitute the regenerated humanity that one day will be all-surpassing in glory. Moreover, *reprobation is in this context not a decree equal in divine energy*, but simply the corollary of election, which establishes that the others, although they belong to the human race as individuals, are not permanently included in the organic whole of the human community, but will cease to be members of it" (*Loc. de Deo* III, 252, dictation; italics supplied). Kuyper calls this reprobation "the dark *shadow* of election for those who are not elected" (253, italics supplied). In Schilder's theology, reprobation and election are equally *highlighted*. Kuyper, who accepts eternal reprobation fully and reverently (142), nonetheless speaks of a "dreadful representation" (174), and calls the text "So ... he hardens whomever he wills" [Rom 9:18] a "hideous testimony" (*Werk van den Heiligen Geest*, 732). He regards the idea of the eternal misery of so many people "shocking and frightful" (*E Voto* II, 216), and asks "the anxious and profoundly heart-rending question: 'Oh my God, why can or may it not be otherwise?'" (*Uit het Woord*, 2nd series I, 261). But for Schilder the glory of God, who is equally great in his righteousness and in his mercy, demands that we glorify God—in his equally balanced actions and thus in election and reprobation (p. 179 above).

And Calvin? He also does not recognize a parallelism. The orientation toward life and toward death are in his view not equivalent in Scripture. There is a proper office and an accidental one in Scripture, and the emphasis falls on *salvation* (p. 272 above). Eternal reprobation is a horrible decree (*Inst.* III, xxiii, 7), a decree that renders us *speechless*. The following statement is also typical of Calvin: "The same mind is capable of being influenced by these two feelings: that when it looks to God it can willingly bear the ruin of those whom he has decreed to destroy, and that when it turns its thoughts to human beings, it shows compassion for the evils that come upon them" (*Comm.* Rom 9:2).

Kuyper puts it somewhat stronger than Calvin; nevertheless, both differ from Schilder. That has nothing to do with an indication of more or less human emotion on their part. Rather, the question is whether reprobation (as shadow) remains in the background, or whether it is displayed, just like election, before the floodlights. Thus it is doctrine that sets the tone.

§ 3. The breadth of predestination

Kuyper depicts predestination in a much broader way than Calvin and Schilder. Kuyper emphasizes especially *organic* predestination, whereas the other two are concerned predominantly with *personal* predestination.

We have seen that Kuyper objects to the position of the Reformed fathers, who almost exclusively interpreted predestination "as a decree of God concerning the eternal weal and woe of his rational creatures" (pp. 34–35 above). For according to Kuyper the decree of predestination must encompass "the totality of history, the entire course that heaven and earth will run, and is directed toward the end, in order that from this entire creation and the entire cosmos

CHAPTER IV. COMPARISON

God may receive the honor due to him" (p. 35 above). For it pleases him "despite Satan's devices and human sin, to actualize what he had put into the world at the time of creation, to persevere in its realization, and to develop it so completely that the full sum of the vital energies of his creation will be disclosed at the consummation of the world" (p. 36 above). In the doctrine of predestination one may not forget *creation*, with which human beings have an organic connection (pp. 34–35 above). The decree of predestination, as we saw, is directed "to the realization in the cosmos as one entity (and more particularly as an organic whole under Christ, as Head and epitome of all things) of what God determined in order to attain his self-glorification" (*Loc. de Deo* III, 252, dictation). It is no wonder that Kuyper labels as *atomistic* the unfolding of a predestination in which the "organic wholeness" is disregarded and the emphasis is exclusively on the election and reprobation of human beings (225).

This organic vision, so central to Kuyper's ideas, is absent in Calvin when he speaks about predestination *(Inst.* III, xxi–xxiv). For him God's decision about human beings individually is central: "We call predestination God's eternal decree, by which he compacted with himself what he willed to become of each person" (*Inst.* III, xxi, 5). I am not forgetting that Calvin also speaks of a general election of the people of Israel, but "still his free election has been only half explained until we come to individual persons, to whom God offers ... salvation" (*Inst.* III, xxi, 7). I am also not forgetting that it is necessary according to Calvin to "ascend to the Head, in whom the Heavenly Father has gathered his elect together, and has joined them to himself by an indissoluble bond" (*Inst.* III, xxi, 7), but this "organic" bond remains personal. Christ is the Head of the *elect*, says Calvin; Christ is the Head of all *things*, says Kuyper, who regards the personal as being organically included in the cosmic.

Schilder also speaks differently about predestination than Kuyper. In predestination God decided to prepare "not only a heaven, but also a hell with an 'infinite' number of variations" (p. 179 above). The personal element clearly dominates. "On the last day" God is concerned "about two outcomes: self-glorification in a full adoption of children and self-glorification in a complete subjection of rebels" (p. 179 above). Everything is subordinated to that: "The conservation of the world and the continuation of history, together with the possibility of culture and the ensuing culture as reality ... are all indispensable, both for building the road that leads to heaven and for traveling down the roads that lead to hell" (p. 182 above; cf. pp. 190–91). It is true that beside double predestination Schilder also posits the "x^n deputations or predestinations of the x^n creatures" (p. 185 above), but he does not develop this anywhere. The x and the n remain unknown. The "breadth" of an organic predestination, as Kuyper sketches it, is not found in either Schilder or Calvin, even though we do read, e.g., in *Wat is de hemel?*, passages that are strongly reminiscent of Kuyper (op. cit., 67–69, 178, 184 ["organic" new humanity]). But when Schilder discusses the doctrine of predestination explicitly (in his *Heidelbergsche Catechismus*), such passages are absent.

§ 4. The concept of development from bud to bloom

The theme of the development of all created existence from bud to bloom as a distinct aspect in God's predestination (beside the realization of the kingdom of heaven) is characteristic of Kuyper. The *specifically* cultural attention that it displays is typical for Kuyper, it is missing in Calvin, and appears in a more modest form in Schilder.

Within predestination, no matter how "organically" it is depicted, Kuyper makes a clear distinction between the function of particular grace, which has as its goal "the realization of the kingdom of heaven" and the function of common grace, which is directed to "bring to light all that was hidden as seeds in our race, to the glory and praise of God's name" (p. 61 above). For according to Kuyper there is so much that has nothing to do with the matter of the kingdom or the content of our faith, and yet "none of it can be spared, because it pleases God ... to actualize what he had put into the world at the time of creation, to persevere in its realization, and to develop it so completely that the full sum of the vital energies of his creation will be disclosed at the consummation of the world" (p. 36 above). Kuyper's reflections on the image of God clarify for us what he means by the idea of the development of created existence: In creating human beings in his image, God placed "an endless multitude of seeds in our nature," that "cannot develop except by way of the social relationships among people.... Seen in this light the broad subdivision of human development attains a significance of its own, an independent goal, a reason for existence apart from the matter of salvation" (pp. 36–37 above). For also—and often *especially* (*Pro Rege* I, 191–92)—the reprobate make their positive contribution to this development, although they are not included in the new humanity.

However, Kuyper's distinction in predestination does not become a separation, for created existence and its re-creation both have their root in Christ (pp. 68–71 above). *But then again with a distinction*: As Mediator of creation he leads common grace, and as Mediator of redemption he leads particular grace, to their respective goals. Thus it is clear that in the foundation of Kuyper's system, common grace retains its own place, which demands independent attention for culture. The attention for an all-inclusive world culture (with its general and special aspects, pp. 47–49 above) remains an independent theme, no matter how interwoven it is with particular grace. Designed from eternity, the cultural plan reaches its full execution in the course of the centuries. At the end of time, the full sum of the vital energies of

CHAPTER IV. COMPARISON

God's creation will be disclosed and our human race will end only "when all possibilities of the reflection of God's image in our race will have been exhausted" (p. 36 above). The seed in field of the world will then have reached its *full* flowering (pp. 29–30 above).

We shall look in vain for such a theory of culture in Calvin's doctrine of predestination, for it is not "broad" (§ 3) and certainly does not place an independent emphasis on culture. The entire idea of the development of creation's potential, in which created existence reaches its flowering and full development in accordance with God's plan, is foreign to Calvin. He does value the achievements and virtues of the Gentiles as gifts of God (pp. 263–64 above). In that respect he is "broad." But which motifs does Calvin adduce for God's gracious dealings with the Gentiles? When we review them (pp. 260ff. above), we will at most find something in the third motif (of restraint) that is reminiscent of Kuyper. But even then, the essential Kuyper is absent in Calvin. For we can compare this restraint only with the *negative* or unchanging operation of Kuyper's common grace, whereas the essence of common grace (its development from bud to bloom) lies in its *positive* or progressive operation (pp. 30–32 above).

Schilder differs from Calvin. Schilder also does not recognize a broad predestination, as we saw, but the concept of development, although it is not derived from predestination, is clearly present in his thought (pp. 187ff. above). We must take from the world what is in it. The world of Paradise was a beginning, in which (in principle) everything was given "that had to be there potentially in order to let it develop into a completed world of perfect order" after a historical *process* of many centuries (p. 188 above).

Nonetheless, and apart from other differences that will be discussed later, Schilder's specific attention to culture is much more modest. Schilder does not give us a philosophical history of culture, in which culture gradually reaches its culmination. On the contrary! Although the command concerning the one culture with its "systematized striving for the sum-total of labor" (p. 188 above) remains, sin snaps the blossoming of culture and, as a result, we receive only cultural *fragments*, both from the side of the world and those from the side of the believers (p. 201 above). A truncated pyramid is all that the Antichrist gives culture (*Christ and Culture*, 122).

The agreement between Kuyper and Schilder with respect to the concept of the development of creation's potential becomes strikingly evident in the exegesis they both give, in contradistinction from Calvin, of Gen 1:28: "Be fruitful and multiply and fill the earth and subdue it, and have dominion over the fish of the sea...," etc. For Kuyper (*G.G.* II, 274–75; *Pro Rege* I, 129–30, 133ff.; III, 457; *Loc. de Christo* III, 170–71) and Schilder (pp. 187–88 above) this text contains a cultural *mandate* with perspectives into the future. This agreement between Schilder and Kuyper draws our attention to Schilder's remark about those "who let their theory of 'common *grace*' speak *only and exclusively* about what by God's charter has still been left to us as being *permissible*" (p. 191

above). This remark is undoubtedly not applicable to Kuyper. For Kuyper was particularly motivated by the task, the mandate, that was maintained also after the Fall. In my opinion he would not have objected to Schilder's term "common mandate."

However, with respect to Gen 1, for Calvin the emphasis falls on the *enjoyment* of what God created: "And hence [because of the dominion that human beings exercise, J.D.] we infer for what purposes all things were created, namely, that none of all the conveniences [! J.D.] and useful things of life might be wanting to humankind. In the very order of the creation the paternal solicitude of God for human beings is conspicuous, because he furnished the world with all things needful, and even with an immense profusion of wealth, before he formed humanity" (*Comm.* Gen 1:26). Everything *has* already been made ready for human *use*. "Humankind had already been created with this condition [the dominion, J.D.], that they should subject the earth to themselves; but now, at length, they are put in possession of their right, when they hear what has been given to them by the Lord: and this Moses expresses still more fully in the next verse, when he introduces God as granting to them the herbs and the fruits. For it is of great importance that we touch nothing of God's bounty but what we know he has granted us" (*Comm.* Gen 1:28). Gen 2:15 (where we read that human beings were placed in the garden to work it and to keep it) also does not impel Calvin to an exegesis of a broad cultural scope. Certainly, people must labor, for "nothing is more contrary to the order of nature than to consume life in eating, drinking, and sleeping." The limited scope of this labor in Calvin's exegesis is apparent from his explanation of the "keeping" of the garden: We only possess the things God has given us on the condition that we are satisfied with an economical and modest use of them and guard the rest well—if possible, in such a way that we leave our field to our descendants in an even better condition than it was ("Let those who possesses a field, so partake of its yearly fruits, that they may not suffer the ground to be injured by their negligence; but let them endeavor to hand it down to posterity as they received it, or even better cultivated" [*Comm.* Gen 2:15]). For Calvin, Psalm 8 also features in the happiness and pleasure of humankind. One quotation: "The world was originally created for this end, that every part of it should tend to the happiness of humankind as its object" (*Comm.* Ps 8:6).

The purpose of this section must be kept in mind. I do not at all suggest that Calvin fails to discuss our task in cultural life but speaks only about our enjoyment of culture. We have seen that the contrary is the case (pp. 282–83 above). But the issue we are now exploring is whether Calvin accepted the idea of a cultural *plan* pursuant to Gen 1:28 in the way that Kuyper and Schilder explained this text. My conclusion is that what Kuyper unfolds and Schilder partially endorses is missing in Calvin.

CHAPTER IV. COMPARISON

§ 5. The place of Christ

The work of Christ in fulfilling the mandate of developing creation is indispensable and *stimulating* for Kuyper and *foundational* for Schilder. In Kuyper's theology we find a duality (Mediator of creation and Mediator of redemption) that explains many (insolvable) contradictions in his definition of the relationship between common grace and particular grace. The difference between Kuyper and Schilder must not, however, obscure their agreement about Christ's place in culture. In Kuyper the emphasis must therefore be placed more on "indispensable" than on "stimulating."

There is no longer a need to defend the proposition that in Kuyper's depiction of culture, Christ occupies an *indispensable* position. For the general operation of common grace is dominated completely by him (pp. 47–48 above); nature would never have been unlocked without his appearance as the restored humanity (p. 51 above); in the church as organism, the "leaven" of particular grace has permeated the "flour" of common grace (p. 66 above). There is no Anabaptist isolation in Christ (pp. 82–83 above), nor of a striving of culture oriented toward secularization (pp. 107–09 above). Kuyper's "Not a square inch ... of which Christ, who is sovereign over all, does not cry out: 'Mine!'" (p. 108 above) did not remain a hollow phrase, neither in his doctrine nor in his life.

Indispensable – But we have to add that other word to it again: indispensable and *stimulating*. For the influence of Christ works as an *exponent* in common grace. Common grace is thereby "tripled in power" (p. 51 above). Thus there is a clear continuity in culture, even though the curve of cultural achievements shoots upward quickly because of Christ's work. What would otherwise languish, now begins to flourish. But the *line of the one culture is being continued*. We are to note here that according to Kuyper the general operation of common grace did not begin with Christ but in Babylon and Egypt, and was only then, via Greece and Rome, taken up by Christianity (pp. 47–49 above)!

These data agree completely with what we saw in the previous section concerning the independence of the cultural process. That is *founded* in the work of the Mediator of creation and is "only" *stimulated* by the Mediator of redemption.

Schilder expresses himself in a very different way. He does not recognize Kuyper's two lines in predestination (the salvific and the cultural lines), and he has overriding objections to the concept of a Mediator of creation (*Heid. Cat.* II, 87–103; III, 190–96). But quite apart from that, while Kuyper believes that culture continues itself (thanks to common grace) despite the Fall, Schilder regards the Fall as causing a *rupture*. The command to be engaged culturally

CHAPTER IV. COMPARISON

has remained, but the fulfillment of it has become impossible. Only through the Word made flesh, Jesus Christ, who again fixes the foundations of the world and, in this corrupt world, prepares the community that he purchased for the labor and service of God, are new perspectives opened (p. 194 above). Christ not only stimulates culture but is the foundation of culture, i.e., of true culture. For, "strictly speaking, there is no such thing as culture in general, culture as such" (pp. 201, 203 above). *The* one culture does not exist, for there is a great antithesis between culture that is from God and that is not from God. Cultural *koinōnia* is at bottom a matter of a *faith* community, while cultural *sunousia* means no more than that people labor on both sides of the dividing line with the same nature, on the same terrain, with identical cultural passion. Consequently, "the products of the believer's labor and the unbeliever's will always show great similarity" (p. 210 above).

We already saw earlier (pp. 85–86 above) that Kuyper also confessed the antithesis on the cultural terrain. And therefore the identification by Noordmans and Van Ruler of a deep and fundamental difference between Kuyper and Schilder is in my opinion far off the mark (p. 200 above). For in Kuyper particular grace does not remain stored away in the soul, as Van Ruler believes. That is why we can clearly see the antithesis also in *Kuyper's* view of culture. Noordmans rebukes Schilder for telescoping faith and culture into one, but I ask whether a similar rebuke should not also apply to Kuyper with his view of the *church* as organism. Besides, what principial difference is there between Schilder's "pure human race" (which causes Noordmans to recoil because it reminds him of the *Deutsche Christen*) and Kuyper's "new humanity," which actually does not just make its appearance on the new earth?

Nonetheless, when we examine the foundations on which the antithesis rests for both, there is a clear difference between Kuyper and Schilder. Schilder does not present a problem for us here. For him cultural labor is religion from the outset. "More than incense," petroleum has been "an express theme in the Bible," and in Paradise "everything is included within cultivation: the ground that one treads upon as well as the heart in all its depth, vegetation as well as the meditative spirit. There undefiled hands as well as souls are washed in righteousness; the one thing cannot be separated from the other" (p. 190 above). Thus faith and culture can never be two separate things. The reconciliation in Christ must touch culture in the root. Being for or against Christ is therefore also determinative for true or false culture. And herewith the antithesis has been presented.

But now let us turn to Kuyper: Also for him, faith and culture are *ultimately* never two separate things: "There is not a square inch of which Christ does not say: 'Mine.'" But that faith and culture are one is not apparent from Kuyper's *independent* view of culture in predestination. For this independence does bring faith and culture into diastasis! If we follow the line of particular grace, we will end with Kuyper's antithesis. But if we follow the line of common grace, we will end up with Van Ruler's image of concentric circles without any incisive

CHAPTER IV. COMPARISON

antithesis (p. 85 above). With the Mediator of creation as final ground we retain the one culture. But with the Mediator of redemption, we get the conquest of culture for Christ and with it the rupture, the antithesis (pp. 108–09 above). *It is this duality from which arise the difficulties that are again and again caused by the relationship between particular grace and common grace in Kuyper* (cf. pp. 58–59, 69–70, 91–92 above).

Here the following inconsistency is to be noted: On the one hand Kuyper speaks in such exalted tones about the development and completion of common grace that "involuntarily the necessity of the enrichment and completion of common grace takes a back seat to particular grace" (Van Ruler, op, cit., 55). Kuyper's argument clearly flows from the independent cultural motif in predestination ("Mediator of creation"). On the other hand, he speaks of "frightful" grace (pp. 28–29 above) and of a progression in which only the intellectual-artistic and *not* the moral-religious function of common grace (in accordance with its *deepest* operation, G.G. I, 423) is included (pp. 31–33 above). But in that way the concept of "culture" is clearly curtailed (p. 111 above; Van Ruler, op. cit., 59), so that its full content only functions again within the church as organism, among regenerate people ("Mediator of redemption"). Here progression acquires a deeper meaning: Kuyper is optimistic about the future of *Calvinistic* culture (p. 113 above).

It is thus necessary in our characterization of the place that Christ's work receives in Kuyper's cultural views (its being indispensable and stimulating) to double-underline "indispensable." The word "stimulating" points to the distance between Kuyper and Schilder; in the *indispensable* they meet each other.

§ 6. General grace – orientation and end result

In contradistinction from Schilder, both Calvin and Kuyper speak about grace in a more general sense. For Calvin this grace is directed to the knowledge of God; however, for Kuyper it is directed to cultural development. Connected with this is the fact that also its end result differs: For Kuyper general grace triumphs; according to Calvin it is sullied and suppressed. This profound distinction did not attract the attention of H. Kuiper and others.

No one will deny that Kuyper taught a general grace and that Schilder objected to the use of this term if "grace" was intended in a scholarly sense (pp. 130, 145, 185 above) rather than employed in a "sloppy, imprecise" way (p. 131 above) or "loosely" (p. 150 above). But how ought we to judge Calvin? Does he agree

CHAPTER IV. COMPARISON

with Kuyper or with Schilder? We cannot give a simple answer to this question, because an either-or response is unsuitable here.

First I shall point out that Schilder is incorrect when he places Calvin in opposition to Kuyper (pp. 134–35 above).

(a) It is incorrect to argue that Calvin only speaks of grace toward Gentiles "so long as it is not in earnest." Many references have confirmed that Calvin does not use the word "grace" just occasionally, but employs it *in a general sense, consciously* and *continuously* (pp. 243–44 above).

(b) Schilder improperly draws important and far-reaching conclusions from just one reference to Calvin, *Inst.* II, iii, 4: "these are not common gifts of nature, but special graces of God" (pp. 135–36 above). Calvin does mention "special" *here*, but that does not prevent him from being much more "general" elsewhere. For we read also of a "general grace" (p. 245 above), and of "universal grace" (p. 246 above, *Comm.* Isa 44:3). Even the mountains and the animals are included in it (p. 248 above). Schilder also reads too much into the use of the plural *gratias* in the quotation cited by him. In that quotation the emphasis is indeed on the *gifts* of grace, but elsewhere the content of the singular is much richer, as evidenced by the alternation of "grace" with words such as "love," "goodness," "clemency," and "compassion." Calvin then calls attention to God's *gracious* heart. In those instances the translation of *gratia* with the French concept of (elegant) "*grâce*," about which Schilder speaks, does indeed not work. Finally, in the above passage Calvin does speak about special grace in preference to gifts of common nature, but in other places common gifts are referred to as "grace" (see, e.g., pp. 244–45 above).

(c) It is incorrect to regard Kuyper's appeal to Calvin in explanation of the virtues of the Gentiles as being "completely immaterial," as Schilder argues (p. 136 above). For the formulation of the question and the answer are the same in Kuyper (pp. 3ff. above) and Calvin (p. 243 above). Both ask the question how, in spite of total corruption, we can still observe so much good in the virtue, learning, and art among the Gentiles. Both also answer that God's grace is the explanation. Their ways clearly part in the *elaboration* of the answer, but that is a different matter, which is to be discussed below. *At this point* I maintain over against Schilder what I already asserted (p. 126 above) about Kuyper's Calvinistic background. On Kuyper's appeal to Calvin, see also G. C. Berkouwer, *Gereformeerd Weekblad*, 7 (1951), 41,

One may ask how a scholar of Schilder's stature could make such a mistake. This calls for a twofold answer. In the first place, insofar as I could ascertain, Schilder did not subject H. Kuiper's dissertation, *Calvin on Common Grace*, to thorough study. Had he done so, he would have spoken about Kuyper in a more nuanced way than became apparent above. For those who have thoroughly examined the material collected by Kuiper *must* conclude that Schilder lacked adequate knowledge of Calvin on this point. For one can hardly call well-founded his analysis of Calvin on the basis of four or five references. But even so, this does not present the full picture. Even without a complete knowledge

CHAPTER IV. COMPARISON

of Calvin, Schilder knew intuitively that Calvin's circumstances were totally different from Kuyper's. But a too hasty conclusion appears to have prevented him from acquiring knowledge of the precise facts in such a way as to do full justice to Calvin (and Kuyper).

I maintain that Calvin spoke of grace in a general sense consciously and continuously. Nonetheless, there is a deep-seated difference between Calvin and Kuyper, and thus Schilder's criticism whereby he rejected Kuyper's appeal to Calvin was not without merit. To this end I will consider the focus of grace in Kuyper and Calvin. In what direction does it go? What is its purpose?

For Kuyper, common grace clearly has a *cultural* focus. See § 4. It is all about the development of the world. The full sum of the vital energies of God's creation must become evident at the close of the age, and that is how the cultural plan reaches its execution. In Kuyper's common grace we have seen an unfolding of a panorama of cultural history (pp. 41–58 above). But those who read Calvin discover a different image. When he discusses grace in a general sense, this grace focuses on *the knowledge of God's* judgment, i.e., it seeks to bring people to this knowledge. All human beings are born and live subject to the condition that they should learn to know God, writes Calvin (p. 260 above). For him it is a matter of this *cognitio*. Human beings are *invited* to the knowledge of God (pp. 260–61 above, the invitation motif); they are called to praise their Creator consciously. They can know God and hence they will later be found guilty in the judgment (p. 262 above, the critical motif). For Calvin, this reveals the focus of God's grace toward the Gentiles.

The difference with Kuyper is tangible. We can state with confidence that the invitation and critical motifs play no role whatsoever in Kuyper. And that is understandable! For in Kuyper it is all about the development of culture, to which also the unbelieving majority among humankind make their *constructive* contribution and can do so without consciously praising God's name. The knowledge of God does not come into view so long as Kuyper restricts himself to common grace. The knowledge of God can and must influence culture in a stimulating way, but then it is a knowledge of God flowing from the spring of *particular* grace. God's general revelation—which calls to repentance, extends an invitation to the true life, and subjects everything to the decision that must be made for or against God—lies beyond Kuyper's cultural horizon of common grace. When he speaks in *De Gemeene Gratie* of general revelation, the first (and the last) thing we hear is that no "aversion to the sciences and no indifference toward nature and the arts" may exist (III, 140–41). Common grace, general revelation, and even natural theology (!) (*Loc. de Deo* I, 72ff.), all receive a cultural content.

The fundamental difference between Kuyper and Calvin becomes even more apparent when we take note of the fact that both write about the *end result* of God's display of grace. Kuyper lets common grace *triumph*. Even if we keep in mind that Kuyper speaks of a frightful grace, that common grace can shrink (pp. 32–33 above), and that only its intellectual-artistic operation is included

CHAPTER IV. COMPARISON

in a complete progression (see § 5), the references to the development of the *totality* created existence remain. Satan will suffer defeat, also on this terrain (pp. 33-34 above). Despite everything, it appears that common grace remains a triumphant matter. Kuyper's optimism about the resilience of a future that will be governed by Calvinism confirms this (p. 112 above). Calvin, on the other hand, recognizes a grace toward the Gentiles that is disdained and kept at bay. That is the "fruit" by which human beings later, and often also already now (p. 272 above), subject themselves to God's righteous judgment. The world spoils his gifts. It is *not* better than expected (pp. 238ff. above) and we must guard ourselves against the semblance of things (pp. 241-43, 260 above).

I have already pointed out that Kuyper nowhere refers to the portions of the Belgic Confession, art. 14, and the Canons of Dort, III/IV, which discuss the fact that human beings are inexcusable because they wholly pollute the light of nature and suppress it (p. 25 above). That no longer surprises me. What receives full attention in Calvin is omitted in Kuyper. Whoever judges common grace so optimistically will have difficulty in perceiving what the Belgic Confession and the Canons of Dort confess in agreement with Calvin.

It is regrettable that H. Kuiper's dissertation is not helpful here. It demonstrates irrefutably that Calvin spoke with emphasis about grace in a general sense. That connects Kuyper with Calvin. But what distinguishes them? H. Kuiper did not answer this question. That would have been difficult in any event, at least in a critical sense, because his study was intended to "help one decide whether the charges lodged against Kuyper and Bavinck [by Haitjema and others, J.D.] are warranted by the facts in the case, yes or no" (op. cit., 2-3). The study, defended at the Free University, was directed toward a particular conclusion, as is apparent from its beginning: Calvin is called "the discoverer of common grace" (2). But then one soon fails to pay attention to the truly *essential* distinctions between Calvin and Kuyper. One is then intent on proving that there is continuity. And it does indeed exist. But then the discontinuity is no longer noticed. But this is even more clearly evident and extends into the root of the matter. Is grace directed toward the knowledge of God, or toward culture? The difference is surely not insignificant. Also S. J. Ridderbos argues that Kuyper "continued the lines drawn by Calvin" (*De theologische cultuurbeschouwing van Abraham Kuyper*, 373). But the true state of the matter is different.

In this way we get a good insight into Schilder's critique in which he rejected Kuyper's appeal to Calvin. I have explained already in what respects Schilder in my opinion erred. But he clearly understood the difference in approach between Kuyper and Calvin. He knew that Kuyper failed to let the complete quotation about the "light of nature" function (*Ref.* 19, 66), and that is why he sharply recognized Kuyper's distance not only from Trigland (pp. 132-33 above) but also from Calvin. The Reformed confession "has applied the brake to every fiery spirit that wants to show that the light of nature is the foundation on which one could build, as the basis upon which proud buildings of learning and art could be constructed, and so on" (*Ref.* 19, 67).

Schilder rightly also does *not* want to sever *Inst.* II, iii, 3, where Calvin speaks of the virtue among the Gentiles, from II, iii, 4, where he says that we must deny all value to everything that seems to be praiseworthy in ungodly people. In the marketplace and by the great mass of people those "virtues" may be praised, but before God's heavenly judgment seat they have no value whatsoever (p. 136 above).

In the article referenced above, Berkouwer pointed out that Schilder did not quote Calvin fully. For it says: "before the heavenly judgment they shall be of no value *in earning righteousness*" (*Inst.* II, iii, 4). Indeed, Schilder does not quote the words italicized here. But it actually makes no difference. For one could ask Berkouwer in what respect the virtues of the Gentiles would have value in the judgment (evidently the definitive judgment!). The phrase "in earning righteousness" is, in my opinion, not restricted. Looked at from God's perspective, the virtues of the Gentiles have no value. A few lines earlier we read that "before God they lose all favor" because of human ambition. Calvin recognizes but one criterion for judging the virtues of the Gentiles: the knowledge of God—and that is why the Gentiles are condemned, for "when there is no zeal to glorify God, the most important part of uprightness is missing" (*Inst.* II, iii, 4). But Kuyper recognizes more than just the one criterion: also the cultural one, and for that reason the virtues are valued by God on account of their place in his cultural program. Over against Schilder, Berkouwer remarked that one may not play off II, iii, 4, against II, iii, 3 (op. cit., 41). Quite so, for Schilder minimizes the breadth of Calvin's speaking about *grace* shown to the Gentiles. But on the other hand, one must also not *abstract* II, iii, 3, from II, iii, 4. The danger then is that from clippings cut out of the *Institutes* a complete Kuyper of common grace emerges.

In conclusion it is yet to be noted that Calvin's *restraint motif* (pp. 263–64 above) also has the same orientation as the first (invitation) and the second (critical) motifs. The third motif does not function in isolation. See, e.g., what was quoted on pp. 263–64 above. By justice, modesty, friendship, moderation, courage, and prudence, people as God's instruments maintain human society. But in which context does Calvin apply these words? "For even though they are God's instruments for the preservation of human society, ... yet they carry out these *good* works of God very badly. For they are restrained from evildoing not by genuine zeal for good but either by mere ambition or by self-love, or some other perverse motive.... In short, when we remember the constant end of that which is right—namely, to serve God—whatever strives to another end already deservedly loses the name 'right.' Therefore, because they do not look to the goal that God's wisdom prescribes, what they do, though it seems good in the doing, yet by its perverse intention is sin" (*Inst.* III, xiv, 3). Here one finds everything that I postulated: the orientation toward the knowledge of God, the bad consequence, and the single criterion for judging. *Everything*

CHAPTER IV. COMPARISON

that pursues a different goal than the conscious service of God loses the name "righteousness." It is easy to check that Calvin's fourth motif (help for the church) also harmonizes with what was said above about the other motifs (pp. 264–66 above).

§ 7. General grace – a doctrine?

In distinction from Kuyper, Calvin did not recognize a doctrine of general grace. This is made clear by his varied terminology and concrete definition of grace in a more general sense. He recognized *a* general grace, but not common grace *as such*.

God shows grace to the Gentiles. Calvin did not use the word "grace" inadvertently in this context. He spoke of it *consciously*. But what was his aim? It became clear to me that the aim and fruit of this grace differs markedly from that of Kuyper's common grace. This raises the following question: Does Calvin's theology recognize a "general grace" as an *independent* theme? Or even stronger: as *doctrine*?

It was a doctrine for Kuyper. He not only says so (p. 5 above), he demonstrates it. Whatever one may think of Kuyper's common grace, no one will deny that in his theology he expanded this grace. The huge domain of the entire history of culture is assigned to common grace. When in this connection we realize that for Kuyper culture functions as an independent theme in God's Counsel, we can hardly deny him the right to speak of a doctrine.

In Calvin we find none of these things; he knows of no culture in predestination and no independent attention to the cultural process. He does not recognize a doctrine of general grace. Surely we cannot really speak of a doctrine solely because he gives an *explanation* of the virtues of the *Gentiles*? As a matter of fact, Kuyper does not do so for this reason either. He would not have written a three-volume work about common grace if he had believed that this grace contained no *calling* for Christians to practice culture. For the first case (the explanation), a reference in the *Locus de Peccato* would have sufficed for the maintenance of the radical Fall; for the second case (the calling) we get an explanation of common grace (interwoven with particular grace) in which virtually all the *loci* of systematic theology are investigated. (Cf. *De Gemeene Gratie* II.) This unveils the following important difference between Kuyper and Calvin. Calvin does not at all recognize a calling that would be based on a "general grace." Hence, nowhere in his writings does such a general grace become an independent theme, let alone a doctrine.

This is apparent also from the *terminology*. For if Calvin had taught general grace *as such*, he would undoubtedly have demarcated it more distinctly from particular grace. But it is a fact that neither the one nor the other kind of

CHAPTER IV. COMPARISON

grace is fixed terminologically. Calvin uses different adjectives for God's grace toward the Gentiles. For this, see the quotations in chapter III: "general" (p. 245), "special" (pp. 243–45), "heavenly" (p. 244), "universal" (p. 246), "common" (p. 247). Thus "special" is truly not used solely for particular grace. Similarly, "compassion," "love," "tenderness," etc. (p. 247), appear as designations of grace in particular and general senses. H. Kuiper rightly says: "We must pay close heed to the context in which Calvin uses the word 'grace' before we can come to a decision as to its precise content" (op. cit., 178). See also C. B. Hylkema, *Oud- en Nieuw-Calvinisme*, 210ff.

On the basis of this, I question whether Calvin really recognized a "double" grace. Is it not rather the case that he recognized but one kind of grace of God, which can, however, differ in extent and effect? *In extent* in that God extends his grace within the church, but also in a more general connection to the world outside of the church. Sometimes he uses the word "grace" very "particularly" and concretely as peculiar or special grace. *In effect*, because it can lead to repentance (for the elect), but it can also be inefficacious (for the others, pp. 268–69 above).

Thus it becomes clear that in Calvin's theology we must not look for general grace *as such* in addition to particular grace *as such*. He recognizes a grace with many gradations. *All* grace, both within the church and outside of it, is directed to the knowledge and praise of God, although its effect may differ. For the Gentiles are also invited to the knowledge of God, although none among them attain salvation without Christ.

Consequently it is dangerous to speak of "Calvin and general grace as such." Calvin recognized general grace. God's display of grace is not limited to the church. But that is something different from adhering to a *doctrine* of general grace in which this grace inevitably becomes an independent entity (as in Kuyper). It should be noted again how greatly Kuyper and Calvin differ. While I concluded first that their ways parted with respect to the direction and the fruit of grace, now I conclude that its *nature* also differs significantly. For Kuyper, common grace is "*of a totally different nature* than particular or covenant grace" (p. 7 above; cf. pp. 61–62). That is not the case for Calvin. For him the effect can differ; grace is efficacious or it is not. But the nature of grace is determined by *salvation*: God extends his invitation even to Gentiles. But they will be found guilty because they despised the invitation to bliss.

Schilder has remarked that Calvin did not recognize a common grace as a *generally valid* category (p. 135 above). This statement is partly incorrect. Indeed, Calvin uses the term "special grace," and also the plural "graces" when he identifies concrete gifts of grace. Schilder also rightly pointed out A. Sizoo's incorrect translation of *peculiarem Dei gratiam* (*Inst.* II, ii, 14; see p. 218 above) as "*the* (instead of *a*) special grace of God." Cf. the French edition, in which it is "*une grâce spéciale de Dieu* (3, 315). But Schilder draws too many conclusions from too few data. For besides "special grace" the much broader terms "general grace" and even "universal grace" are used. In addition to the plural "graces," we find the singular "grace" more often, and it can indeed encompass more than only a reference to the *gift* of grace (see also the next section). And further, in addition to the indefinite article *une*, Calvin also uses the definite article *la* on more than one occasion in the French edition. See, e.g., the quotations from *Inst.* II, ii, 17, and II, iii, 3, on page 245 above, in both of which the definite article *la* is used in the French version. In his "grace" quotations, Calvin is often more general than Schilder would have us believe.

On the other hand, there is much truth in Schilder's remark that Calvin does not use the term "(general) grace" in the categorical sense that Kuyper does. In Calvin's *oeuvre* it definitely is not an independent category that constantly absorbs our attention. One can closely read an entire book of "grace" quotations (H. Kuiper's *Calvin on Common Grace*!) and still maintain that Calvin did not teach a general grace. It never becomes a *theme* in his immense legacy. "General grace" as a generally valid category? It is sometimes generally valid even for angels, wild animals, and mountains (pp. 247–48 above). But a category? Surely then one might expect that "general grace" would form a constitutive factor in Calvin's doctrinal explications. But such is not the case. *Grace*, sometimes all-inclusive, is constitutive—with many gradations, but without such sharp demarcations that one grace is delimited from another as being of "a totally different nature."

After everything that has thus far been adduced, I believe that we must be very skeptical of the following strong statement by S. U. Zuidema: "In his dissertation *Calvin on Common Grace*, Dr. H. Kuiper demonstrates with all his data that the doctrine of common grace is already at least included in Calvin's ideas. Hence those who do not accept the idea of common grace must understand that they attack not only Kuyper and Bavinck. They also attack Calvin on the essential point in question in his Christian thought, and also all of Amsterdam, Kampen, and Geneva" (op. cit., article in *A.R. Staatkunde* 24, 1). Whoever reads Calvin unencumbered by the doctrine of Abraham Kuyper will conclude that general grace (Calvin) and common grace (Kuyper) are *different* entities.

§ 8. *God's wrath*

The previous sections already lead one to suspect that Kuyper does not really discuss the wrath of God in connection with the topic under discussion. However, Schilder and Calvin do so emphatically. Besides a similarity (*inter alia*, the glorification motif), there are also differences between Calvin and Schilder.

Kuyper certainly does not want to eliminate the wrath of God from his doctrine of common grace. "Those who are not converted to life remain children of

CHAPTER IV. COMPARISON

wrath." They find no rest, "because God's wrath does not cease." On the terrain of common grace, therefore, this wrath will always operate "in and through all things" (p. 26 above). But those who would think that Kuyper would therefore constantly point to God's wrath are mistaken. He hardly mentions it.

This is not surprising after what we saw in the previous sections. For Kuyper's common grace is directed to the development of culture, in which the children of wrath make their contribution as positive co-workers of God. In accordance with God's Counsel they contribute to "that entirely different work of God in the domain of common grace." Then we can hardly expect that God's wrath would constantly be drawn to our attention. Kuyper himself says in a telling way that God's wrath always operates *in* and *through* all things. Unbelievers remain children of wrath when we consider God's work in *particular* grace. But that work, at least as key theme, is not the focus of *De Gemeene Gratie*.

God's wrath is referred to when Kuyper speaks of the *shrinking* of common grace, e.g., in I, 415ff. But it has already become clear to me that Kuyper did not write three volumes to demonstrate how common grace shrinks, but rather how it *"expands."* It is typical in this regard that Kuyper can write many pages about the *curse*, but then in such a way "that God and his Christ themselves rage against [the] consequence of the curse; they scold and punish, they break, stem, and resist" (*G.G.* II, 480). The curse *must* break out as punishment and revelation of God's wrath (II, 418ff); but also, "once it has broken out, it *must* be attacked, restrained, and in due course conquered once and for all by God" (II, 498). Consequently common grace arms us against death and suffering and gives us precautionary measures against all this (II, 481–608).

It is striking that Kuyper speaks very impersonally about the curse and does so without referring to the concrete, actual fury of God against the life of the wicked. It is quite different from what we read in Calvin (pp. 250–51 above). See also C. B. Hylkema, op. cit., 243, in this regard.

Those who read Schilder will see another image appear. That is to be expected. If election and reprobation run in parallel and it is impermissible to add a "pre" to God's mercy; when heaven and hell have God's equal attention, and continuation of history forms the substrate of the administration of blessing and curse, then Schilder *must* warn against all one-sidedness (pp. 148–50 above). Not only grace, but also wrath creates its own objects (p. 180 above). *Both* are important in culture. There is a culture that originates from Jesus Christ as its source (p. 198 above), a culture that lives out of grace. There is also a "culture" that gets no further than the number 3½ (Babylon and the Antichrist), which is subject to God's *wrath* (p. 203 above). For Schilder does not recognize a single culture as the development of the totality of created existence in accordance with the independently functioning plan of God in his predestination. In culture, Christ is therefore both Savior-Redeemer and Savior-Judge (p. 194 above).

Calvin also clearly draws attention to the wrath of God (pp. 250–51, 246–47 above). In accordance with Prov 16:4, God glorifies himself also in his wrath (p. 273 above).

The agreement between Schilder and Calvin is striking in more than one respect. Although the one does and the other does not use the word "grace" for God's gifts to the Gentiles, both emphasize that these gifts are *misused*, so that God's wrath against them is revealed (Rom 1:18). In Kuyper we from time to time come across the idea that human beings *reject* common grace (*G.G.* I, 412), or *misuse* it (I, 449–50). But in Calvin and Schilder this idea is central: the light is rejected and extinguished (pp. 132, 165ff., 204–05, 238ff., 252, 262 above). They also both recognize the *glorification motif* in accordance with Prov 16:4. There are people who are destined for certain death from their mother's womb, so that by their destruction they may glorify God as instruments of his wrath (p. 273 above). To that end, God can make the reprobate even more blind and foolish by the proclamation of his Word.

This is said by the same Calvin who characterizes the judgment as a concomitant function of proclamation, using the term "accidental office"! He did not relinquish or diminish this—in our opinion also not when he inserted the words "so to speak" and "as it were" (see the texts on p. 272 above), as J. Kamphuis believes (*Ref.* 41, 61–62). For these additions are repeatedly absent. Cf. the quotation with reference to John 12:47 (p. 272), where we find the expression "as we have said several times before." The reservation that "so to speak" and "as it were" suggest is not connected with the *content*, but with the *manner* in which Calvin conveys this content. Calvin normally has an aversion to scholastic distinctions, but now he uses one: accidental–essential.

But more needs to be said. As accidental office, the preaching is very real in its character as judgment. It can blind and make foolish and it has this effect also on those whom God has *rejected*. Kamphuis rightly pointed this out in opposition to C. Veenhof, who maintained too strongly that the deadening and condemnatory operation of the gospel is always "something accidental, something occasional, something that *conflicts directly with its nature*" (*Zicht op Calvijn*, 100). For "not from its nature" [*non ex eius natura*] (cf. p. 272) means something different than "against its nature [*contra eius naturam*]." And even when in his explanation of Matt 16:19 (p. 272) Calvin speaks of "beyond nature" [*praeter naturam*] that phrase means no more than "other than what nature desires." See Lewis and Short, *A Latin Dictionary*, s.v. *praeter*. The glorification of God's name through the ruin of the reprobate and, in this, through the revelation of God's wrath, does not (always) occur outside of the preaching, even though this function of the Word is also accidental.

Calvin and Schilder have different opinions about the latter, as we saw in § 2. But there are other differences as well.

In the first place, Calvin does not speak of an eternal wrath of God, as Schilder does. It is also not included in the glorification motif. The reprobate are indeed created to be instruments of God's wrath, but this does not extend beyond a predestination *to* wrath [*ad iram*]. Schilder takes it a step further: God's wrath creates its own objects and in that way it unveils a predestination *out of* wrath [*ex ira*].

In the second place, Calvin points out God's wrath in history in a more concrete way than Schilder. I have pointed out that Calvin depicts the general revelation of grace and wrath as very real, dynamic, and personal (pp. 250–51, 272–74 above). Calvin maintains the rule (although he recognizes many exceptions) that all prosperity is a blessing of God, while disaster and adversity are a curse (p. 251 above). In contrast, Schilder warns against drawing a conclusion regarding God's disposition (of grace or wrath) from the facts (pp. 143–45, 184 above). Thus, with respect to the continuation of life after the Fall, he says: "So long as it seems pleasant to us, we call it 'grace,' but when the reality of wrath and punishment occupy us, we say: take it away, take it away, cursed be the day I was born. But neither the one nor the other impression is capable of expressing God's truth in and of itself" (p. 146 above). Indeed, in the strict sense, the disposition of God "is only expressed "in 'the *books*' that *are above*" (p. 183 above).

"In the strict sense"—that is what the theologian says when he wants to speak in a scientific way. But at the same time we remember that the pastor and prophet Schilder *preached* God's wrath (p. 229 above; cf. the entire section on pp. 223–32) as real, dynamic, and personal. And in this the agreement with Calvin becomes apparent again.

§ 9. *God's disposition*

The issue of a general grace in its relation to God's (eternal) disposition barely occupied Kuyper, Calvin now and then, but Schilder continuously.

As has become evident, Kuyper paid little attention to common grace as *disposition* of God. What concerned him was the deed, the gift in common grace (pp. 25–27 above). It functions as *factor* in God's governance of the world. As we already saw, in the first place this concerned God's honor over against Satan. In God's struggle against Satan, human beings may share in his grace, which often is nonetheless a *frightful* grace (pp. 28–29 above). Further, it became apparent from the previous section that, for Kuyper, God's wrath as disposition only becomes a theme in the treatment of particular grace. Common grace demands attention for other topics. We also saw that we must not draw too many conclusions from what Kuyper writes about the patience of God. I posited that this patience combined with "mercy" and "compassion" was depicted inadequately *by itself*. Postponement of wrath, even its maintenance, appeared to me to be indispensable components of God's patience (p. 26 above). When S. J. Ridderbos asserts that Kuyper in his common grace "may not place a favorable disposition toward all people in the foreground, but does presume it," and wants to support this assertion with the argument that "we heard him speak about divine patience from which also the gifts of common grace proceed" (*De theologische cultuurbeschouwing van Abraham Kuyper*, 310), then this argumentation is weak. The patience of God has more aspects. Those who collect Kuyper's meager material on this point must not forget that in God's disposition toward the unbelieving world his wrath never abates.

In my opinion the entire issue of grace as act or as disposition dates from a later period. Kuyper himself hardly mentions it, for the setting in which he was occupied with common grace was entirely different from a context in which questions of eternal life and eternal death, and grace and wrath become urgent. Terminologically, Kuyper does not recognize common grace as a "general favorable disposition of God," but in practice those who do discuss it go further than Kuyper. J. Kamphuis rightly pointed this out in opposition to S. J. Ridderbos (*Ref.* 31, 335; see also *Ref.* 26, 393).

For that reason Schilder's criticism of common grace as general favorable disposition is not really directed at Kuyper, although Schilder would probably have thought: "Whoever reads Kuyper's outpourings about 'common grace' knows that he brings 'anything and everything' into the discussion when it concerns a *paraphrase* of the concept of 'grace.'" God's *disposition, use* of nature, Gentiles who are *"better than expected,"* science, art—these all become *a*bstractions (a form of art or science, or use of nature, or general ethical decency, or divine disposition, all "hovering" above individuals)" (*Heid. Cat.* IV, 66).

I am of the opinion that it was not via Kuyper but via the struggle around *Kalamazoo* that the issue of God's disposition in common grace became a point of discussion. The Synod of Kalamazoo (of the Christian Reformed Church in America, 1924) made the following declaration: "Concerning the first point, touching *the favorable attitude of God toward mankind in general, and not only alone toward the elect*, synod declares that it is certain, according to Scripture and the Confession, that there is, besides the saving grace of God, shown only to those chosen to eternal life, also a certain favor or grace of God which he shows to his creatures in general" (quoted from A. C. de Jong, op. cit., 11–12).

This issue subsequently also to a large extent dominated the debates about common grace in the Netherlands. Cf. V. Hepp, "De kwestie van de Algemeene Genade," three articles in *Ref.* 4, 344ff. (1924). K. Sietsma (*Ref.* 18, 208) rightly stated that Hepp and his followers were thinking principally about the dealings and gifts of God that are of benefit to the entire human race. In contrast, Schilder and De Graaf, proceeding from the term *"grace"* in their critique, "have in view God's *disposition* and his *relationship* with the creature, and then they ask whether these descriptions arrive at the right solution." In this connection Sietsma says that "the parties in the debate do not understand each other." This assertion is too bold in its generality. But it should have resonated more. For then the clear differences between Kuyper and Kalamazoo would have become apparent. Now I sometimes get the impression, also in Schilder's critique, that

CHAPTER IV. COMPARISON

the weapons are directed against Kuyper in a sham battle. What is presumed to be Kuyper's view is actually that of Kalamazoo.

In saying this I am not suggesting that Kuyper was *right* in barely addressing the issue of God's disposition. I merely note the *fact*. And S. J. Ridderbos, Schilder, et al., did not fully recognize this fact or take it into account.

Also in Calvin we find nothing about the question whether grace is act or disposition. But he does differ from Kuyper. Grace as disposition is hardly mentioned in Kuyper. But for Calvin, grace as gift and as disposition are entirely interwoven. That is apparent when he places designations such as "grace," "mercy," "favor," and "love" (p. 247 above) next to each other. This is what we generally find in Calvin. But there are exceptions (pp. 274ff. above). There Calvin speaks clearly from the perspective of election and reprobation, which confront him with a *question*: How it is possible that the elect can (for the time being) be subject to God's curse and wrath, and how can the reprobate receive grace?

The answer was a multiple one:

(a) Let us reverently allow the above to stand side by side. There *is* unity in the manifestation of both (grace and wrath), but in the weakness of our understanding we cannot grasp it;

(b) God is angry with the elect "in a certain sense," just as the reprobate, "strictly speaking," do not receive grace; and

(c) We must distinguish between sinner and creature.

It is abundantly clear that the concomitance of grace and disposition in answer (b) has become problematic. We hear of a "*sense* of grace" and of "strictly speaking." But we must not overemphasize this solution. Calvin maintains the word "grace," even though he regards only those things as "blessings and tokens of God's favor and grace *in the fullest and deepest sense* of these terms in case they proceed from the fountain of God's redeeming love and are subservient to the eternal salvation of men" (H. Kuiper, op. cit., 221; italics supplied). "In the fullest and deepest sense." But that does not prevent Calvin from continuing to speak constantly about grace, mercy, favor, and love—of grace that is not (as in the elect) salvifically effective, but nonetheless remains *grace*.

What we see on the periphery of Calvin's argument is central in Schilder: God regards every individual person very specifically before him "in an absolute disposition of love or of grace." It would conflict with God's simplicity to suppose a general and a special grace toward the same persons (p. 185 above). For a denial of an indifferent working of God (Paraeus, pp. 134–35 above) demands the "recognition that, with respect to every individual, God's disposition, also in the distribution of what we, in apperceptive language, call manifold gifts, is determined by his predestination." Then, when we hold fast to an individual wrath of God, we cannot accept an attitude of God that is favorable toward all people. "Does wrath particularize love?" (Schilder, *Heid. Cat.* IV, 66).

In my view it is clear that we cannot continue to speak that way about grace (as "a fixed disposition," p. 149 above) toward the reprobate. Schilder rejects *general* grace and accepts only a *communal* grace ("for more than one") and a *communal* curse ("shared by more than one"). The first is the portion of those whom Christ calls his own; the second, the portion of all other people (*Christ and Culture*, 92). The wrath of God rests on all of the latter "at all times," while the patience of God toward them is "a controlled permission that allows those who deserve punishment to become more deserving of it; a continuation of the wrathful 'disposition' that waits for its proper time (*Heid. Cat.* IV, 119).

Schilder connects his views about God's disposition especially to the question whether or not the continuation of history after the Fall was grace. On the basis of double predestination and the double disposition of love and hate, he rejects the "subjectivistic qualification that it is *only* grace" (e.g., p. 185 above). Certainly, in "colloquial speech" (p. 130) and in "apperceptive language" (p. 145) one can continue to speak about grace in an "imprecise" way (p. 130). But whoever formulates concepts in "scholarly, precise" language (pp. 129–30, 145–46), "strictly" (p. 140), in a "theological" way (pp. 178–79), must avoid such imprecision. In this context "theological" means: *not* "childlike" (pp. 143–45), "anthropocentric" (p. 145), and "anthropomorphic" (pp. 145–46). In my opinion Schilder's views about God's "*absolute* disposition of love or of hate" have the direct consequence that we cannot speak of grace toward the reprobate in any way if we express ourselves strictly and theologically. But I do emphasize that Schilder nowhere expressly draws the conclusion that there is no grace *whatsoever* for *any* reprobate.

Finally, it is to be noted that Schilder, like Calvin, recognizes the difference between sinful creatures and that which is creaturely in them. God loves the personhood of his creatures, also in the reprobate. But his wrath rests on them as persons (p. 186 above).

§ 10. Grace and necessity

With predestination as their point of departure, Kuyper and Schilder both ascribe the character of *necessity* to the continuation of history. Despite this, Kuyper continues to speak of common grace. That is why Schilder attacks this characterization of Kuyper's. The issue does not arise in Calvin, for predestination remains in the background in his work.

Despite all the differences between Kuyper and Schilder, there are also clear areas of agreement. I will mention one in this section: proceeding from predestination, both ascribe the character of necessity to the continuation of history.

First Kuyper: "In all previous centuries there was nothing among the

CHAPTER IV. COMPARISON

Egyptians and Greeks, in Babylon and Rome, and there is nothing today among the peoples of whatever continent that was or is not needed, that does not all form an indispensable part of the great work that God is doing to bring the world's development to its consummation" (p. 36 above). When sin entered the world, the curse on the one hand had to begin its work, but on the other hand God, if he wanted to be and remain God, could for the same reason not desist from opposing the curse. For the self-destruction by the curse could not have been God's intention. God *had to* stem it and destroy it, for "creation has a *purpose*, and because the self-destruction opposes that purpose, it opposes God" (p. 39 above). God cannot let his plans be destroyed by Satan. He must triumph over him (pp. 33–34 above). Since the Fall was included in God's Counsel, "also common grace, as powerful motive, must be included. For if the Fall had not been followed also by common grace, the entire continuation of the world would for all time have been withdrawn from God's self-glorification." That would be unthinkable. It is *necessary* that the world be maintained, and to that end common grace is an *indispensable link* in predestination (pp. 39–40 above). God wanted to create the world and to permit the Fall, and from this it necessarily follows that common grace was included in God's Counsel.

Schilder also uses the word "necessary" more than once, although in a different sense. Predestination, in its double aspect of election and reprobation, governs history and makes it necessary: "The conservation of the world and the continuation of history, together with the possibility of culture and the ensuing culture as reality ... all are indispensable, both for building the road that leads to heaven and for traveling down the roads that lead to hell" (p. 182 above). God maintains himself in the continuation of history; he remains true to himself in order to carry out his Counsel concerning heaven and hell (p. 179 above). It is for this reason that the prolongation of history is necessary (pp. 141, 143–44 above).

It must strike us that in Schilder's view the entire history of the world and its cultural development is subordinated to God's predestination. This is already apparent from *Wat is de hemel?*: "When in due course the sum of humanity has been gathered and the last elect has been born and regenerated, is it not in this way that history comes to its reward and its completion? The entire world will have been necessary to bring the last elect person to his last temptation and his last triumph, i.e., to bring God to the acme, the high point, of his re-creative work" (219). With this quotation we are still clearly in Schilder's second period, since the "last reprobate" does not yet appear beside the "last elect." But that is a side issue at this point.

Both Kuyper and Schilder apply the concept of "necessity" and do so because of predestination. However, the content of predestination differs for them. For Kuyper, history receives its necessary character because God intended that in predestination there would be culture. For Schilder, the continuation of culture is necessary because God intended that in

CHAPTER IV. COMPARISON

predestination (with the deployment of culture) there would be elect and reprobate.

It is remarkable that despite this necessity Kuyper continues to speak of common *grace*, whereas Schilder, especially because of this necessity, bans the word "grace" as a one-sided characterization. In Kuyper we keep reading about grace, but the question, "Necessary—and yet grace?" that I posed (p. 40 above) is not addressed by him and receives no answer. We need to think only of his exegesis of Gen 2:17 (pp. 14ff. above). In contrast, Schilder rejects the word "grace" as one-sided. The continuation of history is "actually not *grace*. Nor is it *condemnation*, strictly speaking. But it is the *condition* for both." It is *substrate* for the administration of blessing and curse (p. 150 above).

It remains unresolved why Kuyper did not see or discuss the question that inevitably arises when he speaks of both necessity and grace. Why Schilder did so is clear. When you emphasize that election and reprobation, and heaven and hell, receive the same attention, then the continuation of history must also be considered under both aspects and then the leap to this continuation as *substrate* for the administration of blessing and curse is not a great one.

Kuyper has an entirely different doctrine of predestination. It is culturally directed, as we saw. And therefore, despite its "frightful" aspects (pp. 28–29 above), it is a much more "agreeable" matter than predestination is for Schilder. Kuyper was able to incorporate those "frightful" aspects of common grace into *grace* (pp. 28–29 above). In that way the duality of necessity and grace did not become problematic for Kuyper.

Calvin treats the term "grace" in the most uninhibited way. In his argument we find no discussions that flow from predestination. Hence, the word "necessity" does not appear either. One can indeed say that when he speaks of general grace, Calvin does not look backward (to predestination), but forward (to the judgment). The invitation to the knowledge of God is the means that makes people inexcusable (p. 262 above). The righteous judgment presumes the display of grace. It gives depth to the wrath and the curse of God.

Of Gen 2:17, Calvin says that the death that was announced sets in immediately: "Superfluous is the question how it was that God threatened death to Adam on the day in which he should touch the fruit, when he long deferred the punishment. For then was Adam consigned to death, and death began its reign in him, until supervening grace should bring a remedy" (*Comm.* Gen 2:17). This contradicts Kuyper but does not therefore imply that Calvin agrees with Schilder. He does not know of the substrate idea. Thus in an uninhibited way he can say: "This life, however it may abound in endless miseries, is still rightly to be counted among those *blessings* of God that are not to be spurned." Cf. what follows: "For believers especially, this ought to be a testimony of divine benevolence" (*Inst.* III, ix, 3).

CHAPTER IV. COMPARISON

§ 11. Culture and pilgrimage

The recognition of common grace (Kuyper), of pilgrimage (Calvin), and of office (Schilder), respectively, are determinative for the attitude of the three theologians toward and in culture.

Kuyper discovered in the doctrine of common grace the foundation for his appeal to Christians not to avoid culture (p. 118 above). Without common grace, Christians would have to "draw themselves back entirely into the service of the church and isolate the church from the world." Their only calling would then be "to condemn the world while shut up in the ark of God with all God's elect" (*G.G.* III, 16). But over against all dualism stands the "*confession of common grace* that teaches us how God in his mercy has lifted up his hand also over that sinful world in order to preserve it and to arrest sin and curse. And especially because of this, the world again offers God's children the opportunity to serve their God in it to his honor. That immediately changes our calling. Otherwise our calling would have been: to leave the world and lop it off. But now this becomes our calling: to go into that world and to maintain ourselves in the world. And this, in contrast to the Anabaptist claim, is now the stance of all who are Reformed" (op. cit., III, 19).

Does Calvin also regard this as the foundation for the calling of Christians in this world? We have seen that he does not recognize a doctrine of common grace (§ 7). Hence, it cannot possibly serve as foundation for the Christian life in all its breadth. But we also noted that Calvin does recognize a general grace. Does *this* perhaps form the basis for a Christian pursuit of culture? That is also not the case.

This is demonstrated in what is Calvin's strongest statement against those who deny God's gifts of grace toward the Gentiles: "If we regard God's Spirit as the only source of truth, we shall neither reject the truth itself, not despise it wherever it shall appear, unless we wish to dishonor the Spirit of God. For by holding the gifts of the Spirit in slight esteem, we disdain and despise the Spirit himself" (*Inst.* II, ii, 15). Does this recognition become the point of departure for determining what a Christian must do in the world? Not at all, for according to Calvin:

(a) This general grace is a gift to *Gentiles*, to the great jurists, philosophers, rhetoricians, medical doctors, mathematicians, and poets (*Inst.* II, ii, 15). It is not a foundation upon which Gentiles and Christians stand together, as it is for Kuyper; and

(b) We must not despise these gifts of the Holy Spirit to the Gentiles, because the Lord wants to see us *benefit* from the effort and service of the godless. ("If the Lord has willed that we be helped in physics, dialectic, mathematics, and other like disciplines, by the work and ministry of the ungodly, let us use this assistance," *Inst.* II, ii, 16.) Thus Calvin does speak of *enjoyment* of culture (the world serves us, cf. pp. 264–65 above in the context of the fourth motif: help for the church), but not of a Christian *foundation* of culture. It is not a task in culture but the benefit of God's general grace that demands our attention here.

For the rest we can leave Calvin's general grace out of consideration. For it does not tell us what is foundational for his attitude toward and in culture. For that, we must make use of the data collected above on pp. 279ff., in which the idea of *pilgrimage is central*. We travel as pilgrims on the earth to use its goods—also those conferred by God's general grace—in such a way that they help, rather than hinder, our course (p. 281 above). Our homeland is elsewhere and therefore we in our abstinence, frugality, moderation, and modesty stand detached from the present life. We cannot feel at home in this world; we are on duty at a sentry post and must desire to be relieved soon: "No one has made progress in the school of Christ who does not joyfully await the day of death and final resurrection" (p. 281 above).

This eschatological focus can truly not simply be characterized as contempt of the world. I have already rejected this view (p. 283 above). For this see H. Quistorp, *Calvin's Doctrine of the Last Things*, 51ff., in opposition to the opinion of M. Schultze. But on the other hand, it amazes me that after reading *Inst.* III, 6–10, one can possibly call Calvin the founder of common grace. On *this* foundation, with its contemplation of the life to come, the imposing edifice of culture that Kuyper erected with his common grace simply does not fit. How can culture possibly receive any *independent* appreciation, apart from its modest task as a means of helping us on our pilgrimage, when our awaiting the future life with Christ so *governs* our present life as is the case in Calvin? The things that appear to be impressive become transparent in their *pretense* (pp. 241ff. above). Here comes to mind what H. Berger wrote concerning Calvin's judgment about ancient Rome: "With astonishing tenacity he repudiated ... the merely superficial great admiration and sympathy." His account of the Roman empire "shows no trace of any enthusiasm for [its] achievements," and: "As far as the empire in its totality is concerned, it was [in his view] a dreadful chaos" (*Calvin's Geschichtsauffassung*, 170–71). Calvin characterizes the Roman empire as haughty and full of hubris toward the true God (op. cit., 177). This is surely a different appreciation than that which I. A. Diepenhorst regards as (rightly) included in Kuyper's common grace: "Even pagan civilizations that know nothing of particular grace can make God great" (*Algemeene Genade en Antithese*, 19). See, e.g., *Van de Voleinding* IV, 288–89.

I pointed out this radical difference between Kuyper and Calvin earlier when discussing the focus and fruit of God's more general grace (§ 6). Now this difference acquires a new depth. In the light of the coming glory, everything here below that does not live from out of Christ becomes even more relative.

I do not, however, deny that Kuyper also spoke about the concept of pilgrimage. For this, see p. 112 above. But the question is: how does pilgrimage function in Kuyper? And then the huge difference between him and Calvin becomes apparent. For example, Kuyper writes as follows: Calvinism calls

CHAPTER IV. COMPARISON

Christianity back "to the original ordinance of creation: 'Fill the earth and subdue it, and have dominion over ... every living thing that moves on the earth.' So one remains a pilgrim, *but a pilgrim who, on the way to the eternal homeland, still has to fulfill an immeasurable task on earth*. For and under and above humanity, the cosmos with all its realms of nature broadly expanded. All of this immense field must be cultivated. We should throw ourselves into this labor with enthusiasm and resilience. The earth and everything in it must be subjected to humankind" (*Het Calvinisme*, 116; italics supplied). Did Calvin also call people back to the original *creation* ordinance with the immense centuries-long task that is included in it, or was his program for every day marked by the expectation of what is *to come*? The following statement is characteristic for Calvin: "No science is in conflict with the fear of God and the doctrine that he gives us *to lead us to eternal life*, provided that we do not put the cart before the horse, i.e., that we, *while passing through this world*, are so prudent as to make use of the liberal and mechanical arts in order always to direct our steps toward the heavenly kingdom" (*Corpus Reformatorum* 35, 540). In the Latin translation the word "always" is rendered as *velis remisque* [with sails and oars], i.e., "by every means in one's power" (see *Opera*, ed. Schipper, VIII, 509).

Kuyper posits the idea of pilgrimage, but it does not permeate his views on common grace at all. That is not surprising, because he (as distinct from Calvin) calls the Christian a citizen of two kinds of homeland. Heaven is then the better homeland (*Tweeërlei Vaderland*, 13, and "for *both* the earthly and the higher homeland, a separate law and rule exist" (op. cit., 31). Thus as citizen of this earthly homeland, one is *at home* there, and consequently the reservation toward this life that characterizes Calvin is absent. The Christian is a pilgrim, for it is only later that "the seeds that were already hidden in the hearts of God's children, but could not open in the chilly atmosphere here on earth, will bud and flourish" (op. cit., 14). But Christians are evidently not pilgrims when engaged in the labor of contributing to the germination of the seeds that God had placed in creation. Kuyper does mention pilgrimage here and there, but it never becomes constitutive for ethics, as it was for Calvin.

Of Schilder we can say that he takes up a position between Kuyper and Calvin. For him, common grace is also not foundational in our cultural calling. He believes this doctrine to be unsound because it finds the point of departure for its problematics in what was left to us after the Fall, while Schilder wants to go back to before the Fall (p. 191 above). Human beings were placed in Paradise as *office-bearers* with a task, a mandate, to let the world of Paradise develop into a completed world (pp. 187–88 above). Despite the Fall, the task to engage in culture (the common mandate) remains, although it can only be fulfilled in Christ (p. 192 above). But therefore Christ takes up "the great reformational task of *returning to the ABC* of the order for life and for the world." And by his service as office-bearer he now also "makes people again what they were 'in the beginning': God's people," office-bearers in accordance with Lord's Day 12, Answer 32, of the Heidelberg Catechism. That is how "the alpha is joined to the omega; the talents handed out by God to his laborers in the early morning of creation were by evening to have earned a profit equal to the number distributed at daybreak" (p. 196 above). We cannot speak of one culture, says Schilder, so long as we can observe only fragments of culture, both on the part of the unbelievers and on the part of the believers. The difference with Kuyper is obvious. Common grace is dropped as foundation, and the *office*, as it functioned from the beginning in Paradise, takes its place.

It is true that we also read things in Kuyper that clearly correspond with what Schilder argues. See especially *Loc. de Christo* III, 3–39, 177ff. But while for Kuyper there is after the Fall still something left of the office on account of common grace (op. cit., 30), and Christ's work on the terrain of common grace has a *stimulating* effect on these remnants of the office (pp. 47–48 above; cf. § 5 above; *Loc. de Christo* III, 177–78), for Schilder the office remains decisive, also after the Fall. According to Schilder, the common mandate is maintained, but only the work of those regenerated by Christ in the fulfillment of their office may truly bear the name of culture. Thus it is not a matter of "general" grace, but of "particular" grace. Jesus Christ is the *foundation*, also of all that can truly be called culture, for it was *redeemed* in him. That is why for Schilder the church is of such great significance for culture: "Take away the church, and the essentially human element will disappear, while a humanism that boasts about its ruins will come back" (p. 202 above).

Calvin is also of opinion that cultural life must be connected to Christ and to his congregation. The totality of life must be Christocentric. We can read that in the *Institutes*: After Scripture "has taught that we have degenerated from the true origin and condition of our creation, it also adds that Christ, through whom we return into favor with God, has been set before us as an example whose pattern we ought to express in our life.... For we have been adopted by the Lord as his children with this one condition: that our life express Christ, the bond of our adoption" (*Inst.* III, vi, 3).

Nevertheless, this quotation already causes us to surmise that Calvin's and Schilder's ways part when it becomes necessary to determine what is meant by the Christocentric life as far as its *content* is concerned. Then Calvin speaks of Jesus Christ and our pilgrimage, while Schilder deals with the topic of Christ and culture. Culture with its program (taking "out of the world all that it has in it," p. 188 above); with its alpha that despite the Fall will nonetheless be joined to its omega; and thus with its progression. All this brings Schilder back in Kuyper's vicinity. All the sounds are more muffled (§§ 4 and 10), but the music is the same. Together with Calvin, he has little good to say about everything that is culturally active and alive apart from Christ. But together with Kuyper he can be theologically penetrating and engaged with petroleum that "more than incense" has been "an *express* theme in the Bible."

This also shows how great the affinity between Schilder and Kuyper is. The Genevan reformer with his pilgrimage idea and his ascesis, which are sometimes very close to a contempt of earthly life, has had disciples who disputed with each other about truly fundamental points. Once the smoke of battle clears, however, we see that they also traveled *together*—sometimes along other routes than their master. *At the very least*, the emphases have changed. They shifted from the life to come to the task of today: the talents distributed in the morning of creation still had to gain many more before evening.

§ 12. Summary

The opinions of Kuyper and Schilder, when compared to those of Calvin both together and individually, demonstrate differences from the reformer on important points.

I will now do an inventory. For my comparison I will measure the opinions of Kuyper and Schilder against those of Calvin. In doing so, I will as a matter of course consider any agreement and difference between Kuyper and Schilder to be a given.

The most important point in which Kuyper and Schilder stand together over against Calvin is the *broad cultural attention* that derives from their exegesis of Gen 1:28. Taking out of the world what is in it, a cultural program and progression, the connection of the alpha and the omega—all these ideas are unfolded by Kuyper and Schilder, but not by Calvin (§§ 4 and 11). For Calvin, but not for Kuyper and Schilder, *pilgrimage* is central.

For Calvin, culture is more about the gift and the enjoyment of it than about the worldwide task: we may enjoy the gifts of culture as long as we remember that we are passing through this world and must therefore with all our power direct our steps toward the heavenly kingdom (§§ 4 and 11).

Also individually, Kuyper and Schilder differ significantly from Calvin. To begin with Kuyper: his doctrine of common grace distinguishes itself fundamentally from what Calvin confesses about God's general grace. Calvin does not project this grace back into predestination, as Kuyper does (§§ 3 and 4). He also does not let it triumph culturally but, since it is focused quite differently (on the knowledge of God), it delivers a very different "fruit": this grace is sullied and suppressed (§ 6). Its modest place in Calvin's *oeuvre* stands out against the dominant place that Kuyper gives to common grace as doctrine (§ 7) and as the indispensable constitutive factor in God's eternal Counsel (§ 10). While for Calvin "grace" includes God's favorable *disposition*, for Kuyper, God's disposition in common grace is practically left undiscussed (§ 9). Finally, together with grace, Calvin also demands special attention for God's wrath, for which no parallel is to be found in Kuyper's doctrine of common grace (§ 8).

Schilder diverges from Calvin in the following respects: The continuation of history is an indispensable condition (substrate) for Schilder, both for the administration of God's curse and of his blessing. That is connected with

CHAPTER IV. COMPARISON

Schilder's doctrine of predestination, in which election and reprobation run strongly in parallel: we are not entitled to emphasize the one self-glorification more than the other. In contrast, Calvin does not recognize this parallelism and ascribes a "pre" to grace above judgment. This differing insight between Schilder and Calvin is most apparent when Calvin speaks of a general grace (toward the Gentiles), while Schilder rejects "grace" as characterization for this (§§ 2, 6, 10).

As for the *similarities*, both Kuyper and Calvin leave double predestination out of consideration in the investigation of the theological concept of common grace (general grace). Moreover, there is no question that both theologians recognize God's grace toward the Gentiles. For both, this was the answer to the question how it can be reconciled that the Gentiles are totally depraved and yet have virtues (§§ 2 and 6).

Schilder and Calvin agree that there is a personal double predestination, but not in addition also a "broad" cultural predestination, such as Kuyper developed (§ 3). Further, they do not subscribe to a doctrine of common grace, and both describe the fruit of God's gifts (of grace) as bitter: human beings do not use God's gifts properly and are therefore inexcusable (§ 6). They also emphasize God's wrath (§ 8) and desire to be Christocentric in their ethics: pilgrimage and office are governed by Christ (§ 11).

When comparing Kuyper with Schilder, apart from the already noted differences between them and Calvin, it is striking that the work of Christ in the task of developing the totality of created life is indispensably *stimulating* for Kuyper, but *foundational* for Schilder. Both speak of the *indispensable* continuation of history, but Kuyper clearly does not reject its being characterized as "grace," while Schilder definitely does (§ 10). Finally, both have in common that they recognize the calling of Christians to develop culture. In that respect, Schilder's perspectives are more modest that Kuyper's (§ 4). For Schilder, culture is subordinated to, and not coordinated with, the execution of double predestination (§ 10). While in Kuyper the calling of Christians finds its foundation in common grace, for Schilder it is based on the *office* in accordance with Lord's Day 12 (§ 11).

We can still raise the question *how* great the distance from one another is among the three theologians. The answer will necessarily be subjective, for in order to determine the distances, the points of controversy will have to be evaluated. That is the task to which chapter V is devoted.

V

EVALUATION

§ 1. Double predestination

Without yet addressing the significance of this concept for our topic, I want to continue to confess double predestination together with Calvin, Kuyper, and Schilder. I maintain, on the basis of a discussion of Romans 9–11, what the Canons of Dort I, 6 and 15, say about it.

The Canons of Dort describe election as "the unchangeable purpose of God whereby, before the foundation of the world, out of the whole human race, which had fallen by its own fault out of its original integrity into sin and perdition, he has, according to the sovereign good pleasure of his will, out of mere grace, chosen in Christ to salvation a definite number of specific persons, neither better nor more worthy than others, but involved together with them in a common misery. He has also from eternity appointed Christ to be the Mediator and Head of all the elect and the foundation of salvation" (I, 7). The Canons say further that Holy Scripture illustrates and commends this election to us "that not all men are elect but that some have not been elected, or have been passed by in the eternal election of God. Out of his most free, most just, blameless, and unchangeable good pleasure, God has decreed to leave them in the common misery into which they have by their own fault plunged themselves, and not to give them saving faith and the grace of conversion. These, having been left in their own ways and under his just judgment, God has decreed finally to condemn and punish eternally, not only on account of their unbelief but also on account of all their other sins, in order to display his justice. This is the decree of reprobation" (I, 15). I realize that this confession is rejected not only outside of the Reformed world, but even in whole or in part by a large segment of Calvin's heirs. Can what Dort said about election and reprobation be maintained? I answer this question in the affirmative.

As is readily apparent (see ch. IV, § 1), a critical treatment of the topic of "general grace" would lead me in a totally different direction if I could not speak of eternal election and reprobation. In that case my critique of *all* three theologians who were reviewed in the first three chapters would have to be much more thoroughgoing.

In this study I am not giving a detailed defense of Canons of Dort, I, 7 and

CHAPTER V. EVALUATION

15, for it does not have predestination as its theme; but a short exposition of my views is required here. I believe that the best method for that purpose is to examine Romans 9–11. Because challenges to the maintenance of this *locus classicus* as proof for Dort arise from all sides today, I will deal with a few decisive points by considering the following questions:

1. *Is Romans 9–11 concerned with God's sovereign decree also regarding personal salvation and condemnation?* I do not for a moment deny that Paul speaks in this portion of Scripture about the salvation-historical position of the *people* of Israel. While it mentions the names of persons (Isaac, Jacob, Esau, Moses, and Pharaoh), these undoubtedly represent more than a personal scope. "What is being shown here is that the *holy line* of Abraham's seed continued with Isaac and not with Ishmael.... The electing intention of God with respect to Esau and Jacob of which [Paul] speaks, consists in this, *that the elder shall serve the younger* (v. 12). Here it is thus a matter of their election and reprobation in accordance with what God decreed in Gen 25:23.... Similarly, in the citation from Mal 1 the mention of Jacob and Esau is clearly intended to refer not to just a few individuals but also the peoples that sprang from them.... Finally, the same applies *mutatis mutandis* to the examples of Moses and Pharaoh in vv. 14ff. These also do not have a merely personal, exemplary significance ... but represent two important figures who were of decisive significance *in the history of Israel* and through whom *God's intention for his people Israel* becomes visible" (Herman Ridderbos, *Commentaar Romeinen*, 228–29).

I acknowledge this wholeheartedly, and it is gain that more recent exegesis concerning the salvation-historical line supports this view better than the earlier (including Calvin's exegesis) did. But pointing out this line does not exhaust the explanation of Rom 9–11. For God sends his salvation and condemnation, his mercy and the hardening of hearts, very individually within the framework of the history of salvation. This is apparent from the fact that the personal is so often in view in Rom 9–11. To be mentioned are the following texts (not even all): 9:15: "I will have mercy on *whom* I have mercy and I will have compassion on whom I have compassion"; 9:16: "So it depends not on *human* will or exertion..."; 9:18: "So then he has mercy on *whomever* he wills, and he hardens *whomever* he wills"; 9:19, 20: "who can resist his will? But who are *you*, O man...? Will what is molded say to its molder, 'Why have you made *me* like this?'"; 9:21: The potter has the clay at his disposal "to make out of the same lump *one* vessel for honorable use and *another* for dishonorable use"; 9:22–23 speaks about vessels of wrath and vessels of mercy; 9:24: "even *us* whom he has called, not *from* the Jews only but also *from* the Gentiles." In particular the preposition "from" makes clear how the choice falls individually on specific (those who are called!) Jews and Gentiles. Hence, 9:27: "only a *remnant* of [the sons of Israel] will be saved"; 11:4: "I have kept for myself *seven thousand* men ..."; 11:5: "So too at the present time there is a *remnant*, chosen by grace"; 11:7: "Israel failed to obtain what it was seeking. The elect obtained it, but *the rest*

CHAPTER V. EVALUATION

were hardened"; 11:14: Paul hoped by his preaching to make his fellow Jews jealous and thereby to save *"some of them."*

All of these texts confirm what Paul already expressed in Rom 8:28–30, namely that God's loving attention is personal toward those who are his: "And we know that for *those* who love God all things work together for good, for those who are called according to his purpose. For *those* whom he foreknew," etc.

It would be superfluous to mention these data if modern exegesis did not constantly emphasize the salvation-historical aspect at the expense of the personal salvation or condemnation aspect. Those who pay attention to both do not pose false dilemmas. Is it a true dilemma when Berkouwer argues that Rom 9:22 is not concerned with "an independent analysis of the lot of individual people, but with the ways of the electing God in history"? (*De Verkiezing Gods*, 254). It is true that the "analysis of the lot of individual people" in Rom 9:22 is not an independent aspect beside the salvation-historical argument, but it is very clearly included in it. Is it a true dilemma when the same writer argues that Paul in Rom 9:17 "does not suddenly demand attention for the individual lot of Pharaoh, but portrays him because of his place in salvation history" (op. cit., 252)? That personal interest certainly does not come up suddenly, for it is constantly present in the apostle's argument. Therefore I deem it necessary to change Berkouwer's "not–but" into a "not only–but also." Is it a true dilemma when Ridderbos, who states correctly that "the general salvation-historical point of view may *not be separated* from the personal" (op. cit., 229), remarks a page later (when speaking about the holy line of Abraham's seed): "*Thus* we must understand the designation 'Israel,' 'children,' 'children of God' in a salvation-historical sense, and not in a personal, soteriological sense" (op. cit., 228; italics supplied)? What it should say is not "either–or," but "both–and." Such is also the case with respect to Jacob and Esau. They are representatives of two peoples, but they were depicted earlier as two children about whom God made a decision before *they* had done either good or evil.

One can certainly not accuse Dort of speaking so individually; at most one can say that if the salvation-historical aspect (the special and continuing place of Israel in accordance with God's foreknowledge, Rom 11:2) had been included, the Canons of Dort would have been the richer for it. This confession does not deal with its material exhaustively. Who, indeed, can do so when it concerns a theme in God's Word?

2. *Does Rom 9–11 deal with eternal salvation and eternal ruin?* This question is also important. Does God's election and reprobation concern temporal and earthly blessings, in which one person is preferred over the other (e.g., Jacob over Esau)? Does it perhaps concern (only) the administration of an office in salvation history, in which personal and eternal salvation or ruin remain excluded from the discussion? Or also: are election and rejection a matter of "presenting, repeating, and depicting" *Christ's* being elected and rejected but in such a way that the reprobate *are not* truly rejected and do not face eternal

CHAPTER V. EVALUATION

ruin? "The elect are always the ones who have to *testify* to the positive, the *telos* of the divine will, God's mercy. And always the reprobate have to be at their side to testify to the negative, to that which God—almighty, holy, and merciful as he is—does not want, and thus they *testify* to his judgment as such" (K. Barth, *Kirchliche Dogmatik* II/2, 389; italics supplied). But the "testimony" of the "reprobate" can "*as long as it seems to point to their own Godforsakenness and forlornness,* in the end be only a lie because to stand in the actual and real Godforsakenness and to be actually and truly lost is not really possible for them, because only Jesus Christ can be in this situation" (388, italics supplied).

One is inclined to say that according to Barth the reprobate play a role in the *drama*: "Thus the ungodly '*are*' ... the *rejected ones,* inasmuch as they then yet, also with their false testimony concerning man's reprobation, do *present, repeat,* and *depict* the death of the one who was rejected, Jesus Christ" (382, italics supplied). For in actual fact both elect and reprobate stand "in the light or in the shadow of his merciful will" (245).

It is impossible for me to agree with the above. For Rom 9–11 does treat eternal salvation and eternal ruin very personally. Indeed, Paul's entire letter does so. It speaks of decisions that affect eternal salvation (1:16; 2:7; 5:9ff., 17, 21; 6:22; 8:17, 18–30), and also eternal ruin (1:20, 32; 2:3ff., 8; 3:8; 8:6, 13). This is also very clear from Rom 9–11, if we read 9:22–23 honestly. For in these verses the vessels of wrath prepared for destruction (σκεύη ὀργῆς κατηρτισμένα εἰς ἀπώλειαν) stand next to the vessels of mercy, which [God] has prepared beforehand for glory (σκεύη ἐλέους, ἃ προητοίμασεν εἰς δόξαν). Neither ἀπώλεια [destruction] (Matt 7:13; John 17:12; Phil 1:28; 3:19; 2 Thess 2:3; 1 Tim 6:9; Heb 10:39; 2 Pet 2:1, 3; 3:7, 16; Rev 17:8, 11; cf. S. Oepke in *ThWB* I, 396); nor δόξα [glory] (Rom 5:2; 8:18, 30; 2 Cor 3:18; 4:17; 1 Thess 2:12; 2 Thess 2:14; 2 Tim 2:10; 1 Pet 5:4, 10; cf. G. Kittel in *ThWB* II, 253) are susceptible of two different interpretations. They speak of destruction and glory that are lasting and eternal. Barth's entire argument about the elect and reprobate who *together* share God's mercy is demolished by this Scriptural evidence. It must also be apparent that in his extensive exposition of Romans 9 (op. cit., 222–56), Barth says not a word about the horrifying ἀπώλεια [destruction] (cf. 248). Hence there is no reason whatsoever to moderate or delimit other expressions in this pericope. Thus God's wrath toward Esau does not amount "merely" to a "passing-by" in which Jacob is preferred, but to a real hatred that, just like God's love, will not allow itself to be diminished or explained: "The love of God is the mystery of his electing, the hatred of God the riddle of his hardening.... Hatred is here separation and rejection, punishment and judgment" (O. Michel in *ThWB* IV, 695). Here punishment and judgment are not restricted to the absence of temporal and earthly blessings but have eternal consequences: Esau is not ἐξ Ἰσραήλ [from Israel]! (cf. G. Doekes, *De beteekenis van Israels val,* 60). Similarly, Pharaoh is portrayed not only because of his place in the history of salvation, in which he holds a (woeful) office, but also because of his individual, definitive ruin: as vessel of wrath prepared for destruction.

CHAPTER V. EVALUATION

Here, too, I agree with Dort: Rom 9–11 speaks of individual salvation and destruction with eternal consequences.

3. *Must Rom 9–11 be considered in light of predestination (eternal election and reprobation)?* We saw above that salvation and destruction extend into eternity. But is God's decree about this weal and woe also *from* eternity, at least according to Rom 9? Many deny it: "In what Paul says about Moses and Pharaoh he is not speaking about what God decreed about them from eternity, but about what God did with them in history: he showed mercy and hardened hearts.... One can then ask whether Pharaoh's destruction, just as Israel's redemption, did not hark back to God's eternal intention. Of this question, no matter how legitimate it may be in itself, it must be said that *the exegesis of Rom 9* can provide no answer, because it is concerned with another connection between God's sovereignty and Pharaoh's destruction than that of which Paul speaks in Rom 9. For there Paul speaks of God's sovereign power to *harden sinful* Pharaoh and to cast him into destruction, not of God's sovereign power to destine Pharaoh from eternity for destruction and ruin" (Herman Ridderbos, op. cit., 230).

It is also impossible for me to subscribe to Ridderbos' "not–but." For Rom 9 does speak of God's decree from eternity. A compound with the preposition "προ" [before] appears twice in Rom 9, namely in v. 11: ἡ κατ' ἐκλογὴν πρόθεσις [the purpose according to election] and v. 23: σκεύη ἐλέους, ἃ προητοίμασεν εἰς δόξαν [vessels of mercy prepared beforehand for glory]. Since it appears so soon after Rom 8:23, we need not doubt the meaning of this προ. It belongs with those portions of Scripture in which προ with regard to Christ and election has a weighty significance: 'before the foundation of the world,' John 17:24; Eph 1:4; 1 Pet 1:20; 'before the ages,' 1 Cor 2:7; 'before eternal times,' 2 Tim 1:9; Titus 1:3; 'before all eternity,' Jude 25" (B. Reicke in *ThWB* 685). See also C. Maurer, *ThWB* VIII, 167–68. Cf. Eph 2:10 for προητοιμασεν [prepared beforehand].

In Rom 9, this little word προ receives confirmation in the histories of Jacob and Esau and that of Pharaoh. For *in* their histories is revealed what was "intended" *before* their histories. The twins were not yet born when Rebekah received the message that was decisive for their lives, while in the case of Pharaoh it was before he had hardened his heart that God decided, "I will harden his heart" (Exod 4, 21; cf. 3:19). God raised him up in order to show his power in him (Exod 9:16, Rom 9:17). It says ἐξήγειρα, which can legitimately be translated as "called into existence" (see A. Oepke, *ThWB* II, 337). This already shows clearly that God's electing and rejecting becomes visible in history. Cf. 2 Tim 1:9b, 10a. Both aspects are clearly visible in 9:22, 23. "Here suddenly appears in the background the dark possibility of a *praedestinatio ad iram* when Paul (Rom 9:22) speaks of σκεύη ὀργῆς κατηρτισμένα εἰς ἀπώλειαν [vessels of wrath prepared for destruction], where God 'desires' to show the power of his wrath" (G. Stählin, *ThWB* V, 444, citing 1 Thess 5:9; for καταρτίζω, see also G. Delling *ThWB* I, 475). Is it not already included in 9:18 ("he has mercy on whomever he wills, and he hardens whomever he wills"), in which θέλειν [to will],

CHAPTER V. EVALUATION

corresponding to βούλημα [will] in v. 19 (cf. Eph 1:11!), points to "that unsearchable eternal destiny"? (G. Schrenk in *ThWB* I, 634ff.; III, 57; cf. also θέλων [desiring] in v. 22).

Such an exegesis does not at all mean that Rom 9 is interpreted in a deterministic way, as Ridderbos (op. cit., 217, 222, 229–30) and Berkouwer (*Geref. Theol. Tijdschrift* 63, 18) contend. Bavinck already pointed out that the determinist does not know how to deal with God's Counsel. There room is left only for "an unconscious fate, a blind nature, an irrational will" (*Reformed Dogmatics* II, 369). But the Reformed religion "on the basis of Scripture, believingly" trusts "in the absolute, sovereign, and yet—however incomprehensible—wise and holy will of him who will some day cause the full light of heaven to shine on those riddles of our existence" (op. cit., 394). "Sovereign"—that is what Rom 9 deals with, and the mode of God's election and reprobation is unveiled as sovereign in the most pointed way in the προ: *before* all ages. God's judgments (κρίματα) are incomprehensible and his ways are unsearchable. No one has been his counselor (σύμβουλος, Rom 11:34).

God's decisions are also holy and righteous. Rom 9:1–29 is followed by Rom 9:30–10:21, in which faith and unbelief are depicted in their *decisive* significance for salvation and destruction. "The question concerning the human responsibility of Israel, the other side of the same truth, does not follow till Rom 9:30–10:21. To start with, it is intentionally stopped in view of the free divine action" (G. Schrenk in *ThWB* IV, 217). The Bible contains more about Ishmael, Esau, and Pharaoh than Rom 9 relates, and the same is true of Isaac, Jacob, and Moses. Predestination and human responsibility go hand in hand. The connection between the two cannot be explained, but must be *confessed.* Predestination without determinism—in this respect, too, the Canons of Dort follow Scripture.

4. *May we on the basis of Rom 9–11 (also) speak of a numerus clausus [fixed number]?* I quote Ridderbos again: "Being vessels of wrath by virtue of God's sovereignty does not necessarily mean that one can no longer become a vessel of mercy, cf. 11:12." The hardening of Israel by God (11:7ff.) does not close the way to the Lord's salvation (11:11). "Particularly because of this teleological character of God's sovereignty, the way remains open. Consequently, Paul's line of reasoning does not end in establishing on the basis of predestination that there are two fates and two futures, but in a renewed pointing to *the way of faith* as the only way to salvation by virtue of God's sovereign grace" (op. cit., 230). Ridderbos calls this *"not a closed but an open situation."* God's historical action is teleologically directed to the goal that "all Israel" that will be saved.

I quite agree with Ridderbos' exegesis of Rom 11:25, which differs from that of Calvin, Greijdanus, et al. But I have to add something. This *historical* acting with its dynamics (faith that can turn into unbelief, 11:19ff., and unbelief into faith, 11:23; indeed, "rejection," ἀποβολή, that turns into "acceptance," πρόσλημψις, 11:15) continues to be anchored in God's predestination. For:

CHAPTER V. EVALUATION

(a) The people of Israel were and remain God's people. Here we cannot speak of an open situation (11:1, 28–29). Being foreknown from eternity as a *people* (11:2), they progress from "remnant" (λεῖμμα, 11:5, "according to election," κατ' ἐκλογήν!) to "all *Israel*" (πᾶς Ἰσραὴλ, 11:26).

(b) Like λεῖμμα [remnant], also πᾶς Ἰσραὴλ [all Israel] is determined personally: "the full number of Israel, *determined* by God, which will in due course be saved from all sin and decay and in which God's promises to Israel are fulfilled" (Ridderbos, op. cit., 263; italics supplied). But this individual salvation cannot be separated from individual predestination. Here, too, it is not a matter of an open situation; "Israel" and "out of Israel" are fixed.

(c) Also with respect to the "fullness of the Gentiles" (τὸ πλήρωμα τῶν ἐθνῶν, 11:25), we must pay attention to both elements: the Gentiles (τὰ ἔθνη) are saved, for God has reconciled the world (ὁ κόσμος) to himself, 11:15, and the fullness of the Gentiles, their full number as the fullness determined by God, will be saved. Cf. G. Delling, *ThWB* IV, 330–31; Schrenk, op. cit., IV, 218; Ridderbos, op. cit., 254. This *determined* fullness can again not be separated from the electing intention of God. This situation can also not be called "open."

These data must prevent us from interpreting Rom 9:22 in the way Ridderbos does above. Besides, it is dangerous to explain this text, the context of which is God's sovereignty, on the basis of 11:11–24, in which the responsibility of Jews and Greeks receives such emphasis. My conclusion: I will continue to maintain also a *fourth* component of the Canons of Dort I, 7 and 15 (where mention is made of "a definite number of specific persons").

I emphasize that I criticized Ridderbos' exegesis but not his view of the Canons of Dort, which he does not explicitly give anywhere in his *Commentary*. I do, however, ask the question whether an exegesis such as that offered by Ridderbos, an exegesis of one of the most important pillars of the Canons of Dort, still makes it possible to maintain in unabridged form what Dort confessed. A broader exposition in which more than Rom 9–11 is taken into consideration would be able to give an answer to this question.

I note further that I considered Ridderbos' commentary with its many excellent qualities to be the most useful for a critical confrontation with the modern exegesis of Rom 9–11. From my criticism it is clear that I also differ on more than one point with exegetes such as B. Holwerda, *Dictaten Historia Revelationis* I, 26–37; D. Holwerda, *O Diepte des Rijksdoms*, 47–66; and H. Venema, *Uitverkiezen and Uitverkiezing in het Nieuwe Testament*, 105–25, 136–37.

To clarify my exegesis I have made constant use of articles in Kittel's *Theologisches Wörterbuch zum Neuen Testament*. I realize that one can also use the *ThWB* to attack my position. See, e.g., G. Schrenk, *ThWB* IV, 184 (ἐκλογή) and C. Maurer, op. cit., VII, 363ff. (σκεῦος). But many other articles can prevent the formation of a myth that the modern exegesis of Rom 9–11 has become the accepted view. I discovered that the contrary is the case.

CHAPTER V. EVALUATION

§ 2. Non eodem modo [not in the same manner]

The confession of double predestination may, however, not lead us to speak of an eternal hate toward the reprobate in addition to the eternal love of God toward his elect. Holy Scripture does not allow us to do so. And neither Dort (its *phrases duriores*, hard sayings), nor Reformed theology in its entirety support Schilder on this point. We are on safer ground if we speak infralapsarically about double predestination in the line of Dort. For the treatment of our topic this means that eternal rejection cannot be emphasized independently in parallel with election as Schilder does.

Perhaps unnecessarily, but nonetheless as desirable for the correct delineation of what I shall argue below, I declare that the deepest ground also of rejection must find its basis in God's good pleasure (cf. Canons of Dort, I, Rejection of Errors, 8). That the reprobate are *rejected* takes account of their sin and guilt; that *they* are rejected (and not also others) rests entirely in God's good pleasure. Those who speak of a parallelism between election and reprobation *here* will find me on their side. Behind *both* questions, why the one is elected and why the other is rejected, lies God's eternal good pleasure. However, may we extend this parallelism so far that we must speak of an equilibrium in God's decisions and actions of electing and rejecting in the manner that Schilder does, in which we may not ascribe a "pre" to God's mercy above his wrath? Are we allowed (and this is where the parallelism is unveiled the strongest) to speak of an eternal hate (wrath) of God toward the reprobate beside the eternal love of God toward his elect?

The proofs that Schilder adduces for this hate and wrath from eternity (pp. 179–82 above) do not need to occupy us for long. They are few in number and unconvincing. Rom 1:18 does not point to an eternal wrath that reveals itself in time over the world of the Gentiles, but speaks rather of a wrath that follows upon the wickedness of the people. Cf. the thrice-repeated "therefore" or its equivalents "for this reason" and "since" in vv. 24, 26, 28. Also Sirach 14:17, "The covenant from eternity is this: You shall surely die," as quoted in the *Ziekentroost* [Comfort for the Sick], cannot (even apart from the fact that this text appears in an apocryphal book) serve as proof for an eternal hatred in which God "as judge infinitely loves and desires himself and *also* for that reason 'calls' the world into existence." The expression ἡ γὰρ διαθήκη ἀπ' αἰῶνος mean no more than: "For this is the covenant *of old*," and ἀπ' αἰῶνος in this text encompasses the time as of Gen 2:17: "You shall surely die." See the Annotations to the Dutch States Bible, and for ἀπ' αἰῶνος [from of old], see also Luke 1:70 and Acts 3:21. Cf. H. Sasse, *ThWB* I, 198–99: "a far-off, long, uninterrupted period of time." Also Rom 9:22: ("vessels of wrath prepared for destruction") cannot serve as proof. At most this

CHAPTER V. EVALUATION

text speaks of a predestination *for* wrath [*ad iram*] (see § 1), of "vessels" over whom God's wrath *will* rage (θέλων ... ἐνδείξασθαι τὴν ὀργὴν).

Further, the parallelism in the "preservation" of the heirs and the wicked, as 1 Pet 1 and 2 Pet 2 speak of it, cannot have as consequences what Schilder suggests. 2 Pet 2 speaks especially of false prophets who had arisen in the congregation of Christ and who later denied him who had bought them (v. 1). Their eternal judgment flows from their demonstrated wickedness, but nowhere in 2 Pet 2 is this connected in parallel with an eternal election to an eternal rejection and eternal wrath of God. However, it is not these texts that are conclusive for Schilder in speaking of an eternal wrath of God. The motive for that lies elsewhere. Schilder cannot accept that God's wrath is an affect [feeling or emotion]: God "is not moved, not '*affected*,' as if he were one thing today and something else tomorrow, and as if what happens apart from him could cause change in him" (p. 179 above). God's wrath is an *effect*, just as his hate is: "Actually the hatred is not aroused by the creature" (p. 181 above).

In my view this theological construct of Schilder's is untenable. For it should rest on proof from Scripture, but *textual* proof is never evident. And those who read the texts ask, as H. M. Kuitert does: "Where does the Bible speak about wrath or hatred of God that is 'actually not' aroused by the creature? The way the Bible speaks about it, God's wrath is aroused by the sins of human beings. Wrath is a divine reaction to their preceding sins." For this, Kuitert points to the "striking Old Testament word *ka'as* (*Hiphil*): 'to provoke him to anger,' "to offend,' "to provoke,' with human beings as subject and God as object. In this sense it occurs twenty-five times in the Old Testament. See, e.g., Deut 4:25; 1 Kgs 14:9" (*De mensvormigheid Gods*, 20–21). Indeed, Scripture says many times that God's wrath is provoked and is aroused when people sin (Exod 4:14; 22:24; 32:10–11; Num 11:10, 33, etc.; Eph 5:6; Col 3:6 [ἔρχεται ἡ ὀργή]; cf. H. Bavinck, *Reformed Dogmatics*, II, 222–23).

Over against Schilder, I subscribe to what J. Ridderbos remarks about God's wrath: "It is provoked by human sin.... Thus, the wrath does not arise spontaneously in God, but is a reaction, a taking a stand over against the actions of humans" (*Het Godswoord der Profeten* III, 173). It follows that the same author says that wrath is *not an attribute of God* (172–73). In passing, I note that art. 1 of the Belgic Confession also does not mention God's wrath as one of his attributes. See further what Joan van den Honert, in *Verhandelingen van Gods niet algemeene, maar bezondere genade* (1726), writes about the hatred, wrath, and avenging righteousness of God. They do not flow from God's nature or being in this context. Otherwise they would also need to have existed before creation. God's avenging righteousness is not an *essential* attribute, but a *relative* one that God displays in connection with his works (op. cit., 123–26).

Thus God's wrath is indeed an affect. God is moved by human wickedness. But this does not mean that his wrath is fate "that he can do nothing about, a force that sweeps him along also, or, whether in first or second instance, restricts him in such a way that his absolute sovereignty, his good pleasure,

CHAPTER V. EVALUATION

his peace and delight, would be onerously affected by it," as Schilder states (p. 180 above). For while it is true that "wrath, punishment, destruction ... only arise in the second or third place" when creatures "turn themselves against God and refuse to take advantage of his life, peace, and salvation" (S. Greijdanus, *Congres van Gereformeerden, Referaten-Bundel*, 37), we do not thereby fall into the Remonstrant doctrine of God's wrath as affect. "The Remonstrants cannot be condemned for speaking about God's affects, but they can be condemned for attacking the sovereignty, the immutability, of God in their doctrine of affects, including God's wrath. Consequently, we should not contradict the Remonstrant proposition that 'there are affects in God' with an anti-Remonstrant proposition that 'there are no affects in God.' Rather, we must attack them in the root from which their doctrine concerning the affects in God springs, namely the attack on the sovereignty of God. They teach that God in his wrath is *dependent* upon the sinful actions of human beings. They think in an earthly, in a human way about God's wrath. For with us human beings, becoming angry is often—not always!—a lack of self-control, an inability to overcome the anger. But that is never the case with the LORD. For when he rages against sin, it is never because he can no longer control the situation. On the contrary, when he rages against sin, he maintains himself over against the sin and the sinner" (G. Visee, *Ref.* 28, 314). See also J. Ridderbos: "Although kindled by human beings, the wrath originates in God, in the depth of his divine being. The wrath against sin does not proceed from human beings but from God" (op. cit., 174).

In his wrath God is divine and not human. "It has pleased him to create human beings who were not *allowed* 'to raise his ire' ... but who were *able* to raise his ire" (G. Visee, *Ref.* 28, 321). And in his wrath he *remains* sovereign in accordance with Rom 9:22 (where we read that the vessels of wrath were prepared, that God *desires* to show his wrath). This text does not conflict with the continual references in Scripture to God's being provoked to anger. This usage is not "just" anthropomorphic, nor is it "just" apperceptive language. For as we "perceive" him in Scripture, that is how he reveals himself. That is how he *is*, affected in his sovereignty, in his effect sovereign. Affect and effect go together, without devaluation of either term. But when Schilder declares the former to be anthropomorphic, he, by making the latter, God's wrath as effect, independent (by abstraction), ends up positing a wrath from eternity.

Also Rom 9 does not permit this. For there we cannot abstract God's hatred and wrath from *fallen* humanity that has earned God's hatred and provokes his wrath. In his explanation of 9:13 ("Esau I hated"), G. Doekes writes: "God's wrath always applies to the sin or the sinner. In most places, sin appears as object [of the verb 'to hate], both with *sane'* (Deut 16:22; Ps 45:8, etc.) and with μισέω (Heb 1:9; Rev 2:6 and 15). But sometimes also the sinner, as is apparent from Ps 5:6; 11:5; Hos 9:15, and especially from Mal 1:3 and these words of Paul. In fact, it is closely related to the ὀργή [wrath] and the θυμός [wrath] which, according to this

CHAPTER V. EVALUATION

epistle, presuppose sin. This ἐμίσησα [I hated] is thus understandable only from an infralapsaric point of view" (*De beteekenis van Israels val*, 61–62).

What Doekes writes with respect to 9:21–22 is significant: "Entirely in agreement with the argument in the first chapters of the epistle, which states that the entire world, Jews as well as Gentiles, are cursed by God, the apostle here discusses the Lord's sovereign power to mold the one for salvation and the other for destruction from that corrupt lump, that *massa damnata* [condemned mass]. This already became apparent to us from the ἐμίσησα [I hated] in v. 13, which does not have the human being but the sinner as object. And it is no less clear from the words ἐλεεῖν and οἰκτείρειν [to have mercy] in vv. 15 and 16, which, of course, also apply to fallen humanity, the wicked. A third proof is provided by v. 18, in which the *hardening* as well as *having mercy* are again focused on the human race in its fallen state" (op. cit., 89).

When you read Schilder it is striking that, despite his critique of the dilemma of infra- and supralapsarism (*Heid. Cat.* III, 455–80), he speaks in a very supralapsaric way. Particularly by depicting God's eternal wrath as being in parallel with his eternal love, he spoke more often and with a stronger supralapsaric emphasis than was previously done in Reformed theology.

First of all think of Dort. Was it possible in its infralapsaric climate that delegates would have thought about rejection in the way Schilder did? The *Decisions* of the foreign and national delegates speak continuously about God's rejection in terms of not electing, not having mercy, passing over, leaving in the fall and misery (*Acta ofte Handelinghen*, ed. Canin, 1621 [shorter edition]), II, 13–14, 25–26, 46, 49, 55–56, 72, 84, 109, 111; III, 10–11, 13–14, 41, 48, 55–56, 63, 68, 76, 87, 98, 113, 125). Over against election, rejection is called *negative* (op. cit., II, 47, 63; III, 15, 43). Cf. K. Dijk, *De strijd over infra- en supralapsarisme*, 163.

Contrast that with Schilder's description of God's *positive* will to reject, in which God's wrath creates its own objects. The theologians from Great Britain formulated the matter quite differently when they said of the elect that God made them as what they were not, namely, vessels of mercy, but declared of those rejected that God made them as what they *already* were, i.e., vessels of wrath (op. cit., II, 15). There is no reference to parallelism; it is not even mentioned by Molinaeus, who dared to say that impenitence existed before the rejection, but that faith came after election (op. cit., I, 389).

The Canons of Dort display a similar picture. They are clearly infralapsaric, just like all the Reformed confessions (H. Bavinck, op. cit., II, 368). The Canons I, 7 and 15, speak about the rejection of fallen humanity and *thus* they do not mention a divine wrath that creates objects for itself from eternity. This can also not escape our attention: the Canons of Dort do not praise God's electing and rejecting equally; but election clearly has a "pre," while rejection, *as shadow*, highlights election all the more. Canons of Dort, I, 15, says: "Holy Scripture illustrates and recommends to us this eternal and undeserved grace of our election, especially when it further declares that not all men are elect," etc. Therefore I cannot support C. Trimp when he remarks that Canons of

CHAPTER V. EVALUATION

Dort, I, 15, here begins "to speak with uplifting words about God's breathtaking decision of rejection" (*Ref.* 31, 261). For this article speaks with profound words of thankfulness and praise of God's *election*. "The hymn in praise of the Light remains. It is intensified and made more intimate when we regard the darkness as also belonging to the sovereign expression of God's will.... The Canons of Dort are thus far removed from making election and reprobation parallel. Certainly, they bow to the good and sovereign will of God as revealed in both election and reprobation, but they know that the Lord does *not* desire the ruin and the salvation of sinners *in the same manner*. And when they speak of rejection, their goal is to arouse greater praise for the electing God" (J. Kamphuis, *Verkenningen* I, 212–13; italics supplied).

"Not in the same manner," *non eodem modo*. The fathers of Dort laid this down expressly in their *Conclusion* that follows the Canons, in which they, among other things, reject the following: "that God has predestined and created the greatest part of the world for eternal damnation by a mere arbitrary act of his will, without taking into account any sin. *In the same manner* in which election is the source and cause of faith and good works, reprobation is the cause of unbelief and ungodliness."

We would do Schilder an injustice if we were to ascribe to him the view that is condemned here. But the question is nonetheless legitimate whether Schilder escaped the danger of the *eodem modo* and, in this respect, refrained "from all those expressions which exceed the prescribed limits of the true meaning of Holy Scripture" (Canons of Dort, *Conclusion*). For the doctrine of eternal wrath makes it unclear why, parallel to election without consideration of faith, there would not be a rejection without consideration of sin. One of the *phrases duriores* [hard sayings] reads as follows: "That God hates human beings without respect of sin, without [considering] the deserts of evil works, absolutely, solely on account of his will." See K. Dijk, op. cit., 188; H. Bavinck, op. cit., II, 369.

Dort spoke carefully and also wisely. From the final formulation of the *Conclusion*, which was the result of a great deal of effort, it is clear that the fathers of Dort did not want to condemn supralapsarism. It is also possible to be too ready to speak carefully and thereby conceal or remove many "hard sayings" that Holy Scripture leaves in place. The delegates from Overijssel pointed this out when the *Conclusion* was adopted: "And in fact will Scripture not say that God blinds people's eyes and hardens their hearts lest they see with their eyes and understand with their heart and turn; that God removes speech from the truthful, prudence from the aged, makes error efficacious, draws people into wantonness and the heart's unclean desires, fattens hearts, roused Pharaoh, commanded Shimei to curse David, caused Absalom to defile his father's concubines, has prepared the wicked for the day of evil so that he might laugh at them on the day of their disaster and mock them when what they fear comes over them, sent a deceiving spirit to the mouths of all the prophets of Ahab, corrupted the hearts of the Egyptians so that they would hate the Israelites, made the Israelites go astray, incited David to count Israel,

CHAPTER V. EVALUATION

etc.?... By this line of reasoning Scripture itself would not be immune—horrible thought—to the charge of blasphemy" (K. Dijk, op. cit., 199-200).

See also L. Doekes, who opposes J. Kamphuis on the one hand when the latter maintains with Schilder that there is an eternal hatred in God, but also writes: "On the other hand, I regard it as no less dubious when ... it is boldly declared that *there is no* eternal hatred in God toward specific persons. What is meant by that? That before the foundation of the world God did not concern himself intensely with the future revolution of Satan, with the wickedness of the Antichrist, and with the entire horrible development of sin in the history of the world? Those who maintain this, picture a blind God, or a God who is concerned only for the time being with the future lot of his elect. Both ideas do not do justice to what Scripture reveals to us about the living God. We are not entitled to say that in his Counsel, God took a 'neutral' position regarding our future actions. Scripture does not permit us to think and speak in that way" (*Ref.* 29, 349).

Consequently it is all the more striking that also strict supralapsarians did not teach an eternal hatred in God. For example, Beza. In discussing God's hatred of Esau, he distinguishes between a predestination to hate and the hate itself. "Nor does it follow from this [Rom 9:13, J.D.] ... that Esau had been hated before he was born, or evil, since God hates nothing except evil. For being destined by hatred from eternity since thus it seemed good to God is different from, following the execution of his [Esau's] eternal predestination, being hateful to God on account of corruption and its fruits. For God comes upon [! J.D.] the cause of hatred of God as something totally inherent in human beings themselves." There are, says Beza, people who claim, "If the vessels of mercy are loved before they have done any good, also the vessels of wrath are hated before they have done any evil. But in fact none of us has ever come to such a conclusion" (*Tractationes Theologicae*, III, 419). No Reformed theologian appears to have argued what Schilder did on this point. Cf. also Calvin, *Inst.* III, xxiv, 17: "God is said to have ordained from eternity those whom he wills to embrace in love, and those upon whom he *wills* to vent his wrath." Beza wants to maintain a determining of *future* hatred as well as a determining of future love (op. cit., I, 342-42): God "decided to hate" Esau (I, 342).

Schilder sharply criticized Beza's idea that God's hate is not a cause but an effect of his decision to reject (*Heid. Cat.* III, 463ff.). It is of course easy to make critical comments about this, particularly when there are so few data, which limits all discussion of the sequence of God's decisions and actions. But it is incorrect to accuse Beza and his followers of "overconfidence," as Schilder does (op. cit., III, 465). For their hesitation to speak of an eternal wrath of God is what marks them as being careful, *despite* the sketchy nature of their depiction of God's decisions. I prefer an imperfect caution that leaves many inconsistencies unresolved to the strong language about God's eternal hatred that causes even greater difficulties.

For that matter, an infralapsarian such as Walaeus remarked that the

CHAPTER V. EVALUATION

descriptions of God's hatred in Rom 9:13 in the sense of a "foreordaining to righteous hatred and wrath" are unnecessary. Those who do so, are "certain teachers who reach beyond the Fall" and therefore "seek to soften these words in chapter 9 of the letter to the Romans"! But, continues Walaeus, "that is not necessary for those who remain under the Fall, in keeping with the National Synod and our Confession" (*Opera* II, 489). For according to infralapsarians God's wrath is directed to *fallen* humanity.

Also in Gomarus' *Opera* one will search in vain for the doctrine of God's eternal hatred or wrath. That is why Schilder's appeal to this theologian in speaking about God's wrath not as affect but as *effect* (pp. 179–80 above) is dubious. For Gomarus is not speaking about wrath as effect from eternity, but about wrath that shows itself to be effect as punishment (and therefore in time): "For the wrath does not denote an affect in God, but an effect or just punishment" (*Opera* I, 420b, cf. 404b). See also I, 83a, where God's wrath is described as follows: "It indicates his just will with respect to the punishing of those who violate his command."

In addition, other Reformed writers, such as Calvin (*inter alia, Inst.* I, xvii, 13) and Trigland (*Meditationes*, 73: "for love and hatred are affects of his will," cf. also op. cit., 155), do speak of affects, although they clearly demarcate these against undisciplined human affects (Calvin, loc. cit.: "beyond every affect of perturbation"; Trigland, op. cit., 128: "but God does not act without purpose, on account of a disorderly affect"). Calvin does not hesitate to say that the wrath of God is provoked: "The impious, who of their own accord by their sinning provoke God's wrath against them, at that time already, for an indeed just but unknown reason, will have been divinely rejected" (*Corpus Reformatorum* 8, 342). Cf. also *Inst.* III, xxiii, 12.

I presumed (p. 329 above) that no other Reformed theologian spoke in such a strong supralapsaristic way as Schilder did on a number of occasions. Even H. Hoeksema uses different language, at least in his early writings. Readers of *De Plaats der Verwerping in de Verkondiging des Evangelies* will be struck by the fact that Hoeksema clearly assigns a "pre" to election. Election has its "obverse" in rejection (op. cit., 13). The decision about election is most important in predestination, says Hoeksema, "not only because election is positive and rejection negative, but also because election is served by the rejection and exists because of rejection" (14). In his view rejection is certainly subordinate to election (14, 23): God does "not have pleasure in the reprobation in the same way as he has pleasure in the salvation and glory of his elect children" (17). Rejection is the dark side of election, and therefore God's love must always remain the main point (21).

It is strange that Berkouwer in *this* publication of Hoeksema's finds a symmetry that is only broken "briefly" (*De Verkiezing Gods*, 292–93). Contrary to what Berkouwer suggests, in this publication Hoeksema does not speak a word about an eternal hatred of God. He does do so in later publications, e.g., *Het Evangelie*, 243–44; *Dat Gods goedheid particulier is*, 21. But one may not deprive Hoeksema's above-mentioned ideas of their power by reference to his later publications. At most one can say that these ideas lie isolated in an *oeuvre* in which are found many symmetrical expressions that Berkouwer contests correctly (*inter alia*, regarding God's eternal hatred beside his eternal love).

I align myself with the Reformed tradition, which does not speak in a symmetrical way about election and reprobation and in which God's *electing* acts clearly receive a "pre." Cf. Bavinck, op. cit., II, 395ff. The confession of Dort followed Scripture with regard to this asymmetry. For from Gen 3 to Rev 22 there is a struggle concerning the fulfillment of God's *promises*. Despite blood, fire, and tears, despite God's wrath, which, real as it is, does not permit an *apokatastasis* doctrine [a doctrine that holds that all things will in time be restored, i.e., that everyone will be saved], Christ will attain his victory: the new Jerusalem, bathed in *light*. Outside will be darkness (Rev 21:27; 22:15; Matt 8:12, and elsewhere). This defines our view. Darkness can only accentuate the light.

This is also clearly apparent from Rom 9, which I have often referred to already. God desires to show his wrath and make known his power "*in order* to make known the riches of his glory to the vessels of mercy, which he has prepared beforehand for glory" (9:23). This *locus classicus* for eternal damnation directs us to what God sets in motion in history—toward his *opus proprium*: the granting of *salvation*. We heard Calvin say, "God punishes, but he does not do so gladly" (p. 272 above), following Lam 3:33. See also Ezek 18:23; 1 Tim 2:4; 4:10. We shall discover that all of this has consequences for the balance of this chapter.

§ 3. The breadth of predestination

Predestination, a decree that is part of God's Counsel, is not solely about election and reprobation of persons as individuals. By and through Jesus Christ, God again reconciled *all things* to himself, both on earth and in heaven (Col 1:20). In him God loved the *world* (John 3:16); in him as the second Adam, the new *humanity* is comprehended (Rom 5). "Not just a bouquet of elect persons will eventually spread its lovely aroma before God. Rather, the *plant* of redeemed *humanity* itself will eventually bloom before God in eternity" (p. 67 above). Kuyper's call to be a Christian in the *world*, founded as it is in the confession of the all-encompassing predestination, deserves our agreement. Here we meet Kuyper in his strength.

We shall never be able to discuss predestination unless we speak about Christ—not simply to mention him but to point to his pre-eminent and central

CHAPTER V. EVALUATION

place. Read Col 1:15–20. In this pericope, Christ is called "the firstborn of all creation," πρωτότοκος πάσης κτίσεως, not to identify him "as the first of all creatures; for this is followed immediately by the statement that all creation is in him, through him, and for him (v. 16), so that he himself does not form part of it. Rather, this qualification expresses Christ's pre-existence with respect to all created things and consequently his position *above* all created things. Christ exercises over them, as it were, the right of the firstborn" (Herman Ridderbos, *Commentaar Colossenzen*, 135).

Thus there is a very close connection between Christ and creation: All things are created in him, αὐτῷ ἐκτίσθη (v. 16), whereby "ἐν" (in the local sense) tells us that "God placed creation in communion with and at the disposal of Christ with a view to the goal determined by God.... Christ occupies the pre-eminent place in all of creation, because God, in accordance with the rule of primogeniture, has given him possession of and authority over all of creation" (H. Ridderbos, op. cit., 140). All things, τὰ πάντα, hold together, συνέστηκεν, in Christ (v. 17), i.e., "not merely their simple existence, but also their existence together, the mutual connectedness of all things [rests] in Christ" (op. cit., 142). There is a "system" in it (in the etymological sense); there is an organic coherence, as Kuyper would say. This coherence reveals itself not only in creation, but also in re-creation. For the same Christ who assumed a place of all-embracing importance in creation is now, as the firstborn from the dead, the head of the congregation, again pre-eminent in everything (vv. 17 and 18). For God, making his dwelling in Christ, has reconciled himself, ἀποκαταλλάξαι, pacified, all things through Christ's blood. In that respect, it is not only about, "as is often supposed, the personal relationship between God and human beings ... but also about the place and meaning of Christ in the whole of God's creation. While the order and relationships established by God were disrupted by sin ... God again placed all things in the right relationship to himself through Christ" (op. cit., 147). It is also clear in this pericope that Paul views creation and re-creation in one perspective: "All the work of Christ in creation and redemption are here brought mutually and completely in relationship to each other and, corresponding with each other, under one perspective, namely that of the cosmic glory and might of Christ" (op. cit., 136).

Here I draw a number of consequences.

First, we come to the heart of predestination when we speak of Christ. For it is all about him. All things are not only created by him, but also for him, τὰ πάντα δι' αὐτοῦ καὶ εἰς αὐτὸν ἔκτισται (v. 16). And *predestination* is about him (εὐδόκησεν, v. 19, and especially Eph 1:9–10).

Second, the sequence of things is also telling: first Christ, then τὰ πάντα, in which people, in particular Christ's congregation (vv. 18, 21), are included. The cosmic character of τὰ πάντα, embracing heaven and earth (vv. 16, 20), encompasses the personal element in predestination.

Third, when weighing the first two consequences, we may say plainly that Christ is the cause or foundation of election. For one does not at all need to

CHAPTER V. EVALUATION

follow K. Barth's theses in order to take a critical position, as he does, over against the depiction of Christ as merely the first *means* of election in executing the decree of predestination. Cf. *Kirchliche Dogmatik* II, 2, 119ff. Scripture does recognize both views. The Father gave those who are his to Christ (John 6:37, 39; 10:29; 17:6ff.; 18:9), who finishes the works of his Father (John 5:36). To that extent Walaeus is correct and can be used to oppose Barth when he writes: "The elect were the Father's before they were Christ's" (cited by Barth, op. cit., 120), and to that extent the view of Reformed theology, which speaks about Christ as the "first means of election" and as the "executor of the decree," is indeed understandable. But we are permitted to say more. Among other things, Col 1 also entitles us to regard Christ as the "foundation of election." For election is included in the overall context of cosmic reconciliation, which matches in breadth Christ's work of creation, in which all things are through and for him. But why then would the decision of reconciliation and *in it* the decree of election not have been taken for the sake of *Christ*, who is God's beloved Son from eternity? Therefore we may not deny Christ, as the *causa impulsiva et movens* [agent initiating the process] of election, the honor of being its foundation. The dilemma "the foundation *not* of the decree of salvation, *but* of decreed salvation" (quoted by C. Trimp, *Tot een levendige troost*, 53) is wrong. Christ is the foundation not only of the decreed salvation, but also of the decree itself. For the decree as well as the decreed salvation are directed to the reconciliation of *his* cosmos.

This broad cosmic aspect does not appear only Col 1 and Eph 1. John 3:16 speaks of the world, ὁ κόσμος, that God loved; Matt 19:28 speaks of a palingenesis that, in light of Isa 65:17; 66:22; 2 Pet 3:13; Rev 21:1, 5, encompasses a regeneration of heaven and earth (F. W. Grosheide, *Commentaar Mattheüs*, 298). Christ has been given all power (Matt 28:18; 1 Cor 15:27–28; Heb 2:8). He is King of kings and Lord of lords (Rev 17:14; 19:16).

Thus in this all-embracing work of Christ, redeemed human beings have their place. That means very specifically *in* it, as the body connected to Christ its head (Col 1:18; 2:19; 3:15; Eph 1:22–23; 2:16), and connected to each other as members of the same body (Rom 12:5; 1 Cor 12:12ff.; Eph 4:4), to form together the new humanity under the second Adam (Rom 5:12ff.; 1 Cor 15:45ff.). For the great multitude that no one can number is gathered from *every* tribe and language and people and nation (Rev 5:9; 7:9), as the "πλήρωμα τῶν ἐθνῶν (Rom 11:25). And because this new humanity is one in Christ, it shares in his dominion over τὰ πάντα, ὁ κόσμος (1 Cor 3:22; 10:25–26; Eph 1:20ff., and other places). Human sin was not only catastrophic for humanity, but also all of creation in all its parts had to suffer and groan because of the Fall of humankind. *Their* punishment became the punishment of all creation; their glory will also free all creation from its bondage to corruption (Rom 8). Humanity and creation are from the beginning and for all time riveted together.

Christians do not repudiate the world, for it is Christ's world. Kuyper deserves honor in that he discussed the coherence of all things in his doctrine of predestination. One can certainly object to the philosophical excess baggage that accompanies the word "organism" (p. 97 above), as long as the Scriptural core of what Kuyper argues is valued. I will offer a critique in the following section, but *here* I express appreciation for the man who fought the Anabaptist avoidance so fundamentally and defended the calling of Christians (rooted in predestination) so *radically*.

§ 4. Speculation in the concept of development from bud to bloom

In the doctrine of predestination we encounter Kuyper in his strength, but also in his weakness. For Holy Scripture does not speak at all about a development of the totality of created existence as an independent motif in God's predestination beside the actualization of the kingdom of heaven. *In principle* this speculative idea amounts to a secularization of predestination, although *in fact*, in accordance with Kuyper's intention (cf. the church as organism) it nowhere in his writings leads to a dechristianization of culture.

Kuyper radically defended the calling of the Christian in this world, as noted at the end of the previous section. He did this radically, for it is rooted in predestination. He wanted to point out the coherence of "all things" and to assign a calling to all Christians in this. Kuyper was able, rightly, to appeal to Scripture for this coherence.

But what follows from that? Where does it say in Scripture that the development of the totality of created existence forms an *independent* goal beside the actualization of the kingdom of heaven? And where does Scripture address a development of humanity in creation that will exhaust all the possibilities of the one image of God in its societal aspect? We read about a new humanity, of which Kuyper says (and about which we can enter into a discussion on the basis of Rev 5:9; 7:9) that it includes the integral part of the old humanity (pp. 36–37 above). But where in Scripture does the unfolding of the *old* humanity have the function that Kuyper assigns to it? Here we clearly encounter the *speculative* Kuyper. And we must part with him, because here he leaves behind the Bible as foundation.

But it is difficult to part with him! For Kuyper's worldview contains much that is attractive. Everything had to have a place in it. The driving force of his brilliant ideas impelled Kuyper (almost automatically!) Think of the range from "the life of the Bantu peoples in Africa, of the Mongols in China and Japan, and of the Indians south of the Himalayas," etc., pp. 35–36 above) toward constructing a doctrine of predestination in which, beside salvation as aim,

CHAPTER V. EVALUATION

a social-cultural objective also had to find a place: the development of all of creation's potential.

Here speaks not only the brilliant theologian, but also the man who wants to give a positive answer to the existential question whether the life of many hundreds of millions in the past and also at present has *meaning* (although it was and is lived apart from Christ). In doing so, he does not wish to confine himself to the remark that everything has God's glory as aim but wants to determine the *content* of the glory of God (*G.G.* II, 639). *This is where we find the reason why Kuyper distinguishes common grace so sharply from particular grace.* When Kuyper speaks of a "totally different work," a "totally different goal," "two sharply distinguished spheres" between which "a fundamental difference exists that is undeniable" (p. 61 above), this has nothing to do with an Anabaptist dualism. Kuyper wanted to oversee *the whole* with his eagle eye. For him, the meaning of "all things" demands (in order to satisfy the thought process) more categories than just salvation and condemnation, election and reprobation. For this purpose Kuyper makes use of philosophical ideas of his days, for example, about humanity as organism to which all persons make their own necessary contribution. See, e.g., Schleiermacher's *Reden über die Religion*, ch. 2! "Each individual is as regards his inner essence a necessary complement for a complete view of humanity" (157).

As I said, we have to part with Kuyper at this point. For in this cultural philosophy and anthropology the terrain of Scripture has been abandoned. We must exchange "rich speculation" for the sober restraint of Scripture, which indeed does not lift the veil beyond what Prov 16:4 says: "The LORD has made everything for its purpose, even the wicked for the day of trouble." The wicked for the day of trouble—can we say no more than this about the mass of people who are excluded from salvation? God keeps the answer to this question to himself. "For from him and through him and to him are all things." This is a *confession* that follows upon the acknowledgment of God's unsearchable judgments and his inscrutable ways (Rom 11:36, 33).

Hence I would suggest that with his doctrine of development as *independent* aim, Kuyper gave predestination a *secularized* shape. That does not confirm Rothuizen's account of Kuyper. I maintain everything that I raised against his views (pp. 104–114 above). Here, too, I say: from the *fact* of the independent aim of the development in predestination Kuyper does not distill a *mandate* (not even in part or anywhere) to dechristianize culture. I need only point to his doctrine of the church as organism (pp. 66–68 above). In chapter I, my concern was with what Kuyper had in mind with his doctrine: secularization, yes or no? There I answered: no, certainly not. But now the question becomes urgent whether Kuyper with his secularized doctrine of predestination, and despite his own intentions, can still offer a *principial* defense against Rothuizen's secularization ideas. I think not. Speculative ideas gained a place in the heart of Kuyper's theology. We shall see that accidents must then follow.

CHAPTER V. EVALUATION

§ 5. Christ and the covenant of grace

The division of the terrain between a Mediator of creation and a Mediator of redemption does not accord Christ's redemptive work the all-encompassing place that Col 1, John 1, and other passages describe for us. Everything in the world (also governments, Rom 13) is activated in the work of Christ. All grace that the world receives and has received it owes to him. Hence Kuyper's explanation of Gen 9, Gen 2:17, and Gen 3 cannot be mine.

With an eye to Christ's all-embracing redemption, in which he took possession of all things, I must also criticize Schilder's *substrate idea*. In my view, the correct position is that both the continuance and the materials included in the continuance are very much qualified by the covenant of grace.

I must raise serious objections to the distinction between a Mediator of creation and a Mediator of redemption. Schilder demonstrated clearly that the name "*Mediator* of creation" is incorrect (*Heid. Cat.* II, 87–103). His most important objection is that it invalidates the word "Mediator" itself. "For a Reformed person who reflects on the relationship between God and the world will not be able to, and may not, accept a *contrast* between those two, as gnosticism always did." It is from the turbid spring of gnosticism "that all those un-Reformed ideas of a *contrast* between God and world (even aside from a later Fall) arose, and consequently also the idea of a *go-between* or *mediator* in creation" (91). Whenever a mediator takes action, there must be at least two parties. "But where then is the 'other party,' who supposedly stands *over against* God in creation? There is none; ... when God creates the world, the second party, the creature, is not available; the second party only comes into existence through him" (92). See also Berkouwer, *Werk van Christus*, 314ff.

I share this criticism. Schilder also speaks more clearly here than Calvin (pp. 247–48 above), who remarked about sinless human beings that "even if they had remained free from all stain, their condition would have been too lowly for them to reach God without a Mediator" (*Inst.* II, xii, 1). All three theologians say that human beings, though sinless, were nonetheless *weak* in Paradise. For Schilder, see *Heid. Cat.* I, 325, on "the image of unstable human beings, weak, though sound; mortal, (also spiritually), though alive"; for Kuyper, *G.G.* II, 198. But this does not lead Schilder, correctly in my view, to posit a Mediator between God and human beings as essential.

But aside from the incorrect *distinction* between a Mediator of creation and a Mediator of redemption, I have insurmountable objections to Kuyper's *division*

CHAPTER V. EVALUATION

of the terrain between what belongs to the Mediatorship of creation and of redemption: common grace and particular grace, two "sharply distinguished spheres" between which "a fundamental difference exists that is undeniable"; the rule of Christ over the nations on the one terrain and over the church on the other, etc. This entire division is an *abstraction* that rests on an exegetical error. For while Kuyper constantly leads us from the "broad" work of creation to the much "narrower" work of redemption, the New Testament leads us constantly in the opposite direction. The redemptive work of Christ leads us, because of its breadth, to his all-embracing work of creation.

Through Christ's work of redemption, the New Testament gives us a perspective on Christ's pre-existence and his work of creation. This pre-existence confirms and safeguards the all-embracing reconciliation. See Eph 1; Col 1; John 1; Heb 1:2–3; 1 Cor 8:6. None of these texts contains an abstracting attention for a "Mediator of creation" who has his *own* creation aim, but they refer us to Jesus Christ as the one who reconciles "all things" (Col 1:20). It is impossible to conceive of powers in this τὰ πάντα that were supposedly withdrawn from Christ's dominion, since everything was already under his control before and through creation (Col 1:16, 20). That is how Christ's reconciliation is first disclosed in its fullness by a view of his work in creation as the work of the eternal Logos (John 1), the firstborn of all creation (Col 1:20). Cf. G. Kittel in *ThWB* IV, 134 on John 1: What came to pass on earth in the person of Christ "is set in its eternal frame, is questioned about its origin and background, the rays of which become visible in him; but the background by itself alone, without this happening that occurred or was experienced, is never the subject of any debate." See further Herman Ridderbos, *Commentaar Colossenzen*, 135–36, 138, 143, 145ff.; O. Cullmann, *Die Christologie des Neuen Testaments*, 253–323.

This so obvious thrust of the correct exegesis of the Scripture passages referred to does not at all mean that we must follow the explanation of Barth *cum suis*, which contains an "unmistakable tendency to rationalize all *pretemporal* aspects of John 1 into a peculiar soteriological direction" (Berkouwer, *De algemene openbaring*, 205). Further, my agreement with Kittel (s.v. λόγος) and with Cullmann does not imply that I accept all the consequences that they draw. Hence I cannot accept the exclusively soteriological exegesis, which in reality is about the relationship between *Jesus of Nazareth* and creation. "One can say that the prologue is about Jesus of Nazareth, but this means that it is about *that Jesus of Nazareth* who is the *Word* made flesh, *that* Word, that Logos who was *in the beginning* with God and was God, and in whom *was* the life and light of humankind, and *through* whom all things were made" (Berkouwer, op. cit., 207). Also with respect to Col 1:16: "No one who reads these words in their context, will reach the conclusion that Paul here suddenly jumps from the soteriological text [vv. 13–14!] to an abstract cosmological view. On the contrary: everything he says here is *connected* with salvation, but it is connected with it as *that* reality known to us only through revelation: all things *are created by him*" (loc. cit.). This a balanced exegesis.

CHAPTER V. EVALUATION

We may say: to be avoided are the Scylla of Kuyper with his often abstracting attention for the Son of God as Mediator of *creation* and the Charybdis of Barth and his followers, who have attention only for Jesus of Nazareth and creation. The soteriological is not distinct from the cosmological (see § 3), but the cosmological may also never be abstracted from the soteriological.

Hence it is also impossible to create a division somewhere between a governance "by the grace of God" and "by the grace of Christ," as Kuyper does. For according to Matt 28:18, all power, πᾶσα ἐξουσία in heaven and on earth has been given to Christ. This power is soteriologically directed, as v. 19 makes clear. The total ἐξουσία of Christ enables his apostles to bring the gospel to all nations. "Go therefore and make disciples of all nations." What is taught in Rom 13:1, Tim 2:1-6, and Phil 2:10-11 is no different. For one can surely not lift Rom 13 out of the framework of the gospel of Christ that Paul speaks about in his letter to the Romans. When he "poses the question of authority and obedience, he does so only *from out of the redemptive work in Christ Jesus*. Hence for Paul government also forms part of the entirety of this *particular* grace" (B. Holwerda, *De crisis van het gezag*, 7). Governments are God's servants, λειτουργοὶ θεοῦ (Rom 13:6), and so, in light of 1 Tim 2, Holwerda can write: "*Which God is that?* Paul says: pray for kings and all who are in high positions, for this is good, and it is pleasing in the sight of God our *Savior*. There is only one God, who desires all people to be saved and to come to the knowledge of the truth; there is also only one mediator between God and men, the man *Jesus Christ* (1 Tim 2:2-5). Thus Paul *founds this prayer for governing authorities on the first commandment*: there is but *one God*, the God of the whole world. And that is not just the God of *creation* and *providence*, it is God the *Savior*, the God who in his sovereign redemptive will seeks the salvation of the world, and who works that redemption in Christ Jesus, the only Mediator.... And in the great plan of redemption, all *governing authorities* also have their limited task" (op. cit., 8).

Governments are liturgists of *Christ*. This has nothing to do with an abdication by the Father (p. 58 above). If Jesus is the Son of God, "so also the power given to him is not to be thought of as a limited commission, but is rather to be understood as an administration in free unity of will with the Father" (W. Foerster in *ThWB* II, 565).

I do not want to speak of a Christological foundation of the state. The power that Jesus Christ now possesses was *given* to him (Matt 28:18). "In full agreement with our confession, we can say that God instituted government and at the same time see the specific relationship between Christ and government come to the fore through Christ's ascension" (Berkouwer, *De Voorzienigheid Gods*, 125). Cf. op. cit., 136ff., on the dangers of positing a Christological foundation.

Since the whole cosmos is subjected to Christ after he made peace by the blood of his cross (Col 1:20), the whole world receives all grace that flows to it thanks to him. Not only after, but also before his ascension. For those who believe in the unity of Scripture accept that the entire history of salvation in all its phases is governed by the Word (not yet) made flesh (Luke 24:27; 1 Pet 1:10ff.).

CHAPTER V. EVALUATION

The phases in this history are phases of the covenant of *grace* that encompasses all the ages from Paradise via Noah, Abraham, and Christ's advent until his return.

We must reject all abstractions here—also with respect to the Noahic covenant. For one can surely not lift it out of the covenant of grace, as Kuyper does (pp. 8–9 above), and say of the content of this covenant that it "concerns *temporal* and not eternal goods," and that "the true promise of the Noahic covenant does not extend further than to confirm again the result of the first creation and to ensure the *ordinary course of nature*" (*G.G.* I, 26).

I am not forgetting that Kuyper on the same page expressly lays the connection between Christ and his people (stating that it goes without saying "that the *goal* of this act of grace by God cannot lie in the *reprobate*, but must lie in the *elect* and is thus to be found in Christ, and in his people and their future"). But the way Kuyper expresses this transition is characteristic: "*You only arrive at* the *spiritual* meaning of the Noahic covenant when you abandon its content," etc. (italics supplied). How can we, with John 1 and Col 1 before us, only arrive at Christ later and disregard him for the determination of the content of the Noahic covenant? That would be a topsy-turvy world (see above).

Consequently Kuyper's arguments for making the Noahic covenant a covenant of grace do not convince at all (pp. 8–13 above). Why can this covenant not be particular when all living souls and the entire world are *included* in it? Is Christ's reconciliation, in which all things are included in accordance with Col 1, also not particular? The covenant of grace "was universal, it sought humanity as the assembly of all who are truly alive. And God makes everything subject to this assembly in the covenant with nature [Noahic covenant]" (K. Schilder, *Wat is de hemel?*, 187). Noah stands "within the framework of one covenant history, in which the entire creation has always been included. Hence the revelation to Noah is just as much the disclosure of God's Counsel in the Lord Christ. For we know of no other disclosure!" (G. van Dooren in *Geschiedenis der Godsopenbaring* I, 225).

Kuyper can also not adduce as argument the use of the name "God" instead of "LORD." The use of these names varies without suggesting that the name "LORD" has a special function. Why, for example is it "LORD" in Gen 4:3 and 6, and 6:5, and "God" in Gen 5:22 and 6:13? It is also apparent from *G.G.* I, 498–99 that in his reasoning Kuyper uses the text for his own purposes (p. 9 above). There he connects Ps 46:6, in which the name "God" is used when (in connection with Jerusalem) the name "LORD" might have been expected, with Ps 93, which speaks of "LORD" although the use of the name "God" would seem to have been the obvious choice. Kuyper explains that is "a seeming contradiction, to be explained from the fact that Holy Scripture always points to the close connection between common grace and particular grace" (op. cit., 499). But this solution will convince no one.

I will leave out of consideration much (also many good things) that Kuyper wrote about the Noahic covenant. But I want to draw attention to one other

CHAPTER V. EVALUATION

point. According to Kuyper, the prohibition against eating raw meat with the still warm blood is directed against the brutalization of human life (p. 10 above). A different exegesis seems more probable to me: "Blood being the bearer of life, the blood of a sacrificial animal serves with respect to God as means of propitiation" (J. Behm in *ThWB* I, 172). See also C. Vonk, *De Voorzeide Leer* I b, 46; W. H. Gispen, *Commentaar Leviticus*, 258. This view reinforces my explanation of the Noahic covenant as covenant of particular grace.

On the basis of the above I can also not accept Kuyper's exegesis of Gen 2:17 and Gen 3 (pp. 14ff. above). For now I will leave out of consideration the question whether the continuation of life (Gen 2:17) and the protection of that life (Gen 3) can be regarded as grace. If we may speak of grace here, then also this grace comes from Jesus Christ.

Schilder criticized Kuyper's exegesis of the Noahic covenant, and I agree with his criticism to a large extent. In particular, I gladly adopt his rejection of the dilemma "particular or universal" (pp. 152–53 above). He also rightly does not follow Kuyper in the latter's exegesis of Gen 6:5, 8, 21, but the explanation of Aalders that Schilder adopted (pp. 154–55 above) does not satisfy me. Cf. J. P. Lettinga, who for good reasons proposes the following translation of Gen 8:21: "I shall not again curse the ground because of man, *even though* [*ki*] the product of the heart of man is evil from his youth." Lettinga rightly states that in this way "the difficulties for exegetes and dogmatists" vanish just like that (*Ref.* 32, 232). Cf. Th. C. Vriezen, "Einige Notizen zur Übersetzung des Bindeswortes *ki*," in *Von Ugarit nach Qumran: Beiheft zur ZAW* 77, 266–73.

But I already had my questions also about Schilder's views (pp. 153–54 above). They concern the point of Schilder's *substrate idea*. Schilder accepts the Noahic covenant as a phase of the covenant of grace. But *in* the Noahic covenant he draws a distinction between grace and substrate: "Noah's *being* federal *co-knower with God*, that is ... grace, a very particular grace. But the knowledge itself, the guaranteed projects of divine providence, those are not grace, but substrate for blessing and for curse" (*Heid. Cat.* IV, 141). Schilder speaks of the "covenant of retardation and of the providentially guided balanced structures" as "substrate for the other covenant history, in which human beings are called participants in God's grace" (ibid.). In other words: the real covenant of grace with Noah is encompassed by the much broader covenant of retardation, which has *two* goals: administration of grace and of judgment.

It seems to me that Schilder engages in abstraction here. He draws a distinction in the one Noahic covenant that renders dubious the characterization of this covenant *in its totality* as covenant of *grace*. To obtain a clearer picture, I place the above-quoted passages from his *Heidelbergsche Catechismus* next to the following passage from *Wat is de hemel?*, written in Schilder's second period: The Noahic covenant "was universal; it was concerned with humanity as the assembly of all who are truly alive. And in the covenant with nature God makes *everything subordinate* to the work of those gathered

CHAPTER V. EVALUATION

together; all of 'nature' is involved in the growth and the development of the new Jerusalem designed by God. *It becomes God's shop floor, so that he can in due course lay down his church floor*" (187–88, italics supplied; see p. 223 above). Here the content of the covenant is clearly characterized in accordance with its *salvation* aspect—a "one-sidedness" (covenant of *grace*) that agrees completely with Scripture. For John 1 speaks of the Word who brings *life and light*; and Col 1 speaks of the firstborn of creation who made *peace*. This does not detract at all from Christ's judging. On the contrary. His blessing strengthens the power of his cursing. To put it as Schilder does: the covenant does not run aground on hell, but maintains itself in it (op. cit., 176). For the rejection of grace calls for judgment. Covenant *wrath* comes about as payment for covenant *breach* (loc. cit.). But then in that order! The cursing of Ham arises *within* the covenant of grace; people are guilty because they have despised the *light* (John 1; Rom 1).

This is not a "one-sidedness" that tends toward a universal reconciliation. When Col 1:20 says that "all things" are reconciled, we must think "of the restoration of the right relationship toward God, be it willingly, *or by subjection*" (Herman Ridderbos, *Commentaar, Colossenzen*, 149; italics supplied). And when the same verse speaks of "making peace," this "refers to a peace that bears an all-encompassing, eschatological character and also consists of the subjection of the powers that are hostile to God and humanity. Cf., e.g., Rom 16:20: 'The God of *peace* will soon *crush* Satan under your feet'" (loc. cit.).

Heaven and hell do not stand in such an equilibrium as Schilder suggests (see § 2). Hence it would be better to drop the substrate idea (cf. also p. 136 above) and maintain the "one-sided" characterization of Christ's total, *gracious* redemptive work. The judgment, the curse, and hell, follow upon and are the consequence of scorning this grace. "The guilt resulted from rejecting Christ. Thus Christ took action as the Savior-Redeemer and as the Savior-Avenger. The constitutive element in both functions is his evangelical work of redemption, which is never satisfied with being a negligible quantity" (p. 194 above). This quotation from *Christ and Culture* (94)—in which, in my view, the equilibrium was rightly broken (Christ's *redemptive* work is constitutive!)—explodes the substrate idea of the same Schilder. How does he differ *here* from Calvin and his *opus proprium* [proper work] (pp. 271–72 above)?

I called Schilder's depiction of the Noahic covenant in *De Heidelbergsche Catechismus* abstractive. The "guaranteed projects of divine providence" in this covenant are called *substrate*. Over against this I posit that all things included in or serviceable for the covenant of *grace* are very much qualified in this covenant as materials of *grace*. "Christ purchased the world with his blood. Hence all that it contains belongs to him and those who believe in him. For the world is the LORD's, that is, it belongs to the God of the covenant in Christ, the world and those who dwell therein (Ps 24:1). And all things, both present or future, are yours, says Paul, but you are Christ's, and Christ is God's (1 Cor 3:21–23). That which unbelievers use in their way and in their own lives, they steal from Christ" (S. G. de Graaf, *Christus en de wereld*, 100). They therefore do not want to hear about "a certain common, neutral workplace for believers and unbelievers and common materials" that are as yet unqualified (op. cit., 99). Stealing—that is what unbelievers do. They misuse the materials that Christ has appropriated.

Schilder wrote things worthy of consideration about the significance of the covenant for the punishment and judgment of unbelievers. See, for example, *Wat is de hel?*, 194ff. There he says that "Reformed *covenant* theology [is] the indispensable foundation for all doctrine about hell" (194). Hell, death, and punishment are proclaimed on the terrain of the covenant and are "only imposed as judgment on covenant breakers *as such*. And the 'economy' of the covenant of *grace* can therefore posit this relationship between covenant and repudiation with all the more definition" (195). We cannot speak about punishment separate from grace; the "no" from before the Fall rejected the Creator, while the "no" after the Fall rejects the Re-creator (29, 54). People will be judged according to the measure of the light and grace that was offered to all (110). I fully agree with this. But Schilder did not allow his ideas in this book (third edition, 1932) to be governed by what he would later write about God's balanced actions in blessing and curse, heaven and hell. He wanted to go back "to the beginning," but it strikes me that this beginning comes after Gen 1:31: "God saw everything that he had made, and behold, it was very good." "Hell did not yet exist when God, the supreme Architect, called his own riches into being and beheld ... the work of his hands" (43). Hell presupposes sin; it cannot be the same age as heaven (43, 46). Later Schilder would go back "even further." But then (at least in his opposition to the doctrine of common grace) a fully developed parallelism between heaven and hell was such a dominant theme that, in my view, the clearly depicted coherence between covenant and hell in *Wat is de hel?* was no longer presented with sufficient clarity.

§ 6. *Wrong focus of Kuyper's common grace*

While I am not yet considering the question whether we can speak of grace in a more general sense, I can already defend the proposition that Kuyper's doctrine of common grace is unacceptable because he focuses this grace not on *salvation* and the *knowledge of God*, but on culture. Consequently Kuyper's exegesis of John 1 and Rom 1 is untenable. It is to be commended in Calvin that his discussion of grace in a general sense is focused correctly. The invitation motif and the critical motif make this sufficiently clear.

The Prologue to the gospel of John was discussed in the previous section. In fact, what is most important in connection with our topic has already been stated. The New Testament focuses on Christ's pre-existence and his work in

CHAPTER V. EVALUATION

creation as Logos *from the perspective* of his work of redemption. Calvin does not give us a cosmology in addition to a soteriology. The universal aspects are *focused* on salvation in Christ, also in John 1. This has consequences. The meaning of the words "life" (ζωή) and "light" (φῶς) in the Prologue are particularly significant. We can understand these words properly only by following Christ's own exegesis, which is clearly presented later in the gospel of John.

What is that *life*? Or "eternal life" (which expression is its indiscriminately used variant; cf. 6:47, 48, 53, 54; 11:25, 26; 20:31)? According to what Christ himself said, "This is eternal life, that they *know* you the only true God, and *Jesus Christ* whom you have sent" (17:3). Thus this life has a clear theo-logic and soterio-logic content. Cf. also 3:15, 36; 5:24; 6:27–58; 8:12; 10:28; 11:25; 12:25, 50; 14:6; 20:31. Therefore one does not *have* this life without faith (3:15, 36; 5:24; 6:35, 40, 47, etc.). Cf. Bultmann in *ThWB* II, 871ff.

And what does John means when he speaks of *light* in 1:4ff.? It is the light that brings *salvation*, since no one needs to walk in the darkness anymore (9:5; 12:35–36, 46) and since it reveals life to human beings (8:12). One also does not *have* this light without faith, (1:7; 12:36). How would that be possible when Jesus Christ himself is called the substance of life and light? He *is* life (5:26; 11:25; 14:6), and he *is* light (3:19; 8:12; 9;5; 12:35, 46).

Armed with this knowledge, I cannot accept Kuyper's explanation. For he describes *life* and *light* much too generally: Human beings "live by means of the eternal Word. The eternal Word that gives them existence is their life. And that life brightens in their consciousness so that there is *light*, light shining in all directions: light in their understanding, light in the exercise of their will, light in their communal life, light in their moral existence, light in their art and science, light in the eye of their souls by which they see their God" (p. 19 above). It is characteristic of Kuyper that the light "by which they see their God" comes last.

Our ways part even more clearly when Kuyper, following the Annotators of the Dutch States Bible (and also Calvin), speaks about the light as the *light of reason* (p. 20 above). For that way the *revelation* of the light *in* the darkness becomes in fact a condition *of* the darkness: The people who, according to the gospel, are "darkness," hate the light (3:19, 20; cf. 1:5; 1:9) but would, according to the explanation of Kuyper and others, have the light (of reason). The entire question of the light of reason and of other things that are still "good" in the world, falls outside of the theme of John 1. Of the "world" it can only be said that it exists in darkness, in blindness (9:39–41; 12:40; 1 John 2:11) and in the lie (John 8:43–45; 1 John 2:21–22).

My criticism of Kuyper applies in part also to the exegesis of Greijdanus and Schilder, who describe the light of John 1:5 as "the light of all kinds of gifts, goods, and knowledge, of what provides enjoyment and help, of whatever freedom and development people on earth may still be able to share in" (p. 155 above). Here, too, every mention of the light as *salvation* that is hated by the darkness, is lacking. The generality of Greijdanus' definition blurs the *particular*

CHAPTER V. EVALUATION

of the pericope. For the Prologue is concerned with light *or* darkness, with eternal life *or* eternal death. Consequently the light of 1:5 is concerned with more than "whatever freedom and development people on earth may still be able share in." Happily, Greijdanus provides a much stronger view with respect to v. 9. There he speaks of the true light as the light of the "*Savior* promised by God who, already in the time before the incarnation, [performed] his *work of salvation*" particularly in Israel and, radiating from there, to all the nations (p. 157 above).

We can disregard the question whether Greijdanus was right in connecting "coming into the world" with "the true light" (correctly, in my view), and taking ἐρχόμενον εἰς τὸν κόσμον [coming into the world] as referring to his coming ever since the mother promise in Gen 3:15 (too contrived, in my view). I am grateful to observe that *here* the light is focused on *salvation*: "And that which God gave to and wrought in Israel also issued an appeal to other peoples to turn themselves to Israel and to recognize Israel's God" (p. 156 above).

This indication of the direction of "life" and "light" is missing from Kuyper's exegesis of John 1:1-10. For his common grace is searching for something different. It does not ask about re-creation but about creation, and consequently about *culture*. However, the pillar of the Prologue, just as the pillar of the Noahic covenant, fails to provide sufficient support for Kuyper's culture-forming common grace.

What are we to think of the exegetical material that serves as evidence for common grace and that Kuyper believes he has found in *Rom 1 and 2*? The remarkable fact is that this Scripture passage, even in Kuyper's own eyes, could not possibly have been a strong pillar. For how does Kuyper use it? First he draws from Rom 1 and 2 all the data that can prove that this world has not become a hell. The Gentiles still have knowledge of God and knowledge of justice, their consciences work, and they act in accordance with the law (pp. 20-22 above). *Thereafter* Kuyper tells us that the "little sparks are being extinguished" (*G.G.* I, 415ff.). In shrill colors he is able to depict how much common grace can shrink (I, 415, 421ff.), how it is misused (I, 449-50), and how unrighteousness will become apparent in its most refined form under the Antichrist (I, 447-48).

One would expect that every paean on common grace would fall silent under the burden of Rom 1 and 2, 2 Thess 2, and Rev 19. But just before the candle threatens to go out, Kuyper introduces his distinction between the ethical-religious and the intelligent-artistic operation of common grace (I, 421, 427, 456). A *spiritual* fruit is not born of the natural knowledge of God (I, 415), but the "giving up" of the nations "to a debased mind" (Rom 1:28) is said to refer exclusively to "their withdrawal from the common grace extended to the nations on the *religious* and *moral* terrain. On *this* terrain, and only there, God gave the nations over to a debased mind, but meanwhile his common grace had probably never shone forth as strongly as it had formerly on various other terrains" (I, 421). What is the evidence for *this* brilliantly shining common grace?

CHAPTER V. EVALUATION

The content of Rom 1 confirms it for Kuyper. "For when Paul depicts in detail the wicked consequences of this *"giving up" of the nations*, i.e., of the withdrawal of common grace, he points exclusively to manifestations of moral decay" (I, 421; cf. Rom 1:24–32). In other words, Kuyper derives the Scriptural evidence for this blossoming branch of common grace solely from an *argumentum e silentio*!

This provides me with the means to contest Kuyper's views properly. For the silence of Scripture does not support Kuyper but argues against him. The Bible never gives *independent* attention to the culture of the world. Everything that on the basis of Rom 1 and 2 can be said *for* the world serves to illustrate the more strongly what it is *against* (opposition to God). God provided knowledge of himself in his general revelation, but human beings have suppressed this truth in unrighteousness (Rom 1:18ff.). All that preceded it is subordinate to Paul's *devastating* indictment in Rom 3:9–20. Consequently, those who believe that they can still find a progressive intellectual-artistic operation of common grace are guilty of a dangerous *abstraction*. For the direction of these chapters ("no one seeks God," 3:11) is thus easily turned around and changed to a cultural direction when it is said that so much is still being accomplished in the world, and that the "people of the world" often turn out to be better than expected (*G.G.* II, 21).

Schilder's exegesis of Rom 1 and 2 is in more than one respect a *gain* for us. He truly allows 1:20 ("So they are without excuse") to function and contributes many corrections worthy of consideration to the traditional exegesis of 2:14–15, also over against Calvin (pp. 157ff. above). Paul does indeed not speak of *capita communissima* [central truths on which all agree] that are innate in human beings. And Calvin already recognized the impossibility of a natural theology (pp. 255ff. above). Such a theology is a figment of the imagination when we realize how God's revelation in creation *is being suppressed* (1:18).

Nonetheless, Schilder's exegesis does raise questions. In the next section I will discuss whether we may speak of "grace" in connection with Rom 1:19. For now I will focus on two other matters. The first is the difference between ποιεῖν and πράσσειν as Schilder and Greijdanus define it—dubiously, in my opinion (pp. 160–61 above). From what C. Maurer says about these words [which are both normally translated as "to do"] we get quite a different exegesis: Over against the "colorless vocable" πράσσειν stands the much more delineated ποιεῖν (*ThWB* VI, 635ff.). "Thus πράσσειν, in comparison with the more specified ποιεῖν, has in regards to sinning a more general meaning, as the encounter with the law turns human beings in a qualified way into sinners who are in crisis" (637). I believe that caution is demanded here. More than once both these words are used a synonyms; compare Rom 13:4 with 2 Cor 5:10 and Rom 2:14 with 2:25. Further, Rom 1:32; 2:1–3; 7:15–20 also argue against making any distinction in the meaning of the two words. Hence, Schilder (and also Maurer) do not really convince me on this point.

The second question is more important. I believe that Greijdanus and

CHAPTER V. EVALUATION

Schilder incorrectly define νοούμενα [being understood] in Rom 1:20 as conditional. Schilder paraphrases this text as follows: "Scripture says, 'We observe the wisdom of God in his creatures, but only if our eyes are opened for that wisdom by God's Word, *and not otherwise*'" (p. 158 above). If by this he means that we can only perceive God's wisdom *rightly* through his Word, he is correct. But *apparently* he means that νοούμενα cannot function at all without the Word, in which case I disagree. For the revelation of the Word, which is only addressed first in Rom 2, is not at issue in 1:20. It speaks about the *Gentiles* who are guilty because they have misused the principial possibility to know God (νοούμενα καθορᾶται, "being understood, are clearly seen"): "For although they knew God, they did not honor him as God or give thanks to him" (v. 21). See pp. 252–53, 254–55 above for this "knowledge" in its function and ambiguity. Greijdanus rightly says about 1:21: "This γινώσκειν, 'to get to know,' does not refer to a true knowledge that would lead to acknowledgment, as the rest of this verse makes clear. It refers only to a superficial perceiving, so that the consciousness was impinged on and made operative but did not acquire a pure knowledge that manifested itself in a pure service of God that is worthy of him" (*Kommentaar Romeinen*, I, 112).

There *is* a general revelation of God that can be and is perceived. That is why humans are guilty, for in their wickedness they have perverted this knowledge. "Far from referring to the activity of the mind as the natural human instrument for the knowledge of God—the νοῦς [mind] is for Paul not such an instrument ...—the apostle by way of the conclusion of v. 20 ("for them to be without excuse") indicates much more that human beings themselves bear the responsibility for whether or not the possibility of the knowledge of God that is bestowed on them is realized by their νοῦς" (J. Behm in *ThWB* IV, 949). See also Herman Ridderbos, *Commentaar Romeinen*, 44, who rightly states that v. 20 forms the basis of what preceded it (what can be known of God is also indeed φανερὸν, manifest, in the Gentiles), and that v. 21 is linked to v. 20: "For these words proceed from the fact that God is indeed known and therefore do not presuppose a condition in νοούμενα. Consequently I believe it is correct to state that νοούμενα [being understood] is not a conditional, but a modal, temporal, or causal participle: *while* or *because* the νοῦς [mind] is directed toward it."

Thus I maintain the "old exegesis" of Rom 1:20. I am also very much in agreement with what Calvin taught about general revelation (pp. 249ff. above) and about the "knowledge" of the Gentiles (pp. 252–53 above). He does not provide material for a "natural theology" (pp. 255ff. above). The rejection of all natural theology does not at all mean, however, that we can no longer speak of God's general revelation.

In the next section I will discuss whether Calvin uses the word "grace" correctly in this context (pp. 243ff. above). But I can already say now, considering everything that I raised against Kuyper, that I agree with Calvin's *orientation* of this grace. For it invites people to come to know God and to praise him, and it makes them guilty when they fail to acquire this knowledge.

CHAPTER V. EVALUATION

Any independent goal beside this orientation to the knowledge of God, as in Kuyper with his culture-forming common grace, is foreign to Calvin. Thus he remained within the bounds of Scripture.

As we saw, S. J. Ridderbos also criticized what Kuyper says about the independent goal of common grace. However, in my view his objections remain superficial. He asserted that Kuyper "over-emphasized" this independent goal, but that all the elements of his doctrine of common grace can be maintained, "even if we do not regard this independent goal of common grace as highly as Kuyper did" (*De theologische cultuurbeschouwing van Abraham Kuyper*, 274). Not as highly? But if we, with Calvin, remain within the bounds of Scripture, we will not recognize an independent goal of common grace at all. And then, as we saw above, the criticism of Kuyper's doctrine becomes fundamental, and therefore it is impossible to retain "all its elements."

Consequently my position is closer to that of Th. L. Haitjema, whose point of view was criticized by Ridderbos. Haitjema does go too far when speaking about Kuyper's generalizations and calling him a "cultural philosopher" (op. cit., 272). His qualification "cultural optimism" (p. 104 above) is also insufficiently nuanced. For Kuyper constantly corrected this optimism, as Ridderbos rightly pointed out (op. cit., 214ff.) and as we already saw (p. 111 above). But this is where the difficulty arises. Kuyper (and Ridderbos) do make *corrections*, but they maintain the point of departure: the independence of common grace, valued highly to a greater or lesser degree. And with that point of departure, cultural optimism necessarily surfaces, as it were, time and again.

Over against the independence of common grace, Haitjema posits strongly, but correctly: "The idea did not even occur to Calvin and the other Reformed fathers." In Calvin, general grace is "focused on the particular—and causes God's righteousness to become apparent in the fact that it denies Gentiles all ground of excuse outside of Christ" (*De Cultuur-waardeering van het Nieuw-Calvinisme*, 98). See Ridderbos, op. cit., 271. In general I agree with Calvin. I have objections to certain details. Thus, with Schilder (pp. 159–60 above), I reject any habitus [predisposition] *in* a human being that presupposes an inborn knowledge of God as seed of religion (e.g., p. 234 above), or an inborn knowledge of laws as "seeds of laws" (p. 236 above). Scripture does not teach such static constructs. Over against that, however, I fully agree with what Calvin writes about God's *actual, dynamic*, and *personal* general revelation (pp. 250–51 above). Human beings can never escape from this revelation with its primacy and transparency. It is sufficient to make them inexcusable.

Calvin ought to have limited himself to this dynamic depiction of God's general revelation. Scripture does not speak of "general concepts," of "seeds" that should be arranged as "habits" *in* human beings pursuant to God's general revelation. The word "revelation" is too precious to permit us to recognize "seeds" in it that would germinate "by natural means," automatically, as it were.

CHAPTER V. EVALUATION

§ 7. Grace – also toward the reprobate

When, summarizing Scripture, I speak of "grace," I refer exclusively to the *one* grace of God in Jesus Christ. My objection to what Greijdanus and Schilder postulate when they say, "Only when something promotes eternal salvation can we truly speak of grace," focuses on the word "truly." The differing *effect* of God's manifestation of grace toward the elect and the reprobate does not deprive this manifestation of the common character of *grace*. Holy Scripture clearly speak of grace toward the reprobate within the covenant. Further, it does not anywhere contradict the use of the word "grace" for God's patience outside of the circle of the covenant. I follow Calvin on this point. But he does not do justice to the Christocentric character of all grace. Here we can learn from S. G. de Graaf, although my agreement with his views is only partial. Reformed theology has followed Calvin in its use of the word "grace."

The word χάρις has different meanings in Scripture. Both the Hebrew *khen* and the Greek χάρις can be translated as "handsomeness," "gracefulness," "graciousness," "charm" (Ps 45:3; Prov 4:9; 5:19; 11:16; 31:30; Luke 4:22; Col 4:6. Also the meaning "favor," or "mercy," occurs frequently (Gen 18:3; 30:27; 33:8; Ruth 2:2; Esth 2:15; Prov 21:10; Luke 2:52; Acts 2:47; and other places). In addition, χάρις can be translated as "thanks," "thankfulness" (Luke 17:91, Cor 10:30) and in a few places comes close to meaning "reward" (Luke 6:31ff.; 1 Cor 9:16 in some manuscripts). Cf. W. Bauer, *Wörterbuch zum Neuen Testament*, s.v. χάρις.

All of these translations of χάρις, also "profane" ones, do not yet render what Scripture means by grace as such. "It is the New Testament that fixed its meaning and determined the whole range of this meaning. It used the word precisely to characterize the new regime established by Jesus Christ and to set this over against the previous economy: the latter was governed by the law, the former by grace" (Jean Giblet in *Vocabulaire de théologie biblique*). The grace of God is revealed in Christ (John 1:16–17); in him it appears salvifically to all human beings (Titus 2:11ff.); in him dwells the fullness of God (Col 1:19). The grace of God exists in the grace of the one man Jesus Christ (Rom 5:15; cf. Eph 1:6; 2:7; 1 Tim 1:14; 2 Tim 1:9). That is why Scripture often speaks of the grace of Christ in addition to the grace of God (Rom 5:15; Gal 1:6; 2 Cor 8:9; Acts 15:11).

This indissoluble unity between God's grace and its revelation in Christ makes it impossible for me to accept Kuyper's distinction between particular grace as such and common grace as such, in which the latter supposedly has a

CHAPTER V. EVALUATION

"totally different nature" (p. 7 above). There is but one grace of God in Christ. God loved the *world* (Kuyper), but *in* Jesus Christ (John 3:16). The use of the word "grace" in Scripture does not support Kuyper's distinction anywhere.

The meaning of "grace" as God's grace in Christ therefore also marks many words that are used in their *context*, such as ἔλεος, οἰκτιρμός, σπλάγχνα, χρηστότης, ἀγάπη [mercy, compassion, tender mercy, kindness, love]. Hence, if you deny that there is grace toward unbelievers, it is incorrect to speak nevertheless of a "certain love," a "certain goodness," of God toward them, as S. G. de Graaf does (*Christus en de wereld*, 102). *Either* the one word is to be used sparingly—but then we must also be careful with the others. With respect to God's love that is very obvious, in my opinion; but also God's goodness, or kindness, χρηστότης, reveals itself in Christ (Rom 11:22; Eph 2:7; Titus 3:4). *Or* those who dare speak of a "certain love" and a "certain goodness" of God ought also to be able to speak of a "certain grace." Kuyper wrongly makes a distinction in the concept of grace, whereas De Graaf draws too strong a distinction between the word "grace" and its *synonyms* (at least, considered globally).

For that matter, even when De Graaf speaks of a "certain *patience*" of God (loc. cit.), this raises questions. For patience, μακροθυμία, can also have the tint of "grace." Cf. Ps 103:8: "The LORD is merciful and gracious, slow to anger and abounding in steadfast love." Also see Exod 34:6; Neh 9:17; Ps 86:15; 145:8; Joel 2:13. I do understand De Graaf's discomfiture when he speaks of a *certain* love, goodness, and patience, but this discomfiture has wrongly caused him less concern than his difficulty with the word "grace."

I can understand that not only De Graaf, but also Schilder, wants to use word "grace" sparingly (pp. 129–35 above). But Schilder uses it *too* sparingly—for example, when he says that grace is "always insuperable." And he sees "no reason at all" to make an exception to that rule (p. 168 above). I already noted that in an earlier period Schilder expressed himself differently. Then he wrote: "One may not say of grace in general what is indeed true of *regenerating* grace, namely, that it is irresistible" (p. 169 above). In my view Schilder thereby not only, as he himself said, adhered to the historical line, but also remained in line with Scripture. For the Bible does not restrict the granting of grace to persons who believe and are elected. How otherwise are we to understand that people can "despise God's grace" (Heb 12:15); that Paul can adjure people "not to receive the grace of God in vain" (2 Cor 6:1); or that people can begin with the Spirit and be perfected by the flesh" (Gal 3:3)? Who can, even though the word "grace" is not used, deny that Rom 9:4–5; 1 Cor 10:1–4; and (even stronger) Heb 6:4–6, list many spiritual gifts of grace, given to those in whom for the most part God has had no pleasure?

This grace of Christ (1 Cor 10!) was granted within the *covenant*, in which God many times showed his faithfulness (*khesed*, mercy as faithfulness to his covenant) toward unfaithful persons (Ps 51:3; 25:6–7; Isa 64:7ff.). I think here also of Isa 26:10: "Though grace is shown (*yukhan rasha'*) to the wicked, he does

CHAPTER V. EVALUATION

not learn righteousness." Even by a display of grace the wicked among God's people cannot be moved to learn righteousness. It is clear from the context (vv. 7ff.) that this grace is God's grace. Besides, the form of the verb is not irrealis (non-factual).

Given these data, I cannot agree with Schilder when he follows Greijdanus in his definition: "Only when something promotes eternal salvation can we truly speak of grace" (p. 170 above). As I see it, this statement also conflicts with what both theologians defended in 1942 and following years over against those who began to distinguish between the benefactions for the elect and the non-elect in the covenant. Then Greijdanus wrote: "When water runs up against a dam that stems the flood, the water is not increased if someone makes an opening in the dam through which it can flow. But if no opening is made, the water will soon run over the dam and will probably breach it and cause all kinds of destruction. But that water is not increased by either the one or the other, nor changed in its nature. Similarly, the flow of the grace God displays and of the privileges he offers is also not changed in nature or quantity when he finds either open or closed hearts among people. But in the one case he works blessing and in the other, ruin" (*De openbaring Gods in het Nieuwe Testament over Zijn genadeverbond*, 32).

An excellent image, enlightening in more than one respect! But it also gives me the confidence to attack Greijdanus' own definition of what is "truly" grace with *this* weapon. For in the just-quoted passage Greijdanus says that the grace that God shows to human beings whose hearts are closed does not differ "in nature or quantity" from the grace shown to his elect, for whom it does promote their "eternal salvation."

Schilder expresses himself in a similar way. "Covenant is the mutual agreement between God and his people, his in origin, and maintained (by virtue of his gracious work) by himself and his people as two 'parties.' It is, to the extent that it concerns *his* contribution, determined by *his speaking*, by his *Word* (promise and demand). And in this speaking he carries out his Counsel (of election)—as well as that of his rejection (insofar as it is a predestination to punishment) specifically for despising the administration of the covenant of grace." In discussing the "synodical sophistry" of the *Praeadvies* [preliminary report to General Synod] of 1943, Schilder calls this "its disastrous and fundamental mistake: it confuses God's *speaking* with God's *thinking*. It observes that God 'draws' two lines. If only it had been satisfied with that. But it [the *Praeadvies*] says itself that *it* 'draws' two lines. That is a fiction in this case. It had to follow only the line of the things that have been revealed. Then it would not have to presume anything. But then it could *entice* and *threaten*, since God's speaking also did both, while leaving the hidden things to God himself" (*Looze Kalk*, 66).

But the remarkable fact is that unsound artillery in one battle zone can be used in another. For Schilder keeps the "hidden things" outside the battle on one occasion, while assigning them a role again in the struggle against common

CHAPTER V. EVALUATION

grace: One can speak "properly" of grace only when something leads to eternal life, i.e., of grace to the elect! This idea, which in my opinion would not find a place in Schilder's publications about the covenant, *fits* his critique of common grace. For here I recall how much Schilder (as well as Greijdanus; see his "Waartoe het kwaad in deze wereld?" *De Wachter* 40, no. 40) was influenced in this by the doctrine of election and reprobation. In my view it is not possible to have their one view (about the covenant) run parallel with their other view (about common grace).

Also in one of his later publications, *Bovenschriftuurlijke binding: een nieuw gevaar*, Schilder did not answer the questions that arise here. In this brochure he confronts H. Hoeksema but does not become enmeshed in the latter's web by speaking of the *covenant* from the perspective of election and reprobation. The duality in Schilder's approach is not exchanged for the simplistic argument of Hoeksema, who has but one theme throughout, namely, election and reprobation. Schilder's estrangement from Hoeksema was never resolved (op. cit., 32–33, 41ff., 46–47, 53, 67ff., 77–78, 81).

Thus far I have discussed grace for the reprobate *within* the church. I agree with what Calvin said about this (pp. 293ff. above). This same grace is offered to all. Think of the integrity of the sacrament. But all grace is not efficacious. The effect differs, even though this does not detract from the genuineness of all offered *grace*—genuineness also with regard to a disciple such as Judas. It would have been better for him if he had not been born, says Jesus (Matt 26:24). But this does not contradict, but rather underscores, that God's grace was revealed to him in his life. Just as for Chorazin, Bethsaida, and Capernaum (Matt 26:20ff.), so for Judas the judgment must be horrifying, precisely because he and they encountered and despised *Christ*.

May I take this a step further? Does God also show grace to people *outside of* the church, outside of the sphere of influence of the written Word of God? Without being blinded by the word "grace," I believe that we must consider the matter by reference to the following texts:

1. *Ps 145:9*: "The LORD is good (Hebrew: *tob*; LXX: χρηστός) to all, and his mercy (Hebrew: *rakhamayw*; LXX: οἱ οἰκτιρμοί) is over all that he has made." In v. 8, "The LORD is gracious and merciful, slow to anger and abounding in steadfast love," we find the same Hebrew word as in v. 9: *rakhum* [merciful]. Since it is used in v. 8 together with *khannun* [gracious] without a clear distinction between the two, it is difficult to explain why in v. 9 *khannun* could not have been used instead of *tob* [good]. The second half of v. 9 and the entire context indicate that God's goodness toward all is not restricted to Israel. "All live from his goodness, in which this Lord shows mercy not only to Israel but indeed to his whole creation, to all his works " (H. Lamparter, *Das Buch der Psalmen*, II, 367).

2. *Jonah 4:2*: "That is why I made haste to flee to Tarshish; for I knew that you are a gracious God and merciful, slow to anger and abounding in steadfast love,

CHAPTER V. EVALUATION

and relenting from disaster" (Hebrew: *'el-khannun werakhum 'erek 'appayim werab khesed wenikham 'al-hara'a*; LXX: σύ ἐλεήμων καὶ οἰκτίρμων μακρόθυμος καὶ πολυέλεος καὶ μετανοῶν ἐρι ταῖς κακίαις). We cannot dismiss this text with the remark that God's gracious and merciful actions followed upon Nineveh's repentance. For:

(a) Already before he went to Nineveh with his threatening message, Jonah knew that God was gracious and merciful (1:2; 3:4). He apparently knew of God's mercy even toward the Gentiles;

(b) Verse 4:2 must also be connected with 4:11. God spared Nineveh not only because he could be gracious after Nineveh's repentance, but also because he was gracious toward a city with 120,000 persons and much cattle. His *mercy* is what moved him to send Jonah to Nineveh. It strikes me again that we cannot make a principial distinction between the word "gracious" and the other words. For this list of attributes, see also Exod 34:6; Ps 86:15; 103:8; 145:8; Neh 7:17; Joel 2:13. In those places they are used for God's attitude toward his people; here in Jonah 4:2 they are used for his attitude toward the Gentiles.

3. *Matt 5:44–45*: "Love [ἀγαπᾶτε] your enemies ... so that you may be sons of your Father who is in heaven. For he makes his sun rise on the evil and on the good [ἐπὶ πονηροὺς καὶ ἀγαθοὺς], and sends rain on the just and on the unjust [ἐπὶ δικαίους καὶ ἀδίκους]." It is especially these words that Calvin quotes many times to confirm that God displays grace toward the Gentiles. Cf., *inter alia*, *Corpus Reformatorum* 25, 18; 31, 198; 32, 415; 36, 104; 36, 263; 43, 37; 52, 266; 52, 266; 52, 296, and 55, 258. In my opinion he was correct in so doing. This text surely does not allow us to interpret it as H. Hoeksema suggests. He maintains that πονηροί and ἄδικοι as well as ἀγαθοι and δίκαιοι refer to the elect. "Sinners can only love those who love them; they are unable to love their enemies. God can do that. Were that not so, we would all be lost; for all people are by nature enemies of God. However, God can love people that do not love him. And therein lies in that sense the possibility of our salvation. *God loved us while we were still enemies*. That is why we can now also love" (*Dat Gods goedheid particulier is*, 190, italics supplied). Cf. also *The Protestant Reformed Churches in America*, 317ff.

Here Hoeksema is engaged in reading things into the text, not in exegesis. We would want to ask him whether the reprobate do *not* walk in the sun and the rain. The parallel reference in Luke 6:35 makes it even clearer that we must not engage in selecting: God is good toward the ungrateful and the evil (ἐπὶ ἀχαρίστους καὶ πονηρούς). The simple meaning of Matt 5:44–45 therefore is that God's love toward his enemies is given us as an example. This love is apparent in the sun and the rain, for they benefit also the πονηροί and ἄδικοι, the wicked and the unjust.

It is also incorrect to say of Matt 5:45 that the sunshine and the rain are not unmixed blessings: "The sun's rays can also be scorching, so that everything dries and burns up; and the rain can become torrential, so that everything is drowned and rots" (*Dat Gods goedheid particulier is*, 186). Schilder also presents a similar argument, but then on the basis of Acts 14:17, where Paul says that

CHAPTER V. EVALUATION

God has given "rains [ὑετοὺς] from heaven and fruitful seasons" to the Gentiles. According to Schilder, God gives, "among other things, *huetous*, i.e., in addition to the spring rain, also threatening rain squalls, storms, *plural*" (*Heid. Cat.* IV, 183). What Hoeksema and Schilder say is, of course, true. But that is not relevant *here*. And Matt 5 and Acts 14:17 speak of a nurturing sun and mild rains. Scripture does indeed speak elsewhere of a scorching sun and torrential rains. But the texts I am referring to have God's goodness as theme, not his wrath. Matt 5:45 stands "beside Isa 5:6 and Amos 4:7," according to Schilder (op. cit., 121). Correct. But then we must also truly place *beside* each other Matt 5:45 and Acts 14:17 on the one hand and Isa 5:6 and similar texts on the other.

4. *Luke 6:35*: "Love your enemies ... and you will be sons of the Most High, for he is kind [χρηστός] to the ungrateful and the evil." I point to this text, which finds its parallel in Matt 5:45, only to draw attention to χρηστός, an indication of God's actions that we also found in Ps 145:9.

5. *Acts 14:16-17*: "In past generations he allowed all the nations to walk in their own ways. Yet he did not leave himself without witness [οὐκ ἀμάρτυρον αὐτὸν ἀφῆκεν], for he did good [ἀγαθουργῶν] by giving you rains from heaven and fruitful seasons, satisfying your hearts with food and gladness." This is a text of the utmost importance, also for an understanding of the preceding passages of Scripture.

First, it is clear that God did *good* to the nations. They were even able to enjoy life ("food and gladness").

Second, this goodness has a *purpose*: "With all these gifts that enriched life, God made an 'appeal' to human beings to worship not the creature, but himself only" (K. Schilder, *Ref.* 20, 36). For God gave all his gifts as witness of himself as the Creator of heaven and earth, to whom the inhabitants of Lystra must now turn (v. 15), as they ought to have done already before. The general revelation was directed to the knowledge of God, to repentance, and renders people guilty in the judgment if they despise such great goodness on the part of God (cf. Calvin's invitation and critical motifs!).

Third, Acts 14:15ff. also makes clear what kind of "fruit" God's goodness among human beings has yielded: They have fallen into the "vain things" of idolatry (v. 15). This text truly keeps us far away from cultural speculation. The Gentiles did not walk in God's "cultural" ways, but in their *own* sinful ways, in which *idolatry* flourished.

Fourth, God did good to all (also, according to Paul, "in past generations," v. 16) and spared their lives until the day of Paul's preaching in Lystra, so that they would repent of their vain things and turn to the living God. I am thinking here of Rom 3:25, where Paul speaks of God who "in his divine forbearance [ἐν τῇ ἀνοχῇ τοῦ θεοῦ] ... passed over former sins." God did not ignore those sins, but restrained himself "in order not fully to punish the sin, human beings, and the world and to destroy them.... Only God could, in merciful love that wanted to work salvation, so tolerate and bear with them and refrain from imposing the punishment that was deserved" (S. Greijdanus, *Kommentaar Romeinen*, I, 200). Paul speaks of God's forbearance "τοῦ θεοῦ and not αὐτοῦ in order to indicate the greatness and graciousness of this ἀνοχῇ" (loc. cit.). God displays his gracious forbearance to keep the way of Christ in the world open. We must not fail to note this facet in regard to the texts we are discussing.

6. *Acts 17:30*: "The times of ignorance God overlooked [τοὺς μὲν οὖν χρόνους τῆς ἀγνοίας ὑπεριδών], but now he commands all people everywhere to repent." This passage confirms what we discovered in Acts 14. Here, too, there is the *seriousness* of God's doing good. They could have known God, for he is "not far from each one of us" (v. 27). The Athenians are also guilty because of their idolatry. And here, too, God passes over the times of ignorance for the sake of Christ (v. 31).

7. *1 Pet 3:20*: "... when God's patience [ἡ τοῦ θεοῦ μακροθυμία] waited [ἀπεξεδέχετο] in the days of Noah, while the ark was being prepared." The imperfect ἀπεξεδέχετο is used "to indicate the protracted, incessant waiting; cf. Gen 6:3. Hence also the compound ἀπ – εξ – εδέχετο, in which is pictured the stretching to be able to see what is longed for. It expresses the ardent desire for repentance as well as the great exertion to bring it about and also to postpone judgment and, if possible, to avert it.... God did not desire the death of those wicked ones. That is why he spared them as long as possible, worked many years in a special, unmistakable way to lead people to repentance, and waited to see whether judgment could perhaps be avoided" (Greijdanus, *Kommentaar 1 Petrus*).

It is not my intention to engage in a complete discussion of the concept of "patience" in Scripture. Nor do I, in contrast to Schilder, want to "soften," or even eliminate the element of God's wrath in his patience. For those who wish to try this, I recommend that they first read what J. Horst writes in *ThWB* IV, 378–90, after which they will abandon the task. But I do wish to draw attention to an aspect of God's patience that is often evident but that remains in the background in Schilder. It is the "kindly color," to use an expression of Horst's (op. cit., 385).

This "kindly color" of the patience of God, who sympathizes with his creatures and does not desire the death of the wicked, often strikes me. Note Jonah 4, where, as we saw already, the word is used in the same breath as "gracious," "merciful," "abounding in steadfast love," and "relenting from disaster." See further all the parallel passages already identified above. I think also of Rom 2:4, where not only "kindness" gives patience a "kindly color," but especially the "*riches* of his kindness, forbearance, and patience." The same is true of 1 Pet 3:20, according to Greijdanus' exegesis that we have just considered. The same mercy shines forth in 2 Pet 3:9: "The Lord ... is patient toward you, not wishing that any should perish, but that all should reach repentance." Greijdanus gives this explanation: "Thus, out of mercy, to give occasion for repentance, and to achieve the salvation of all who were bought by

CHAPTER V. EVALUATION

the Lord Christ ... God has not yet caused the day of judgment to arise, and the Lord has not yet appeared on the clouds.

In his not yet coming, the scoffers greatly fail to recognize the Lord's compassion and grace" (op. cit.).

Schilder has pointed especially to the patience in which God "waits" until the measure is full in order then to strike (p. 183 above). God's *wrath* receives full attention. But the Bible also says that *love* is patient (1 Cor 13:4). The one thing can be connected with the other. God (still) restrains his wrath because he is patient in his love. Nineveh came to realize this. God does not like to break things off. But if it *must* come to that, people are that much more guilty. Jonah's divine message for Nineveh is followed by that of Nahum: "The LORD is a jealous and avenging God ... and keeps wrath for his enemies. The LORD is *slow to anger and* great in power, and the LORD will by no means clear the guilty" (Nah 1:2–3). God went far in his mercy. It will justify his wrath in the judgment.

8. *1 Tim 4:10*: "... the living God, who is the Savior [σωτήρ] of all people, especially of those who believe." These last words are clear. For the believers share in salvation. But what about the preceding words? In what way is God, albeit not "especially" [μάλιστα], nonetheless also σωτήρ for *all* people? C. Bouma refers to God's care in giving "to all mankind life and breath and everything" (Acts 17:25). God maintains "already in general all his rational creatures" (*Korte Verklaring I Timotheus*, at the verse cited). This may well be included. "This opinion is not to be rejected entirely, in view of the estimation of the natural order of life in the pastoral epistles as determined by false teachers; but it is better not to separate this point from 1 Tim 2:3–4. God is therefore called σωτήρ ... μάλιστα πιστῶν [Savior especially of believers] since the believers have accepted salvation, whereas for the others he only becomes σωτήρ when they accept it," states W. Foerster in *ThWB* VII, 1017–18.

I agree with Foerster, except for the last words. For the text does not say that God can become σωτήρ for all people, but that he *is*. In my opinion one ought to think here about the orientation of God's redeeming work in Christ. He is involved with the entire world, with all people. That is why believers must pray for all people, including kings and all who are in high positions. For God regards this as good and it is pleasing in his sight, for he desires all people to be saved and to come to the knowledge of the truth (1 Tim 2:1–4). The text also does not teach a universal reconciliation, but it does teach a universal well-being that is also intended for kings. God wants the best for all, and that is why he can be called σωτήρ even though true well-being is extended only to believers, who thereby enter into a special relationship with God. The things listed by C. Bouma ("life and breath and everything") must not be regarded as separate from the foregoing. All help is directed toward the *well-being*.

When we examine the material collected in points 1–8, it is impossible to maintain that the word "grace" does not apply in identifying the gifts that

CHAPTER V. EVALUATION

God gave and still gives to the world. Although I did not come across the word χάρις, I did consider the Hebrew word *khannun* (LXX: ἐλεήμων) and also referred to God's goodness, mercy, lovingkindness, and the love of God as Savior. Precious words. Hence, we must use them sparingly, not forgetting, among other things, that they will irrevocably become worn-out small change if we fail to consider them with God's wrath in mind. But we should also not use them more sparingly than God himself does. They are precious words, but what God does for the world is indeed precious and decisive. In connection with Acts 14:16-17, Schilder says: "The world with fruits and trees and yearly seasons is not presented as a place of Arcadian rest, but as a court room in which to plead, a unit of the Building of the Great Court of Justice. The rain showers are still *signs* and the sun's rays still *proof*; but when the hearing concludes and the presentation of evidence is finished, there are only *two* exits from the hall of justice: the one leads to heaven, the other to hell" (*Ref.* 20, 36). To this I add that the justice of the righteous verdict is most strongly revealed when we see the verdict as punishment for the contempt shown for all the pains that God took in his precious grace.

In this section I am not yet considering (at least not expressly) the question of God's disposition, about which Schilder speaks constantly. I will deal with that question in § 9. Here the focus is particularly on grace as *gift*. Scripture also knows of both aspects. For grace as disposition, see Rom 3:24; 4:4, 16; 5:15; Eph 2:8; 2 Tim 1:9, etc. For grace as gift, see, e.g., Rom 1:5; 12:6; 1 Cor 15:10; 2 Cor 8:1; 9:14; Eph 4:7. I will also leave for § 9 the question whether grace as gift can be separated from grace as disposition. Since on the basis of Scripture, I do not have to remove the word "grace" from the list, even when it concerns what God does for the Gentiles, I can without hesitation follow general usage as found among Reformed theologians such as Calvin. However, I do not subscribe to everything they wrote. This applies also to Calvin. Thus it is in my view incorrect to speak of God as Father of humanity (p. 261 above). Acts 17:28, which Calvin refers to, does not permit this. And Scripture does not permit it elsewhere either. "According to Matt 5:43-45 the great benevolence of the Creator applies to all people. But that is not yet a matter of his Fatherhood. Therefore the crucial question is posed whether or not one wants to be the Father's son. Thus here is not spoken of a natural static Fatherhood in a general sense.... The word 'Father' pertains to those who accept from Jesus what is expressed in the words 'your Father'" (G. Schrenk in *ThWB* V, 990-91). Nor can 1 Cor 8:4ff.; Eph 3:15; and 4:6 serve as proof (op cit., 1013-14, 1019ff.). We cannot speak about God the Father apart from Jesus Christ.

This brings us to a second point of criticism regarding Calvin. At the beginning of this section I said that there is one grace of God *in Christ*. This Christocentric character of all grace must be maintained also when we deal with *general* grace. Acts 14:16-17 and 1 Tim 4:10 made it clear to us that God kept the way open for Christ and that he bestows his gifts as Savior so that human beings would acknowledge salvation in Christ. Moreover, in our discussion of Eph 1,

CHAPTER V. EVALUATION

Col 1, and John 1 in §§ 5 and 6, we saw that Christ's central place in re-creation is connected with his central place in creation. *He* held and holds all things in his hand. But this means that the display of general grace also does not come about apart from him. He directs that also. The whole earth will in due course be judged by *Christ*, as, *inter alia*, Acts 17:31 tells us. For the revelation of life and light has always been from *him*, as the Prologue to John says.

Calvin did not speak of these connections in this way. Neither did the theologians who will be mentioned below. Calvin looked at the gifts to the Gentiles more in the framework of the cosmic work of the Holy Spirit. Cf. especially *Inst.* II, 15 and 16, and W. Krusche, op. cit., 119ff., 340 (with cautious criticism, also that of J. Faber, *Ref.* 35, 277). It was especially to the credit of S. G. de Graaf that he, in speaking about the theme of my study, pointed to the unity of all grace in Christ. Cf. *Christus en de wereld*, 72–113; *Philosophia Reformata* 1, 17–29; *Het ware geloof*, 67–68. De Graaf, as we already saw at the end of § 5, also posited, correctly in my opinion, that unbelievers render themselves guilty of the theft of God's goods when they misuse the material of which he has claimed possession. De Graaf had an eye for the all-encompassing position that Christ occupies in the cosmos.

Still, my agreement with De Graaf's ideas is not without reservation. For there is a very artificial element in them. I already pointed out that De Graaf does admit of a "certain love, goodness and patience" of God toward the unbelieving world, but wants nothing to do with a "certain grace." To me this seemed inconsistent. Certainly when De Graaf speaks of God's general goodness as "an offshoot of that gracious love by which God, for Christ's sake, turns again to a world fallen into sin" (cf. p. 169 above; quotation in *Ref.* 18, 111). I do not want to fall into the mistake made by V. Hepp, who argued that an "offshoot" of particular grace must therefore also be irresistible (p. 169 above). But I do not share the view that an "offshoot" of particular grace may not be called a "certain grace."

But of greater concern to me is this speaking of an "offshoot." Even if the *word* is not used, the *idea* comes back again and again. According to De Graaf (*Christus en de wereld*, 79), God displays grace only to those who are his, but the wicked *share* in the fruits of this grace. The covenant *concerns* all people (op. cit., 92); it contains a universal blessing in which unbelievers also *share* (94). The *indirect* character of this blessing becomes even more apparent when De Graaf writes that we "must recognize the central place of believers in this life. It is all about their salvation in all relationships in which they live on earth. However, the people of God still live here in an organic relationship with unbelievers, a relationship that may be compared to the organic relationship between the core and the husk of ripening fruit. Pursuant to that relationship there is still a certain working of the Spirit of Christ in the life of unbelievers" (100).

I think more has to be said about this. God also acts *directly* and actively toward unbelieving people in such a way that they cannot escape his revelation and will in due course be found inexcusable. It is a revelation of God and his

CHAPTER V. EVALUATION

Son Jesus Christ outside of the circle of light cast by his written and proclaimed Word, outside of "particular" grace (Rom 1:16ff.; John 1:4–5). Think, for example, of what Calvin wrote about the actual, dynamic, and personal aspects of this (pp. 250–51 above). Consequently all of this can hardly be subsumed under the passive image of an "offshoot."

I have yet a third objection that is connected with the second. For De Graaf, God's "certain goodness" is overmuch a matter of culture. In this I recognize Kuyper, although the idea is presented in a Christological form: "That the unbelievers are able to achieve a certain culture, although it is not subjected to obedience in faith to the Lord, does mean that the power of the root [Christ as the new root on which the world stands, op. cit., 92, J.D.] is driven out of them. To put it very strongly: it is the Christ who works in them.... Since God still recognizes the power of Christ in the works of the unbelievers, those works can, regardless of the motives that drove them, still be pleasing to him" (101). The unbelievers "were allowed to take part in the building of the totality of the world that is being saved. Despite their defection from and enmity toward the totality of God's work, their lives have not been totally in vain" (102). "To take part in the building of the totality of the world"—here Kuyper's cultural idea comes to the fore, although it is developed more modestly. We read of a "not totally in vain." Cf. also op. cit., 105: "This does not at all hint at cultural optimism." Nonetheless, the direction of God's display of goodness is clearly cultural. In contrast, I maintain what we discovered in § 6: God's general grace invites knowledge and love, and it renders persons guilty where this knowledge is missing. The texts discussed above confirm what we discovered earlier.

The objections I have against De Graaf also apply in the main to H. Dooyeweerd. He does continue to speak of general *grace*, but it is "not grace for a *particular* apostate, but for *humanity in Christ*" (*Vernieuwing and Bezinning*, 38). That is too general for me. For grace toward the Gentiles is indeed "particular" (not in the sense of particular as "regenerating,") but) as *concrete* revelation of God, who invites people to come to know him and renders them inexcusable. However, for Dooyeweerd, just as for De Graaf, general grace is concerned principally with maintaining the *ordinances of creation*. "These ordinances are the same for Christians and non-Christians. And it is due to God's general grace that even the ruler who is most hostile toward God has to submit to these ordinances and must *capitulate* in order to see a lasting positive result in his work" (op. cit., 37). When Dooyeweerd in addition also speaks of "individual gifts and talents" given by God "to specific persons," we again miss a reference to the direction and "fruit" of this grace, i.e., the glorification of and thankfulness to God (Rom 1:21), and to the misuse of his gifts. God by his grace desires human beings *actively* to bring him honor and glory. But the unbelieving world does not do this. It extinguishes the light, misuses God's gifts, and walks in ignorance.

In the passages from the *Institutes* cited by Dooyeweerd, Calvin also speaks of this balance derived from Scripture: I, xvii, 7 and 11; I, v, 14; II, ii, 16; III, iii, 25;

CHAPTER V. EVALUATION

III, xx, 15, 24, 2. But what these passages contain is more than and different from what Dooyeweerd finds in them: "Calvin himself subordinated *gratia communis* to *gratia particularis* and to 'the honor and glory of God'" (*A New Critique of Theoretical Thought* I, 523).

Not only Calvin, but also other Reformed theologians, use the word "grace" both for what "promotes eternal salvation" and for the gifts that God bestows on the Gentiles. It was not only the Remonstrants who, at the time of the National Synod of Dort, spoke of "common grace." Schilder already referred to Trigland (p. 135 above). We can also use the *Acts* of Dort as proof. The delegates from Nassau speak in one breath about the light of nature and of the "more common grace" (op. cit., II, 216). God is said to enlighten every person with "that common and natural grace," and the delegates of Embden subscribe to that view (II, 252). Paraeus, who knew very well how to oppose the Remonstrants and their indifferent general grace, points out clearly that the word "grace" "is in other ways differently interpreted" (I, 294). The delegates from Bremen say that the word "grace" extends "far and wide" (II, 232) and that certain forms of grace are rejected by the reprobate (II, 233). The Embden delegation speaks of "grace that restrains" (II, 237). The delegates from South Holland teach an "external grace that arises from the book of nature" and that is common to all people. Overijssel speaks of "general grace" (III, 284). The delegates from Drenthe also recognize a "common grace," although they speak of it principally in connection with the general calling by the Word (III, 310–11). They describe the goal of this common grace as follows: "... so that the human community and civil order might be maintained and thereby in different ways all helpfulness might be rendered to the elect, and so that they might thereby be prepared for the inward call" (III, 311).

When we consult the dogmatic publications from those days, we hear the same sounds. Gomarus even speaks of a double grace by which sin in general is restrained: "one [is] inward grace: the light of the mind and the restraint of cupidity; another outward: the repression of the fury of Satan and of the world" (*Opera* II, 137b). The reprobate are deprived of their *grace*, says the same writer: "God, however, in order to preserve the human race and society, to render the reprobate all the more inexcusable by his kindness, and to preserve the elect has withdrawn the remnants of [his gifts] and has distributed knowledge, consciousness, and civil virtues for the public benefit.... By taking away his grace, God is not in a proper sense the cause of hardening and is not in any way unjust to human beings" (op. cit., 427b).

The *Synopsis* also plainly teaches a general grace: "So then, no one contributes anything to this grace [i.e., regenerating grace, J.D.]. In fact, man has no more power to prepare, dispose, and apply himself to that grace than he does to contribute anything to his own conception and birth—neither by the benefit of universal grace and the light of nature [note that they are treated as equivalent, J.D], nor by the benefit of particular grace, namely the law (which is

CHAPTER V. EVALUATION

imprecisely and loosely included in the word 'grace')" (*Synopsis, Disputatio* XVII, 31).

Looked at historically, Schilder's assertion that the Remonstrants identified the light of nature with "common grace" while the Reformed did *not* (pp. 131-32 above) is untenable. Of course the Reformed and the Remonstrants assigned quite a different effect to general grace, as is apparent from the quotation from the *Synopsis*. It is to be noted that it does say of the particular grace that the law brings, but not of the universal grace, that it is "imprecisely" and "loosely" called grace.

I want to refer to a few other theologians (although I am not striving for completeness). W. a Brakel differentiates grace into "*common* or *particular*: God displays common grace to all people by the distribution of physical benefactions. Acts 14:1.... To these belongs also the good that God does to all he calls, giving them the Word, the means to repentance and salvation. Titus 2:11.... By this means, God gives general illumination, historical faith, convictions, and motivations to become a Christian. See Heb 6:4, 5, 6" (*Redelyke Godts-dienst* I, Cap. XXX, 26). See also cap. III, 33ff., where he classifies God's goodness, love, grace, mercy, and patience as either "common" or "particular."

Beside saving grace, Johannes a Marck recognizes also a general grace, which in his explanation is, however, restricted to grace within the church (*Het Merch der christene Got-geleertheit*, IV, 42; VII, 31ff.). See also H. Kuiper, op. cit., Appendix III–IV). Finally I refer to P. van Mastricht, because Schilder also speaks of him. Van Mastricht distinguishes three types of grace:

(a) universal grace, "by which God dispenses natural gifts to his creatures, all and sundry." He supports this grace by reference to 1 Tim 4:10; Ps 36:7; and Matt 5:45. To it he ascribes free will and all kinds of powers by which the natural good is attained. However: "these are all allowed by the gracious love of God and so far as they may spring from grace: nevertheless, according to the usage of Scripture, and also of all orthodox antiquity, they are rarely and less properly called grace because nature is distinguished from grace, contrary to the Pelagians";

(b) common grace, "by which God dispenses moral gifts to human beings especially, but without distinction to the elect and the reprobate." These include the intellectual virtues: mental power, wisdom, and prudence (Exod 31:3), and also the volitional, ethical virtues (Luke 18:11); virtues that are shared by Gentiles and unbelievers. Also to be included are the gifts of grace "that seem to come quite close to what belongs to salvation," as mentioned in Heb 6:4, 5; Isa 58:2; 1 Cor 13:1. Think of the outward call and also of the inward call (distinguished from the efficacious, regenerating call, J.D.), and further of all the gifts that are evident in those who have a temporary faith (Matt 13:20–21);

(c) particular grace that leads to salvation.

For all of this, see P. van Mastricht, *Theoretico-Practica Theologia*, II, 15–16. Schilder referred to this passage more than once—and particularly to call attention to what it says about universal grace, which is there referred to as

CHAPTER V. EVALUATION

"less properly" called grace. "'Less properly'—i.e., the word 'grace" is not meant seriously; it has no *scholarly* value" (*Heid. Cat.* I, 494; cf. also IV, 48). For Van Mastricht recognizes the threatening danger that nature and grace will be confused in a Pelagian way.

However, I question whether Schilder can dispute the doctrine of common grace with his appeal to Van Mastricht. For Van Mastricht does refer to universal grace as what is "less properly" called grace, but he does *not* say this of the common grace [*gratia communis*]. But for his doctrine of common grace, Kuyper specifically adopted this *gratia communis* with its "ethical gifts" and its "intellectual and volitional virtues," a grace in which all of humanity shares.

Besides, in my opinion, Kuyper would probably have agreed with Van Mastricht's remark about the "less proper" use of the word "grace" in "universal grace." For Kuyper also does not want to confuse nature and grace in a Pelagian way. Schilder says that "Pelagius already considers a 'possibility' *conferred* in creation, in nature, to be 'grace' as such" (p. 130 above; italics supplied). But *Kuyper* regards as grace only what in creation is still *left to us* as a *forfeited* "possibility." Surely that makes a difference! Consequently the passage in Van Mastricht does not disagree with Kuyper anywhere.

Schilder is quite correct when he states that common grace as such was never previously taught in the church. I have demonstrated this, I think, in connection with Calvin. But none of the other theologians I referred to teach an independently functioning doctrine of common grace. Generally they switch quickly to the common grace that reveals itself in the outward call (and even in the inward one) and thus in the church. I did not ascertain anywhere an independent attention for the development of culture. The restraint of sin receives attention, but we do not read of a progressive operation of common grace.

Nonetheless, in my view, a decline is noticeable after Calvin. While Calvin spoke in a terminologically flexible and dynamic way about general grace, the later schematic approach appears to be very rigid, such as, for example, that of Van Mastricht. Schilder says of this theologian: "The desire to draw distinctions is too apparent and quickly overburdens itself. This is evident when he categorizes not only love and grace, but also the 'goodness' of God as 'general, common, and particular'" (op. cit., I, 495). Van Mastricht and others constantly draw from the fresh spring of Calvin, but they *channel* the water. This schematic approach lacks vitality. To use Schilder's expression, the wave is enclosed and isolated in a can.

In fact, a great difference in terminology remains. What one person calls "common grace" (Van Mastricht), another refers to as "universal grace" (*Synopsis*); one person applies the term "general grace" to what another calls "common grace" (respectively, Overijssel and Drenthe at Dort). While Marck restricts "common grace" to those who are called by God's Word (p. 139 above), Van Mastricht, as we saw, extends "common grace" to *all* people.

"Common" and "general" are distinguished less sharply than Schilder suggests (pp. 138–39 above). This certainly applies to Calvin. He expresses what he means by general grace variously using the words "special," "general," and "universal," as we saw in the previous section. But he does not do so with "common grace." Calvin does not employ it as a technical term (cf. H. Kuiper, op. cit., 177–78). But what Schilder means by "common," namely in describing the "grace that everyone *in the church* receives" (p. 139 above) is referred to in Calvin as "universal" or "general." Cf. *Inst.* III, xxii, 10: "in inviting *all* without distinction while he elects only a few...." See also *Inst.* III, xxiv, 8: "for there is a *universal* call." Also *Inst.* III, xxiv, 17: "for however *universal* the promises of salvation may be...." This is further proof that Calvin did not really consider the later schematic of "general" (or "universal"), "common," and "special." For him the *effect* of grace differs. For the elect it leads to salvation, but not for the others. That is a clear distinction. But it remains grace, also for the reprobate. The boundaries that were fluid in Calvin (general grace) were demarcated strictly by his descendants (*the* general grace), after which Kuyper demarcated and guarded them as boundaries of *two kingdoms* (common grace as *dogma*).

Finally, I also note that it seems more correct to me not to speak of grace before the Fall, as Calvin does (p. 221 above). Then, too, human beings lived from God's *unmerited* love, but after the Fall that love was also *forfeited*. Both elements are found in χάρις: "unearned and unmerited ... or indeed demerited." This word is used in "reference to the *sins* of men" (R. C. Trench, *Synonyms of the New Testament*, 169). Cf. Kuyper, *E Voto* II, 537.

§ 8. Judgment and wrath of God

Schilder rightly drew attention to the judgment and the wrath of God. The church can be thankful for his prophetic critique of common grace, even though Schilder's theological formulation of this critique raises concerns, as we have already seen. The world provokes God's wrath by its contempt for him. That must never be pushed into the background in the treatment of our topic.

After the "Davidic" period under Kuyper, followed the "Solomonic" years in Reformed life, which attained great flowering. The struggle and lack of recognition in the days of the Secession and *Doleantie* became history. At one time the Reformed part of the nation was like Saul hiding among the baggage, and later, under the leadership of Kuyper, it grew to greatness like a second David, but now it could enter into its Solomonic period. It was recognized, respected, and sometimes called to assume the highest functions in the land. But within the renown a spiritual decline lay concealed. Would antithesis and common grace, so clearly intertwined by Kuyper (pp. 66, 85, 93–94, 109–10

CHAPTER V. EVALUATION

above), *remain* united, or would the antithesis become more and more the theory and common grace more and more the practice?

There were warning signs already during Kuyper's life. The names of D. P. D. Fabius and J. C. Sikkel are well-known in this connection. Seven years after Kuyper's death, Seerp Anema wrote a brochure from the title of which, *Davidisch of Salomonisch*, I have borrowed (see above). It signaled a decay, and the protests against it became constantly stronger in the following years. That made a critical evaluation of Kuyper's theology inevitable. This required boldness, considering that it was said as late as 1939: "Let us rally around Kuyper! That is the only way to preserve the Lord's cause in our land" (V. Hepp, quoted in *Ref.* 19, 183). It is to Schilder's credit that he resisted the secularization of Reformed life so strongly (pp. 223-24 above) against all lazy, anthropocentric use of common grace (pp. 145, 224-25 above: what God has "still" left to us; p. 191 above: "what is and what is not permissible"). In his criticism he was *forced* to include Kuyper himself too. That became clear after § 4. For the disintegrating seed of secularization (which Kuyper did not have in mind and did not at all strive for during his life) is included in his theological system. It was Schilder's intention to make the ground of Kuyper's foundational ideas "theoretically more secure" (p. 217 above).

In my view the most valuable aspect of the criticism to which Schilder subjected the doctrine of common grace is the attention he drew to the judgment and the wrath of God. Beside the "may" he places the "must" (pp. 188-90 above), beside the "glory," the "dreadfulness" of the cultural question (p. 224 above).

It is necessary to criticize the development of Schilder's theology. I have done so as well (§ 2). But such criticism may never have the effect of silencing Schilder's prophetic voice. He drew attention to God's wrath (and does that still) in a time in which much was said about grace and love, but little about God's wrath and hatred. But those who ignore the latter, lose the former. Only the seriousness of the wrath can reveal to us the depth of the grace. Otherwise the grace becomes cheap. Consequently I have with great approval followed Schilder from his first to his second period (pp. 223-29 above).

It is therefore very regrettable that in his third period Schilder spoke about God's balanced actions in such a way that God's eternal hatred is placed beside God's eternal love and that predestination to life and to death are treated as running in parallel—even to such an extent that I could speak of a predestination from wrath [*ex ira*] to characterize Schilder's portrayal of reprobation. There were adverse reactions to Schilder's view. See T. J. Bakker, *Coram Deo*, 200-01; H. M. Kuitert, *De mensvormigheid Gods*, 19ff.; G. Visee, *Ref.* 28, 314.

It is not necessary for me to return to the criticism expressed in § 2. In this section I am concerned with the place of God's wrath which, according to Calvin and Schilder, must *rightly* take a central position when we speak about God's work in an unbelieving world. God's wrath descends upon the Gentiles

CHAPTER V. EVALUATION

because they despise the revelation of God's power and divinity, δύναμις and θειότης, in creation (Rom 1:18, 21ff.) "As in the Old Testament ... so also in the New, all motives for divine wrath can be traced back to people's contempt for God " (G. Stählin in *ThWB* V, 442). Because this contempt for God is a fact that is as large as life, God's wrath must perforce enter the picture. The Canons of Dort (III/IV, 4) underline this. Human beings may possess a certain light of nature. But "although they 'have' it, 'possess' it, whatever it may be, it is always besmirched; even worse, totally besmirched; yet worse than that, totally besmirched in various ways; and the very worst: they 'have' it as truth suppressed in iniquity" (C. Veenhof, *Kracht en doel der Politiek*, 23). Truth is violated and thereby God's wrath is provoked. Therefore one cannot, as Kuyper did, say of this wrath that it operates "under and through" everything and then, in spite of this, develop a dogma of the progressive doctrine of common grace in which God's wrath apparently does not tear apart the edifice of common grace.

God's wrath does not run parallel with his love and grace. That is what I maintained over against Schilder. However, this Scriptural truth may not, in my view, oust another, namely that God is able to glorify himself also in his wrath (Ps 137:8, 9; Prov 16:4; Rom 9:17; 1 Thess 5:9). In this respect Schilder and Calvin, and actually also Kuyper (but outside of the topic of common grace, e.g., *Loc. de Deo*, III, 147) repeat what Scripture says. This aspect may not be ignored by those who want to take into account all of God's work in a godless world.

Finally, another comment about the *concrete*, and also a concretely demonstrable, revelation of God's wrath. I realize how dangerous it is to come to a conclusion about God's attitude of grace or wrath on the basis of the *facts*. "No single fact allows us to draw a conclusion about God's disposition, unless God himself reveals that his disposition finds expression *in* that fact" (G. C. Berkouwer, *De Voorzienigheid Gods*, 207). Calvin stated that all prosperity is a blessing, while calamity and adversity are a curse, as we saw. But this statement raises questions. Scripture teaches that the opposite is often the case—so often that it would be difficult to make this statement into "a rule subject to exceptions" (cf. Job; Pss 49, 73; Eccl; Jer 12:1ff.; Rom 5:3ff.; 1 Pet 3:14ff.).

On the other hand, Scripture does make many facts transparent. Here I think, *inter alia*, of Rom 1, in which Paul writes that the contempt of the Gentiles for God brings punishment in the form of God's giving them up to the lusts of their hearts, to impurity, and to reprehensible thinking. God's wrath is revealed in this. Hence, we must be careful with Schilder's assertion that, strictly speaking, God's disposition is expressed only in "the 'books' that are above." Strictly speaking, that would then preclude recognition of all *concrete* indications of God's judgment (and blessings) that we so often find in Calvin. About the disposition of God we may not draw conclusions from the facts alone, beyond what Scripture promises and threatens. But we may, because Scripture does promise and threaten, frequently in faith point to God's concrete grace and wrath as shown in the facts. There are significant difficulties in doing so; these require a broader discussion than is possible at this point. See, e.g., G. C. Berkouwer, op. cit., 190–228; M. C. Smit, *The Divine Mystery in History*; and J. Kamphuis, *De hedendaagse kritiek op de causaliteit bij Groen van Prinsterer als historicus*. In my view, the truth lies somewhere between the positions of Calvin and Schilder. We must not lose the *concrete* speaking about God's guidance in history, but our conclusions will never be easy.

§ 9. God's disposition – grace and wrath

The doctrine of election and reprobation does not allow us to conclude that in the life of the elect no wrath, and in the life of the reprobate no grace, can become apparent. It is also not possible to speak about the manifestation of grace and wrath apart from the corresponding disposition of God, which can vary in and regarding the same person's life. Besides, it is incorrect to speak of one of these terms ("grace" and "wrath") to the detriment of the other by characterizing it as non-scientific (apperceptive language, anthropomorphism, etc.). We must, as so often, use *both* words.

The doctrine of a "favorable attitude of God toward humanity in general" (Kalamazoo, 1924) and also the concept of a "general offer of grace" contain the danger of abstraction.

Grace and wrath are revealed in the life of God's elect. By their gross sins David, Peter, and other saints "greatly offend God, incur the guilt of death, grieve the Holy Spirit, suspend the exercise of faith, severely wound their consciences, and sometimes for a while lose the sense of God's favor—until they return to the right way through sincere repentance and God's fatherly face again shines upon them" (*Canons of Dort* V, 4, 5).

Scripture speaks clearly of God's turning from wrath to love and from love to wrath, but such turning away does not become problematic (e.g., Exod 32:12; Deut 13:17; Josh 7:26; 2 Chr 29:10; Ps 30:6; Isa 54:8; Hos 14:5; Mic 7:18; John 3:36; Eph 2:3). The last text is particularly instructive: "among [the sons of disobedience] we all once [ποτὲ] lived ... and were by nature [φύσει] children of wrath [τέκνα ὀργῆς], like the rest of mankind." We should not make this "turning" into a problem as, in our opinion, Calvin does with his "in a certain sense," and Schilder also with his "absolute disposition of love or of hate" (p. 308 above). For that raises the question whether God's wrath, which is revealed in the history of God with his people, is still a divine reality. Designations such as "in a certain sense," "apperceptive language," and "anthropomorphic" do not do the matter justice, in my opinion.

CHAPTER V. EVALUATION

The most beautiful example that Scripture gives of God's wrath in its dreadfulness, but also in its *yielding* dreadfulness, is the suffering and death of Jesus Christ. He shares in the eternal love of his Father, but nonetheless undergoes his wrath, even to the point of being deserted by God. This wrath on Golgotha is not a drama; it is real, horrifying in its depth. I do not subscribe to a doctrine of subjective reconciliation, "in which the suffering of Christ is regarded as a *sign* of God's love that is directed toward evoking a reciprocal love in our hearts in order to realize the 'reconciliation.... Every element of God's wrath and righteousness is [in such a doctrine of reconciliation, J.D.] eliminated on the way of reconciliation. The cross becomes a *knowledge principle* of God's love.... The mistake of the noetic, subjective doctrine of reconciliation is that it denatures God's love to an unaffected, impassive sentiment that cannot be offended and is invulnerable, a love that merely needs to be 'unveiled,' without any struggle, without *sacrifice*, and without *action* in history. This 'unveiling' then stands in opposition to God's wrath which, as a human construct, must be eliminated from our thinking about God" (G. C. Berkouwer, *Het Werk van Christus*, 301–02). This "elimination" is not permissible. Christ has "presented himself in our place before his Father, appeasing God's wrath by his full satisfaction" (Belgic Confession, art. 21; cf. Canons of Dort, I, 4; V, 7). The views that regard Christ's suffering as a "sign" of God's love "come into conflict not only with the church's confession, but also with many testimonies of Scripture, which do not regard the cross of Christ as only a sign, an illustration, an unveiling, but as a historical event, a historical act by which guilt is taken away" (Berkouwer, op. cit., 301; cf. Isa 53:5ff.; Rom 3:25; 5:9ff.; 2 Cor 5:18–19, 21; Heb 2:17; 5:7ff.; 13:12; 1 Thess 1:10).

Undoubtedly, Calvin and Schilder would have been pleased to subscribe to all of this. In *Christ in His Suffering*, Schilder clearly shows how real and deep God's wrath was in the life of Christ. The "in a certain sense" idea is not part of it, and rightly so. How can the man Jesus Christ, recognized by God in love from eternity, now be subjected to God's wrath? That remains a mystery. Calvin and Schilder do not provide an "explanation." They hold fast to both love and wrath, without weakening wrath by using the expression "in a certain sense." But what happens *here*, ought to have made Calvin's "in a certain sense" superfluous elsewhere also. We are always confronted with a mystery and must therefore use *both* words. Eph 1:4–5: God "chose us in [Christ] before the foundation of the world" and "*in love* predestined us for adoption." And Eph 2:3: previously we "were ... children of *wrath*." The first text is not scholarly theology compared to the second, which supposedly uses anthropomorphic, apperceptive language. Both are true, for they rest on divine reality. He did love his own in Christ and he was angry with them. He loves his own, but can nonetheless display his wrath toward them (Eph 5:6; Col 3:6). It is still a fearful thing to fall into the hands of the living God (Heb 10:31).

We must continue to use both words. For that matter, there are more topics in Christian doctrine where such an approach is necessary. This is true, for

CHAPTER V. EVALUATION

example, in respect of God's election and our responsibility, and of the temptation by Satan and the testing by God. Questions remain, and we can say with K. J. Popma that on this point we venture into mysteries that remain closed to us and that we therefore necessarily ask unanswerable questions, "i.e., questions that are not questions" (*Levensbeschouwing* I, 231).

That is how I want to continue in Schilder's line. He constantly hammered home the idea that we must not be one-sided and that we must use both words. Well then, love and wrath, *two* "dispositions" of God (cf. Canons of Dort V, 5!) are revealed in the life of one and the same person. They make themselves count in that life in full seriousness, even though God's eternal love for his children always has the first and last word.

In that way God's wrath is not weakened so that it becomes an affect (wrath that arises and then gives way, is stilled) in the *powerless* sense of the word, as Schilder feared. That is apparent also in God's wrath toward Christ. The wrath is kindled and discharges itself fully on Golgotha. It is affect, but also effect. For "all this is *from* God, who through Christ reconciled us to himself" (2 Cor 5:18). "The divine initiative is not at all shrouded in darkness when the way to Christ's sacrifice is opened. On the contrary: exactly in that way the loving and sovereign acts of God are fully revealed. It is true that Christ is the means for reconciliation, but it is *God* who has presented him *as the means of reconciliation*" (Berkouwer, op. cit., 299).

I cannot enter into a broad examination here of the questions surrounding God's "anthropomorphic" speaking. That topic presents far-reaching and difficult questions, which I do not underestimate. For this, see G. Visee, *Over het "anthropomorphe" spreken Gods in de Heilige Schrift, Ref.* 28, 273ff.; J. Kamphuis, *Katholieke Vastheid*, 69ff.; H. M. Kuitert, *De mensvormigheid Gods*; P. den Ottolander, *Deus Immutabilis*. I will limit myself to a few remarks in connection with God's wrath. Schilder says of this: "Particularly ... when God's wrath is mentioned, its depiction in Scripture is often anthropomorphic or anthropopathic. There is no dispute about that, but there *is* about the question whether there is a real boundary between anthropomorphic and non-anthropomorphic expressions in the description of God's attributes, such as, e.g., wrath and mercy, hate and love" (*Heid. Cat.* I, 472).

But I am not going to analyze even this question (called "a *sorely needed* question" by J. Kamphuis, *Katholieke Vastheid*, 89). Actually, I am concerned with only one aspect of that question. When Scripture teaches us that God turns from wrath and to love (and the reverse), is this turning anthropomorphic in nature or not? And, if we want to speak "perfectly" about God, should the anthropomorphic description of God's wrath as *a*ffect then make room for a depiction of God's wrath as *e*ffect? We could only give a positive answer to these questions if *in* Scripture itself we were to "move out of the way" (to use a term of Schilder's, p. 146 above) the anthropomorphic way of speaking about divine wrath that can change. But there is no evidence of that. Scripture nowhere speaks of such a "separation." The particulars discussed on pp. 326–28, and

CHAPTER V. EVALUATION

especially those mentioned above, demonstrate the contrary. No one has ever seen God except his one and only Son; *he* has made him known (John 1:18). *Also in his wrath*? Wrath that is kindled and then averted?

I want to hold on to what Schilder envisioned. We may not lose sight of God's decrees. But on the other hand, eternity should not take away our perspective of the temporal, in which we observe God's decisive actions and the changes in them." History is more than a large notice board of eternity. We must constantly use *both* words, of which the first (about eternity) may never swallow up the second (about the temporal) as naïve, anthropomorphic, and apperceptive language (pp. 145–46 above).

The latter point also applies when I call attention to God's attitude *toward the reprobate*. His wrath rest on them, for "whoever does not obey the Son shall not see life, but the wrath of God *remains* on him" (John 3:36). But is this attitude of God the only attitude that is revealed in the life of unbelievers? I deny that. For although the wrath, which has the last word, rests on them, there is more to be said. How could the grace of God, as Rom 9:4; 1 Cor 10:1–4; Heb 6:4–6; and other places speak of it, have been bestowed apart from his merciful disposition? "All day long I have held out my hands to a disobedient and contrary people" (Rom 10:21). What remained to be done in God's vineyard that he did *not* do in it? (Isa 5:4). The unbelievers will stand guilty in God's judgment, for they have despised the evidence of God's *love*, and therefore their transgression is doubled. They do not respond to God's great *kindness* and *goodness* (Calvin, p. 268 above).

But also with respect to the *Gentiles*, God's disposition is not fully described if we point only to God's wrath. What comes to mind are the Scripture passages discussed in § 7. Ps 145:9 speaks of God's goodness and mercy toward all and over everything that he has made. A comparison with v. 8 taught us that we cannot draw a sharp distinction between the anger and mercy mentioned there.

But is it possible, for example, to think of God's mercy separate from his kind attitude? We know of Schilder's exegesis in which he says that Ps 145:9 is "not yet a scientific pronouncement about God's favorable *disposition* toward humanity in general. In his *disposition* God's thoughts, which I never find adequately expressed in his works, come back in their unity; in it the one meets the other" (*Ref.* 20, 28). If Schilder by "never ... adequately expressed" means that we can say more about God's attitude toward the Gentiles than Ps 145:9 tells us, he is entirely correct. But Schilder goes further. In answering the question about God's attitude he pushes Ps 145:9 aside as not-scientific. It seems to me that this is unjustified. For Scripture itself interprets the *facts*, the *works* of God, and then it places them in the light of God's merciful disposition. It is not *we* who reach this conclusion on the basis of our naïve experience, but that is how Scripture speaks. Just as Paul in Rom 1 connects the facts in the world of the Gentiles with God's wrath, so also the poet in Ps 145 connects the facts with God's mercy. We must let both stand.

Here, too, we use both words. God's disposition does not remain hidden

CHAPTER V. EVALUATION

behind the clouds when Scripture itself explains the facts. And it does so in a very nuanced way. A. Janse has pointed out that we must not make God in the image of human beings. "When I am angry with someone, then I am completely angry. It is then impossible to be (*at the same time*) merciful toward that person." But we may not measure God by this portrayal of human behavior. "We are commanded to point prophetically to all of Scripture and to accept all it says" (A. Janse, quoted in *Opbouw* 6, 175).

Matt 5:45 and Luke 6:35 are also instructive on this point. Schilder says of the former that disciples of Christ may not turn their *attitude* of disapproval and anger into *deeds* of punishment or vengeance. "The attitude that lives in their hearts toward concrete human beings with their concrete acts of enmity and even persecution, may not be expressed in actions, in their attitude. In their *attitude* they must express their position over against the Lord. And *that* attitude (toward the Lord) is certainly not the opposite of the anger at sin, nor of the excommunication (at the Lord's command) of those who persecute the church (Gal 4:30), nor of the later jubilation over God's justice as shown in the ruin of those who hate him" (*Ref.* 20, 28). In summary, the disciples must hide their true attitude of anger behind acts of *love*.

This exegesis seems untenable to me. For it breaks the connection between the command, "Love your enemies," and the loving disposition. It has been stated, correctly, that this compels us to act: "This love does not *just* mean an inner sentiment or disposition, but a loving activity, an active display of love in action. In that way there is also a connection with what follows, which also speaks of actions that must proceed from a loving heart," writes S. Greijdanus in connection with the parallel passage in Luke 6:27 (*Korte Verklaring Lucas*, I, 163; italics supplied).

Thus action and disposition go together. You are children of the Most High when it is apparent "that you have his spirit and that your heart, your mind, and your inner being are in agreement with his inner being, as determined by his Spirit." God's actions arise "from his being or, as it were, his inner being, as also the actions that have been prescribed for us must arise from an inner display of love" (Greijdanus, op, it., 166). I share this view. Schilder's explanation becomes even more improbable when we consider that in Matt 5 Christ challenges the sentiment expressed in v. 43: "You shall love your neighbor and *hate* your enemy." Christ actually is opposed to a wrong disposition, one that cannot bear good fruit and must therefore be replaced with a disposition marked by love, which does bear such fruit and, in doing so, responds to God's disposition.

I can also not subscribe to what Schilder writes about God's goodness as it is spoken of in Luke 6:35. Schilder views this text as a pronouncement about God's "works in the way they speak to the addressees. But not about his *disposition* as it is known to himself and of which he is aware" (*Ref.* 20, 36). Greijdanus, as we saw, took a different approach. But quite apart from that, in Luke 6:35 it is not *we* who give an interpretation of God's works (Schilder: "in the way they speak to the addressees"), but Christ himself, who makes

CHAPTER V. EVALUATION

the Father known. "When Schilder argues that we cannot legitimately reach a conclusion about God's attitude from the facts, we reply that we are specifically told that God's attitude is revealed in those facts. This is not to deny for a moment that, throughout it all, the rain and sunshine are means by which the wicked adds to his final punishment" (C. Van Til, *Common Grace*, 32). In Luke 6:35 we also have "a direct statement about the attitude of God, in the light of which the facts are interpreted" (loc. cit.).

I state emphatically that the Bible contains more about God's attitude toward the Gentiles than Matt 5:44 and Luke 6:35 relate. What Schilder writes about the wrath of God and about that of the believers and their "later jubilation over God's justice as shown in the ruin of those who hate him" must be taken into account. But again, we need to use more than one word.

A further remark about Acts 14:16–17: Schilder places all emphasis on "rains ... and fruitful seasons" as proof of God's judgment, so that human beings are rendered inexcusable. I heartily agree with what Schilder says about this, as is apparent from what I said about the direction and fruit of God's grace toward the Gentiles. But just like Van Til, I do not see that the one excludes the other: "We cannot understand why the one cannot be true as well as the other. To be a witness of God, of the whole God, these gifts must show his mercy as well as his wrath. God's judgment is threatened because men reject God's mercies" (op. cit., 33).

Both with respect to Acts 14:16–17 (*Ref.* 20, 36) and many other places (p. 186 above) Schilder draws a distinction between what is creaturely and the creature. God is favorably disposed toward the former, but not toward the latter (as rejected human beings). As we have seen, this distinction is also not foreign to Calvin (pp. 277–78 above). At the Synod of Dort it was used by S. Lubbertus, *Acta ofte Handelinghen* III, 17.

This distinction incorporates the correct idea that God has a certain attention for his creatures despite their sin. For example, Nineveh is (also) spared because it had 120,000 persons and much cattle. But I consider it incorrect to abstract the attention for personhood from the persons themselves. In Rom 11:28 we find an example of how God can be disposed differently toward the same persons, even though this does not lead to a distinction between their creatureliness and the actual human beings. According to the gospel, the Jews are *enemies* (blameworthy before God) for the sake of those who are Gentiles in origin because they are beloved (by God) for the sake of the fathers. *The same persons*, considered under the one aspect, are blameworthy before God, but, considered under the other aspect, they are beloved in his eyes. Both times *they* are ἐχθροί, ἀγαπητοί [enemies, beloved]. See also Matt 5:44–45. Undoubtedly God loves his enemies, the evil and unrighteous (also) because in them he sees his creatures. But he loves (not the creatureliness in his enemies, but) his *enemies*. He is merciful, kind, and loving toward *them*. Therefore, when Calvin and Schilder by abstraction separate the creaturely aspect from actual human beings, I deem this distinction to be incorrect.

CHAPTER V. EVALUATION

Furthermore, I wonder whether God *always* loves his own creatures, also Satan and the Antichrist (p. 186 above). Can we continue to say this as we remember that God will cast Satan and all the reprobate from his presence into *outer darkness* (Matt 8:12; 22:13; 25:30; 2 Pet 2:4, 17; Jude 13; Rev 22:15), in which he surrenders his creatures to pain and fire, i.e., to destruction, for all eternity (Isa 66:24; Matt 8:12, and other places)? It would surely be an abstraction that is foreign to God's *actions* if we were still to speak of his love toward what is creaturely in these hideous creatures.

I can also, using both words, not subscribe to the pronouncement of Kalamazoo about "the favorable attitude of God toward mankind in general, and not alone toward the elect" (see p. 307 above). For in the Three Points of 1924 (for the complete text, see C. Van Til, op. cit., 19ff.), we find the same defect as in Kuyper with respect to common grace: it becomes an *abstracted entity*. This favorable attitude is treated separately, leads to a doctrinal statement, and functions as the first of the Three Points, in which restraint of sin in the life of the individual and society as well as civil righteousness are discussed only in positive terms. It does not mention that God loves *human beings* who despise his love and misuse his gifts, so that the conclusion of Canons of Dort III/IV, 4 (not referred to by Kalamazoo, nor by Kuyper), receives no attention. Here the expression "*the* favorable attitude" so easily glosses over the reality of God's wrath, to which all who live without Christ *remain* subject. The *tension* that marks texts such as Matt 5:44-45 and Acts 14:16-17 disappears as soon as no attention is paid to God's touching engagement with the world, with those who despise his favorable disposition and thus make themselves inexcusable. "The favorable attitude," taken out of context, thus becomes a cheap affair.

C. Van Til also engaged this topic. He speaks of God's love toward humanity in general, before the Fall. But "a little later God hated mankind in general. That was after mankind had sinned against God. Is there any doubt that the elect, as well as the reprobate, were under the wrath of God? Calvin says that the whole human race is 'individually bound by the guilt and desert of eternal death, as derived from the person of Adam....' So the elect and the reprobate are under a *common wrath*" (op. cit., 74). Thus Van Til takes a corporate, "organic" view. "It was *mankind*, not some individual elect or reprobate person, that sinned against God. Thus it was mankind in general, which was under the favor of God, that came under the wrath of God" (loc. cit.). After that comes Christ with his redeeming work for humanity—even though he did not die for all human beings, but only for his people: "His people are not yet his people except in the mind of God. They are still members of the sinful mass of mankind. It is with them *where they are* that contact is to be made. The offer or presentation [of Christ, J.D.] is not to those who believe any more than to those who disbelieve. The offer comes to those who have so far neither believed nor disbelieved. It comes before that differentiation has taken place. It comes thus generally, so that differentiation may have meaning" (op. cit., 78). First comes "the common,"

CHAPTER V. EVALUATION

the "general," and after that, "in each case, comes the conditional. History is a process of differentiation" (op. cit., 74).

It is to be appreciated that Van Til dares to speak of a change in God's attitude: "We need at this point to be fearlessly anthropomorphic" (op. cit., 73). But then he should also *continue* to speak anthropomorphically and not begin to engage in abstractions. Where does Scripture teach us that God first loved *humanity*—of which, save for two, none had yet been born—and a short while later hated them? Van Til opposes abstractions (op. cit., 34ff.), and often with effect; but does he not fall on his own sword here? Besides, in continuing the corporate argument, humanity in Christ would have progressed from the "common wrath" into "the common grace." Apparently Van Til did not want to draw this conclusion: "There is a *certain* attitude of favor on the part of God toward a generality of mankind, and a *certain* good before God in the life of the historically undeveloped unbeliever" (op. cit., 94; italics supplied). Besides, Scripture does not permit such a "general" turning from wrath to grace. God's wrath *remains* on all who are disobedient to the Son (John 3:36). It does not say: *comes* (again) over all.

For Van Til the common grace after the Fall flows from the common grace before the Fall: "All common grace is earlier grace. Its commonness lies in its earliness. It pertains not merely to the lower dimensions of life. It pertains to all dimensions, and to these dimensions in the same way at all stages of history. It pertains to all dimensions of life, but to all these dimensions ever decreasingly as the time of history goes on. At the first stage of history there is much common grace. There is a common good nature under the common favor of God. But this creation-grace requires response. It cannot remain what it is. It is conditional. Differentiation must set in and does set in. It comes first in the form of a common rejection of God. *Yet common grace continues*; it is on a 'lower' level now; it is patience that men may be led to repentance.... Common grace will diminish still more in the further course of history" (op. cit., 82–83; italics supplied).

This is not clear to me. Why does common grace continue after "common vengeance," about which we heard above, entered the picture? Does it not then become an abstract entity? What is its relationship to Christ? I believe that Van Til is too schematic and fails to provide proof from Scripture.

I also regard the term "general and well-meant offer of grace" as dangerous. It can be understood in a good sense. I point to what Calvin wrote about God's genuine, earnest offer of grace (pp. 266ff. above). See also C. Veenhof, *Ref.* 28, 380–81. Hoeksema wrongly attacked this *good* use of the term, for example in what he wrote about the promises being only for the elect, and about his "shell-kernel" construction, in which the promises to Israel (the church) are directed entirely, not to the shell of the reprobate, but only to the kernel of the elect. See H. Hoeksema, *Een kracht Gods tot zaligheid*, 25–26, 73–74. Cf. A. C. de Jong, op. cit., 38ff.; L. Doekes, *Ref.* 22, 182–83, 333; J. Kamphuis, *Ref.* 29, 293.

However, the "general offer of grace" can easily become just as *cheap* an affair as the talk about God's favorable attitude toward humanity in general. Greijdanus already pointed out in 1931 that while the term "does not necessarily have to be interpreted incorrectly," that can easily happen, "especially because it does not speak of the demand for faith and repentance. The Canons of Dort, III/IV, 8 and 9, speak otherwise. Besides, it makes a difference whether the term is used in everyday conversation or in a theological dispute, in which precision is demanded" (quoted in Hoeksema, op. cit., 181).

This careful criticism later increased in volume, especially in Schilder. The Reformed did not want to relinquish the word "offer" (*Heid. Cat.* II, 248), but it is easy to think of the promise "by itself, as if it were not most closely connected to the *demand*" (*Ref.* 20, 78). "The blessings of the covenant are so easily abstracted from the wrath of the covenant" (loc. cit.). "And, as far as I am concerned, I am happy to give up the word 'well-meant;' it reminds me too much of a tea party. But I will not give up the word "earnestly" [Canons of Dort III/IV, 8, J.D.].... In that word "earnestly" [*serio* in Latin] I hear more than that friendliness of Kalamazoo.... In the expressions '*serio ostendere*' ('to reveal earnestly' in his Word) and '*serio promittere*' ('to promise earnestly' the content of the gospel) I see *also the flaming wrath of God*" (*Bovenschriftuurlijke binding*, 69–70). Every thought of a "weak invitation" and a "gentle suggestion" must be considered taboo (J. Kamphuis, *Ref.* 31, 319). I agree. Also the term "well-meant offer of grace" functions properly only in a *context*. By itself it gives rise to dangers.

§ 10. Grace and necessity

The execution of God's decrees should not cause us to speak of a "necessity" in the continuation of history, so devaluing the word "grace" (Kuyper) or rejecting it as one-sided (Schilder).

In his treatment of predestination, Kuyper looked behind the scenes. He discovered that God, were he to remain God, *had* to let common grace come about. I already raised the question (pp. 40–41 above) how this "necessity" is compatible with Kuyper's doctrine of common *grace*. I answered this question negatively. If Kuyper had correctly introduced the concept of "necessity" here, so that God was constrained to let history continue, the concept of "grace" would be devalued.

For how can we continue to speak of "grace" when we realize that the threat of death in Gen 2:17 (according to Kuyper's exegesis) *cannot* have been a true threat? God *had* to triumph over Satan, says Kuyper. That is why history *had* to be continued. To remain God, God could not let the works of his hands fail. But, according to Kuyper's view, Adam and Eve could not die immediately. For God desired a human race! But how can Kuyper then still maintain that God

CHAPTER V. EVALUATION

granted Adam and Eve *grace* by letting them live? Granting them something out of necessity can surely not be called grace. For "grace" must (in Kuyper's own words) be *free* (pp. 40–41 above). In my view Kuyper here undermines the validity of the title of his trilogy. *Common Grace*: that title is unmasked as anthropomorphic when we (following Kuyper's argument, to be sure) move from Gen 2:17 to predestination—an anthropomorphism that we can apparently overcome. I will disregard the naïve stage of the interpretation of Gen 2:17 (and what follows from that) in order to sketch the true state of affairs as based on predestination.

As we saw, Schilder rejected the use of the word "grace" in this context, arguing as follows: The continuation of history is not grace, also not judgment, but it is a condition, the substrate, for grace as well as for judgment. It is necessary in order to arrive at a full heaven and a full hell. This continuation of history can make a certain impression on us (that of "grace"); it can also *seem* as if God postpones his judgments (in his patience), and Scripture conforms more than once to this "perception." But in addition to apperceptive language, Scripture speaks in terms of *final conclusions*, "in order to cut off all anthropomorphic speech" (p. 145 above). Scripture itself overtakes the "perception." From "as it appears" we apparently come to "as it is," to the final conclusion, in which the continuation as *necessity* is proved incorrect.

I want to make the following observations about this element of necessity in the views of Kuyper and Schilder:

(a) First something about the distinction Schilder draws between apperceptive and scientific language in our speaking about God, about his disposition, about the continuation of history, etc. We are to remind ourselves that this perception or "observation," to the extent that it is found in Scripture also according to Schilder, is not our observation, but the observation of Scripture itself. I have already pointed to that in connection with Matt 5:44 and Luke 6:35, where it is *Christ* who interprets the observation (p. 372 above). But then it becomes particularly hazardous to try to rise above this observation by speaking in a clearer "scientific" way in which we can observe the true state of the matter (e.g., in connection with the continuation).

How hazardous this distinction is, becomes apparent in Schilder's exegesis of 2 Pet 3:9: "The Lord is not slow to fulfill his promise as some count slowness, but is patient toward you, not wishing that any should perish, but that all should reach repentance." I have already quoted what Schilder wrote about this: "The expression 'patience' looks at God's actions from our *perspective*, and the *apperceptive* language chooses that expression. But the expression '*the Lord is not slow*' harks back to the scientific *discussions* with false teachers. In that context (to speak conceptually now) it rejects the *concept* of retardation *as such*" (p. 184 above). We just heard Schilder say that Holy Scripture, speaking in terms of "final conclusions," cuts off all anthropomorphic speech. But then it is remarkable that the author of 2 Pet 3:9 progresses from conceptual language to apperceptive language: The Lord is not slow, *but* he is patient! The distinction

CHAPTER V. EVALUATION

between scientific and apperceptive language is completely foreign to this text. We need to provide a different explanation than Schilder gives. Ridderbos rightly says: "Peter does reject the retardation concept of *false teachers*, but does not deny that judgment is being postponed; οὐ βραδύνει means no more than that the Lord *is not slow*, not *tardy*, in fulfilling his promise" (*De theologische cultuurbeschouwing van Abraham Kuyper*, 311, with a reference to the exegesis of S. Greijdanus).

(b) We have already noticed (pp. 339ff., 345–46 above) that Scripture does not speak about prehistory in an abstract way. So, for example, the preexistence of Christ receives attention in the context of Christ's redemptive work. One could say that the "apperception" of salvation (and sometimes also of condemnation) obtains its certainty and depth in what was decided by God before its revelation. Thus we do not receive something deduced from God's Counsel, but we are more than once directed to God's Counsel. But when Kuyper and Schilder speak of *necessity*, is the direction not the reverse? Do they not draw conclusions from God's Counsel about what happens in history? And as for Schilder, is it not the case that our "perception" must constantly be *corrected* on the basis of what God decided in his Counsel?

(c) When we examine the texts that speak of God's Counsel, it becomes apparent that the reference to this Counsel seeks to comfort or to admonish and frighten us. See Eph 1:11; Matt 11:26; Rom 8:28–30; Acts 15:18; Heb 6:17. The *salvation* that is given to God's people is certain and fixed, for God's Counsel cannot be broken. See also Isa 14:27; 46:10; Prov 16:4; 1 Pet 2:8. The *condemnation* will certainly strike all who resist God. He has his audacious enemies in his grasp, and thus they will not, to their terror, escape what he has decreed in his Counsel. That is how God's Counsel functions in the *preaching*. Thus a text such as Prov 16:4, "The Lord has made everything for its purpose, even the wicked for the day of trouble," can legitimately be interpreted as, "We must not forget that the goal of this proverb is to move the ungodly to repentance by fear of the judgment" (W. H. Gispen, *Korte Verklaring Spreuken*, II, at the verse cited).

But in the views of Kuyper and Schilder, as summarized above, we more than once see *speculations* about God's Counsel that fall outside of the boundaries of what Scripture actually says. And this then leads, *inter alia*, to positing that the continuation of history is *necessary*. A passage from the Bible can clarify the difference I have in mind.

Exodus 32 tells us of the LORD's wrath over the sin with the golden calf. He even says to Moses: "I have seen this people and behold, it is a stiff-necked people. Now therefore let me alone, that my wrath may burn hot against them and I may consume them, in order that I may make a great nation of you" (vv. 9–10). One could *argue* that what God wills here is impossible. Did he not decide in his Counsel to choose Israel and to prepare for the coming of Jesus Christ from the tribe of Judah? And is *therefore* the continuation of Israel's history and of Judah's tribe not necessary? Does it not follow that God's Counsel cannot be executed if he destroys Israel and creates a great nation descended

CHAPTER V. EVALUATION

from Moses? Is Exod 32:9–10 thus not remarkably anthropomorphic? I think that it is not legitimate to argue this way. Moses does not do so either. He recognizes the full seriousness of God's words (Exod 32:11ff.; 33:12–13, 15–16; 34:8–9; Deut 9:19, 25ff.). And he has to wrestle for God's *grace*. When he does so, it is particularly striking that he appeals to God's promises to Abraham, Isaac, and Jacob (Exod 32:13; Deut 9:27), which God swore *on oath*. But this appeal to God's earlier decisions does not lead to the proposition that Israel's continued existence is necessary, but forms an occasion for Moses to plead with the LORD, to move him to grace, so that he will not do what he had truly determined to do.

God's promises of old testify to his grace, but so also does the entire path leading to their fulfillment. God's *faithfulness* remains surprising and never becomes something that speaks for itself, something that is a necessity, on the basis of which *we* in our reasoning can arrive at conclusions.

This seems to me also important for the evaluation of the question whether the continuation of history after the Fall may be called grace, yes or no. Gen 2:17 can hardly provide the answer, for in my view the exegesis of this text will remain uncertain. One person maintains that the announced punishment was fulfilled; another says that it was not fulfilled (immediately). Thus J. de Fraine states that mortality befell human beings on the actual day that they ate of the fruit of the tree of the knowledge of good and evil (*Genesis*, at the text cited). Giving the words "on the day" a conditional flavor (with reference to, *inter alia*, Num 30:6, 9, 13) and translating the Hebrew *mot tamut* as "certainly die," not as "die immediately," Paul Humbert states : "Thus it is not a matter in Gen 2:17 of immediate death, but of certain death" (*Études sur le récit du paradis et de chute dans la Genèse*, 140). Others believe that Gen 2:17 was not fulfilled immediately. This is the very strong position of H. Gunkel: "This threat is not fulfilled subsequently: they do not die immediately, This fact cannot be explained away but must simply be acknowledged" (*Handkommentar Genesis*, at the verse cited). Gerhard von Rad writes more moderately: "We must indeed be satisfied with the fact that with the threat of 2:17 things cannot be made completely congruent, for human beings did not die in accordance with their deed" (*Das erste Buch Mose*, comment on Gen 3:19). This last opinion cannot be dismissed with the assertion that it was impossible after the Fall because of the *necessity* of the continuation of history. Then this is the line of reasoning: God wanted a *human race* of elect and reprobate and *thus* history had to continue. Exod 32 admonishes us to be careful here. For, leaving the correct exegesis of Gen 2:17 aside for now, we may say of the continuation of history after the Fall that God wanted to remain faithful to his eternal plan in Christ Jesus. It was his *will* (*and that was grace*) to remain faithful to his decision and therefore he did not cut short his relationship with humanity. Thus it is not correct to state: God continued history because he was forced to do so (Kuyper). Thereby Kuyper devalues his own use of the word "grace." And this statement is also not correct: it was not possible otherwise, because God's decree of election and reprobation rendered history necessary as substrate for the administration of blessing and curse, so that this continuation cannot "strictly speaking" be characterized as either blessing or curse (Schilder). For both § 2 (*Not in the same manner*) and § 5 (*Christ and the covenant of grace*) as well as what this section has shown, give me the confidence to regard the continuation of history as *grace*. We must exclude the entire concept of "necessity," in my opinion. We have a sound Scriptural footing in the *faithfulness* of God. But whoever refers to God's faithfulness also always refers to God's grace. It is a faithfulness that is never self-evident or necessary but constantly and surprisingly reveals itself as grace.

From the above and the previous sections it is clear that I maintain Calvin's explanation of the achievements and virtues of the Gentiles (pp. 203ff. above). Therefore a detailed discussion of Schilder's explanation with its four factors (pp. 203ff. above) has become superfluous. Schilder makes valuable remarks in that explanation. But they do not prevent me from recognizing as *grace* God's maintenance of his "advantageous" law (1st factor), the remnants of the original gifts (2nd factor), and God's preservation of the world and humanity (3rd factor) in maintaining *time* for the development of his creation. For the sake of Christ and his grace ("proper office"!), God does not cut short his relationship with humanity.

§ 11. Culture and our being sojourners

I question where Holy Scripture supports the fascinating idea that in Paradise a task was given (made executable again in Jesus Christ) for the development all of creation's potential as a program for the ages. In addition to the objections that I have already raised against the doctrine of common grace, I draw attention to the fact that it does not do justice to what Scripture says about our being sojourners here on earth.

I have disputed Kuyper's doctrine of common grace in the preceding sections. In this dispute I have taken a strong stand against his proposition that the development of the totality of created existence is an independent aim of God's predestination, beside the actualization of the kingdom of heaven. I rejected this proposition as speculative (common grace in predestination, § 4) and as abstractive (Mediator of creation beside Mediator of redemption, § 5) Further, the entire concept of "common grace" appeared to me to be untenable (§§ 6 and 7). Consequently, I cannot regard common grace as constitutive for our labor as Christians in this world. I deem Kuyper's foundation for the calling of the Christian in the world to be unacceptable.

But what exactly does Kuyper have in mind? He wants to draw the attention

CHAPTER V. EVALUATION

of Christians to a *cultural task* as a calling of God. What must we think of this *cultural task* which, as commission of God, was supposedly given already in Paradise for the development of all of creation's potential?

I note first that not only Kuyper and Schilder, but also many others, connect this cultural task with Gen 1:28. With regard to Kuyper and Schilder I have noted this already (pp. 292–93 above). H. Dooyeweerd also speaks of "the cultural commandment of Gen 1" (*A New Critique*, II, 262). H. Berkhof takes the same tack: "As God's image, i.e., as God's representative and caretaker-manager, man is called to unlock and exploit the possibilities that lie hidden in nature and in being human. Paradise in which, according to Gen 2, humanity began its existence was not at all an ideal situation. It was not an end point, but a point of departure. Man was called to work and preserve the garden. Subsequently, humanity was to expand from there in order to continue this work over the whole earth. And this work does continue. The end point is not a garden or a forest, but a city, nature developed, a completed culture, the new Jerusalem" (*De mens onderweg*, 37–38).

This great unanimity cannot prevent me from asking a few questions. The expositions, especially by Kuyper and Berkhof, captivate me immensely and therefore it is difficult for me to dismiss them. But even though what they write is fascinating, is it also true? I pose the following questions:

1. *Do Gen 1:28; 2:15; 3:23; and Ps 8 imply a mandate "to develop creation's potential"?* What comes to mind here is that in his exegesis of Gen 1:28 and 2:15 Calvin places all emphasis on the *enjoyment* of what God created (p. 266 above). This explanation might, at first blush, seem excessively Arcadian. But it must nonetheless be tested seriously. Gen 1:28 does command humankind to *subdue* the earth. But is that the same as bringing about the development of created existence"? Is it not rather the case that human beings take possession of what they already have from God (Gen 1:26), namely power over the animals? I think of Ps 8:6ff.: "You have given him *dominion* over the works of your hands; you have *put all things under his feet*:" (and then follows a detailed description of this having dominion and subjecting) "sheep and oxen and also the beasts of the field, the birds of the heavens and the fish of the sea, whatever passes along the paths of the sea." Cf. also Gen 2:19ff. Human beings were placed in a world that God had already *prepared* for them. This is something different than a task imposed on them "to take out of the world what it is in it."

It is true that Gen 2:15 says that human beings were placed in the garden of Eden to *work* it. But to what end? The Hebrew verb *'abad* means: to work (the field). Cf. 2 Sam 9:10; Isa 30:24; Zech 13:5; and especially Gen 4:2, which refers to Cain as *'obed 'adamah*, i.e., farmer. The purpose of this work was to provide humans with food (cf. Gen 1:29; 2:5–6). Does Gen 3:17ff. cast light on this too? The ground was cursed, so that thereafter humans had to eat of it by the sweat of their brow. The connection between working and eating and the command to work in order to "eat" remained (3:23), but the circumstances in which humankind subsequently had to labor became arduous.

This explanation does not mean that I want to keep culture out of the discussion. But culture as development of what God had placed in his creation in the form of seeds is thus more a *consequence* of Gen 1:28 than a *task* assigned there. Culture as such, which is more than "being able to eat and drink," comes into perspective because human beings must multiply and because humanity may begin to enjoy God's wide world.

Psalm 8 has also been advanced to prove that we have a cultural task. But does it concern the task of humankind to develop creation? Or does this psalm call attention to God's glorious works (vv. 2, 4), while the poet then marvels at the dominion human beings enjoy over animals? And is it not in particular a dominion for the purpose of providing them with the means of sustaining life? "Here the hidden backgrounds of everyday life are disclosed. The pasturing and slaughtering of animals, the hunting and catching of wild animals is a royal prerogative proceeding from God, by which figuratively becomes manifest man's superiority over all created things" (H. J. Kraus, *Psalmen* I, 70–71). It seems to me that I may rightly place a question mark after Kuyper's exegesis of this Psalm, an exegesis that was followed by many others.

2. *Does our developing of nature form an extension of Christ's marvelous power?* Kuyper's opinion is well-known: "In Jesus restored humanity appears before us, and in this humanity appears the highest expression of the power of which the human spirit is capable over against nature, matter, and demons once this power has reached its culmination" (p. 54 above). This power of Christ receives an extension: "No matter how great *his* miracles were, the fruit of his entry in the world would cause a yet still *greater* and more miraculous work to result when the dominion over nature would begin—the dominion that we now enjoy through the unveiling of nature's secrets and of the knowledge of its latent powers" (p. 55 above).

This idea of Kuyper's must also be tested critically. In this respect I do not consider it overly significant that some call into question the coherence between the unlocking of nature (technology) and the de-demonization of the world by Christ's work (p. 56 above) on the basis of the *facts*. For example, J. C. Hoekendijk remarks: "It is indeed apparent in 'real history' that beside the bio-morphic and socio-morphic models (that apply to an ontocratic pattern), from the beginning there were also techno-morphic models in use in the 'East' (Topitsch) even without the world's having been denuded of magic. Of course, this does not explain why only in the 'West' technology could take flight; but it does suggest that the ultimate emergence of technocracy will have to be explained on the basis of entirely different factors than the functioning of a theocratic idea" (*Wending* 19, 812).

What concerns me is something different. Can we, even disregarding the facts, argue from out of faith as Kuyper did? He relies on Ps 8, stating that in

CHAPTER V. EVALUATION

Christ "Psalm 8, about the dominion God gave to human beings over nature, has been fulfilled." I agree wholeheartedly. But does this fulfillment now have its extension in our dominion over nature? I place a question mark here too. For the majesty of Christ, which *he* according to Ps 8 already possesses, we, according to Heb 2:5–9, receive only in the world to come, τὴν οἰκουμένην τὴν μέλλουσαν. "Since Chrysostom people have often attempted to understand the concept ἡ οἰκουμένη ἡ μέλλουσα [the world to come] from the perspective of the Old Testament and hence to interpret it as pointing to the scope of the New Testament deliverance; however, this contradicts the usage of the epistle. As ἡ μέλλουσα πόλις, "the city that is to come" (13:14), designates the city that Christians do not have on earth but rather desire as a future good, so is ἡ μέλλ. οἰκουμένη also for Christians still the future abode and arrangement, with the preparation of which the state of consummation will come to pass and the μέλλουσα ἀγαθά, "the good things to come" (9:11; 10:1), will be received. Thereby it is not excluded that what is to come already occasionally reaches into the present, as believers already now enjoy the powers of the age to come (6:5) and in faith are assembled in the city to come (13:14), yes, have their citizenship there (12:22–23); only the essentially eschatological character of the mentioned concept is thereby not done away with." (E. Riggenbach, *Der Brief an die Hebräer*, at the verse cited).

But how then can the development of creation *by us* surpass even Christ's actions in accordance with Ps 8? My objections to Kuyper do not touch on what he says about Christ, but what he says about *us*. He can be very impressed with human technology and human dominion over creation, but does that allow him and us to be tempted to *see* in this dominion the (partial) fulfillment of what we, according to Heb 2, must *believe* as reality in the world to come?

Also John 14:12 ("Truly, truly, I say to you, whoever believes in me will also do the works that I do; and greater works than these will he do, because I am going to the Father"), cited by Kuyper as evidence (p. 55 above), does not at all convince me. For what matters here is *which* works Christ is referring to. John 14:12 speaks of the salvific acts of God in Christ. "As long as Jesus lived on earth, his actions were not limited solely by his earthly existence, but also by the will of God, who sent him only to the Jews. But as soon as he enters the glory of his Father, his influence will become greater and will extend much farther. That is why the works of his disciples will be greater than those that he performed personally" (J. Keulers, *Het evangelie volgens Johannes*, at the text cited). They are "the works of preaching and miracles (Mark 16:17–18) and therefore of regeneration and faith" (C. Bouma, *Korte Verklaring Johannes*, at the text cited). Surely that is something different than "having dominion over nature." By means of preaching and regeneration, *Christ's* powers become evident and demons are cast out. But does that happen also in technology in general and culture as such? We must not forget that in culture and technology throughout the ages demons can make themselves at home and the Antichrist will make himself great (Rev 13:17–18)!

CHAPTER V. EVALUATION

3. *Is the meaning of the "interim period" also found in the full development of created existence?* Kuyper argues expressly that it is: "I am convinced ... that the Consummation must bring us not only a transition from the church militant to the church triumphant, and not only a gathering of the kingdoms of the world into the Kingdom of heaven, but also that in the life of nature and the world whatever God concealed in them must be made manifest to the praise of his name *before the end can come*" (*Van de Voleinding* II, 507; italics supplied). We heard Berkhof say that the point of departure was the garden, while the end point "is not a garden or a forest, but a city, nature developed, a *completed* culture, the new Jerusalem" (op. cit., 38; emphasis supplied). Schilder declares that the alpha will be joined to the omega by Christ's work, and that the talents handed out in the early morning of creation will by evening have earned a profit equal to the number distributed at daybreak (p. 315 above). "Cultural grace" (Kuyper, op. cit., 179), "cultural mandate" (Schilder), dominion over nature as "divine calling" (Berkhof)—all of these point to a program that God has instructed human beings to carry out for the development of creation's potential. May we indeed say with Kuyper that the significance of the time between Christ's ascension and return also lies in the completion of a cultural program? Is it a program that must be completed before the end can come?

I believe that this, too, must not be left undisputed. When we review the relevant passages in the New Testament, we nowhere find any indication that the interim period is given the above-mentioned significance. They do say that God creates and makes room for penance and repentance (2 Pet 3), and room for the proclamation of the gospel. "That life in its continuation is directly connected with the intention of God, our Savior. Both 2 Pet 3:9 (the patience of God) and in 1 Tim 2 (government in its preserving and protective functions) are concerned with God's intention in the continuation of time" (G. C. Berkouwer, *De Wederkomst van Christus* I, 156–58). The gospel must first be proclaimed to all nations, and *then the end will come* (Matt 24:14; cf. Matt 28:19–20; Acts 1:8). Berkouwer quotes Cullmann, who says of Matt 28:20 that it is "a clear allusion to the eschatological character of mission, which is to take place precisely in the present interim *and which gives it its meaning*" (op. cit., 167; italics supplied by Berkouwer). It is remarkable that Berkouwer, who wrote a chapter in the book just referred to on "the meaning of the interim period" (122–75), makes no mention at all of the meaning that Kuyper assigned to the interim period. To me it is an argument from silence that the New Testament texts about the "end" and the "interim period" examined by Berkouwer evidently do not give any occasion to connect them to a "cultural" interpretation. Kuyper failed to support from Scripture what was conclusive for him (see the above quotation from *Van de Voleinding*).

4. *Does today's culture provide building blocks for the new earth?* Kuyper argued on the basis of Rev 21:24, 26 that the gain of common grace "will not simply perish and be destroyed in the universal conflagration." Even though the *forms*

CHAPTER V. EVALUATION

will not continue, "the powerful *seed* which underlies all this" certainly will. It will receive a new form "that is in holy harmony with the glory of [God's] kingdom" (p. 24 above). Schilder contested this opinion by means of, *inter alia*, Greijdanus' exegesis, stating that the "bringing in" of the glory and honor of the kings and nations into the new Jerusalem is happening "now, in this age," and besides, is done by *converted* kings and nations (p. 163 above). I, too, believe that Kuyper's "form and seed" idea is speculative. Rev 21 does not speak about the world's culture as such that will be saved (be it in seed form) for the new earth. Culture also does not receive independent attention in Rev 21. Kings and nations will subject themselves to Christ and apply "their might and knowledge, competence, and industriousness" to "the well-being, edification, and expansion of the Lord's congregation," and will "increase the beauty of this heavenly city with their talents and powers" (S. Greijdanus, *Korte Verklaring Openbaring*, 322).

In addition, 2 Pet 3:5–13 demands that we be cautious. The "heavens and earth that now exist" are "stored up for fire, being kept until the day of judgment and destruction of the ungodly" (v. 7). The elements will be destroyed by fire (στοιχεῖα δὲ καυσούμενα λυθήσεται, v. 10). We must not tamper with the drastic λυθήσεται [will be destroyed] (cf. John 2:19; Acts 27:41)—not by using Kuyper's "form and seed" idea and, in my view, also not by using what H. Berkhof says about this passage: "No matter how drastic its [i.e., the fire's, J.D.] destructive operation may be, it purifies but does not destroy" (*Christus de zin der geschiedenis*, 171). In my opinion, 2 Pet 3 in fact places all emphasis on the total dissolution of the old world (including its culture), which must make room for the *new* heavens and the *new* earth, καινοὺς δὲ οὐρανοὺς καὶ γῆν καινὴν (v. 13). The use of not only λυθήσετα, but also καυσούμενα [with intense heat] (vv. 10, 12) and τήκεται [will melt] (v. 12) point to a radical change that will come about with the new.

However, I do not at all deny that there is a connection between the old and the new. For we await the new *heavens* and a new *earth*. But this connection between the old and the new earth does not permit us to conclude that there is a continuity between what will be found *on* the old and new earth in the form of culture—neither with a "form and seed" scheme, nor with Berkhof's distinction (also employed by others) "that we do not await a destruction of the *essence*, but a change in *appearance*" (loc. cit., emphasis supplied). The word "melt" in 2 Pet 3:12 prevents me from formulating the connection between old and new. We are not likely to get any further than *non liquet* [it is not clear].

Verse 10b ("and the earth and the works that are done on it will be exposed [or found]") also does not help us. For in the first place this reading is not certain. Beside εὑρεθήσεται [will be found], κατακαήσεται [will be burnt up] is also found here in the manuscripts. And second, even if we maintain the above translation, it is not obvious that this refers to works (of culture) *that will survive the "burning."* Greijdanus provides the following attractive explanation: "*The earth* itself in its entire existence, mountains, hills, *and the works* of human

CHAPTER V. EVALUATION

beings *on it*, their deeds, no matter how hidden, *will be found*, come to light, and be rewarded or punished according to their essence. Another reading of this verse is 'will be burnt up.' In that case what is meant by those works on earth are the buildings and other products of human knowledge and skill. There are still other translations. But the fact that 'will be found' is the most difficult reading favors the view that it is the original one. But determining the exact reading in these verses remains somewhat difficult, so that sometimes no more can be said than that it is 'most likely' correct" (*Korte Verklaring 1 en 2 Petrus*, at the text cited).

We must also not read too much into Rev 14:13, which says of the believers that "their deeds follow them." This refers the labor of believers only, and that labor cannot properly be described by using the overtaxed word "culture." The works are "the revelations and tokens of their love for and their faith in the Lord, and of their faithfulness, perseverance, and effort" that will receive "the reward of grace" (S. Greijdanus, *Korte Verklaring Openbaring*, 227). Works such as those described in Matt 25:35–40 are surely not cultural labor in the broad sense of the word that Kuyper, Berkhof, and others ascribe to it. On the basis of the foregoing, I believe that I had good reason to raise also my fourth question.

Meanwhile, in asking my four critical questions, my purpose is not to propagate a kind of cultural avoidance. But it is important to explore where the *emphases* fall in our acceptance of "culture." Do we have a task in culture because we must carry out a God-given cultural program before the end comes? Or must we, so long as Christ's parousia tarries (because the proclamation of the gospel is not yet complete), work in order to be able to eat?

The latter undoubtedly sounds less grand than the former, and it also requires supplementation. But this *modest* cultural ordinance is what we find in Scripture. To the Thessalonians, who expected the return of Christ in the near future and therefore did not work, Paul presented this sober rule: "If anyone is not willing to work, let him not eat" (2 Thess 3:10). Which does not mean that this work is incorporated into a cultural program, but into the proclamation of the gospel: "so that you may walk properly before outsiders and be dependent on no one" (1 Thess 4:12). By living as loafers they would make "not only themselves but also the gospel contemptible in the eyes of unbelievers" (J. Keulers, *De brieven van Paulus* I, 44).

I spoke of emphases that may differ. In chapter IV, § 11, I ascertained a distinction between Kuyper and Schilder on the one hand and Calvin on the other that was based on the issue of the sojourning and pilgrimage of Christians in this world. In Calvin pilgrimage is central. In Kuyper and Schilder it functions on the periphery of their cultural views (pp. 312ff. above). H. J. Meijerink has strikingly demonstrated the differences by placing a quotation from Calvin beside one from S. G. de Graaf. Calvin writes: "If we must simply pass through this world, there is no doubt we ought to use its good things in so far as they help rather than hinder our course" (*Inst* III, x, 1) (see p. 281 above). In

CHAPTER V. EVALUATION

contrast, De Graaf (a Kuyperian, as we saw on p. 360 above) gives the following formulation: There are also "strong indications that Paul was a person who enjoyed life. They are found in his most principial opposition to ascesis when he says: 'Everything created by God is good if it is received with thanksgiving.' Then nothing remains of being but a stranger and sojourner here on earth, as it is often interpreted. Rather, by faith in Christ he has a rightful claim to created things. That does not conflict with what Scripture says elsewhere about being a stranger and sojourner. Believers are strangers and sojourners *insofar as* sin still reigns here" (*Christus en de wereld*, 34; emphasis supplied). In my opinion Meijerink rightly remarks on this that according to De Graaf we are actually not strangers: "We are not strangers; but only 'insofar' as sin still rules here, Holy Scripture applies the image of 'the stranger' to us" ("Vreemdeling en Erfgenaam," in *Handboek ten dienste van de Gereformeerde Kerken in Nederland* [1948], 200).

We now face the question whether the concept of strangers in Scripture has such an important place that it must also permeate our cultural views. If the new theology, as portrayed by J. Sperna Weiland, is to be believed, then the answer is no: "The new theology is marked by a farewell to a Christianity that views the earth as a vale of tears in which the soul longingly looks toward the *Urbs Syon aurea* of Bernard of Morlaix, the 'golden heavenly city' of Hymn 126 in the Reformed [state church] Hymnal, and sees life as a pilgrimage to eternity.... Marx and Nietzsche, the first with his remarks about opium, the second with his call to be true to the earth, have made an impression, together with the Old Testament. The eschatology of the new theology ... is an earthly theology; the horizon is not heaven, but human history, the history of human freedom" (*Wending* 20, 636–37).

This portrayal of the Old Testament as temporal, this-worldly, is untenable in view of Heb 11. It says that the believers in the Old Testament "not having received the things promised, but having seen them and greeted them from afar, ... acknowledged that they were strangers and exiles on the earth. For people who speak thus make it clear that they are seeking a homeland. If they had been thinking of that land from which they had gone out, they would have had opportunity to return. But as it is, they desire a better country, that is, a heavenly one. Therefore God is not ashamed to be called their God, for he has prepared for them a city" (Heb 11:13–16). The New Testament believers join in saying this: "Here we have no lasting city, but we seek the city that is to come" (Heb 13:14). This eschatological ordinance has decisive, positive meaning for life in this world. That is why Calvin could legitimately choose Titus 2:11–14 as point of departure for his ethics. In that passage Paul enjoins his readers to live self-controlled, upright, and godly lives, "waiting for our blessed hope, the appearing of the glory of our great God and Savior Jesus Christ." Cf. *Inst.* III, vii, 3ff.

Of these "strangers and exiles," who have their "home" elsewhere (2 Cor 5:9), Abraham is "the first and classic example in Holy Scripture. Abraham, the

CHAPTER V. EVALUATION

stranger, the *ger wetoshab* among the sons of Heth, has become rich, but he *owns no land*.... In Abraham's situation in his 'world' the author of Hebrews finds a striking and typical image of every believer who seeks a heavenly country, of whom the patriarch owning but a *grave* is the classic example.... And the fact that believers, the seed of Abraham, do not truly possess anything in this world—this is now the reality also maintained throughout the entire history of revelation. Think only of the laws regarding redemption and the year of jubilee, which also concerned this idea: not Israel is the real owner of Canaan, but Yahweh. Israel remained a stranger, also in Canaan, 'before the face of the LORD.' That is why David still had to say in Ps 39:12: 'For I am a sojourner with you, a guest, like all my fathers'" (H. J. Meijerink, op. cit., 205–06).

The same author points to the scope of these data: "In the days of his sojourning in Canaan, Abraham was *promised* that he would gain possession of that land (Gen 15:17–18). Thus the situation would change radically for Abraham's seed. But nonetheless, the people living in fear of the Lord continued to confess in Canaan, in obedience to Lev 25:23: 'We are *also still* strangers, just like our fathers.' The sojourning therefore did not end, also not for Israel in the land of promise. And according to Heb 11 this means that, like Abraham, Israel also did not receive the actual promise. For them, too, it had to remain a searching for the better, i.e., the heavenly, country" (op. cit., 206). This corresponds with what the New Testament says about the believers as heirs of the world. As children of God they *are* heirs (Rom 8:17; cf. Rom 4:13; Titus 3:7; Heb 9:15), but the inheritance will only be given them later. "'Being children' contains the idea of being heirs, and this is not only a matter of the future, but certainly also of the present time (as becomes apparent particularly in Galatians). However, the gift that flows from being heirs, and which will also cause the 'being children' to be (fully) 'revealed' (Rom 8:19), is still a matter of hoping and waiting" (Herman Ridderbos, *Paulus*, 221–22). Cf., Matt 5:5; 1 John 3:2; Titus 3:7. The inheritance is kept in heaven, and salvation is ready to be revealed in the last time (1 Pet 1:4–5).

The sojourning of the Christian demands a corresponding walk of life (1 Pet 1:17. For my purposes in this study, the following is important:

(a) In sojourning, the *antithesis* is implied. For those whose citizenship is in heaven (Phil 3:20) there exists henceforth "the relationship of mutual strangeness and alienation between Christians and the world. That is indicated in John 3:8 by the comparison with the πνεῦμα; those born of the Spirit are, like Christ himself, unknown according to origin and goal. In the fact that they because of their ἄνωθεν γεννηθῆναι ['you must be born again'] (John 3:7) are, in distinction from the people of the world (cf. 1 John 4:5), not ἐκ τοῦ κόσμου [of the world] but rather, like Christ, are ἐκ τοῦ θεοῦ [of God] (cf. John 15:19; 17:14, 16) lies the mystery of their being strangers" (G. Stählin in *ThWB* V, 29, s.v. ξένος). This "separateness" is not an invention of Abraham Kuyper but already attracted attention in the days of Nero, when Christians were accused of *odium*

CHAPTER V. EVALUATION

humani generis, "hatred for the human race" (Tacitus). The church does not seek the antithesis, but it accepts it: "That is not the way you learned Christ" (Eph 4:20). The conflict between church and world is consequently unavoidable and should not even surprise Christians (1 Pet 4:12). "How could Christians let themselves be surprised? After all, the hostility of the world is in a certain sense natural for those who live in it as strangers" (Stählin, loc. cit.).

I have no difficulty with Kuyper's doctrine of the antithesis, but, even more than in the previous sections, I do have difficulty with his doctrine of common grace. *Is it not the necessary consequence* of this doctrine with its focus on culture, its own program, its own cultural grace, that it destroys what Scripture says about sojourning? Are we citizens of "two kinds of homeland" (p. 314 above), or of the *one*, the heavenly, homeland that also determines our conduct "in this foreign land," here on earth? I prefer Calvin's ethics, in which our sojourning also *remains* sojourning, to Kuyper's ethics, in which common grace constantly threatens to cause the concept of being "strangers and sojourners" to fade.

(b) The Christian walk of life must not display the evil of Anabaptist world avoidance, against which Kuyper warned. However, this evil does not flow from the correct confession of our sojourning. We are strangers, but strangers in a world that is subject to Christ's dominion and in which he gives us a task. Although we are not yet "home," we are where we belong. The proclamation of the gospel and the gathering of Christ's church have not yet been completed. Until they are, Christians have their calling in these earthly relationships. Besides, every kind of dualism that wants to flee the earthly life as inferior, forgets that God is busy with a cosmic redemption that envisions a new *humanity* gathered from out of the old. See § 3 of this chapter.

(c) Our calling toward the world is not fleeting in character: "You are the salt of the earth, ... you are the light of the world" (Matt 5:13–14). When the gospel is accepted by many, this can have the effect that also political, social, and cultural life will be influenced by it in a salutary way. The church does not exist (solely) in the catacombs. For that reason, it is in my view better to speak not of pilgrimage but of sojourning. Of these two words Calvin often uses the former, but not without danger. "Pilgrimage" is easily conjoined with the wrong idea of a fleeting contact between the pilgrims and their surroundings, as distinct from "sojourning." Pilgrims pass through a world that they want to leave behind as quickly as possible. Their calling *in* the world is then liable to be quickly pushed aside. Scripture nowhere speaks expressly about a "pilgrim's *journey* to eternity." As prototype of our sojourning the New Testament also does not have in mind the *nokri* of the Old Testament, the *migratory* stranger, but the *ger wetoshab*, the resident alien (H. J. Meijerink, op. cit., 204). We are strangers who, like the classic example of Abraham, are intensively involved with the world (pp. 42–44 above).

(d) But this intensive labor may never cause the church to forget its sojourning and to cease praying for the speedy return of Christ. Also (and especially!) in days of peace and prosperity the church must remember that Scripture characterizes it as church in the wilderness for the entire interim

CHAPTER V. EVALUATION

period (Rev 12). However, the doctrine of common grace, which does not include sojourning among its central tenets, is also confronted with the danger of secularization. Kuyper certainly did not have this in mind. But S. Greijdanus once pointed out ironically how easy it is to interpret texts such as 1 Cor 3:21ff. ("For all things are yours") in a worldly sense when it is forgotten that the enjoyment of all things will be given to us after this life: "All things are yours. Thus, Christian dance clubs and Christian dancing. Christian news cinema and movies. Christian theatre. Christian film. All is yours, and you are Christ's. And therefore we must get to work. Present things and things to come are yours, the entire world, everything. There is not a square inch in all of our human life of which Christ does not say: Mine! Well then, stand up, roll up your sleeves, get busy, young and old; establish societies, make alliances, put together organizations" (*Ref.* 23, 54).

But such reasoning, which may seem logical, is wrong, says Greijdanus. For the same Paul of 1 Cor 3 writes in 1 Cor 15:19: "If in Christ we have hope in this life only, we are of all people most to be pitied." And Christ says to his disciples: "I have overcome the world," but this is preceded immediately by: "In the world you will have tribulation" (John 16:33). "The good of the believers, the enjoyment of all things that is theirs in and through Christ, is not to be found here on earth, on this side of death and grave, but in eternity. Here there is tribulation, deprivation, suffering. Here we are guests and strangers (Heb 11:13; cf. also Phil 3:20); there liberation, glory, enjoyment will be ours" (loc. cit.).

Lofty plans for the conquest of the world (of culture) for Christ will result in the conquest of Christians by the world.

(e) The church which, as heir of "all things," will continue to be acquainted with struggle and fasting, often receives here below a foretaste of eternal *pleasure*. It may rejoice in the breadth and length and height and depth of the love of God and of Christ in the work of redemption (Eph 3:18). It may also delight, in accordance with Ps 8, in God's glorious name in all the earth. We must continue to work on this earth so that we may eat, as we heard Paul say. I place this modest cultural ordinance over against the broad cultural program of Kuyper and his followers (p. 385 above).

This doing "whatever your hand finds to do" (Eccl 9:10), which for the sake of the gospel is still necessary, allows us to eat and live not just in troubles and strife but often also already for the enjoyment of God's great works. This enjoyment (as well as the troubles and strife, Rom 5:3-4) are given to us to *praise* the name of God. Everywhere and at all times. Apart from their church attendance on Sundays, Christians do not make their way through the world anonymously. They *praise* the name of their God. "The glorifying and praising of the Lord's name as often as thankfulness is to be shown" is "always in the foreground" in Scripture; namely such glorifying and praising in which the *sincere* heart brings as sacrifice the bullocks of the *lips*" (Kuyper, *E Voto* III, 361). The Christian school offers more than "here and there" a "retouching of the material that is being taught" (Van Ruler, see p. 78 above). For it connects the name of God to his works. That is nothing "new," but it does pave the way for the most important thing: that human beings will glorify their God for his great works. The "exiles" already enjoy and sing of this, so that they may later at "home" on the new earth continue to do so without troubles and strife. Also the enjoyment of today calls for fulfillment: "Come, Lord Jesus!" (Rev 22:20).

In the foregoing I have aligned myself in a broad sense with Calvin. I agree with the point of departure of his ethics and the development of it according to Titus 2:11–14. In contrast, Kuyper's doctrine of common grace appeared to me to be unsound as the guideline for our labor in the world. I can agree much more with the views of Schilder. He also rejected common grace as foundation for our task in the world. He discerned clearly the danger of secularization that arises when Kuyper's doctrine is employed (pp. 223–24 above).

In addition, it greatly appeals to me that Schilder took his point of departure in Lord's Day 12 of the Heidelberg Catechism (about the Christian as officebearer), and that he identified the central place of the church as "fiery hearth," where Christians must be "charged" with power from on high for all their activities (pp. 202, 209 above).

I also pointed out already that the *specifi*cally cultural attention that is so typical of the doctrine of common grace appears in a much more modest form in Schilder (pp. 291–92, 310, 314–16 above). This explains also, I think, why he considered the above-quoted article by H. J. Meijerink to be "instructive" (*Ref.* 23, 264).

Various aspects of Schilder's own views on "Christ and culture" (pp. 186–210 above) were left undiscussed in this study because I had to concentrate on the topic of general grace." But the four questions I posed above also have a bearing on *Schilder's* positive appraisal of culture. I will summarize my objections briefly: Did Schilder not give an explanation of Lord's Day 12 (think of his definition of "culture," p. 188 above) that is strikingly congruent with what Kuyper wrote about God's cultural program and that for this reason rightly raises questions for us? Furthermore, did the concept of sojourning not lose in Schilder's exposition the central place that it had in Calvin? I have already remarked that when we compare Schilder and Kuyper with Calvin, the affinity between them is striking on more than one occasion (pp. 315–16 above).

§ 12. General grace?

I believe that the theologoumenon of general grace can maintain a legitimate place in theology provided that one speaks of it the way Calvin did. I have also noted the restricted nature of this theologoumenon when I was compelled to reject "general grace" in the sense of Kuyper's "common grace."

CHAPTER V. EVALUATION

The question mark following the heading of this section indicates that the answer to the question what "general grace" is depends on what the proponents of the term mean by it.

A theologoumenon is a topic in theology "about which theologians must still carry on discussions and about which they may differ among themselves" (V. Hepp, *De algemeene genade*, 8). It has become apparent to me that authors in Reformed theology have written in very different and very contradictory ways (sometimes it was the same author) about the topic dealt with in this study. This makes it impossible for me to answer with a simple yes or no the question whether we can speak of a general grace.

Contrary to what Kuyper maintained, there is *no* doctrine involved here—also not *the* doctrine of common grace, which supposedly was the "the sound point of view of all good Reformed people," as Hepp, quoting Bavinck, remarked in order to dismiss the suggestion that Kuyper's doctrine was to be characterized as a theologoumenon (loc. cit). The doctrine of general grace does not exist. We have seen how radical the differences between Kuyper and Calvin were. Both spoke of grace in a more general sense. But this grace was so different in orientation and fruit that I found it impossible to identify Kuyper with Calvin, although such identification was posited or suggested by Kuyper himself (pp. 4–5 above) and by S. U. Zuidema (p. 275), H. Kuiper (p. 271), and S. J. Ridderbos (p. 271).

But this divergence between Kuyper and Calvin must not let us forget that both speak of "general grace." In contrast, Schilder maintains that in scientific and semi-scientific usage the terms "common grace" and "general grace" "must be abandoned" (*Heid. Cat.* IV, 21)—in other words, that the theologoumenon of general grace has no right to exist, that it no longer deserves a place in theological literature, at least not once one begins to speak thetically.

In summary, our evaluation in this chapter has led to the following result:

1. Over against Schilder I maintain the *right* to speak of general grace. I have come to the conclusion, with a legitimate appeal to Scripture, that I can subscribe to the essentials of what Calvin says about our topic. In my view the consideration of Schilder's arguments yet remains to be completed. I have shown appreciation for the *motives* that drove Schilder to criticize the (use of the) doctrine of common grace (see pp. 211ff. above). But I believe that in the theological *formulation* of this criticism Schilder went too far. It *does remain* possible to use the term "general grace" legitimately.

2. Over against Kuyper, I posit the *limited nature* of the theologoumenon of general grace. Kuyper expanded it into a doctrine. Common grace, rooted in predestination, became the foundation of the whole of cultural history and also the principial basis for the cultural task of Christians in this world. Over against this I posited that, according to Scripture, general grace does not permit

CHAPTER V. EVALUATION

such an expansion. The direction and fruit of this grace, as Calvin portrayed it in accordance with Scripture, assign a much more modest place to the theologoumenon referred to than Kuyper did. In my opinion, Calvin's "general grace" does not lead to Kuyper's "common grace."

It is a legitimate question whether a heavily loaded term such as "general grace," which is often indiscriminately used together with "common grace," can then still be employed. *Verba valent usu* [words get their meaning in their use], and we live after Kuyper. It will be difficult to find a better designation, one that is less likely to be misunderstood. As is the case with other concepts in theology, the explanation of what one means by "general grace" will have to have the decisive last word.

My criticism of Schilder and Kuyper must remain within proper boundaries. Not only because I have discussed just one theme from the extensive *oeuvre* of both theologians. But especially because, in the treatment of this theme, I have come to know them as confessors of Christ who wanted to serve church and nation with the gospel and who also did so.

Those who keep this in mind will gladly conclude their examination the way J. P. A. Mekkes concluded his discussion of *Christus en cultuur*. After *far-reaching* criticism of this book of Schilder's, the reviewer says that he has pointed out "a few *deficiencies*" (emphasis supplied). This characterization was not a misplaced pleasantry but offered a correct evaluation. We can, according to Mekkes, "read Prof. Schilder's book in no other way than to share in his faith enthusiasm, which ... is *filled with the glory of the Christ*, and this is precisely what he intends to communicate to us."[1]

"The glory of the Christ." We really do not need to relativize the great mutual *differences* between Calvin, Kuyper, and Schilder in order constantly to recognize their mutual *harmony* in the praise of Christ.

---

1. J. P. A. Mekkes, "*Christus en cultuur*," review in *Polemios* 9, 29.

Bibliography

This bibliography contains only those works that have been cited in this study.[1]

Anema, S. *Davidisch of Salomonisch.* Kampen, 1927.
Aalders, G. Ch. *Het Boek Genesis.* Vol. 1. 2nd edition. In *Korte Verklaring der Heilige Schrift*, edited by G. Ch. Aalders et al. Kampen, 1949.
Acta et Scripta synodalia Dordracena ministrorum Remonstrantium in Foederato Belgio. Herder-vviici, 1620.
Acta ofte Handelinghen des nationalen Synodi. Edited by I. J. Canin. Shorter edition. Dordrecht, 1621.
Bakker, J. T. *Coram Deo.* Kampen, 1956.
Barth, K. *Die Kirchliche Dogmatik:*
  II/2 *Die Lehre von Gott.* Zurich, 1942.
  III/3 *Die Lehre von der Schöpfung.* Zurich, 1950.
  IV/1 *Die Lehre von der Versöhnung.* Zurich, 1953.
  IV/3 *Die Lehre von der Versöhnung.* Zurich, 1959.
_____, *Die Menschlichkeit Gottes.* Theologische Studien, Heft 48. Zurich, 1956.
_____, *Nein! Antwort an Emil Brunner.* Munich, 1934.
_____, *Der Römerbrief.* Reprint of first edition, 1919. Zurich, 1956.
_____, *Die Römerbrief.* 6th edition. Munich, 1933.
Barth, P. *Das Problem der natürlichen Theologie bei Calvin.* Munich, 1935.
Bauer, W. *Griechisch-Deutsches Wörterbuch.* 4th edition. Berlin, 1952.
Bavinck, Herman, *De Algemeene Genade.* Kampen, 1894.
_____, *Reformed Dogmatics.* Vols. 1 and 4. Edited by John Bolt. Translated by John Vriend. Grand Rapids: Baker Academic, 2003.
Berger, H. *Calvin's Geschichtsauffassung.* Zurich, 1955.
Berkhof, H. *Christus de zin der geschiedenis.* Nijkerk, 1958.
_____, *De mens onderweg.* The Hague, 1960.
Berkouwer, G. C. *Conflict met Rome.* 3rd edition. Kampen, 1955.
_____, *Dogmatische Studiën:*
  De Voorzienigheid Gods. Kampen, 1950.
  De Algemene Openbaring. Kampen, 1951.
  Het werk van Christus. Kampen, 1953.
  De Verkiezing Gods. Kampen, 1955.
  De Wederkomst van Christus. Vol. 1. Kampen, 1961.
_____, "Kuyper's beroep op Calvijn." *Gereformeerd Weekblad* 7, 41. Kampen, 1951.
_____, "Vragen rondom de belijdenis." *Gereformeerd Theologisch Tijdschrift* 63, 18ff. Kampen, 1963.
Beza, Th. *Tractationes Theologicae.* Vols. 1 and 3. Geneva, 1576 (1582).
Bohatec, J. *Calvin und das Recht.* Feudingen, 1934.
Bouma, C. *De brieven van den apostel Paulus aan Timotheus en Titus.* 2nd

---

1. If it is not mentioned in this study, the correct edition of a particular work to which reference has been made can be found in this bibliography.

edition. In *Korte Verklaring der Heilige Schrift*, edited by G. Ch. Aalders et al. Kampen, 1953.

_____, *Het Evangelie naar Johannes*. Vol. 2. 3rd edition. Also in *Korte Verklaring*. Kampen, 1950.

Brakel, W. a. *Redelyke Godts-dienst*. Vol 1. Rotterdam, 1707.

Bremmer, R. H. "De beteekenis van de vrijmaking voor theologie en leven." *De Reformatie* 25, 233ff. Goes, 1950.

Brunner, E. *Dogmatik*. 3rd edition. Vol. 1: *Die Christliche Lehre von Gott*. Zurich/Stuttgart, 1960.

_____, *Natur und Gnade: Zum Gespräch mit Karl Barth*. 2nd edition. Tübingen, 1935.

Calvin, John. *Institutes of the Christian Religion*. Edited by John T. McNeill. Translated by Ford Lewis Battles. 2 vols. Philadelphia: Westminster, 1960.

_____, *Commentaries*. 22 vols. Translated by John King et al. Calvin Translation Society, 1847–1850. Reprint, Grand Rapids: Baker Academic, 1999.

Cullmann, O. *Die Christologie des Neuen Testaments*. Tübingen, 1958.

Denzinger, H. *Enchiridion Symbolarum*. Edition 31. Barcelona, 1957.

Diepenhorst, I. A. *Algemeene Genade en Antithese*. Kampen, 1947.

Dijk, K. *De strijd over infra- and supralapsarisme in de Gereformeerde Kerken in Nederland*. Kampen, 1912.

Doekes, G. *De beteekenis van Israëls val*. Nijverdal, 1915.

Doekes, L. "Gevaarlijk kruispunt."*De Reformatie* 29, 341. Goes, 1954.

_____, "Kinderen des verbonds." *De Reformatie* 22, 333, 398–99. Goes, 1947.

_____, "Om het verbond." *De Reformatie* 22, 182–83. Goes, 1947.

Dooren, G. van., and I. de Wolf, *De Geschiedenis der Godsopenbaring*. Vol. 1. Enschede [n.d.].

Dooyeweerd, H. *A New Critique of Theoretical Thought*. Vols. 1 and 2 (1953). Amsterdam/Philadelphia, 1955.

Faber, J. "Kosmisch Geesteswerk." *De Reformatie* 35, 277–78. Goes, 1960.

Fraine J. de. *Genesis*. In *De Boeken van het Oude Testament*, edited by A. van den Born et al. Roermond/Maaseik, 1963.

Gispen, W. H. *Het boek Leviticus*. In *Commentaar of het Oude Testament*, edited by G. Ch. Aalders et al. Kampen, 1950.

_____, *De Spreuken van Salomo*. Vol. 2. In *Korte Verklaring der Heilige Schrift*, edited by G. Ch. Aalders et al. Kampen, 1954.

Gomarus, F. *Opera Theologica Omnia*. Amsterdam, 1664.

Graaf, S. G. de. *Christus en de wereld*. Kampen, [1939].

_____, "De genade Gods en de structuur der gansche schepping." *Philosophia Reformata* 1, 17ff. Kampen, 1936.

_____, *Het ware geloof*. Kampen, 1954.

Greijdanus, S. "Kerk en Koninkrijk Gods." In *Congres van Gereformeerden*, March 30–April 1, 1948. *Referaten-bundel*. Kampen, [1948].

_____, *De brief van den apostel Paulus aan de gemeente te Rome*. Vol. 1.

BIBLIOGRAPHY

In *Kommentaar op het Nieuwe Testament*, edited by S. Greijdanus et al. Amsterdam, 1933.
_____, *De brieven van de apostelen Petrus en Johannes, en de brief van Judas*. Also in *Kommentaar op het Nieuwe Testament*. Amsterdam, 1929.
_____, *Het Evangelie naar Lucas*. Vol. 1. 2nd edition. In *Korte Verklaring der Heilige Schrift*, edited by G. Ch. Aalders et al. Kampen, 1955.
_____, *De tweede brief van den apostel Petrus*. 2nd edition. Also in *Korte Verklaring*. Kampen, 1950.
_____, *De openbaring des Heeren aan Johannes*. 3rd edition. Also in *Korte Verklaring*. Kampen, 1955.
_____, *De openbaring Gods in het Nieuwe Testament over Zijn genadeverbond*. Enschede, [1946].
_____, "Verovering der wereld." *De Reformatie* 23, 54–55. Goes, 1947.
_____, "Waartoe het kwaad in de wereld." In *De Wachter* 40, no. 40. Kampen, 1942.
_____, *Wezen van het Calvinisme*. Franeker, 1941.
Grosheide, F. W. *Het heilig Evangelie volgens Mattheus*. In *Commentaar op het Nieuwe Testament*, edited by S. Greijdanus and F. W. Grosheide. Kampen, 1954.
Gunkel, H. *Genesis*. In *Göttinger Handkommentar zum Alten Testament*, edited by W. Nowack. Göttingen, 1910.
Haitjema, Th. L. "Boekbespreking: Ds. A. A. van Ruler, *Kuyper's idee eener Christelijke cultuur*." *Onder eigen Vaandel* 16, 159–60. Wageningen, 1941.
_____, "De Cultuur-waardering van het Nieuw-Calvinisme." *Onze Eeuw* 19, part 4, 83ff. Haarlem, 1919.
_____, "De Gereformeerde Theologie in Nederland." *Vox Theologica* 3, 69ff. Assen, 1932.
_____, "Zestig jaren Nederlandsche theologie." *Onder eigen Vaandel* 6, 34ff. Wageningen, 1931.
Hepp, V. *De algemeene genade*. In *Dreigende Deformatie*. Vol. 4: *Symptomen*. Kampen, 1937.
_____, "De kwestie van de Algemeene Genade." *De Reformatie* 4, 152–53, 344ff. Goes, 1924.
Hoekendijk, J. C. "Het Christendom in de wereldgeschiedenis." *Wending* 19, 808ff. The Hague, 1965.
Hoeksema, H. *Het Evangelie, of De Jongste Aaanval op de Waarheid der Soevereine Genade*. Grand Rapids, 1933.
_____, *Dat Gods goedheid particulier is*. Grand Rapids, 1939.
_____, *Een kracht Gods tot zaligheid*. 2nd edition. Grand Rapids, 1931.
_____, *De Plaats der Verwerping in de Verkondiging des Evangelies*. Grand Rapids, 1927.
_____, *The Protestant Reformed Churches in North America*. Grand Rapids, 1927.
Holwerda, B. *De crisis van het gezag*. Groningen, [1947].
_____, *Historia Revelationis Veteris Testamenti*. Vol. 1. Lectures. Kampen, 1954.

Holwerda, D. *Commentatio de vocis quae est 'phusis': VI atque usu praesertim in graecitate Aristotele anteriore.* Groningen, 1955.
_____, *O Diepte des Rijkdoms.* Utrecht, 1949.
Honert T. Hzn., J. van den. *Verhandelingen van Gods niet algemeene, maar besondere genade.* Leiden, 1726.
Humbert, P. *Études sur le récit du paradis et de la chute dans la Genèse.* Neuchatel, 1940.
Hylkema, C. B. *Oude- en Nieuw-Calvinisme.* Haarlem, 1911.
Janse, A. "Een brief van broeder Janse." *Opbouw* 6, 175. Zeist, 1962.
Jong, A. C. de. *The Well-Meant Gospel Offer.* Franeker, 1954.
Jongeling, P. *Terwille van het Koninkrijk.* Groningen, 1956.
Kamphuis, J. "De algemene genade bij dr. A. Kuyper." *Jeugd en Politiek* 1, no. 6, 1ff. Utrecht, 1964.
_____, *De hedendaagse kritiek op de causaliteit bij Groen van Prinsterer als historicus.* Goes, 1962.
_____, *Katholieke vastheid.* Goes, 1955.
_____, "De langzame haast des Heeren." *De Reformatie* 26, 361ff. Goes, 1951.
_____, "Over: het 'aanbod der genade.'" *De Reformatie* 31, 289ff. Goes, 1956.
_____, (using Leo Dregt as pseudonym). "Over 'de gemene gratie.'" *De Reformatie* 33, 39ff. Goes, 1957.
_____, *Verkenningen.* Vol. 1. Goes, 1963.
_____, "Zicht op Calvijn." *De Reformatie* 41, 53ff. Goes, 1965.
Kasteel, P. *Abraham Kuyper.* Kampen, 1938.
Keulers, J. *Het evangelie volgens Joannes.* Roermond/Maaseik, 1951.
_____, *De brieven van Paulus.* Vol. 1. Roermond/Maaseik, 1953.
Kittel, G., et al. *Theologisches Wörterbuch zum Neuen Testament.* 2nd edition. Vols. 1–8. Stuttgart, 1953–1966.
Kolfhaus, W. *Vom christlichen Leben nach Johannes Calvin.* Neukirchen, 1949.
Kraus, H. J. *Psalmen.* Vol. 1. In *Biblischer Kommentar Altes Testament*, edited by Martin Noth. Neukirchen, 1960.
Krusche, W. *Das Wirken des Heiligen Geistes nach Calvin.* Göttingen, 1957.
Kuiper, H. *Calvin on Common Grace.* Goes, 1928.
Kuitert, H. M. *De mensvormigheid Gods.* Kampen, 1962.
Kuyper, A. *Antirevolutionaire Staatkunde.* Vols. 1 and 2. Kampen, 1916–1917.
_____, *Bedoeld noch Gezegd.* Amsterdam, 1885.
_____, *Calvinism: Six Lectures Delivered in the Theological Seminary at Princeton.* Grand Rapids, Eerdmans, 1931. Reprint, Edinburgh: T&T Clark, 1999.
_____, *Calvinisme en Revisie.* Amsterdam, 1891.
_____, *De Christus en de sociale noden.* Amsterdam, 1891.
_____, *Confidentie.* Amsterdam, 1873.
_____, *Dictaten Dogmatiek.* 2nd edition. Kampen, [1910–1911].
N.B. Kuyper dealt with the *Loci* in his lectures in the following order (see J. C. Rullmann, *Kuyper-bibliografie* III, 266):
  De Sacra Scriptura. 1881–1888.

De Creatione (not included in the Lecture Notes). 1884.
De Creaturis. 1884.
De Homine. 1885.
De Peccato. 1885–1886.
De Christ. 1886–1888.
De Salute. 1889.
De Sacramentis. 1890.
De Consummatione saeculi, 1891.
De Ecclesia. 1892.
De Magistratu. 1893.
De Deo. 1894–1897.
De Providentia. 1898.
De Foedere. 1899.
De Creatione (2nd ed.). 1900.
_____, *Uit het diensthuis uitgeleid*. Kampen, 1912.
_____, *Drie kleine Vossen*. Kampen, 1901.
_____, *Eer is teer*. Amsterdam, 1889.
_____, *Encyclopaedie der Heilige Godgeleerdheid*. Vol. 2. Amsterdam, 1894.
_____, *Idem*. Vols. 1–3. 2nd edition. Kampen, 1908–1909.
_____, *De Gemeene Gratie*. 4th edition. Kampen, [n.d.].
N.B. The pagination of the *first* edition (Amsterdam/Pretoria: Höveker and Wormser, 1902–1905) differs from that of the 2nd to the 4th editions (Kampen: J.H. Kok).
_____, *IJzer en leem*. Amsterdam, 1885.
_____, *Maranatha*. 5th edition. Amsterdam, 1891.
_____, *De Meiboom in de kap*. Kampen, 1913.
_____, *Niet de Vrijheidsboom maar het Kruis*. Amsterdam, 1889.
_____, *"Ons Program."* Large edition with appendices. Amsterdam, 1879.
_____, *Pro Rege*. Vols. 1–3. Kampen, 1911–1912.
_____, *Revisie der Revisie-Legende*. Amsterdam, 1879.
_____, *Rome en Dordt*. Amsterdam, 1879.
_____, *Scolastica*. Vol. 1. Amsterdam, 1889.
_____, *Het sociale vraagstuk en de Christelijke religie*. Amsterdam, 1891.
_____, *Souvereiniteit in eigen kring*. 3rd edition. Kampen, 1930.
_____, *Tweeërlei Vaderland*. Amsterdam, 1887.
_____, *Uit het Woord*. 1st series. Vols. I–3. 2nd edition. Amsterdam, [n.d.].
_____, *Uit het Woord*. 2nd series. Vols. 1–3 (vol. 1: *Dat de genade particulier is*; vol. 2: *De Leer der Verbonden*). Amsterdam, 1884–1886.
_____, *De Vleeschwording des Woords*. Amsterdam, 1887.
_____, *Van de Voleinding*. Vols. 1–4. Kampen, 1929–1931.
_____, *Volharden bij het ideaal*. Amsterdam, 1901.
_____, *Voor den Slag*: Utrecht, 1909.
_____, *Het Werk van den Heiligen Geest*. 2nd edition. Kampen, 1927.
_____, *Wij Calvinisten*. Kampen, 1909.
_____, *De wortel in de dorre aarde*. Kampen, 1916.
Kuyper, H. S. S., and J. H. Kuyper, eds. *Herinneringen van de oude garde aan den persoon en den levensarbeid van Dr. A. Kuyper*. Amsterdam, 1922.

Lamparter, H. *Das Buch der Psalmen*. Vol. 2. In *Die Botschaft des Alten Testaments*. Stuttgart, 1959.
Lang, A. "The Reformation and the Natural Law." In *Calvin and the Reformation*. London/Edinburgh, 1909.
Langman, H. J. *Kuyper en de Volkskerk*. Kampen, 1950.
_____, "De moderne cultuur." *Trouw*, 2 February 1963.
Leeuwen, P. A. van. *Het kerkbegrip in de theologie van Abraham Kuyper*. Franeker, 1946.
Léon-Dufour, X., et al. *Vocabulaire de théologie biblique*. Paris, 1962.
Lewis, Charlton T., and Charles Short. *A Latin Dictionary*. Oxford: Clarendon Press, 1962.
Lettinga, J. P. "Van een oud 'kruis.'" *De Reformatie* 32, 232. Goes, 1957.
Marck, J. a. *Het Merch der christene Got-geleertheit*. Rotterdam, 1758.
Mastricht, P. van. *Theoretica-Practica Theologia*. Vol. 2. Amsterdam, 1724.
Meijerink, H. J. "De leer der 'gemeene gratie' bij de remonstranten." *De Reformatie* 24, 157ff. Goes, 1949.
_____, "Vreemdeling en Erfgenaam. " In *Handboek ten dienste van de Gereformeerde Kerken in Nederland (onderh. art. 31 K.O.)*, edited by K. Schilder. Goes, 1948.
Mekkes, J. P. A. Review of *Christus en cultuur*, by K. Schilder. *Polemios* 9, 20 (1953/54).
Noordmans, O. "De algemeene genade." *De Reformatie* 16, 115ff. Goes, 1936.
Ottolander, P. den. *Deus Immutabilis*. Assen, 1965.
Polyander, J., et al. *Synopsis Purioris Theologiae*. Edited by H. Bavinck. 6th edition. Leiden, 1881.
Popma, K. J. *Levensbeschouwing*. Vol. 1. Amsterdam, 1958.
Plooy, C. P. "De openbaring van Johannes en het sociale leven." *Contact* 2, no. 8, 4ff. Groningen, 1952.
Quistorp, H. *Calvin's Doctrine of the Last Things*. London, 1955.
Rad, G. von. *Das erste Buch Mose*. In *Das Alte Testament Deutsch*, edited by V. Herntrich and A. Weiser. Göttingen, 1952.
Rahner, K. "Natuur en genade volgens de leer van de Katholieke Kerk." In *Brandpunten van de hedendaagse theologie*. Hilversum/Amsterdam, 1962.
Ridderbos, H. N. *Aan de Romeinen*. In *Commentaar op het Nieuwe Testament*, edited by S. Greijdanus and F. W. Grosheide. Kampen, 1959.
_____, *Aan de Kolossenzen*. Also in *Commentaar op het Nieuwe Testament*. Kampen, 1960.
_____, "Eerherstel voor cultuur theologie." *Gereformeerd Weekblad* 14, 74. Kampen, 1958.
_____, *Paulus*. Kampen, 1966.
Ridderbos, J. *Het Godswoord der Profeten*. Vol. 3: *Van Nahum tot Jeremia*. Kampen, 1938.
Riessen, H. van. "De uitdaging van de moderne cultuur." In *De moderne cultuur en de christelijke school*. Kampen, 1962.
Riggenbach, E. *Der Brief an die Hebräer*. In *Kommentar zum Neuen Testament*, edited by Th. Zahn. Leipzig, 1913.

Rothuizen, G. Th. *Primus usus legis*. Kampen, 1962.
_____, *Tweeërlei ethiek bij Calvijn?* Kampen, 1964.
Ruler, A. A. van. *Kuyper's idee eener Christelijke cultuur*. Nijkerk, [n.d.].
Rullmann, J. C. *Kuyper-bibliographie*, Vols. 1–3. The Hague/Kampen, 1923–1940.
Schilder, K. *Bij dichters en schriftgeleerden*. Amsterdam, 1927.
_____, *Bovenschriftuurlijke binding:een nieuw gevaar*. Goes, 1952.
_____, *Christus en cultuur*, 3rd edition. Franeker: T. Wever, 1953. 4th edition. Annotated by Jochem Douma. Franeker: T. Wever, 1978. Translated as *Christ and Culture*, by William Helder and Albert H. Oosterhoff. Hamilton: Lucerna CRTS Publications, 2016.
_____, *Christus en Zijn lijden*. Vols. 1–3. Kampen, 1930. Translated as *Christ in His Suffering*, *Christ on Trial*, and *Christ Crucified* by Henry Zijlstra. Grand Rapids: Religious Publications, 1938. Reprint, Minneapolis: Klock and Klock, 1978.
_____, *Christus in Zijn lijden*. Vols. 1–3. 2nd edition. Kampen, 1949–1952.
_____, *Geen duimbreed*. Kampen, [1936].
_____, "De Gemeene Gratie." In *Congres van Gereformeerden* (March 30–April 1, 1948). *Verslag*. Kampen, [1952].
_____, "'Gemeene Gratie' en verwereldlijking." *Gereformeerde Kerkbode van Delft*, 14 and 21 February 1925. Delft, 1925.
_____, *Heidelbergsche Catechismus*, vols. 1 and 2 (to the extent published), 1st edition. Goes: 1938–1940.
_____, *Heidelbergsche Catechismus*, 2nd edition, vols. 1–4. Goes, 1947–1953.
_____, "Jezus Christus en het cultuurleven." In H. L. Both et al., *Jezus Christus en het menschenleven*. Culemborg, 1932.
_____, *De Kerk*. Vols. 1–2. In *Verzamelde Werken*, Part 3. Goes, 1960–1962.
_____, *Licht in de Rook*, 3rd edition. Delft: 1951.
_____, *Looze Kalk*. Groningen, 1946.
_____, *Om Woord en Kerk*. Vols. 1–4. Goes, 1948–1953.
_____, *Ons aller moeder anno Domini 1935*. Kampen, [1935].
_____, *De Openbaring van Johannes en het sociale leven*. 3rd edition. Delft, 1951.
_____, *Preken*. Vols. 1–3. In *Verzamelde Werken*, Part 1. Goes, 1954–1955.
_____, *De Reformatie: Weekblad tot ontwikkeling van het Gereformeerde Leven*. Vols. 8–27. Goes, 1927–1952.
_____, *Schriftoverdenkingen*. Vols. 1–3. In *Verzamelde Werken*, Part 2. Goes, 1956–1958.
_____, *Tusschen "Ja" en "Neen."* Kampen, 1929.
_____, "Twee bijdragen tot de bespreking der 'Gemeene-Gratie'-idee." In *Almanak Fides Quaerit Intellectum 1947*. Kampen, 1947.
_____, *Wat is de hel?*, 2nd edition. Kampen, 1932.
_____, *Wat is de hemel?*, 2nd edition. Kampen, 1954.
Schleiermacher, Fr. *Reden über die Religion*. Edited by S. Lommatzch. Gotha, 1888.
Sietsma, K. "Bespreking van: V. Hepp, *De algemeene genade*," reprinted in part in *De Reformatie* 18, 208. Goes, 1938.

Smit, M. C. *The Divine Mystery in History*. Kampen, 1955.
Sperna Weiland, J. "Er is iets aan het gebeuren." *Wending* 20, 617. The Hague, 1965.
Spier, J. M. "Iets over de methode van de vierde brochure van Prof. Hepp." *De Reformatie* 18, 84ff. Goes, 1937.
Trench, R. C. *Synonyms of the New Testament*. Grand Rapids, 1958.
Trigland, J. *Meditationes in opiniones variorum de voluntate Dei et gratia universali*. Leiden, 1642.
Trimp, C. "Heimelijke aanslag op het lofoffer van Dordt." *De Reformatie* 31, 380–81. Goes, 1956.
_____, *Tot een levendige troost Zijns volks*. Goes, 1954.
Van Til, C. *Common Grace*. Philadelphia, 1947.
Veenhof, C. "Aanbod van genade." *De Reformatie* 28, 380–81. Goes, 1953.
_____, "Calvijn en de prediking." In *Zicht op Calvijn, Christelijk Perspectief*, vol. 7. Amsterdam, 1965.
_____, "God wil dat alle mensen behouden worden." *De Reformatie* 30, 321–22. Goes, 1955.
_____, and A. Zijlstra, eds. *Kracht en doel der Politiek*. Goes, 1948.
_____, "Over Christus' 'wezen' en 'eigenlijke' ambt en woord." *De Reformatie* 30, 289ff. Goes, 1955.
_____, *Predik het Woord*. Goes, [n.d.].
_____, *Souvereiniteit in eigen kring*. Kampen, 1939.
_____, *De volkomenheid der Sacramenten*. Goes, [n.d.].
Velema, W. H. "De genadeleer in de theologie van Kuyper." *Kerk en Theologie* 11, 207ff. Wageningen, 1960.
_____, *De leer van de Heilige Geest bij Abraham Kuyper*. The Hague, 1957.
Venema, H. *Uitverkiezen en Uitverkiezing in het Nieuwe Testament*. Kampen, 1965.
Vonk, C. *De Voorzeide Leer*. Vol. 1b. Barendrecht, 1963.
Visee, G. "Over het 'anthropomorphe' spreken Gods in de Heilige Schrift." *De Reformatie* 28, 273ff. Goes, 1953.
Vriezen, Th. C. "Einige Notizen zur Übersetzung des Bindeswortes *kî*." In *Von Ugarit nach Qumran*, edited by J. Hempel and L. Rost. *Zeitschrift für alttestamentliche Wissenschaft* 77. Berlin, 1958.
Walaeus, A. *Opera*. Leiden, 1647–1648.
Zanden, L. van der. *De mensch als beeld Gods*. Kampen, 1939.
Zuidema, S. U. "Gemene Gratie en Pro Rege bij Dr. Abraham Kuyper." *Antirevolutionaire Staatkunde* 24, 1ff. Kampen, 1954.

Name Index

Aalders, G. Ch., 151, 154–55, 342
Andel, L. van, 159
Anema, S., 365
Aquinas, Thomas, 34 (fn. 142), 121, 227
Aratus, 235
Aristides, 238 (fn. 29), 246, 278
Aristotle, 79, 236, 240
Augustine, 129ff., 134, 135, 219, 248, 278

Bakker, T. J., 365
Baltus, P., 82
Barth, K., 158, 199 (fn. 320) 255–58, 286–87, 322, 335, 339–40
Barth, P., 233, 258
Bauer, W., 350
Bavinck, H., 6, 37, 96, 107, 146, 169–70, 299, 303, 324, 327, 329–30, 333, 391
Behm, J., 342, 348
Bellarminus, R. F. R., 120
Berg, M. van den, 99
Berger, H., 234, 313
Berkhof, H., 60, 380, 383, 384–85
Berkhof, L., 139
Berkouwer, G. C., 120, 142–43, 185 (fn. 241), 229 (also fn. 376), 231–32, 297, 300, 321, 324, 332–33, 338–40, 366–67, 368–69, 383
Bernard of Morlaix, 386
Beza, Th., 331
Boethius, 209

Bohatec, J., 257
Bonhoeffer, D., 107, 109
Bouma, C., 357–58, 382
Brakel, W. a, 362
Bremmer, R. H., 91, 127
Bronsveld, A. W., 118
Brunner, E., 255ff.
Bultmann, R., 155 (fn. 115), 345

Calvin, John, 1–2, 4–5, 42, 121, 123, 126–27, 135–36, 138, 159, 186, 197–98, 227, 233–392 *passim*
Caligula, 238, 242, 272
Camillus, 238, 242, 243
Catiline, 238, 243
Cato, 242
Chrysostom, 382
Cicero, 234, 236
Cock, Hendrik de, 227
Crates, 281
Cullmann, O., 339, 383
Curius, 238 (fn. 29), 243

Darwin, C., 79
Dee, S. P., 254
Delling, G., 323, 325
Demosthenes, 236
Denzinger, H., 286
Descartes, R., 136–37
Diagoras, 272
Dionysius, 272
Dibbets, H. J., 127
Diepenhorst, I. A., 313
Dijk, K., 329–31
Doekes, G., 322, 328–29

NAME INDEX

Doekes, L., 331, 374
Domitian, 238, 242
Dooren, G. van., 341
Dooyeweerd, H., 360–61, 380
Dorotheus, 150

Faber, J., 359
Fabius (Cunctator), 243
Fabius, D. P. D., 365
Fabricius, 243, 272
Foerster, W., 340, 357
Fraine, J. de, 378

Giblet, J., 350
Gispen, W. H., 342, 377
Gogarten, F., 107
Gomarus, F., 180, 332, 361
Graaf, S. G. de, 60, 168–69, 307, 343, 350, 351, 359–60, 386
Greijdanus, S., 141 (also fn. 57), 142, 155ff. (also fns. 115, 118, 122), 161 (fn. 144), 163–64, 170, 184, 206, 324, 328, 345, 347–48, 350, 352–53, 356–57, 371–72, 375, 377, 384–85, 389
Groen van Prinsterer, G., 109, 110, 367
Grosheide, F. W., 169, 335
Gunkel, H., 378
Gunning, J. W., 109–10, 113
Gunning, J. H., 233 (fn. 1)

Haitjema, Th. L., 50, 104, 117, 211, 299, 349
Heidegger, J. H., 154
Hepp, V., 95–96, 137, 168–69, 228, 234 (fn. 4), 307, 359, 365, 391

Hitler, A., 197, 200
Hoedemaker, Ph. J., 77, 79
Hoekendijk, J. C., 381
Hoeksema, H., 229, 231–32, 332–33, 353, 354–55, 374
Holwerda, B., 325, 340
Holwerda, D., 163, 325
Honert T. Hzn, J. van den, 327
Horst, J., 356
Humbert, P., 378
Hylkema, C. B., 302, 304

Isodore of Pelusium, 150

Janse, A., 371
Jong, A. C. de, 285, 307, 374
Jongeling, P., 115 (fn. 411)

Kamphuis, J., 82–83 (also fn. 314), 91, 305, 307, 330, 331, 367, 369, 374
Kant, I., 24, 79
Kasteel, P., 115
Kittel, G., 322, 325, 339
Keulers, J., 382, 385
Kolfhaus, W., 283
Kooiman, W. J., 228
Kraus, H. J., 381
Krusche, W., 233–34 (also fn. 4), 254, 256, 257, 259, 263, 264, 359
Kuiper, H., 136, 233–34 (also fn. 4), 245, 247, 262, 264, 288, 296, 297, 299, 302, 303, 308, 362, 364, 391
Kuitert, H.M., 327, 365, 369
Kuyper, A., 1, 3–232 *passim*, 233, 285–392 *passim*

NAME INDEX

Lamparter, H., 353
Lang, A., 257
Langman, H. J., 60, 83 (fn. 321)
Leeuwen, P. A. van, 88 (fn. 355), 91, 95 (also fn. 373), 97
Lettinga, J. P., 342
Lewis, C. T., 305
Limborch, Ph. à, 132
Lingen, F. Ph. L. C., 227
Lubbertus, S., 372
Luther, M., 11, 197–98, 227

Marck, J. à, 139, 362, 363
Marx, K., 386
Mastricht, P. van, 362ff.
Maurer, C., 323, 325, 347–48
Meijerink, H. J., 286, 385–86, 387, 388, 390
Mekkes, J. P. A., 392 (also fn. 1)
Michel, O., 322
Molinaeus, P., 329
Moor, B. de, 139 (also fn. 49)

Nero, 238, 242, 388
Niesel, W., 234
Nietzsche, Fr., 386
Noordmans, O., 200, 217, 295,

Oepke, A., 322, 323
Ottolander, P. den, 369

Paraeus, D., 134 (also fn. 25), 135, 169, 185, 308, 361
Pelagius, 130–31, 132, 134, 135, 363
Pierson, A., 110

Plato, 79, 234, 235 (fn. 10), 236, 238, 239, 286
Plooy, C. P., 223
Popma, K. J., 369
Plutarch, 235
Prins, P., 137, 206

Quistorp, H., 313

Rad, G. von, 378
Rahner, K., 286
Reicke, B., 323
Ridderbos, H. N., 117, 320, 321, 323–25, 334, 329, 343, 348, 387
Ridderbos, J., 327, 328
Ridderbos, S. J., 16, 59, 70, 85, 91, 92–93, 95, 104, 107, 111 (also fn. 408), 168, 173 (fn. 180), 299, 306–07, 308, 349, 377, 391
Riessen, H. van, 60
Riggenbach, E., 382
Rothe, R., 97
Rothuizen, G. Th., 96, 99–114, 258–60, 337–38
Ruler, A. A. van, 49, 57, 71ff., 110, 114, 117, 122, 200, 295–96, 389
Rullmann, J. C., 117

Sasse, H., 326
Schilder, K., 1–2, 17, 81, 129–232 *passim*, 233, 285–392 *passim*
Schleiermacher, Fr., 97, 337
Schrenk, G., 324, 325, 358
Schultze, M., 313

NAME INDEX

Scipio, 238 (fn. 29), 243
Short, C., 305
Sietsma, K., 307
Sikkel, J. C., 365
Smit, M. C., 367
Socrates, 238 (fn. 29)
Sperna Weiland, J., 386
Spier, J. M., 169
Stählin, G., 323, 366, 387
Suarez, F., 131

Tacitus, 388
Tagore, Rabindranath, 211
Tiberius, 238, 242
Titus, 238, 242
Trajan, 238, 142
Trench, R. C., 364
Trigland, J., 132, 135, 166, 169, 204 (fn. 340), 299, 332, 361
Trimp, C., 329–30, 335

Uittenbogaert, J., 166
Ursinus, Z., 185 (fn. 248)

Van Til, C., 372ff.
Veenhof, C., 55 (fn. 230), 95, 96, 268 (fn. 195), 272, 274, 305, 366, 374
Vespasian, 238, 242
Velema, W. H., 17, 33, 85, 91, 105, 121, 125
Venema, H., 325
Visee, G., 328, 365, 369
Vitringa, C., 153 (fn. 113)
Vonk, C., 342
Vriezen, Th. C., 342

Walaeus, A., 331, 335

Xenocrates, 238 (fn. 29)

Zahn, Th., 155 (fn. 115)
Zanden, L. van der, 168
Zuidema, S. U., 91, 93–94, 96, 303, 391
Zwier, D., 218

CULTURE AND OUR BEING SOJOURNERS

What follows is a revised version of a paper I delivered on 27 September 1968 at the 21st lustrum [quinquennial celebration] of *Fides Quadrat Intellectum*, a fraternity of theological students in Kampen, the Netherlands. Original title: *Cultuur en vreemdelingschap*.

It is almost two years ago that I published my study *Algemene Genade* [General Grace] and defended it as my dissertation at the Theological Seminary of the Reformed Churches in the Netherlands (Liberated) in Kampen.[1] It was to be expected that the dissertation would draw criticism.

There was indeed criticism—in addition to much appreciation for the whole dissertation and various parts of it. Actually I can hardly use the phrase "in addition to," for the criticism was for the most part so courteous and appreciative that I have no cause to complain. Besides, the dissertation received much publicity through reviews both within and outside of the Netherlands. Hence I may surmise that it will not end up in the mausoleum of libraries for the time being.

I had no cause to complain, but neither did I have cause to rest on the laurels of the "highest honor" received along with the doctoral degree. The topic of my study was too all-embracing and the criticism too fundamental to permit this.

Accordingly, I am glad to resume the thread of 1966 and it is a pleasure to cross swords again on a topic that deserves more in-depth investigation.

I shall have to limit myself somewhat. This discussion will concentrate principally on the fundamental issue of culture and sojourning that became the focus of the discussion after the dissertation was published. Further, I shall limit my answer to those who raised criticisms from within the Reformed Churches.

By means of seven propositions, I am pleased to provide a further account of my views.

---

1. J. Douma, *Algemene Genade: Uiteenzetting, vergelijking en beoordeling van de opvattingen van A. Kuyper, K. Schilder en Joh. Calvijn over "algemeene genade"* (Goes: Oosterbaan & Le Cointre, 1966).

APPENDIX – CULTURE AND OUR BEING SOJOURNERS

1. *In my response to the criticism that was received from within the Reformed Churches against my views on "culture and our being sojourners" (Dissertation, Chapter V, § 11), I continue to maintain that in the reciprocal rejection of cultural avoidance, the mutual differences are focused on the question where the emphases fall in our acceptance of culture (Dissertation, p. 385).*

It is not a bad thing to begin with this proposition. Differences have become apparent, but we must not make too much of them either. In the current ecclesiastical situation there is a serious need for deeper reflection about various theological questions that are of great significance for the life of the Reformed Churches. But this discussion must take place in an atmosphere of mutual trust. And that is possible when we recognize each other in our desire to let Holy Scripture and its interpretation in the confession of the church have the final say.

The testing of one's own ideas, which have sometimes become fixed, is necessary and possible within a properly functioning church community. We will never finish this process. I acknowledged this for myself in chapter V, § 11, by raising four *questions*, the answers to which, as point of departure for further discussion, could also serve to instruct *me*.

Besides, we all unanimously reject cultural avoidance that would place us outside of the world and within the walls of monasteries. To bear one's cross joyfully is something different than taking pleasure in isolation. The church has a message for her members and for the world. The message is not only for the heart, but from out of that heart it demands of its hearers that it be given shape in all of life.

The unanimity on this point makes our discussion a pleasure. For that reason it was more than a mandatory courtesy that caused Professor Kamphuis to write at the conclusion of a number of critical remarks that he is firmly of the opinion that he and I find agreement "in the belief in our calling to, and the love for, this *Christian* life—the life that submits itself to the dominion of him who is coming."[2] I concur in this without reservation.

2. *De Reformatie* 41, 258 (incorrectly identified as p. 158), (Goes, 1967).

Our differences are *differences of emphasis*. I continue to maintain this in respect of all criticism from within our own circles. In fulfilling our calling as church in this world we heartily cooperate in various organizational relationships. But in the matter of the *theoretical foundations* of our calling we differ on where we place the emphases. What should be the basis of our cultural endeavor? What are its perspectives and limits?

"Differences in emphases"—those are the words I used in my dissertation. But these differences are nonetheless important enough to discuss. To make that clear, allow me to draw a parallel. When in 1935 Schilder raised significant criticisms about the doctrine of common grace in *Wat is de hemel?* he called the distinction between Kuyper's views and his own "more a matter of word choice and especially of method ... than of content."[3] But history moved on. The clash of opinions does not always lead to the truth, but often to a hardening in established opinions, and even to ruptures in the church. That is what happened in the Reformed world. And when the impure elements of the doctrine of common grace became more and more evident in practice, it became impossible after the Liberation to tolerate new wine in old leather wineskins. At the Congress in Amersfoort in 1948, the same Schilder declared that the thesis of common grace "conflicts with Scripture and the confession" and must be abandoned.[4]

I hope that God will grant the Reformed Churches many years of peace in which the binding to the confession of these churches will serve as the basis for united Christian cultural effort. Then the *differences* in emphases, which will keep open the possibility of a *shift* in emphases, will truly not cause us to become estranged from one another.

2. *Despite all the differences between Schilder and Kuyper regarding "common grace," there is clear agreement about the cultural mandate that was given in Paradise in order to achieve "the systematized striving for the sum-total of labor that in a gradual process is to be attained by the*

---

3. *Wat is de hemel?* 2nd edition, 213 (Kampen, 1954).
4. *De Gemeene Gratie*, in *Congres van Gereformeerden* (March/April 1958), Report, 100 (Kampen, [1952]).

sum-total of humanity." This profound convergence prevents us from characterizing Schilder's life struggle for the reliability of revelation and the history of Paradise as one of the backgrounds of Schilder's opposition to the doctrine of common grace, as J. Kamphuis does.

One of the most exciting discoveries during my study was the profound harmony between Schilder and Kuyper regarding the cultural task that human beings have. It caused me consciously to identify with the time of the Liberation. During those years all the emphasis was on the *contrast* between Schilder and Kuyper. When something like that happens, the harmony between these great theologians is quickly obscured.

The image that was given of the doctrine of common grace was often no more than that it legitimized junkets in the world, in which one could "still" appreciate and enjoy so many good things. But when one reads Kuyper himself, one is impressed with the grand perspective of his cultural views. God gives a task for the development of the world. This task is fixed and established in his eternal Counsel. The decree of predestination encompasses "the totality of history, the entire course that heaven and earth will run, and is directed toward the end, in order that from this entire creation and the entire cosmos God may receive the honor due to him."[5]

Satan failed in his attempt to frustrate the goal of creation: the development of all of creation's potential. For God, who maintains his work from eternity to eternity, had already decided in his Counsel to uphold and carry out his program by the operation of a common grace that began after the Fall. What is in the earth will be exploited. That is strongly put. But for Kuyper it was a certainty "that the Consummation must bring us not only a transition from the church militant to a church triumphant, and not only a gathering of the kingdoms of the world into the Kingdom of heaven, but also that in the life of nature and the life of the world whatever God concealed in them must be made manifest to the praise of his name *before the end can come*."[6]

5. *De Gemeene Gratie*, vol. II, 108, 4th edition (Kampen, [n.d.]). Cf. Dissertation, 34ff. Page references to the dissertation apply to the translated version as presented above in this volume.
6. *Van de Voleinding*, vol. II, 507 (Kampen, 1929); italics supplied.

In this work of common grace Christ also has a place. He came to accelerate the process of the development of creation by his power over nature. From then on, an exponent by which it is "tripled" in power began to operate in common grace. The enormous technological development in Europe, the possession human beings assumed over nature, would have been impossible without Christ.[7]

Schilder's position is often different, often on fundamental points. Thus he in his writings about the cultural mandate does not proceed from God's eternal Counsel but from creation. But he does speak of the same mandate that was also maintained after the Fall to achieve "the systematized striving for the sum-total of labor that through a gradual process is to be attained by the sum total of humanity."[8]

This clearly calls to mind what Kuyper had already expressed. The one may speak of a "task," the other of a "mandate," but they connote the same thing. Despite the wiles of Satan, God does not abandon the work of his hands. The mandate, the program, the development, continues.

The work of the development of culture is given its foundation by Christ and is made possible again through him. According to Schilder, he came to restore the ABCs of the order for life and for the world.[9] The original service of God is made possible again for human beings. Christ's struggle delivers to the new humanity "rich powers of the outpouring of the Spirit, powers of sanctification, of church conquest, of world maturation, of cultural action."[10]

When one pays closer attention to these things, it will be obvious (to say it again) that there are significant differences from Kuyper. This is apparent already from the foregoing brief summary. Kuyper regards Christ's work in culture as *stimulating*, as giving culture great momentum. Schilder views Christ's work as *foundational*, so that true culture is *Christian* culture. Kuyper recognizes this as well, but Schilder drew a clearer antithesis in culture. Moreover, Kuyper's view of culture is much more optimistic than Schilder's. The latter

---

7. Cf. Dissertation, 51ff.
8. *Christ and Culture* (Hamilton: Lucerna CRTS Publications, 2016), 77.
9. Ibid., 60.
10. Ibid., 64.

is much more reserved about the results of cultural labor. In his view unbelievers will not be able to complete a tower of Babel by their labor. The curse of a crumbling culture remains and the cultural structure of the last days is a truncated pyramid. Even faithful cultural labor remains fragmentary.[11]

But it is striking that both theologians maintain the cultural mandate from Paradise until the last day. The unity of history cannot be broken. God remains God in maintaining his mandates.

Kuyper emphasizes this as much as Schilder. For Kuyper traces the cultural task back to God's eternal Counsel. The mandate given before the Fall continues to have the same force after the Fall.

That is why I do not consider it correct when J. Kamphuis reproves me for failing to point out Schilder's struggle for the reliability of revelation and the history of Paradise as background to his dispute with the doctrine of common grace.[12] In his view, Schilder's struggle against Barth for this reliability, which recognizes *one* history with a historical Paradise and a historical Fall, with norms from the beginning that are also determinative for what follows, actually marked Schilder's attack on the doctrine of common grace.

I am pleased to give the following response:

1. If you speak of common grace, you speak of Kuyper. But if you then want to talk about the reliability and unity of history in opposition to Kuyper, you are tilting at windmills. A few passages from volume I of *De Gemeene Gratie* demonstrate clearly how fundamental Kuyper regarded the historicity of the first chapters of the Bible for his view of culture. If you tamper with that historicity "in whatever way, you can save yourself and others all further consideration of the matter of general grace. For then all certainty escapes you and the ground under your feet will disappear."[13] Or also: "The origins of everything that still inspires you today, surrounds your personal life, and about which you cogitate in your heart, lie exposed for you in this book of Genesis."[14] "Literally *every* word, *every* letter" of it is relevant for that purpose.[15]

---

11. Ibid., 124ff. See also Dissertation, 294ff.
12. *De Reformatie* 42, 242 (incorrectly identified as p. 142).
13. *De Gemeene Gratie*, vol. I, 95.
14. Ibid., 105.
15. Ibid., 101. Cf. the entire section, 95–108, in which Kuyper opposes ethical theology.

2. It is possible that Schilder misunderstood Kuyper on this point, so that Kamphuis might still be correct in his remark that it is "abundantly obvious on virtually every page that Schilder devoted to the cultural mandate" how he mobilizes the reliability of the first chapters of the Bible also in his struggle against Kuyper.[16] I have investigated the matter, but have not been able to find this anywhere. Not in *Christ and Culture*; not in both *rectoral lectures*, which were dedicated to the doctrine of common grace; and also not in *Wat is de hemel?* whenever he speaks of Kuyper.

Certainly, Schilder fought for the reliability of the Scriptures with the full dedication of his theological strength. But that was against Barth and Geelkerken. In Kuyper's doctrine of common grace the unity of world history, both before and after the Fall, was anchored in the eternal Counsel of God. This was so fundamental to Kuyper that a serious attack on his doctrine requires something other than contesting him about the historicity of the first pages of the Bible. And Schilder never did that.

Because my dissertation concerned the differences between Schilder and Kuyper, and not those between Schilder and Barth, Kamphuis discovered a lacuna that does not exist.

3. *The criticism that I mounted principally on the basis of Calvin's views on the cultural mandate, draws attention to the following:*
(a) Christ's (first) coming as the "last times" (cf. Heb 1:1; 1 Pet 1:20; 1 John 2:18). This notion makes it dubious whether we, with Schilder, can speak about Christ as office-bearer in the "middle" of history, who takes upon himself "the great reformational task of returning to the ABCs of the order for the world and for life";
(b) the fruitlessness of all of creation that will continue until the last day (Rom 8), over against the dominion, according to Ps 8, over all created things that exists in Christ but is not yet visible to us (Heb 2:5ff.);
(c) a more nuanced exegesis of Gen 1:28 and a more proportional application of this text in Christian ethics.

In my second proposition I already pointed to the place of Christ

---

16. *De Reformatie* 41, 242. See footnote 13.

in culture according to Schilder's views. The creation mandate remained in force after the Fall and can be fulfilled again through Christ's work.

For, as second Adam, in the *middle* of history he returned to the beginning.[17] He fixed the foundations of the earth again. He equips "the work community and office community of God, which he himself has purchased, for the work and service of God, in order that all its living members may enter into the city of perfected glory."[18] "Christ connects the beginnings of the world with the end, the primeval history with final history, the first things with the *eschata*, the alpha with the omega, the ABC of God's efficacious legislative speaking in the *beginning* with the XYZ of his once again efficacious evangelical word at the *end* of time."[19]

In the New Testament we do not find any reference to Christ as office-bearer in the *middle* of history. It does depict him as coming at the *end* of time. Think for example of Heb 1:1–2: "Long ago, at many times and in many ways, God spoke to our fathers by the prophets, but in these last days he has spoken to us by his Son." Also of 1 Pet 1:20: Before the foundation of the world Christ was already known, but he was "made manifest in the last times" for the sake of the believers. Similarly John can tell his "children" that it is "the last hour" (1 John 2:18).

In view of these texts, is it legitimate to speak of Christ in the middle of history? Is the unnoticed effect of making the quantitative distance in years between his first and second coming the reason for a qualitative description of Christ's work, in order to give the development of culture in the time between Christ's ascension and return its own place?

Further, I question whether by accepting a cultural program expressly determined by God as it comes to the fore in the idea of the cultural mandate also for the centuries between Christ's first and second coming, it is still possible to let Romans 8 function sufficiently. That chapter testifies of the groaning of all creatures and the entire creation that continues to be subjected to futility until last days. A program of development envisions fruits; but what

---

17. *Christ and Culture*, 60.
18. Ibid., 64.
19. Ibid., 67–68.

then must we do with the image of total futility sketched here? Does this permit a taking out of creation what it in it? Do human beings thus achieve dominion over creation? Or does the result of such cultural labor arise outside of the futility of creation referred to in Rom 8?

It is true that the New Testament speaks about the total subjection of all things to human beings. But that refers to the subjection to the man *Jesus Christ*. Think for example of Heb 2:6–8, where the author quotes Ps 8: "What is man that you are mindful of him...? you ... have crowned him with glory and honor, putting all things under his feet." This (obviously) legitimate application of Ps 8 surely transfers us *from* human beings and their cultural possibilities of *gaining* dominion over creation *to* the man Jesus Christ, who in accordance with Ps 8 *has been given* dominion over all creation. Ephesians 1 and Colossians 1 say the same thing. The fullness of God dwells in the image of the invisible God, Jesus Christ, to whom dominion over all rule and authority and power and dominion and every name *has been given*.

Human beings are not en route to the triumph over all creation. With good reason we may ask whether it was especially the technological innovations of the past centuries that gave Kuyper and his followers this idea and that thereby the *command* of Gen 1:28 began to predominate over its fulfillment in Christ.

I believe that we can certainly ask that question in Kuyper's case. But also, though to a lesser extent, in the case of Schilder. He states correctly that human beings are unable to complete the tower of Babel. His speaking of truncated pyramids and torsos in all of culture are heartening and remind us of the language in Rom 8. But do his *ideas* also not fail to give sufficient attention to the fulfillment in Christ when the agenda of the beginning, the task of taking out of creation everything that it contains, is assumed by Christ and is presented as a program for those who are his?[20]

One thing leads to another. When you regard Ps 8 as fulfilled in Christ, you will then also ask whether Gen 1:28 can function as foundation for Christian ethics.

I must admit that my criticism on the accepted exegesis of this

---

20. Ibid., 69.

text, as I gave it in my dissertation, was incorrect. It was too forced. The text does speak of a cultural mandate. I am grateful to Kamphuis for his correct comments on this component of my study.[21]

Nonetheless, I should like to continue to argue for a more nuanced exegesis of Gen 1:28. It certainly speaks of a task, a mandate to subdue the world. But the text also presents *words of blessing*. For we read: "And God blessed them and said...." This blessing is expounded in the wording that follows. One exegete explains it as follows: "This text is not a wish, not even a task, but power that is granted to human beings. Just as a curse contains calamity that will sooner or later burst out, so also the blessing connotes a latent power that will be revealed over time."[22]

I believe that the dilemma "a blessing but not a task" is incorrect. But I call attention to both. By the power of the blessing human beings are endowed with the impulse that is necessary for procreation, and with the inclination to investigate and the intelligence to cultivate the earth and to subdue it. Those are creation gifts that were not taken away after the Fall, for *humanity* remains. The power to subdue and the strength to multiply are "commanded," just as the sea creatures and the birds are told, "Be fruitful and multiply and fill the waters of the seas, and let birds multiply on the earth" (1:22).

The gift and the task are conjoined. Human beings are different from fish and birds. It is not automatic, but since they as creatures are included in the covenant with God, their being equipped becomes their calling and the enjoyment and acquisition of their position of authority in the world will also be conjoined. They hear the command in the blessing that God spoke to them.

I also gladly call attention to a more proportional application of Gen 1:28 in Christian ethics. For we must keep pace with the clock of salvation history. When Christ came at the end of days, he did not abandon the norms of the beginning. On the contrary! He, and his apostles in his footsteps, confirmed them. Marriage remained an institution in which two are one and the husband remained the

---

21. *De Reformatie* 42, 241–42 (see footnote 13).
22. J. L. Koole, *De Tien Geboden*, 115 (Baarn, 1964).

head of his wife.[23] But that is something different from a return to the program of the beginning: "Be fruitful and multiply and fill the earth." Indeed, for many believers this still contains a blessing and a command: Paul writes that the woman "will be saved through childbearing" (1 Tim 2:15). But the same apostle states in 1 Cor 7:8 that it is good for a person to remain single. It is the end time, the last hour in which woes are expressed over those who are pregnant and who are nursing infants (Matt 24:19) and in which persons who made themselves eunuchs for the sake of the kingdom of heaven will find a place in that kingdom (Matt 19:12).

With reference to cases of sexual immorality, Scripture says that each man should have his own wife and every woman her own husband (1 Cor 7:1, 2). When you read such a sober injunction—just as sober as the injunction "If anyone is not willing to work, let him not eat" (2 Thess 3:10) in motivating people to work—you will not forget in your Christian ethics that the orientation of Gen 1:28 reminds you how much further salvation history has advanced.

4. Their being strangers and sojourners marks Christians as people who, in their short and difficult life, know that they are on their way to a better, heavenly homeland (cf. Gen 47:9; Lev 25:23; 1 Chr 29:15; Ps 119:19, 54; Heb 11:13ff.; 13:14; 1 Pet 1:1. See also Heidelberg Catechism, Lord's Day 9 about "this life of sorrow" and the Form for the Baptism of Infants, which calls this life "no more than a constant death"). We maintain this description of our sojourning over against W. G. de Vries.

In developing the idea of the cultural mandate, people are in my view easily faced with the danger of so directing their attention to the *beginning* (Genesis) that the perspective on the *end*, as Scripture speaks of it, hardly functions anymore. That is the perspective of the stranger or sojourner here on earth, who in his short and difficult life looks forward to a better, a heavenly homeland.

When you examine the above-mentioned texts, you will find three elements that determine the concept of "stranger" or

---

23. Cf. Matt 19:4ff.; 1 Tim 2:13–14.

"sojourner": the brevity of life; the troubles and opposition in it; and the being en route to a better homeland.

King David confesses to God that he and his subjects are strangers and sojourners before God. For "our days on earth are like a shadow, and there is no abiding" (1 Chr 29:15). Everything comes from God and everything is given back to him. He remains, but human beings depart from the earthly stage (1 Chr 29:14ff.). God is the owner, while human beings are only entitled to possess for a time what has been bestowed on them in the form of land and goods (Lev 25:23).

In other places the state of being strangers and sojourners testifies to the difficulty that the service of God causes in relationships with other people. The poet of Psalm 119 calls himself a "sojourner on the earth" among the godless and insolent who scorn and despise him (vv. 19ff.). The house of his sojourning is surrounded by other houses in which the Lord is not being served. He feels the antithesis because the faithful service of God implies isolation.

The status of the stranger and sojourner is described as temporary in the texts that testify of believers being en route to a better, heavenly homeland. That is undeniably the case in Heb 11:13ff., which harks back, *inter alia*, to Gen 47:9. The author of Hebrews says that the patriarchs confessed that they were strangers and exiles on the earth and thereby made it clear that they sought a homeland that could not be found here on earth, but in heaven.

De Vries has contested my exegesis of "being strangers and sojourners" principally with the argument that the governing element of the concept of sojourning is our relationship to God. He writes: "Our sojourning is not determined by human beings among whom we live, but by God to whom the entire earth belongs. *We are never our own master*. That is why God says to Israel: 'The land shall not be sold in perpetuity, for the land is mine. For you are strangers and sojourners with me'" (Lev 25:23).[24]

God remains the Owner and therefore we remain strangers who have to reckon with the commandments of the Owner.

---

24. *Petah-ja*, Journal of the Federation of Men's Societies Based on Reformed Principles, 21, 7 (January 1967).

This position is so permanent that De Vries remarks: "The sojourning that we are discussing, always remains, even though we are continuously in the homeland. For the homeland is *the land of our Father*. And to him belong all things, also this earth. We are already in the homeland, for we shall inherit the earth" (Matt 5:5).[25] Because of our permanent relationship toward God—on this earth and on the new earth—in which we must regard "our" goods as belonging only to him and in which we will always be subject to his command, human beings remain "strangers and sojourners."

This logical reasoning immediately betrays the weakness of my opponent's argument. N. Bruin has pointed out correctly that 1 Pet 1:17 speaks about the "time of your exile"; a time that passes by, just like the time "of your former ignorance" and "the rest of the time in the flesh" (1 Pet 1:14; 4:2).[26] Moreover, it is clear from Heb 11 that the sojourning of the patriarchs is contrasted with having as home a better, that is a heavenly homeland. We should not blur the perspective of the patriarchs with the remark that they were *and would remain* strangers!

When De Vries turns the word "fatherland" [homeland] into the land of the Father, I consider that to be no more than a play on words, for based on it he then concludes that because this earth is the Father's land we are now already in the "fatherland" [homeland].

Of course I acknowledge what De Vries says about strangers in their obedience to God's commandments. But the relationship with and obedience to God that De Vries makes into the *condition* of the concept of "sojourning" is only its *supposition*: it is matter of being no stranger without a relationship with God, but *in* that relationship a stranger, because by our obedience toward God we encounter resistance in this world (Ps 119) and learn to look forward with longing to a better, a heavenly homeland (Heb 11). To put it schematically, De Vries points to the vertical line but forgets that it is actually the horizontal line (Christians among other people) and the diagonal line (Christians en route to their heavenly home) that depict their being "strangers." Again, it is impossible to think

25. Loc. cit.
26. *Petah-ja* 21, 47 (March 1967).

of this apart from what De Vries correctly says about it. But being strangers and sojourners encompasses more. The enmity of the world and the journey toward the homeland to come lend their *color* to the concept.

The view that Christians are strangers and sojourners also finds expression in our confessions and ecclesiastical formularies. Very well known (and therefore often not well-considered) is the characterization in Heidelberg Catechism, Lord's Day 9, of this life as a "life of sorrow." And in the prayer before baptism, in the Form for the Baptism of Infants, this life is referred to as "no more than a constant death." We all accept the confession of Guido de Brès as expression of our faith. In the hour of his ordeal this man concludes his confession by expressing our faith as follows: "Therefore we look forward to that great day [of the last judgment] with a great longing to enjoy to the full the promise of God in Jesus Christ our Lord" (art. 37).

These things are not mere *additions* but form an integral part of the faith that marks us. At least that was the effect on Calvin, who did not fall into the Anabaptist error. He was not a fanatic, but in his sober-minded instruction he has made clear that we must *learn* to confess that part of our confession.[27]

Earlier I said that we must keep pace with the clock of salvation history, that we live in the last hour. "By the official work of the Lord Jesus Christ we are directly connected with the rest of the age to come. In comparison with it, in this creation we remain strangers and exiles. We have no lasting city here, but we await the city whose designer and builder is God, just as Abraham did in his time" (N. Bruin).[28]

5. *The confession of our being strangers and sojourners does not deny the regenerating power of the gospel, also for culture (cf. Matt 5:13ff.; Col 4:5–6; Eph 4:17ff.; 5:22–6:9; and other texts). But the oases accentuate the wilderness (Rev 12; Mark 10:30) and what has been tossed to us in culture (Matt 6:33) is something different from an aspect of a cultural program in*

---

27. Dissertation, 279ff.
28. *Petah-ja* 21, 50 (April 1967).

which the garden is supposed to develop into a completed culture of the city, the new Jerusalem of Rev 22.

The confession of our being strangers and sojourners does not force us into an attitude of passivity that makes us indifferent to this world. I do not defend a pilgrimage à la John Bunyan, which lets us, whether or not packed up and ready to go, depart from the world and make our way to a heavenly homeland.

My fifth proposition suggests something else. The prospect of the future does not paralyze activity for the here and now!

In my dissertation I formulated this in brief as follows. "Although we are not yet 'home,' we are where we belong."[29] The expectation of Jesus Christ must fill us with a burning zeal. For the instruction of the nations has been entrusted to the church as the salt of the world, the light of the earth, the pillar and buttress of the truth. She must work while it is day, take advantage of opportunities, and in doing so must do good to all people.

For the gospel brings *salvation* and frees believers from the coming wrath of God. With a perspective on Christ—"My desire is to depart and be with Christ" (Phil 1:23)—but with their hand on the plow, Christians have a task here on earth. Focused on what is to come, but fully active in the here and now—that is how the church, proclaiming the Word, is busy. The preaching of the gospel with all its consequences fills the time between the ascension and the return of Christ. The end can come only when the gospel of the kingdom has been preached in the whole world, as a witness to all nations (Matt 24:14).

This preaching bears rich fruit, also for culture. The new life of which Paul writes to the Ephesians does not remain hidden in society. Family relationships are restored and political situations are changed. When you examine world history after Christ's incarnation, you would have to be blind if you do not notice how the gospel has drawn deep furrows in the field that is called the earth.

No one can deny that the prayer for those in authority (1 Tim 2) has often been heard, so that the church could lead a quiet and

---

29. Dissertation, 388.

peaceable life—a life in which the impact of the gospel on society often produced splendid results. We will not hate this quiet and peaceable life in order to seek struggle and martyrdom.

Only: when we examine the entire time between Christ's ascension and his return, we see that the church finds itself as the woman in the *wilderness* (Rev 12). The true church (taken globally) discovers, when she does not wear blinders, that there is no place for her on earth. She preaches in the streets of the city, but she is not accepted. Persecution is her lot; she knows herself to be a stranger here below.

To become concrete: things are going well for us in the Netherlands and we have our *lustra* [quinquennial celebrations], but how many are not being persecuted before or behind iron curtains, both where they are in hiding and where they function in public? The quiet and peaceable life that *we* enjoy is like an oasis in the wilderness. But it does not cause us to forget that such oases are located in the *wilderness*. Blinders can prevent us from losing sight of the church in its entirety and forgetting her suffering because of our prosperity and peace. The one church of Jesus Christ must continue to cry out: "Come, Lord Jesus."

The good things that we receive here bring joy. Received with thanksgiving, they enable us to make free use of them. We shall not forget the word of Christ that we shall receive back a hundredfold already here of what we have given up: houses, brothers and sisters, mothers and children, and lands. But ... with persecutions (Mark 10:30)! The mark of being strangers, which causes us to miss out on much but which also causes us to receive back very much in the church, identifies us in this life.

We may not assign a negative content to our being strangers and sojourners. When the kingdom of God is sought and when we look forward to the coming of Christ, there is more. "Seek first the kingdom of God and his righteousness, and all these things will be added to you" (Matt 6:33): food and drink and clothing.

Added to you! That sounds less programmatic than what is often said to be included in arguments about our cultural task. In those arguments we hear about a *garden* in Gen 2 that must develop into the *city* of Rev 22, the new Jerusalem.[30] But this city is God's creation. *We* may enter it, and the glory and honor of the nations and the treasures of nature will be gathered in it. But the city is already prepared. Humanity, not even a new humanity, is involved in building it in this dispensation. It already accommodates the patriarchs among its citizens, for God had already prepared a city for them (Heb 11:16).

I know, of course, that we must be careful with our interpretation of the images in Revelation. But those who teach a cultural progression from the "garden" to the "city," will have to explain to us where in Rev 21–22 human hands build the walls of this city and pave its streets.

6. *A confrontation with the Guidelines Program of the Gereformeerd Politiek Verbond [Reformed Political Alliance], explained by Dr. A. J. Verbrugh in "De politieke partijen in Nederland" and in "Hoe wij het verkiezen," can clarify my objections against founding our (political) task on the cultural mandate. For this I refer to the place of Christ, to the origin and the task of government (both of which were depicted more clearly by B. Holwerda in his "Crisis van het gezag") and to the meaning of human existence as the Guidelines and/or Dr. Verbrugh's explanation speak about it.*

By engaging with the Guidelines of the *Gereformeerd Politiek Verbond* (G.P.V.) I yet want to make more concrete my objections to using the cultural mandate as theoretical foundation of our calling. It is abundantly clear that the Guidelines assign a dominant place to the cultural mandate.

The G.P.V. says in art. 3 that governments must strive "toward the cultivation and development of our own country" and thereby contribute "to the development of the whole earth."[31] The idea of progression is not missing from the Guidelines. The cultural task

---

30. K. Schilder, *Wat is de hemel?*, 181; H. Berkhof, *De mens onderweg*, 37 (The Hague, 1960); A. J. Verbrugh, *Hoe wij het verkiezen*, 46–47 (Groningen, 1966).
31. *Hoe wij het verkiezen*, 40.

begins in the garden and reaches its fulfillment in the city of the future (Rev 22).[32]

Governmental authority has its origin in creation. That argument is logical! For the task that government must carry out with respect to the development of the country in the execution of the cultural mandate is not at all incidental, but essential.[33] If the mandate exists from the beginning, then so does its executor! The government is "the head of public society" (arts. 13 and 14), for the realization of "development projects."[34]

The government must have a specific goal. We read in art. 3: "Governments that ... contribute their share to the execution of the task that humanity possesses for the development of creation, must do so with the public objective of giving all honor to the righteous and merciful God."[35] What does the G.P.V. mean by the words "righteous" and "merciful"? In his explanation Dr. Verbrugh says the following:

The government must in its actions practice the righteousness "to which the Bible points.... Doing righteousness means in general and in a positive sense doing all that God commands, which includes submitting comprehensively to the cultural task, insofar as this conforms with everyone's office."[36]

Also universal is the duty "to demonstrate God's mercy. Human beings must know well that it is the merciful God who enables them, mere human creatures, to accomplish much and to receive much, in consequence of which they may possibly occupy a favorable position. It is then the duty of human beings in their turn to give a helping hand to their neighbors, in order to bring them also into a favorable position. Such is the Christian duty to love one's neighbor."[37]

The government and the nation are called to "show love and honor to God, who made heaven and earth with all the sources of

---

32. Ibid., 46–47.
33. Ibid., 45.
34. Ibid., 116, 120.
35. Ibid., 41.
36. Ibid., 49–50.
37. A.J. Verbrugh, *De politieke partijen in Nederland*, vol. II, 10–11 (Rotterdam, 1962).

life and prosperity" (art. 1), to the "Creator of all things" (art. 2).[38] How must that be done?

"At important stages of its work, the government ought to acknowledge God publicly in appropriate, Scriptural phraseology" (art. 13).[39] As put another way in Dr. Verbrugh's explanation : "When a major project is completed, or when people are rescued from a great danger, etc., the government must not give glory to human accomplishments, nor speak of fate, but give praise to God. In carrying out its official duties, this praise must be its goal and the crown on its work.[40]

Can the government carry out this task? Yes, if it is governed by the law of God, the universal law of God "expounded in the Ten Commandments and summarized by Christ as the command to love God and the neighbor" (art. 6).[41] This moral law is meant not only for believers; for not only they, "but *all* people after all [have] a certain awareness of the moral law ... so that we can appeal to this awareness."[42] The government must accompany its help to underdeveloped areas with efforts to enlighten them about the meaning of the universal law for the governance of those regions (art. 10).[43]

I also refer to yet another element regarding the cultural mandate. Its fulfillment "gives a future to human beings who live on the earth. Their existence will thus become meaningful and give them joy."[44] To put it more strongly: those who follow the calling that God gives them "have the certainty that it is not they, human beings with their limited capacities, who are at work, but that it is the Eternal One himself who, in covenant with them, executes his plan for this world. Those who submit themselves to God's will ... are governed by the Holy Spirit of God and of Christ and know that the angels support them and that all the saints pray with them for the success of their labor and their struggle."[45]

The following song about labor sounds serene: "The attention

38. *Hoe wij het verkiezen*, 14, 33.
39. Ibid., 116
40. Ibid., 36.
41. Ibid., 57.
42. *De politieke partijen in Nederland*, vol. I, 32–33 (Rotterdam, 1959).
43. *Hoe wij het verkiezen*, 83.
44. Ibid., 97.
45. *De politieke partijen*, vol. II, 12–13.

of human beings can be diverted from the unpleasantness of the difficulties that they perhaps experience in fulfilling their task to the good feelings that they will enjoy when they remember that they are following their life's goal before which the God of all light and brilliance placed them.... When you know that you are truly following the right way, you will be able to carry on and stay the course until the end and you will discover that the deep undertone of happiness will not leave you."[46]

Creator, creation, cultural mandate, cultural progression, a life of happiness for human beings—these are some of the catchwords that stuck in my mind when I examined the Guidelines.

But they raise pressing questions for me:

1. Where in the Guidelines do we find a discussion of the dominion of Jesus Christ as Lord of lords and King of kings? Certainly, his name is mentioned. But that happens in *subordinate clauses*, not in the *principal clause*. Art. 1 is a telling example of this: "In accordance with the universal and eternal gospel of the coming Christ, the King of kings, the *Gereformeerd Politiek Verbond* calls on government and people to give praise and honor to God, who made heaven and earth with all the sources of life and prosperity."[47] Christ's kingship is mentioned, but it does not function here. And that would also be difficult if the following remark by Dr. Verbrugh is determinative for the background of the Guidelines: "The other forms of labor [namely, those other than the ministry of the Word and the sacraments, the supervision of which has been entrusted by Christ to specified ecclesiastical office-bearers, J.D.] came to belong to the non-ecclesiastical area of office. And everything that belongs to the latter, Christ radically separated from the church with the words: 'My Kingdom is not of this world.'"[48]

Another remark by Dr. Verbrugh demonstrates the extent to which Christ's kingship has been pushed to the margins of political confession. In *De politieke partijen in Nederland* he speaks about the universal moral law that applies to all. "If people do not have faith in Christ, they are not inclined to see God's revelation in nature in the clarifying light of Holy Scripture and will also not be inclined to

---

46. Ibid., 14–15.
47. *Hoe wij het verkiezen*, 14.
48. Ibid., 41–42.

be led to the true life in God's service by this revelation of God."⁴⁹ This already raises questions that become more urgent when we read further: "Consequently, a Christian party that calls people to organize society according to the norms of the moral law that is both universal and Christian, will in many cases find it appropriate to provide certain illustrative explanations that can promote the knowledge of Christ ... so that the significance of Christ for the people who want to lead a sound and uplifting political life becomes clearer."⁵⁰

It must strike us that while the universal moral law remains the foundation for political action, the Christian faith, and thus also the confession of the Christ, merely functions to *clarify* and *illustrate*. That is indeed a different aim than one in which the confession of Christ's kingship functions as the point of departure for political discourse.

2. A second question is connected with the first: Where do the Guidelines take into account the continuation of salvation history? Surely politics is not excluded from that? To put it another way: does art. 36 of the Belgic Confession function adequately? That article points, on the one hand, to the *preservative* task of the government "by laws and statutes, in order that the lawlessness of men be restrained and that everything be conducted among them in good order." But the government's task also has a *progressive* element. The Kingdom of Jesus Christ must be promoted. The government is called into service to safeguard the advancement of the proclamation of the gospel.

I believe that this confession is richer that what the Guidelines have made of it. Dr. Verbrugh is correct when he says that art. 36 "is not a political program but a confession of the church. This article does therefore say that the government must protect the church and its ministry, that it must ensure that the gospel may be preached, and that it must cause the kingdom of Christ to be promoted, etc.... But it does not say *how* the government must do so."⁵¹ Agreed! But *that* the government has to do this is hardly apparent from the Guidelines. And as for the *how*, one can surely

---

49. *De politieke partijen*, vol. 1, 35.
50. Ibid., 35–36.
51. *Hoe wij het verkiezen*, 55.

say more than that governments must maintain "the constitutionally guaranteed freedom of religious worship and the related spiritual freedoms" (art. 5, Guidelines), [52] or that by guaranteeing civil order and peace they must protect the true proclamation of God's Word.[53] For while this takes into account the first part of art. 36, the second part is left out of consideration. Order and peace also guarantee the right of *Muslims* in the Netherlands to practice their religion.

In this context I wonder why the Guidelines say nothing about *mission*. In the passage where we might expect it, we read only: "Help by the Netherlands to underdeveloped countries ought to be accompanied by education about the significance of the universal law of God for the governance of those countries" (art. 10).[54] I think that is a very meagerly expressed. This is where the mention of mission work with its confession of Christ as King over all of life ought to have found a place.

3. Why did the G.P.V. not make use of what B. Holwerda said about the task of government? His address *De crisis van het gezag*, delivered in 1947, made a deep impression at the time. In it, Holwerda wanted to make it clear that we must say more about government than that it is founded in creation, or that it exists "because of sin." He takes another point of departure: "Government exists ... *for the sake of redemption.* It does not exist for the continuation of the world, but solely with an eye to *building* the world to come. All authority is included and involved in the *eschatological salvific work of God.* And as often as the Lord does something new, it is not just something new for his people, but something new for all earthly powers. All governments are involved in the dynamic intervention by God for redemption and each new act of God is thereby characterized further. Every step that Christ takes and every 'stage' that he reaches in his exaltation, touches also the government directly!"[55] It is true that the government has another liturgy than the church, "but it is nonetheless just as much *liturgy of Christ.* Its power to bear the sword is also in the service

52. Ibid., 54.
53. Ibid., 56.
54. Ibid., 83.
55. *De crisis van het gezag*, 6 (Groningen, 1947).

of God, who comes in Christ to redeem the world. Hence both the death penalty and war *are instruments of eternal life—eschatological powers of redemption*, which lend their meaning to this: that God so loved the world, that he gave his only Son, that whoever believes in him should not perish but have eternal life."[56] We miss this Christocentric definition of the task of the government and its focus on the *eschata*. That is regrettable!

4. Where do the principles of the G.P.V., as they have been formulated, rise above the Kuyperian mindset? Where in the Guidelines (and its explanation) do we find, in distinction from Kuyper, a satisfactory formulation of the *unity* of creation and redemption, of law and gospel. Where do they give concepts such as "righteousness" and "mercy" the meaning that they have *in Christ*? Where is the connection between the robust song of labor and the confession of our being sojourners, which knows that only labor in Christ avoids the stigma of "vanity"?

1. With my sixth proposition I am not forgetting the first! I regard the theoretical foundation of the G.P.V. as weak, but I am thankful for what this party is accomplishing in the life of our nation. I also cherish the clear language that P. Jongeling speaks in the Second Chamber [of Parliament]. No one can doubt that the kingship of Jesus Christ is being confessed in it. In fact, the calling to do so also appears in the explanation of Dr. Verbrugh: "Our government must acknowledge that Christ is King of kings and that it therefore also has its own calling among the nations" (*Hoe wij het verkiezen*, 84). But what becomes apparent in the practice of political speech and action and what is mentioned in a fragmentary and incidental way in the theoretical foundation ought to *pervade* the Guidelines. There is a deficiency in that respect.

2. The discussion that followed the delivery of my address in Kampen was also instructive for me. Among other things, it was mentioned that we must be careful with posing dilemmas, saying that it is *either* this *or* that. Those who criticize the cultural mandate as Kuyper, Schilder, and others spoke of it are then inclined to reject the concept altogether, along the lines of thinking it must be one or the other: cultural mandate *or* sojourning. In proposition 3 above, I already mentioned that Gen 1:28 does contain a cultural task. And the rest of the Bible confirms this task. For example, in the building of the tower of Babel, humanity clearly contravened the mandate it had received. The proclamation of the gospel to all nations presupposes that those nations formed themselves in accordance with Gen 1:28. There could have been no "multitude that no one could number" if it had not been for that task in Paradise; nor could mothers

---

56. Ibid., 9.

have been declared blessed if there had been no children born in conformity with the command to "be fruitful and multiply."

But none of this changes the fact that taking the cultural mandate into account is something different from basing a (political) program on it. The Guidelines of the G.P.V. have confirmed my opinion on that point. It has become clearer to me since I studied the Guidelines that we may not remain silent about Gen 1:28, also not after Christ's incarnation. But at the same time, I have become more convinced than before that we must begin and end with Christ and his return for the definition of our calling. And in defining that calling, the cultural mandate must form part of our deliberations. We must keep pace with salvation history (Holwerda) and that means more than the Guidelines suggest.

3. I question whether Schilder's views of culture do not differ somewhat from the view that (according to the explanation) forms the foundation of the Guidelines. For Schilder, culture properly considered, is *Christian*, as he maintained very strongly over against all other "culture" (*Christ and Culture*, 129ff.). In my opinion, this antithetical view is not as clearly expressed by Dr. Verbrugh.

4. A few days before my address in Kampen, I was able to review the objections against the Guidelines that the electoral association of Schiebroek-Hillegersberg-Terbregge sent to the council of the G.P.V. in a submission dated 6 April, 1965. On more than one point it appeared that my objections paralleled those of that electoral association. In my opinion this letter deserves more attention than it received at the time.

7. My criticism of the "cultural mandate" is dated: Over against the horizontalism of present-day theology with its vain expectations it asks for conversion to the living hope of the glory of God (Rom 5:2) and to the inheritance that is kept in heaven for us (1 Pet 1:4).

Those who study, delve into books. But in studying Calvin, Kuyper, and Schilder they do not forget the times they live in.

These are times in which people want to close heaven and exploit (rather than develop) the earth. Those who still believe in Jesus Christ, who preached more than human solidarity, are not able to keep up with the pace of their times.

It is considered backward to find Christ above, seated at God's right hand.

It is considered backward to seek the things that are above.

It is considered backward to regard the earth as a vale of tears and not as "home" that we must make livable and maintain as such.

It is considered backward—but it is the backwardness of strangers—to await the coming Christ. But they are constantly being taught by the Spirit and the bride to say: "Come!" Because of our sluggishness we gladly want to feel completely at home "in a foreign country." But the one church, above and in many places below, cries out: "How long?"

God gives us times of refreshing and we delight in them. But satiation must remain foreign to us if the hope of the inheritance that is preserved above against moth and rust, is to be a *living hope*: the hope of seeing God and his Son. We must *mean* it when we say—not in a pietistic, but in a Scriptural way—that it is *not* be found here below.

Over against the lie of horizontalism, we shall not be ashamed of the confession of our being strangers, a confession that is a cause of offence—also in our own lives. For who can escape the attractions of modern thinking? May we be kept watchful by that word of Christ, "When the Son of Man comes, will he find faith on earth?"

J. Douma
Brunssum, The Netherlands

www.ingramcontent.com/pod-product-compliance
Lightning Source LLC
Chambersburg PA
CBHW071139300426
44113CB00009B/1019